Use the attached order cards to order your own or extra subscriptions to **SPECIAL EDUCATION AND THE HANDICAPPED** ... the monthly newsletter service reporting the very latest special education school law cases and late-breaking legislation.

Order an extra subscription for the Assistant Superintendent, the school Personnel Officer, a board member or the faculty lounge. The attached order cards may be removed from the book for your order.

Yes, please send me _____ subscriptions to **SPECIAL EDUCATION AND THE HANDICAPPED**... the monthly newsletter service reporting the very latest special education school law cases and late-breaking legislation.

☐ Send two years at $177.00 (your best price)

☐ Send one year at $97.00

Name _____

Title/School _____

Address _____

City _____ **State** _____ **Zip** _____

Purchase Order Number _____ **Telephone Number** _____

Send order and check payable to: DATA RESEARCH, INC., P.O. Box 490, Rosemount, MN 55068

Yes, please send me _____ subscriptions to **SPECIAL EDUCATION AND THE HANDICAPPED**... the monthly newsletter service reporting the very latest special education school law cases and late-breaking legislation.

☐ Send two years at $177.00 (your best price)

☐ Send one year at $97.00

Name _____

Title/School _____

Address _____

City _____ **State** _____ **Zip** _____

Purchase Order Number _____ **Telephone Number** _____

Send order and check payable to: DATA RESEARCH, INC., P.O. Box 490, Rosemount, MN 55068

OUR GUARANTEE: If you are not satisfied with **SPECIAL EDUCATION AND THE HANDICAPPED,** for any reason, we will refund the unused portion of your subscription payment.

HANDICAPPED STUDENTS
AND
SPECIAL EDUCATION

EIGHTH EDITION

Published by
Data Research, Inc.
P.O. Box 490
Rosemount, Minnesota 55068

Library of Congress Cataloging-in-Publication Data

Handicapped students and special education. — 8th ed.

    p.   cm.
  Includes index.
ISBN 0-939675-24-2 (pbk.)
    1. Special education—Law and legislation—United States.
2. Handicapped children—Education—Law and legislation—United
States. I. Data Research, Inc. (Rosemount, Minn.)
KF4210.H36   1991   344.73´0791—dc20   91-55252
                            [347.304791]   CIP

PREFACE

Federal law requires that school districts provide each handicapped child with a free appropriate education. This volume has been published in response to the need of school administrators and others involved in providing special education services to have a reference available when confronted with any of the multitude of problems in the special education area. The Seventh Edition represents a completely reorganized treatment of special education cases which we believe will be even more useful and easier to use than previous editions. This volume contains the full text of the Education of the Handicapped Act of 1970, as amended through 1990, as well as the full text of the major federal regulations governing the education of handicapped children. This volume also contains the text of five U.S. Supreme Court decisions dealing with special education. *School Board of Nassau County v. Arline*, has been included because of its impact on cases involving students and employees with AIDS. The full legal citation is given for each case reported, and all cases have been indexed and placed in a Table of Cases following the Table of Contents. A Subject Matter Table of Recent Law Review Articles is also included.

The intent of this volume is to provide professional educators and lawyers with access to important case, statutory and regulatory law in the field of special education and handicapped student rights.

EDITORIAL STAFF
DATA RESEARCH, INC.

INTRODUCTORY NOTE ON THE JUDICIAL SYSTEM

In order to allow the reader to determine the relative importance of a judicial decision, the cases included in *Handicapped Students and Special Education, Eighth Edition,* identify the particular court from which a decision has been issued. For example, a case decided by a state supreme court generally will be of greater significance than a state circuit court case. Hence a basic knowledge of the structure of our judicial system is important to an understanding of school law.

Almost all the reports in this volume are taken from appellate court decisions. Although most education law decisions occur at trial court and administrative levels, appellate court decisions have the effect of binding lower courts and administrators so that appellate court decisions have the effect of law within their court systems.

State and federal court systems generally function independently of each other. Each court system applies its own law according to statutes and the determinations of its highest court. However, judges at all levels often consider opinions from other court systems to settle issues which are new or arise under unique fact situations. Similarly, lawyers look at the opinions of many courts to locate authority which supports their clients' cases.

Once a lawsuit is filed in a particular court system, that system retains the matter until its conclusion. Unsuccessful parties at the administrative or trial court level generally have the right to appeal unfavorable determinations of law to appellate courts within the system. When federal law issues or Constitutional grounds are present, lawsuits may be appropriately filed in the federal court system. In those cases, the lawsuit is filed initially in the federal district court for that area.

On rare occasions, the U.S. Supreme Court considers appeals from the highest courts of the states if a distinct federal question exists and at least four justices agree on the question's importance. The federal courts occasionally send cases to state courts for application of state law. These situations are infrequent and in general, the state and federal court systems should be considered separate from each other.

The most common system, used by nearly all states and also the federal judiciary, is as follows: a legal action is commenced in **district court** (sometimes called a trial court, county court, common pleas court or superior court) where a decision is initially reached. The case may then be appealed to the **court of appeals** (or appellate court), and in turn this decision may be appealed to the **supreme court**.

v

Several states, however, do not have a court of appeals; lower court decisions are appealed directly to the state's supreme court. Additionally, some states have labeled their courts in a nonstandard fashion.

In Maryland, the highest state court is called the Court of Appeals. In the state of New York, the trial court is called the Supreme Court. Decisions of this court may be appealed to the Supreme Court, Appellate Division. The highest court in New York is the Court of Appeals. Pennsylvania has perhaps the most complex court system. The lowest state court is the Court of Common Pleas. Depending on the circumstances of the case, appeals may be taken to either the Commonwealth Court or the Superior Court. In certain instances the Commonwealth Court functions as a trial court as well as an appellate court. The Superior Court, however, is strictly an intermediate appellate court. The highest court in Pennsylvania is the Supreme Court.

While supreme court decisions are generally regarded as the last word in legal matters, it is important to remember that trial and appeals court decisions also create important legal precedents. For the hierarchy of typical state and federal court systems, please see the diagram below.

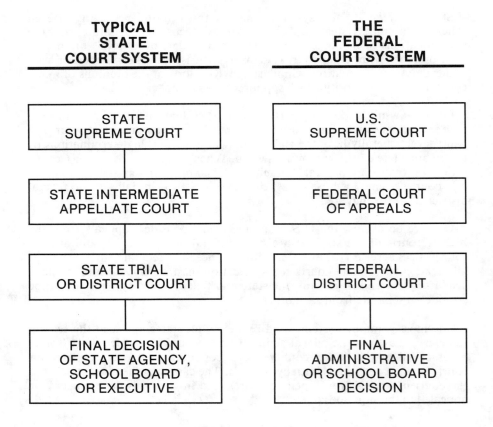

TYPICAL STATE COURT SYSTEM	THE FEDERAL COURT SYSTEM
STATE SUPREME COURT	U.S. SUPREME COURT
STATE INTERMEDIATE APPELLATE COURT	FEDERAL COURT OF APPEALS
STATE TRIAL OR DISTRICT COURT	FEDERAL DISTRICT COURT
FINAL DECISION OF STATE AGENCY, SCHOOL BOARD OR EXECUTIVE	FINAL ADMINISTRATIVE OR SCHOOL BOARD DECISION

Federal courts of appeals hear appeals from the district courts which are located in their circuits. Below is a list of states matched to the federal circuits in which they are located.

First Circuit	— Puerto Rico, Maine, New Hampshire, Massachusetts, Rhode Island
Second Circuit	— New York, Vermont, Connecticut
Third Circuit	— Pennsylvania, New Jersey, Delaware, Virgin Islands
Fourth Circuit	— West Virginia, Maryland, Virginia, North Carolina, South Carolina
Fifth Circuit	— Texas, Louisiana, Mississippi
Sixth Circuit	— Ohio, Kentucky, Tennessee, Michigan
Seventh Circuit	— Wisconsin, Indiana, Illinois
Eighth Circuit	— North Dakota, South Dakota, Nebraska, Arkansas, Missouri, Iowa, Minnesota
Ninth Circuit	— Alaska, Washington, Oregon, California, Hawaii, Arizona, Nevada, Idaho, Montana, Northern Mariana Islands, Guam
Tenth Circuit	— Wyoming, Utah, Colorado, Kansas, Oklahoma, New Mexico
Eleventh Circuit	— Alabama, Georgia, Florida
District of Columbia Circuit	— Hears cases from the U.S. District Court for the District of Columbia.
Federal Circuit	— Sitting in Washington, D.C., the U.S. Court of Appeals, Federal Circuit hears patent and trade appeals and certain appeals on claims brought against the federal government and its agencies.

TABLE OF CONTENTS

Page

TABLE OF CONTENTS

TABLE OF CASES

TABLE OF CASES

TABLE OF CASES

TABLE OF CASES

CHAPTER ONE
THE EDUCATION OF THE HANDICAPPED ACT

I. THE EDUCATION OF THE HANDICAPPED ACT

The Education of the Handicapped Act (EHA)* was enacted by Congress to assist the states in providing handicapped children with a free appropriate public education. Local school districts and states may be sued by handicapped children, or their parents or guardians, if a free appropriate public education is not provided. A recent amendment to the EHA, the Handicapped Children's Protection Act of 1986 (HCPA), encourages the handicapped to bring such lawsuits by requiring the losing defendants in EHA cases to pay attorney's fees and/or money damages to handicapped children. The Education of the Handicapped Act Amendments of 1986 brought handicapped infants and preschool children within EHA coverage.

A. Background

The EHA establishes minimum requirements which must be complied with in order for states to be eligible to receive financial assistance. First, each state must have "in effect a policy that assures all handicapped children the right to a free appropriate public education" [20 U.S.C. § 1412(1)], and must develop a plan which details the policies and procedures which insure the provision of that right [§ 1412(2)]. Each state must also establish the requisite procedural safeguards [§ 1412(5)], and must insure that local educational

---

*Also referred to as the EAHCA (Education for All Handicapped Children Act), and changed by act of Congress to the Individuals with Disabilities Education Act (IDEA) as of October 30, 1990.

agencies in this state will establish the individualized educational programs (IEPs) required by the Act [§ 1412(4)]. Individual states are responsible for establishing and maintaining education standards for the handicapped [§ 1412(6)]. The Act additionally requires that each state must formulate a plan for educating its handicapped children which must be submitted to and approved by the Secretary of Education before the state is entitled to federal assistance.

States receiving federal assistance under the EHA must prepare an IEP for each handicapped student and review the program at least annually. Both the preparation and review processes must be conducted with participation by the child's parents or guardian. The EHA and its accompanying regulations, the full text of which are reprinted in the appendix, also require that a participating state provide specified administrative procedures by which the child's parents or guardians may challenge any change in evaluation and education of the child.

Even severely handicapped students are entitled to EHA protection. A New Hampshire student was multiply handicapped and profoundly mentally retarded. His mother attempted to obtain appropriate education for him but the local school district refused. It stated that because of the student's severe handicaps he would not benefit from education and was therefore not entitled to receive it. The student filed a complaint with the New Hampshire Department of Education for immediate educational placement. The department ordered placement, but the district again refused. The district then appealed the department's order. Meanwhile, the local school board found that the student was not entitled to special education. The student then sued the district in a U.S. district court, seeking special education services and damages under the EHA. Two years later, the district court ruled that the student had not exhausted his administrative remedies. A hearing officer then found for the student and the school district appealed to the district court, which ruled that the student was not capable of benefitting from special education services. Thus, the district was not obligated to provide educational services. The student then appealed to the U.S. Court of Appeals, First Circuit.

The court of appeals held that the EHA was intended to ensure that all handicapped children receive a free appropriate education regardless of the severity of the handicap. The court noted that severely handicapped students had priority under the act. The student was mentally retarded and multiply handicapped and unquestionably was entitled to a free appropriate public education. The appeals court reversed the district court's decision, and remanded it for a determination of a suitable IEP and damages. The student was entitled to an interim special education placement until a final IEP was developed. *Timothy W. v. Rochester, N.H. School Dist.*, 875 F.2d 954 (1st Cir.1989).

The EHA was enacted in order to vindicate the rights of handicapped students, not to provide a general forum for claims in federal court. A three-year-old Pennsylvania child suffered severe head injuries in a traffic accident. As a result, she required special education services for which her parents sued their insurance company. After making initial payments for educational services, the insurer refused to provide further benefits. The parents sued the insurance company in a federal district court. The insurer then filed a third-party complaint against the student's school district under the EHA. The insurer alleged that the school district was primarily responsible for providing special education services. The district court ruled that the EHA did not provide general jurisdiction for special education issues in federal courts. Only students seeking special education services could invoke the EHA. Federal regulations under the statute (34 CFR § 300.301(b)) stated that insurers were not relieved from paying for services to handicapped students. Accordingly, the insurer had no standing to bring an EHA lawsuit against the school district. There was no connection between the insurance company's obligation to satisfy its claim and an appropriate education for the student under the EHA. The EHA provided a minimum educational opportunity level for handicapped students, not a clearly defined entitlement or benefit. The court dismissed the insurance company's third-party complaint. *Gehman v. Prudential Property and Cas. Ins. Co.*, 702 F.Supp. 1192 (E.D.Pa.1989).

In order to invoke the EHA, litigants must exhaust their administrative remedies. Several mentally impaired students at a Michigan school alleged that they received inappropriate discipline ranging from bodily humiliation and the withholding of food and medicine to repeated physical assault. The students sued the teachers, administrators, and the school district in a federal district court. The students asserted causes of action under the Education of the Handicapped Act (EHA), § 504 of the Rehabilitation Act, 42 U.S.C. § 1983, and Michigan tort law, seeking compensatory damages, costs and attorney's fees. The defendants moved to dismiss the case.

The court ruled on four matters. First the court stated that a previous case, *Sanders by Sanders v. Marquette Public Schools*, 561 F.Supp. 1361 (W.D. Mich. 1983), held that a damages remedy is not available under the EHA unless there are exceptional circumstances. Since there were no exceptional circumstances in this case, the court determined that no damages could be awarded under the EHA. Second, the court determined that the plaintiffs had failed to exhaust their administrative remedies as required under the EHA. The plaintiffs contended that because they sought monetary relief, not available under the EHA, the lawsuit should be allowed to proceed. The court, however, determined that to allow the lawsuit to proceed would open up the courts to numerous lawsuits and allow other plaintiffs to circumvent the EHA procedural process. Therefore, it remanded the case to the Michigan Department of Education. Third, the court ruled that the school district and the Michigan Department of Education had concurrent EHA jurisdiction over child abuse cases which arose in the context of classroom discipline. And finally, the court ruled that the Department of Education afforded the appropriate remedy, to return for exhaustion of administrative remedies. The court remanded the case to the Department of Education. *Waterman v. Marquette-Alger Intermediate School Dist.*, 739 F.Supp. 361 (W.D.Mich.1990).

Georgia's local educational agencies (LEAs) sought a declaratory judgment in a federal district court that the Georgia Department of Education (DOE) and Georgia Department of Human Resources (DHR) were obligated under the EHA to provide all handicapped children in Georgia with a free appropriate public education, including residential placement services. The two state educational agencies had originally entered into an interagency co-operative agreement which required the DHR to assist the DOE with the placement of severely handicapped children in twenty-four-hour residential programs in Georgia state-operated facilities. The DOE and the DHR later amended their agreement and placed sole responsibility for providing residential services on the LEAs. The LEAs alleged that the state agencies had failed to uphold their duty. The LEAs claimed that without the assistance of the DOE and DHR they were unable to provide appropriate daycare programs for severely handicapped children. The district court dismissed the LEAs' motion and they appealed to the U.S. Court of Appeals, Eleventh Circuit.

The court of appeals held that the LEAs did not have standing to sue under the EHA in order to force the state agencies to provide needed services. The court noted that nothing in the statute itself and no case authority construed the act to support the LEAs' authority to sue. Under the act, LEAs had the right to challenge handicapped children's IEPs, including appealing state educational agencies' administrative hearing decisions regarding such provisions. However, there was no indication that Congress intended to grant LEAs standing to bring suit to compel a state agency to fulfill its statutory duty. The court of appeals affirmed the district court's decision. *Andrews v. Ledbetter*, 880 F.2d 1287 (11th Cir. 1989).

B. Overview

"Special education means specially designed instruction, at no cost to parents or guardians, to meet the unique needs of a handicapped child, including classroom instruction, instruction in physical education, home instruction, and instruction in hospitals and institutions" [§ 1401(16)]. The term *handicapped children* is defined in the EHA as any children who are "mentally retarded, hard of hearing, deaf, speech impaired, visually handicapped, seriously emotionally disturbed, orthopedically impaired, or other health impaired children, or children with specific learning disabilities, who by reason thereof require special education and related services" [§ 1401(1)]. The public schools must provide all handicapped children with a *free appropriate public education*, which means "special education and related services which (A) have been provided at public expense, under public supervision and direction, and without charge, (B) meet the standards of the State educational agency, (C) include an appropriate preschool, elementary, or secondary school education in the State involved, and (D) are provided in conformity with the individualized education program required under section 1414(a)(5) of this title" [§ 1401(18)].

Related services are defined as "transportation, and such developmental, corrective, and other supportive services (including speech pathology and audiology, pyschological services, physical and occupational therapy, recreation, and medical and counseling services, except that such medical services shall be for diagnostic and evaluation purposes only) as may be required to assist a handicapped child to benefit from special education, and includes the early identification and assessment of handicapping conditions in children" [§ 1401(17)]. While medical services are excluded from the definition of related services, insofar as they may be needed by a child for diagnostic and evaluative purposes, medical services must also be provided free of charge.

Section 1401(17) states that psychological services are related services and thus are to be provided free of charge by school districts to handicapped students who require such services. While it is clear that not all services involving psychotherapy are related services, if the psychotherapy required by the child is of the type that could be provided by a social worker, school psychologist, nurse or counselor, it will be considered a related service. Where the required psychotherapy is of such a nature that it can only be competently administered by a licensed psychiatrist, then it will be considered a medical service and the school district will not be required to furnish it. Thus, a U.S. district court in New Jersey held that a school district was required to pay $25,200 for a child's stay at a day school which provided individualized psychotherapy, family therapy, group therapy, and individual and group counseling. The court held that the psychotherapy provided here was an integral part of the child's special education. See *T.G. v. Board of Education*, 576 F.Supp. 420 (D.N.J.1983). It is important to remember that under section 1401(17), even medical and psychiatric services must be provided free of charge if such services are required for evaluative or diagnostic purposes. See *Darlene L. v. Illinois State Bd. of Educ.*, 568 F.Supp. 1340 (N.D.Ill. 1983).

Section 1415 of the EHA contains mandatory procedures designed to safeguard the rights of handicapped students. The safeguards emphasize, among other things, notice to parents and an opportunity for parental participation in the development of a child's special education program. Most important, the various subsections under § 1415 require that parents be informed of all available procedures and methods by which any grievances or dissatisfaction may be resolved. Written notice must be given to parents if a school proposes to change or refuses to initiate a change in a child's educational program, or if the school refuses to perform an initial evaluation and placement of the child [§ 1415(b)(1)(C)].

In case of any dispute over their child's IEP, EHA § 1415 states that parents have the right to an impartial hearing before a hearing officer who is neither an employee of the school district nor of the state education department [§ 1415(b)(2)]. If either the parents or the school are unhappy with the hearing officer's decision, appeal may be taken to the state education department [§ 1415(c)]. During pendency of a dispute over any aspect of a special education program, the child must remain in his or her "then current" program [§ 1415(e)(3)]. The Supreme Court held that indefinite suspensions of handicapped students is a violation of this provision. See *Honig v. Doe*, 108 S.Ct. 592 (1988), in Chapter Two. A lawsuit may be commenced in either state or federal court after a decision has been reached by the state education department [§ 1415(e)(2)]. If the parents or guardians are successful in a special education lawsuit, the defendant will be liable for their attorney's fees. However, parents or guardians who are unsuccessful will not be required to pay the school district's (or state's) attorney's fees [§ 1415(e)(4)(B)]. Money damages, in addition to tuition reimbursement, may be awarded on behalf of a handicapped child [§ 1415(f)].

II. STATE AND LOCAL RESPONSIBILITIES TO HANDICAPPED CHILDREN: *BOARD OF EDUCATION v. ROWLEY.*

The U.S. Supreme Court case of *Board of Education v. Rowley* established the following standard for evaluating the appropriateness of a handicapped child's education: the child's program must be reasonably calculated to allow him or her to receive educational benefits. However, states may enact higher standards for educating handicapped students.

Parents of an eight-year-old child, deaf since birth, claimed the child was entitled to have a sign language interpreter in her classroom to enable her to have the same educational opportunity as her classmates. The district court held that the child was entitled to have a sign language interpreter in her classroom (483 F.Supp. 528). The case was appealed to the U.S. Court of Appeals, Second Circuit, which affirmed the district court (632 F.2d 945). The school board then made a final appeal to the U.S. Supreme Court, which reversed the two lower courts. The Supreme Court held that the EHA is satisfied when a school provides personalized instruction with sufficient support services to permit the handicapped child to *benefit educationally* from that instruction. The court went on to state that the IEP should be reasonably calculated to enable the child to achieve passing marks and to advance from grade to grade. The EHA does not require a school to provide a sign language interpreter as requested by a child's parents. The court stated that the EHA was not meant to guarantee a handicapped child a certain level of education but merely to open the door of education to handicapped children by means of special educational services. Under the EHA a school is not required to maximize the potential of each handicapped child, nor is it required to provide equal educational opportunity commensurate with the opportunity provided to nonhandicapped children. However, several states have education laws which surpass EHA standards. In such cases the state standard is incorporated into the EHA and such states are required to meet the standard in educating handicapped students. *Board of Education v. Rowley*, 458 U.S. 176 (1982).

Although schools are not required to provide equal educational opportunities to handicapped students, they are required to provide facilities that are substantially equal.

A class action was brought by handicapped Pennsylvania students seeking declaratory and injunctive relief under § 504 of the Rehabilitation Act and the EHA against the Secretary of Education of the Commonwealth of Pennsylvania. In Pennsylvania, handicapped students who needed special education programs which could not be provided by the district were referred to the intermediate unit (IU) serving that district. The IUs did not own or operate regular schools. Instead, IUs obtained classroom space from member school districts or from other sources. The Carbon-Lehigh Intermediate Unit (CLIU) served the students instituting this class action. The secretary of education had admitted that a number of problems existed with the CLIU program. The problems stemmed from inadequate classroom space for handicapped students enrolled in the program. Thus, the CLIU had to place students in facilities that were not comparable to those furnished to nonhandicapped students. It also had been required to shift handicapped students from one district to another and from one school to another, had placed students in facilities that were excessively restrictive and separate from the facilities for nonhandicapped students, and was unable to open new classes needed by handicapped students assigned to it. The students sued the secretary of education in a federal district court seeking summary judgment.

The court stated that the EHA and § 504 of the Rehabilitation Act both prohibit funding recipients from providing objectively inferior facilities and services to handicapped individuals. Although the acts do not require that the classroom space afforded CLIU students be precisely equivalent to that of nonhandicapped students, the CLIU classrooms were unequal to those furnished nonhandicapped students in several important areas including size, sanitation, ventilation, noise level and furnishings. The court held that the secretary had violated the students' statutory rights by failing to ensure that their educational facilities were comparable to those of nonhandicapped students. It further held that interschool or interdistrict CLIU classroom relocations, resulting from the failure of the school district to provide adequate space for CLIU classes, constituted a violation of the secretary's duty to assure that handicapped students were educated to the maximum extent appropriate in a regular educational environment. In addition, the court pointed out that the failure to open classes necessary for the appropriate special education of class members violated the state's duty under the EHA and § 504 to ensure that handicapped students received a free appropriate education. The court granted the class members' motion for summary judgment and ordered the secretary to submit a plan as a remedial order to ensure that the violations were remedied. *Hendricks v. Gilhool*, 709 F.Supp. 1362 (E.D.Pa.1989).

A New York student's teacher noticed that he was experiencing problems with handwriting, organization, and following instructions. She recommended that he be referred to the child study team in an attempt to ascertain if he had any learning problems. The team determined that the child was not learning disabled but did suffer from some remedial problems which might be addressed with modifications in his current classroom programs. After receiving a letter from the parent's lawyers, the child study team agreed to label the child as handicapped to avoid litigation and instituted an IEP. The mother rejected the IEP and requested an administrative hearing. The hearing officer found that the child was not handicapped and the student was not entitled to receive special education services. The parents then instituted this action in a federal district court.

The court determined that a child who exhibited weak attention span and handwriting difficulties was not handicapped within the meaning of the EHA. Furthermore, the program instituted by the school was reasonably calculated to enable the child to receive educational benefit and thus complied with the EHA. Therefore, the court found for the school district. *Hiller v. Bd. of Educ. of Brunswick Central School Dist.*, 743 F.Supp. 958 (N.D. N.Y.1990).

In 1978, the state of New York agreed to pay the tuition costs of a schizophrenic boy who had been placed in a residential psychiatric hospital which operated an accredited academic high school. Behavioral problems prevented the boy from attending the high school, but he continued to reside at the hospital. His doctors hoped that the behavior problems could be overcome. The boy's parents, after petitioning state officials in vain, sought to compel the state to pay the cost of the boy's residential care at the hospital from the time of his placement, July, 1978, through June, 1983.

The state contended before a U.S. district court that as long as the child's behavioral problems prevented him from attending the high school at the institution, he was in effect uneducable and therefore the state had no responsibility for any of his expenses. The court ruled that once the state placed the boy at the psychiatric hospital, it became obligated to pay the entire expense of the placement. The state could not escape its responsibility for costs of the boy's residential care simply by stating that those costs did not directly address educational problems. As long as the boy could be educated (however little) through a residential placement, the state remained responsible for the cost of that placement. *Vander Malle v. Ambach*, 667 F.Supp. 1015 (S.D. N.Y.1987).

An Indiana case demonstrates the proposition that although state education departments are the primary parties responsible for special educational services, states may require local school districts to assume responsibility for such services and related expenses. Here, the parents of a mentally retarded boy sued their school board and the State Board of Education seeking reimbursement for the tuition and transportation costs involved in their son's placement in a private residential facility in Kansas. The boy was first identified in 1975 as being in need of special educational services, and in 1976 the school board concurred with the parents' decision to place the child in the Kansas facility. Pursuant to Indiana law the school board sought and was granted State Board approval for such placement. The school board therefore made transfer tuition payments to cover the cost of the boy's special education. State Board approval was similarly granted for the 1976-77 school year.

However, for the 1977-78 year the school board neglected to forward an application to the State Board but nevertheless assumed that it concurred in the school board's decision to continue the boy's placement at the Kansas school. When the school board forwarded its application for approval for the 1978-79 school year, the State Board rejected it and furthermore refused to meet with the parents' attorney to discuss its decision. The child's parents then sued the school board and the State Board contending that under state law they were entitled to tuition and transportation expenses. An Indiana trial court ruled that the school district was liable for the boy's transportation costs and that the State Board was liable for transfer tuition fees. On appeal, the Court of Appeals of Indiana reversed the trial court and held that under Indiana law the local school board is primarily liable for all special education expenses. The case was remanded to the trial court to determine whether the State Board was obligated to reimburse the school board for the excess transfer tuition. *Weesner v. Baker*, 477 N.E.2d 337 (Ind.App.2d Dist.1985).

Three school districts in Pennsylvania brought suit against the state's Department of Education challenging a change in the special education plan of an "intermediate unit" which had been educating handicapped children. The unit proposed to suspend operation of classes for the educable mentally retarded (EMR). The unit's decision placed responsibility for operation of all

EMR classes on each individual school district, with the unit providing support services and supervision for the classes. The adopted changes affected four school districts, one of which acceded to the plan changes. The remaining three districts argued in the Commonwealth Court of Pennsylvania that the unit had an obligation to continue to operate EMR classes in their districts unless each district consented to the cessation of the classes.

The court disagreed stating "that the primary responsibility for identifying all exceptional children and developing appropriate educational programs to meet their needs is placed on the local school districts." Because the unit was not bound to continue EMR classes absent a showing that the districts could not "efficiently and effectively" provide appropriate educational programs for EMR children in the districts, the proposed changes were upheld. *Bermudian Springs School Dist. v. Dep't of Educ.*, 475 A.2d 943 (Pa.Cmwlth. 1984).

The Human Rights Authority of the State of Illinois Guardianship and Advocacy Commission appealed an order of an Illinois district court denying the enforcement of a subpoena issued by the Commission. Acting on a complaint which alleged that a local school district was not providing occupational and physical therapy for its students, the Commission started an investigation and asked the district superintendent to produce the students' educational program records. The records were to be masked so as to delete any information by which students could be identified. When the school district failed to turn over the information, the Commission issued a subpoena for the masked records. Again, the school district refused to comply. The Commission then sought judicial enforcement of the subpoena.

A trial court ruled that the Commission had no right to examine the records because it did not satisfy the access requirements of Illinois state law regarding student records. On appeal to the Appellate Court of Illinois, the school district argued that the Commission was somehow usurping the role of the State Board of Education by investigating the special education program of the school district. According to the school district, the Commission's inquiry was "tantamount to the control and direction of special education which makes local school authorities accountable to the [Commission] rather than the State Board of Education as required by the School Code."

The Appellate Court disagreed. The statutory authority of the Commission to investigate complaints concerning violations of the rights of handicapped persons, including the right to special education programs, was not subordinate to that of the State Board of Education. Further, the Commission's investigation of the school district's overall special education program and not merely individual students was within the bounds of the Commission's statutory authority. *Human Rights Authority v. Miller*, 464 N.E.2d 833 (Ill.App.3d Dist.1984).

In order for a handicapped child to receive educational services from a school district he/she must be a resident of that school district.

A New York child with Down's Syndrome resided at a home certified by the State Department of Social Services to provide care. The child had resided at the home since he was two weeks old. His parents resided in a different county whose school district reimbursed the school district where the child attended school. The parents moved to another state and their former school district ceased tuition payments. The child's school district then informed the parents that tuition would have to be paid if the child was to continue attending school. The parents appealed to the commissioner of education who concluded that the school district where the child lived was not the "actual and only residence" and therefore he was not a resident of that school district. The parents sued the commissioner in a federal district court challenging the constitutionality of the residency requirement. After the district court found for the commissioner, the parents appealed to the U.S. Court of Appeals, Second Circuit. The U.S. Court of Appeals, Second Circuit, determined that the meaning of actual and only residence was a matter of state law. The parents then instituted this action in a New York trial court asking that the child be declared a resident. The trial court granted summary judgment to the parents, concluding that because the child had spent his entire life in the residence home, this satisfied a simple reading of the "actual only residence" clause. The commissioner appealed to the Supreme Court, Appellate Division.

The court noted that the child's residence was presumed to be the same as the parents and could be rebutted by showing that the child had lived at a residence home for virtually all his life and had never visited the parent's home. The court affirmed the trial court's decision and determined that the child was a resident of the school district where the resident home was located and was thus entitled to a free education in that district. *Catlin by Catlin v. Sobol*, 553 N.Y.S.2d 501 (A.D.3d Dep't 1990).

A child born in Yuma, Arizona, to Mexican parents was significantly hearing impaired. Her parents resided in Puerto Penasco, Mexico, where the child was raised until 1984, when she was sent to live with long-time family friends in Ajo, Arizona. The friends attempted to enroll her in Ajo public schools but were advised by school personnel that they did not have a suitable program for the student. The school recommended the Arizona State School for the Deaf and Blind (ASDB). The ASDB informed them that a guardianship would be necessary so that a responsible person living in the United States could make decisions for the child's welfare. The friends obtained the guardianship and the child was admitted to the ASDB. After obtaining guardianship of the child, the friends received no financial support from her natural parents. The guardians maintained health and dental insurance. Following an action by the attorney general's office, ASDB officials ordered the removal of six children from the school because they were allegedly not U.S. citizens. As a result of legal action initiated by their guardians, however, the removal was stopped due to the violation of their due process rights under the EHA. At an administrative hearing, the hearing officer determined that the child was entitled to the benefits of U.S. citizenship as a minor child of non-citizens. An appeals hearing officer determined that the child's residence was that of her parents. The guardians appealed to a federal district court.

On appeal, the ASDB contended that the guardianship was invalid because it was a sham and obtained only in order to evade tuition. The court, however, found that the guardianship was validly granted after a full hearing and full disclosure of the child's Mexican parentage. To qualify for federal assistance a state must submit a detailed plan which demonstrates a policy assuring all handicapped children the right to a free appropriate public education. The state is obligated to identify, locate and evaluate all children residing in the state who are handicapped. If states are to accept funding under the act, then they have an obligation to educate the handicapped children within their borders. The only way that the child can claim the benefits of her U.S. citizenship before reaching adulthood is if a guardianship is established for her. The court found that the guardians had demonstrated that the child had been an Arizona resident entitled to free education services since she came to live there. *Sonja C. by and through Olivas v. ASDB*, 743 F.Supp. 700 (D.Ariz. 1990).

III. DUTY TO PROVIDE A FREE APPROPRIATE EDUCATION

The EHA does not define free appropriate education, and in practice, parents and schools do not always agree on what is appropriate to the education of a particular handicapped child. The *Rowley* case, above, provides the standard to which courts are to look in determining whether an education is appropriate.

The parents of a seven-year-old deaf Illinois student disagreed with the IEP proposed by their school district. The district proposed placement in its self-contained classroom for hearing-impaired students for at least half the school day. The parents wanted education in a regular classroom near their home with the assistance of a full-time speech instructor. The proposed IEP called for integration into regular classrooms where possible. The parents requested and received due process hearings at local and state levels at which hearing officers affirmed the placement. The parents then filed a lawsuit in a federal district court, alleging that the district failed to provide their son with a free appropriate public education under the EHA. The court applied the U.S. Supreme Court test for a school district's obligation to provide handicapped students with a free appropriate education under *Board of Education v. Rowley*, 458 U.S. 176 (1982). The *Rowley* test determined whether the state complied with procedures under the EHA, and whether the IEP was reasonably calculated to enable a child to receive educational benefits. Finding that the school district had satisfied these requirements, the court dismissed the complaint. The parents then appealed to the U.S. Court of Appeals, Seventh Circuit.

The appeals court noted that the district court had properly applied the *Rowley* test. The EHA preference for mainstreaming must be balanced against the possibility that some students could be better educated in segregated facilities. The EHA granted school districts the primary responsibility for formulating IEPs. Although parents have an important role to play in proposed IEPs, this dispute was primarily over the appropriate methodology, which was within the school district's primary discretion. The appeals court affirmed the district court's dismissal of the lawsuit. *Lachman v. Illinois Bd. of Educ.*, 852 F.2d 290 (7th Cir.1988).

A handicapped Alabama student was manic-depressive. The illness caused the student substantial academic difficulty. His district provided the student with a three hour per week home tutoring program until he began attending special education and regular academic classes at a junior high school. The student again began to experience emotional disturbances and he was suspended at the end of the school year. The next year, after attending only one day of classes, the student refused to return to the high school. His parents then unilaterally decided to enroll him in a residential school. The student attended this residential school for two weeks and again refused to return to school there. Later that year, the parents and the school district developed an IEP which called for the student to attend classes five days a week for three hours a day and to receive counseling services to bolster his self-esteem. The student was unable to complete that school year. The following year the school proposed a schedule which called for several revisions during the year so that the student would gradually be required to spend more time in school until by the end of the year he would spend a full day.

The parents rejected the proposed IEP and obtained an independent evaluation by a clinical psychologist. The psychologist recommended residential school placement for the student. The parents then unilaterally placed the student at a private residential school in Georgia. The student did relatively well at the school, but was expelled in April for sharing his medication with a fellow student. After the student returned to the school district, the school officials and the parents met to discuss a new IEP for the student. However, an IEP was not agreed upon and the student did not begin school in the fall. At another IEP meeting in December, the school was to provide someone to coordinate the student's program of education. The parents sought and received a due process hearing to challenge the IEP proposed by the school. The hearing officer determined that the IEP was reasonably calculated to provide the student with a free appropriate education. The parents filed suit in a federal district court. After the district court upheld the hearing officer's determination, the parents appealed to the U.S. Court of Appeals, Eleventh Circuit.

The parents contended that the school district violated the student's substantive right to a free appropriate public education. In particular, they alleged that the only appropriate education for the student was in a residential setting. The court noted that the state must provide a child with a basic floor of opportunity, consisting of access to specialized instruction and related services. The court determined that the proposed schedule for the school year met the student's psychological needs; it provided for the student's school day to begin with a counseling session. Further, the court noted that the residential facility where the student spent part of his school year was an inappropriate placement for him because it did not provide the facilities necessary to deal with the student's psychological and emotional needs. The nearest residential school that even approached the full benefits sought by the parents was in Texas and experts testified that sending the student so far from his home would be counterproductive to his development. Therefore, the court affirmed the trial court's decision and determined that the IEP provided the student with a free appropriate education. *Doe v. Alabama State Dep't of Educ.*, 915 F.2d 651 (11th Cir.1990).

A five-year-old District of Columbia multiply-handicapped student was eligible for special education services under the EHA. Her parents requested private special education from the District of Columbia Public Schools (DCPS). They unilaterally placed her in a private daycare center. Each week the student received speech and occupational therapy from an outside source. The DCPS completed an IEP for the student, identifying her as multiply-disabled with motor and speech communication problems. The DCPS placed the student in a public school program for handicapped children. The student's parents challenged the public school placement and requested two due process hearings under the EHA. The hearing officer refused to award tuition expenses to the parents, and later determined that the school district's placement was appropriate. The hearing officer also stated that the student's placement at her private daycare program was inappropriate and did not provide the services described in her IEP. The hearing officer held that the DCPS should pay for the student's outside occupational and speech therapy because they were appropriate and because the DCPS had failed to timely place the student.

The parents appealed the decision to the U.S. District Court, District of Columbia, claiming that the DCPS placement was inappropriate. The district court ruled in the parents' favor because the DCPS program was inadequate and the district was completely incapable of providing occupational therapy. The district lacked adequate funding and had a lengthy waiting list for occupational therapy. The court approved the educational alternative proposed by the parents, which was a private special education school in Maryland specializing in educating children with severe sensory integration deficiencies and occupational therapy. *Kattan by Thomas v. Dist. of Columbia*, 691 F.Supp. 1539 (D.D.C.1988).

Parents of handicapped children who lived in a New York Jewish community requested that their local school district furnish special education services at their private schools. The parents and children adhered to the practices of Hasidism which generally requires that males and females be separated. The male and female Hasidic students attended separate private schools. Initially the district provided special education services at the individual schools. It later determined that it would only furnish special education services at the public schools. The parents refused to allow their children to attend public school to receive special education services. They sought administrative review of the school district decision.

A New York trial court ordered the district to provide services to the Hasidic children in a "mobile or other appropriate site not physically or educationally identified with but reasonably accessible to the [Hasidic] children." The school district appealed this decision to a New York appellate court which overturned the trial court decision because it had the primary effect of advancing religion. After the appellate court determined that the school district only need provide handicapped services at the public schools, the parents appealed to the New York Court of Appeals.

The New York high court determined that a school district must offer the same services to nonpublic school students as it does to public school students. It noted that the Education for All Handicapped Children Act declared that each handicapped child is to have a free appropriate public education. Congress had recognized that not all services could be furnished in regular public school classes. In effect, the high court held that the district was not required to provide services at the private school or at a neutral site. It simply had to make the services available to all students residing within district boundaries. It modified the appellate court decision that the district was not allowed to provide services outside of the public school. *Bd. of Educ. v. Wieder*, 527 N.E.2d 767 (N.Y.1988).

A Maryland case illustrates that when a local school district fails to implement a hearing officer's decision, its inaction may result in a failure to provide an appropriate education. In October, 1984, a hearing officer found four procedural violations of the EHA by the Baltimore City Schools relating to an eighteen-year-old handicapped student. The hearing officer found that the student was a seriously emotionally disturbed adolescent who required a residential placement and ordered the Baltimore City Schools to permanently place the student in a residential setting by November 20, 1984. On December 5, 1984, the student and his mother sued the city in a U.S. district court because the student had not received any change in his educational program. The district court dismissed the student's claims and he appealed to the U.S. Court of Appeals, Fourth Circuit.

The student claimed that he was denied a free appropriate public education when the city school system failed to implement the decision by the hearing officer in a timely manner. The district court had dismissed the complaint, holding that the student failed to exhaust his administrative remedies under the EHA. The court of appeals disagreed, noting that the student had received a final administrative decision under the EHA and that the student had neither the responsibility nor the right to appeal the favorable decision by the local hearing officer since he was not an aggrieved party.

The court of appeals also concluded that since the EHA did not contain any provision for enforcing final administrative orders by a hearing officer, the student was entitled to a claim under § 1983 of the Civil Rights Act. When the Baltimore City Schools refused to enforce the hearing officer's decision to put the student in a residential placement the Baltimore City Schools had, under color of state law, violated the EHA. The district court was therefore wrong in dismissing the student's § 1983 claim. The student's § 1983 claim was remanded to the district court for further proceedings. *Robinson v. Pinderhughes*, 810 F.2d 1270 (4th Cir.1987).

A nine-year-old Florida boy who lived with his parents suffered from juvenile autism. For three years the boy was enrolled in the Hendry County School Class for the Trainable Mentally Handicapped. Because the boy had made limited progress toward the educational goals set for him during the three-year period, both the school and the boy's parents agreed that the boy needed a different individualized educational plan (IEP) for the 1985-86 school year. Subsequently the boy was labeled severely emotionally disturbed (SED) and found to be in need of a program for the severely handicapped. In May, 1985, the school held a planning conference to develop a new IEP for the boy. As a result of the conference, which was attended by the boy's mother and her attorney, the school's director of exceptional student education approved a new IEP for the boy.

When the new IEP was issued the parents rejected it. They contended that the boy needed residential placement if he was to reach necessary educational goals. In June, 1985, the parents asked for a due process hearing to determine the appropriateness of the IEP. In July, 1985, the hearing officer issued his order, rejecting the school's proposal and ordering residential placement for the boy. The school appealed the hearing officer's decision to the Florida District Court of appeal.

The issue before the court was whether the IEP provided the boy with an appropriate education even though residential placement was not part of the plan. The court observed that for Florida to receive federal assistance under the EHA it must demonstrate that it had a policy in effect that guaranteed all handicapped children the right to a "free appropriate education." It also observed that the IEP is to be developed at a meeting between a qualified representative of the local educational agency, the child's teacher and his parents or guardian. Noting that the proper procedure was followed in this case, the court ruled that the school did not have to provide services designed to maximize each child's potential. A residential placement was not necessary for the boy to benefit from his instruction. Additionally, the court concluded that a hearing officer is limited to determining the appropriateness of an IEP. The hearing officer's decision was reversed and the case was remanded for further proceedings. *Hendry County School Bd. v. Kujawski*, 498 So.2d 566 (Fla. App.2d Dist.1986).

The parents of an Oklahoma youth brought suit in U.S. district court after their local school district refused to fund their son's placement at a residential facility. The youth, who was classified as "educable mentally handicapped," had been enrolled at the age of eighteen in his local school district's EMH program. An IEP was developed at this time with the approval of his parents. Although his educational program included both high school instruction and vocational instruction, he was soon expelled from the vo-tech program due to his emotional outbursts. When these outbursts continued at the high school, school officials notified his parents that an alternative to classroom placement was necessary. Homebound instruction was suggested, but the parents rejected the proposal.

For the next several months the parents considered residential placement; during this period the youth received no educational services. His parents also failed to bring him to school for testing to aid in the formulation of a new IEP, as requested by school officials. At the beginning of the next school year they appeared once again at the high school to enroll their son, and school officials, who had not expected the youth to enroll, requested a week to formulate an IEP. Several days later school officials attempted to arrange a meeting with the parents to discuss a new IEP for the youth, but the parents refused because a new teacher had not yet been hired to instruct him. This impasse caused the parents to unilaterally enroll their son in the out-of-state residential facility. A due process hearing resulted in approval of the school district's decision not to reimburse the parents for the cost of his placement, and the parents sought judicial review. The U.S. Court of Appeals, 1st Circuit, upheld the denial of tuition reimbursement and found that the district had taken all steps necessary to provide the child with a free appropriate public education. *Cain v. Yukon Pub. Schools, Dist. I-27*, 775 F.2d 15 (10th Cir.1985).

The parents of a child in Virginia who suffered severe head trauma when she was injured in an automobile accident and who became mentally impaired as a result, alleged that the child was denied a free appropriate public education. The parents contended that their local school district's refusal to implement an educational program proposed by the parents and its decision to implement its own program in the public school system was in violation of the EHA. The parents brought suit in a U.S. district court, which found the parents' plan to be unreasonable and the school's plan appropriate, saying:

"The State is not required to pay all of the expenses incurred by parents in educating a child, whether the child be handicapped or non-handicapped. The State is also not required to provide a perfect education to any child . . . Rather, the Court must ascertain in the light of educational theories over which experts often disagree if the education provided plaintiff was, under the law, 'appropriate.' " The court relied on the standard for an appropriate education enunciated in *Board of Education v. Rowley,* which held that an "appropriate" education is not necessarily one that enables a child to achieve his or her full potential. The court concluded that "An appropriate education is not synonymous with the best possible education. [P]arents [do not] have the right under the law to write a prescription for an ideal education for their child and to have the prescription filled at public expense." *Bales v. Clarke*, 523 F.Supp. 1366 (E.D.Va.1981).

The following cases demonstrate that states may establish higher standards for special educations than the EHA's "appropriate" standard. In the first, a handicapped student received special education through a California school district. Her parents were not satisfied with the child's individual education plan (IEP) and requested a due process hearing. The California hearing officer set forth the standard for review set out under the Education of the Handicapped Act (EHA). The parents, however, appealed the decision to a federal district court, moving for a higher standard.

To provide an appropriate education the school need only comply with the EHA. The school district must develop an IEP reasonably calculated to enable the child to receive educational benefits. Some states, however, have enacted a higher standard for the education of the handicapped. California Code of Regulations § 3001(b) requires education programs for the handicapped to "provide the equal opportunity for each individual with exceptional needs to achieve his or her full potential." California's standard for the education of the handicapped is higher than that required under the EHA. The court adhered to the higher standard for handicapped education because the EHA sets out the minimum required under federal law but leaves the states at liberty to require a higher standard. The district court then remanded the case to the Department of Education for a new hearing. *Pink by Crinder v. Mt. Diablo Unif. School Dist.*, 738 F.Supp. 345 (N.D.Cal.1990).

In the second case, the parents of a seventeen-year-old child with Down's syndrome became dissatisfied with their child's IEP because they felt it did not adequately address his sexual misbehavior. They believed that the child required a twenty-four-hour residential program. A U.S. district court found that the child was entitled to twenty-four-hour residential school placement to attempt to correct his sexual misbehavior. The court noted that under Massachusetts law a special educational program must "assure the maximum possible development of a child with special needs." Accordingly, the child was entitled to the more comprehensive behavior therapy available in a residential program, especially in light of the degree of his sexual maladjustment. On appeal by the school district, the U.S. Court of Appeals, First Circuit, upheld the district court's decision. The appellate court held that where state law sets a minimum educational standard for handicapped children, those standards are incorporated by reference into the federal EHA. The U.S. Supreme Court declined to review the decision. *David D. v. Dartmouth School Comm.*, 775 F.2d 411 (1st Cir.1985). *Cert. denied*, 106 S.Ct. 1790(1986).

A U.S. district court in Illinois found that handicapped children in Illinois were not receiving an appropriate education by reason of delays of the Illinois Superintendent of Education in resolving placement appeals. The case arose after a severely emotionally disturbed twelve-year-old child was recommended for placement by his school district in a self-contained classroom for behavior disordered students. His mother objected to the recommendation and said that she had been advised by experts that a highly structured residential program would be an appropriate placement for the child. The mother appealed the decision but after five months the superintendent had made no decision. The mother claimed that the superintendent was obligated to decide within thirty days. She alleged that the long delay and inappropriate educational setting had caused the deterioration of the child's condition to the extent that the child had to be placed in a mental hospital.

The mother then brought suit against the superintendent on behalf of her child and all handicapped school children in Illinois. The superintendent sought to dismiss the suit on the basis that the EHA creates no substantive rights for handicapped children. The U.S. district court disagreed saying that the EHA is the source of a federal statutory right to a free appropriate education in every state electing to receive financial assistance, and that is more than merely a "funding statute." The passage of time, said the court, caused the deprivation of a child's substantive right to an appropriate education. *John A. by and through Valerie A. v. Gill*, 565 F.Supp. 372 (N.D.Ill.1983).

IV. INDIVIDUALIZED EDUCATIONAL PROGRAMS

An individualized education program (IEP) is a statement of a handicapped child's present education level, future educational goals for the child, future educational services to be provided, and the extent to which he or she will be able to participate in regular educational programs [§ 1401(19)]. At the heart of the EHA's "individualized educational program" provision is the idea that each handicapped child's particular needs are unique and thus require an educational program specifically tailored to a child's particular handicap. Courts have viewed the failure to provide a program specifically designed to meet the unique needs of a child as a failure to provide a free appropriate education.

A fourteen-year-old Virginia public school student suffered from a severe learning disability in reading. The school developed an individualized education plan (IEP) for the student which provided for public school placement. The student's parents refused to keep him in a public school and enrolled him in a private residential school. The parents requested a due process hearing demanding that the public school pay for the student's private residential schooling. The hearing officer found that the proposed IEP did not provide the student a free appropriate education. The school board appealed the hearing officer's decision to a reviewing officer. The reviewing officer affirmed the hearing officer's decision. The school board then brought an action in a Virginia trial court challenging the reviewing officer's decision. The trial court reviewed the evidence presented to the hearing officer and found the public school the most appropriate placement for the student. Residential placement was not necessary. The trial court reversed the hearing officer's decision and the student appealed to the Court of Appeals. The court of appeals reversed the trial court's decision and the school board appealed to the Supreme Court of Virginia.

The supreme court held that the appellate court erred when it redetermined facts and then reversed the trial court's decision. The trial court's decision was not plainly wrong or without evidence. It had found that the evidence led to the inescapable conclusion that the IEP was reasonably calculated and designed to provide the student educational benefits. It offered the student a program appropriate to his needs. He had received benefits from the program and would continue to benefit in the future. The supreme court reversed the court of appeals' decision and found that the school board had offered the student a free appropriate public education. *School Bd. of Campbell County v. Beasley*, 380 S.W.2d 884 (Va.1989).

A Pennsylvania student participated in a school district's gifted program from the time he began school. When the student was in sixth grade, a hearing officer included a math program in his IEP. By the time the student was in eighth grade he had completed all appropriate math courses offered by the school district. The student's parents then arranged for his transportation and paid tuition for his college-level math classes. The district accommodated the student's high school class schedule so he could attend the college courses. When the student entered twelfth grade, the school district's IEP excluded math. The student and his parents then requested a due process hearing to determine whether college level math courses should be included in his high school grade point average and whether his IEP should include math courses. A special education hearing officer ordered the district to develop an IEP to include the college courses. He also recommended that the student's college grades be incorporated into his high school grade point average. The school district challenged the hearing officer's recommendation to include the student's college coursework in his high school grade point average. The district later amended its petition, challenging the inclusion of college courses in the student's IEP.

The Pennsylvania education secretary agreed with the school district's petition to disallow inclusion of college course grades in the high school grade point average, as grading policy was a matter of local school district discretion. However, the secretary agreed with the hearing officer's other findings, and the district filed a petition for review in the Pennsylvania Commonwealth Court. On appeal, the district argued that the hearing officer's recommendation to include college math courses in the student's IEP was unsupported. The student filed a motion to strike the district's petition because it had failed to timely file an exception with the education secretary. The court agreed with the student, ruling that a new theory of recovery cannot be advanced on appeal. It quashed the school district's appeal, resulting in inclusion of the college courses in the student's IEP. *Gateway School Dist. v. Dep't of Educ.*, 559 A.2d 118 (Pa.Cmwlth.1989).

A learning disabled Ohio student who suffered from dyslexia attended public schools until sixth grade. The student was handicapped according to the EHA definition. The IEP developed for the student's fifth grade education was never used and the school failed to comply with EHA requirements. The student's parents unilaterally removed him to a private school without requesting a due process hearing or complying with school district requests to discuss an IEP for seventh grade. The student returned to the public school for ninth grade, during which the parents requested a due process hearing to determine whether the school district was complying with the EHA and state law. They also requested reimbursement for private school tuition for seventh and eighth grades. An independent hearing officer ruled that the student had received a free appropriate public education during the sixth and ninth grades and that the school district had developed an appropriate IEP for tenth grade. The parents were not entitled to reimbursement for private school tuition. A state level review officer upheld the independent hearing officer's decision and the parents appealed to the U.S. District Court for the Southern District of Ohio.

The court applied the two-step inquiry developed by the U.S. Supreme Court in *Board of Education v. Rowley*, 458 U.S. 176 (1982), and ruled that the school district had provided the student a free appropriate education in the sixth grade, despite its lack of complete compliance with the EHA. The student had advanced academically and the district had followed the significant provisions of the IEP. The parents had failed to request a due process hearing before the student's entry into seventh grade and had also failed to comply with requests by school officials to discuss the seventh grade IEP. The court denied reimbursement for private school tuition during the seventh and eighth grades.

The court noted that there had been delays in formulating the tenth grade IEP, but that EHA procedural requirements had been essentially satisfied. Because experts who testified at the due process hearing had agreed that the student should be placed in regular classrooms and that mainstreaming would not have presented a great burden for the district, the court ruled that the IEP for the tenth grade was insufficient. Because the district had failed to provide the student a free appropriate education, and because the IEP was not presented to the parents until immediately before the student's tenth grade school year, the unilateral placement of the student in the private school was the only remaining alternative for obtaining an appropriate education. Because the student was now in twelfth grade, it was not feasible to develop an appropriate IEP for the remainder of the student's high school career, and the student could remain at the private school with tuition reimbursement for the eleventh and twelfth grades. *Gillette v. Fairland Bd. of Educ.*, 725 F.Supp. 343 (S.D.Ohio 1989).

In a second case involving a dyslexic student, a California student attended public school through the fifth grade and was eligible for its special education services. He received speech and articulation therapy in first and second grade and performed in the average range. When his poor reading and writing progress became evident in the third grade, the school developed an IEP for him including one hour per day of special education services. The student continued to study in the special education class for one period per day in fourth and fifth grades. He showed steady progress in reading, spelling and math. As the school's IEP team prepared a transition program for the student to advance to middle school, the team found that the student was functioning a full grade above his grade level in reading comprehension. The mother notified the school that she had enrolled her son in a private school for summer session. Because the parents were pleased with the student's progress at the private school, they reenrolled their son at the private school for the following school year. The parents then unsuccessfully approached the school district about funding the private school placement. They rejected the school district's offer to provide the student with two periods of public school special education. The parents then requested a hearing at which the hearing officer decided that they were not entitled to reimbursement for the private school tuition.

The hearing officer held that the student's appropriate placement was in the public school's special education class. The student's parents appealed the decision to a federal district court, alleging that the student had been denied a free appropriate public education and that the public school placement was inadequate. They also sought reimbursement for private school tuition. The school district brought a motion for summary judgment, stating that the hearing officer's decision was correct. The court determined that the state had complied with procedures set forth in the EHA and that the IEP was reasonably calculated to benefit the student. The public school special education placement class was appropriate, as was the mainstreaming from which the student would benefit during the remainder of the school day. The hearing officer's determination that the student was functioning a full year above his grade level was correct. A free appropriate public education did not mean that school districts need to find the best or potentially most maximizing education for a student or to select the placement preferred by the family. The court granted the school district's motion for summary judgment, and denied the parents' motion for a rehearing. *Bertolucci v. San Carlos Elem. School Dist.*, 721 F.Supp. 1150 (N.D.Cal.1989).

A U.S. Court of Appeals held that an IEP must be developed prior to placement. A severely retarded nineteen-year-old student possessing the functional skills of an eighteen-month-old child was placed at a Pennsylvania residential facility. The county public school paid the full cost of the student's education at the residential facility, where his individualized education program (IEP) concentrated on basic skills. The student went to school throughout the year and received after school training and care. County officials began focusing on a new placement for the student at a local public school. At the public school he would attend class five and a half hours per day during a nine month school year and four hours daily during a six week summer session. After a series of letters and meetings between school officials and the student's parents, a new IEP was drawn up for the student to attend the public school.

The student's parents appealed the placement decision to the local hearing officer. The hearing officer found that there were no procedural violations of the EHA and that the new IEP was appropriate, but that the student required placement at the residential facility. The state reviewing officer affirmed the procedural compliance, but found that the student should be placed in the public school. The student's parents appealed this decision to a federal district court. The district court found that the school system had complied procedurally but had the burden of proof to show that the student would receive educational benefits at the public school. The court ordered the continuation of the residential placement. The student's parents appealed the finding of procedural compliance and the school appealed the decision regarding placement. On appeal, the U.S. Court of Appeals, Fourth Circuit, upheld the district court's order to have the student remain in his placement at the residential facility. Under the EHA regulation, placement should be based on the IEP. Placing the student at the public school before developing an IEP violated the EHA, which emphasized parental involvement. Involvement after the fact was not sufficient. The county failed to provide the student the free appropriate public education to which he was entitled. The district court's order requiring the student to remain at the residential facility was affirmed. *Spielberg v. Henrico County Pub. School*, 853 F.2d 256 (4th Cir.1988).

A severely retarded teenage student had the capacity of a two-year-old for most functions. His parents placed him in a private dayschool for the handicapped, and arranged residence at a group home at their own expense. The family moved and sought special education placement for their son through their new public school district. The district formulated an IEP as required by the EHA. The IEP proposed placement in a day program at a public special education facility. The parents objected, claiming that the student's only possible appropriate placement was education at the private school and residence at the group home.

The district held a hearing under the EHA and found that the proposed placement at the public special school was inadequate. However, the hearing officer also rejected the parents' alternative proposal. The hearing officer then approved the district's proposal to add additional services to its proposed public school placement. The parents appealed to a federal district court, which ruled that the district's proposed IEP was inadequate. It ordered the district to reimburse the parents for private school expenses. The district appealed to the U.S. Court of Appeals, District of Columbia Circuit. The appeals court ruled that the district court had used an impermissible standard under the U.S. Supreme Court's decision in *Bd. of Educ. v. Rowley*, 458 U.S. 176.

The *Rowley* decision held that states were required only to provide a basic floor of opportunity, reasonably calculated to enable students to receive educational benefits. It rejected the argument that special education must maximize the handicapped student's potential. It also ruled that reviewing courts must give due weight to hearing officer determinations. According to the appeals court, the district court below had failed to properly apply *Rowley*. The lower court had not given due deference to the hearing officer's decision and had inappropriately overturned the hearing officer's determination. The appeals court reversed and remanded the case to the district court to determine whether the district's IEP was appropriate. *Kerkam v. McKenzie*, 862 F.2d 884 (D.C.Cir.1988).

A Pennsylvania school district devised an individualized education program (IEP) for an exceptional student. It recommended that the district include the student in its "enrichment" program. The enrichment program added certain materials to the regular curriculum but did not attempt to provide accelerated instruction. The student's parents requested a due process hearing in which they asserted that the enrichment program was insufficient.

The hearing officer concluded that the student should be given specialized instruction in addition to the enrichment program. Both the state secretary of education and the Pennsylvania Commonwealth Court affirmed the hearing officer's decision. The school district appealed to the Pennsylvania Supreme Court.

The issue before the supreme court was whether the secretary and the commonwealth court had exceeded the provisions of the Pennsylvania Public School Code in requiring the school district to provide the student with an IEP beyond the enrichment program. The code required that schools provide gifted students with plans for individualized instruction designed to meet the "unique needs of the child." The school district argued that this subjective standard would lead to its bankruptcy. It argued that providing a program for exceptional children which addressed their needs to some degree was sufficient. The supreme court affirmed the lower court and administrative decisions. Public school code regulations promulgated by the state education board required individualized planning and education for exceptional children. School districts were required to prepare an IEP for each exceptional child. However, districts were not required to provide individual tutors for exclusive individual programs outside the school district's existing special education curriculum. The student was entitled to specialized instruction beyond the enrichment program. *Centennial School Dist. v. Commonwealth Dep't of Educ.*, 539 A.2d 785 (Pa.1988).

Pursuant to his IEP a ten-year-old autistic boy attended the Cooperative Behavior Center, a facility operated by the Garland, Texas, Independent School District (GISD). He attended school during regular school hours and spent the remainder of his time at home. Dissatisfied with the placement, his mother supplemented his IEP by unilaterally obtaining after school and summer educational services for him. She also appealed GISD's IEP to a hearing officer who ordered residential placement. GISD appealed to a U.S. district court which overturned the hearing officer's decision because the family had moved out of the school district. The U.S. Court of Appeals, Fifth Circuit, vacated this decision and remanded the case to the district court.

Whether the mother was entitled to reimbursement for expenses she incurred by unilaterally obtaining supplementary care for her son was the issue before the court. GISD argued that it was not liable for such reimbursement for two reasons: 1) the mother's unilateral action, without consulting GISD and without specifically requesting after school care at the due process hearing, foreclosed reimbursement, and 2) the mother failed to exhaust administrative remedies regarding the expenses for which she sought reimbursement. The court observed that generally, a parent's unilateral action in obtaining supplemental education for a handicapped child, in lieu of that provided by the school district, did not constitute a waiver of the right to reimbursement. The court noted that the EHA permits reimbursement if a court determines that such placement, rather than the IEP, is appropriate under the EHA. Here, the evidence clearly indicated that the boy had made little or no progress under the IEP developed by GISD. The mother was entitled to reimbursement for the supplementary after school education since the IEP developed by GISD was not "reasonably calculated to enable the child to receive educational benefits." *Garland Indep. School Dist. v. Wilkes*, 657 F.Supp. 1163 (N.D.Tex.1987).

During the 1983-84 school year the teacher of a first grade student referred him to a psychologist for testing in order to determine if the student was in need of special education. In January, 1984, a psychologist for the Roanoke (Virginia) County Schools (RCS) tested the student and informed his mother that he did not require testing for a learning disability (LD). On March 1, 1984, RCS conducted an eligibility meeting to determine if the student was handicapped and to discuss an appropriate educational placement for him. A private school psychologist, who had evaluated the student on the mother's behalf, testified that the student should be placed in an LD classroom. However, RCS placed him in a "behavioral adjustment" (BA) classroom. The student's mother then removed him to a private school for learning disabled children.

Prior to the student's second grade year (1984-85) RCS held another eligibility meeting. RCS recommended a dual placement IEP in which the student would spend a part of each day in a BA classroom, an LD classroom and a regular classroom. The mother sued RCS seeking tuition reimbursement for the student's private school placement. After a U.S. district court concluded that she was entitled to reimbursement for the last three months (beginning March 1) of the 1983-84 school year only, she appealed to the U.S. Court of Appeals, Fourth Circuit.

The court of appeals agreed with the district court that the mother was entitled to tuition reimbursement for the last three months of 1983-84 but not the 1984-85 year. It reasoned that the 1984-85 dual placement was a reasonable judgment by RCS. It agreed with the district court's conclusion that the 1984-85 IEP enabled the student to benefit from the IEP. The mother was also entitled to reimbursement for the costs of the evaluation by the private school's psychologist. *Hudson v. Wilson*, 828 F.2d 1059 (4th Cir. 1987).

A U.S. district court in Texas faced the difficult task of determining the appropriate IEP for a child exhibiting maladaptive behavior, which the parents of the child contended was autistic behavior and the child's school district asserted was the result of severe mental retardation. The court stated that "In formulating the IEP . . ., the district and those involved with the development of the IEP should bear in mind that one of the aims of educational . . . programming is to achieve the highest level of self-sufficiency possible; the ultimate goal of education programming for [the child] is, of course, the complete avoidance of institutionalization." *Stacey G. v. Pasadena Indep. School Dist.*, 547 F.Supp. 61 (S.D.Tex.1982).

The U.S. Court of Appeals, Ninth Circuit, has held that a homebound program for a handicapped child was not an appropriate IEP. A girl in Hawaii suffered from cystic fibrosis and tracheomalacia. After the child was certified by the Hawaii Department of Education as eligible for special education services under the EHA, the child's school district proposed a homebound program because of the unavailability in the public schools of medical services which the child required. The child's parents rejected this IEP and the child remained in the private school. The school district then proposed for the following year a public school program whereby it would train its staff to see to the child's medical needs. The parents also rejected this IEP, enrolled their child in the private school for the following year, and brought suit against the school district to compel it to pay for the child's private education. A U.S. district court in Hawaii held in favor of the parents, and the school district appealed.

The U.S. Court of Appeals, Ninth Circuit, held that the proposed homebound program was decidedly inappropriate for the child's needs. Because the school district was unable to offer an appropriate public school program, it was liable for the child's tuition expenses for the year the proposed IEP was to be implemented. However, the alternative program offered by the school district wherein it would train its staff to take care of the child's medical needs was appropriate. Thus, the parents were not entitled to tuition reimbursement for the following year. *Dep't of Educ. v. Katherine D.*, 727 F.2d 809 (9th Cir. 1983).

The parents of a twelve-year-old hearing impaired child sought review of a Kentucky Department of Education decision regarding the educational program for their child. The child's IEP required that he be taught using the "oral/aural" method of instruction. His school district sought to place him in a classroom where, along with several other oral/aural children, another child was being taught using the "total" method of instruction. The difference between these two methods of instruction is that the oral/aural method avoids the use of sign language and focuses on speech communication skills, while the total method relies upon sign language, residual hearing, and lip reading. The child's parents contended that the mixing of methods would result in him picking up sign language and neglecting his speech communication skills. A U.S. district court rejected the parents' claims, and they appealed to the U.S. Court of Appeals, Sixth Circuit. Agreeing with the lower court, the appeals court refused to overturn the school district's decision to mix the methods of instruction in one classroom. All other children in the child's classroom were making satisfactory educational progress and none of the children being taught using the oral method had begun picking up the total skills. *Age v. Bullitt County Pub. Schools*, 673 F.2d 141 (6th Cir. 1982).

When a school district wishes to conduct an evaluation of a child for the purpose of developing an IEP, under the EHA the district must notify the parents of the child of its intention to conduct the evaluation and the type of evaluation to be administered.

A Rhode Island case dealt with the issue of whether, once an IEP has been formulated, parental consent is required for a re-evaluation of the child. A mother of a handicapped child sought to prevent the child's school district from making a second educational assessment of her child. The school district had based the boy's IEP on an evaluation conducted by a private school formerly attended by the child. The mother maintained that the assessment sought by the school district would constitute an original evaluation and, therefore, the school was barred from conducting it without her cooperation. The school district contended that its assessment would be a re-evaluation and under the law, a parent's consent was unnecessary. It further stated that any change in placement resulting from the re-evaluation would be subject to challenge by the parent in a statutorily mandated hearing. A U.S. district court agreed with the school district's position, stating that the private school assessment on which the IEP was based did not legitimately constitute an original pre-placement evaluation. Thus, the court held in favor of the school district and the case was dismissed. *Carroll v. Capalbo*, 563 F.Supp. 1053 (D.R.I.1983).

CHAPTER TWO
PLACEMENT

I. MAINSTREAMING

An additional component of an "appropriate" education is the requirement that each handicapped child be educated in the "least restrictive environment." Section 1412(5)(B) of the EHA requires that states provide procedures to ensure that handicapped children are educated "to the maximum extent appropriate" with nonhandicapped children in regular classes. This is known as mainstreaming.

A mentally retarded Pennsylvania student's educational placement was in a classroom with an educable mentally retarded classification and a socially and emotionally disturbed classification (EMR/SED). During the 1987-88 school year, the school district officials recommended that the student continue his fulltime educational placement in the EMR/SED at the public school. The mother objected to this recommendation because it did not provide for any interaction between the student and his nonhandicapped peers. The student already had extracurricular activities with nonhandicapped peers including Cub Scouts, football and ballet classes, in which he functioned well and enjoyed the interaction with the other children. Therefore, the mother requested that her son be placed in an EMR classroom in a regular district school to enable him to be mainstreamed with his nonhandicapped peers. The school district refused and the mother invoked a due process hearing. During the prehearing conference, the district offered to integrate the student into an EMR class for one period per week. Under this proposal, integration would be increased gradually. The mother rejected this proposal and again requested a due process hearing pursuant to the EHA.

The hearing officer determined that the student's appropriate placement would be in the less restrictive environment of the EMR class. A transition from the EMR/SED to the EMR class would begin with two periods per day and lunch. Eventually, the hearing officer hoped the student would be placed in the EMR classroom on a full-time basis. The mother filed exceptions to the hearing officer's decision to the Secretary of Education. She specifically objected to the recommendation that the student be required to attend classes at both schools during the transition period. The secretary issued a decision ordering the district to place the student in the EMR class on a full-time basis. The school district appealed to a federal district court.

Pending the ruling of the district court, the mother and the school district agreed to an interim placement. The student was placed in an EMR class and mainstreamed to other nonhandicapped classes where he appeared to behave satisfactorily. The student made no progress, however, in the EMR class. He had difficulty completing assignments and did not interact socially with the other students in the EMR class. The school officials recommended that it was in the student's best interests that he be returned on a full-time basis to the more structured EMR/SED. The court noted that under the EHA the district court must make an independent determination based on the evidence presented. Applying this standard to the present case, the court concluded that a free appropriate public education required the placement of the student in the EMR/SED for academic subjects and the mainstreaming of the student in nonacademic subjects to the maximum extent possible. *Liscio v. Woodland Hills School Dist.*, 734 F.Supp. 689 (W.D.Pa.1989).

A sixteen-year-old profoundly deaf student was eligible for special education. He had been enrolled in Virginia public school special education programs since the age of two. From first grade on, the student had participated in the school system's cued speech programs and advanced in school with the aid of a cued speech interpreter and other support services. The district increasingly mainstreamed him into regular classes so that by high school he was taking academic classes with nonhandicapped students with the assistance of a cued speech interpreter. He also played on the high school baseball and basketball teams. The student's public school support services included one period per day in a special resource class taught by a fulltime staff teacher for the hearing impaired and several weekly speech and language therapy sessions taught by a therapist. The cued speech program was one of three different educational methods used by the school system in serving its three hundred hearing-impaired students and the district was one of only a few in the nation which offered a cued speech program.

The district established its hearing-impaired programs at centrally-located schools close to major arterials. Many participating students came from across the county and from other Virginia counties. Participating schools were located close together to allow program interpreters to easily travel to different schools. The high school which the student attended was located 5.1 miles farther from his home than the neighborhood high school he would have attended in the absence of his hearing impairment. Despite the success of the school district's mainstreaming efforts, the student's parents felt that the program should be offered at the closer school and they requested an administrative hearing. The local hearing officer required the school system to provide the cued speech service at the neighborhood high school. The district appealed to a state administrative hearing officer who determined that the student's placement constituted a free appropriate education in the least restrictive environment. The district was not required to duplicate its cued speech services at the neighborhood high school. The parents sued the district in a federal district court on a number of grounds, and the court issued two separate opinions.

In the first opinion, the court considered the student's request for $100,000 for alleged mental and emotional distress from his inability to attend the neighborhood school. The court granted the school district's motion for summary judgment. Apart from tuition reimbursement, the EHA did not authorize compensatory damage awards. To allow damages such as these would create a cause of action for educational malpractice, which was not the EHA's intent. The court also rejected the student's Rehabilitation Act § 504 complaint as another impermissible educational malpractice complaint. *Barnett v. Fairfax County School Bd.*, 721 F.Supp. 755 (E.D.Va.1989).

In the second opinion, the court considered the student's request for an order to provide cued speech services at his neighboring high school. The district had provided the student an appropriate public education as he had advanced academically and maintained a B average in regular classes while participating in two interscholastic sports. The school system had lived up to the EHA mainstreaming requirement. The cued speech program was offered at a regular public high school and constituted the least restrictive environment for handicapped students under the EHA. The EHA did not create an absolute duty to place a student in the neighborhood school, and the district was free to locate its special education programs at a central site. While the EHA provided the minimal requirement for school districts, they were free to determine the particular method of providing services. The school district had employed a successful method for providing interpreters in hearing-impaired special education programs and had provided a free appropriate public education under the EHA. The district had also complied with § 504 of the Rehabilitation Act. The court granted the district's motion for summary judgment. *Barnett v. Fairfax County School Bd.*, 721 F.Supp. 757 (E.D.Va. 1989).

A Connecticut preschooler suffered from speech and hearing impairments. The student's parents requested a student evaluation by the Board of Education. The board recommended placement in a public preschool program for hearing-impaired children. The program was attended by seven children, all of whom had hearing disabilities. The parents objected to the recommendation and placed the student in a private preschool program. Most of the students at the preschool were not handicapped. The preschool provided a twenty-minute session of speech and language therapy during each four-hour school day. The student's parents requested an impartial hearing officer to review the board's decision. The hearing officer concluded that although the student had benefitted from the private program, the public program was appropriate. The parents sued the State Board of Education of Connecticut in a federal district court, seeking reimbursement for the private school placement.

The court held that the educational program offered by the board was not appropriate under EHA § 1412(5), which provides that to the maximum extent possible, handicapped children should be mainstreamed with nonhandi-capped children. There is a strong EHA preference for mainstreaming. The board's recommended program should have been offered in a much less seg-regated setting. The benefits to the student in obtaining the services in a mainstream setting outweighed any marginal loss of the effectiveness of those services. Thus the student had been denied his right to a free public educa-tion. The student's parents were entitled to reimbursement for the cost of the private preschool program. *Briggs v. Bd. of Educ. of The State of Conn.*, 707 F.Supp. 623 (D.Conn.1988).

A multiply-handicapped Idaho student was classified as trainable mentally retarded. He was placed in a public school's handicapped contained class-room, taught by special education teachers. The student's parents then de-cided to place him in a private school, but all the schools contacted required a full-time aide as a prerequisite. The parents enrolled him in a parochial school for the following school year. They then commenced an administrative proceeding to obtain reimbursement for the aide. The district's child study team met to determine financial responsibility for the full-time aide. The team was advised by its counsel that it had no financial responsibility and it then informed the parents about the public education system's educational opportunities. The district offered placement in a segregated special educa-tion program. The parents argued that the student was entitled to main-streaming under the EHA. The district then offered to fund educational services in a private school, but refused to pay for the aide. The parents kept their son in the parochial school and began an administrative appeal for the cost of the aide and tuition. The hearing officer ruled in favor of the school district, and the parents appealed to an Idaho county court. The court over-turned the hearing officer's determination and ruled in favor of the parents. The district then appealed to the Idaho Supreme Court.

The supreme court noted that the district had failed to rebut the parents' argument that mainstreaming was appropriate. Free appropriate education must be provided in the least restrictive environment and there was a strong preference for mainstreaming in conformity with the EHA. The court noted that school district documents did not qualify as an IEP, because they set forth no goals or other evaluation procedures for determining whether EHA educational objectives were being met. Because there was no appropriate IEP, the district was not in compliance with the EHA and the hearing officer's determination was erroneous. The court ordered the school district to reim-burse the parents for their son's tuition and for his aide. *Thornock v. Boise Indep. School Dist. 1*, 767 P.2d 1241 (Idaho 1988).

A Pennsylvania student was classified as educable mentally retarded (EMR). His school district placed him in an EMR program operated by Cen-tral Intermediate Unit 10 (CIU 10). His parents objected to the EMR classifi-cation, claiming that he was either learning disabled (LD) or brain damaged (BD). The school district recommended placement in a mixed category LD/EMR class and proposed a new IEP. His parents were not satisfied and re-quested a due process hearing. The parents contended that a mixed category placement was inappropriate. The hearing officer found that the student was BD and qualified as a BD/LD student under Pennsylvania school law. Both the school district and the parents contested the hearing officer's decision.

The Pennsylvania Secretary of Education dismissed the case, finding that the student was properly classified LD and that the school district's proposed placement was appropriate.

The parents sued the school district and the secretary in a U.S. district court, alleging that they had violated the EHA. They sought a full-time private school residential placement. The school district sought a reversal of the secretary's classification and claimed that the court had no authority to rule on the matter since the school district did not receive EHA funds. It also contended that the student was receiving sufficient educational benefits to satisfy EHA requirements. The court ruled that it had authority over the school district and upheld the secretary's LD classification. The student was not EMR under Pennsylvania school law because his IQ was above eighty. However, the court upheld the school district's placement. The EHA indicated a clear congressional preference for "mainstreaming." EHA regulations required state established alternative placements for handicapped children giving priority to the least restrictive environment. Placement in a private school program was sixth on the state's priority placement list. The student was to be placed in a private school program only if placement in one of the less restrictive programs was inappropriate. The record did not support that conclusion here. The student's classification and placement were appropriate. *Garrick B. v. Curwensville Area School Dist.*, 669 F.Supp. 705 (M.D.Pa.1987).

A learning disabled child who attended New York City's public schools through the fourth grade (the 1979-80 school year) received resource room assistance and language therapy to augment his mainstream educational placement. When the city's COH recommended the same placement for the 1980-81 school year his parents disagreed and unilaterally enrolled their child in the Churchill School, a private school for disabled children. A hearing officer upheld the COH's recommendation. For the 1981-82 school year the COH made the same placement recommendation, but this time a hearing officer ruled that it was inappropriate and awarded the parents reimbursement for the child's tuition at the Churchill School for 1981-82. For subsequent school years the COH included a regular program of speech and language therapy in its public school mainstreaming recommendation for the child. The parents, however, kept him at Churchill and continued to contest the appropriateness of the COH's public school mainstreaming recommendations. A hearing officer found that despite the addition by the COH of speech and language therapy, its proposals were still inadequate and she awarded tuition reimbursement to the parents. The New York City Board of Education appealed to the State Education Commissioner, who reversed the hearing officer's decision. The parents sought review in federal district court.

The district court noted that the EHA encourages the mainstreaming of handicapped children with nonhandicapped children to the maximum extent possible. This preference for mainstreaming, combined with the district court's view that the dispute in this case was essentially over two appropriate educational placements, induced the court to uphold the State Education Commissioner's decision in favor of the COH. The witnesses for the COH had testified credibly that the COH's educational proposals were calculated to allow the child to receive "educational benefits," and the parents' witnesses testified conversely that the COH's proposals would be "disastrous"

to the child. Stating that the federal courts "must be careful to avoid imposing their view of preferable education methods upon the states," and that the
primary responsibility for designing the handicapped child's education is left
to state and local agencies along with the child's parents or guardians, the
district court deferred to the State Education Commissioner's judgment. Tuition reimbursement was denied. *Manuel R. v. Ambach*, 635 F.Supp. 791
(E.D.N.Y.1986).

In a New Jersey case, the parents of a hearing impaired girl with an I.Q. of
120 brought suit under the EHA to prevent their daughter from being assigned to a program for hearing impaired children. The girl, whose hearing
loss was profound in the left ear and severe in the right, had attended her
local school district's hearing impaired preschool program. Her parents,
however, believed that she should be educated with her nonhandicapped
peers. The superintendent of schools decided to accommodate the parents
and he temporarily assigned their daughter to a regular kindergarten class.
Later the school district child study team (CST) disagreed with the decision to
mainstream the child. The CST formulated an IEP for the child which proposed that she be placed in a hearing impaired special education class.

The girl's parents brought suit in U.S. district court and successfully
blocked her removal from the regular classroom. The court noted that due to
the EHA "status quo" provision, the girl had remained in the regular class
through kindergarten and first grade. She had made excellent progress socially and the other children in the class had helped her cope with her hearing
impairment. In fact, the court felt that the girl's presence in the regular class
benefited both her and her classmates. Also, the CST's evaluation methods
were "woefully inadequate" because they had employed only one procedure:
teacher evaluations. The court held that the girl should be placed in the regular classroom for homeroom, gym, art, music, lunch and free period, with
part-time one-to-one instruction in a learning disabilities resource room.
Bonadonna v. Cooperman, 619 F.Supp. 401 (D.N.J.1985).

In the following cases mainstreaming was found to be inappropriate for
students whose needs could only be met in special educational settings.

The parents of a Downs Syndrome student enrolled him in a Texas public
school system's half-day special education program. The following school
year, the parents requested mainstreaming for their son in a half-day regular
prekindergarten class. The school district's admissions committee met and
agreed to combine a regular and special education program for the student.
The student was unable to participate in classroom activities without individual supervision from the teacher or her aide. The school's committee met
again and changed the student's placement to special education only. However, the committee made arrangements for the student to have contact with
nonhandicapped students during lunch and recess. The student's parents appealed the committee's decision to a hearing officer under the EHA. The
hearing officer determined that regular education was not appropriate since
the student could not participate in a class without constant supervision and
the curriculum was beyond his ability. The parents appealed the hearing officer's decision to a federal district court. The court ruled in favor of the school

district, and the parents appealed to the U.S. Court of Appeals, Fifth Circuit.

The court of appeals held that because the prekindergarten curriculum was not within the student's reach, the school district was not required to mainstream him. It noted that the primary purpose of the EHA was to provide handicapped students with meaningful access to education, sufficient to confer some educational benefit to the student. The district had taken creative steps to provide regular education access to the student and had mainstreamed him to the maximum extent appropriate. The appeals court affirmed the district court's decision in favor of the school district. *Daniel R.R. v. State Bd. of Educ.*, 874 F.2d 1036 (5th Cir.1989).

In May, 1980, the parents of a Missouri boy with Down's syndrome attempted to enroll him in a public elementary school. The public school recommended that he be placed at a private institution and referred him to the Missouri Department of Elementary and Secondary Education for evaluation and services. The department concluded that the boy was severely handicapped and was eligible for placement in State School No. 2, a school exclusively attended by and designed for handicapped children. Questioning his "severely handicapped" classification, the parents requested a due process hearing. The hearing panel concluded that it was inappropriate to place the boy in State School No. 2, and ruled that an appropriate educational program would include interaction with nonhandicapped peers. The parents appealed to the state board of education which agreed with the department's "severely handicapped" label. It ruled that the boy should be placed in State School No. 2 and the parents appealed to a U.S. district court, which decided against them. The parents then appealed to the U.S. Court of Appeals, Eighth Circuit.

The parents took issue with the district court's interpretation of EHA mainstreaming provisions. They argued that the court was wrong in considering the cost of a mainstreaming placement to the school district. The court of appeals observed that EHA § 1412(5) provides that "to the maximum extent appropriate, handicapped children . . . are to be educated with children who are not handicapped, and that . . . removal of handicapped children from the regular educational program [should occur] only when the nature . . . of the handicap is such that education in regular classes . . . cannot be achieved satisfactorily." The court noted that the EHA preference for mainstreaming is not absolute because regular classrooms are not suitable for many handicapped students. It held that the district court was correct in concluding that the marginal benefit of the boy's mainstreaming was outweighed by the deprivation of benefits to other handicapped children. The boy's placement at the public elementary school would have required the hiring of at least one special education teacher, thus diminishing funds available to other students. The district court decision was affirmed and the school district was not required to mainstream the boy. *A.W. v. Northwest R-1 School Dist.*, 813 F.2d 158 (8th Cir.1987).

A handicapped child was placed in a private nonprofit daycare center for children ages one through six. The daycare center's educational program was designed to promote relationships between handicapped and nonhandicapped children. The child's school district recommended that she be placed in a preschool development class in a public elementary school. The child's parents objected, believing that the child's placement at the private daycare center was more appropriate due to its commitment to the integration of handicapped and nonhandicapped children. A hearing officer of the Iowa Department of Public Instruction affirmed the placement decision and the parents appealed to a U.S. district court. The district court upheld the decision and the parents appealed to the U.S. Court of Appeals, Eighth Circuit.

The issue before the court was whether the decision to place the child in a public educational program teaching handicapped children only, rather than in a private program serving both nonhandicapped and handicapped children, violated the EHA's mainstreaming requirement. The EHA requires that states are to educationally integrate handicapped and nonhandicapped children "to the maximum extent appropriate." The child's parents alleged that the mainstreaming requirement was violated when she was placed in a program for handicapped students only. The district court, however, rejected the idea that mainstreaming requirements are met only when the handicapped child is educated in the same classroom as nonhandicapped children. It observed that the child could be educated in the same school as other handicapped children, and that this did not necessarily violate the "maximum extent appropriate" requirement. The court further observed that while the private facility may have offered the best educational opportunity for the child, the EHA does not require states to provide parents with the best possible option. *Mark A. v. Grant Wood Area Educ. Agency*, 795 F.2d 52 (8th Cir.1986).

A Florida high school student who was handicapped by a special learning disability brought suit against a local school district under the EHA and the Rehabilitation Act, alleging that her involuntary transfer from high school to an alternative learning center violated her right to a publicly financed appropriate special education. The student requested a preliminary injunction to allow her to attend high school during pendency of the proceedings. A U.S. district court denied the student's request and she appealed to the U.S. Court of Appeals, Eleventh Circuit. She argued that the hearing officer who upheld the decision to transfer her denied her the right to lay representation in the administrative proceedings. The student also contended that the record of the administrative proceedings contained uncontested evidence that the school district violated her procedural right to remain in the high school during the pendency of the action as guaranteed by the EHA. Finally, she claimed that neither the hearing officer nor the district judge determined whether the alternative learning center was the least restrictive environment in which she could be educated.

The court of appeals held that the Rehabilitation Act was not the appropriate provision under which to bring suit since the EHA provides the exclusive avenue for asserting rights to a publicly financed special education. Further, the student had no right under the EHA to lay representation in the administrative proceedings. The hearing officer's examination of the student's chosen representative revealed his almost complete ignorance of state administrative procedure. Thus, the hearing officer did not violate the EHA in limiting his role to offering advice. The uncontradicted evidence left no doubt that the student's behavior at the high school posed a threat to both students and school officials. Thus, the court found that the school district properly exercised its authority to transfer the student to the alternative learning center and the district did not violate her right to remain in the high school during the pendency of the action. Finally, the court held that because the student introduced no evidence that the proposed placement was inappropriate or that a less restrictive environment existed in which she could receive the special education she needed the proposed placement was appropriate. *Victoria L. By Carol A. v. Dist. School Bd. of Lee County, Florida*, 741 F.2d 369 (11th Cir.1984).

The parents of a handicapped child in Arizona brought suit against their local school district because of the district's proposed plan to relocate the child at a school which could provide assistance from an instructor specially qualified to train her. The child suffered from cerebral palsy and physical handicaps but possessed normal intelligence. However, because of her handicaps she had difficulty in learning to read and write. For this reason the child's school believed the child could best be served in a school which had teachers certified in physical disabilities. The parents objected to the move because they feared that moving the child from her neighborhood and friends would create emotional problems and would stigmatize her as "handicapped."

The U.S. Court of Appeals, Ninth Circuit, held that the school district's decision was reasonable under the circumstances. In affirming a U.S. district court decision, the Court of Appeals stated that the importance of mainstreaming a handicapped child must be balanced with the primary objective of providing handicapped children with an "appropriate education." The court found that the objective of mainstreaming would not be "thwarted" by requiring the child to be instructed for a period of time by a physical disabilities teacher at another school. At issue here, said the court, is a school district's ability, after determining that a handicapped student is not making satisfactory progress, to transfer that student to a school which can provide assistance from an instructor especially qualified to train a student with that particular disability. The court found that the school district's proposal complemented state and federal law by "providing the child with a teacher particularly suited to deal with her learning problems," and held that the transfer should be allowed. *Wilson v. Marana Unified School Dist. No. 6 of Pima County*, 735 F.2d 1178 (9th Cir.1984).

A parents' association in Missouri brought suit against Missouri education officials on behalf of a group of handicapped children challenging the state's alleged policy of labeling certain handicapped children "severely handicapped" and automatically educating them in schools separate from non-handicapped children. The parents claimed that this practice violated the EHA, the Rehabilitation Act, the Equal Protection and Due Process clauses of the U.S. Constitution and Missouri law. A U.S. district court in Missouri held that the policy was consistent with the EHA. The court found evidence of an elaborate system for formulating IEP's and making a placement decision for each handicapped child on an individualized basis. It noted that if it were to order the wholesale transfer of all the children in separate schools to regular schools it would be committing the same wrong as the plaintiffs were alleging, which was not treating each child as a unique individual.

The court also found that the complained-of educational policy was consistent with the EHA mainstreaming requirement. The court held that it is possible to provide an appropriate educational environment to children attending a separate educational facility. The court was not persuaded by testimony from the plaintiffs' witnesses that a separate setting was inadequate because it could not provide sufficient interaction opportunities with non-handicapped peers and that the quality of instruction was not as high in a separate school.

The plaintiffs also asserted no valid Rehabilitation Act claim in their argument that placing the profoundly handicapped in separate schools excluded them from the benefits of regular public school placement. The court stated that the availability of organized school activities is meaningless when the evidence indicated that most, if not all, of the handicapped children in separate schools had severe problems preventing them from participating in these activities anyway. Resources are too scarce, said the court, to provide the handicapped with activities or personnel from which they cannot benefit. Finally, the court found no violations of equal protection or due process and concluded that the plaintiffs' claims were without merit. *St. Louis Developmental Disabilities Treatment Center Parents Ass'n v. Mallory*, 591 F.Supp. 1416 (W.D.Mo.1984).

The parents of a fifteen-year-old trainable mentally retarded child with a neurological impairment brought suit against a New Jersey school district. They challenged the district's determination to remove the child from a residential school and place him in his home and local schools. A hearing officer had found that the child required a structured specialized program with major assistance in the development of communication skills and that such a program could be provided in the local public schools. It had not been established, noted the hearing officer, that the child required a twenty-four hour residential placement in order to learn.

A U.S. district court in New Jersey disagreed. The court found both the program offered in the public school system and the residential program to be excellent. However, it concluded that the residential program was best for this particular child. The court found that continued attendance at the residential school would enable the child to best achieve success in learning and that placing him in his home and in local schools would have an adverse effect on his ability to learn and develop to the maximum possible extent. Accordingly, the hearing officer's determination was overturned. *Geis v. Bd. of Educ. of Parsippany-Troy Hills*, 589 F.Supp. 269 (D.N.J.1984).

II. PLACEMENT IN SPECIAL EDUCATION PROGRAMS

Placements of handicapped children in special education programs provided by public schools are generally upheld if the educational program offered by the school is appropriate and responsive to the particular child's needs. However, parents often challenge the school district's proposed IEP and seek an alternative placement.

A. Disputes in Placements

Two moderately retarded Missouri brothers, ages twenty and eighteen, functioned between a kindergarten and third grade level. At a hearing before the Missouri State Board of Education, the school district and the students' parents could not agree on an educational program for the brothers. The parents filed a lawsuit in a Missouri trial court contesting the students' placement. Meanwhile, in response to the parents' request for vocational services, the school district held a meeting in which a vocational school representative was present. Educational plans for each student were drafted at the meeting. The vocational school rejected the plans, which would have required the vocational school to enroll the students for part of their education. The parents wanted their sons trained at the vocational school. The vocational school was not a party to the ongoing lawsuit. The school district filed a motion to add the vocational school as a party. It also filed a motion to require the state board to order the vocational school to accept the plans which had been discussed at the meeting. Approximately one month later an order was issued that added the vocational school as a party and ordered the board to direct the vocational school to accept the students based on the educational plans drafted at the meeting. The vocational school sought relief in the Missouri Court of Appeals, Western District.

The court of appeals held that the trial court lacked authority to add the vocational school to the litigation between the parents and the school district. It also lacked the authority to order the vocational school to provide part of the students' education without first remanding the case to the state board of education. The vocational school should have been provided proper notice and a hearing at the administrative level in order to be properly joined. Once the vocational school's ability to provide training became apparent, it should have been brought into the case. The vocational school could not be joined in the lawsuit. *Clinton Area Vocational School v. Dandurand*, 766 S.W.2d 169 (Mo.App.1989).

B. Public vs. Private School Placement

Private school placements are made when public schools are unable or unwilling to offer a program responsive and appropriate to a handicapped child's unique needs.

An autistic Virginia student attended a private special education school. The local school district paid his tuition. Public school officials developed an IEP which provided for the student's continued attendance at the private school. The student's mother requested that her son be transferred to a neighborhood public school where he could be mainstreamed with nonhandicapped students. When the district denied the request, the mother initiated an administrative hearing. A hearing officer affirmed the private school placement. The mother appealed the decision to a state reviewing officer who affirmed the placement. She then filed a lawsuit in a federal district court. The court dismissed the lawsuit because, in the interim, another IEP had been developed. The student's mother also contested the second IEP but the placement was affirmed by a local hearing officer and a state reviewing officer. The U.S. Court of Appeals, Fourth Circuit, then remanded the case to the district court to consider the second IEP. In the meantime, the student's mother filed another action in the district court contesting the second IEP. The district court consolidated the cases and held that the student had been properly placed in the private school. The mother appealed the district court's decision to the U.S. Court of Appeals, Fourth Circuit.

The court of appeals held that the IEP complied with EHA requirements. The court noted that the district court had fully considered the EHA's mainstreaming requirements and correctly concluded that the student could not be satisfactorily educated in regular classes even with the use of supplementary aids and services. The IEP which placed the student in the private school provided an appropriate education in the least restrictive environment. The court of appeals affirmed the district court's decision. *Devries by DeBlaay v. Fairfax County School Bd.*, 882 F.2d 876 (4th Cir.1989).

The parents of a learning disabled District of Columbia student requested that he be evaluated for special education services. An IEP meeting was held and the District of Columbia Public Schools (DCPS) assigned the student to a public school program designed for learning disabled students. The student's parents requested a hearing, arguing that a private school was the appropriate placement. The student's parents then enrolled the student at a private school for the 1985-86 school year. Because the hearing officer found that the DCPS had committed procedural violations, and in light of the student's attendance at the private school, the hearing officer ordered the student to remain in the private school for the academic year. All costs incurred were to be paid by the DCPS. The DCPS was to begin to plan for the student's return to a public school for the following school year. In June, the DCPS erroneously sent a letter to the student's parents which stated that the DCPS intended to continue to pay the student's tuition at the private school for the following school year. However, approximately one month later, the DCPS sent a correction letter which stated that the student would be placed at the public school for the following school year. The student's parents then requested a due process hearing to determine whether the DCPS could legally place the student at the public school after issuing the June letter and whether the public school was an appropriate placement for the student. The hearing officer found no procedural violations and found the public school appropriate. The student continued to attend the private school throughout the 1986-87 school year. During this time the student's parents challenged the hearing officer's determination in a federal district court. The district court affirmed the hearing officer's decision and the parents appealed to the U.S. Court of Appeals, District of Columbia Circuit.

The appeals court held that the public school placement was appropriate. There was no prejudice to the parents where they were inadvertently notified that the private school tuition would be paid. The corrective notice was mailed well in advance of the school year. The hearing officer had initially found the public school appropriate and allowed the student to complete the year at the private school only because of the procedural violations committed by the DCPS. The parents were on notice that the private school would cease to be the student's "current educational placement" after the 1985-86 school year. The DCPS was not required to pay for the student's private school tuition while the placement decision was being challenged. The court of appeals affirmed the lower court's decision. *Leonard by Leonard v. Mc-Kenzie*, 869 F.2d 1558 (D.C.Cir.1989).

In a California case, the proposed IEP for a nine-year-old boy was challenged by his parents in federal district court. The boy was severely handicapped in three major categories: he had deficiencies in cognitive abilities; he had difficulties in language and communication; and he had severe physical problems resulting in his being very small and fragile for his age and making it difficult for him to walk. The boy functioned at the overall level of a child three to four years of age.

Previously, the child's parents and their local school district had provided for the boy's special educational and physical needs, and until 1983 the boy had been placed in the district's severe disorders of language (SDL) program. At that time all parties agreed that SDL was no longer appropriate, and a new IEP was formulated by the district which proposed to place the child in the district's program for the trainable mentally retarded (TMR). However, the parents objected to this placement on the grounds that the TMR program would not serve their child's physical or language needs. They contended that private school placement was required because the district maintained only SDL and TMR programs.

After a state hearing officer ruled that the district's proposed IEP was appropriate the parents brought suit in U.S. district court seeking review of the hearing officer's decision as provided by the EHA. The court found that the TMR program would be an inappropriate placement because the child would be endangered by the presence of physically larger children with Down's syndrome, and that since the program was mainly directed to children with cognitive deficiencies the child would also receive inadequate language assistance. The court reversed the hearing officer's determination that the TMR program was appropriate and ordered that the district provide a program that addressed all three of the child's areas of deficiency, or alternatively, that the district comply with the parents' request for funding of the private school placement. *Russell v. Jefferson School Dist.*, 609 F.Supp. 605 (N.D.Cal.1985).

A five-year-old District of Columbia multiply-handicapped student was eligible for special education services under the EHA. Her parents requested private special education from the District of Columbia Public Schools (DCPS). They unilaterally placed her in a private daycare center. Each week the student received speech and occupational therapy from an outside source. The DCPS completed an IEP for the student, identifying her as multiply-disabled with motor and speech communication problems. The DCPS placed the student in a public school program for handicapped children. The student's parents challenged the public school placement and requested two due process hearings. The hearing officer refused to award tuition expenses to the parents, and later determined that the school district's placement was appropriate. The hearing officer also stated that the student's placement at her private daycare program was inappropriate and did not provide the services described in her IEP. The hearing officer held that the DCPS should pay for the student's outside occupational and speech therapy because they were appropriate and because the DCPS had failed to timely place the student.

The parents appealed the decision to the U.S. District Court, District of Columbia, claiming that the DCPS placement was inappropriate. The district court ruled in the parents' favor because the DCPS program was inadequate and the district was completely incapable of providing occupational therapy. The district lacked adequate funding and had a lengthy waiting list for occupational therapy. The court approved the educational alternative proposed by the parents, which was a private special education school in Maryland specializing in educating children with severe sensory integration deficiencies and occupational therapy. The court also awarded attorney's fees to the parents under the EHA. *Kattan by Thomas v. Dist. of Columbia*, 691 F.Supp. 1539 (D.D.C.1988).

A Virginia student was of average to above-average intelligence. Because of a reading disability, however, he was deemed handicapped and was eligible for special education services. For five years the student participated in special education programs. The student's progress in improving his reading skills was minimal. In the seventh grade the student was identified as being a nonreader. The county school board recommended the student continue in the same public school special education program for the following school year. The student's parents, however, placed the student at a private school. The student made significant progress in reading during his first year at the private school. A hearing was then conducted by the school board to consider the student's appropriate educational placement for the following school year. The hearing officer concluded that because of the student's lack of progress in reading at the public school, only "exceptional" circumstances would justify a change in placement. The school board appealed to a reviewing officer who upheld the hearing officer's decision. The reviewing officer found the student required residential placement at the private school. The school board challenged the decision of the reviewing officer in a Virginia circuit court. The circuit court reversed the decision of the administrative hearing officer and the student appealed to the Court of Appeals of Virginia.

The appeals court held that the public school had not provided the student with free and appropriate public education. The student had remained a nonreader after nearly five years in the public school program. The proposed education plan by the public school was a continuation of that which had not benefited the student. The student had demonstrated an ability to learn to read while attending private school which offered a program not available within the public school system or a state facility. The Court of Appeals reversed the circuit court's decision. *Beasley v. School Bd. of Campbell County*, 367 S.E.2d 738 (Va.App.1988).

Two hearing-impaired Pennsylvania students attended DePaul Institute, a private school that specialized in educating the hearing-impaired. The school district evaluated the students and formulated an IEP for each student. Based on each student's IEP, the school district recommended that one be placed in a special program for the hearing-impaired at a public school and the other placed in a different program for the hearing-impaired at another public school. The students' mother rejected both proposals and requested an administrative hearing regarding the placement of both students. A hearing was held at which the hearing officer agreed with the school district's decision to transfer the students from DePaul. The hearing officer's decision was appealed by the students' mother and affirmed by the secretary of education. The mother rejected the secretary's decision and sued the school district in a federal district court.

The court held that the students were entitled to remain at DePaul. In determining a "free appropriate education" under the EHA, it was necessary to consider the individual requirements of each student along with the potential harm a program change might present. The court found that a change in schools for either student would mean a change in the educational method used to teach them. Both students were making satisfactory progress in their present educational environment and the risks of a program change outweighed the possible benefits. The court ordered the students to continue their education at DePaul. The district was required to continue to fund the students' education at DePaul. *Visco by Visco v. School Dist. of Pittsburgh*, 684 F.Supp. 1310 (W.D.Pa.1988).

An Alabama student was injured in an automobile accident which resulted in physical and emotional problems. She was placed in several public and private schools with marginal success. Her mother requested that the board of education suggest appropriate placement for the student. The board recommended that she be enrolled at a public high school. While at the school, she attempted suicide by drug overdose. The student's doctor then recommended placement at a private facility where she could receive twenty-four hour therapeutic and educational services. Her mother again asked the school board to propose appropriate placement for the student. The mother rejected the board's proposal of public school placement and requested a hearing to determine whether the board was obligated to pay for the student's care at the private facility. The hearing officer upheld the student's current placement. Its decision was affirmed by a state administrative review officer. While the administrative proceedings were pending, the student had returned home. Thereafter, the board filed a lawsuit against the student under the Education of the Handicapped Act in a federal district court, seeking to place the student in a state mental hospital. The district court found for the student and the board appealed to the U.S. Court of Appeals, Eleventh Circuit.

The court of appeals held that the state mental hospital lacked the facilities to provide the student with an appropriate education. The private facility, however, provided the student with the educational and support services she needed. The board was required to reimburse the mother for the private facility expenses. The court also found that the student was entitled to two additional years of compensatory education to preserve the student's right to a free education. This was necessary because the board had failed to provide an appropriate education prior to the court's order. The court of appeals affirmed the trial court's decision. *Jefferson County Bd. of Educ. v. Breen*, 853 F.2d 853 (11th Cir.1988).

A private day school education was ordered for a child by a U.S. district court in Massachusetts after that court found a learning disabled child's IEP offered by a public school system to have fallen "far short of meeting his unique needs." The parents of the child had brought suit against the school district responsible for the child's education alleging that the IEP proposed by the district was inadequate. The district court agreed. The court found that the school district, which was aware of the child's inability to work independently and also aware that the child had to be placed in an environment with few distractions, nevertheless failed to structure a program designed only to improve his basic skills.

Although it was well known in the school that the child's poor self-image and "defeatist" attitude were obstacles to his learning progress, no program was structured whereby the child might realize some success in his weaker subjects. In contrast, the program offered at the private school was specifically designed to provide children having severe learning disabilities and problems of low self-esteem with sufficient skills to return to a normalized educational program. The court ordered the school district to fund a private residential education for the child. *Norris v. Massachusetts Dep't of Educ.*, 529 F.Supp. 759 (D.Mass.1981).

The U.S. Court of Appeals, Fourth Circuit, held that a Maryland school district was under no duty to consider private school placement where an appropriate public education could be provided. In this case, a handicapped student and her parents brought suit seeking tuition reimbursement when the parents placed their child in a private school, which they deemed a more appropriate placement than that offered by their county board of education. They contended that the county board improperly failed to consider placing their child in a private school when formulating a special education program for her.

The court noted that, while state law permits placement of handicapped students in an appropriate nonpublic educational program, such a placement is limited to those instances in which public educational services appropriate for the handicapped child are not available. Thus, under EHA regulations, the duty of a state to pay for nonpublic schooling does not attach "if the handicapped child has available a free appropriate public education and the parents choose to place the child in a private school or facility. . . ." Of course, parents retain the right to challenge the placement. In this case such a challenge resulted in the state board of education upholding the public school placement. *Hessler v. State Bd. of Educ. of Maryland*, 700 F.2d 134 (4th Cir.1983).

In a Rhode Island case a U.S. district court found that a proposed public school placement of two learning disabled children violated the children's right to a free appropriate education. The proposed placement involved pupil/teacher ratios possibly as high as ten to one and provided for some mainstreaming. The children's father brought suit against the school district which had made the placement decision seeking a permanent injunction compelling the district to fund the children's placement at a private residential school.

The district court, persuaded by evidence that the children were severely learning disabled and that both children had significant accompanying emotional problems, found that the district's proposal to educate the children in a "self-contained" classroom for learning disabled children would not serve the children's needs and that only a residential placement would provide the children with the type of education anticipated by the EHA. The school district appealed the case to the U.S. Court of Appeals, First Circuit, which upheld the district court ruling. *Colin K. by John K. v. Schmidt*, 715 F.2d 1 (1st Cir.1983).

C. Residential vs. Day School Placement

A Massachusetts school proposed an IEP which called for a disabled student to attend a dayschool program. The parents consented to the IEP. The school prepared a new IEP for the following school year which provided that the student continue his education at the dayschool. The student's parents rejected the proposed IEP and requested that the student be placed in a residential program. The parents then requested the state bureau of special education appeals to determine whether the recommended IEP was the least restrictive adequate and appropriate placement for the student. Meanwhile, the parents enrolled their son in an unapproved Arizona residential program. The bureau found that the school's proposed IEP provided an appropriate educational placement. The parents appealed this decision to the State Advisory Commission on Special Education. The commission reversed the decision of the bureau and remanded the case to the bureau for further hearings. The bureau then found that the student was entitled to residential placement in an approved educational program that provided the services he had been receiving at the Arizona residential school. The bureau denied the parents' request for reimbursement for the prior unapproved residential placement costs as the facility was not an "approved school."

The parents sued the Commissioner of Education in a Massachusetts trial court. The parents then moved for summary judgment, seeking reimbursement for the student's educational costs. The court denied the motion and found that reimbursement was unauthorized because the placement was not at an approved school. The parents appealed the decision and were granted direct review by the Supreme Judicial Court of Massachusetts. The court found that the bureau could order reimbursement when a student was placed in an unapproved school while contesting his IEP. The Arizona school was an appropriate school, although it was not a state approved school. The bureau had only specified the type of program for the student. The student's parents were not precluded by regulation from choosing an unapproved school. The court further found that reimbursement was essentially an equitable remedy. Whether to order reimbursement, and in what amount, were questions which must be determined by balancing the equities. The case was reversed and remanded to the bureau for further proceedings to determine if equity required reimbursement. *Carrington v. Comm'r of Educ.*, 535 N.E.2d 212 (Mass.1989).

An autistic and severely mentally handicapped student attended a special education program in a Georgia school. The student's parents withdrew him from the school and placed him in a residential center for the severely mentally retarded. While at the center the student was evaluated and it was determined that he should be placed in a residential center with facilities for autistic children. The school district refused to pay for the student's placement. The student's parents requested an administrative hearing. A regional hearing officer found that the student did not require residential placement in a facility for autistic children and denied reimbursement for the center's costs. The parents appealed to a state hearing officer who affirmed the regional officer's decision. The student's parents then sued the school district in a federal district court. In the meantime, the student was placed in a residential center for autistic children in Tokyo, Japan. Thereafter he was transferred to a Boston sister school. The district court held that the student's educational needs had not been met by the Georgia school district. The court ordered the district to provide the student with residential treatment in a facility for autistic children until the age of twenty-one, and reimbursement for past educational expenses and attorney's fees. The district appealed to the U.S. Court of Appeals, Eleventh Circuit.

The court held that the student needed placement in a residential treatment facility for autistic children in order to provide him with a setting in which he could receive an educational benefit. The court further held that the student's parents should be reimbursed for past private school placement expenses in the Tokyo and Boston facilities and for their attorney's fees. The court noted that reimbursement was proper under the EHA if the court determined that the student's placement was proper. The student's parents were justified in placing him in the residential facilities for autistic children. The court further noted that if at the yearly IEP meeting the school district demonstrated that the student no longer needed residential placement, a new IEP reflecting this decision would control. The court of appeals affirmed the district court's decision. *Drew P. v. Clarke County School Dist.*, 877 F.2d 927 (11th Cir.1989).

A Virginia student suffered serious emotional disabilities such as lack of self-esteem and an inability to check his aggressive impulses or accept responsibility for his actions. His performance on various tests placed him in the low-average range of intelligence. School reports and tests indicated that the boy performed well in reading but was learning disabled in math. After a circuit court reversed an administrative decision which suggested residential placement for him, his parents appealed to the state court of appeals.

The EHA requires placement in residential programs only when local school districts are unable to educate handicapped children in either regular or special education classes. Virginia special education law further mandates that local school boards pay for reasonable tuition costs and other costs that result from residential care.

In December, 1983, the boy's parents had requested that the local school board place the boy in a residential setting with special education services. In March, 1984, the local school proposed an IEP of segregated emotionally disturbed instruction in one of the local schools. The boy's parents rejected the proposal and requested a due process hearing. The hearing officer ruled that the local school's proposed placement was deficient and suggested that the boy be placed in a residential setting. On appeal the court of appeals ruled that the hearing officer's concern, well-intended as it was, improperly focused on the total social and behavioral needs of the boy. The local school was not required to address social and psychological problems. By offering the boy a placement in a self-contained classroom for emotionally disturbed students, the school district had met its obligations under both the EHA and Virginia law. The court of appeals affirmed the circuit court decision. *Martin v. School Bd. of Prince George County*, 348 S.E.2d 857 (Va.App.1986).

A learning disabled child who also suffered from emotional problems had been educated in private day schools for over nine years. The local school district, the District of Columbia Public Schools (DCPS), had found that his placement at these private day schools was appropriate and funded his education. However, when the child reached the age of fourteen, officials at the private school determined that due to his increasing emotional problems the child required a full-time residential educational placement. Accordingly, at the close of the school year the private school notified DCPS that the child had completed his program of instruction and that he needed a new educational placement. On July 15, 1982, a review session was conducted by DCPS which resulted in a revised IEP for the child.

Under the new IEP, which called for placement in a public high school learning disabilities program, the child was to spend no time in regular classes but would receive twenty-five percent of his instruction in regular education. The parents rejected this proposed IEP on the grounds that their child required residential placement, and they requested a due process hearing. Prior to the hearing the parents unilaterally enrolled the child in a private residential school. On September 28, 1982; a hearing officer concluded that due to the child's status as a multihandicapped individual (i.e., emotional and learning disabilities), a change in placement from a private day school to a public high school would be detrimental to the child. The hearing officer noted that the child had never been enrolled in a public school program. He ordered DCPS to propose an appropriate placement by November 3, 1982. DCPS took no action with regard to the child's placement but instead it filed suit on January 7, 1983, to vacate the hearing officer's order. A federal court ruled against DCPS, and appeal was taken to the U.S. Court of Appeals for the District of Columbia Circuit.

The appellate court held that the hearing officer's recommendation of residential placement was correct, noting that the alternative proposal by DCPS was clearly unacceptable. The "unique needs" of the child were not adequately considered by DCPS, which had made its recommendations on preprinted forms using "boilerplate language." The court ordered that DCPS fund the child's placement at the residential school and reimburse the parents for the costs incurred in their unilateral placement decision. The lower court's award of attorney's fees to the parents was, however, reversed. *McKenzie v. Smith*, 771 F.2d 1527 (D.C.Cir.1985).

An emotionally disabled Alabama twelve-year-old boy received educational placements designed to address his behavioral difficulties. He was placed in the Davis Learning Center, a public school offering only special education programs. He made substantial progress during the year and had no major behavioral incidents. He was therefore mainstreamed into a public school with some behavioral classes being offered. He had a number of behavioral incidents including a few in which the police were called to restrain him. He was then returned to the Davis Learning Center. He again had many behavioral incidents in which the police were called. His mother requested that the school place the boy in a residential school. The school refused, instead offering either homebound instruction or a return to the learning disabled school. The mother sued the board in a federal district court.

All parties agreed that the placement of the child in the Davis Learning Center was inappropriate. The child had behavioral problems only in the classroom. Therefore, the intervention must take place in these settings in order to be effective. The court ruled that the homebound instruction would be ineffective since there would be no students around and the behavioral problems would not occur. It then determined that the residential school would meet the two essential requirements under the EHA. First, the residential setting would provide the student with his basic educational needs. Second, the placement would also offer an environment in which the school staff could work effectively with the student in controlling his behavior in the least restrictive environment. The court ordered the school to place the student in a residential school. *Chris D. v. Montgomery County Bd. of Educ.*, 743 F.Supp. 1524 (M.D.Ala.1990).

A Tennessee student suffered from brain damage since birth and was afflicted with a serious emotional disturbance and mental retardation. Her condition was aggravated by a severe behavioral disorder which caused bizarre and uncontrollable outbursts endangering both herself and others. These outbursts were unpredictable and could last for hours. The student's behavior included ingestion of foreign objects, head banging, public masturbation, assault, feces smearing, object throwing and window breaking. The student's behavior rendered placement in mainstream educational facilities provided by the school district impractical. Therefore, the student's parents and special education personnel worked together for years to find an appropriate individualized education program. The student had received educational services at four different schools. None were successful in meeting the student's specific educational goals or improving the student's behavior. Since an effective residential program could not be found, the student's IEP consisted of homebound instruction. The student's parents learned of Cedarbrook's Fresh Approach Program. Cedarbrook is a residential rehabilitation facility in Tennessee for brain injury victims. The Fresh Approach program addresses significant behavioral problems which interfere with the student's rehabilitation. After placement in the program, the student's behavior improved significantly.

After the parents were denied reimbursement, they instituted this action in a federal trial court. The court determined that the IEP offered by the district did not provide educational benefit to the student. The student deteriorated rather than benefitted under the IEP which consisted of three hours per week of homebound instruction. The court then determined that Cedarbrook represented an appropriate educational placement for which the district was liable. The issue in determining the appropriateness of Cedarbrook placement was whether it was educational or medical in nature. The occupational therapy, psychological services, recreational therapy, physical therapy and medical evaluations provided by Cedarbrook were all specifically listed as special education and related services in the EHA. Therefore, the residential placement was educational and not medical in nature. Finally, the court determined that the school district was not required to provide compensatory education because neither the student nor the district were previously aware that the Cedarbrook program existed. Thus, a compensatory education was not warranted. *Brown v. Wilson County School Bd.*, 747 F.Supp. 436 (F.D. Tenn.1990).

Parents are generally responsible for educational costs of a student if the parents place the student in a nonapproved private institution. In an Illinois case, the parents of an emotionally handicapped student challenged their school district's recommendation that their son be placed in a day-only special education program. The parents based their challenge on the findings of a private psychologist who recommended twenty-four hour residential placement for the boy. They were granted a due process hearing at which the hearing officer found the school district's proposed placement of the boy in the day program to be adequately supported by a case study done on the student. Also, the hearing officer found that the day program met the student's educational and psychological needs.

Prior to the hearing the parents had placed their son at the Grove School, a private facility in Madison, Connecticut. The Grove School was not approved by either the Illinois Governor's Purchase Review Board or the State Board of Education. The parents appealed the hearing officer's decision and requested reimbursement for the cost of placing their son at the Grove School. The State Superintendent denied the request because the Grove School was not approved by the state of Illinois. The parents appealed the State Superintendent's decision to an Illinois circuit court, which ruled for the parents.

The school district appealed the circuit court's decision to the Appellate Court of Illinois, claiming that the parents were not entitled to tuition reimbursement for the child's Grove School placement. The parents claimed that their son's needs constituted an "exceptional circumstance" upon which the circuit court had correctly based its decision. However, the appellate court held that a parent cannot be reimbursed for tuition at a nonapproved school even if there were exceptional circumstances. Regardless of the right of tuition reimbursement under section 1415(e)(2) of the EHA, the appellate court observed that the Illinois School Code prohibits the placement of a student in a nonapproved institution. Since the school district did not have the authority to place students in nonapproved facilities, the court reasoned that the district could not be responsible for such placements when made by parents. *Taglianetti v. Cronin*, 493 N.E.2d 29 (Ill.App.1st Dist.1986).

In Massachusetts, the parents of a seventeen-year-old child with Down's syndrome became dissatisfied with their child's IEP because they felt it did not adequately address his sexual misbehavior. The child, who had been receiving special educational services from his public school system in a highly structured day school program, exhibited no significant behavioral problems during the school day. However, after school he appeared preoccupied with sex, touching young girls in an inappropriate manner and attempting to sexually abuse animals. The boy's parents believed that in order to correct this misbehavior and instill in the child proper attitudes toward sex, thus enabling him to enter into private employment as an adult, the child required a twenty-four-hour residential program.

School officials rejected this proposal, stating that the child was progressing satisfactorily at school and that his sexual misbehavior after school did not mandate his placement in a residential facility. They agreed to address the parents' concerns only by adding individual therapy and family counseling to the child's IEP. After a hearing officer ruled in favor of the school district the parents brought suit in U.S. district court.

Reversing the hearing officer's decision, the court found that under the EHA, the child was entitled to twenty-four-hour residential school placement to attempt to correct his sexual misbehavior. The court noted that under Massachusetts law a special educational program must "assure the maximum possible development of a child with special needs." Accordingly, the child was entitled to the more comprehensive behavior therapy available in a residential program, especially in light of the degree of his sexual maladjustment.

The school district appealed to the U.S. Court of Appeals, First Circuit, contending that the district court had erroneously applied the requirements of Massachusetts state law to the case. This argument was rejected by the court of appeals. Where state law sets a minimum educational standard for handicapped children, those standards are incorporated by reference into the EHA. Thus a Massachusetts child suing a school district will be able to hold it to the same educational standards regardless of whether the suit is brought in state or federal court. The court of appeals approved the federal district court's application of Massachusetts law, and the residential placement was upheld. *David D. v. Dartmouth School Comm.*, 775 F.2d 411 (1st Cir.1985), *U.S. cert. denied*, 106 S. Ct.1790 (1986).

The parents of a handicapped child challenged a local school district's decision denying tuition funding for residential placement of their child. The parents argued that a free appropriate education would not meet their child's needs unless it were a twenty-four-hour residential program. A U.S. district court in Delaware disagreed with the parents and held that the educational program offered by the public school system could provide an adequate free appropriate public education.

The court found that although the child was better off emotionally because of her attendance at a private facility, the school district offered a free appropriate program which could confer educational benefits. The court also held that delays in the administrative and due process hearings did not violate the parents' right to due process and that there was no due process violation in the school district's unilateral appointment of a hearing officer and the seating of educators as hearing officers. The court held in favor of the school district. *Ahren v. Keene*, 593 F.Supp. 902 (D.Del.1984).

A California court also found that a residential placement was necessary to serve the needs of an emotionally handicapped child. The school district charged with placing the child in a special education program disputed that the child was entitled to a special education. The school asserted that the child's emotional disturbance was linked exclusively with his home environment and, therefore, did not qualify as a "handicap" under the EHA.

The California Court of Appeal disagreed with the district's characterization of the child's problem saying that merely because his emotional disturbance may have stemmed from his home environment, this did not preclude a finding that the child was entitled to special education services. Further, only a program calling for a residential placement was appropriate for this particular child's needs. A residential setting would remove the child from his turbulent home environment and provide consistency which would not otherwise be possible. The court found that without removal from his home situation the child would be unable to learn. The school district was ordered to fund a residential placement. *San Francisco Unified School Dist. v. State*, 182 Cal.Rptr. 525 (Cal.App.1st Dist.1982).

In a similar case, the parents of a multiply handicapped child brought suit against a Texas school district over a dispute involving the district's proposed placement of the child. The district formulated an IEP which called for a six-hour-day program to be augmented by home support. The parents claimed this did not constitute a "free appropriate public education" as required by the EHA. Complicating the situation was a dispute between the child's parents and the school district as to the nature of the child's handicap. The parents maintained she suffered from organic childhood schizophrenia and the district contended that its evaluation of the child showed she suffered from severe mental retardation. A U.S. district court held in favor of the parents. The court deemed the dispute over whether the child was schizophrenic or mentally retarded to be irrelevant. What mattered, said the court, was whether the child was receiving an education suited to her unique needs. Finding the proposed public school placement inadequate to meet the child's needs, the court said residential placement is required under the EHA when necessary for educational purposes. Here, residential placement was required where the child's social, emotional, medical, and education problems were so intertwined that it was impossible to separate them. *Gladys J. v. Pearland Indep. School Dist.*, 520 F.Supp. 869 (S.D.Tex.1981).

The U.S. Court of Appeals, First Circuit, has affirmed a U.S. district court decision which upheld the right to a residential education program where an alternative public school program failed to meet a handicapped child's particular needs. The parents of a severely retarded child in Massachusetts brought suit under the EHA, challenging the school district's placement of their child in a day school training program. The parents sought residential placement as well as a day educational program. When the parents' proposal was rejected, they appealed to the Massachusetts Bureau of Special Education Appeals. It found that the day school training would provide an appropriate education and that, while the child required residential care, such needs were not "educational" under the EHA, and thus not the responsibility of the school board.

The court of appeals disagreed, saying that the only way this child would make any educational progress would be through a combined day school and residential program. The court noted that under EHA regulations, if a public or private residential program (including nonmedical care and room and board) is necessary in order to provide services to a handicapped child, such services must be provided at no cost to the parents of the child. Here, the lower court properly concluded that not only would the child fail to make educational progress without a residential program, he would very likely regress without one. The combined day school-residential placement was upheld. *Abrahamson v. Hershman*, 701 F.2d 223 (1st Cir.1983).

The allegedly inordinate cost of residential placement, according to a U.S. district court in Illinois, did not preclude it from being the appropriate placement. This case arose after a hearing officer exonerated an Illinois school district from liability for all but "purely educational" expenses of a severely multiply handicapped child and determined that residential expenses should be borne by another agency. The child's mother responded to this determination by placing the child in a residential school in Kansas. She then brought suit against state educational officials seeking an injunction to prohibit the district from adhering to its policy of distinguishing between "educational" and "noneducational" components of "related services" needed to enable handicapped children to perform adequately in school. The court, finding that the child could be best served by placement in a residential facility, ordered the school district to fund the child's placement at the school in Kansas. *William S. v. Gill*, 572 F.Supp. 509 (E.D.Ill. 1983).

Where a state elects to provide state-subsidized residential care for handicapped children, the U.S. Court of Appeals, Second Circuit, has held that the state may require the parents of the children to transfer temporary custody of the children to the state. The parents in this case claimed that the temporary custody transfer requirement violated their right to privacy and family integrity without sufficient justification and that it discriminated against handicapped children solely on the basis of their handicaps.

The court of appeals, in upholding New York's custody transfer requirement, placed great emphasis on the voluntary nature of New York's benefits program and stressed that the state, while under no constitutional obligation to provide residential treatment for handicapped children, elected to do so. Consequently when the state provided voluntary social services, it could administer the program without having to consult and satisfy the individual concerns of each of the recipients.

The court dealt with the handicap discrimination issue by saying that "*all* parents whose children need state-subsidized home substitutes must transfer custody to the state, regardless of whether the child is or is not handicapped." Therefore, New York's foster care scheme discriminated between children only as to the type of assistance needed and not solely on the basis of their handicaps. The court upheld the constitutionality of the New York law. *Joyner By Lowry v. Dumpson*, 712 F.2d 770 (2d Cir.1983).

Residential placement was held to be inappropriate for a profoundly handicapped child in the following Virginia case. The child's parents asked the U.S. Court of Appeals, Fourth Circuit, to reverse certain administrative decisions made by a local school district and to issue both a preliminary and permanent injunction requiring the state of Virginia and county school officials to provide a twenty-four-hour residential placement for their son. The child had been placed in a residential program but local school officials later recommended that the child be placed in a day education program and live at home. The parents rejected this decision and applied for tuition assistance for the residential school. Tuition assistance was denied by a county special education committee on the ground that the day program could meet the child's needs.

The parents appealed to the Superintendent of Public Education of the Commonwealth of Virginia, who concurred in the committee's decision. After exhausting their administrative remedies, the parents brought suit in a U.S. district court, which released the school district from its obligation to provide twenty-four-hour residential care and education for the child.

The child and his parents appealed to the U.S. Court of Appeals, which upheld the district court ruling. The court of appeals was persuaded by testimony which indicated that the child had reached the point in his education at which a continuation of the residential program would at best yield only marginal results and probably none at all. Testimony by the school district's witnesses also indicated that basic living skills could easily be taught at home by teaching the child's family the cues the child had developed for implementing such skills. *Matthews v. Davis*, 742 F.2d 825 (4th Cir.1984).

III. CONTAGIOUS DISEASES AND PLACEMENT

In *School Board of Nassau County v. Arline*, 107 S.Ct. 1123 (1987), the U.S. Supreme Court ruled that tuberculosis (and any other contagious disease, such as AIDS) is a "handicap" under § 504 of the Rehabilitation Act so long as the individual suffers some physical impairment from the disease. The Court refused to accept the school board's argument that the teacher was not protected by § 504 because her tuberculosis was contagious and therefore dangerous to her students. The Court remanded the case to the U.S. district court to determine if the teacher was "otherwise qualified" for her job. In light of *Arline*, students with AIDS should be considered handicapped under § 504 and cannot "solely by reason of [their] handicap, be excluded from participation in any program receiving federal financial assistance."

Courts have generally held that students with AIDS are handicapped and must be admitted to public school programs if their enrollment is not a health threat to the school community. A federal district court held that three brothers who were hemophiliacs and who had tested positive for the HIV virus could not be excluded from public school classes. The school district contended that although no actual physical harm had been done to their classmates or teachers due to the brothers' class attendance, there was the possibility of future harm. This future harm allegedly included transmission of the HIV virus in the classroom setting and liability of the school district for allowing the brothers to attend the classes.

The court also cited the Supreme Court's decision in *School Board of Nassau County v. Arline*, 107 S.Ct. 1123 (1987). (See Appendix C for complete opinion.) In *Arline*, the Supreme Court held that tuberculosis was a handicap under § 504 of the Rehabilitation Act of 1973. The district court in the present case held that the HIV virus was also a handicap within the meaning of § 504. Because § 504 prohibits recipients of federal funds from discriminating against the handicapped solely because of their handicap, the school district could not exclude the three brothers from class. *Ray v. School Dist. of Desoto County*, 666 F.Supp. 1524 (N.D.Fla.1987).

A girl born with respiratory distress received 39 blood transfusions during the first four months of her life and was diagnosed as having AIDS-Related Complex (ARC) at the age of three. The girl was evaluated as having significant neurological impairment. It was not known how much damage was due to ARC, an AIDS precursor. The girl had attended schools for the handicapped prior to the ARC diagnosis and spent parts of two years in health care facilities. She was classified as trainable mentally handicapped (TMH). At the age of six the girl had a mental age of between one and one-half years in expressive language and three and one-half years in perceptual motor skills. The girl was incontinent and was observed by doctors to drool and suck her thumb continually. In the past the girl had developed skin lesions. When these occurred, her mother kept her home.

When the girl approached school age her mother attempted to enroll her in a Florida public school. The school district operated two schools which each maintained classes for TMH children. However, the school district excluded the girl from public schools based upon her incontinence. The school district recommended that the girl be educated in its homebound program.

The girl appealed to the Florida State Division of Administrative Hearings. The school district prevailed after an evidentiary hearing. After the hearing was held, but before the decision was announced, the girl began treatment with azidothymidine and showed significant progress in her developmental and neurological skills. An evaluating physician reported that her progress would be enhanced by social interaction and that her development could not be enhanced in isolation. A specialized educational setting such as the public school TMH program would be the appropriate supportive environment for further development. Other physicians testified that the girl's presence in an integrated classroom presented only a "remote theoretical possibility" of transmitting the AIDS virus.

The administrative decision was appealed to a federal district court which held in favor of the school district. The court stated that to grant an order to enroll the girl in public school it would have to find that she was likely to prevail on the merits of her claim, that her claimed injuries were irreparable and that others attending the school would not be harmed. The court ruled that potential harm to others clearly outweighed the girl's interest in attending classes. This conclusion was primarily due to conflicting expert testimony before the district court. The court also relied upon publications by the Center for Disease Control and other sources which indicated that students who lack control of body secretions increase the risk to others attending school. *Martinez v. School Bd. of Hillsborough County, Florida*, 675 F.Supp. 1574 (M.D.Fla.1987).

In 1988, the U.S. District Court for the Middle District of Florida held a full trial on the matter of placing the student. The court allowed the student to join the school's TMH classroom with heavy restrictions. The court noted that the student was still incontinent and sucked her thumb and fingers continuously. Because there was a remote theoretical possibility of transmitting AIDS through bodily secretions the court again ruled that the student could not be mainstreamed. The court also noted that medical evidence indicated that, as an AIDS sufferer, the student was at great risk of developing complications from other diseases transmitted by other students.

The court ordered the school district to construct a separate room within the TMH classroom conforming to the court's order. The room was to have a separate entry from the main classroom. The separate room was to be no less than six by eight feet and secure from intrusions. It was also required to provide a clear view of the main classroom through a large picture window, with an adequate sound system so that the occupant could hear everything occurring in the main classroom. The room was also to be equipped with toilet facilities, an appropriate work area, and necessary furniture. The school board was also required to provide a full-time aide to remain with the student in her room at all times. The TMH teacher and the aide, as well as the student's family, were ordered to attempt to toilet train the student and teach her not to put her fingers in her mouth. The court also held that as soon as the student became toilet trained and no longer mouthed her fingers she could be removed from the special room and taught in the general TMH classroom. Other children in the TMH class who had written parental waivers could be allowed into the separate room during class time. *Martinez v. School Bd. of Hillsboro County, Fla.*, 692 F.Supp. 1293 (M.D.Fla.1988).

The student's mother then appealed to the U.S. Court of Appeals, Eleventh Circuit. The appeals court stated that two federal statutes applied for determining appropriate educational placement for handicapped children—the Education of the Handicapped Act (EHA) and § 504 of the Rehabilitation Act. The EHA required schools to provide a free appropriate public education to handicapped children. Section 504 of the Rehabilitation Act stated that handicapped students should not be excluded if otherwise qualified for the activity. The court first determined that the student in this case was entitled to a free appropriate education under the EHA. She suffered from two handicaps under § 504 as she was both mentally retarded and had AIDS. The appropriate educational placement was the regular TMH classroom. The district court's finding of a "remote theoretical possibility" of transmission of AIDS was insufficient to exclude her from the TMH classroom. Because the district court had failed to make findings concerning the overall risk of transmitting AIDS through bodily secretions, it had failed to determine whether the student was "otherwise qualified" to attend the TMH classroom. If the court found on remand that the student was not "otherwise qualified" to attend the TMH classroom, it was bound to consider whether reasonable accommodations would qualify her. The lower court would also be required to hear evidence concerning the stigmatizing effect of segregating the student in a separate room. The appeals court vacated the district court's decision and remanded the case for rehearing. *Martinez v. School Bd. of Hillsboro County, Fla.*, 861 F.2d 1502 (11th Cir. 1988).

On remand, the mother asserted that an unmodified TMH classroom was the appropriate placement for her daughter. She also asked the school district to begin work on an AIDS education program in the school district. The court considered new evidence which had become available since the case was remanded. The court noted that the American Academy of Pediatrics had eliminated its recommendation that students who could not control their bodily secretions be placed in more restrictive environments. It also noted that the Center for Disease Control had stated that the risk of transmission of HIV and HBV from feces, nasal secretion, saliva, sweat, tears, urine and vomit was extremely low or nonexistent unless visible blood was actually present.

The court also reevaluated a treating physician's testimony that segregation from the TMH students was more for his own comfort than the degree of risk involved. The student's behavior had changed since the initial consideration of the case. She sucked her fingers less often and was becoming toilet trained. The court ruled that the student could join the TMH classroom, although the school's nurse should be consulted if there was any question of the advisability of her attendance on any particular day. The student was otherwise qualified to attend the TMH classroom which was therefore the most appropriate placement under the EHA. The court also required the school board to provide an educational program for parents whose children would be in the classroom. *Martinez v. School Bd. of Hillsborough County, Fla.*, 711 F.Supp. 1066 (M.D.Fla. 1989). In 1989, Eliana Martinez died at the age of six from complications attributable to her affliction with AIDS.

A twelve-year-old student contracted the AIDS virus through blood transfusions when he had undergone open-heart surgery as a child. When the board of education of an Illinois school district learned that the student was infected with the AIDS virus, it excluded him from attending the school's regular education classes and extracurricular activities. The student filed a complaint in a federal district court, seeking an order to allow him to return to his regular classes as a full-time student. The student's claim was primarily based on § 504 of the Rehabilitation Act of 1973. In order for the student to prevail under this section, he must be a "handicapped individual" and "otherwise qualified" to attend school.

The court found that the student would likely be considered a handicapped individual. As an AIDS victim, he was regarded as being impaired and this impairment substantially limited one or more of the student's major life activities. The court also deemed the student "otherwise qualified" to attend school. Medical authorities found no significant risk of transmission of AIDS in the classroom setting. The court found that the student had been harmed by loss of self-esteem which could be partially alleviated by returning him to the normal classroom environment. Any injury that might occur by issuing the order was insufficient to outweigh the harm to the student. In addition, the public interest would not be disserved by allowing the student to return to school since the threat of the student transmitting the AIDS virus to others was minimal. The court held that the student was entitled to return to school. The court also required carefully-drawn procedures to ensure that any potential risk of harm to the student's classmates and teachers was eliminated. *Doe v. Dolton Elementary School Dist. No. 148*, 694 F.Supp. 440 (N.D.Ill.1988).

A California school district learned that an eleven-year-old hemophilic student in the district had been exposed to the AIDS virus. The district instructed the student not to enroll in school and required him to study at home until the district formulated an AIDS policy. The student's guardian was unhappy with the home tutor program and repeatedly requested to have the student returned to regular classes. On each occasion the district told her that the student could not attend school until an AIDS policy had been formulated. The guardian filed a complaint in a California trial court, seeking both a preliminary and permanent order to allow the student to return to school. The guardian also sought attorney's fees. The school district stated that it was developing an AIDS policy and requested verification from the student's doctor and county health officials that his attendance at school would pose no health risk to students or staff members. Meanwhile, the guardian filed a motion for a temporary order and a permanent order for the student's admittance to school.

The court ordered the school district to allow the student to attend a regular school within its district, subject to the reevaluation of his medical condition every six months. Shortly after the court's order, the district's policy on AIDS and infectious diseases became effective. The matter then proceeded to trial where the court found for the guardian. An order was granted which required the school district to allow the student to attend a regular school, subject to periodic medical examinations. The guardian was also awarded attorney's fees. The school district appealed the decision to the California Court of Appeals, Fourth District.

On appeal, the school district argued that the trial court abused its discretion in issuing a permanent order. It insisted that a permanent order was not necessary because the student had been attending school. Alternatively it contended that even if the order was proper, attorney's fees were not warranted. The court of appeals ruled that the district had unreasonably delayed the formulation of its AIDS policy for more than five months. The permanent order was proper even though the school district had decided to allow the student to attend class. The record suggested that the student was allowed to attend solely because it was mandated by the court order. The court also found that attorney's fees were appropriately awarded as the lawsuit was instrumental in motivating the school district to address the issue of AIDS and to effectuate an appropriate policy without impairing the rights of students. *Phipps v. Saddleback Valley Unified School Dist.*, 251 Cal.Rptr. 720 (App.4th Dist.1988).

A seven-year-old hemophilic student was diagnosed as having AIDS-related complex (ARC). Prior to enrollment in public kindergarten his mother requested home instruction, as she believed mainstreaming would be inappropriate. After conducting a home instruction evaluation, the school district agreed. It developed an individualized educational program (IEP) for the student in compliance with the EHA and Illinois education statutes. After the school year began, the mother requested mainstreaming for her son. The school district placed the student in a separate "modular" classroom where he was the only student. It refused to mainstream the student even after an Illinois federal district court ordered mainstreaming of another AIDS-afflicted child.

The mother filed a lawsuit against the school district in a federal district court. She sought an order to declare the district in violation of the Rehabilitation Act and Equal Protection Clause. The district argued that the student had failed to exhaust his EHA administrative remedies. The court noted that the EHA applied to ARC victims only if the condition affected their classroom performance and ability to learn. The district's IEP stated that the student's learning and behavioral problems were not the result of ARC. Because his learning and behavioral problems did not result from his condition, he was not "handicapped" under the EHA. The court noted the considerable harm done to the student by placing him in a separate classroom. He did not pose any significant health threat to others at the school. A trial would commence on the issue of the Rehabilitation Act violation. In the meantime, the court ordered the district to mainstream the student. *Robertson v. Granite City Comm. School Dist. No. 9*, 684 F.Supp. 1002 (S.D.Ill.1988).

An Oklahoma hemophilic child tested positive for the HIV virus (AIDS) and was handicapped within the meaning of the EHA due to his emotional disorders. A placement team determined that a placement within the emotionally disturbed class of his local public school was the least restrictive environment for him. A group of parents whose children attended the child's school sought a temporary restraining order from a state court to prevent his class attendance. They sought to bar the child from school on the basis of a state law regarding contagious diseases. The child's parents then asked a U.S. district court to disallow the temporary restraining order. The court held for the child's parents. When states accept federal funding as in this case, they accept limitations or restrictions on state statutes or regulations which conflict with federal statutes. Because the child was handicapped under the EHA due to his emotional disability, the court did not need to address the issue of whether AIDS was a handicap. Procedures were conducted under the EHA between the local school district and the child's parents, resulting in an unappealed placement decision. That decision was enforced by the court. The child could attend class. *Parents of Child, Code No. 870901W v. Coker*, 676 F.Supp. 1072 (E.D.Okl.1987).

After a kindergarten boy, who was infected with the AIDS virus, bit a fellow student's pant leg, his California school district instructed the boy's parents to keep him at home until the school district considered "whether [his] potential for again biting another student posed any danger to the health of others in the class." Following an examination a psychologist determined that the boy would behave aggressively in a kindergarten setting. The school district then recommended that the boy be kept out of class and in home tutoring for the rest of the academic year. The boy's parents sued the school district in a U.S. district court seeking an order allowing the boy to attend his kindergarten class.

The court observed that the boy was "handicapped" within the meaning of § 504 of the Rehabilitation Act of 1973. It also noted that the school district had failed to demonstrate that the boy was not "otherwise qualified" to attend kindergarten. Specifically, the school district had failed to prove that the AIDS virus could be transmitted in the classroom setting through biting or otherwise. Therefore, it could not exclude the boy from his kindergarten class on the ground that he posed a risk of transmission of the AIDS virus to his classmates or teachers. The court also observed that the boy had been subjected to discrimination and had been excluded from class solely because of his handicap. Section 504 triggered statutory protection for the boy. The court ordered the school district to allow him to attend his regular kindergarten class once again. *Thomas v. Atascadero Unified School Dist.*, 662 F.Supp. 376 (C.D.Cal.1987).

The Superior Court of New Jersey held that a neurologically impaired student who was afflicted with AIDS could be refused admittance to school until proper state guidelines on AIDS were developed and the school board could hold a hearing on the child's case. It noted that children should receive a regular classroom education where possible but held that classmates, faculty and staff have an equally important interest in being free from a communicable disease in the public school system.

When she was an infant, the girl had received a blood transfusion containing the AIDS virus. She had attended a public preschool program, but the school requested that she be withdrawn from class upon learning that she had AIDS. Two leading physicians specializing in children afflicted with AIDS advised the board that the girl did not pose a threat to others. The board, however, still refused to accept the girl into the school system. A child study team then evaluated the girl and recommended that she be given a special education designed for a neurologically impaired student. According to the report, the appropriate placement would be in a "Pre-K-Handicapped Program." The school board rejected the recommendation and voted to keep her in a home study program.

On the same day as the school board vote, the New Jersey Commissioner of Education promulgated regulations on AIDS. The regulations allowed a student with AIDS admittance to school if he or she was toilet trained, did not drool excessively and was not aggressive toward others. A suit filed on the girl's behalf claimed she was being denied an appropriate education. The commissioner and a medical panel reviewed the case and found that the girl should be admitted to school. The commissioner cautioned the board not to use the educationally handicapped classification as a means of denying her a regular classroom environment.

The school board appealed the decision to a state Chancery Division judge who upheld the decision to admit the girl. The Superior Court of New Jersey reversed that decision. It held that the AIDS regulations were improper because the commissioner had not allowed comment from school boards and others before promulgating the regulations. Also, the court held that a school board should be allowed to conduct a hearing before admitting a student having AIDS. Until the rules governing students afflicted with AIDS were properly made and a new hearing conducted, the court held that the girl should remain in a home study program.

On further appeal, the New Jersey Supreme Court rejected the school board's argument that the power to exclude students for health reasons was held solely by local school boards. The commissioner's AIDS policy was valid, but "the right to call witnesses with the attendant right of cross-examination must be provided automatically upon request of the parties." However, because the burden of proof fell on the local school board seeking to exclude the child, the child should be admitted pending a final decision to exclude. The decision of the appellate court was affirmed as modified. *Bd. of Educ. v. Cooperman*, 523 A.2d 655 (N.J.1987).

Another case involving AIDS arose when two public school boards in New York City sought to prohibit a child thought to have AIDS from attending class. Although the child was later found to have HTLV-III/LAV rather than AIDS, the New York Supreme Court nonetheless addressed the issues because of the likelihood of their recurrence and the desirability of resolving the issues. The court ruled that neither the New York City Commissioner of Health nor the Chancellor of the Board of Education, nor any other city or state education officials, were required by law to exclude children afflicted with AIDS, AIDS-related complex (ARC) or HTLV-III/LAV from public school classrooms. The court reasoned that since neither city nor state health or education codes had defined AIDS and its related afflictions as "communicable diseases," provisions in the laws requiring exclusion of children with communicable diseases did not apply. The court cited expert testimony regarding Centers for Disease Control (CDC) studies showing that the risk of infection from AIDS is "apparently nonexistent" in the classroom setting. CDC studies have also shown that only about ten percent of adults infected with HTLV-III/LAV have progressed to ARC, and that approximately thirty percent of ARC patients thereafter developed AIDS. The court also held that the proposal in this case to exclude only children with AIDS from the classroom and not those afflicted with ARC or HTLV-III/LAV would be a denial of equal protection of the laws, because all three groups are carriers of the same virus. Although public education is not a "fundamental right" granted to individuals by the U.S. Constitution, "the right to an education must be made available to all on equal terms." The proposal, stated the court, would also violate the rights of AIDS-infected children under § 504 of the Rehabilitation Act for the same reasons. *Dist. 27 Comm. School Bd. v. Bd. of Educ. of City of New York*, 502 N.Y.S.2d 325 (Sup.Ct.1986).

The Appellate Court of Illinois considered the question of what is the appropriate educational placement of a trainable mentally handicapped child with Down's syndrome who is also a carrier of an infectious disease, Hepatitis Type B. Local school officials contended that because of the risk of the child transmitting the disease to other children, the appropriate placement for her was in a "homebound" setting. The child maintained that the risk of transmission of the disease was remote and therefore not a sufficient reason to exclude her from classroom participation.

A hearing officer, the State Superintendent of Education and a lower court agreed with the child. So did the Appellate Court of Illinois. The question on appeal was whether the child's homebound placement was mandated by the school district's health and safety obligations to its students so that she was being educated in the least restrictive environment as required by Illinois law and the EHA. The court held it was not. Using the *Rowley* case as its guide, the court first noted that the trial court gave due deference to the state agency's determination of educational policy under the present circumstances.

Next, the court noted that there is a strong congressional preference in favor of mainstreaming wherever possible. A major goal of the educational process is the socialization process that takes place in the regular classroom, with the resulting capacity to interact in a social way with one's peers. The superintendent of education recognized this and determined that the risk of transmission of the disease did not outweigh the injury to the child if she remained isolated from her peers. After a thorough examination of the testimony of expert witnesses, the court concluded that the trial court's decision was not against the manifest weight of the evidence and thus the child could be integrated into the classroom if appropriate sanitary procedures were followed. *Comm. High School Dist. 155 v. Denz*, 463 N.E.2d 998 (Ill.App. 1984).

IV. CHANGES IN PLACEMENT

Recognizing that a school district's unfettered discretion to change a handicapped child's placement could result in a denial of a free appropriate education to the child, EHA § 1415(b)(1)(C) requires that prior written notice of any proposed change in the educational placement of a child be afforded to the parents or guardians of the child. A hearing must be granted to parents wishing to contest a change in placement of their child. Under the EHA "stay-put" provision, school officials are prevented from removing a child from his or her current placement over the parents' objection pending completion of review proceedings.

A profoundly retarded teenager was admitted to the District of Columbia's mentally retarded facility. In accordance with his IEP, the student was bused to instruction programs at the district's hospital for sick children. The student was suffering from foot injuries which his doctor stated were aggravated by the long daily bus trips. Without notifying the student's surrogate parent, the school district bused the student to his program only eleven days during a two month period. At an IEP conference district officials notified the parent about the student's sporadic attendance. The parent approved the IEP, but the district refused to bus the student for the following three months due to his injuries. The parent then filed a lawsuit in the U.S. District Court for the

District of Columbia complaining that the student had been deprived of a free appropriate education under the EHA. She also complained that she had been deprived of an opportunity to contest a change in his educational program. She sought an order to continue his instruction at the hospital. The district court dismissed the complaint. Despite signing a consent form approving the student's IEP for the following year, the parent appealed the court's decision to the U.S. Court of Appeals, District of Columbia Circuit.

The appeals court ruled that the EHA required prior written notice for any change in educational placement, a description of available procedural safeguards, and explanation for the proposed change. The parental right to a hearing was preserved by the notice requirement and the district had failed to comply with it. By failing to implement the student's IEP during his confinement, the district also failed to provide free public education as required by the EHA. The fact that the student could not be safely bused did not excuse the district from its duty to notify the parent in writing of the discontinuance of his educational benefits. However, the parent had consented to the child's new IEP and could not complain about the change in his instruction after the three month interruption. The student was entitled to a declaration that the district had violated the EHA and the case was remanded to the district court to determine whether the parent was entitled to attorney's fees. *Abney by Kantor v. Dist. of Columbia*, 849 F.2d 1491 (D.C.Cir.1988).

The District of Columbia Public Schools (DCPS) found a child to be eligible for special education and placed him at the Brent Public Elementary School. His parents were dissatisfied with the placement and asked for a due process hearing. The hearing officer concluded that the Brent placement was inappropriate and gave DCPS a deadline of November 25, 1985, to provide a new placement. On November 27, 1985, DCPS proposed a placement at the Prospect Learning Center. However, the parents were also dissatisfied with the Prospect placement and requested a second due process hearing. In the meantime, they unilaterally placed the child in the Lab School, a private special education facility.

The second hearing officer determined on March 24, 1986, that both Prospect and the Lab School were appropriate and that DCPS was responsible for the child's placement at the Lab School for the 1985-86 school year until April 7, 1986, because it missed the November 25, 1985, deadline. The hearing officer also determined that the child should be placed at Prospect after April 7, 1986. The parents sued DCPS seeking a court order that DCPS place the child at the Lab School retroactive from April 7, 1986, during the pendency of the court proceedings. They argued that the Lab School was his current educational placement and that DCPS was required to maintain this "status quo" under the EHA. DCPS contended that only after April 7, 1986, was Prospect his placement.

The U.S. district court concluded that there was substantial evidence that the Lab School was his current educational placement during the court proceedings. First, the child never had a true placement in the public school system. The Brent placement was aborted after one day and the first hearing officer found that DCPS could not prove that the Brent placement was appropriate. Second, the second hearing officer found that DCPS did not have an appropriate program in place for the child until November 27, 1985, and therefore he concluded that DCPS was responsible for the Lab School placement from the beginning of the 1985-86 school year until April 7, 1986. Based upon the above facts, the court held that the parents were justified in unilaterally placing the child at the Lab School. It declined to order DCPS to fund the child's Lab School placement from April 7, 1986, to May 1, 1987, since a later court could find that the Lab School was not the child's current educational placement for that period. However, the court held that effective May 1, 1987, DCPS had to fund the child's education during the pendency of the court proceedings. *Cochran v. Dist. of Columbia*, 660 F.Supp. 314 (D.D.C.1987).

In January, 1976, a Washington state boy was found to be eligible for special educational service having scored 70 on an I.Q. test. The district developed an IEP for him which recommended placement in an "educable handicapped classroom." After further testing the school district recommended continued placement in a special education class, but his parents chose to have him repeat first grade in a regular class during the 1976-77 school year. In May, 1979, another assessment by the district found the boy's I.Q. to be 69 and his academic performance less than half the expected grade level. The parents again refused the district's placement in an "educable handicapped classroom" for mildly retarded students and placed him in a private school.

In the summer of 1981, a school district employee began tutoring the boy. When the parents placed the boy in a public school in the fall of 1981 they asked that the tutoring continue. After the tutor resigned, the district told the parents that a new tutor would instruct the boy. The parents alleged that this constituted a change of placement in violation of the EHA's "status quo" provision. The parents chose to remove the boy from school three hours daily to be tutored by the original tutor at their own expense. Another test was then performed by the school district which revealed that the boy's I.Q. was 66 and that he was "mildly mentally retarded." After two hearings favored the school district's position the parents appealed to a U.S. district court which ruled in their favor. The school district appealed to the U.S. Court of Appeals, Ninth Circuit.

The school district challenged the district court's ruling that the boy had a learning disability and was not mentally retarded. In 1982, a neurologist had concluded that the boy was dyslexic, not mildly retarded. The court of appeals agreed with the school district noting that the trial record provided no support for the district court's conclusion that the boy had a learning disability, not mild retardation, according to state regulations. It refused to accept the neurologist's subjective conclusion that the boy could not benefit from placement in the school district's special education classes. State regulations required placement to be based upon objective criteria such as the I.Q. test. The boy's eligibility for special education was correctly based on "mild mental retardation." The district court decision was reversed. *Gregory K. V. Longview School Dist.*, 811 F.2d 1307 (9th Cir.1987).

A thirteen-year-old student residing in the District of Columbia suffered from learning disabilities. He was injured in an automobile accident which resulted in multiple physical handicaps. The student was of above-average intelligence, but also suffered from gender-identity disorder and other emotional difficulties. The District of Columbia Public Schools (DCPS) placed the student in a private facility near the student's home pursuant to the EHA. A social worker at the school advised the DCPS that the school would not be an appropriate educational placement for the student during the following school year. His teachers, therapists and parents developed an IEP for the following school year and the DCPS recommended placement in a public day school.

The parents disagreed with the proposed IEP. They suggested placing the student at a private special education school for learning disabled students of average to above-average intelligence. They then asked for a hearing to challenge the student's placement under the EHA. The hearing officer upheld the DCPS's public school placement. Shortly thereafter, the student was enrolled in a private school. The parents then filed a lawsuit in the U.S. District Court, District of Columbia. The court ruled that the DCPS did not comply with the EHA. School districts are restricted from taking students from a private facility by the act's "stay-put" provision, "which directs that a disabled child 'shall remain in (his or her) then current educational placement' pending completion of any [administrative or judicial] review proceedings, unless the parents and state or local educational agencies otherwise agree." This required the DCPS to maintain the student at his current private placement until the resolution of the lawsuit. The parents were entitled to retroactive reimbursement for the student's private placement by the school district. *Knight v. Dist. of Columbia*, 691 F.Supp. 1567 (D.D.C.1988).

An emotionally disabled New York student attended a vocational school as a part of his mainstreaming. His parents were notified that the school district intended to graduate him at the end of the school year. When the vocational school notified the parents that the student should continue in its program for another year, the parents requested an impartial hearing. They objected to their son being graduated because he had not attained targets established by the vocational school. Following the hearing but prior to the hearing officer's decision, the student was graduated. The hearing officer agreed that graduation was appropriate and the parents appealed to the Commissioner of Education. They requested that their son be allowed to continue the vocational program until a final decision was reached. The commissioner denied the request and determined that the student had been properly graduated.

The parents sued the school district in a New York federal district court. They asserted that the school district violated the EHA's stay-put provision by graduating their son. They sought to have their son reinstated to the vocational program pending a final decision. The court noted that one of the purposes of the stay-put provision was to prevent school officials from removing a child from the classroom over the parents' objection pending completion of review proceedings. It then noted that what had to be determined was whether graduation constituted a change in placement. The court equated graduation to a long-term suspension because it resulted in the total exclusion of the student from his educational placement. Therefore, EHA procedural safeguards should be enforced. The court ordered the school district to reinstate the student to the vocational program during the pendency of the proceedings. *Cronan v. Bd. of Educ. of East Ramapo Cent. School Dist.*, 689 F.Supp. 197 (S.D.N.Y.1988).

School officials conducted an assessment of a Minnesota child. They found that the child was excessively active, did not conform well to rules, was argumentative and did not actively interact with adults. An individualized education program (IEP) team, which included the child's mother, met to discuss the assessment. Although the mother was reluctant to classify the child as handicapped, she consented to special education in May, 1985. In January, 1986, the mother approved an annual IEP that placed the child in Level IV special education which included mainstreaming and separate special education classes. In March, 1986, the school district modified the child's IEP to allow him to attend regular classes as a special education student. In May, 1986, the school district recommended full mainstreaming as a special education student on a trial basis in the fall. However, the child went to live with his father and enrolled in another school system where he was placed in regular education classes. After one month the child returned to his mother's custody. In December, 1986, she attempted to reenroll the child in the original school district as a regular education student. The school district asserted its right to continue the child's Level IV special education program.

In January, 1987, the mother sued the school district in a federal district court. She moved for a preliminary injunction under § 1983 of the Civil Rights Act to forbid the school district from placing the child in special education. A § 1983 claim arises when a school district acting under authority of state law violates rights secured by the Constitution or federal laws. She claimed that the school district changed the child's educational status without affording her a hearing. This violated due process and the EHA's stay-put provision. The court denied the mother's motion and she appealed to the U.S. Court of Appeals, Eighth Circuit. The mother argued that the district court wrongly concluded that a § 1983 claim was not available to correct violations of the EHA or the Due Process Clause of the U.S. Constitution. She also contended that the child should be in regular classes because he transferred as a regular education student. The school district claimed that the child was a continuing student at the original school district in Level IV special education. Although the child was mainstreamed as a special education student, his permanent placement in regular education was contingent on an IEP assessment.

The court of appeals held for the mother on her § 1983 claim. The Handicapped Children's Protection Act of 1986 (HCPA) permits due process challenges to procedures employed by school districts under § 1983 in the EHA context. The HCPA provides that nothing in the EHA limits the rights of handicapped students under other federal statutes. However, the court of appeals held for the school district on the stay-put issue. The child's one-month enrollment in regular classes at the second school system did not negate his history as a special education student. Although the Level IV program involved mainstreaming, the original school district had not taken the child out of the special education program. Furthermore, placing him in a special education program pending a determination of his proper educational program would not irreparably harm the child. The district court decision was affirmed. *Digre v. Roseville Schools Indep. Dist. No. 623*, 841 F.2d 245 (8th Cir. 1988).

A U.S. district court has ruled that the party who proposes to change the placement of a handicapped child bears the burden of proof in demonstrating the propriety of such a change. This case arose when a Georgia school district proposed to change a child's residential school placement to placement in a self-contained learning disabilities classroom in the county school district. The district had placed the boy in a residential facility under his IEP and had paid all costs associated with his attendance there since 1979. However, in June 1982, the district reevaluated the boy and recommended a change from residential placement to special class placement in a regular school system. The child's parents objected to this change and two administrative hearings were held. The parents then brought suit in U.S. district court challenging the standard of proof used in the hearings. While stating that it would not address the results of the administrative hearings, the court agreed to order that the school district should bear the burden of proof in the administrative hearings because it was the party seeking to change the boy's placement. The residential placement, which had been previously agreed to by both the school and the boy's parents, was therefore presumed to be the child's appropriate placement until the school district was able to prove otherwise. *Burger v. Murray County School Dist.*, 612 F.Supp. 434 (N.D.Ga.1984).

The parents of a handicapped child brought a complaint against their Massachusetts school district after a privately-run after-school day care program refused to continue accepting their child. The parents alleged that the school district had deprived them of due process by failing to notify them in advance of this so-called change in placement. After the Massachusetts Bureau of Special Education Appeals ruled in favor of the parents, the school district appealed to the federal district court arguing that it had not changed the child's placement. Here, the child's IEP had included two afternoons per week at a BASS program, and three afternoons per week at a private day care center located at Driscoll Public School. Unfortunately, the following fall the day care center decided that the child was too old to attend. The parents then requested of school officials that he be allowed to attend the BASS program five days per week. The school responded by proposing that the child attend the BASS program three days per week and spend the remaining two days at an individualized public school program at the Driscoll Public School. The one-on-one aides for the child while at the Driscoll public school program would be the same persons who were involved in Driscoll's private program.

The district court ruled that such a minor alteration in the child's program (the change from two days at BASS and three days at Driscoll to three days at BASS and two days at Driscoll) was not a "change in educational placement" under EHA section 1415(e)(2). This was especially true where the private day care group, which was composed of parents at the Driscoll school, was the entity responsible for the change in the child's schedule. Because no change in placement had occurred, the school district had no duty to notify the parents. The court reversed the Bureau of Special Education Appeals and ruled in the school's favor. *Brookline School Comm. v. Golden*, 628 F.Supp. 113 (D.Mass.1986).

The U.S. Court of Appeals, Third Circuit, held that a change in the method of transportation of a severely handicapped child to and from school did not constitute a "change in educational placement." A Pennsylvania school district changed the method of transportation from a system whereby the child's parents were reimbursed for their expenses in driving the child to school to a "combined run" involving other children and a small increase in travel time. The parents objected to the combined run on the ground that the increase in transportation time would be detrimental to the child's education. The school district denied the parents a due process hearing because it did not consider the change in transportation to be a "change in educational placement."

The Court of Appeals agreed, finding that the change in the method of transporting the child did not constitute a "change in educational placement" under the EHA and thus could be implemented without a prior due process hearing. It is clear, said the court, that the "stay put" provision under the EHA does not entitle parents to demand a hearing when minor administrative decisions alter the school day of their children. The question is whether the school district's decision is likely to affect in some significant way a child's learning experience. Here, the parents' objections were merely speculative. *DeLeon v. Susquehanna Comm. School Dist.*, 747 F.2d 149 (3d Cir. 1984).

In a similar case, the U.S. Court of Appeals, District of Columbia Circuit, held that a change in the feeding program that a profoundly handicapped child would receive as a result of a transfer from a private hospital to a government-run institution did not constitute a "change in educational placement" within the meaning of the EHA. The child's guardian sued the District of Columbia Board of Education alleging that the change in residence from the private hospital at which the child had been placed to a government-run institution where the child would live but continue to receive a day education at the private hospital, constituted a "change in educational placement" triggering the requirement of a due process hearing. The guardian specifically alleged that differences in the feeding programs of the private hospital and the public institution constituted a sufficient change in the child's individual education program to warrant the child's retention in the private hospital until resolution of the matter.

The court of appeals disagreed, finding that an individual voicing objections to a handicapped child's educational program must identify, at a minimum, a fundamental change in, or the elimination of, a basic element of the education program in order for the change to qualify as a change in educational placement. Here, although the child's transfer from one facility to another was decidedly a "change in placement," it was not alone sufficient to constitute a change in educational placement requiring the board of education to keep the child at the private hospital or a comparable facility until the hearings were completed. A move from a "mainstream" program to one consisting only of handicapped students, said the court, would constitute a change in educational placement; a move from one mainstream program to another, with the elimination, for instance, of a theater arts class, would not be such a change. Here, the board of education, using the residential services of the public institution and the out-patient education program of the private hospital, had fulfilled its obligation under the EHA to maintain the child's educational placement pending the resolution of any complaint proceedings brought on the child's behalf. Thus, the court of appeals held that the child could be discharged from the private hospital prior to his guardian's consent and prior to a hearing. *Lunceford v. Dist. of Columbia Bd. of Educ.*, 745 F.2d 1577 (D.C. Cir. 1984).

In Massachusetts, parents of an eleven-year-old boy who suffered from acquired encephalopathy challenged in U.S. district court a proposed change in their son's educational placement. For seven years the child had attended a special education center for brain-injured children. This center offered special teaching techniques which would not be available to the child at the new location. The parents argued that the transfer of their child from the center to the new program would halt his progress and cause him to regress. In deciding whether the placement change was appropriate, the court relied on language set forth by the U.S. Supreme Court in *Board of Education v. Rowley.* That case held that handicapped children are to be provided a "basic floor of opportunity" and that educational services must be sufficient to confer some educational benefit upon them. Here, the court stated that the relative validity of the differing techniques used by the two institutes was a matter of dispute among special education experts. In light of the court's unwillingness to make educational policy and insufficient evidence that the child would regress at the new institute, the court refused to hold that the change of placement would be inappropriate. Judgment was rendered in favor of the school district. *Doe v. Lawson*, 579 F.Supp. 1314 (D.Mass.1984).

A dispute in Michigan resulted in a U.S. district court determination that the proposed transfer of an eleven-year-old girl with cerebral palsy from a traditional elementary school to an elementary school specially designed to meet the needs of handicapped children did not violate the EHA. The mother sued the school district which had proposed the transfer alleging that her daughter was denied a free appropriate education in the least restrictive environment without due process of law. The court was persuaded that the child could not receive a satisfactory education in the traditional school, even with the use of supplementary aids and services to the maximum extent possible. Further, the mother had exhausted all of the administrative remedies available to her. Thus, the mother's due process claim was without merit because she had been afforded and had availed herself of every EHA procedural safeguard. In addition, the court held that the mother's equal protection claim asserted on behalf of her child was unfounded, because there was no showing that the child was treated any differently from other handicapped children who were being evaluated by procedures mandated by state and federal law. *Johnston v. Ann Arbor Pub. Schools*, 569 F.Supp. 1502 (E.D.Mich. 1983).

The Supreme Judicial Court of Massachusetts held that the decision to graduate a child with special education needs is a "change in placement," triggering mandatory EHA procedural safeguards. In this case a twenty-one-year-old male suffering from multiple cognitive and motor disabilities, emotional and behavioral difficulties, and also confined to a wheelchair, brought suit against a Massachusetts school district alleging that his graduation, which terminated his right to special education services, violated EHA procedural provisions. In the fall of 1980, the boy's teachers had met to formulate his IEP for the 1980-81 school year. The teachers agreed that the child was to graduate at the end of the school year, although his IEP did not state this. Neither the student nor his parents were invited to the meeting at which this decision was made. The student signed the IEP but the parents did not. At no time were the parents provided formal, written notice of their right to challenge the IEP or of the procedural avenues open to them to make that challenge. Neither were they told that graduation would terminate their son's eligibility for special education services. In June, 1981, the boy was presented with a high school diploma; his eligibility for special education services was thereby terminated. In the time between the student's graduation and the commencement of this lawsuit, no special education services were afforded to the boy. Evidence showed that he failed to adapt either to sheltered workshops or independent living settings. Furthermore, at the time of the lawsuit, the boy was hospitalized in a chronic care unit.

The Massachusetts Supreme Judicial Court reversed a lower court decision in favor of the school district, holding that the failure to provide to the parents a formal, written notice concerning the decision to graduate the student, the failure to provide notice regarding the rights of the parents to involvement in that decision and the failure to notify them of their rights to a hearing and administrative review violated state and federal statutory law. This was true even though the parents had actual notice of the student's graduation and had participated to a limited extent in the transitional planning surrounding the graduation, and even though the student signed the IEP. *Stock v. Massachusetts Hospital School*, 467 N.E.2d 448 (Mass.1984).

A local school district and concerned parents of handicapped students objected to the New York City Board of Education's refusal to renew its contract with a special school on the ground of claimed financial mismanagement. The board had conducted an audit of the school and discovered that large sums of money were being misspent and that serious educational deficiencies existed in the programs offered. Upon termination of the contract with the school, the board of education offered an alternative "location" for the majority of the students and was seeking placement for the balance. The school district and the parents argued that the placement of the handicapped children from one school to another involved a change in educational placement which triggered the requirement of a court order preventing the immediate closing of the school.

The court disagreed, holding that a change of school is not *per se* a change in educational placement of a handicapped student. Further, for the court to order a temporary stay of the school closing, the students must show irreparable injury resulting from the closing. This could be shown by demonstrating the educational uniqueness of the school or by showing that another school would not similarly aid such students. No such potential injury was shown. Thus, although it is conceivable that the placement of a child from one school to another may involve a change in educational placement which would then trigger the requirement of an order preventing the immediate closing of a school, no sufficient proof of the required irreparable injury to the student was shown. *Cohen v. Bd. of Educ. of City of New York*, 454 N.Y.S.2d 630 (Sup.Ct.1982).

A New York case resulted in a ruling that handicapped children should be periodically reevaluated. The case arose in 1983, when the family court of Nassau County found that a young boy was handicapped within the meaning of state law and ordered the county of the boy's residence to pay the cost of tuition and maintenance for the boy at a summer camp for the handicapped. The $2,450 award was payable directly to the boy's mother. One year later the mother again petitioned the family court to order the county to pay the cost of the boy's stay at the camp during the summer of 1984. She contended that since all the facts were the same as in the previous year there was no need to hold a second trial. The county, however, believed that the boy's condition had changed and that he was no longer entitled to reimbursement for summer camp expenses under New York law. The family court disagreed and held in favor of the mother. On appeal by the county to the New York Supreme Court, Appellate Division, the decision in favor of the mother was reversed because of the possible changes in her son's condition as a handicapped child. The appeals court remanded the case to the family court for a full trial, where the question of whether the boy's condition had materially changed since the preceding summer could be answered. *Schwartz v. County of Nassau*, 489 N.Y.S.2d 274 (A.D.2d Dept.1985).

V. SUSPENSION AND EXPULSION OF HANDICAPPED STUDENTS

Whether suspension or expulsion of handicapped students from school constitutes a "change in placement" for purposes of the EHA is an issue which has been presented before the courts. The U.S. Supreme Court has clarified the issue in *Honig v. Doe*, 108 S.Ct. 592 (1988) (reprinted in the Appendix of U.S. Supreme Court Cases in this volume). Indefinite suspensions violate the EHA's "stay put" provisions. Suspensions up to ten days do not constitute a change in placement. The Court seemed to leave intact the principle that where a student's misbehavior is caused by his or her handicap, any attempt to expel the student from school will be turned aside.

Honig v. Doe involved two emotionally disturbed children in California who were given five day suspensions from school for misbehavior which included destroying school property and assaulting and making sexual comments to other students. Pursuant to state law, the suspensions were continued indefinitely during the pendency of expulsion proceedings. The students sued the school district in U.S. district court contesting the extended suspensions on the ground that they violated the EHA's stay put provision, which provides that a student must be kept in his or her "then current" educational placement during the pendency of proceedings which contemplate a change in placement. The district court issued an injunction preventing the expulsion of any handicapped student for misbehavior which arises from the student's handicap and the school district appealed.

The U.S. Court of Appeals, Ninth Circuit, determined that the indefinite suspensions constituted a prohibited change in placement under the EHA and that no "dangerousness" exception existed in the EHA's "stay put" provision. It ruled that indefinite suspensions or expulsions of disabled children for misconduct arising out of their disabilities violated the EHA. The court of appeals also ruled, however, that fixed suspensions of up to thirty school days did not constitute a "change in placement." It determined that a state must provide services directly to a disabled child when a local school district fails to do so. The California Superintendent of Public Instruction filed for a review by the U.S. Supreme Court on the issues of whether a dangerousness exception existed to the "stay put" provision and whether the state had to provide services directly when a local school district failed to do so.

The Supreme Court declared that the intended purpose of the stay put provision was to prevent schools from changing a child's educational placement over his or her parents' objection until all review proceedings were completed. While the EHA provided for interim placements where parents and school officials were able to agree on one, no emergency exception for dangerous students was included. The Court concluded that it was "not at liberty to engraft onto the [EHA] an exception Congress chose not to create." The Court went on to say that where a disabled student poses an immediate threat to the safety of others, school officials may temporarily suspend him or her for up to ten school days. The court held that this authority insured 1) that school officials can protect the safety of others by removing dangerous students, 2) that school officials can seek a review of the student's placement and try to persuade the student's parents to agree to an interim placement, and 3) that school officials can seek court rulings to exclude students whose parents "adamantly refuse to permit any change in placement." School officials could seek such a court order without exhausting EHA administrative remedies "only by showing that maintaining the child in his or her current placement is substantially likely to result in injury either to himself or herself, or to others."

The Court therefore affirmed the court of appeals' decision that indefinite suspensions violated the EHA's stay put provision. It modified that court's decision on fixed suspensions by holding that suspensions up to ten rather than up to thirty days did not constitute a change in placement. The Court also upheld the court of appeals' decision that states could be required to provide services directly to disabled students where a local school district fails to do so. *Honig v. Doe*, 108 S.Ct. 592 (1988).

On January 9, 1986, after a severe temper tantrum at school, an eight-year-old boy was suspended for thirty-five days until a February 13, school board meeting. The boy was readmitted on January 13, but was suspended again after another disruptive incident on January 15. A January 20, examination by a psychologist found that the boy suffered from a learning disability. The school board was notified of the child's learning disability and the school psychologist began testing him on February 3. His parents requested on two occasions that in light of his learning disability he be readmitted to school. The school board suggested both times that they allow their child to receive homebound instruction and refused to lift the suspension until February 13. On February 4, the parents sued the school board seeking a temporary restraining order ordering the boy's readmission and a hearing. A U.S. district court ordered the school board to provide the boy with an appropriate educational program after which the board began devising an appropriate IEP for him. The school board then moved to dismiss the parents' lawsuit.

The parents argued that leaving the boy under disciplinary suspensions for twenty-nine days with no educational services caused irreparable harm. The court observed that the facts of the case required a two-part examination: first, the child's due process rights had to be considered as those of a nonhandicapped child facing a twenty-nine day disciplinary suspension since the school officials did not at first perceive him to be handicapped. Second, once school officials were notified of the child's learning disability, his due process rights had to be considered in light of the EHA. The court ruled that both examinations revealed that the boy had due process rights. The U.S. Supreme

Court held in *Goss v. Lopez* that a disciplinary suspension for even a non-handicapped child gives rise to due process rights. *Goss* stated that notice of suspension proceedings must be sent to a student's parents and a hearing held with the student present "as soon as practicable." The district court ruled that under *Goss* a due process hearing twenty-nine days after an incident would not be adequate. Such a time lapse would result in irreparable harm to the boy which justified the initiation of the civil lawsuit before February 13. Since his civil rights were violated he was entitled to relief under § 1983 including an award of attorney fees. Because the school board was in the process of devising a proper IEP, other measures of relief requested by the boy were denied. The boy was entitled to summary judgment in his favor. *Doe v. Rockingham County School Bd.*, 658 F.Supp. 403 (W.D.Va.1987).

A fourteen-year-old Virginia boy who had been identified by his school district as having a serious learning disability was suspended from school in March, 1983. The boy had acted as a middleman for two nonhandicapped girls who desired to buy "speed" from another student. He made no money doing this and took no drugs himself. The boy was suspended, but during his suspension the school district's committee on the handicapped held proceedings which culminated in the determination that the boy's handicap was not the cause of his involvement with drugs. The school board then voted to expel the boy for the remainder of the school year. One month later the parents requested and received a due process hearing at which the hearing examiner ordered the expulsion reversed because he found that the boy's misbehavior was related to his learning disability. A state reviewing officer affirmed this decision.

The school board then filed suit in U.S. district court contending that in situations like this, the EHA allows expulsions without review. The district court dismissed the school board's complaint and the U.S. Court of Appeals, Fourth Circuit, affirmed. The appeals court noted that it is settled law that any expulsion of a handicapped student is a change in placement for EHA purposes, triggering the Act's procedural safeguards. Also, the district court's determination that the boy's involvement in drug sales was caused by his handicap would not be overturned on appeal unless it was "clearly erroneous." The dismissal of the school board's complaint was therefore affirmed. *School Bd. of Prince County v. Malone*, 762 F.2d 1210 (4th Cir.1985).

In 1978, a handicapped girl obtained a preliminary injunction from a federal district court in Connecticut which prevented her school board from expelling her from high school. The board was also ordered to conduct an immediate review of her IEP under the EHA. The girl's class action suit continued in district court for the next five years, with the girl seeking a declaratory judgment that the school board "was bound by the procedural requirements of the EHA if it desired to exclude a handicapped student from class attendance for longer than a ten day period." In 1984, the class action suit was dismissed because the girl graduated and was no longer a member of the class she purported to represent. She then petitioned the district court for an award of attorney fees pursuant to section 1988 of the Civil Rights Act.

The court, while noting that attorney fees are rarely justified in cases involving the EHA, ordered the school board and state department of education to pay the full amount of the girl's attorney fees ($57,631). Although plaintiffs in EHA cases often allege violations of the Civil Rights Act, the U.S. Supreme Court held in *Smith v. Robinson*, 104 S.Ct. 3457 (1984), that substantive claims made under the EHA will not justify the use of section 1988 as a basis for attorney fees. The Supreme Court held however, that where a plaintiff is successful in proving that a school board or other state entity has deprived the plaintiff of procedural protections, attorney fees may be awarded. In the present case, the girl proved that the board, by excluding her from class attendance for longer than a ten day period, had failed to provide her with the procedural safeguards mandated by the EHA. These procedural violations gave rise to an award of attorney fees under section 1988 of the Civil Rights Act, and the court ordered that the school board, as the primary party at fault, pay eighty percent of the award and that the state department of education pay twenty percent. *Stuart v. Nappi*, 610 F.Supp. 90 (D.Conn.1985).

In a Mississippi case, a student's sexual misconduct prevented his return to the classroom. The behaviorally handicapped student admitted to school officials that while in a special education class he had unbuttoned a girl's blouse and touched her breast. As a result, the school suspended him for three days and he was sent before the County Youth Court. Because this was the boy's third instance of school-related sexual misconduct, the Youth Court sent him to a state hospital for one month of treatment. After he lived at home for seven months following his hospitalization, the boy's mother sought to re-enroll him at his school under his former IEP program. However, school officials claimed that the old IEP was inapplicable in light of the boy's continuing sexual misconduct and proposed that he be placed in a closely supervised group home.

The boy's mother then brought suit in U.S. district court seeking a preliminary injunction to compel school officials to allow her son to attend class under his former IEP. The court ruled in favor of the school district, noting that in order to grant a preliminary injunction there must be an immediate threat of irreparable harm to the plaintiff. However, in this case the boy's mother had delayed for seven months before seeking to once again enroll her son in the school. Also, school officials had evidenced a genuine concern for the boy's welfare by offering to provide home tutoring during the time in which a new appropriate IEP could be formulated. The court held that because the boy had neither a current IEP nor a current educational placement, and because of the danger that he presented to others, there were insufficient grounds to order that he be returned to the classroom.

On appeal by the boy's mother, the U.S. Court of Appeals, Fifth Circuit, affirmed the district court, holding that when a handicapped student presents a substantial danger to himself or others, immediate removal from the classroom may be justified. The school's decision to provide the boy with home tutoring was upheld. *Jackson v. Franklin County School Bd.*, 765 F.2d 535 (5th Cir.1985).

The boy and his mother appealed again to the court of appeals. They argued that the district court was wrong in not finding that the boy's due process rights were violated by being excluded from school during the spring of 1984 and the first two months of the 1984-85 school year.

The court of appeals held that when the school failed to convene an IEP conference in the spring of 1984 it had violated the EHA. The EHA specifically required that "written prior notice to the parents or guardian" be provided whenever a school "proposes to initiate or change . . . the identification, evaluation, or educational placement of the child or the provision of a free appropriate public education to the child." The court observed that the U.S. Supreme Court has held that even a short suspension of up to ten days required notice of charges and some type of informal hearing. It stated that a failure on the part of the school to follow the procedural requirements of the EHA amounted to a failure by the school to provide a free appropriate education for the boy. The court concluded that, under the EHA, the burden rested on the school or agency to safeguard handicapped children's rights by informing the parents or guardians of those rights. It also noted that the writers of the EHA intended that students and parents should participate as much as possible in outlining the educational program of the handicapped student. Both the EHA and the Fourteenth Amendment required the school to provide the boy with notice and a hearing regarding his continued exclusion from school.

The case was remanded to the district court to determine the extent of the boy's loss caused by the school's failure to provide notice and a hearing in April and August, 1984. The court of appeals also instructed the district court to determine what damages, either monetary or in remedial educational services, would be appropriate for the boy. *Jackson v. Franklin County School Bd.*, 806 F.2d 623 (5th Cir.1986).

A U.S. district court in Ohio issued a preliminary injunction ordering that two violently disruptive students, ages twelve and fifteen, be allowed to return to their classrooms. Both boys, wards of the state, had been evaluated as severely behaviorally handicapped (SBH) and were placed in a residential facility. The local school district conducted classes at the facility to provide the students with an appropriate education under the EHA. During the 1983-84 school year the boys were involved in several episodes of destructive and violent classroom behavior at the residential facility.

The school district decided that for the 1984-85 school year it would conduct the SBH classes at a regular school building. During the first week of classes the fifteen-year-old boy violently attacked another student and began throwing books and a ruler around his classroom; the twelve-year-old boy, after telling his teacher, "I'm going to kick your ass," picked up a plastic baseball bat and generally destroyed the classroom. The school district removed the students from the SBH classes and instead provided the boys with one hour per day of personalized tutoring at the residential facility. The school district then caused the boys to be prosecuted for their misbehavior and each was adjudged delinquent under Ohio law.

The boys sued the school district in federal court claiming that the school district had violated the EHA by changing their placement. The EHA provides that whenever a school district proposes to change a child's educational placement there must be a hearing before an impartial hearing officer and, most importantly, that during the pendency of these proceedings the child must remain in his then current educational placement unless the child or his guardian agrees to a change in placement. The school district argued that because of their behavior the boys presented a danger to themselves and others, and that their education could not be safely continued even in an SBH class.

The district court rejected this reasoning and granted a preliminary injunction allowing the students to return to the SBH classroom. The court was disturbed that the school district had not used its normal disciplinary procedures, which included a one to two week suspension or expulsion, before it decided to prosecute the boys and change their educational placements. It further held that although the students must be allowed to return to their classroom, and thus to their "then current" educational placements as required by the EHA, the school district would not be precluded from using normal disciplinary procedures to deal with any future disruptive conduct by the students. *Lamont X v. Quisenberry*, 606 F.Supp. 809 (S.D.Ohio 1984).

In an Illinois case when a seventeen-year-old "exceptional" child told his teacher, "I'm not serving your fucking detention. Fuck you," he was promptly suspended for five days. His parents contested the suspension and he was given a hearing at which an impartial hearing officer upheld the suspension. On appeal to the Department of Education, the State Superintendent of Education overturned the suspension saying that the child's emotional outburst was evidence that the system had misplaced this child in a class setting too advanced. The school district appealed to a U.S. district court, which reversed the state superintendent's decision. The court stated that if the seventeen-year-old had managed to complete eleven years of education and had advanced to the point where he was placed in a mainstream educational course, it was nonsense to suggest that his shameful outburst was somehow the fault of the system. The child knew, or should have known, that his behavior was unacceptable. Further, the court pointed to the U.S. Supreme Court decision *Goss v. Lopez*, 419 U.S. 565 (1975), which held that "suspension is considered not only to be a necessary tool to maintain order but a valuable educational device." The court concluded by noting that a five-day suspension should not be equated to expulsion or termination, and that federal law permits the enforcement of ordinary classroom discipline through such suspensions. *Bd. of Educ. of the City of Peoria, School Dist. 150 v. Illinois State Bd. of Educ.*, 531 F.Supp. 148 (C.D.Ill.1982).

The following case illustrates that a suspension can constitute a "change in placement" if it is to last for an indefinite period. Here a school for the blind in New York suspended a deaf, blind and emotionally disturbed residential student who engaged in persistent self-abusive behavior. The reason for the suspension was that the school lacked the staff to supervise the fourteen-year-old girl, who needed to be watched continually. Without the proper supervisory staff the girl was a danger to herself. In fact, at one time during her enrollment at the school the girl had to be hospitalized because of self-inflicted injuries. The suspension was to last "until such time it appeared to be in the best interests of the child and the school to revoke the suspension." The student's mother brought suit against the school to compel it to reinstate her daughter as a residential student and to force it to provide a hearing in compliance with the EHA. Shortly after the suit was commenced the girl was reinstated in the school and the school argued that the mother's claim was then moot.

The U.S. district court disagreed with the school's claim, saying that the actions of the school were unlawful. The court observed that the time during which the child had been hospitalized as a result of self-inflicted injuries stemming from her self-abusive behavior did not constitute a "change in placement" triggering procedural safeguards. However, the indefinite suspension period which was to last until such time as "it appeared to be in the best interests of the child and the school to revoke the suspension" was unlawful within the meaning of the EHA. The indefinite suspension constituted a "change in placement" within the meaning of the EHA and thus required a hearing. *Sherry v. New York State Educ. Dep't*, 479 F.Supp. 1328 (W.D.N.Y. 1979).

The following cases illustrate that expulsions are not viewed in the same light as suspensions. Expulsions trigger the procedural safeguards of the EHA and require a showing that the behavior leading to the expulsion was not the result of an expelled child's handicap.

A law student at the University of Wisconsin completed his first semester with below standard grades. He was dismissed during his second semester because he failed to furnish certification of his undergraduate degree. The school allowed him to return the following spring despite knowledge that he was an alcoholic. Sensing that he was doing poorly, the student asked to withdraw. The school later learned that while drunk, he had harassed and threatened a classmate. The school readmitted the student for a third time the following spring. He completed the semester with below standard grades and the school expelled him. The student sued the school in a Wisconsin federal court alleging § 504 violations of the Rehabilitation Act, by discriminating against him on account of alcoholism. The district court granted the school's dismissal motion because the student was not "otherwise qualified" to continue as a law student. He then appealed to the U.S. Court of Appeals, Seventh Circuit.

The appeals court noted that § 504 provided that an institution receiving federal funds may not discriminate against an "otherwise qualified handicapped individual." It also noted that previous cases had held that "[a]n otherwise qualified person is one who is able to meet all of a program's requirements in spite of his handicap." The Rehabilitation Act did not forbid decisions based on the actual attributes of the handicapped individual. It also recognized that the school's decision was based on evaluations of how the student had previously performed and how he could be expected to perform in the future. In this case the school acted on the basis of the student's past performance rather than his alcoholism. The appeals court upheld the district court decision to dismiss the case. *Anderson v. Univ. of Wisconsin*, 841 F.2d 737 (7th Cir.1988).

A learning disabled Mississippi high school student was found with marijuana cigarettes and knives at school. A local school district recommended that he be expelled for the remainder of the school year and that he receive no academic credit for the year. It also offered the student homebound instruction during the expulsion period. A hearing officer concluded that the expulsion was impermissible because the student did not present an immediate danger to himself or other students, and the school district appealed.

The Mississippi Supreme Court held that a handicapped student could be expelled based upon a reasonable conclusion that the student would otherwise disrupt the educational process of other students. The school district, however, would have to provide quality educational services to the handicapped student during the expulsion period. The test in expelling a student, stated the court, was whether the behavior for which the student was expelled was caused in some way by his handicap. It held that school districts could expel handicapped students so long as less harsh forms of discipline are considered and proper procedures are followed under the EHA. *Bd. of Trustees v. Doe*, 508 So.2d 1081 (Miss.1987).

A Kentucky case arose after a fifteen-year-old ninth grade student, identified and evaluated since kindergarten as a handicapped or exceptional child, defied the authority of his teacher. He refused to do assigned work, destroyed a worksheet, destroyed a coffee cup, and pushed and kicked the teacher while leaving the classroom. The following day the child was suspended. A hearing regarding the suspension was held by the school board which did not convene nor consult the Administrative Admissions and Release Committee (AARC), a multi-disciplined group which, in Kentucky, is the organization responsible for reviewing challenged placement decisions. In addition, the board did not address the relationship, if any, between the child's handicap and his disruptive behavior. Expulsion followed. The child, through his parents, then sought legal help in the federal courts.

The U.S. Court of Appeals, Sixth Circuit, affirmed a U.S. district court decision which held than an expulsion from school is a "change of placement" within the meaning of the EHA, thus requiring certain procedural protections prior to expulsion. The Court of Appeals also determined that an expulsion must be accompanied by a determination as to whether the handicapped student's misconduct bears a relationship to his handicap. The lower court injunction requiring the expungment of expulsion records from the board minutes and school attendance records was upheld. *Kaelin v. Grubbs*, 682 F.2d 595 (6th Cir.1982).

The Nebraska Supreme Court has held that the expulsion of a disruptive handicapped student violated the EHA. In this case a student expelled for disruptive behavior from a school for the trainable mentally retarded was found by the court to have been denied a free appropriate education. After the expulsion the student, who suffered from autism, mental retardation and epilepsy, was placed in regional institutions by his parents. While in the institutions, many of the skills the child previously learned were lost, but the school district made no attempt to relocate the student. The Nebraska Supreme Court held that the expulsion constituted a change in placement which was subject to the procedural protections of the EHA. It further stated that under the Act, local school officials were prohibited from expelling students whose handicaps were the cause of their disruptive behavior. The school's only course of action in such circumstances was to transfer the disruptive student to an appropriate, more restrictive environment. The court ordered that the school district reimburse the parents for the cost incurred in the institutionalization of their child. *Adams Cent. School Dist. No. 690 v. Deist*, 334 N.W.2d 775 (Neb.1983).

In a similar case arising in Indiana, the mother of a handicapped child sued a local school district challenging the child's expulsion from school. The child had been expelled for disciplinary reasons. The mother sued the school district in U.S. district court which held that the school was prohibited from expelling students whose handicaps caused them to be disruptive, but was allowed to transfer the disruptive student to an appropriate, more restrictive environment.

The court noted that the EHA does not prohibit all expulsions of disruptive handicapped children. It only prohibits the expulsion of handicapped children who are disruptive because of their handicap. The distinction between a handicapped child and any other child is that, unlike any other disruptive child, before a disruptive handicapped child can be expelled, it must be determined whether the handicap is the cause of the child's disruptiveness. This must be determined through the change of placement procedures required by the EHA. In this case the school district was found to have violated the due process provisions of the EHA when it expelled the student without first determining whether his propensity to disrupt was the result of his inappropriate placement. *Doe v. Koger*, 480 F.Supp. 225 (N.D.Ind.1979).

A U.S. district court in Florida granted a preliminary injunction against state and local school officials preventing them from enforcing the expulsion of nine handicapped students. The students, expelled for alleged misconduct, were all classified as "educable mentally retarded," "mildly mentally retarded," or "EMR/dull normal." The Florida school district which had expelled the students did so on the ground that the students knew right from wrong.

The students sued the school district alleging they were denied a free appropriate education under the EHA as a result of their expulsions. The district court agreed with the students finding that under § 504 of the Rehabilitation Act and the EHA, no handicapped student could be expelled for misconduct related to the handicap. The court found that no determination was made as to the relationship between the students' handicaps and their behavioral problems. The court also found that an expulsion is a change in educational placement. The students' request for an injunction was granted.

The school district appealed to the U.S. Court of Appeals, Fifth Circuit, which affirmed the district court ruling. The court of appeals held that the determination that a handicapped student knows the difference between right and wrong is not sufficient to support a determination that his misconduct was or was not a manifestation of his handicap. Only a trained, knowledgeable group of persons should determine whether a student's misconduct bears a relationship to his handicapping condition. Because no such determination was made in this case, the court found the expulsion of the nine students to have constituted a change in placement invoking the procedural protections of the EHA and § 504 of the Rehabilitation Act. *S-1 v. Turlington*, 635 F.2d 342 (5th Cir.1981).

CHAPTER THREE
EHA PROCEDURAL SAFEGUARDS

I. ROLE OF THE HEARING OFFICER

The procedural safeguards of the EHA are designed to ensure that parents and children are able to enforce their rights under the Act. The safeguards include the right to an "impartial due process hearing" when parents or guardians are dissatisfied with their child's IEP [section 1415(b)(2)]. These hearings are to be conducted by the state or local educational agency responsible for providing services. The hearing must be conducted by an impartial hearing officer. The initial due process hearing may be provided at the state or local educational agency level. If the initial hearing is held at the local level, either party may appeal "to the State educational agency which shall conduct an impartial review of such hearing" [section 1415(c)]. The decision of the initial hearing officer is final unless appealed; the decision of the state officer is likewise final unless either party brings an action in state court or federal district court [section 1415(e)(1)].

The first cases in this section define some procedural aspects of an appeal.

A multidisciplinary team proposed an individualized educational program (IEP) for an Oregon student. It included eighty-five percent of each day in regular classes and fifteen percent in a resource room where the student would receive special assistance in math. His mother contested the proposed IEP and the recommended placement. She requested a hearing pursuant to Oregon law. A local hearing officer approved the IEP. The mother then sought review of the hearing officer's decision. The Superintendent of Public Instruction appointed a reviewing officer. Oregon law provided that the hearing officer's decision could be reversed only if the reviewing officer found that the hearing officer's decision was not supported by "substantial evidence in the record." The reviewing officer affirmed the hearing officer's decision. The mother then appealed to the Oregon Court of Appeals.

The court of appeals observed that EHA § 1415(c) required reviewing officers to make independent decisions upon completion of their case review. It also noted that the federal regulation governing review procedures required reviewing officers to "make an independent decision on completion of the review." The court of appeals reversed the reviewing officer's decision because his review wrongly relied on state law. The reviewing officer merely reviewed the local hearing officer's decision to determine whether there was sufficient evidence in the record to support his decision. He failed to make an independent decision based on the record. The court of appeals remanded the case to the superintendent so that he could independently review the record and make appropriate findings of fact consistent with the EHA and the regulation. *Tompkins v. Forest Grove School Dist.*, 740 P.2d 186 (Or.App.1987).

A boy entered a New York school district at the fifth grade level in 1985. His teacher requested that he be evaluated by the school psychologist for the presence of a learning disability because he demonstrated writing and attention problems. A school psychologist evaluated the boy and decided not to refer him to the local Commission on Special Education (CSE). The boy's parents were not notified of their procedural rights as required by New York regulations. The boy was subsequently evaluated at the Boston Children's Hospital, which concluded that he had a learning disability and recommended remedial help outside the classroom. In September, 1986, the CSE held a hearing and found the boy to be learning disabled. An Individualized Educational Program (IEP) was then developed for the 1986-87 school year. The boy's parents, however, appealed this IEP and a hearing officer found that the school district had "violated nearly all of the parents' procedural rights under New York and federal law." The contested IEP was remanded to the CSE and revised. In January, 1987, the parents appealed the IEP again, alleging that it did not provide the boy with an appropriate education. The boy's status as a learning disabled child was not contested by the parents or the school district in this appeal. In considering the appeal, however, the Commissioner of the New York State Department of Education reclassified the boy as not handicapped under either state or federal law. The CSE, in turn, declared the boy ineligible for special educational services because of this reclassification.

The boy's parents sought a declaration from a U.S. district court that the commissioner lacked authority to review the uncontested CSE finding that the boy was handicapped. The court noted that the EHA provided that "[a] decision made in a hearing . . . shall be final, except that any party involved in such hearing may appeal such decision." It observed that the decision in *Antkowiak v. Ambach*, 638 F.Supp. 1564 (W.D.N.Y.1986) held that the decision of an impartial hearing, such as that held by the CSE in this case, was final as to issues not appealed.

The court disagreed with the commissioner and the school district who argued that in considering an IEP the commissioner has discretion to review the "nature and existence of the handicap itself." The court declared that allowing the Commissioner to reconsider the handicap issue in an IEP appeal would "remove all the procedural safeguards from the process, which the EHA was enacted, in part, to provide. It would mean that the commissioner could, as he did here, completely alter the outcome of the hearing." It would also mean, declared the court, that decisions by the CSE with respect to labeling a child handicapped would never become final, which was a violation of the finality requirement of the EHA. The court determined that the Commissioner lacked the power to reclassify the boy as not handicapped because the issue of the boy's handicap was not before him. It ruled in favor of the boy's parents. *Hiller v. Bd. of Educ.*, 674 F.Supp. 73 (N.D.N.Y.1987).

The Michigan Court of Appeals reversed on procedural grounds a state review officer's decision in favor of the parents of a handicapped child, citing a lack of impartiality on the part of the review officer. The court's opinion also indicated that it was displeased with the review officer's disregard of financial burdens on school districts. In this case a girl suffered a stroke at the age of ten which left her with a full scale I.Q. of forty-seven and a potential I.Q. of sixty-four. When her parents approached their local school district requesting a free appropriate public education for their daughter, the district evaluated her and proposed placement in a classroom for the "educable mentally impaired." The parents disagreed and a due process hearing was held. The hearing officer, rejecting the parents' claim that the girl required a two-to-one student-teacher ratio, approved the school district's proposed EMI placement. The parents appealed to the state review officer, who exercised his statutory power to allow neither the school nor the parents to file written briefs or present oral arguments. After examining the evidence which had been presented to the hearing officer, the review officer ruled that the girl was entitled to a student-teacher ratio of not more than three to one, and the school district appealed.

The state court of appeals held that because the parents had written arguments attacking the hearing officer's decision on the appeal form they filed with the review officer, the review officer had, in effect, allowed the parents to file a written brief. The review officer had therefore been obligated to allow the school district to present its position as well. Since the review officer had improperly allowed only one side to file a brief, his decision was vacated and the case was remanded to the review officer with instructions that oral arguments be allowed. *Nelson v. Southfield Pub. Schools*, 384 N.W.2d 423 (Mich.App.1986).

The New Hampshire Supreme Court decided a case in which a fourteen-year-old girl, who suffered from a severe learning disability coupled with speech and language disorders, was placed in a private residential school in Massachusetts. The reason for this placement was the inability of the girl's New Hampshire school district to provide an appropriate educational program for her. During the summer, after the child's second year at the school in Massachusetts, the local school district in New Hampshire formulated an IEP for the child which utilized public resources. The girl's mother appealed the school district's decision to place the child in a public program, which resulted in a determination that the public program offered was both "free and appropriate," and that the school district would no longer be obliged to pay for the child's education at the school in Massachusetts or any other private facility. The determination also denied tuition reimbursement to the mother for the four month period following the proposed IEP. (The mother had enrolled the child for a third year at the private school pending the resolution of the appeals process.) The mother then asked the New Hampshire

Supreme Court to order the school district to pay the expenses incurred for the four months.

The court declined to rule on the matter since the child's mother had not appealed the final administrative decision to a state trial court or federal district court. Petitioning the supreme court of a state is not the appropriate method for seeking review of a decision of a state board of education. Although the court declined to hear the merits of the mother's complaint, it noted that if a school district can provide satisfactory assurance that its programs meet EHA standards for "free appropriate public education" of handicapped children, it will only be liable for the costs resulting from the placement of handicapped children in its own public programs and not for the cost incurred in private placements. *Petition of Darlene W.*, 469 A.2d 1307 (N.H.1983).

The remaining cases in Section I deal with the power of, and appropriate selection criteria for, a hearing official.

A nine-year-old Florida boy who lived with his parents suffered from juvenile autism. For three years the boy was enrolled in the Hendry County School Class for the Trainable Mentally Handicapped. Because the boy had made limited educational progress both the school and the boy's parents agreed that the boy needed a different IEP for the 1985-86 school year. Subsequently the boy was labeled severely emotionally disturbed (SED) and in need of a program for the severely handicapped. In May, 1985, the school held a planning conference to develop a new IEP for the boy. As a result of the conference the school's director of exceptional student education approved a new IEP for the boy. It provided for a profoundly handicapped class program, a mainstreaming opportunity with first grade students, an aide to accompany the student to music class, and an SED class placement in a varying exceptionalities class.

When the new IEP was issued the parents rejected it contending that the boy needed residential placement if he was to reach necessary educational goals. In June, 1985, the parents asked for a due process hearing to determine the appropriateness of the IEP. In July, 1985, the hearing officer issued his order, rejecting the school's proposal and ordering residential placement for the boy. The school appealed the hearing officer's decision to the Florida District Court of Appeal.

The court concluded that a hearing officer is limited to determining the appropriateness of an IEP. Here the hearing officer overstepped his authority when he ordered a residential placement for the boy. The most the hearing officer could do was to remand the matter to the school district for further deliberation with an attached recommendation for residential placement. The court held that the school's proposed program met the needs of the boy and that a residential placement was not necessary for the boy to receive an appropriate public education. The hearing officer's decision was reversed and the case was remanded for further proceedings. *Hendry County School Bd. v. Kujawski*, 498 So.2d 566 (Fla.App.2d Dist.1986).

Where state law regarding the role of a hearing officer contradicts the EHA, the EHA controls. Following the private evaluations of their two children, North Carolina parents informed the principal of the public school in which the children were enrolled that the children were being placed in a private educational facility for half of each school day. Subsequently, the parents asked that the board of education provide the children with an IEP comparable to that of the private institution or, alternatively, that the board provide transportation and tuition for the children to continue at the private facility for the 1984-85 school year. They asked to be reimbursed for expenses incurred by them resulting from the children's private school placement during the 1983-84 year. The board of education denied their request and the parents requested a due process hearing. The hearing officer determined that he had no authority under North Carolina state law to grant an award of reimbursement and no hearing was held. When the state board of education denied a request by the parents that the hearing officer be granted such authority, the parents appealed to a U.S. district court.

The parents claimed that the board of education, through the appointed administrative hearing officer, deprived them of their EHA procedural rights. They also contended that the state board of education refused to interpret or amend state regulations to be consistent with the EHA. The state board argued that reimbursement costs were monetary penalties that could only be imposed by the courts.

The district court noted that the EHA contained a detailed procedural component with which local and state boards were required to comply. It concluded that to allow a state hearing officer to conduct a hearing on the issue of reimbursement and to enter findings of fact based on that hearing, but to refuse to order reimbursement even when appropriate, made the EHA less than complete. To the extent North Carolina's interpretation of the authority of a hearing officer contradicted the EHA, the terms of the EHA must control. The local board of education was ordered to conduct another hearing and order reimbursement costs if appropriate. *S-1 v. Spangler*, 650 F.Supp. 1427 (M.D.N.C.1986).

A hearing officer is not charged with the responsibility of choosing between an educational program offered by a school district and counterproposals submitted by parents. To give the hearing officer such powers would be to diminish the role of the school districts in selecting the best possible educational program appropriate to the needs of handicapped children. This ruling was handed down by a federal district court in the District of Columbia in a case in which the parents of a handicapped child challenged District of Columbia hearing procedures. The court observed that the EHA requires a due process hearing if the parents of a handicapped child objected to the placement of their child in a program they deemed inappropriate to the child's needs.

Here, the parents were dissatisfied with the program offered by the school district. They asked the court to order the hearing officer to weigh the proposals of both the school district and the parents and then to determine which of the two proposals was most appropriate for their child. The court refused to grant such powers to the hearing officer. Instead the court reiterated the duties of the hearing officer in such cases—the officer was required to hear the school district's proposal. If the parents were dissatisfied with that proposal they could offer alternative suggestions to the school district. If, after hearing the proposal and the counterproposals, the hearing officer deemed the school district's proposal to be inadequate, the hearing officer was required to remand the district's proposal to the district with instructions to submit a new proposal within 20 days. *Davis v. Dist. of Columbia Bd. of Educ.*, 530 F.Supp. 1215 (D.D.C.1982).

A U.S. district court in Connecticut has dealt with the procedural problem of whether testimony of a hearing officer regarding her mental processes while making a decision could be allowed in a case involving an administrative determination that a minor's placement in a private residential facility was not necessary for educational reasons. The case arose on appeal of a state administrative determination to the district court. The defendant school board was excused from any financial obligation in excess of tuition costs by the administrative determination and the minor, through his parents, appealed.

At the appeal stage the state listed as its sole witness the hearing officer whose decision was being appealed. The minor's motion to preclude her testimony at trial was granted. The court noted that in reviewing a decision of an administrative agency, it was not the proper function of the court to probe the mental processes of the agency or its members, particularly if the agency made a considered decision upon a full administrative record. Such probing should ordinarily be avoided and there must be a strong showing of bad faith or improper behavior before such inquiry may be made.

In this case, the state based its opposition to the motion on the premise that the mental processes rule had little or no application in a case where the officer was testifying voluntarily and the purpose of the testimony was not to contradict or impeach the record which had already been established.

The court stated that this proposition was supported neither by logic nor authority. The objectivity and independence of the hearing officer in her role as administrative adjudicator would likely be undermined by her being offered by the state as a probative witness in support of its case. Cross examination and the court's assessment of the testimony would involve, necessarily, a review of the mental processes of the adjudicative officer. Such an examination of a judge would be destructive of judicial responsibility. Just as a judge's mind should not be subjected to scrutiny, so the integrity of the administrative process must be equally respected. The court, therefore, granted the motion to exclude the hearing officer's testimony. *Feller v. Bd. of Educ. of State of Connecticut*, 583 F.Supp. 1526 (D.Conn.1984).

Two handicapped children in Alabama, dissatisfied with the educational plans that had been prescribed for them, sought and were afforded due process hearings. Prior to the hearings, the children, through their parents, filed written objections to the method used by the state for selecting due process hearing officers. They alleged that the selection of hearing officers who were officers or employees of local school systems in which the children were enrolled or who were university personnel involved in the formulation of state policies concerning special education violated the EHA and its implementing regulations. Despite these objections, due process hearings were conducted and in each case a determination adverse to the children was reached. The children's claims were then evaluated by a review panel which was selected by the same method as the due process panel. Prior to the second hearing the children filed a second set of written objections to the method of selecting hearing officers. The review panel affirmed the adverse ruling of the due process panel and the children brought suit in federal court.

A U.S. district court enjoined the local school superintendent from selecting, as due process hearing officers under the EHA, individuals who were officers or employees of local school systems which the children attended, or university personnel who had been or were involved in the formulation of state policies on educating handicapped children.

The school district appealed to the U.S. Court of Appeals, Eleventh Circuit, which affirmed the district court ruling. The court of appeals found that officers and employees of local school boards in Alabama were employees of agencies "involved in the education and care of the child" with a personal or professional interest in the type of educational assistance extended to handicapped children, and thus were not eligible to serve on due process hearing panels. Further, university personnel involved in the formulation of state policies for the education of the handicapped were not sufficiently impartial to serve as due process hearing officers under the EHA. *Mayson v. Teague*, 749 F.2d 652 (11th Cir. 1984).

A hearing officer in Rhode Island ordered a school district to fund the special education of two learning disabled children at a private school in Massachusetts. A U.S. district court upheld the hearing officer's order. The school district appealed claiming that because the hearing officer was an employee of the Department of Education, the hearing did not satisfy the EHA requirement that it not "be conducted by an employee of [the local or state educational] agency . . . involved in the education or care of the child." The U.S. Court of Appeals, First Circuit, upheld the district court ruling saying that the school district was not within the "protected class" of handicapped children and their parents that Congress envisioned when it prohibited employees of a state educational agency from acting as review officers. *Colin K. v. Schmidt*, 715 F.2d 1 (1st Cir. 1983).

A thirteen-year-old child afflicted with dyslexia attended a private school in New Hampshire. The school district offered an IEP which was to be implemented by placing the student in one of the district's public schools. Her parents rejected the plan and requested an impartial due process hearing to resolve the dispute. A prehearing conference was held and all parties were represented by counsel. The hearing officer took notes and tape recorded the proceeding. Thereafter, he issued an order stating that the district could employ a court reporter to supplement the hearing officer's effort to record the hearing. At the hearing, the district's counsel brought a private court reporter certified by the state of New Hampshire to record the proceedings at the district's expense. The parents announced their intention to appeal the prehearing order allowing the district to employ a court reporter. A complaint was filed in a federal district court. The district court dismissed the action and the parents appealed to the U.S. Court of Appeals, First Circuit.

The court noted that there had been gaps and inaudible tapes at previous administrative hearings. Therefore the court concluded that in order to secure its entitlement to a verbatim record of the hearing, the district had a right to ensure that a quality recording was made. The attendance of a court reporter was a reasonable and necessary means for the district to secure its statutory right. The parents contended that the use of the court reporter denied them their rights under the EHA. By statute, public access to a special education hearing is permitted only with the permission of the parents or child. The court, however, found no meaningful distinction between permitting a court reporter to attend a hearing to make a verbatim recording and exposing that same person to the recording at the completion of the hearing in order to make a transcript of the proceeding. Therefore, the court affirmed the trial court's decision allowing the court reporter to attend the administrative hearing. *Caroline T. v. Hudson School Dist.*, 915 F.2d 752 (1st Cir. 1990).

A thirteen-year-old Connecticut student with Down's Syndrome received special education in the public schools of Groton, Connecticut. The student's mother's native language was Danish, making it difficult for her to follow written and spoken English. Pursuant to the EHA, the mother, the teacher, and others participated in the development of the individualized education program (IEP) for the student at a yearly meeting. Because of her difficulty with English, the mother requested to tape record the meeting. She believed that a recording would let her listen to the meeting again along with a dictionary. The teacher, however, did not wish to be taped. She felt that it would make her uncomfortable and create unnecessary tension. The board of education then denied the mother permission to tape record the meeting. After the mother requested a due process hearing, the board of education ruled that the mother would be permitted to take notes of the teacher's statements and could tape record the others if they did not object. The mother felt, however, that the notes of the meeting were unsatisfactory. The teacher then refused to attend an annual review meeting when she learned that the mother intended to tape record the meeting. The mother refused to proceed without the teacher present and requested a due process hearing. The hearing officer concluded that the mother did not as a matter of law have a right to tape record the meetings. Further, the hearing officer found that there was no evidence that the tape recording was necessary for the student to receive an appropriate education. The mother appealed to a U.S. district court. Both parties moved for summary judgment.

The EHA, the court noted, emphasized the importance of parental participation in developing the IEP. The EHA provided safeguards "that guarantee parents both an opportunity for meaningful input into all decisions affecting their child's education and the right to seek review of any decisions they think inappropriate." However, the Office of Special Education Programs (OSEP), had addressed this issue stating that "although taping is clearly not required, it is permissible at the option of either the parents or the agency," 34 CFR Part 300, Appendix C 1989. The OSEP noted, however, that it did not have authority to require or prohibit recordings. The court determined that the EHA is "designed to help implement individualized and personalized educational plans for handicapped children and their parents." Since the mother had difficulty understanding what took place at the meetings, a tape recording would allow the mother to go home and review what was said at the meeting until she was clear what her child's IEP entailed. The court determined that the tape recording was an essential part of her participation in the planning and evaluation of the IEP. The court then addressed the second issue, whether the teacher could refuse to be taped. The court determined that since the teacher's participation is extremely important to the success of the meetings, she would have to have an objective reason why her comments should not be taped. Her argument that such taping would make her uncomfortable, the court determined, was completely self-serving. The parents' summary judgment motion was granted and the mother was allowed to tape record the meetings. *E. H. v. Tirozzi*, 735 F.Supp. 53 (D.Conn.1990).

The Hawaii Department of Education appealed from a Hawaii trial court order dismissing its appeal of a hearing officer's decision. The appeal was prompted by the decision and order of an administrative hearing officer in favor of the parents of a handicapped student who had complained that the Department had not provided him with a free appropriate public education as required by the EHA.

The Supreme Court of Hawaii held that under the EHA, the Department was not entitled to appeal from the administrative decision. Section 1415(e)(2) of the Act provides only that "any party aggrieved by the findings and decision made pursuant to the hearing process may bring a separate civil action in a state or federal district court." The court noted that the standard of review in such an action "is very different" from the standard of review in an appeal. This was discussed in the case of *Board of Education v. Rowley*. In a separate civil action the state court or federal district court "shall receive the records of the administrative proceedings, shall hear additional evidence at the request of a party and, basing its decision on the preponderance of the evidence, shall grant such relief as the court determines appropriate." The court concluded that the EHA did not confer the right of appeal upon state agencies. The district court's dismissal of the appeal was reversed, however, on the ground that a claim for relief in a separate civil action was presented, even though misdesignated on appeal. *Matter of Eric G.*, 649 P.2d 1140 (Hawaii 1982).

II. EXHAUSTION OF ADMINISTRATIVE REMEDIES

The doctrine of exhaustion of remedies provides that "no one is entitled to judicial relief for a supposed or threatened injury until the prescribed administrative remedy has been exhausted." This was pointed out by the U.S. Supreme Court in the case of *Myers v. Bethlehem Shipbuilding Corp.*, 303 U.S. 41 (1938). The reasons supporting the exhaustion of remedies doctrine were advanced in a later Supreme Court case, *McKart v. U.S.*, 395 U.S. 185 (1968). Among the reasons given were the development of an accurate factual record, thus allowing more informed judicial review, encouraging "expeditious decision making," and furthering Congressional intent.

A. Operation of the Exhaustion Doctrine

EHA Section 1415 provides for an initial independent review of a contested IEP at the agency level. Section 1415(e)(2) provides that an "aggrieved party" may bring a separate civil action in state or federal court to challenge the final decision of a state educational agency. Normally the parents or guardians of a handicapped child have the duty to exhaust all administrative channels before resorting to a state or federal court. However, some courts have excused the "exhaustion" requirement under certain exceptional circumstances.

A District of Columbia student had severe language, emotional and behavioral problems. Her parents sent her to a private school. The student's parents then contacted the District of Columbia Public Schools (DCPS) for special education placement. However, the DCPS's first evaluation concluded that the student required no special education. The DCPS also failed to develop an individualized education program (IEP) or recommend placement by the beginning of that school year. The parents then enrolled their daughter in a private school where she had attended summer school. The district then developed an IEP for the student, recommending that twenty-five percent of her school hours be mainstreamed with nonhandicapped students. The parents disagreed with the IEP and requested a due process hearing before an administrative hearing officer. The parties were unable to reach a settlement and three hearings were held.

As the following school year approached, the parents requested a fourth due process hearing but then withdrew the request in favor of a federal lawsuit filed in the U.S. District Court for the District of Columbia. The court granted the DCPS's summary judgment motion. The parents filed a motion to amend the judgment, and the court reversed itself, vacating its prior opinion and ruling for the parents. The court held that further administrative appeals by the parents would have been futile. The private school was an appropriate placement for the current and following school years because the DCPS had failed to participate in IEP meetings for that year. Because the DCPS had already paid for the student's private school tuition for the current school year, the court ordered the DCPS to reimburse the parents for the upcoming school year. The DCPS then appealed to the U.S. Court of Appeals, District of Columbia Circuit. According to the court, the law clearly required that all administrative remedies be exhausted before an EHA lawsuit could be filed in a federal district court. An exception existed if exhaustion of remedies would be futile or inadequate. The parents had not exhausted their administrative remedies in this case because the administrative hearings had ended in only a determination for the prior school year, whereas the final order had pertained to the current and upcoming academic years. The court reversed the district court's decision. *Cox v. Jenkins*, 878 F.2d 414 (D.C.Cir. 1989).

A learning disabled Rhode Island student with attendance and behavior problems required special education services and speech therapy. He was placed in a self-contained classroom in a local school where he continued to have tardiness and behavior problems. The school district developed an IEP, which the student's mother approved. The IEP called for the student's enrollment as a special education student. He continued to miss classes and was frequently placed on suspension. Because of the school's policy regarding absences, the student did not receive academic credit for any of his courses. The student's mother claimed that she was never informed of her right to challenge the school's disciplinary system through an administrative process. The student filed a complaint with the Rhode Island Department of Education, alleging that the department had failed to comply with federal and state regulations regarding procedural safeguards. The department notified the school's superintendent that the disciplinary actions taken against the student violated the law because the school had not met to determine whether there was a causal relationship between the student's misbehavior and his handicap. The superintendent stated that the school had determined that the student was behaviorally disordered but that not all of his inappropriate behavior was due to his handicapped condition. The student continued to experience attendance problems and eventually quit school. He then sued the school board in a federal district court under the EHA, the Rehabilitation Act and the Civil Rights Act, challenging the school's disciplinary sanctions. The court found that it lacked jurisdiction because the student had failed to exhaust state administrative remedies. The student appealed to the U.S. Court of Appeals, First Circuit.

The court of appeals noted that the student would have to exhaust the administrative remedies outlined in the EHA before proceeding with any action in the district court. The student had not pursued any administrative remedies, other than his initial complaint. No evidence was presented which suggested that asking for a due process hearing would have been futile. The student would not be irreparably harmed in the absence of immediate action by the federal court. The student was required to exhaust his administrative remedies before he could bring an action in the district court. The court of appeals affirmed the district court's decision. *Christopher W. v. Portsmouth School Comm.*, 877 F.2d 1089 (1st Cir.1989).

In a district court proceeding brought in Maine, a fifteen-year-old student was an exceptional child within the meaning of Maine education laws. He attended public school special education classes, but began to suffer from severe psychological problems. He eventually had suicidal thoughts, and was admitted to a medical center for depression. He then attended a children's hospital in Boston and underwent psychiatric diagnosis, care and treatment. While the student was still in the children's hospital, the school district considered placement for the upcoming school year. The student's parents supported the recommendations of the doctor who had treated the student at the children's hospital, but the school district refused to do so. The Maine Department of Mental Health and Mental Retardation then funded a sixty-day evaluation at a New Hampshire rehabilitation facility. While the student was at the New Hampshire facility the parents twice attempted to reconvene the IEP meeting and then requested an impartial due process hearing under Maine education statute and the EHA.

Meanwhile, the New Hampshire facility's staff attempted to develop an appropriate IEP. The school district refused to attend the meeting. The facility's IEP team recommended residential treatment and placement at the facility for six to twelve months. The district refused to comply with the IEP and the student returned to Maine. The student's parents then sued the district in a federal district court, requesting a temporary restraining order to prevent the district from denying placement at the New Hampshire facility. The school district argued that the student had failed to exhaust his administrative remedies as required by the EHA.

The court ruled that the EHA required exhaustion of administrative remedies unless an administrative proceeding would be futile, severe harm would result, the administrative procedure would not bring adequate relief or the issue was purely legal. In this case, the student's parents failed to show that the student would be severely harmed by a failure to be placed in the New Hampshire facility. While the parents alleged that there had been significant developments following the development of the IEP, this was no reason to avoid the administrative remedies doctrine. The court denied the parents' motion and dismissed the lawsuit. *Harper v. School Admin. Dist. No. 37*, 727 F.Supp. 688 (D.Me.1989).

In the course of locating an alternative placement for a handicapped child, the District of Columbia Public Schools (DCPS) requested a due process hearing on the grounds that the mother had failed to cooperate with its placement efforts. A hearing was held in which testimony was presented on behalf of the mother which focused on the need for residential placement. The hearing officer, believing that it was beyond her power to order residential placement, remanded the case to DCPS with the direction that it was to submit the matter to the Residential Review Committee and propose a placement. Subsequently, the mother received a letter advising her that the Committee had declined to recommend residential placement and that the child was to be placed at a day school. The mother filed suit in federal district court and unilaterally placed the child in a school.

The court found that the mother was "aggrieved" as that term is used in the EHA and thus her claims were properly before the court. The argument that the mother had failed to exhaust her administrative remedies was also rejected. Resorting to the administrative process would have been futile in light of DCPS's blanket rejection of residential placement without setting forth the criteria upon which it based its decision. The court held that DCPS should place and fund the child at the residential school.

Further, the court rejected the argument that the Residential Review Committee had official status and that parents seeking to have their children considered for residential placement must satisfy criteria established by the Committee. Finally, the mother's claim for compensatory and punitive damages was denied since Congress intended the EHA to be the exclusive avenue through which a plaintiff may assert a claim to publicly financed special education. However, the court granted the mother's claim for attorney fees because of bad faith on the part of the school district, which had commended her for her cooperation and then the following day initiated a hostile due process hearing. *Diamond v. McKenzie*, 602 F.Supp. 632 (D.D.C.1985).

The remaining cases in this section involve situations which seem to alter the exhaustion requirement but do not.

A sixteen-year-old student with a language disorder attended a Tennessee public school. His parents became dissatisfied with the implementation of his IEP and requested a due process hearing. The hearing officer found that the school had provided the student with an appropriate education as required by the EHA. The parents did not appeal this decision. The following year a meeting was held to develop a new IEP. The parents requested that the student be placed in a private school but their request was denied. They later enrolled the student in a private school and sued the public school in a federal district court, alleging that it had failed to provide the student with an appropriate education. In the meantime, the parents sought another due process hearing requesting reimbursement for the student's private school costs. The hearing officer denied their request because they had bypassed the EHA's procedural requirements. The school proposed another IEP, which the parents rejected. Rather than requesting a due process hearing, they filed a supplemental complaint and requested the district court to find the private school an appropriate placement. They also sought tuition reimbursement. The district court held that the private school was an appropriate placement and ordered the public school to pay the student's private school tuition. The state appealed this decision to the U.S. Court of Appeals, Sixth Circuit.

The court of appeals held that the parents had not waived their right to seek reimbursement under the EHA by unilaterally removing the student from the public school and placing him in the private school. Although the parents had not waived their right to seek redress under the EHA, they were required to exhaust administrative procedures before seeking reimbursement for the student's private school costs. The parents were procedurally required to request a due process hearing instead of going directly to the district court. The court of appeals reversed the district court's decision and remanded the case for further proceedings. *Doe by and through Doe v. Smith*, 879 F.2d 1340 (6th Cir.1989).

A fourteen-year-old Indiana student had serious emotional handicaps. His IEP called for regular class attendance with outside counseling for his behavioral problems. The junior high school which the student attended used a demerit system for regular students which imposed a maximum sanction of expulsion. The student was suspended several times during one semester and received a sufficient number of demerits to justify expulsion. The school suspended the student under procedures for regular students, but when school administrators learned that he was receiving special education services, the suspension was lifted. A case conference was held, but the parents walked out of the meeting. The school later determined that the student's conduct was related to his emotional condition. As a result, the student was not expelled. Prior to the conference, the parents had requested a due process hearing. The hearing officer ordered a new IEP conference. The parents made a written request for review of this decision before the state Board of Special Education Appeals. The board held a hearing and upheld the hearing officer's order.

The parents then sued the school district in a federal district court, claiming that the IEP was inadequate. The court noted that the EHA explicitly required the use of administrative remedies and procedures and required states to develop adequate procedures for providing due process to handicapped students. The parents and student had failed to exhaust their administrative remedies and were precluded from review in a federal court. The court granted the school district's motion to dismiss the case. *Browning v. Evans*, 700 F.Supp. 978 (S.D.Ind.1988).

The Association for Retarded Citizens of Alabama sued the Alabama Superintendent of Education on behalf of 6,000 handicapped children. The association asserted that the superintendent violated the EHA by failing to provide sufficient funding to support necessary facilities and programs for the handicapped children. It also contended that the superintendent had violated the Due Process Clause of the Constitution because he failed to establish an effective administrative review process. The association claimed the children were entitled to relief under § 1983 of the Civil Rights Act. The association did not employ EHA administrative remedies before it initiated the lawsuit. A U.S. district court held for the superintendent and the association appealed to the U.S. Court of Appeals, Eleventh Circuit.

The association claimed that the administrative remedies were inadequate. The state was unprepared to handle thousands of individual administrative hearings. Furthermore, the hearings would be unlikely to produce the necessary funding for new programs and facilities for the handicapped children. The association also alleged that the administrative remedies were a "sham" and incompetent. The court of appeals observed that under the EHA, complaining parties were required to utilize the act's elaborate administrative scheme before challenging the actions of local school authorities in the courts. This administrative review process provided for a factual record and full development of technical issues. It also prevented deliberate disregard of congressionally-established agency procedures.

The court of appeals affirmed the district court decision. Initial review at the administrative level was required to determine whether the superintendent was providing the educational facilities and programs to which the handicapped children were entitled. Permitting the association to bypass EHA administrative procedures would violate Congress' mandate that parents and school officials formulate individualized educational plans together. The due process claim did not require exhaustion of administrative remedies since it was brought under § 1983. However, the association produced no evidence to support its allegation that the superintendent's administrative remedies were a "sham." The association was required to exhaust the EHA administrative procedures if it desired to contest the alleged insufficient funding and facilities. *Ass'n for Retarded Citizens of Alabama v. Teague*, 830 F.2d 158 (11th Cir.1987).

A handicapped Rhode Island child was enrolled in a hospital's special education facility where he was to receive both medical and educational services. In August, 1984, the hospital allegedly requested that the Rhode Island Department of Children and Their Families (DCF) consider the child eligible for services under Rhode Island's Mental Health Services for Children and Youth Program. If a child is eligible for the program his parents are required to contribute to the cost of medical services through any insurance they have. The child's parents challenged the child's eligibility under the program. They alleged that they were never notified by anyone that the child's benefits under a $50,000 lifetime major medical policy were being used under the program until September 1, 1986. At this time, they were allegedly informed by the insurer that their child's benefits had been exhausted. The parents sued the school board in a U.S. district court. They claimed that the child's right to an education had been violated since his expenses at the hospital were educational.

The parents argued that it was "futile" for them to exhaust their administrative remedies because the school board failed to notify them of their rights regarding use of the insurance proceeds to pay for the child's special education and related services. They also contended that they were not required to exhaust their administrative remedies because they were "inadequate." The district court held for the school board. At no time after the parents learned that their insurance coverage had been applied to the child's special education did they request a due process hearing or file a complaint with the state department of education. The parents failed to give administrative agencies a chance to resolve their claims. The administrative remedies were adequate since the parents only needed to obtain an administrative ruling that some of the insurance benefits were paid toward the cost of the child's special education and related services. The school board could then be required to reimburse the insurer for the money improperly paid under the child's policy. The case was dismissed. *Laura v. Providence School Bd.*, 680 F.Supp. 66 (D.R.I.1988).

A handicapped child was confined to a juvenile detention center in Florida. He sued the local school board in a U.S. district court under § 504 of the Rehabilitation Act and the EHA. He alleged that the detention center was overcrowded, unsanitary, lacked adequate staffing and was deficient in special education opportunities. The school board moved for dismissal. It contended that the child's claims under § 504 were invalid because the EHA provided all the remedies and procedures which Congress afforded handicapped children. It also claimed that the child's lawsuit should be dismissed because he failed to exhaust administrative remedies. The child contended that exhaustion of administrative remedies would be futile. The court held for the child with respect to his § 504 claim. Under the Handicapped Children's Protection Act the child could assert claims under both § 504 and the EHA. However, the court held for the school board regarding its exhaustion of administrative remedies argument. The child failed to show that exhaustion of administrative remedies would be futile or cause him irreparable harm. The school board's motion to dismiss the child's claim was granted. *G.C. v. Coler*, 673 F.Supp. 1093 (S.D.Fla.1987).

The father of a handicapped student in Virginia sued the county school board in a U.S. district court alleging that it had failed to develop a proper IEP for his son. He argued that because the school board had violated federal and state law in its failure to provide appropriate educational services for his son, he did not need to exhaust EHA administrative remedies prior to commencing court proceedings. The school board asked the court to dismiss the father's lawsuit, claiming that he had failed to first seek all of his remedies at the administrative level.

The court observed that according to § 3 of the Handicapped Children's Protection Act, administrative remedies must be exhausted prior to any lawsuit filed to vindicate the rights of handicapped students. When the father sought to bring suit under other laws he was required to exhaust EHA administrative remedies to the same extent that this exhaustion would be required if the suit had been brought under the EHA. This exhaustion doctrine, observed the court, serves the "interest of accuracy, efficiency, agency autonomy, and judicial economy." Here, although the father disagreed with the IEP developed for his son by the school board, he had made no attempt to invoke the administrative procedures available to him. Further, he had not shown that the exhaustion of administrative remedies would be futile. The court granted the school board's motion for dismissal and ruled that the father could seek relief in federal court if he was still dissatisfied with the IEP after he had fully exhausted his administrative remedies. *Davenport v. Rockbridge County School Bd.*, 658 F.Supp. 132 (W.D.Va.1987).

In a New York case, an eleven-year-old handicapped student who was transferred by his school district to a special school for disabled students objected to the transfer because it separated him from his classmates and friends. The student claimed that the school district could have made his original school accessible and, through reasonable accommodation, could have permitted him to attend that school. The student asked a New York supreme court to issue an injunction compelling the school district to reverse its transfer decision and return the child to his original school. The school district argued that the student had not exhausted his administrative remedies, a prerequisite to requesting judicial relief. The court agreed, finding that the injunction requested by the student was not proper until EHA administrative remedies were fully pursued.

In its ruling the court stated: "Congress intended that the complaints of . . . handicapped students should be handled expeditiously by administrative law procedure and the educational agency is to keep the student in the facility where he was when the complaint was made." Congress wanted such complaints to be resolved in a matter of weeks; otherwise, students such as the plaintiff would be in high school before the controversy was resolved by the courts. The court dismissed the student's complaint until completion of administrative proceedings. *Robideau v. South Colonie Cent. School Dist.*, 487 N.Y.S. 2d 696 (Sup.Ct.1985).

A fourteen-year-old emotionally disturbed and mentally handicapped student and his parents sued in U.S. district court in Wisconsin, arguing that the child's school district had failed to provide a free appropriate public education in violation of the EHA. They also argued that the district had failed to properly evaluate and identify the severity of the child's handicap and had failed to provide special education and related services to enable the child to meaningfully benefit from his education.

The U.S. district court held that the failure of the parents to exhaust their state administrative remedies precluded an EHA lawsuit. A federal court lawsuit can be brought only if state administrative remedies have been exhausted or if to pursue such remedies would be futile. Here, the parents had not shown that pursuing state remedies would have been futile. In addition, the parents' allegation of procedural inconsistencies between the EHA and Wisconsin's use of county boards to make decisions related to handicapped education conflicted with the EHA requirement that local agencies make all such decisions. The court found that the parents misread the EHA since the Act clearly applies to both local educational agencies "or an intermediate educational unit." The Wisconsin Department of Public Instruction's motion to dismiss the parents' claims was granted. *Brandon v. Wisconsin Dep't of Pub. Instruction*, 595 F.Supp. 740 (E.D.Wis.1984).

In another Wisconsin case, a severely handicapped child, through her parents, brought suit in U.S. district court against the local school district and its special education director, alleging that her right to an appropriate special education and other constitutional rights had been violated by the school district. The child's IEP called for one-to-one instruction which the parents claimed was suspended without notice to them. The school district responded that this action was an "experiment" designed to determine whether the child would benefit by a program change. The parents appealed the child's IEP to the state superintendent of instruction.

Pending the result of the appeal the parents, dissatisfied with the child's instruction, had her independently evaluated and enrolled her at a special rehabilitation facility. When the superintendent finally ruled on the parents' claim, he concluded that the child was entitled to a full-day educational program. The case was tried and the court held that the parents' suit would be dismissed for their failure to exhaust state administrative remedies. The parents were not entitled to reimbursement for the expenses they incurred in having their child independently evaluated and for unilaterally enrolling their child in a special facility. This, said the court, was "self help" activity precluding reimbursement.

The court also found that the parents were not denied due process of law with regard to the change in the child's IEP without notification to the parents. The court stated that although the imposition of a change in an IEP without parental consent may deprive them of "liberty with finality," it was apparent in this case that the alleged damage as a result of the change was minimal. The parents' claim that their equal protection rights under the U.S. Constitution had been violated was without merit because the child had never been totally excluded from any program offered by the school district. The court noted that the parents' argument that exhaustion of remedies should be excused on the ground that the superintendent had failed to reach a final decision within thirty days as required by law was also without merit. This, the court said, would not excuse the parents' failure to exhaust their administrative remedies. The case was dismissed. *Williams v. Overturf*, 580 F.Supp. 1365 (W.D.Wis.1984).

A Virginia case illustrates the rule that the exhaustion of administrative remedies doctrine cannot be waived absent a clear showing of futility. Here the mother of an emotionally disturbed child sued Virginia education officials, alleging that her son had been denied a free appropriate education. Specifically, the mother claimed that local school officials had wilfully withheld educational opportunities from her child. To support her argument the mother noted that the child, at the time the suit was brought, was at home receiving no educational services whatsoever.

A U.S. district court held that the mother's claims should be dismissed because of her failure to exhaust available administrative remedies prior to bringing suit in federal court. The child was receiving a homebound education and the school district had formulated an IEP. The IEP called for placement at a private residential school. The problem was that shortly after this proposal was made no openings were available in the selected school. The court stated that had the facts conclusively shown that the child was not receiving any education whatsoever and that the defendant school district had not taken any steps to provide him with an appropriate education, the school district's violation of the EHA would be clear. Under such circumstances, prior resort to administrative remedies would not be a prerequisite to bringing suit in federal court because "administrative remedies need not be pursued when to do so would be futile." Here, however, the mother was required to exhaust the available administrative remedies prior to bringing suit. *Harris v. Campbell*, 472 F.Supp. 51 (E.D.Va.1979).

A U.S. district court in Louisiana held that the parents of handicapped and exceptional children were not entitled to bring suit in federal district court because of their failure to seek EHA administrative review. The parents claimed that a local school district had in effect a policy which constituted a failure to provide a meaningful, appropriate education to their handicapped children. The parents alleged that there was no division of the students based on age or handicap. The court held that the parents must have exhausted their administrative remedies prior to bringing suit in federal court. The court next had to determine whether to dismiss the case or stay the case pending exhaustion of administrative remedies. The court decided to dismiss the case, noting that courts will retain jurisdiction where not to do so would cause irreparable harm to the plaintiffs. Here, the court found no such potential irreparable harm. *Sessions v. Livingston Parish School Bd.*, 501 F.Supp. 251 (M.D.La.1980).

In an action brought in Puerto Rico, the U.S. Court of Appeals, First Circuit, has held that the mother of a handicapped child was required to exhaust the administrative process prior to bringing suit in federal court, despite the fact that a state agency initially failed to provide the mother with an internal remedy. The child, severely learning disabled, was placed by her parents in a residential private school in Vermont although the parents resided in Puerto Rico. They then sought funding for the child's education from the Puerto Rico Department of Education. The parents' request was denied because the department was conducting an assessment of the child for purposes of making a placement recommendation. The parents then brought suit in a U.S. district court, which dismissed the case because of the parents' failure to exhaust administrative remedies. The parents appealed, arguing that the department had taken an excessive amount of time to make a placement recommendation. The U.S. Court of Appeals, First Circuit, affirmed the district court ruling and held that despite delays in the placement process, the parents were obligated to pursue administrative channels before bringing suit in federal court. The court noted that courts are free to use their discretion in applying the doctrine. In this case, however, the various interests served by the doctrine weighed heavily in its favor. *Ezratty v. Commonwealth of Puerto Rico*, 648 F.2d 770 (1st Cir.1981).

The exhaustion doctrine was also applied in a New York case which involved a blanket decision by the New York Commissioner of Education that learning disabled children were not eligible for residential placement unless their learning disability was accompanied by an additional problem, such as an emotional disturbance. Eighteen learning disabled children who were denied residential placement sued the commissioner in a U.S. district court without first requesting a hearing. The court enjoined the commissioner from adhering to the policy and did not require the parents of the children to exhaust administrative remedies. The commissioner appealed to the U.S. Court of Appeals, Second Circuit, which reversed the district court ruling.

The Court of Appeals held that the district court acted too hastily, and should have required that the children exhaust state administrative remedies before bringing suit in federal court. The court was not persuaded by the parents' argument that exhaustion might prove "futile." There was, according to the court, always the possibility that, during the hearing process, the commissioner might reverse himself in a compelling case if he were proved wrong and a residential placement was shown to be necessary for a learning disabled child. The court stated that exhaustion may well have afforded relief to the children. Accordingly, the parents were not entitled to judicial relief when administrative relief might be available. *Riley v. Ambach*, 668 F.2d 635 (2d Cir.1981).

A Nebraska case involved a mentally retarded child who also suffered from muscular dystrophy. The child, who eventually became confined to a wheel-chair, was unable to continue his then current educational placement because of the school's inability to accommodate handicapped students in wheel-chairs. The child's parents, dissatisfied with the alternate placement provided, brought suit in federal district court challenging the appropriateness of the placement decision. The boy and his parents never requested a due process hearing prior to bringing suit.

At the time the suit was commenced there existed inconsistencies between state and federal administrative procedures. At that time, therefore, the student was under no duty to exhaust administrative remedies. However, at the time the case went to trial the inconsistencies had been resolved. The court held that because the inconsistencies had been rectified there was no longer any justification for permitting the child to circumvent the exhaustion requirement. The court observed that a state hearing officer is in the best position to make an initial determination on a child's placement. Here, there was no reason to believe that the state would not proceed in an expeditious manner if the parents opted for a due process hearing. The parents appealed to the U.S. Court of Appeals, Eighth Circuit. The court of appeals agreed with the district court ruling. No relief could be provided by a federal court where the child's father had failed to exhaust administrative remedies. The boy and his father never invoked the impartial hearing process provided by state law. *Monahan v. State of Nebraska*, 687 F.2d 1164 (8th Cir.1982).

An epileptic child in Kansas brought suit in the state of Kansas contending that Kansas educational practices violated his right to a free appropriate public education. He did not object to the state's overall special education program, but claimed that the plan was insufficiently enforced against local school districts as to its identification, screening and evaluation requirements. The Kansas Commissioner of Education maintained that, at all times, the plan had been in conformity with the EHA requirements. A U.S. district court denied the child's request for an injunction on the ground that he had failed to exhaust his administrative remedies. In fact, the court found that the available administrative review under the EHA had not even begun. While the exhaustion requirement is generally excused if the exhaustion would be futile, this was not established in this case. Accordingly, the child was not entitled to relief in federal court. *Akers v. Bolton*, 531 F.Supp. 300 (D.Kan.1981).

A blind Kentucky child who suffered from other handicaps, including mental retardation, was not making adequate progress in his current placement. His parents and the school district met to discuss the student's IEP placement. The Admission and Release Committee (ARC) recommended that he be placed in a residential school and specifically the Kentucky School of the Blind (KSB). KSB is an institution for visually impaired schoolaged children. KSB admission criteria requires that a prospective student demonstrate the ability for academic and vocational learning, self-care, and independent functioning. Therefore, the student was denied admission because he required extensive medical care. His parents requested a due process hearing. They sought to have the hearing officer determine if the student should be placed at KSB. In response to the request, the former head of the Kentucky Department of Education's Office of Education for Exceptional Children (OEEC) took the position that KSB was not the proper respondent and also that the hearing officer had no authority to order placement in a particular facility. The parents then instituted an action in a federal district court. Specifically, they asked that the action be styled as a class action for all visually impaired students who have one or more additional handicaps.

The court determined that the action would be certified as a class action. It then decided that if placement at the KSB was the only means by which an appropriate education could be obtained, the school would be required to accept students who did not otherwise meet the school's criteria. The court, however, did determine that the school's admission criteria did not violate due process or equal protection. It also ruled that the parents must exhaust their administrative remedies before filing suit. It then remanded the case so that the parents could exhaust their administrative remedies. *Eva N. v. Brock*, 741 F.Supp. 626 (E.D.Ky.1990).

A New York kindergartner participated in class testing at her school. Because of her poor performance on the psychological and auditory portions, her scores were reported to the district's committee on special education (CSE). The student's mother consented to weekly speech and language services. The school also tried to determine whether the student was handicapped within the meaning of state education laws. The officials did not obtain written consent from the student's parent. Several months later, when the school's speech teacher told the student's mother that the student needed to undergo more evaluations, the mother refused permission. She obtained a psychologist at her own expense. The reports were then submitted to the school district, which determined that the student needed special education services. This required classification of the student as a handicapped child. The mother objected to the classification, and offered to pay for private education for her daughter. Shortly thereafter, the CSE unanimously classified the student as speech impaired, assigning her to regular classrooms. This was to be supplemented by private speech services at the mother's expense.

The mother objected again to the handicapped child designation, and the district's assistant superintendent suggested retesting. The CSE then held another meeting, at which the assistant superintendent discovered that the mother had never previously consented to her daughter's evaluation. The assistant superintendent then nullified all previous CSE findings. The assistant superintendent stated to the mother that he would destroy the student's file if she so desired. When the student's mother did not respond, the assistant superintendent destroyed the file. The mother then filed a civil rights lawsuit in a federal district court, alleging violation of the Rehabilitation Act, the EHA and 42 U.S.C. § 1983. She claimed that the school district had incorrectly classified her daughter without consent. The school district argued that the mother had failed to exhaust her administrative remedies, that the statute of limitations barred her claims, and that the complaint failed to state a claim upon which relief could be granted. The court considered the EHA's requirement for exhaustion of administrative remedies and noted that administrative review was proper if any party was dissatisfied with the results of impartial hearings. Only then could a lawsuit proceed in federal district court. While parties may also seek redress under other acts such as the Rehabilitation Act and § 1983, they are still required to exhaust administrative remedies as if the suit had been brought under the EHA. There were no facts in this case to indicate that the mother should have been excused from exhausting her administrative remedies and the school district was entitled to summary judgment on those grounds. *Buffolino v. Bd. of Educ. of Sachem Central School Dist.*, 729 F.Supp. 240 (E.D.N.Y.1990).

In another New York case the mother of a handicapped child, concerned about her son's lack of progress in his second year of kindergarten, asked that he be evaluated by a psychologist. The mother claimed that a school representative who came to her home with a parental permission form put a check mark on the form in the box indicating that she denied the district permission to conduct an evaluation of her child. The mother later brought suit in a U.S. district court claiming that as a result of being denied the special education to which he was entitled, her son suffered damages to his intellect, emotional capacity and personality, and was impeded in acquiring necessary training. In addition, she alleged that she moved to a different school district to obtain the services her child needed and that she herself had suffered emotional distress. The court held in favor of the mother and the school district appealed. The U.S. Court of Appeals, Second Circuit, held that because the mother had not availed herself of her EHA administrative remedies, she was not entitled to relief under the Act. However, the court did find that the mother had a claim under the Civil Rights Act. *Quakenbush v. Johnson City School Dist.*, 716 F.2d 141 (2d Cir.1983).

B. Exceptions to the Exhaustion Doctrine

The following cases illustrate that exhaustion of administrative remedies is not required when it is clear that the exhaustion of the administrative remedies would be futile or cause irreparable harm. There are cases in which courts deem state administrative remedies inadequate and thus not subject to the exhaustion requirement. Such things as delay by an agency in making a decision, or the fact that the agency may not be empowered to grant relief, will excuse the "exhaustion" requirement. The unavailability of a state or local remedy or a predetermined result by an agency will also excuse the requirement.

A Virginia student attended a private special education school. The local school district paid his tuition. The student's mother requested that her son be transferred to a neighborhood public school. When the district denied the request, the mother initiated an administrative hearing. A hearing officer affirmed the private school placement. The mother appealed the decision to a state reviewing officer who affirmed the placement. The mother and the district met to develop an individualized education program (IEP). The district sought to have the student placed in a program at a different high school.

The mother rejected the change in placement pending the outcome of a lawsuit she had filed in a Virginia federal district court. She sought to have the court overturn the district's original decision to have the student remain at the private school. At trial, the mother informed the court that she no longer wished to pursue the question of whether the private school placement constituted an appropriate education for her son. She wanted the court to decide the appropriateness of placing her son at the new high school. The court refused to hear the case because the IEP for which administrative proceedings had been conducted was not before it. The mother appealed the district court's dismissal to the U.S. Court of Appeals, Fourth Circuit. The appeals court held that the mother did not have to reexhaust all administrative remedies. The new IEP continued to provide for the student's education at a place other than where the mother wished. Therefore, her complaint remained the same. It returned the case to the district court to determine if the student should be placed at his neighborhood high school. *DeVries by DeBlaay v. Spillane*, 853 F.2d 264 (4th Cir.1988).

The mother of a six-year-old boy who had been diagnosed as having hemophilia and AIDS intended to enroll the boy in the first grade in a new Illinois school district for the 1987-88 school year. When the school board learned that the boy had AIDS, it formulated a "Policy Regarding Children With Chronic Communicable Diseases," to serve as a basis for placing the boy. Following the guidelines set forth in the policy, the school board met with the boy's mother and her attorney and thereafter unanimously decided to exclude the boy from the normal classroom and to provide him with a tutor in his home. The boy and his mother filed a lawsuit under the Rehabilitation Act of 1973, claiming that the boy had been discriminated against.

The court applied the definition of "handicapped children" under the EHA to determine whether the boy's diagnosis of AIDS qualified. The court concluded that three tests had to be met before the EHA could be applied to the boy: 1) the boy's strength, vitality, or alertness had to be limited due to chronic or acute health problems, 2) those problems had to adversely affect his educational performance, and 3) the problems had to cause the boy to require special education and related services. The court also quoted a Department of Education opinion which stated, "[c]hildren with AIDS could be eligible for special education programs . . . if they have chronic or acute health problems which adversely affect their educational performance." The court determined that because the boy's educational performance had not been adversely affected, the EHA did not apply and the boy was therefore not required to exhaust administrative remedies before filing his discrimination lawsuit. The court denied the school board's motion to dismiss the case. *Doe v. Belleville Pub. School Dist.*, 672 F.Supp. 342 (S.D.Ill.1987).

The parents of several handicapped students in New York filed a class action lawsuit against the New York State Department of Education, the local school board and other local defendants alleging that they had violated the EHA by failing to properly identify, evaluate and place handicapped students. The parents entered into a consent judgment with the local school board and the other local defendants which provided the parents with the relief they had sought in correcting the violations. The parents then sought attorney fees, which were awarded by a U.S. district court. The local school district appealed this award of attorney fees to the U.S. Court of Appeals, Second Circuit.

The court of appeals considered the local school district's argument that attorney fees could not be awarded under the EHA because the parents in this case were not challenging a final decision of a state administrative agency relating to the evaluation or placement of a specific handicapped student. The court noted that the generalized procedural violations challenged by the parents "lend themselves well to class action treatment," and that administrative remedies need not be exhausted where they would not provide adequate relief. The court of appeals then noted that the consent judgment in this case provided substantial relief to the parents which could not have been obtained through administrative appeal processes. It therefore concluded that the parents were entitled to attorney fees. It decided that since the parents had sought relief under §§ 1983 and 1988 of the Civil Rights Act as well as the EHA, the award of attorney fees would be made under § 1988. The court of appeals also ruled that the award of attorney fees should be reduced by the amount of such fees which were spent by the parents in suing the state since the state had not participated in the consent judgment. *J. G. v. Rochester City School Dist. Bd. of Educ.*, 830 F.2d 444 (2d Cir. 1987).

In October, 1984, a hearing officer found four procedural violations of the EHA by the Baltimore City Schools relating to an eighteen-year-old handicapped student. The hearing officer found that the student was a seriously emotionally disturbed adolescent who required a residential placement and ordered the city to permanently place the student in a residential setting by November 20, 1984. On December 5, 1984, the student sued the city in a U.S. district court because the student had not received any change in his educational program. The district court dismissed the student's claims and he appealed to the U.S. Court of Appeals, Fourth Circuit.

The student claimed that he was denied a free appropriate public education when the city school system failed to implement the hearing officer's decision in a timely manner. The district court had dismissed the complaint, holding that the student had failed to exhaust his EHA administrative remedies. The court of appeals disagreed, noting that the student had received a final administrative decision and that he had neither the responsibility nor the right to appeal the favorable decision by the local hearing officer since he was not an aggrieved party. The student had exhausted all administrative remedies and when the city did not appeal the hearing officer's decision, it became the final administrative decision of the state.

The court of appeals also concluded that since the EHA did not contain any provision for enforcing final administrative orders by a hearing officer, the student was entitled to a § 1983 claim. When the city refused to enforce the hearing officer's decision to put the student in a residential placement the city had, under color of state law, violated the EHA. The district court was therefore wrong in dismissing the student's § 1983 claim. His § 1983 claim was remanded to the district court for further proceedings. *Robinson v. Pinderhughes*, 810 F.2d 1270 (4th Cir. 1987).

A case arising in New York has held that the exhaustion doctrine did not apply to a situation involving the suspension of a multiply handicapped student from a school for the blind. In this case, the parents of the child brought suit against the New York State Education Department and the school for the blind seeking an injunction to reinstate the student at the school. The parents brought suit without first having exhausted the available administrative remedies. This was done, claimed the parents, because of a denial of procedural safeguards when the parents wished to contest their child's suspension. The parents alleged that the state had failed to provide for an impartial hearing officer and that there was no provision requiring the agency to allow the child to remain in the school pending resolution of their complaint. The school argued that it had "substantially complied" with EHA procedural requirements. However, the court disagreed stating that a "person who claims that the state defendants have not even provided the impartial hearing as required by federal law *a fortiori* asserts a claim over which [the] court has jurisdiction." Finding the parents and the child in that position, the court denied the school's motion to dismiss the case. *Sherry v. New York State Educ. Dep't*, 479 F.Supp. 1328 (W.D.N.Y.1979).

The exhaustion doctrine was also inapplicable in a case in Pennsylvania. Here, the parents of an emotionally disturbed son sought special education placement for him after he had been diagnosed as emotionally disturbed. The parents then activated the due process hearing system, but the responsible officials in the child's school district reached no decision in time to place the boy at a special school before the beginning of the following academic year. The parents then found what they believed to be an appropriate school in New York and began paying tuition. A hearing was held after the first year of the child's enrollment in the school chosen by the parents, which resulted in a determination that the placement chosen by the parents was appropriate. The parents raised the matter of tuition reimbursement but this was never resolved.

Believing they had received a favorable ruling from the hearing officer, the parents did not appeal the decision but their attempts to secure reimbursement proved unsuccessful. They claimed that there simply was no reimbursement procedure in Pennsylvania. The parents eventually brought suit in a U.S. district court against the school district, which argued that they were not entitled to do so on the ground that the reimbursement issue was never litigated at the hearing level and thus the parents had failed to exhaust their administrative remedies. The court concluded that the "exhaustion" doctrine was irrelevant where no administrative remedy had ever been available. *Hark v. School Dist. of Philadelphia*, 505 F.Supp. 727 (E.D.Pa.1980).

The parents of a handicapped child in Illinois challenged the failure of various state agencies to assume the full cost of the child's placement at a private residential facility. After being assessed by the state as "responsible relatives," the parents were told they must contribute $100 per month toward their son's placement. The state's reason for excluding this amount from the child's placement at the school was that it was attributable to "clothing, medical supplies and purchased services." An outstanding bill at the school in the amount of $2,154.53 resulted in the issue of a discharge notice to the child which was to become effective prior to the resolution of the parents' appeal of the decision to assess them as "responsible relatives." The parents, without waiting for resolution of the appeal, filed suit in U.S. district court. The state sought to have the case dismissed for failure to exhaust administrative remedies.

The district court excused the exhaustion requirement because the parents had no practical opportunity to obtain the appeal decision. They had done everything possible to obtain speedy administrative review, but were unable to do so through no fault of their own. Because of the state's failure to decide the parents' administrative appeal within the time specified by federal law, the purpose of the exhaustion requirement was undermined; the parents would have been unable to obtain the decision before the time that the school intended to discharge the child. The court stated that "when the press of time makes exhaustion impractical, it is not required by the EHA." The court also found that the parents had no "real administrative remedy" in this case. It was doubtful, said the court, that administrative review could provide the parents with the relief they sought. It appeared that the agency decision had been made pursuant to state law. Thus, by adopting the responsible relatives policy, the agency had already predetermined the result it would reach in the child's case. *Parks v. Pavkovic*, 536 F.Supp. 296 (N.D.Ill.1982).

In another Illinois case, a group of emotionally disturbed children brought suit in a U.S. district court against Illinois state education officials, challenging a rule excluding counseling and therapeutic services from being considered special education or related services. The children admittedly did not exhaust their administrative remedies but argued that an exhaustion attempt would be futile. They claimed that the Illinois State Board of Education was not the "appropriate forum" to address the issues relating to the Illinois Governor's Purchased Care Review Board determinations of allowable cost for related services. Noting that none of the children had attempted to exhaust EHA administrative remedies and that, ordinarily, this would require dismissal, the court excused the exhaustion requirement in this case. The court concluded that Illinois had not established a meaningful process of administrative review. *Gary B. v. Cronin*, 542 F.Supp. 102 (N.D.Ill.1980).

The U.S. Court of Appeals, Second Circuit, reversed a district court's decision to dismiss a case because of the plaintiff's failure to exhaust her administrative remedies. The controversy originally centered on whether a school district was liable for the transportation cost of the plaintiff's son. The school district declined to provide transportation reimbursement, because the tests necessary to determine whether the child was in fact handicapped were never made due to the parent's rejection of the school district's psychologists. A final administrative decision then was rendered in favor of the school district. When the case was appealed to a U.S. district court, the judge held that the plaintiff had not exhausted her administrative remedies because the testing data had not been provided. The Court of Appeals reversed the lower court, stating that the absence of the testing data did not mean that the proper administrative route was not followed by the plaintiff. The court concluded that if a final administrative decision has been rendered, it is to be reviewed on its merits. The case was remanded for further proceedings. *Dubois v. Connecticut State Bd. of Educ.*, 727 F.2d 44 (2d Cir.1983).

The U.S. Department of Education's Office of Civil Rights (OCR) responded to parental complaints about the education of their handicapped children against the Georgia State Board of Education and two local school districts by investigating the districts and the state education department. When county special education administrators and state education department officials refused to cooperate with the investigation, the OCR began an administrative proceeding to terminate federal funding of state and local special education. The state board of education and local districts sued the U.S. Department of Education in a federal district court, alleging that the OCR had acted outside its powers. The OCR argued that the case should be dismissed because the Georgia educators had failed to exhaust their administrative remedies. The district court granted the OCR's motion and the Georgia educators appealed to the U.S. Court of Appeals, Eleventh Circuit.

The appeals court agreed with the OCR, ruling that the Georgia educators had failed to exhaust their administrative remedies. The appeals court then amended its decision, giving further grounds for the judgment favoring the OCR's right to challenge the Georgia educators. According to the court, Congress intended federal agencies to implement § 504 of the Rehabilitation Act by appropriate means of regulation and enforcement. This included investigation and review of federal funding recipients. Termination of federal funding was an appropriate sanction, according to a congressional report. The OCR was not plainly outside its jurisdiction by investigating the Georgia educators. Additional grounds for affirming the district court's dismissal of the Georgia educator's complaint were that the EHA did not prohibit federal supervisory action as taken by the OCR, and that the Georgia educators had failed to exhaust their administrative remedies. The appeals court affirmed the judgment, as modified. *Rogers v. Bennett*, 873 F.2d 1387 (11th Cir. 1989).

A twenty-one-year-old prison inmate in Massachusetts sued state education officials on behalf of himself and other inmates alleging that the failure to provide special education services to inmates who were under age twenty-two, and who had not already received a high school diploma, was a denial of a free appropriate education as required under state and federal law. A U.S. district court held that the incarcerated status of the plaintiffs did not preclude their entitlement to a free and appropriate special education under the EHA and state law. Accordingly, the court issued an injunction enjoining the education officials from failing to provide special education services to the plaintiffs. *Green v. Johnson*, 513 F.Supp. 965 (D.Mass.1981).

III. STATUTE OF LIMITATIONS

The EHA does not specify a time limitation in which parties may bring suit in state or federal court after exhausting administrative remedies or appeal an adverse administrative decision. Administrative procedures are generally governed by state laws which usually specify a thirty-day limitation on appeals. However, state laws for other types of actions usually set a longer time limitation. Conflicts arise when one party files a lawsuit or appeals a decision outside what the other party perceives to be the applicable statute of limitations.

A learning-disabled student completed fourth grade in a mainstream class at a private school. His parents then requested the District of Columbia Public Schools (DCPS) to provide special education services. The DCPS proposed an IEP which included placement in a special education program in their public school in which handicapped students were placed with nonhandicapped students for a quarter of their curriculum. The parents disagreed with the IEP and requested a hearing. They claimed that the private school was an appropriate educational environment because it did not involve contact with nonhandicapped students. A hearing officer approved a modified version of the DCPS's IEP but the parents kept their son at the private school and paid his expenses for the next three years. The DCPS advised the parents that the hearing officer's determination was final but that an appeal could be made to an appropriate court. The notice did not advise the parents of any applicable statute of limitations. Nearly three years later the parents sued the DCPS in a federal district court under the EHA for an order declaring the IEP inappropriate. They also sought approval of the student's current private school placement and tuition expenses. The court applied a local thirty-day statute of limitations, which barred review of the hearing officer's order. The parents appealed to the U.S. Court of Appeals, District of Columbia Circuit.

The appeals court noted that the EHA did not specifically provide a statute of limitations for appeals from final administrative determinations. Where Congress did not establish a statute of limitations for federal lawsuits, federal courts could "borrow" local statutes of limitation provided they did not conflict with underlying federal policies. Whenever the school district made a new placement decision, a new thirty-day period would begin in which parents could file a claim. The court noted that while other federal circuits had approved longer statutes of limitation, the thirty-day period was consistent with federal law. However, the DCPS had failed to advise the parents that they had only thirty days to file an appeal in the appropriate court. For this reason, the court reversed the district court's decision. *Spiegler v. Dist. of Columbia*, 866 F.2d 461 (D.C.Cir.1989).

A mentally handicapped North Carolina student attended a local public school. Due to psychological difficulties, the student was then placed in a Texas private school. In the meantime, the board of education placement committee for the student's North Carolina school district recommended placement at another North Carolina institution. The board informed the parents of their right to appeal the decision and stated that they would not be reimbursed for the Texas private school tuition. The parents paid for the student's private education. The student was insured under a group health insurance policy provided by her father's employer. A special self-insurance plan benefitted the student individually. It provided a $100,000 maximum lifetime benefit for therapeutic services relating to mental and nervous disorders. When the student turned eighteen, a legal guardian was appointed for her. The student then sued the board seeking reimbursement for the depletion of health insurance benefits which had been used to pay for her education. A federal district court granted summary judgment for the board, finding that although the statute of limitations had been tolled, the student lacked standing. The student then appealed to the U.S. Court of Appeals, Fourth Circuit.

The court of appeals held that the district court had correctly determined that the state's three-year statute of limitations was tolled by the student's infancy and incompetence. The student's claim was not time barred. She had timely filed the complaint after she attained majority. The court also held that the student had standing to seek reimbursement for the depletion of health insurance benefits used to pay for her education. Although none of the student's own funds were used, her remaining insurance benefits had been reduced from $100,000 to $36,000. Under state law, the student was deemed a third-party beneficiary of the insurance contract between her father, his employer and the employer's group health insurer. The student had standing to prosecute her claim under the EHA. The court of appeals remanded the district court's decision for further proceedings. *Shook v. Gaston County Bd. of Educ.*, 882 F.2d 119 (4th Cir.1989).

An educationally handicapped New Hampshire student attended a day-school program. The student's parents requested the school district to place the student in a residential program. The district denied their demand and the parents requested a hearing before the state Department of Education. The hearing officer determined that the student should be placed in a residential facility, which was done at the district's expense. At the time, attorney's fees were not available to prevailing parties under the EHA so the parents did not apply for them. In 1986, Congress amended the act permitting prevailing parties in EHA claims to recover attorney's fees. The parents did not apply for them at that time. Two years later, the district sought to place the student in a day program. The parents' attorney discovered that they were entitled to recover attorney's fees for the earlier action and filed a lawsuit in federal district court. Both parties moved for summary judgment.

The district court held that the state's three year statute of limitations for personal actions governed the EHA claim for attorney's fees. The scope of judicial review under the EHA was the same as that required in personal injury actions. The court also ruled that the delay of nearly twenty-seven months was unreasonable, but did not prejudice the city or the school district. The attorneys who participated in the initial action were available for discovery purposes. The court also found that the city and school district had no standing to challenge the retroactive application of attorney's fees. The district court found the parents entitled to attorney's fees and denied the city and school district's motion for summary judgment. *James v. Nashua School Dist.*, 720 F.Supp. 1053 (D.N.H.1989).

A handicapped New York student attended special education classes for which the school district sought tuition reimbursement from another New York school district. The district claiming compensation failed to notify the other school district of any claim or lawsuit until two years after the expenses were incurred. New York education law sets a statute of limitations for an action to recover money from a school district at one year, and requires lawsuits filed after one year to be dismissed. The Supreme Court of Westchester County determined that there was no basis for finding the one year statute of limitations inapplicable. *Bd. of Educ. of the Katonah-Lewisboro School Dist. v. Bd. of Educ. of the Carmel Central School Dist.*, 549 N.Y.S.2d 322 (Sup.Ct.1989).

A mother placed her autistic son in a private school in California from February, 1974, through February, 1975. Her son entered his local school district's program in September, 1977, but was suspended in December, 1978, for disciplinary reasons. Without obtaining her consent the school district

notified the mother that her son would be taught at home pending evaluation. However, the school district delayed his evaluation until May, 1979, and
failed to hold an IEP meeting until June, 1979. The IEP recommended a
special day school for her son but a teachers' strike delayed the school's opening until October, 1979.

Her son continued in the day school until 1985 when he was notified that
he was no longer eligible for public education because he was twenty-two
years of age. The mother requested a hearing to contest the decision to terminate his education. She alleged that the school district had violated § 504 of
the Rehabilitation Act in 1974-75 by excluding her son from the public
school. She requested total reimbursement for all private school expenses or a
compensatory education. She also contended that the school district violated
the EHA in 1979 by not timely providing her son with an appropriate education. After the hearing officer ruled for the school district the mother appealed to a U.S. district court, which upheld the hearing officer's decision.
She then appealed to the U.S. Court of Appeals, Ninth Circuit.

Because § 504 contains no statute of limitations, the court borrowed the
statute of limitations governing similar disputes under California law, which
provided for a three-year limitation. Because the statute of limitations began
to run when the mother knew or had reason to know of the injury she was too
late in filing her claim. Her EHA claim was also barred because she waited
six years to assert it. The district court's decision in favor of the school district was affirmed. *Alexopulos v. San Francisco Unified School Dist.*, 817
F.2d 551 (9th Cir. 1987).

A handicapped nine-year-old New York boy who suffered from speech and
motor difficulties was evaluated by his school district's committee on the
handicapped (COH). The COH then made a recommendation for an educational placement of the boy which his parents believed to be inappropriate.
They appealed the placement decision to the New York Commissioner of
Education, who ruled in favor of the parents. However, the Commissioner
declined to order that the parents be reimbursed for the boy's educational
expenses incurred as a result of the parents' decision to unilaterally place
their child in a private school. The private school had provided an appropriate education for the boy during the ten-month period from the time of the
initial, incorrect COH evaluation to the time the Commissioner's decision
was rendered.

Fifteen months after the Commissioner's decision denying reimbursement,
the parents sued in U.S. district court seeking reimbursement for the private
school tuition. The district court held that the suit was barred by the statute
of limitations, a decision upheld by the U.S. Court of Appeals, Second Circuit. While noting that the EHA contains no statute of limitations, the appeals court stated that the applicable state statute of limitations will be
applied in EHA lawsuits. In this case there was a conflict between a New
York statute governing educational proceedings in state courts which called
for a four-month limit, and a more general New York statute providing for a
three-year limit on any suit "to recover upon a liability . . . created or imposed by statute."

The district court had relied upon the law providing for a four-month limit
because it was the one most closely analogous to the present cause of action
had it arisen under state law. The Court of Appeals sanctioned this ap-

proach, noting that to allow the longer three-year statute of limitations to govern lawsuits seeking reimbursement for educational expenses would conflict with the EHA requirement that a child remain in his current educational placement during the pendency of any proceedings to review the appropriateness of a child's placement. Said the court, "this 'status quo' provision hardly contemplates a period of three years plus pendency of the proceedings. After all, it is a child's education we are talking about." The court therefore refused to allow the three-year general statute of limitations to govern the case and stated that because the parents had failed to appeal the Commissioner's decision within four months, their suit had been properly dismissed. *Adler v. Education Department of State of New York*, 760 F.2d 454 (2d Cir.1985). A New York federal district court has upheld the decision. The statute of limitations for New York EHA cases is four months, based upon state Article 78 proceedings, rather than three years as provided by the state's limitations period for federal civil rights cases. *Gerasimou v. Ambach*, 636 F.Supp. 1504 (E.D.N.Y.1986).

The mother of a twenty-year-old mentally handicapped, speech impaired and emotionally disturbed girl filed suit in U.S. district court against the Board of Education of Wood County, West Virginia. Since 1969, the girl had been enrolled at the Institute of Logopedics, a private school in Wichita, Kansas. For several years the mother paid the entire cost of this education. After Congress enacted the EHA, the Board of Education assumed responsibility for the bulk of her educational and residential costs at the Institute. However, when the girl reached the age of eighteen the board concluded that she could be appropriately educated in the Wood County public school system. The mother was told that the board would no longer pay the cost of her private school education.

The mother objected and requested a due process hearing. The hearing officer agreed with the Board of Education that the girl should be transferred from the private school to the Wood County public school. The mother appealed the hearing officer's decision to the West Virginia State Board of Education which agreed with Wood County's decision to place the girl in the public school system. The mother filed suit in U.S. district court nearly one year after the State Board's decision and the school board asked that the suit be dismissed because it had been filed more than 120 days after the State Board's decision. The 120-day limitation would be applied only to West Virginia special education cases filed after the present decision. *Thomas v. Staats*, 633 F.Supp. 797 (S.D.W.Va.1985).

A twelve-year-old handicapped boy was enrolled at the Achievement Center, a private school for the learning disabled in the Roanoke, Virginia area. Previously, he had been enrolled in the Roanoke County public schools in which he had only taken special education classes in one area, mathematics. His parents were unhappy with a single math class being the only special education class provided. During the 1983-84 school year, the child's academic and social problems became severe and his parents filed a complaint against the superintendent for failure to develop a sufficient IEP.

A hearing officer held that the IEP was adequate and the parents were denied tuition reimbursement. The state review board affirmed the hearing officer's decision. Seventy-six days after the state board's decision, the parents filed a complaint under the EHA against the school superintendent claiming that the school district was denying their son an appropriate education. The school moved for dismissal on the ground that the complaint had been filed too late.

The U.S. district court noted that because the EHA does not specify a time limit in which to bring a lawsuit, the courts must determine the time limit based on the "most analogous" state cause of action. It found the Virginia Supreme Court Rules 2A:2 and 2A:4 analogous to EHA proceedings, but held that the thirty-day limit contained in the Rules was not in keeping with EHA policy. Instead, the court found that the one-year statute of limitations provided for tort actions under a state statute (Va.Code secs. 8.01-248) was the appropriate time limit. Congress' policy in EHA cases was that placement disputes be given as fair and complete a hearing as possible. Finding that the one-year statute of limitations for tort cases was more conducive to fairness, the court denied the school's motion to dismiss the complaint. *Kirchgessner v. Davis*, 632 F.Supp. 616 (W.D.Va.1986).

A thirty-day statute of limitations period did not bar a suit brought against the Pennsylvania Department of Education and a local school district. A handicapped student requiring clean intermittent catheterization to enable her to attend school challenged a school district policy which denied such services. The U.S. Court of Appeals, Third Circuit, affirmed a district court ruling in favor of the child. The court of appeals agreed with the district court's decision to apply either a two-year or a six-year statute of limitations period to the child's claim under the EHA. Finding that the thirty-day limitations period was incompatible with the EHA, the court held that it did not apply. The court of appeals decided that the two-year state statute of limitations which applied to actions to recover damages for injuries caused by the wrongful act or negligence of another, and controlled in medical malpractice cases, was the most analogous statute. Because the child's claim was brought within the two-year period, her action was not barred. *Tokarcik v. Forest Hills School Dist.*, 665 F.2d 443 (3d Cir.1981).

The U.S. Court of Appeals, Sixth Circuit, has ruled that the statute of limitations for EHA tuition reimbursement claims should be three years. In so ruling the court stated its belief that a one-year limitations period would simply be "too short."

Here, the Knox County, Tennessee, school system became aware that one of its male students was emotionally disturbed due to "multiple drug ingestion." On the recommendation of a psychologist the boy's parents sent him to the Brown School, a residential school in Texas, where the boy stayed for nearly three years. After receiving a high school equivalency diploma in April, 1981, the boy permanently left school.

In February, 1985, his parents filed suit under the EHA in U.S. district court seeking reimbursement for their son's tuition at the Brown School. They alleged bad faith on the part of the Knox County School System and claimed that it had failed to advise them of their EHA rights. The parents did not seek a due process hearing prior to filing suit because they believed it would be futile. Knox County moved for dismissal on various grounds, including the Tennessee statute of limitations. The district court granted Knox County's motion and the parents appealed.

The court of appeals agreed with the district court's adoption of the three-year statute of limitations provided by Tennessee law for "services performed but not paid for" [T.C.A. § 28-3-105(3)]. The one-year limitations period provided by Tennessee law for personal injury lawsuits was found to be inadequate, as was the state's sixty-day limitation on appeals for administrative agency rulings. Section 28-3-105(3), which applied to money owed for services rendered, was deemed to be the most analogous statute of limitations consistent with the EHA. Since the parents became aware of their right to tuition reimbursement in May, 1981, and did not file suit until February, 1985, their claims were barred by the Tennessee statute of limitations. The court of appeals upheld the dismissal of the parents' claims. *Janzen v. Knox County Bd. of Educ.*, 790 F.2d 484 (6th Cir.1986).

In a Texas case, a handicapped child was placed by her school district in a public facility which was equipped to treat children with emotional disturbances and autism. She made progress during her first year there. However, during the second year she regressed significantly. The parents removed her from the facility and placed her in another institute. After tuition expenses were denied by the child's school district, the parents sought relief in a U.S. district court which held that because the parents had brought suit nine months after the denial, their claim was barred by a thirty-day statute of limitations. In addition, said the court, the parents forfeited all rights to recover tuition for the private residential facility by unilaterally withdrawing the child from the school district's program. The parents appealed this decision to the U.S. Court of Appeals, Fifth Circuit, which agreed with the district court ruling that the parents were not entitled to reimbursement, but reversed the thirty-day statute of limitations ruling, saying that the limitation was inconsistent with the EHA policy of investing parents with discretion to take action regarding their children's education. *Scokin v. State of Texas*, 723 F.2d 432 (5th Cir.1984).

In Hawaii, a thirty-day statute of limitations period did apply to a suit brought outside that period by the Hawaii Department of Education. The Department had filed two suits in federal court challenging adverse hearing officer decisions on the issue of responsibility for the costs of educating two handicapped children. The U.S. Court of Appeals, Ninth Circuit, held that the Department's suit was barred by its failure to appeal the hearing officer's decision within the thirty-day limitation period set by the Hawaii Administrative Procedures Act. The court found the APA to provide a more comprehensive standard of review than the EHA. Further, the need to avoid delays in resolving disputes over education plans for handicapped children supported the application of a thirty-day statute of limitations period for a state agency to appeal an adverse decision. The court affirmed a U.S. district court decision to dismiss the cases. However, the court noted that it was not being asked to decide whether the same thirty-day rule would apply to parents or guardians seeking judicial review of a handicapped child's placement. The thirty-day rule may not apply in those cases. *Dep't of Educ., State of Hawaii v. Carl D.*, 695 F.2d 1154 (9th Cir.1983).

IV. FAILURE TO COMPLY WITH THE EHA

Due process of law is contingent upon a school district's adherence to EHA procedural safeguards. The failure to adhere to the EHA will generally result in a favorable ruling for the parents or guardians of handicapped students.

A functionally retarded learning-disabled student resided at a Massachusetts private school until he was twenty-years-old. The student and his social worker reached an agreement to terminate the student's placement at the school. The student expressed a desire to live with his mother. He was then discharged from the school and into the custody of his mother. The student's termination occurred without the involvement of either his surrogate parent, appointed by the state, or his mother. Neither party was provided with notice or an opportunity to participate in the termination decision. Within a few weeks, the living arrangement fell apart. The family services agency placed the student in a structured home. The placement lasted twenty-four hours. The student then moved into a homeless shelter and a series of temporary living arrangements. Thereafter, he began supporting himself through prostitution. The student's mother challenged the termination in an administrative hearing. The hearing officer determined that the student terminated the placement himself and was not entitled to compensatory education. The mother then brought an action in a federal district court. The district court dismissed an EHA claim determining that the EHA procedural safeguards such as the stay-put provision are not applicable when a legally competent adult chooses to leave an institution. The mother then appealed to the U.S. Court of Appeals, Second Circuit.

The EHA provides that if there is any proposed change in a child's IEP, the parent or guardian must be notified in writing. The parent or guardian then has the right to contest the matter in an impartial due process hearing conducted by the state educational agency. During the pendency of these proceedings, the child must be allowed to remain in his current educational placement under the stay-put provision of the act. The court determined that the issue was whether the state must comply with the EHA procedural safeguards before terminating the educational placement of a handicapped student who is between eighteen and twenty-one, on the basis of the student's consent. The court noted that the EHA and the U.S. Department of Education make it clear that if a state provides education to an eighteen to twenty-one-year-old handicapped child, the requirements of the EHA apply. Thus, the statute and the relevant state regulations apply to an eighteen to twenty-one-year-old even though there has been no determination of incompetency. The court held that the state was required to comply with the EHA procedural safeguards before it terminated, on the basis of consent, the educational placement of a student. The court reversed the decision of the trial court and remanded the case to determine the amount of compensatory education to which the student was entitled. *Mrs. C. v. Wheaton*, 916 F.2d 69 (2d Cir.1990).

An emotionally disabled New York student attended a vocational school as a part of his mainstreaming. His parents were notified that the school district intended to graduate him at the end of the school year. When the vocational school notified the parents that the student should continue in its program for another year, the parents requested an impartial hearing. They objected to their son being graduated because he had not attained targets established by the vocational school. Following the hearing but prior to the hearing officer's decision, the student was graduated. The hearing officer agreed that graduation was appropriate and the parents appealed to the Commissioner of Education. They requested that their son be allowed to continue the vocational program until a final decision was reached. The commissioner denied the request and determined that the student had been properly graduated.

The parents sued the school district in a New York federal district court. They asserted that the school district violated the EHA stay-put provision by graduating their son. They sought to have their son reinstated to the vocational program pending a final decision. The court noted that one of the purposes of the stay-put provision was to prevent school officials from removing a child from the classroom over the parents' objection pending completion of review proceedings. It then noted that what had to be determined was whether graduation constituted a change in placement. The court equated graduation to a long-term suspension because it resulted in the total exclusion of the student from his educational placement. Therefore, EHA procedural safeguards should be enforced. The court ordered the school district to reinstate the student to the vocational program during the pendency of the proceedings. *Cronan v. Bd. of Educ. of East Ramapo Cent. School Dist.*, 689 F.Supp. 197 (S.D.N.Y.1988).

The procedures outlined in the EHA bind the parents or guardians of students as well as schools.

A Michigan child received special education services under an emotional impaired (EI) label. His school district suspended him in April, 1985, due to the increasing severity of his emotional problems. In May, 1985, the school district convened an IEP meeting for him. His parents approved of the May, 1985, IEP. The child was hospitalized for a suicide attempt in the fall of 1985. He never returned to the district's school. The child's parents independently obtained several professional evaluations which recommended a twelve month residential placement in a highly structured environment. On November 4, 1985, the parents unilaterally placed him in the Devereux Foundation School in Pennsylvania. After numerous procedural steps, a state hearing officer affirmed a local hearing officer's decision which required the child to submit to an evaluation in Michigan. The parents sued the school district in U.S. district court. At a February, 1986, IEP meeting the parents asked the school district to conduct an evaluation of the child in Pennsylvania.

The parents contended that the school district waived its right to compel evaluation since it refused their February, 1986, request to evaluate the child at Devereux. They also argued that the state level decision compelling evaluation violated the child's due process rights. The parents claimed that only the Devereux evaluations should be considered in determining his IEP. The district court held for the school district. It was undisputed that the child was in Pennsylvania when his parents offered him for evaluation. The school district was under no duty to go to Pennsylvania to conduct an evaluation of the child who had been unilaterally removed from the school district without the prior knowledge or acquiescence of school officials. His due process rights were not denied since the school district requested an evaluation of the child before rendering a final decision. Having overlooked EHA procedures, the parents could not now seek to have the school district place the child at Devereux. *Lenhoff v. Farmington Pub. Schools*, 680 F.Supp. 921 (E.D.Mich. 1988).

A fourth grade boy displayed signs of disruptive behavior and his teacher suggested that he receive psychological help. To avoid having such information on his school records, his parents enrolled him in a private school outside of the district. After he was expelled from the private school and had attended a series of public schools unsuccessfully, his grandmother contacted the Seattle school district to ask if the district could help with the costs of his private school enrollment. She was told the school district would have to do a "complete workup" to find out what his needs were and what could be done. The district psychologist contacted the boy's mother and told her that based on his limited information, he could not find the boy eligible for special education services but that the school district would evaluate his needs should he return to the area. The mother requested a hearing. The Seattle superintendent of public instruction reversed the decision and the mother initiated a lawsuit.

The Court of Appeals of Washington stated that the issue was whether a school district must reimburse a parent for tuition costs when the parent unilaterally places a child in an out-of-state private school before the school district has had an opportunity to assess the child's needs and make a recommendation. The EHA authorizes tuition reimbursement, in appropriate cases, when the parents and the district disagree as to which educational placement is appropriate for the child. In this case, however, such disagreement was absent. The mother's unilateral placement of her son in the private school without the district's assessment prevented recovery of her expenses for his private school education. *Hunter v. Seattle School Dist. No. 1*, 731 P.2d 19 (Wash.App.1987).

The next cases deal with the effects of an improper selection of a hearing officer.

The U.S. Court of Appeals, Fourth Circuit, ruled that a school district's failure to fully advise the parents of a dyslexic child of their EHA procedural rights justified unilateral private school placement by the parents. In this North Carolina case, the child, who had been enrolled in his local public elementary school, had extreme difficulty in reading. Although he was required to repeat second grade, the child was thereafter advanced due to the school district's practice of making "social promotions." When the child reached the third grade, an IEP was developed which identified him as having reading deficiencies only and called for placement in a regular classroom ninety percent of the time, and placement in a learning disabilities resource room for the remainder of the time. When the child reached the fifth grade he still could not read. In desperation, his parents enrolled him in a private residential facility. At this time a private evaluation of the child was performed which finally disclosed that although he was of above average intelligence, the child suffered from dyslexia. The parents also discovered for the first time that under federal law their school district might be obligated to pay for their child's placement at the private school. The parents filed suit and a U.S. district court ruled in their favor.

On appeal, the U.S. Court of Appeals upheld the district court's ruling, ordering that the school district pay the cost of the child's placement at the private school. The child had made no educational progress while in the public schools and the IEP developed by public school officials was utterly inadequate, said the court. The school district's contention that the child had achieved educational benefits because he had advanced from grade to grade was dismissed by the appellate court, due to the school's policy of making social promotions. Furthermore, the school district's failure to fully inform the parents of their rights under the EHA constituted a *per se* breach of its statutory duties. The appellate court also noted that the child had finally begun to make educational progress after his placement at the private residential school. The child's parents were thus entitled to recover the costs of his placement from the school district. *Hall v. Vance County Bd. of Educ.*, 774 F.2d 629 (4th Cir.1985).

The parents of a learning disabled boy claimed that the Mississippi Board of Education violated the EHA by not having an impartial state review team decide whether to reimburse them for their son's tuition at a private school during the 1984-85 school year and to provide a private education for the next school year.

The parents had become dissatisfied with the IEP developed for their son, a learning disabled handicapped child. They sought an administrative hearing concerning the child's proper placement and reimbursement for the tuition they had paid at a private school. The hearing officer ruled that the parents should be reimbursed for the 1984-85 school year, but that the child should return to the public school system. On appeal, however, the state review board ruled that the parents should not receive tuition reimbursement and that the boy should return to public school.

The parents filed suit in federal district court, requesting a new hearing before the state review board. The district court granted the request because it found that the State Board of Education had violated the EHA. The court held that officers of local school boards and personnel active in state policy for the education of handicapped children should not serve on the state review panel. These individuals were too closely involved with the State Board of Education and could not provide the parents with an impartial hearing. Also, the court ruled that a state review team must make specific findings of fact in support of their conclusions under the EHA. *Kotowicz v. Mississippi State Bd. of Educ.*, 630 F.Supp. 925 (S.D.Miss.1986).

A Missouri case involved the proposed transfer of two handicapped children from an elementary school district to a state school for the severely handicapped. The parents of the children sued the school district alleging that the children were denied due process of law in violation of the EHA. A federal district court agreed with the parents. The court found that the referral of the children to the State Department of Education for placement was without prior notice to the parents. In addition, the first level hearing was defective because a three-member panel failed to review the facts and make a decision as required by the EHA. Instead, the State Department of Education decided to withdraw the proposed assignment of the children and to conduct further proceedings before making a final determination as to an appropriate educational placement. The court found that the state was thus bound to comply with federal procedural safeguards which became effective as of the date of the hearing. The actions taken by the department were in violation of EHA procedural safeguards which require a determination of the facts and a decision. Finally, the court found that the state level hearing was not conducted by an impartial hearing officer. This hearing was conducted by the Missouri State Board of Education which was an "agency or unit involved in the education or care of the child" within the meaning of the EHA. The Act also requires that the impartial individual who conducts a due process hearing at the state level may not be an employee of the State Department of Education or "of any local or intermediate unit thereof." Here, the parents were entitled to, but did not receive, an impartial hearing officer. *Vogel v. School Bd. of Montrose R-14 School Dist.*, 491 F.Supp. 989 (W.D. Mo.1980).

Another school district was found to have violated the procedural safeguards of the EHA by the failure to provide an impartial hearing officer. This case arose in Iowa and involved a challenge to a local school district's decision to place a child in special education classes. The child's guardian brought suit against the Iowa State Superintendent of Public Instruction alleging that the superintendent violated the "impartial hearing officer" provision of the EHA by presiding over the due process hearing which the child had received. A U.S. district court held that the superintendent violated the EHA provision barring employees of agencies involved in the education of a child from serving as hearing officers in due process hearings required by the Act. The district court remanded the case for a new hearing which was to be presided over by an outside hearing officer and the superintendent appealed to the U.S. Court of Appeals, Eighth Circuit.

The Court of Appeals was asked to decide whether the superintendent, as Superintendent of Public Instruction and an employee of the State Board of Public Instruction, was employed by a direct provider of educational services, the local school board, or whether he merely exercised supervisory authority over the direct provider. The court affirmed the district court ruling, declaring the superintendent to be statutorily disqualified from serving as a hearing officer. The EHA's clear language and history indicate that "no hearing may be conducted by an employee of the State or local educational agency involved in the education or care of the child." *Robert M. v. Benton*, 634 F.2d 1139 (8th Cir.1980).

The parents of an emotionally handicapped, learning disabled child with severe behavioral problems brought suit against an Oregon school district alleging that an appropriate education program was not being made available to their child and that the school district had violated statutes and regulations it was legally bound to follow. They requested and received a complaint hearing before the state Department of Education (DOE). The DOE found that the school district had violated applicable state and federal laws and awarded the parents partial reimbursement of tuition costs they had incurred by enrolling their son in a private school. However, it denied the parents' request for attorney fees.

Both the parents and the school district appealed to the Court of Appeals of Oregon which defined four issues: 1) whether the allegations that the district denied the child a "free appropriate public education" and otherwise violated state and federal laws were properly before the DOE; 2) whether the DOE, after finding that such violations had occurred, had the authority to require the district to reimburse the parents, in part, for expenses they had incurred; 3) whether the DOE was empowered to award the parents attorney fees; and 4) whether the DOE's findings of fact were supported by substantial evidence.

The court held that the DOE was the correct forum in which to bring the complaint. Had the parents' complaint alleged only that they disagreed with the district's IEP or educational placement for their child, the proper forum for resolution of that matter would have been a due process hearing. However, it alleged that an appropriate educational program was not made available to the child and also that the district violated various other federal statutes and regulations. Accordingly, the correct forum was a "complaint hearing." Such a hearing is governed by Oregon state law, which requires that local school districts comply with the EHA, that school districts have complaint procedures available for alleged violations and that sanctions be imposed against noncomplying districts.

However, the DOE, after finding violations, did not have the authority to require the school district to reimburse the parents' expenses. The district had a duty, said the court, to provide the child with a free appropriate education and, its having failed in that duty, the DOE only had the authority to withhold funds from it. The court went on to hold that the DOE had the power to award attorney fees even though it had not done so in this case, and that the DOE's findings of fact were supported by substantial evidence. *Laughlin v. School Dist. No. 1*, 686 P.2d 385 (Or.App.1984).

The final cases are a compilation of various interesting circumstances which change the result of an appeal.

The parents of an eleven-year-old learning disabled child in the District of Columbia, dissatisfied with a local school district's placement of the child, expressed their concern to the school staff. A meeting with school staff followed in which the parents again reiterated the concerns they had expressed earlier concerning the appropriateness of the child's education. After the meeting the school sent the parents a "Notice of Continuing Special Education Services," which stated that the child was to continue in the current program at the school. The notice did not inform the parents of the need to file any form, not did it state any way by which a dissatisfied parent could challenge the school's decision. A hearing was scheduled, but it was later canceled by the school. A letter to the parents' attorney stated that "since the [school was] 'unaware' of the [parents'] desire to change [the child's] program, no formal evaluation procedure had been initiated for the child." Accordingly, the letter continued, "the public schools will not be ready, nor are they required to participate at a hearing until they are given an opportunity to complete the formal evaluation/placement process."

The parents then brought suit against the school in federal court requesting the court to order the school to provide a due process hearing in which their objections to their child's continued placement at the school would be "fully ventilated." Without the hearing, claimed the parents, they were being denied due process guarantees mandated by the EHA and the Act's regulations which require that the parents or guardian of a child be afforded a hearing whenever they have a complaint about a school district's proposal to change or refusal to change a child's educational placement or any matter concerning the child's placement.

The school also argued that the parents had failed to submit a "Form 205" request which would have given the school notice of their objections. Noting that a school must be afforded reasonable notice of any parent's desire for a change of placement before the school is required to act upon the request, the court nevertheless found that the notice of placement to the parents did not inform them that filing "Form 205" was the proper procedure for objecting to their child's placement. Accordingly, the court denied the school's motion to dismiss the case and ordered that a hearing be held within five days of the court's order to address the parents' complaints about their child's IEP. *Pastel v. Dist. of Columbia Bd. of Educ.*, 522 F.Supp. 535 (D.D.C.1981).

A handicapped child and his mother brought suit on behalf of themselves and all handicapped children not receiving an appropriate education by reason of delays of the Illinois Superintendent of Education in resolving placement appeals. A severely emotionally disturbed twelve-year-old child was recommended for placement by his school district in a self-contained classroom for behavior disorder students. His mother objected to the recommendation and said that she had been advised by experts that a highly structured residential program would be an appropriate placement for the child. The mother appealed the decision but after five months the superintendent had made no decision. The mother claimed that the superintendent was obligated to decide within thirty days. She alleged that the long delay and inappropriate educational setting had caused the deterioration of the child's condition to the extent that he had to be placed in a mental hospital. The superintendent sought to dismiss the suit, arguing that the EHA creates no substantive rights for handicapped children.

A U.S. district court in Illinois disagreed, saying that the EHA is the source of a federal statutory right to a free appropriate education in every state electing to receive financial assistance, and that it is more than merely a "funding statute." The court then applied due process analysis and said that the passage of time caused the deprivation of the child's substantive right to an appropriate education and timeliness of review is an essential element of due process. The superintendent's motion to dismiss was denied. *John A. v. Gill*, 565 F.Supp. 372 (N.D.Ill.1983).

A Pennsylvania case resulted in a determination that a local school district failed to meet its legal responsibility to provide an appropriate program of education in training for an exceptional child. The court based its ruling on the fact that the district, instead of making an initial placement recommendation, merely provided the parents with a list of "approved private schools" and took twenty-one months to make an official recommendation of appropriate educational placement. *Pires v. Commonwealth of Pennsylvania, Dep't of Educ.*, 467 A.2d 79 (Pa.Cmwlth.1983).

CHAPTER FOUR
PRIVATE SCHOOL TUITION

I. REIMBURSEMENT FOR TUITION EXPENSES

Parents or guardians of handicapped children who unilaterally change the placement of their child during the pendency of any review proceedings often seek reimbursement from their school district for private school tuition expenses. In *Burlington School Committee v. Department of Education of Massachusetts*, below, the Supreme Court ruled that parents who violate the status quo provision may nevertheless receive private tuition reimbursement from the school district if the IEP proposed by the school is later found to be inappropriate. However, if the proposed IEP is found to be appropriate, the parents will not be entitled to reimbursement for expenses incurred in unilaterally changing their child's placement.

A. Unilateral Placement by Parents

In the *Burlington* case, the father of a learning disabled third grade boy became dissatisfied with his son's lack of progress in the Burlington, Massachusetts, public school system. A new IEP was developed for the child which called for placement in a different public school. The father, however, followed the advice of specialists at Massachusetts General Hospital and unilaterally withdrew his son from the Burlington school system, placing him instead at the Carroll School, a state-approved private facility in Lincoln, Massachusetts. He then sought reimbursement for tuition and transportation expenses from the Burlington School Committee, contending that the IEP which proposed a public school placement was inappropriate.

The state Board of Special Education Appeals (BSEA) ruled that the proposed IEP was inappropriate and that, therefore, the father had been justified in placing his son at the Carroll School. The BSEA ordered the Burlington School Committee to reimburse the father for tuition and transportation expenses, and the School committee appealed to the federal courts. A federal district court held that the parents had violated the EHA status quo provision by enrolling their child in the private school without the agreement of public school officials. Thus, they were not entitled to reimbursement.

The U.S. Court of Appeals, First Circuit, reversed the district court's ruling, and the Burlington School Committee appealed to the U.S. Supreme Court.

In upholding the court of appeals, the Supreme Court ruled that parents who place a handicapped child in a private educational facility are entitled to reimbursement for the child's tuition and living expenses, *if* a court later determines that the school district had proposed an inappropriate IEP. The Court stated that reimbursement could not be ordered if the school district's proposed IEP was later found to be appropriate. The Supreme Court observed that to bar reimbursement claims under all circumstances would violate the EHA, which favors proper interim placements for handicapped children.

In addition, under the School Committee's reading of the EHA status quo provision, parents would be forced to leave their child in what might later be determined to be an inappropriate educational placement, or would obtain the appropriate placement only by sacrificing any claim for reimbursement. This result, found the Court, was not intended by Congress. However, the Court noted that "[t]his is not to say that [this provision] has no effect on parents." Parents who unilaterally change their children's placement during the pendency of proceedings do so at their own financial risk. If the courts ultimately determine that a child's proposed IEP was appropriate, the parents are barred from obtaining reimbursement for an unauthorized private school placement. *Burlington School Comm. v. Dep't of Educ. of Massachusetts*, 105 S.Ct. 1996 (1985).

A Connecticut three-year-old suffered from a sensorineural hearing loss and speech and language delays. A planning and placement team (PPT) recommended that the student be placed in a public preschool program for hearing impaired students and that he attend the school's handicapped summer school program. The student's parents disagreed with the PPT's recommendation and placed him in a summer program at a private nursery school which enrolled both hearing impaired and nonhearing impaired students. After completion of the summer program, a second PPT meeting was held in which the PPT recommended that the student be placed in the public school's segregated preschool hearing impaired program. The parents disagreed with the placement and returned the student to the private school. The parents then requested an administrative hearing before the Connecticut Department of Education. The hearing officer concluded that the program developed by the PPT was reasonably designed to meet the student's special education needs and was therefore appropriate. The hearing officer also found that the parents were not entitled to tuition reimbursement. The parents sued the board of education in a federal district court seeking review of the hearing officer's decision. The district court found that the public school program was inappropriate and ordered tuition reimbursement. The board appealed to the U.S. Court of Appeals, Second Circuit.

The court of appeals held that the district court had failed to give proper deference to the agency experts' judgment when it concluded that the board had failed to offer the student an appropriate educational program. The court noted that the student's IEP was geared toward providing him with the best possible education. The PPT had conducted a thorough analysis of the student's handicap and his special needs with full knowledge of the legislative preference for mainstreaming. The court agreed with the PPT that the proposed program was appropriate to meet the student's special education needs in the least restrictive environment. The public school was an appropriate placement for the student and he was not entitled to tuition reimbursement. The court of appeals reversed the district court's decision. *Briggs v. Bd. of Educ. of State of Conn.*, 882 F.2d 688 (2d Cir.1989).

A mentally-retarded Nebraska child had cerebral palsy and severe behavioral impairment. An IEP was prepared in October, 1984, which was approved by her parents. During the 1984-85 school year the child's behavior posed significant problems. Her most severe tantrums included head banging and screaming. The child's teacher believed a program with stronger behavior management and with a lower pupil-to-teacher ratio might be necessary. The mother expressed some concern about the present IEP. The teacher told the child's parents to contact the state department of education about a different placement. The teacher met with the child's mother in May, 1985, to review her 1984-85 IEP. The mother was given a pamphlet describing her EHA rights. A school district official allegedly advised her of her procedural rights and told her to talk to the appropriate school official about alternative residential placement for the child. The mother informed the official that she was considering a private school placement. The school district learned in the summer or early fall of 1985 that the child was going to be placed by the parents in a private Kansas school.

The parents filed an application for tuition reimbursement with the Nebraska Department of Education but it was denied. The parents then asked the department to order a twenty-four hour private placement for the child at the Kansas school and payment for past and future costs of such care. In July, 1986, a hearing officer denied the relief and the parents sued the school district in a federal district court. The court held for the school district and the parents appealed to the U.S. Court of Appeals, Eighth Circuit. The parents contended that the school district refused to change the child's placement upon their request, failed to give them proper written notice, and that the school district failed to comply with EHA regulations regarding the timing of reevaluations while the child was still in the school district in 1984-85. The court of appeals affirmed the district court decision. The parents' concern about the child's education did not trigger EHA procedural requirements. They unilaterally placed the child in the Kansas school rather than formally asking the school district to make a change in the child's placement. Although the school district failed to give written notice of a refusal to provide tuition reimbursement in the fall of 1985 this violation of EHA requirements was harmless. Even though the school district failed to reevaluate the child within three years, this failure did not harm the child's educational progress. The parents were not entitled to tuition reimbursement. *Evans v. Dist. No. 17 of Douglas County, Nebraska*, 841 F.2d 824 (8th Cir.1988).

The parents of a handicapped Massachusetts child were denied reimbursement for past tuition expenses at a private school which their child attended by the choice of the parents, and the local school district was also absolved from having to pay for any future tuition. The child had attended local public schools through the third grade but the following year, at the suggestion of a learning disabilities specialist, his parents enrolled him in a remedial program at a private school. The student remained there for several years. At approximately the same time as the child began his private schooling, the public school devised an IEP for him. However, the parents rejected the plan, preferring to place the child in the private school. Following an administrative determination, disputed by both the parents and the school district, a lawsuit was brought. A lower court entered judgment dismissing the parents' action for reimbursement and declaring that the school was not responsible for tuition at the private school.

On appeal to the Court of Appeals of Massachusetts, the lower court's determinations were affirmed. After resolving a number of procedural problems the court went on to say that "private placements are authorized only when the appropriate special education program . . . is not available within the public school system. . . . The private placement provisions of [the statute] only apply to a child who seeks services in the public school system and who is then identified as requiring special services which the school system either cannot, or chooses not to, provide." It was noted that parents who undertake a private placement unilaterally assume a financial risk because school authorities very possibly could recommend a different placement.

The court also commented on both federal and state laws which encourage a mainstreaming policy. It stated that the common objective of these laws is the prompt provision of needed services to learning-handicapped children through the free local public school system except where the resources of those schools cannot appropriately meet the childrens' needs. In this case, following that policy required a public school program for the child if one could be developed which would meet his special needs. Here the parents took the position that he would be better served by a private school education. This, of course, was their right but, subject to the limited exceptions, no public obligation to pay for this private education could arise unless a school authority determined that the public school system could not meet the child's special needs. Thus, the parents were obligated to pay their child's tuition costs. *School Comm. of Franklin v. Comm'r of Educ.*, 462 N.E.2d 338 (Mass.App.1984).

The U.S. Court of Appeals, Fifth Circuit, reversed a trial court ruling which granted a preliminary injunction to the parents of a handicapped child who had placed the child in a private school of their choice pending the outcome of the parents' action against a local Texas school district. The parents of the child had requested the district court to issue the injunction ordering the school district to pay, pending resolution of the case, the costs of the private school in which they had placed their child. The Court of Appeals held that under federal law, maintenance of the present placement of a handicapped child (or the "status quo") during the pendency of proceedings demands only that school districts and state educational agencies maintain financial commitments to continue to fund an educational placement that it already funded prior to commencement of proceedings. Nothing requires a school district to pay the costs of parent-chosen private schooling pending judicial review of placement procedures and decisions by a state agency. *Stacey G. v. Pasadena Indep. School Dist.*, 695 F.2d 949 (5th Cir.1983).

In an Illinois case, the mother of an emotionally handicapped child brought an action on behalf of her child. The mother, because of dissatisfaction with her school district's recommendation for educational placement of the child, unilaterally transferred him to a private school of her choosing. Thereafter, the Illinois Office of Education determined the local school district could provide an appropriate education for the child. The mother appealed this decision to the Illinois courts which reversed and ordered reimbursement for educational expenses. Employing a pre-*Burlington* legal standard, the Appellate Court of Illinois held that there generally are two circumstances where a parent should be able to be reimbursed for expenses relating to unilateral placement in a private school without undergoing lengthy administrative processes. One is where a child's physical health is endangered. The other is where a school has acted in bad faith in refusing to assign a child to a special school. Here the court stated that both circumstances could arguably have existed. Therefore, the placement of the child at the special school was proper and the mother was entitled to reimbursement from the child's district of residence. *Walker v. Cronin*, 438 N.E.2d 582 (Ill.App.1982).

B. Residential School Placement

In order for parents to obtain tuition reimbursement when they have placed their handicapped child in a residential home, they must show that the IEP placement was inappropriate and that the residential placement was appropriate. The parents will then be reimbursed for all necessary related costs.

A neurologically impaired New Jersey student was placed in a perceptually impaired program. An IEP was designed with five goals. The following year the IEP was reviewed and the school agreed to provide a more intensive reading and writing program. The student's parents rejected the proposed IEP because they were concerned that the student was still reading at a second-grade level and that he had not received proper training to overcome his dyslexia. The parents enrolled the student at a private Massachusetts school which specialized in teaching students with severe dyslexia. The parents then requested a due process hearing seeking reimbursement for tuition and residential costs at the private school. The hearing officer found that the public school's IEP failed to clearly specify the student's educational goals and objectives or provide a means of measuring his progress. The officer also found that the parents had unilaterally placed the student in the private school without any indication that the student required residential placement. The parents' request for reimbursement was denied and they appealed to a new Jersey trial court. The court found that the school had failed to design an appropriate IEP for the student and that his parents should be reimbursed for tuition but not his room and board. Both parties then appealed to the Superior Court, Appellate Division, which vacated the trial court's order and remanded the case for a new trial. On remand, the trial court dismissed the parents' claim and they appealed to the Appellate Division, which affirmed the dismissal. The Supreme Court of New Jersey granted certification.

The supreme court noted that the school district had the burden to prove that the IEP was adequate. Because the district's IEP was nonspecific in its written aspirations and evaluation of effectiveness, it was incapable of review and inappropriate. The court held that the parents were entitled to tuition reimbursement, but not residential expenses. The student could have remained at the public school if it had provided the level of education provided by the private school. Residency at the private school was unnecessary. The supreme court reversed the appellate division and remanded the case to the trial court. *Lascari v. Bd. of Educ.*, 560 A.2d 1180 (N.J.1989).

A Massachusetts child suffered from learning disabilities which included difficulties with visual motor skills, visual perception, visual tracking and motor coordination. He attended the Concord School but made little progress, especially in his social skills. The parents unilaterally placed the student into a private residential school in Massachusetts and sought to have the child's IEP changed to include placement at the school. The school district refused and the parents instituted an administrative hearing with the Bureau of Special Education which ruled that Concord had offered the student an appropriate education but ordered the parents reimbursed for certain interim expenses including the residential school tuition. The parents brought suit in a federal district court and they assigned an error to the bureau's determination that Concord was an appropriate placement. Concord then crossclaimed contending that the bureau exceeded its authority by ordering any reimbursement. At trial, the district court accepted the administrative record as evidence and prevented the parents from calling certain additional witnesses. The court found that the IEP was appropriate and affirmed the defendant's placement but reversed the bureau's order for reimbursement of the interim costs. The parents appealed to the U.S. Court of Appeals, First Circuit.

The appellate court determined that the issue was whether the trial court's ruling was clearly erroneous. Massachusetts provides that special education programs assure the maximum possible development of handicapped students. The parents contended that because the student had been doing better at the residential school, it was the appropriate placement. The appellate court disagreed, stating that the school district properly determined the appropriate education to assure the maximum possible development of the student under Massachusetts law. The trial court did not abuse its discretion in precluding the testimony of the parents' expert witnesses, because the testimony was deliberately withheld at the administrative level. Therefore, the parents were not entitled to be reimbursed for their costs of the residential placement. *Roland M. v. Concord School Committee*, 910 F.2d 983 (1st Cir.1990).

A severely multihandicapped Ohio student was evaluated at a center for developmental disorders. The center diagnosed the student as "basically retarded with a language delay." The center concluded that the student suffered from a severe language disorder, had difficulty with interactive skills, demonstrated inconsistent eye contact, inconsistent reaching out, and an inappropriate gesturing system. Upon the recommendation of the center, the student was enrolled in several placements based on his IEP, but the parents were consistently unhappy with them. Finally, the center recommended a residential placement and encouraged the parents to investigate residential homes, suggesting a particular residence. The parents decided that the resident home was unsatisfactory. The school district also provided names of other possible residential homes. The parents rejected this IEP and instead enrolled the student in a Japanese resident home. They then commenced a due process proceeding seeking reimbursement for the student's tuition and expenses. The impartial hearing officer rendered an opinion in favor of the district and denied the parents reimbursement for the tuition and expenses. The parents appealed to the state level review officer who also found in favor of the district. The parents then sued in a federal district court.

The court noted that the parents must show that the Japanese school was an appropriate placement and the proposed IEP was inappropriate. The court then found that the Japanese school was not appropriate for four reasons. First, it preferred not to work with severely mentally retarded children. Second, the parents' involvement was minimal due to the distance between the U.S. and Japan. Third, there were language difficulties which would hinder the student's communicative development. And finally, the extreme cost of the Japanese school would act to the detriment of many other students. The parents contended that since the student became more compliant, the Japanese school was appropriate. The court noted that there was no evidence to suggest that the student's behavior was the product of the Japanese school or merely his being in a well-structured residential setting. Under the EHA, the placement need only give some educational benefit, it need not maximize the child's abilities. The district court affirmed the decision of the state level review officer, and held for the school district. *Matta v. Bd. of Educ.-Indian Hill Ex. Vil. Schools*, 731 F.Supp. 253 (S.D.Ohio 1990).

A ten-year-old Washington special education student was seriously emotionally disturbed due to an unstable childhood, including neglect and abuse. After adoption, the student began her public education in Washington; then when the adoptive parents moved to Riverside, California, they enrolled the child in a mental health day treatment program. Shortly thereafter, because of her destructive behavior, she was placed in a mental health residential treatment program. The parents then moved to Fresno. They continued, however, to educate their daughter in Riverside. Then the mental health director of the Riverside facility informed the parents that the child's behavior had deteriorated to such an extent that the staff could no longer control her, even with medication. The staff recommended placement in an acute care facility where the child was eventually placed. The costs were paid primarily through the parents' medical insurance until their policy was exhausted. The parents then asked their school district to provide an appropriate educational placement for their daughter. The district provided a number of options which the parents rejected. Instead the parents requested that the school district fund the student's placement at the acute care facility. When the district refused to do so, the parents sought an administrative hearing to determine whether the student was entitled to be educated at the district's expense at the acute care facility. The administrative hearing officer ruled in favor of the student's parents, ordering the district to pay for the student's hospitalization. The school district appealed to a federal district court. The trial court ruled in favor of the student and ordered the school district to pay all costs. The school district appealed to the U.S. Court of Appeals, Ninth Circuit.

On appeal, the school district argued that it was not required to pay for the student's placement because the child was not hospitalized for purely educational reasons. The court noted that, thus far, the student was hospitalized primarily for medical and psychiatric reasons and therefore the district was not responsible for the costs of placement under the EHA. The court determined that the district was, however, responsible for maintaining placement of the child at the acute care facility through the pendency of court review proceedings. The court of appeals reversed the district court's decision and determined that the school district was not responsible for the residential placement costs. *Clovis Unif. v. Office of Administrative Hearings*, 903 F.2d 635 (9th Cir.1990).

A New York father placed his thirteen-year-old daughter who suffered from anorexia nervosa at the Hedges Treatment Center, a Pennsylvania residential treatment facility. He placed her at Hedges due to several placement delays by a school district's committee on the handicapped (COH). A federal district court denied his request for tuition reimbursement because he had failed to exhaust administrative remedies. He then sought an administrative hearing and the hearing officer ordered placement at Hedges. However, the New York Commissioner of Education refused to provide tuition reimbursement because Hedges was approved only for fourteen-year-olds and older. The father appealed to the same federal district court. It upheld the placement. The daughter received all of the benefits and rights at Hedges that she would have received at a New York school even though Hedges was not approved for her age.

On appeal before the U.S. Court of Appeals, Third Circuit, the commissioner contended that the district court exceeded its authority by ordering the placement. The court of appeals agreed with the commissioner. EHA § 1401(18)(B) required that the daughter receive special education and related services which met the state educational agency standards. EHA section 1413(a)(4)(B)(ii) provided that the state determine whether private facilities like Hedges met those standards. Thus, the EHA incorporated state educational standards. It was the state of New York's obligation (through the commissioner) to ensure that private facilities met applicable state educational standards. No court or agency could approve a placement at a private facility consistent with the EHA unless the commissioner approved the facility prior to the placement. The hearing officer and the district court wrongly placed the daughter at Hedges without the commissioner's approval. The district court decision was reversed and the father was denied reimbursement. *Antkowiak v. Ambach*, 838 F.2d 635 (2d Cir.1988). *U.S. cert. denied sub nom Doe v. Sobel*, 109 S.Ct. 133 (1988).

A New Jersey boy was born in 1971 with a neurological impairment which hindered his ability to walk and communicate. His local school board placed him in the Midland School, a private school for disabled children. However, in 1980, Midland School notified the parents that it was unable to provide an appropriate education for the boy. Because the school board allowed the Midland placement to continue and failed to act on a request for a hearing, the parents removed the boy to a Rhode Island private school in June, 1981. Although the boy was making remarkable progress at the Rhode Island school his parents were forced to place him in the Mercer Special Services School District because the school board refused to reimburse the parents for the private school program. In Mercer (a New Jersey nonresidential program) the boy's condition deteriorated because the program only provided one to one and one-half hours of home instruction per day.

The parents requested another due process hearing in which the hearing officer directed the school board to place the boy in a residential program and to reimburse his parents for all his residential placement expenses. The school board appealed to a federal district court which ruled for the parents, but denied the parents' request for money damages and attorney's fees.

On appeal to the U.S. Court of Appeals, Third Circuit, the school board contended that the district court was wrong in determining that a residential placement was appropriate for the boy and in ordering reimbursement to the parents. However, a psychologist who had observed the boy in the nonresidential setting at Midland testified that the boy's program required a high degree of one-to-one instruction, and that he required behavior modification involving administration of consequences for at least ninety percent of targeted behavior. The court of appeals ruled that the district court was correct in concluding that the Mercer program was inappropriate for the boy's needs.

Both courts rejected the school board's argument that it was obligated by law to provide no more than an education that would be "of benefit" to the boy. The court of appeals observed that under the EHA, the school district was required to provide a "free appropriate education" to the boy which must be tailored to his individual needs by using an IEP. Only a residential program such as the Rhode Island private school program would provide this "appropriate" education for the boy.

The court of appeals also upheld the district court's decision ordering tuition reimbursement. Reimbursement for private school tuition and related expenses incurred pending resolution over a dispute about placement is appropriate relief under the EHA. The matter of money damages was remanded to the district court for further proceedings. The school board was required to reimburse the parents for the boy's past, present and future residential placement. The school district was also ordered to redraft the boy's IEP. *Bd. of Educ. v. Diamond*, 808 F.2d 987 (3d Cir.1986).

A California school district was ordered to pay the tuition and related expenses for a learning disabled boy whose parents had unilaterally placed him in an out-of-state private residential facility. In November, 1976, the boy's first IEP, in which he was classified as suffering from a mild learning disability, was formulated by school district officials. The boy progressed and by June, 1977, he had successfully been partially integrated into regular classes. A new IEP was formulated at this time which provided that he continue in regular classes with minimal supplementary educational services. Three months later, in September, 1977, another IEP was developed which noted the boy's progress and recommended continued regular placement with some special education assistance. However, his performance and behavior suffered greatly during the ensuing 1977-78 school year. School officials observed increased anger, hostility and rebelliousness during this period. The boy's parents were contacted in February, 1978, and a review session was held at which it was agreed that the September, 1977 IEP would remain in effect.

At the close of the 1977-78 school year, the boy was removed from school after slashing the tires on a teacher's car. He also ran away from home in August, 1978, and was consequently made a ward of the juvenile court. His behavior was described as "self-destructive" with "poor impulse control." In the fall of 1978 the boy was enrolled in the local high school where school officials, with the concurrence of his parents, tentatively decided that his September, 1977, IEP would remain in effect. He was thereafter truant from school on numerous occasions and ran away from home again for a week in September, 1978, at which time he committed the offenses of joyriding and marijuana possession. He spent the remainder of the school year in juvenile hall and various youth residential facilities. The school district made no effort to reevaluate the boy or develop a new IEP during this period.

Due to the school district's failure to properly evaluate their son, the parents decided to enroll him in a private residential facility in Utah in March, 1979, and asked that the school district pay the cost of his placement. The district, however, stated that it would pay only educational expenses at the facility. The parents requested a due process hearing on the matter and the hearing panel found that because the parents had acted unilaterally in placing their son at the residential facility, thereby breaching the EHA's status quo provision the school district was not liable for the cost of the placement. The parents appealed and the California Court of Appeal held that the school district was liable under the EHA for the boy's educational and related expenses at the private, out-of-state residential facility.

The court based its decision on the failure of the school district to develop an IEP for the boy annually, as required by the EHA. An IEP had been formulated in September, 1977, but as of April, 1979, a new IEP had not been developed. The court rejected the school district's contention that because the boy had been truant and was frequently involved in the juvenile court system, it would have been difficult to properly evaluate him. The boy's status in the juvenile court system was well known to school officials and their failure to update the "manifestly inappropriate" September, 1977, IEP was characterized by the court as evidence of bad faith. The school district was therefore ordered to pay the cost of the private school placement. *In Re John K.*, 216 Cal.Rptr. 557 (Cal.App.1st Dist.1985).

A special education dispute of fourteen years' duration was settled by the U.S. Court of Appeals, Third Circuit. The court of appeals upheld a federal district court's ruling that the Westfield, New Jersey, board of education was not liable for the cost of nine years of private school placement. The child in this case was first identified as handicapped in 1968. At that time the Westfield Board of Education placed the child at the Midland School, a private facility. In 1972, further testing was performed by outside experts as well as Westfield's child study team. The child was thereafter labeled "mentally retarded-educable" by the child study team, and an IEP was formulated which called for placement at a different institution, the Tamaques School. Objecting to the label "mentally retarded-educable," as well as the change in placement, the parents kept him at Midland and paid the tuition themselves.

In 1975, the parents filed a petition with the New Jersey Department of Education seeking review of Westfield's 1972 reclassification decision. The parents contended that during the pendency of all review proceedings, Westfield was obligated to pay for their child's tuition at Midland, since EHA section 1415(e)(3) requires that a child remain in his or her "then current" placement until review is completed. Due to the department's failure to comply with EHA procedural requirements, a proper hearing on the merits of the parents' claim was not held until June 9, 1983.

At the due process hearing in 1983, the parents claimed that they were entitled to tuition reimbursement for their child's education at the Midland school from 1972 to 1981, since they were entitled to leave their child at Midland during all review proceedings. They also claimed that the Westfield board of education was liable for the period their child attended school in Jerusalem. The hearing officer denied the parents' claims and they filed an action in federal district court, seeking review, but the court upheld the hearing officer's decision. The parents appealed their case to the U.S. Court of Appeals, Third Circuit, which similarly agreed with the hearing officer. The appeals court stated that since section 1415(e)(3) had not become effective until 1977, the Westfield Board of Education was relieved of responsibility for its 1972 decision to change the child's educational placement from Midland to Tamaques. Thus, the parents' decision to keep their child at Midland was not protected by section 1415(e)(3). The appeals court ruled that the parents should have placed the child at Tamaques in accordance with Westfield's 1972 recommendation.

The court also held that under EHA section 1412(2)(B), the Westfield Board of Education would be responsible for the post-graduation education of the child only if the board made it a regular practice to educate children even after they had graduated. Since the board did not, and since the child had already graduated when his parents sent him to the school in Jerusalem, the board was not liable for those expenses. Noting that all the classifications and placements proposed by Westfield's child study team were appropriate, the court of appeals affirmed the prior rulings against the parents. *Wexler v. Westfield Bd. of Educ.*, 784 F.2d 176 (3d Cir. 1986).

A learning-disabled West Virginia child was educated in a public school district for seven years. His parents became dissatisfied with his progress and rejected the individual educational program (IEP) suggested by his teacher. They obtained a loan and placed him in a private school after an unsatisfactory meeting with school officials. They then sought tuition reimbursement under the EHA. Following an unsuccessful administrative hearing and appeal to a state educational agency, the parents sued the school district in a federal district court. The court held for the parents and the school district appealed to the U.S. Court of Appeals, Fourth Circuit.

The school district argued that the parents' administrative appeal was untimely because they had waited approximately ten months before appealing to the state educational agency. The district also claimed that since the parents had received partial reimbursement from the state educational agency they were not an "aggrieved party" for further appeal under the EHA. It further contended that procedural defects found by the trial court were insufficient to prove that it had failed to provide the child with a free appropriate public education. The court of appeals upheld the district court decision. Retroactive imposition of a time limitation on the parents' administrative appeal was contrary to the EHA. The state agency decision did not compensate the parents for all tuition expenses and did not reimburse them for room, board, travel expenses or interest on their loan. These expenses qualified the parents as "aggrieved parties." The district court hearing established that the school district had failed to conduct the required multidisciplinary review for the child. Furthermore, the district did not conduct a placement advisory committee meeting or otherwise adequately involve the parents in the preparation of the child's IEP. The parents were entitled to full reimbursement. *Bd. of Educ. of the County of Cabell v. Dienelt*, 843 F.2d 813 (4th Cir. 1988).

In 1978, the state of New York agreed to pay the tuition costs of a schizophrenic boy who had been placed in a private residential psychiatric hospital which operated an accredited academic high school. Behavioral problems prevented the boy from attending the high school, but he continued to reside at the hospital. His doctors hoped that the behavior problems could be overcome. The boy's parents, after petitioning state officials in vain, sought to compel the state to pay the cost of the boy's residential care at the hospital from the time of his placement, July, 1978, through June, 1983, when the boy turned twenty-one years old. The state argued that as long as the child's behavioral problems prevented him from attending the high school at the institution, he was in effect uneducable and therefore the state had no responsibility for any of his expenses.

The court ruled that once the state placed the boy at the psychiatric hospital, it became obligated to pay the entire expense of the placement. The state could not escape its responsibility for costs of the boy's residential care simply by stating that those costs did not directly address educational problems. As long as the boy could be educated (however little) through a residential placement, the state remained responsible for the cost of that placement. *Vander Malle v. Ambach*, 667 F.Supp. 1015 (S.D.N.Y. 1987).

The town of Henniker, New Hampshire, was not entitled to reimbursement from a local school district for the placement expenses of a handicapped child adjudged delinquent, according to the New Hampshire Supreme Court. When the boy entered the Henniker school system, he was diagnosed as educationally handicapped and an IEP was established for him. When he entered junior high school in the Hillsboro-Deering school district, the district found the boy was emotionally disturbed. It decided that his problem could be addressed within the school system under an IEP that provided for psychological counseling, parent consultations and academic monitoring. The student was later adjudicated a delinquent child by a New Hampshire district court. The court ordered that he be placed in a foster home and put him on probation. He violated probation and was placed by the court in the Chamberlain School. The town of Henniker was billed for the cost of the student's educational and residential fees at the Chamberlain School. The town sought reimbursement for these costs from the Hillsboro-Deering school district in state district court. The court found that the school district was liable for the educational portion of the expenses. The school district appealed the decision.

The Supreme Court of New Hampshire held that the district court had exceeded its authority. When a handicapped child is involved in delinquency proceedings a court can only order a review of the IEP by the school district; it has no authority to order a school district to assume financial responsibility for a placement not addressed or provided for in a child's IEP. Since the child's placement arose out of his delinquency adjudication, his residential and educational cost at Chamberlain had to be paid by the town in which he resided, with a right of reimbursement from the person legally responsible for the child's support. The school district was held not liable for the cost of the child's private residential school placement. *In re Todd P.*, 509 A.2d 140 (N.H.1986).

Reimbursement was denied to the parents of an Oklahoma youth, who brought suit in federal district court after their local school district refused to fund their son's placement at a residential facility. The youth, who was classified as "educable mentally handicapped" and who had serious emotional and behavioral problems, had been enrolled at the age of eighteen in his local school district's EMH program. An IEP was developed at this time with the approval of his parents, in which it was agreed that if the boy became "unmanageable" he would be suspended for three-day intervals. Although his educational program included both high school instruction and vocational instruction, he was soon expelled from the vo-tech program due to his emotional outbursts. When these outbursts continued at the high school, school officials notified his parents that an alternative to classroom placement was necessary. Homebound instruction was suggested, but the parents rejected the proposal. For the next several months the parents considered residential placement; during this period the youth received no educational services. His parents also failed to bring him to school for testing to aid in the formulation of a new IEP, as requested by school officials.

The parents then requested funding for their child's placement at an out-of-state residential facility. When their school district refused they requested a due process hearing under the EHA. The parents, after discovering the name of the hearing officer, believed that he would find in favor of the school district and withdrew their request for a hearing. At the beginning of the next school year they appeared once again at the high school to enroll their son, and school officials, who had not expected the youth to enroll, requested a week to formulate an IEP. Several days later school officials attempted to arrange a meeting with the parents to discuss a new IEP for the youth, but the parents refused because a new teacher had not yet been hired to instruct him. The school officials explained that a new teacher would not be hired unless the parents approved the new IEP and assured them that they would enroll their son. This impasse caused the parents to unilaterally enroll their son in the out-of-state residential facility.

A due process hearing resulted in approval of the school district's decision not to reimburse the parents for the cost of his placement, and the parents sought judicial review. The U.S. Court of Appeals, First Circuit, upheld the denial of tuition reimbursement and found that the district had taken all steps necessary to provide the child with a free appropriate public education. The appeals court stated that "[a]lthough the [residential facility] undoubtedly offered . . . a superior educational program, an education which maximizes a child's potential is not required by the EHA." *Cain v. Yukon Pub. Schools, Dist. I-27*, 775 F.2d 15 (10th Cir. 1985).

In a District of Columbia case, a seventeen-year-old learning disabled boy had spent one year in a private special education boarding school. His parents were notified by the school board that it would not continue financial support of their son's placement at that school during the next year. The school board also informed the parents that it had decided on an alternative school for their boy's placement. The parents became very confused when, a few days after receiving the first notification, a second notice arrived recommending that their son attend yet another school. Letters written by the parents seeking an explanation for the conflicting recommendation went unanswered. When the next school year started, the parents reenrolled their son in the private boarding school. They then sued in a federal district court where they sought to have the school board held financially responsible for the boarding school placement.

The parents contended that since the school board had approved the boarding school during the previous year the EHA dictated that the boy must remain at that school pending all administrative or judicial proceedings and until another appropriate placement was finally determined. The school board maintained that the boy's parents had purposefully delayed the proceedings and frustrated its attempts to find a new placement. The court held that while it was true that the parents had delayed the due process hearing, they did so out of confusion over the conflicting placement recommendations. Further, the notifications sent by the school board did not comply with EHA requirements. The court agreed with the parents' contention that the boarding school was the boy's current placement, and due to the procedural failures of the school board he must remain there pending further appeals. Summary judgment was granted in favor of the parents. *Jacobsen v. Dist. of Columbia Bd. of Educ.*, 564 F.Supp. 166 (D.D.C.1983).

A Massachusetts case involved a Down's syndrome child who, almost since birth, had been living at a private special education school at his parents' expense. When the parents sought an IEP the initial response was to place the child in a nonresidential public school. The parents objected and a long series of hearings and appeals ensued. The boy remained at the private school at his parents' expense pending the outcome of the proceedings. The trial court finally settled the placement question by ruling that the private school was indeed the proper IEP for the child. The district court, however, declined to reimburse the parents for their private school expenditures while the proceedings were taking place.

When the reimbursement question was appealed to the U.S. Court of Appeals, First Circuit, it held that the EHA required reimbursement only under circumstances not met by this case (a pre-*Burlington* decision). It noted, however, that Massachusetts law did call for reimbursement in some situations and remanded the case to the district court to decide this question. The district court held that the parents were entitled to reimbursement under Massachusetts law. *Doe v. Anrig*, 561 F.Supp. 121 (D.Mass.1983).

C. Placement in Unapproved Schools

Tuition reimbursement will almost never be granted when parents place their children in an unapproved school, unless the school district's placement was "woefully inadequate." However, this is a difficult burden for the parents to meet.

The parents of a handicapped New York student unilaterally placed their son in an unapproved school when their son's school district recommended placement which the parents found unacceptable. The parents requested a hearing claiming that the placement was inappropriate and untimely. They also requested tuition reimbursement for expenses at the unapproved school. A hearing officer overruled the district's recommendation, finding it untimely and insufficient. Although the hearing officer found that the placement at the unapproved school was appropriate, he denied tuition reimbursement because the school had never been approved by the state education commissioner. The parents appealed to the commissioner, who upheld the decision denying tuition reimbursement. The parents then sued the school district in a federal district court which dismissed the lawsuit. The parents then appealed to the U.S. Court of Appeals, Second Circuit.

The parents argued that to obtain reimbursement they need only show that the district's proposed IEP was inappropriate, and not that the unapproved school met state educational requirements. The court held that the parents could not obtain tuition reimbursement because the unapproved school was ineligible to contract for the education of handicapped students. Under the EHA, handicapped children may be educated at public expense only where private schools meet state educational standards. Placement in an unapproved school, whether by state officials or parents, was improper under the EHA because it violated the requirement that placement of handicapped students meet state educational agency standards. The court of appeals affirmed the district court's decision denying tuition reimbursement. *Tucker v. Bay Shore Union Free School Dist.*, 873 F.2d 563 (2d Cir.1989).

The mother of a handicapped Fairfax, Virginia, boy unilaterally placed him in the East Hill Farm and School in Vermont. She then requested a due process hearing to resolve the questions of tuition reimbursement and living expenses. Two due process hearings found that the Fairfax County Public Schools' (FCPS) recommendation of placement at the Little Keswick School, Inc., was appropriate and the mother appealed to a U.S. district court. The district court ruled in favor of FCPS and the mother appealed to the U.S. Court of Appeals, Fourth Circuit.

The court of appeals affirmed the district court's decision to deny tuition reimbursement to the mother for the East Hill education. It noted that when a handicapped child is educated at a private school under the EHA, the state or local school district has an obligation to ensure that that school meets applicable state educational standards. Here, East Hill was not approved by Virginia to offer special education. Therefore, FCPS could not place the boy and fund his education at East Hill without violating the EHA's requirement that handicapped children be educated at public expense only in those private schools that met state educational standards. The court of appeals observed that "[w]hen a handicapped child is educated at a private school under the [EHA], the State has an obligation to ensure that the school meets applicable State educational standards." Therefore, the EHA did not require FCPS to place the handicapped boy in the unapproved Vermont school. The district court decision was affirmed. *Schimmel v. Spillane*, 819 F.2d 477 (4th Cir.1987).

An emotionally handicapped New York child and his parents sued their local school district and various state officials under the EHA to recover tuition and costs incurred during the year and one-half the child spent at a private school in Maine. The child had been placed in a private school in New York by his school district but was expelled. He then returned home where he received four months of home tutoring. Then, concluding that no good faith effort was being made to place the child, the parents sent him to the Maine school from which he graduated. Because the out-of-state school was not on New York's list of approved facilities the parents were denied reimbursement for expenses for this placement. Suit was then brought, but a U.S. district court in New York granted the defendants' motion to dismiss. The court said that parents are generally entitled to an impartial due process hearing if they disagree with a local placement recommendation. However, this procedure is not available to review the state Commissioner of Education's refusal to contract with an out-of-state facility. *Smrcka v. Ambach*, 555 F.Supp. 1227 (E.D.N.Y.1983).

II. RELIGIOUS SCHOOLS

Public aid to private religious schools implicates the Establishment Clause of the First Amendment. Such aid must have a secular purpose which neither advances nor inhibits religion and does not entangle the state with religion.

The U.S. Supreme Court ruled unanimously on the issue of state aid to handicapped students at private religious schools. The Court held that the First Amendment to the U.S. Constitution does not prevent a state from providing financial assistance to a handicapped individual attending a Christian college. The plaintiff in this case, a blind person, sought vocational rehabilitative services from the state of Washington's Commission for the Blind pursuant to state law [Wash.Rev.Code sec. 74.16.181 (1981)]. The law provided that visually handicapped persons were eligible for educational assistance to enable them to "overcome vocational handicaps and to obtain the maximum degree of self-support and self-care." However, because the plaintiff was a private school student intending to pursue a career of service in the church, the Commission for the Blind denied him assistance. The Washington Supreme Court upheld this decision on the ground that the First Amendment to the U.S. Constitution prohibited state funding of a student's education at a religious college.

The U.S. Supreme Court took a different, much less restrictive view of the First Amendment and reversed the Washington court. The operation of Washington's program was such that the commission paid money directly to the student, who would then attend the school of his or her choice. The fact that the student in this case chose to attend a religious college did not constitute state support of religion, because "the decision to support religious education is made by the individual, not the state." The First Amendment was therefore not offended. The case was remanded to the Washington Supreme Court. *Witters v. Washington Dep't of Servs. for the Blind*, 106 S.Ct. 748 (1986).

On remand, the Washington Supreme Court reconsidered the matter under the Washington State Constitution, which is far stricter in its prohibition on the expenditure of public funds for religious instruction than is the U.S. Constitution. Vocational assistance funds for the student's religious education violated the state constitution because public money would be used for religious instruction. The court rejected the student's argument that the restriction on public expenditures would violate his right to free exercise of religion. The court determined that the commission's action was constitutional under the free exercise clause because there was no infringement of the student's constitutional rights. Finally, denial of the funds to the student did not violate the Fourteenth Amendment's equal protection clause because the commission had a policy of denying any student's religious vocational funding.

The classification was directly related to the state's interest in ensuring the separation between church and state as required by both state and federal constitutions. The court reaffirmed its denial of the student's tuition. *Witters v. State Comm'n for the Blind*, 771 P.2d 1119 (Wash.1989).

Relying on the EHA's status quo provision, a federal district court ordered the New York City Board of Education to fund a handicapped child's placement at a private educational facility. The city's school system, explained the court, had been operating since 1972 under a federal court order which mandates that an offer of a public school placement must be made by the school system within sixty days of a child's identification as a handicapped individual. Under the court order, if the child is not offered such a placement within sixty days the parents have the right to place the child in a private facility at the board's expense.

The present case arose when a child was unilaterally enrolled by his parents in the Hebrew Academy for Special Children as provided by the order described above. The board agreed to pay for the placement at the academy, but at the beginning of the following school year it once again recommended public school placement. The parents, however, desired to keep their child at the academy, and he remained there during the due process hearings which ensued. The hearings culminated in an order by the state education commissioner that the board was required to fund the child's education at the academy, and the board appealed to a federal district court.

Ruling that the Hebrew Academy had become the child's "then current" educational placement, the court upheld the commissioner's order. By initially failing to offer a placement within the required sixty days, the board had given the parents the unqualified right to place the child in a private facility at the board's expense. That placement then became the status quo, which could not be altered by the board until such time as they offered an acceptable placement. Under the EHA, the board then became unconditionally liable for the resulting tuition and related expenses. The court affirmed the commissioner's order of reimbursement for the parents' cost of placing the child at the Hebrew Academy. *Bd. of Educ. v. Ambach*, 628 F.Supp. 972 (E.D.N.Y.1986).

A Virginia case resulted in a ruling that that state will not fund the education of handicapped students at out-of-state religious institutions. Here, a twenty-year-old handicapped citizen of Vietnam who was a permanent resident alien of the United States graduated from a Virginia high school in 1984. He applied to and was accepted for admission to St. Andrews Presbyterian College, a nonprofit liberal arts college affiliated with the Presbyterian Synod of North Carolina. Its primary purpose is to provide collegiate or graduate education and not to provide religious training through a theological education. The student and his foster father sought financial assistance from the state of Virginia under its program of financial aid to the handicapped, which is 80% federally financed and 20% Virginia financed. Virginia denied financial aid to the student to attend St. Andrews solely because it was a church-affiliated school located outside Virginia.

Until 1969 Virginia could not provide assistance to any church-affiliated schools through tuition grants to students. In 1969, the Virginia Constitution was amended to provide for loans to students attending in-state church-affiliated schools so long as the primary purpose of those schools was to provide collegiate or graduate education. The student sued the state of Virginia in a U.S. district court claiming that the denial of financial aid violated the Establishment Clause of the First Amendment to the U.S. Constitution. He also contended that even if tuition aid was properly denied, he should still receive payments for incidental expenses to attend St. Andrews. The district court ruled for the state and the student appealed to the U.S. Court of Appeals, Fourth Circuit. For a state law to be consistent with the Establishment Clause its primary effect must neither advance nor hinder religion. The student contended that distinguishing out-of-state schools on the basis of religious affiliation violated the primary effect standard because it disfavored church-affiliated schools. The appeals court disagreed, noting that the U.S. Supreme Court has recognized that a decision to fund religious studies, along with other postsecondary education, lies within a permissible zone of accommodation of religion but is not mandatory.

The student also claimed that the Virginia policy infringed upon his right to the free exercise of religion since it forced him to forfeit attendance at an out-of-state religious institution in order to receive tuition aid. The court dismissed this allegation, observing that Virginia was not obligated to provide the student with an ideal learning situation. The state was only prohibited from forcing him to give up essential beliefs and practices in order to obtain tuition aid. The student's free exercise of religion needs and physical needs could be met in Virginia schools.

Further, the court of appeals noted that the Virginia Constitution did not prohibit the student's reimbursement for incidental expenses (books, transportation costs, living expenses, etc.) should he still choose to attend St. Andrews. Such subsidies would be to the student and not to a disqualified school. The appeals court remanded the case to the district court to determine how the state determines the primary purpose of in-state church-affiliated schools and how it provides for their monitoring so as to insure that Virginia is not advancing religion. *Phan v. Commonwealth of Virginia*, 806 F.2d 516 (4th Cir.1986).

In a New York case the U.S. Court of Appeals, Second Circuit, held that a plan to provide remedial education classes on public school property for private parochial school students violates the Establishment Clause. Chapter One of the Education Consolidation and Improvement Act established a federally funded program to provide remedial instruction and related support services to elementary and secondary school children who were "educationally deprived" and who lived in an area having a high concentration of low income families. The purpose of the program was to meet the remedial educational needs of students that could not otherwise be met by the schools they attended. States receiving Chapter One funding were required to provide such remedial services to private as well as public school students.

In order to comply with a 1985 U.S. Supreme Court decision which held that sending federally supported public school teachers to teach in private religious schools violated the Establishment of Religion Clause of the First Amendment [*Aguilar v. Felton*, 105 S.Ct. 3232 (1985)], the city of New York adopted a new plan. One aspect of the plan called for the city to conduct remedial education classes for girls from a Hasidic Jewish school on public school premises. Specifically, the plan provided for a section of the public school to be completely closed off for use by the Hasidic girls by constructing a wall in a previously open corridor. It also provided for the girls to be taught only by women (in accordance with Hasidic tradition) who spoke Yiddish. Before the plan was implemented, a local parents' association sued the New York City School District in a federal district court seeking a preliminary injunction against the plan. When the injunction was denied, the parents appealed to the U.S. Court of Appeals.

The parents contended that the city's plan had the primary effect of promoting religion and excessively entangled the state in religious matters. The city argued that the injunction was properly denied because the plan did not have those effects and was only a reasonable effort to encourage the Hasidic Jews to send their children to the remedial classes conducted in the public school. The court of appeals observed that the U.S. Supreme Court has developed a three-part test for determining whether a given state law is one that "establishes" religion. First, the statute must have a secular legislative purpose; second, its primary effect must be one that neither advances nor hinders religion; third, the statute must not promote an excessive government entanglement with religion. The court of appeals stated that the issue was whether the city's plan had the primary effect of advancing the religious tenets of the Hasidic Jews and whether it fostered an excessive entanglement of the city with religion. The court of appeals observed that the city's plan seemed "plainly to create a symbolic link between the state and the Hasidic sect that [was] likely to have a magnified negative impact on the minds of the youngsters attending P.S. 16."

It also disagreed with the district court's observation that an injunction against the plan would hinder the free exercise of religion on the part of the Jewish girls. "The Free Exercise Clause of the First Amendment . . . does not prohibit a government from forcing a choice between receipt of a public benefit and a pursuit of a religious belief if it can show a compelling reason for doing so." Avoiding a violation of the Establishment Clause that would otherwise result from an apparent endorsement of the tenets of a particular faith was ample reason for compelling that choice. The court of appeals reversed the lower court decision and held that the parents were entitled to preliminary injunctive relief on the ground that the city plan had the primary effect of establishing religion through a federally funded program. *Parents' Ass'n of P.S. 16 v. Quinones*, 803 F.2d 1235 (2d Cir.1986).

Parents of handicapped children who lived in a Hasidic Jewish community in New York requested in 1984 that their local school district furnish special education and related services at the Hasidic community. Both the parents and their handicapped children adhered to the practices of Hasidism which generally requires the separation of males and females. Male and female students in the community attended separate private Hasidic schools.

After providing some services during the 1984-85 school year at one of the Hasidic schools, the school district determined that it could furnish special education and related services to the community's handicapped students only in the public schools, together with public school students. This decision was based upon a New York state law which provided that "[p]upils enrolled in nonpublic schools for whom services are provided . . . shall receive such services in regular classes of the public school and shall not be provided such services separately from pupils regularly attending the public schools." The district's Committee on the Handicapped recommended a public school special education program for each handicapped Hasidic child after conducting individualized evaluations. The parents refused to allow their children to attend the public school programs, employed private tutors and sought administrative review of the individual public school placements.

The school district sought a judicial declaration that it was only required to furnish special education services to the Hasidic children in regular public school classes along with public school students. A trial court, however, ordered the district to provide the Hasidic children with special education and related services in a "mobile or other appropriate site not physically or educationally identified with but reasonably accessible to the [Hasidic] children." The school district appealed.

On appeal, a New York appellate court considered the school district's argument that the trial court's order violated the Establishment Clause of the First Amendment. The court determined that although the trial court's order reflected the clearly secular purpose of providing special education and related services to school children, it violated the Establishment Clause because it had the primary effect of advancing religion. The court pointed out that the "mobile or other appropriate site" that the trial court had ordered to be provided for use in the Hasidic community was necessary "not because of the nature of [the children's] handicaps, but because of their Hasidic faith and socio-cultural background." It found that the creation of a "mobile or other appropriate site" for the Hasidic children posed a "substantial risk that the [school district] will be required to plan and administer its special education curriculum according to the religious requirements of . . . Hasidism." The court ruled in favor of the school district. *Bd. of Educ. v. Wieder*, 522 N.Y.S.2d 878 (A.D.2d Dept.1987).

CHAPTER FIVE
RELATED SERVICES

The EHA requires school districts to provide special education students a free appropriate education. This may include related services, which are defined in EHA § 1401(17) as transportation, speech pathology, psychological services, physical and occupational therapy, medical and counseling services and others, so long as they relate to diagnoses for special education purposes.

I. PSYCHOLOGICAL SERVICES

Although expressly included within the EHA definition of related services, psychological services are not defined in the act. This has made the area of psychological services a highly litigated one.

A Virginia first grade student began to do poorly in school and showed signs of learning and emotional disabilities. His teacher recommended that the student be evaluated to determine if he was handicapped. A child study committee met and, 200 days after the initial referral, the committee determined that the child was not handicapped. The parents requested that the child be referred to an outside professional to be evaluated. The committee agreed and the child was diagnosed as having emotional and learning disabilities. Three days after the report from the outside professional was sent to the school the child became hysterical. That night the child became progressively worse and the parents admitted him to a hospital. While the child remained at the hospital he received educational and psychological counseling as well as medical services. After the child was released from the hospital, the committee met and developed an IEP for the child with the parents' consent. The IEP did not provide for one-on-one counseling but the parents provided the counseling at their own expense. The parents then demanded reimbursement for the psychological counseling and the hospital stay. The school district refused and the parents then requested a due process hearing. The hearing officer found for the school district and the parents appealed to a federal district court. After the court found for the school district, the parents appealed to the U.S. Court of Appeals, Fourth Circuit.

On appeal, the parents contended that the delay in processing of the student's referral caused his need for hospitalization and psychotherapy. As for the psychotherapy claim, the IEP was in effect and did not provide for psychotherapy. Because courts are unwilling to second-guess educators' decisions, the court affirmed the district court's decision to deny reimbursement. As for the hospital claim, clearly the child was not given a free and appropriate education by the school district while he was in the hospital. The court did, however, remand the case to the district court to determine if the placement in the hospital was an appropriate placement and if so to determine which expenses were incurred for special education and related services and to order reimbursement for related services expenses only. *Tice v. Botetourt County School Bd.*, 908 F.2d 1200 (4th Cir.1990).

After failing the seventh grade, a handicapped Tennessee student attended a private school for children with learning disabilities. After one year, the student had outgrown the school academically. The parents and local school officials met and agreed that the student would attend regular classes and receive special support from the school staff. After a short time, the student started having trouble in his classes and began to skip school. His behavior became so irrational that his parents sent him to a psychiatrist. When the student's behavior did not improve, the parents admitted the student into a private psychiatric hospital. The parents requested a due process hearing to determine reimbursement for the hospital expenses. The hearing officer found the placement at the hospital appropriate and necessary for the student to benefit educationally and ordered the school to reimburse the student's parents for all expenses. The school appealed to a Tennessee trial court which reversed the hearing officer's decision, holding that it was not supported by substantial and material evidence. The parents then appealed to the Court of Appeals of Tennessee.

The court of appeals held that payment for the student's psychiatric services was expressly excluded by the EHA. Under the EHA a physician's services are covered only when necessary to provide diagnosis or evaluation. The physician's services were not necessary for diagnosis or evaluation. The court found that the student's placement in the psychiatric hospital was for medical reasons, rather than for educational purposes. The school was not responsible for the student's hospitalization expenses. The court of appeals affirmed the trial court's decision denying reimbursement. *Metropolitan Gov't v. Dep't of Educ.*, 771 S.W.2d 427 (Tenn.App.1989).

A thirteen-year-old girl suffering from anorexia nervosa and various other emotional problems was placed at a Pennsylvania treatment center by her father. This placement occurred after the local school district committee on the handicapped (COH) had determined that the girl could be categorized as an "emotionally disturbed" child with medical problems. The father placed the girl at the Pennsylvania center because of placement delays by the COH. After being denied tuition reimbursement by the New York Commissioner of

Education, the father sued in U.S. district court. The court denied reimbursement because the father had failed to comply with EHA procedures. The father then sought and received a ruling by a hearing officer that his daughter was emotionally handicapped. However, the commissioner refused to provide tuition reimbursement because the Pennsylvania treatment center was approved by the commissioner only for children age fourteen or older. The father once again sought review in the same U.S. district court.

The district court held that the decisions of the hearing officer that the girl was emotionally handicapped, and that she required placement at the Pennsylvania center, were not reviewable by the commissioner. The court also observed that the girl had applied to nine in-state approved institutions, and had been rejected by all nine, indicating that the father had been reasonable in attempting to place her at a school acceptable to the commissioner. The commissioner claimed that under the EHA, the state was required to provide special education and related services which are a part of a "free public education" but that other services, such as medical services, are not provided for in the EHA. The district court ordered a trial to determine what portion of the girl's expenses at the Pennsylvania treatment center were related services to be paid by the state of New York. After trial, the district court concluded that counseling, psychological services and periodic psychiatric evaluations for medication purposes were "related services when provided by a psychologist, social worker, or other professional." The father was entitled to reimbursement for both these expenses and tuition, according to the court.

The commissioner appealed to the U.S. Court of Appeals, Second Circuit. Although the court of appeals did not dispute that the tasks performed for the girl's benefit were related services under the EHA, it reversed the district court decision. It concluded that the court and the hearing officer wrongly placed the girl at the Pennsylvania treatment center without the commissioner's prior approval. *Antkowiak v. Ambach*, 838 F.2d 635 (2d Cir.1988), *U.S. cert. den. sub nom Doe v. Sobel*, 109 S.Ct. 133 (1988).

During the 1983-84 school year the teacher of a first grade student referred him to a psychologist for testing in order to determine if the student was in need of special education. In January, 1984, a psychologist for the Roanoke (Virginia) County Schools (RCS) tested the student and informed his mother that he did not require testing for a learning disability (LD). On March 1, 1984, RCS conducted an eligibility meeting to determine if the student was handicapped and to discuss an appropriate educational placement for him. A private school psychologist, who had evaluated the student on the mother's behalf, testified that the student should be placed in an LD classroom. However, RCS placed him in a "behavioral adjustment" (BA) classroom. The student's mother then removed him to a private school for learning disabled children.

Prior to the student's second grade year (1984-84) RCS held another eligibility meeting. RCS recommended a dual placement IEP in which the student would spend a part of each day in a BA classroom, an LD classroom and a regular classroom. The mother sued RCS seeking tuition reimbursement for the student's private school placement. After a U.S. district court concluded that she was entitled to reimbursement for the last three months (beginning March 1) of the 1983-84 school year only, she appealed to the U.S. Court of Appeals, Fourth Circuit.

The court of appeals agreed with the district court that the mother was entitled to tuition reimbursement for the last three months of 1983-84 but not the 1984-85 year. It reasoned that the 1984-85 dual placement was a reasonable judgment by RCS. It agreed with the district court's conclusion that the 1984-85 IEP enabled the student to "benefit" (as required under the EHA) from the IEP. The mother was also entitled to reimbursement for the costs of the evaluation by the private school's psychologist. *Hudson v. Wilson*, 828 F.2d 1059 (4th Cir.1987).

A federal district court awarded $8,855 to the parents of an emotionally impaired youth as reimbursement for psychological services which their school district admittedly had failed to provide. The court's decision reverses an earlier denial of relief to the parents. The court was able to reconsider its earlier ruling because it had not yet finally disposed of the case. After the U.S. Supreme Court's ruling in *Burlington School Committee v. Department of Education*, 105 S.Ct. 1996 (1985), the parents asked the district court for a new ruling. The district court observed that its earlier ruling that the parents could not be reimbursed for their child's psychotherapy unless the school district had denied it in bad faith, was wrong in light of *Burlington*. In that case the U.S. Supreme Court stated that where a school district fails to provide a handicapped child with a service essential to his special education, the child's parents will be entitled to reimbursement for their efforts to provide their child with the service. Since the parents had spent $8,850 on psychotherapy, the court ordered the school district to pay the parents this amount. Since the school district failed to provide evidence that it could have supplied the psychotherapy for less than the psychiatrist selected by the parents had charged, the parents were entitled to the full $8,855. *Max M. v. Illinois State Bd. of Educ.*, 629 F.Supp. 1504 (N.D.Ill.1986).

The parents of an emotionally disturbed eleven-year-old boy sued a New Jersey school board seeking to have the board pay the cost of psychotherapy allegedly provided for the boy as part of an individualized education plan developed by the board. Both the child's parents and the board agreed that the child should be placed in a therapeutic environment. Thereafter, he was placed in a special education day school for the emotionally disturbed. The school provided an integrated program of individual child psychotherapy, family therapy with the parents, a therapeutic activity group, individual and group counseling and behavior modification, as well as special education on a daily basis in self-contained and departmentalized classes.

Due to the success of the program, the child was able to return to his local school approximately two years later. The parents were informed by the school that the cost of the psychotherapy provided to the child as part of the program would be assessed to them. At the time of the child's discharge the charges had grown to a total of $25,200. The parents sought to have the school board pay the cost of the psychotherapy, which the board refused to do.

The board gave three reasons for its decision. First, it argued that psychotherapy was not part of the IEP agreed to by both the board and the parents. Second, it noted that the New Jersey Department of Education had issued a policy statement to the effect that "psychotherapy," other than that necessary for diagnostic and evaluative purposes, was not a "related service" for which a local school district would be responsible under the EHA. Finally, the board took the position that nothing else in the EHA or its implementing regulations required it to pay for this service.

A U.S. district court in New Jersey held that psychotherapy provided to an emotionally disturbed child as an integral part of that child's special education is a "related service" under the EHA. EHA definitions superseded inconsistent New Jersey regulations and "policy statements." Thus, while no explicit reference to psychotherapy is made in the EHA, the definition of "related services" shows a congressional intent to include it where appropriate among those services which are to be provided at no cost to the parents under the Act. The court concluded that the psychotherapy services should be paid for by the board of education. *T.G. v. Bd. of Educ.*, 576 F.Supp. 420 (D.N.J.1983).

An emotionally disturbed student in Connecticut sought an injunction requiring the state to pay the full cost of her attendance at a private school, including psychotherapy. The student's school district had denied such services on the ground that the psychotherapy was not a "related service" under the EHA because the definition of related service excludes medical services that are not diagnostic or evaluative. A. U.S. district court disagreed with the school district's characterization of related services. The plain meaning of the EHA distinguishes between "medical services" and other supportive services, including speech pathology and audiology, physical therapy and recreation, as well as psychological services. Only medical services are singled out as limited to services for diagnostic and evaluative purposes. Thus, the court concluded that psychological services required to assist the student to benefit from her special education were related services required to be provided by the state, without cost to the student or her parents. *Papacoda v. State of Connecticut*, 528 F.Supp. 68 (D.Conn.1981).

II. MEDICAL SERVICES

Generally, medical services are excluded from "related services" under the EHA unless the services are for diagnostic or evaluative purposes relating to education.

In the following case, the U.S. Supreme Court ruled that clean intermittent catheterization (CIC) is a related service not subject to the "medical service" exclusion of the EHA. The parents of an eight-year-old daughter born with spina bifida brought suit against a local Texas school district after the district refused to provide catheterization for the child while she attended school. The parents pursued administrative and judicial avenues to force the district to train staff to perform the simple procedure. After a U.S. district court held against the parents they appealed to the U.S. Court of Appeals, Fifth Circuit, which reversed the district court ruling. The school district then appealed to the U.S. Supreme Court.

The Supreme Court affirmed that portion of the Court of Appeals decision which held that CIC is a "supportive service," not a "medical service." The court was not persuaded by the school district's argument that catheterization is a medical service because it is provided in accordance with a physician's prescription and under a physician's supervision, even though it may be administered by a nurse or trained layperson. The court listed four criteria to determine a school's obligation to provide services that relate to both the health and education of a child. First, to be entitled to related services, a child must be handicapped so as to require special education. Second, only those services necessary to aid a handicapped child to benefit from special education must be provided, regardless of how easily a school nurse or layperson could furnish them. Third, EHA regulations state that school nursing services must be performed by a nurse or other qualified person, not by a physician. Fourth, the child's parents in this case were seeking only the *services* of a qualified person at the school, they were not asking the school to provide *equipment*. The court reversed those portions of the Court of Appeals ruling which held the school district liable under the Rehabilitation Act and which held that the parents were entitled to attorney's fees. *Irving Indep. School Dist. v. Tatro*, 104 S.Ct. 3371 (1984).

Parents of a seventeen-year-old student with severe mental and physical impairments claimed that a Pennsylvania school district violated the Education of the Handicapped Act (EHA) because it failed to provide their child with adequate special education. For several years the school district had provided the student with direct physical therapy from a licensed therapist. Thereafter a physical therapist came in once a month to train the student's teacher to integrate physical therapy with the student's education. The student's parents acknowledged that the school program had benefited the student to some degree, but argued that his educational program was not providing him a meaningful benefit as the EHA required.

The parents first challenged the student's IEP before a Commonwealth of Pennsylvania Department of Education hearing officer who found that the student was benefiting from his education and that his education was appropriate. The Pennsylvania Secretary of Education affirmed this finding. The parents then appealed to a federal district court which dismissed the case. The district court concluded that because the student had received some benefit from his education the provisions of the EHA had been met. The parents appealed to the U.S. Court of Appeals, Third Circuit. On appeal the court found that the purpose of the EHA is to provide "full educational opportunity to all handicapped children." Congress' use of this phrase indicated an intent to afford more than a trivial amount of educational benefits. One of the chief concerns of the EHA was to foster self-sufficiency for handicapped children. Implicit in this emphasis is the notion that states must provide some sort of meaningful education. Physical therapy was an essential part of the student's appropriate education. The court of appeals ruled in favor of the parents and remanded the case to the district court for a determination of whether the student's physical therapy was meaningful as required under the EHA. *Polk v. Cent. Susquehanna Intermediate Unit 16*, 853 F.2d 171 (3d Cir. 1988).

A Tennessee student suffered from brain damage since birth and was afflicted with a serious emotional disturbance and mental retardation. Her condition was aggravated by a severe behavioral disorder which caused bizarre and uncontrollable outbursts endangering both herself and others. These outbursts were unpredictable and could last for hours. The student's behavior rendered placement in mainstream educational facilities provided by the school district impractical. Therefore, the student's parents and special education personnel worked together for years to find an appropriate individualized education program. The student had received educational services at four different schools. None were successful in meeting the student's specific educational goals or improving the student's behavior. Since an effective residential program could not be found, the student's IEP consisted of homebound instruction. The student's parents learned of Cedarbrook's Fresh Approach Program. Cedarbrook is a residential rehabilitation facility in Tennessee for brain injury victims. The Fresh Approach program addresses significant behavioral problems which interfere with the student's rehabilitation. After placement in the program, the student's behavior improved significantly.

After the parents were denied reimbursement, they instituted this action in a federal trial court. The court determined that the IEP offered by the district did not provide educational benefit to the student. The student deteriorated rather than benefitted under the IEP which consisted of three hours per week of homebound instruction. The court then determined that Cedarbrook represented an appropriate educational placement for which the district was liable. The issue in determining the appropriateness of Cedarbrook placement was whether it was educational or medical in nature. The occupational therapy, psychological services, recreational therapy, physical therapy and medical evaluations provided by Cedarbrook were all specifically listed as special education and related services in the EHA. Therefore, the residential placement was educational and not medical in nature. Finally, the court determined that the school district was not required to provide compensatory education because neither the student nor the district were previously aware that the Cedarbrook program existed. Thus, a compensatory education was not warranted. *Brown v. Wilson County School Bd.*, 747 F.Supp. 436 (F.D. Tenn.1990).

A Pennsylvania child was injured in an automobile accident which resulted in the permanent implantation of a tracheostomy. He required ready access to a trained attendant to maintain the tracheostomy. An insurer paid for the cost of the attendant. When the child returned to school the insurer demanded that the child's school district pay the cost of the attendant during the school day. It contended that the presence of the attendant was a "related service" under the EHA and the Rehabilitation Act. The school district refused to pay.

The insurer sued the school district in a federal district court seeking a declaration that the attendant was a "related service" for which the school district was obligated to pay. The school district contended that the EHA required administrative agency procedures through which "related service" must be determined. The insurer argued that there were no special education issues involved so as to require referral to an agency. It contended that the real issue concerned whether the health needs of the child must be provided for by the school district pursuant to the EHA and Rehabilitation Act. The court held for the school district because the insurer lacked legal standing to press its claim. The insurer's relationship with the child's parents through the insurance contract in no way altered the EHA. The insurer's lawsuit was dismissed. *Allstate Ins. Co. v. Bethlehem Area School Dist. and BB*, 678 F.Supp. 1132 (E.D.Pa.1987).

In Pennsylvania, a severely handicapped child was admitted to a classroom for handicapped children on the condition that her parents would pay the cost of nursing services and related equipment required by the child. The child was profoundly mentally retarded and legally blind. She breathed through a tracheostomy tube and was fed and medicated through a gastrostomy tube. A nurse administered a constant oxygen supply to the child, administered chest physical therapy each day, suctioned mucus from the child's lungs and supervised her positioning for physical and occupational therapy. The child required the constant presence of a nurse to clear her tracheostomy tube in the event that it became plugged by mucus. When this occurred, several times a day, the tube had to be cleared within thirty seconds to prevent injury to the child.

The child's parents and the school district both agreed that the program to which the child was admitted was the most appropriate and least restrictive for the child. When the parents requested that the school district assume the costs of the nursing services as "related services" under the EHA, the school district refused. A hearing officer ruled in favor of the parents, but that ruling was reversed by the Pennsylvania Secretary of Education. The parents appealed to a U.S. district court.

The court began by noting that the purpose of the EHA was to provide a "free appropriate education" to all handicapped children. A free appropriate education is defined as "special education and related services." "Related services" are defined in the EHA to exclude medical services provided for other than diagnostic or evaluation purposes. Regulations implementing the EHA define "medical services" to include only "services provided by a licensed physician."

The court then addressed the parents' argument that the services required by the child could not be excluded as medical services because they were not provided by a physician. It looked to previous decisions which, instead of looking solely to whether the provider of a service was a physician, considered the reasonableness of providing a service to determine whether it was a covered "related service." The court concluded that the nursing services required by the child in this case were so extensive that placing the burden of providing them on the school district did not "appear to be consistent with the spirit" of the EHA and its regulations. The court concluded that "the nursing services required are so varied, intensive and costly, and more in the nature of 'medical services' that they are not properly includable as 'related services.'" *Bevin H. v. Wright*, 666 F.Supp. 71 (W.D.Pa.1987).

A U.S. district court in New York has ruled that school districts are not required to pay for in-school nursing care. The mother of a severely handicapped seven-year-old student requested that her local school district provide in-school nursing care for her daughter. After the school district denied her request she asked for an impartial hearing and the hearing officer found that because the nursing care constituted "related services" under the EHA, the local school district was required to provide and pay for the special nursing services. The school district appealed the decision and the New York State Commissioner of Education reversed the hearing officer's order. The commissioner determined that the in-school nursing care was not a related service. The mother appealed to a U.S. district court.

The district court observed that the EHA mandates a "free appropriate public education," including "related services," and requires that an individualized education program be developed for each handicapped child providing for his or her specific educational needs. The issue before the district court was the extent to which school health support services are mandated by the EHA. The mother contended that the extensive medical attention required by her daughter qualified as a related service under the EHA. The school physician testified that the services required by the daughter would require the expertise of a licensed practical nurse or a registered nurse. The school district argued that the medical care required did not constitute related services because the EHA excludes from the definition of "related services" medical services required for purposes other than diagnosis or evaluation. It asked that the court consider the type of related services required by the EHA as the crucial element in deciding whether the district was required to provide for the medical services. The mother, however, focused on the qualifications of the person performing the services, contending that because the necessary services were to be performed by a qualified person other than a physician, they fell within the description of "school health services," which are not excluded by the EHA. The court concluded that the child's daily medical needs did not qualify as related services and that the EHA does not require that school districts provide a severely physically handicapped child with constant, in-school nursing care. The mother's request for relief in the form of payment for the daily nursing care of her child was denied.

The mother appealed to the U.S. Court of Appeals, Second Circuit. The mother contended that the district court gave "insufficient deference" to the decision in *Department of Education v. Katherine D.*, 727 F.2d 809 (9th Cir. 1983). Although the student in that Hawaii case needed special care, she only required the intermittent services of a lay person. Here, the handicapped daughter needed a full-time person with special training, and thus the decision of the district court was affirmed. *Detsel v. Bd. of Educ.*, 820 F.2d 587 (2d Cir. 1987).

The following case illustrates that courts will generally not order a school district to pay the medical expenses of a handicapped child where the services are not diagnostic or evaluative, and are not aimed at allowing the child to benefit from his education. A public school system in the District of Columbia appealed an order compelling it to pay a profoundly schizophrenic child's medical expenses during her stay at a private psychiatric hospital as a "related service" under the EHA. The child's mother requested special education placement at the private hospital. Treatment at the hospital involved intensive psychotherapy and a drug program. A U.S. district court held that the school system did not have to subsidize the child's medical expenses. The court reasoned that under the EHA, a child who is placed in a residential treatment program must have been placed there to render him educable, not for medical reasons only. Here, the placement in the residential treatment program was primarily for medical reasons and not educational reasons. The stay in the hospital was not related to the child's education but was, rather, for treatment of her condition. Therefore, the public school system, although obligated to provide the child with a "free and appropriate public education" under the EHA, was not obligated to finance the medical expenses. *McKenzie v. Jefferson*, 566 F.Supp. 404 (D.D.C. 1983).

III. INTEGRATED TREATMENT PROGRAMS

Other services, such as occupational therapy, family counseling and extra-curricular activities are sometimes requested by parents or guardians of handicapped children. Whether a court will order a school district to provide such services seems to depend upon the particular facts of the case.

An eleven-year-old South Dakota child, afflicted with Williams Syndrome, had a learning disability, attention deficient disorder with hyperactivity, and scoliosis. His hand-eye coordination and ability to succeed in a traditional school setting were also affected. During the 1988-89 school year the boy attended fourth grade at a public school. He was provided with physical and occupational therapy designed to increase his motor skills and visual perception. In January, 1989, the child's learning disability teacher determined that the child was regressing in his motor skills and visual perception. Therefore, a new IEP was developed which would allow the student to transfer to another occupational therapist. The parents became disenchanted with the new therapist and sought a meeting with the school district administrators. The parents were dissatisfied with the meeting and they moved the student from the school's occupational therapy program to a private program. In June, 1989, a new meeting was held to discuss the students' IEP. The district agreed to transfer the student's occupational therapy program to the private therapist. The parents then sought reimbursement of the costs of the private therapist from April to June, but the school district refused. The parents appealed to the South Dakota Board of Education which determined that the school district was responsible for the costs of the therapist. The school district appealed the hearing officer's decision in a federal district court.

To recover the tuition costs, the parents had to show that the district's IEP placement was inappropriate and that their private placement was appropriate. The court found that the parents presented clear and convincing evidence that the private placement of the student was appropriate and that the IEP placement had been inappropriate. In fact, the school district agreed, at the June IEP meeting, that the parents' private therapist was the appropriate placement for the child. The court upheld the hearing officer's decision to reimburse the parents for their costs of the occupational therapist and also awarded the parents attorney's fees. *Rapid City School District 51-4 v. Vahle*, 723 F.Supp. 1364 (S.D.1990).

The parents of two handicapped children who received physical therapy as related services in conjunction with the mandated education required under the Education of the Handicapped Act (EHA) were covered by health insurance policies issued by the same insurer. The handicapped students attended two intermediate educational units formed as part of the Pennsylvania public school system. Physical therapy was provided by licensed physical therapists either employed by or affiliated with the units. Both sets of parents and the two intermediate educational units sought coverage from the insurer, which was denied. The insurer's basic coverage provided that the policy would pay for "physical therapy prescribed by the attending provider as to type and duration when performed by a duly qualified physical therapist." The parents and educational units filed a class action suit in a Pennsylvania federal district court. The insurer moved to dismiss their case, contending that the policy covered only "medically necessary hospitalization and medical benefits," and that the physical therapy which had been provided to the children would never have been prescribed by doctors without the EHA. It further argued that the policies excluded coverage for services which the insureds were not legally obligated to pay or which they were entitled to receive from a governmental unit or agency without cost. The district court granted the motion for dismissal, and the parents and educational units appealed to the U.S. Court of Appeals, Third Circuit.

The court of appeals refused to accept the insurer's position that the EHA does not authorize shifting of costs to private insurers when intermediate educational units have a statutory duty to provide an appropriate public education for handicapped children at public expense. Under some circumstances, the insurer would be obliged to pay for physical therapy services furnished under a handicapped student's individualized education program. However, the court noted that the parents were entitled under the EHA to the physical therapy services provided, and that the parents were not legally obligated to pay for those services. Since the insurer had contractually excluded coverage for services which were provided free under the EHA, the court refused to hold it liable for the costs of the physical therapy at issue. The court thus affirmed the district court's decision, and dismissed the case. *Chester County Intermediate Unit v. Pennsylvania Blue Shield*, 896 F.2d 808 (3d Cir.1990).

A Pittsburgh child was paralyzed from the chest down as a result of spina bifida. Prior to kindergarten, the child was evaluated by a multidisciplinary team which recommended that he be placed in a program for physically handicapped students and that he receive physical and occupational therapy. However, in September of the following year, the board terminated the physical and occupational therapy without notice to the student's parents. His parents were then notified of the board's intent to reclassify him from exceptional to nonexceptional. The student's mother rejected the intended change. At the request of the board, a due process hearing was held before a hearing officer, who found that the student was an exceptional child in need of special education and related services. He ordered the board to prepare an IEP for the student which included physical and occupational therapy. The secretary of the Department of Education upheld the hearing officer's decision. The board appealed to the Commonwealth Court of Pennsylvania.

On appeal, the board contended that the student was not exceptional, and was not entitled to compensatory physical and occupational therapy. Physically handicapped means orthopedic or other health impairments of sufficient magnitude to limit the classroom accommodation and educational performance. The court noted that the student's paralysis limited his educational performance. The student was unable to perform physical activities which were required of other students. The physical education teacher modified the instructions to the student to accommodate his impairment. The court determined that the child was an exceptional child and that he was in need of a regular physical and occupational therapy program. The court also determined that he was entitled to compensatory physical and occupational therapy as a result of the board's denial of an appropriate program. The court affirmed the Department of Education's decision. *Bd. of Educ. v. Commonwealth Dep't of Educ.*, 581 A.2d 681 (Pa.Cmwlth.1990).

A child in California suffered from mental retardation and infantile autism. The Regional Center for the East Bay (RCEB) was a nonprofit community agency created under the California Welfare and Institutions Code. The child was eligible for the services RCEB provided. RCEB placed the child at the Behavior Research Institute of California (BRI). BRI was licensed as a community care facility by the California Department of Social Services. RCEB funded the child's residential program at BRI and a school district paid his educational costs. In October, 1987, RCEB terminated the child's placement and funding at BRI due to his self-abusive behavior. RCEB claimed that the California Administrative Code permitted it to remove the child when his health or safety was threatened. The child's parents asked a U.S. district court for a temporary order to prevent RCEB from terminating their child's placement and funding at BRI pending a hearing. The court denied their request. The parents then requested a preliminary injunction against the change in placement. At the court hearing RCEB contended that the court had no authority over it because RCEB was not an educational agency, did not receive EHA funding and had no control over the child's educational program. The parents argued that EHA procedural safeguards applied since RCEB was providing "related services" under the EHA.

The court noted that it had authority over noneducational state agencies that provide related services under the EHA. Residential placements qualify as "related services" under the EHA if they are made for educational purposes. Here, the child's residential placement at BRI was not a related service under the EHA. It was an independent residential placement made pursuant to state law. There was no evidence that the child's placement at BRI was made for educational purposes. Because RCEB's placement of the child at BRI was not protected by EHA safeguards the parents' request for a preliminary injunction was denied. *Corbett v. Regional Center for the East Bay*, 676 F.Supp. 964 (N.D.Cal.1988).

The parents then moved for reconsideration, whereupon RCEB expressed concern about the child's safety because he had recently undergone surgery. The parents contended that the child's behavior had dramatically improved at BRI and that his self-abuse was minimal. They also maintained that the child would be irreparably harmed if he could not return to BRI. The district court reversed its previous decision. The child's placement at BRI was made for educational purposes and was therefore protected by EHA "stay-put" provisions. A member of the child's IEP team testified that the child's educational, behavioral, social and developmental needs were all "intertwined." When residential placement is necessary to provide a handicapped child with a free appropriate education, residential placement is a "related service" under the EHA. The child's placement at BRI was jointly recommended by the IEP team and RCEB in part to enable him to receive a free appropriate education. The court had authority over RCEB. The court held that EHA § 1415(e)(3) created a presumption in favor of the child's current educational placement. This presumption could only be overcome by showing that maintaining the child at RCEB was "substantially likely to cause injury either to himself . . . or to others." RCEB failed to overcome the presumption. The parents prevailed and the court vacated its previous denial. The child could remain at

BRI pending any appeals. *Corbett v. Regional Center for the East Bay*, 699 F.Supp. 230 (N.D.Cal.1988).

The U.S. Court of Appeals, Sixth Circuit, has affirmed a district court ruling that the EHA did not obligate school districts to provide continuous occupational therapy to a handicapped student in Ohio. The Court of Appeals also held that the inclusion of nonacademic extracurricular activities once per week was not automatically required. The court observed that the EHA, in and of itself, does not require that states maximize the potential of handicapped children commensurate with the opportunity provided to other children. These programs, the court found, were not necessary to permit the child to benefit from his instruction. *Punikaia v. Clark*, 720 F.2d 463 (9th Cir.1983).

IV. TRANSPORTATION

The EHA expressly authorizes expenditure of public funds for transportation as a related service.

A hearing impaired Ohio student and her parents sued their local school district under the Education of the Handicapped Act (EHA). They sought a determination that the district had to provide the student with transportation to and from a private school for the deaf. An independent hearing officer found that the student met the time and distance requirements for free public transportation. The school district appealed to a federal district court. The court found that because the student had no disability which precluded her from using nonhandicapped transportation services, she was not entitled to free transportation. The student's parents appealed to the U.S. Court of Appeals, Sixth Circuit.

The court held that under the EHA when a student is voluntarily placed in a private school, a public school district does not need to provide a related service to that student if that particular service is not designed to meet the unique needs of the student. In order to obtain transportation as a related service under the EHA, parents must establish that the student is handicapped, that transportation is a related service and that the related service is designed to meet the unique needs of the student caused by the handicap. Parents must also prove that the school district must be responsible under the EHA for providing the related services. In this case, the student was handicapped and, under the statute, transportation was a related service. The need for transportation, although a related service, was no more unique to the student because she was deaf than it would have been had she not been deaf. Since the statute specifically required a relationship between the related service and the unique needs of the student, the requirements were not met. The district was not required to provide the student with transportation to the private school. The appeals court affirmed the district court's decision for the school district. *McNair v. Oak Hills Local School Dist.*, 872 F.2d 153 (6th Cir.1989).

A severely multiply impaired Michigan student was placed at a school within his school district. The student's IEP indicated that the student's education could take place either in his home or at a school but it did not require the district to provide transportation. The student's parents objected to the IEP because it denied the student transportation. A hearing was held and the local hearing officer found that the district was not required to provide transportation due to the student's medically fragile nature. The parents appealed and the state reviewing officer reversed, finding that, given proper training, an aide could place the student in his wheelchair and suction his tracheostomy tube during transportation. The district sought review in a federal district court to determine whether it was obligated to provide the student with transportation to and from school.

The court held that transportation represented a supportive service which the district was required to provide under the EHA. The EHA required schools to provide related services, which included transportation and other supportive services except medical services for diagnostic and evaluation purposes. The court found that the medical services exclusion was limited to services provided by licensed physicians and did not include services of other trained medical professional. There was no evidence which indicated that the complications surrounding transportation of the student required the attention of a licensed physician. The district was required to provide transportation to the student and to use a medical professional, other than a physician, if necessary to safely transport the student. *Macomb County Intermediate School Dist. v. Joshua S.*, 715 F.Supp. 824 (E.D.Mich.1989).

A trainable mentally handicapped student attended a special educational facility in Florida. The school board operated both a southern facility, which the student attended, and a geographically distant northern facility. During the school year, the student's parents became concerned with the possibility of sexual abuse occurring at the southern facility. A counselor at that facility had been arrested and charged with sexual abuse. Although the sexual abuse charges were later dropped, the student's parents withdrew her from the facility for approximately six months. After returning to the southern facility, the parents requested a hearing to determine whether the student was properly classified as a trainable mentally handicapped student. At the hearing, the school board established that the student was properly classified as a trainable mentally handicapped student. However, the hearing officer further found that the student's parents had lost confidence in the southern facility and ordered that the student attend the northern facility. The school board was to also provide transportation for the student to that facility. The school board appealed the hearing officer's decision to a Florida district court of appeal.

The court held that the board was not required to pay the additional expense of transporting the student to the northern facility. The hearing had not been conducted for the purpose of determining whether the student should be transferred from the southern facility to the northern facility. It was conducted for the sole purpose of considering the student's reclassification into a different category of mentally handicapped student. The hearing officer had found that she was properly classified. The student had been provided a free appropriate public education at the southern facility as required by state law. The board was not required to pay the additional expense of transporting the student to the northern facility. *School Bd. of Pinellas County v. Smith*, 537 So.2d 168 (Fla.App.2d Dist.1989).

A hearing-impaired Philadelphia student received a scholarship for bi-weekly hearing treatment at a therapy clinic. His mother requested that the school district provide her son with transportation to the clinic. When the district refused, the mother requested a due process hearing. The hearing officer determined that the district was not obligated to provide transportation to the clinic. The mother appealed to the Pennsylvania Secretary of Education. The secretary determined that additional therapy would allow the student to make better use of his residual hearing. He also held that additional therapy would assist the student in his current classroom and ensure that he continued to function independently and successfully in the future. The secretary determined that the district must provide transportation because the combination of the student's regular education and the additional therapy constituted "sufficient services reasonably calculated to give real educational benefit." The district appealed this decision to the Pennsylvania Commonwealth Court.

On appeal, the district argued that it was already providing the student with an appropriate education. In upholding the secretary's decision, the court determined that the combined therapies constituted services calculated to afford the student real educational benefit. Since the additional therapy program was approved by the Department of Education, the school district was obligated to provide free transportation. The court noted that although the student was progressing satisfactorily, evidence showed that students with the same problem require additional assistance later on in their education and that providing additional therapy now would allow the student to become more independent. Thus, the district was required to provide transportation to the clinic. *School Dist. of Philadelphia v. Dept. of Educ.*, 547 A.2d 520 (Pa.Cmwlth. 1988).

A New York boy was born with severe multiple handicaps. Because his parents lived in Maryland they placed him in the voluntary custody of the Eleanor Roosevelt Developmental Services (ERDS) when he was thirteen months old. The boy began receiving special education and related services from the Cerebral Palsy Center for the Disabled (CP Center) in 1982 as directed by ERDS. When a recommendation by the school district's committee on the handicapped to place the boy in a Board of Cooperative Educational Services school was upheld by the commissioner of education the parents sued the school district in a U.S. district court.

Among other things, the district court ruled that the boy should remain at the CP Center and that his family care provider (employed by ERDS) should be reimbursed for transportation expenses which were adequately documented. *Taylor v. Bd. of Educ.*, 649 F.Supp. 1253 (N.D.N.Y.1986).

A handicapped Virginia child brought suit against a school district alleging that the district failed to provide her with an appropriate education. The child, through her parents, requested reimbursement for the cost of summer programs which the child had attended as well as placement at a private school of the parents' choice. In addition, the child's parents requested reimbursement for their travel expenses incurred while the child was a patient and student at a home for crippled children in Pennsylvania. The U.S. district court held that neither state law nor the EHA required the state to pay all of the expenses incurred by parents in educating a child, whether the child is handicapped or nonhandicapped. Thus, the parents were not entitled to reimbursement for their travel expenses. *Bales v. Clarke*, 523 F.Supp. 1366 (E.D.Va.1981). See also *Helms v. Indep. School District No. 3*, 750 F.2d 820 (10th Cir.1984) (a similar Florida case in which the parents of a handicapped child enrolled in a Georgia residential school were denied reimbursement for their travel expenses incurred as a result of visits to their son in Georgia).

An individualized education program committee meeting was held to review a Michigan hearing impaired student's special education program. The student's mother disagreed with the committee's placement and requested local and state level administrative hearings. Both hearing officers supported the committee's report. They found that the committee's local school placement would best develop the student's potential in the least restrictive environment. The mother however placed the student in the Model Secondary School for the Deaf (MSSD) in Washington, D.C. because she believed that both the EHA and the Michigan Mandatory Special Education Act (MMSEA) required placement there. MSSD is a federally funded program which does not require tuition or residence charges. The student's mother then sought reimbursement from her local school district in the amount of $2,500 per year for transportation expenses to and from MSSD. The district refused and she sued various state and local school officials in a Michigan federal district court.

The central issue was the degree to which the school district program and the MSSD program fulfilled EHA requirements and the MMSEA. Under the MMSEA, school districts were to provide special education programs and services that were designed to develop the "maximum potential" of each handicapped student within the least restrictive environment. The EHA incorporated the MMSEA standard by reference. The school officials contended that the committee's IEP adhered to EHA and MMSEA standards. They further argued that the mother's objection to its IEP rested upon her philosophical disagreement with mainstreaming. She allegedly failed to consider the merits of the education the student would receive at the local district school. The mother argued that the school district's IEP failed to maximize the student's potential as a handicapped student.

The court upheld the hearing officer's decisions. It agreed with the school officials that the mother's argument turned upon a discussion of the merits of mainstreaming versus placement in a segregated setting. The court refused to substitute its judgment for that of the committee on decisions of this nature. Although the state of Michigan had not defined "maximum potential" there were geographical and physical limits to its commitment to educate handicapped students to their maximum potential. Michigan law indicated that "maximum potential" meant neither "utopian" nor the best education possible. Although other hearing-impaired students had been placed at MSSD, their placements were deemed the least restrictive placement for them. This was not the case here. Because the mother had not met her burden of proving that the committee's IEP failed to meet EHA requirements including the MMSEA's "maximum potential" requirement, she was not entitled to transportation costs. *Barwacz v. Michigan Dep't of Educ.*, 681 F.Supp. 427 (W.D. Mich.1988).

A deaf girl in Ohio was provided with special education and transportation at no cost by a school district for three years. The child's parents then unilaterally enrolled the child in a private school for the deaf for the 1985-86 school year. Both the parents and the school district agreed that the child had been provided a free appropriate education in public school as required by the EHA. The parents nevertheless requested that the school district pay for the child's transportation to and from the private school and reimburse them for transportation costs that they had already paid. They asserted that the transportation was a related service for which the school district was liable under the EHA. The school district refused to pay and this refusal was upheld by the state education agency. The child's parents appealed.

A U.S. district court declared that "'special education' means the educational program established and monitored by the state, financed with authorized state and federal funds as expressly mandated by the [EHA] to appropriately educate the handicapped." Required related services therefore "are those required to be provided to the handicapped child with regard to the child's 'special education' program." The court determined that the EHA required the state to provide related services only for programs that the state has designed and offered as "special education." Because the parents unilaterally chose to place the child in private school for their own reasons, that placement was not "special education" within the meaning and intent of the EHA. The court concluded that "Congress did not intend the public to bear the additional expense of a private education for handicapped children where those children have already been provided a free, appropriate special education program and services related to that program by the state." It ruled that the school district did not have to pay for the child's transportation to and from the private school. *McNair v. Cardimone*, 676 F.Supp. 1361 (S.D.Ohio 1987).

The mother of a multi-handicapped girl requested special education and related services for the girl in March, 1986. However, the District of Columbia Public Schools (DCPS) did not propose an educational program for the girl until August, 1986. The mother unilaterally placed the girl in the Lab School (a private special education day school) claiming that because DCPS failed to timely propose an appropriate placement for the girl she was forced to seek an appropriate program on her own. The mother then sought a U.S. district court order that DCPS provide the girl with transportation from home to the Lab School.

The mother argued that a federal regulation implemented pursuant to the EHA [34 CFR § 300.451(a)] required DCPS to provide transportation to the Lab School as a related service even though the girl had been unilaterally placed. DCPS argued that the federal regulation cited by the mother to support her claim only applied to cases where a child was placed in a private school by his or her parents and required a particular program that was not offered by the public school. The district court observed that 34 CFR § 300.451(a) had to be construed in light of § 300.403. The latter section made it clear that when the public agency (DCPS) provided a free appropriate education and the mother chose to place the girl in a private school nevertheless, "the regulations relating to payment for a private school are not involved and therefore the public agency is not required . . . to pay for the child's education at the private school." Section 300.451(a) merely clarified that DCPS was not relieved of *all* responsibility for the girl. The court concluded that neither the EHA nor the implementing regulation required DCPS to provide transportation for the girl to attend the Lab School. *Work v. McKenzie*, 661 F.Supp. 225 (D.D.C.1987).

The individualized education program (IEP) developed for an orthopedically handicapped child recommended that he be educated in a regular class because he was functioning at or above his grade level in all of his academic subjects. It also provided that a special vehicle was needed for his transportation in order to meet his special physical needs. Though the child's local school district offered an appropriate education in and transportation to a public school, his father voluntarily placed him in a private school. After two hearing officers determined that the school district only had to pay $406 per year (considerably less than the actual cost) for the child's transportation to the private school, his father sued the New Jersey Department of Education seeking the actual cost.

The issue before the Superior Court of New Jersey, Appellate Division, was whether the child was entitled to transportation as a "related service" under the EHA even though his IEP did not indicate the need for special education. The court held that the child was not entitled to transportation as a "related service." It reasoned that, although the child had a handicap, he did not have a handicap that required special education. Therefore, stated the court, related services auxiliary to special education were not mandated by the EHA. The court accepted the school district's argument that under New Jersey law, if a school district provided transportation for students to and from public schools, it was also required to do so for private school students. Since the child was being transported as a private school student and not as a handicapped student, he was held to be entitled only to the fixed amount of $406 under New Jersey law. *A.A. v. Cooperman*, 526 A.2d 1103 (N.J.Super. A.D.1987).

The West Virginia Supreme Court of Appeals held that under state law, two handicapped children were entitled to transportation to school. In this case, two families lived on a dirt road, located in rural West Virginia, known as Dry Monday Branch. The road, which was often traversable only by four-wheel drive vehicle, was owned by a timber company which never objected to its use by the two families. The families had, respectively, a seven-year-old boy and a six-year-old girl who were both afflicted with spina bifida. Both children wore orthopedic braces from waist to feet and were unable to walk to the established school bus stop, which was located on a regular road one-half to nine-tenths of a mile from the children's homes. The county school board refused to send a school bus up Dry Monday Branch because of the road's poor condition, and the children's parents did not own a reliable vehicle in which to transport them to the established bus stop. As a result, the children were unable to attend school during the 1984-85 school year.

Throughout the summer of 1985 the children's parents attempted to persuade school officials to provide transportation for their children. Finally the superintendent sent them a letter informing them that because Dry Monday Branch was a privately owned road, was poorly maintained and was unsafe for a school bus, the parents would have to provide transportation themselves.

Because the laws of West Virginia [W.Va.Code 18-5-13(6)(a)] require that county boards of education provide "adequate" transportation to any student living more than two miles from school, the parents sought an order that the board provide their children with transportation down Dry Monday Branch. The West Virginia Supreme Court of Appeals agreed and issued a writ of mandamus directing the county school board to provide proper transportation. The court held that poor road conditions could not excuse the board from providing adequate transportation to all students. Since neither child was able to walk to the established school bus stop, the board's arrangements were inadequate as a matter of law. As further justification for its decision, the court noted that the timber company which owned Dry Monday Branch regarded it as a public road. *Kennedy v. Bd. of Educ., McDowell County*, 337 S.E.2d 905 (W.Va.1985).

V. REIMBURSEMENT FOR OTHER EXPENSES

In addition to tuition reimbursement expenses, parents sometimes request reimbursement for other related expenses.

A multiply-handicapped Idaho student was classified as trainable mentally retarded. He was placed in a public school's handicapped contained classroom, taught by special education teachers. The student's parents then decided to place him in a private school, but all the schools contacted required a full-time aide as a prerequisite. The parents enrolled him in a parochial school for the following school year. They then commenced an administrative proceeding to obtain reimbursement for the aide. The district's child study team met to determine financial responsibility for the full-time aide. The team was advised by its counsel that it had no financial responsibility and it then informed the parents about the public education system's educational opportunities. The district offered placement in a segregated special education program. The parents argued that the student was entitled to mainstreaming under the EHA. The district then offered to fund educational services in a private school, but refused to pay for the aide. The parents kept their son in the parochial school and began an administrative appeal for the cost of the aide and tuition. The hearing officer ruled in favor of the school district, and the parents appealed to an Idaho county court. The court overturned the hearing officer's determination and ruled in favor of the parents. The district then appealed to the Idaho Supreme Court.

The supreme court noted that the district had failed to rebut the parents' argument that mainstreaming was appropriate. Free appropriate education must be provided in the least restrictive environment and there was a strong preference for mainstreaming in conformity with the EHA. The court noted that school district documents did not qualify as an IEP, because they set forth no goals or other evaluation procedures for determining whether EHA educational objectives were being met. Because there was no appropriate IEP, the district was not in compliance with the EHA and the hearing officer's determination was erroneous. The court ordered the school district to reimburse the parents for their son's tuition and for his aide. *Thornock v. Boise Indep. School Dist. 1*, 767 P.2d 1241 (Idaho 1988).

A five-year-old District of Columbia multiply-handicapped student was eligible for special education services. Her parents requested private special education from the District of Columbia Public Schools (DCPS). They unilaterally placed her in a private daycare center. Each week the student received speech and occupational therapy from an outside source. The DCPS completed an IEP for the student, identifying her as multiply-disabled with motor and speech communication problems. The DCPS placed the student in a public school program for handicapped children. The student's parents challenged the public school placement and requested two EHA due process hearings. The hearing officer refused to award tuition expenses to the parents, and later determined that the school district's placement was appropriate. The hearing officer also stated that the student's placement at her private daycare program was inappropriate and did not provide the services described in her IEP. The hearing officer held that the DCPS should pay for the student's outside occupational and speech therapy because they were appropriate and because the DCPS had failed to timely place the student.

The parents appealed the decision to the U.S. District Court, District of Columbia, claiming that the DCPS placement was inappropriate. The district court ruled in the parents' favor because the DCPS program was inadequate and the district was completely incapable of providing occupational therapy. The district lacked adequate funding and had a lengthy waiting list for occupational therapy. The court approved the educational alternative proposed by the parents, which was a private special education school in Maryland specializing in educating children with severe sensory integration deficiencies and occupational therapy. The court also awarded attorney's fees to the parents under the EAHCA. *Kattan by Thomas v. Dist. of Columbia*, 691 F.Supp. 1539 (D.D.C.1988).

The United States brought this suit because the University of Alabama, Board of Trustees (UAB) denied auxiliary aids to hearing impaired handicapped students because of their financial ability to pay or their enrollment in noncredit courses. UAB adopted a policy that provided aids such as note-takers and transcriptions of tape recordings of classes, but would not provide costly aids such as interpreters. UAB directed such handicapped students to the Vocational Rehabilitation Service to provide the costly aids. Then the students were directed to apply for financial aid. If the students could demonstrate the financial need and an inability to pay they would receive the free interpreter or aid. The policy excluded students taking noncredit or nondegree courses from receiving auxiliary aids. The federal district court ruled that the UAB policy violated § 504 of the Rehabilitation Act when it failed to provide an interpreter to students who were unable to procure such services elsewhere free of charge and when it failed to provide any auxiliary aids to students in nondegree programs. UAB appealed to the U.S. Court of Appeals, Eleventh Circuit.

On appeal, the court sought to determine the statutory intent and the legislative history of § 504. The court noted that the Department of Health, Education and Welfare published a notice of proposed rules which indicated that universities could refer students to state vocational rehabilitation agencies as a first step in obtaining auxiliary aids. However, where no resource exists the university must provide the needed auxiliary aid. Next, the court analyzed the reasonableness of the auxiliary aid policy. Other courts have determined that § 504 does not impose an affirmative action on the part of universities who receive federal funds. However, the court determined that in this case it was not an affirmative action on the part of the university to provide an interpreter because the lack of an interpreter effectively denies the handicapped person an opportunity to learn. The court also determined that non-credit and nondegree courses are also covered by § 504 because they are a part of "all of the operations of . . . a college, university, or other post-secondary institution." The court of appeals affirmed the trial court's decision requiring UAB to provide aids to hearing impaired students free of charge. *U.S. v. Bd. of Trustees for Univ. of Ala.*, 908 F.2d 740 (11th Cir. 1990).

CHAPTER SIX
ATTORNEY'S FEES

Prior to 1986 there was no provision in the EHA for attorney's fees. Accordingly, the U.S. Supreme Court held in *Smith v. Robinson*, 468 U.S. 992 (1984), that attorney's fees were not recoverable for special education claims made under the EHA. It also held that attorney's fees were not recoverable under § 1983 or the Rehabilitation Act. With the passage of the Handicapped Children's Protection Act (HCPA) of 1986, Congress expressly provided for attorney's fees to a prevailing parent or guardian in cases that were pending on or after July 4, 1984.

I. COURT PROCEEDINGS

Under the Handicapped Children's Protection Act (HCPA), attorney's fees are recoverable where a student or guardian prevails in a court proceeding pending on or after July 4, 1984.

A Minnesota sixth-grader began to experience academic and emotional problems. His school district requested permission to conduct an assessment of his ability, achievement and social-emotional skills. Eventually, the district conducted three evaluations, which resulted in a program of complete mainstreaming. The student still received poor grades, but the IEP team saw no need to modify the program. The team decided to mainstream the student for the eighth grade. However, before the school year, the student moved to a different town to live with his father. The new school district then sought to place him in special education. The student's mother refused to give her consent to special education placement, and the student attended regular classes. Soon, the student returned to live with his mother. The district attempted to make another assessment for special education services, but the mother refused to give her consent. She requested a conciliation conference, then obtained an attorney and requested a due process hearing. The hearing officer held that the proposed fourth assessment of the student was appropriate, and its decision was affirmed by a deputy commissioner of education. The mother then filed a lawsuit under the EHA and 42 U.S.C. § 1983, seeking an order to reverse the hearing officer's decision and a declaratory judgment that the EHA permitted her son to obtain a full due process hearing on any issue relating to his evaluation or placement. A federal district court granted the mother's motion. The mother then made a motion in the court for an award of attorney's fees under the EHA. The court held that the mother was a prevailing party under the EHA and awarded attorney's fees in excess of $10,000. This represented only one half of the fees requested.

The mother then failed to appear for court-ordered depositions, and the district court issued a final order dismissing the complaint. The school district then appealed the attorney's fees award to the U.S. Court of Appeals, Eighth Circuit. The court noted that an award of attorney's fees under the EHA could only be reversed for an abuse of discretion. It rejected the school district's argument that special circumstances existed which made the attorney's fees award unjust. The court noted that the school district had continually opposed the mother's request for a due process hearing, effectively denying her an opportunity to present her objections. The district had operated under an unreasonable interpretation of state law, which, like the EHA, provided parents an opportunity to present their complaints about evaluation and placement of special education students. The district court had not abused its discretion by awarding attorney's fees as there were no special circumstances in support of the district's argument. The court of appeals affirmed the district court's order awarding attorney's fees. *ISD 623, Roseville, Minnesota v. Digre*, 893 F.2d 987 (8th Cir. 1990).

The parents of a handicapped Texas student appealed the student's IEP by filing a request for a due process hearing before a special education hearing officer. The parties settled their dispute before the hearing was held. One week after the settlement, the student sued the school district in a federal district court to recover attorney's fees and costs. The district court granted the student's summary judgment motion and awarded him $30,533.62 in attorney's fees. The school district appealed to the U.S. Court of Appeals, Fifth Circuit.

The court of appeals found that summary judgment was inappropriate. The school district had submitted affidavits supporting its contention that the attorney's fees were unreasonable based on the prevailing fees in the community. The contradictory evidence presented by the school district created material issues of fact which precluded summary judgment. The court further held that attorney's fees were recoverable under the Handicapped Children's Protection Act (HCPA) where settlement was reached prior to a due process hearing. The language of the HCPA implied that attorney's fees were recoverable when a written settlement offer was made and accepted more than ten days before a due process hearing. Congress intended prevailing parents to recover fees for legal services performed in connection with an administrative proceeding, including services rendered in anticipation of a due process hearing. The court of appeals reversed the district court's decision and remanded the case to determine if the student was entitled to attorney's fees. *Shelly C. v. Venus Indep. School Dist.*, 878 F.2d 862 (5th Cir. 1989).

A California school district decided to transfer a severely handicapped student to another school. After a hearing officer upheld the district's decision, the student sued it in a federal district court under the Education of the Handicapped Act (EHA). Before trial the parties settled the case. The district agreed not to transfer the student to a different school, and to create a special day class for the student at her current school. The settlement did not mention attorney's fees. At the time of the settlement, the U.S. Supreme Court had determined that attorney's fees were not available to prevailing parties. *Smith v. Robinson*, 468 U.S. 992 (1984). After that decision, Congress enacted the HCPA which overruled *Smith*, and provided for recovery of attorney's fees retroactively to the date of *Smith*.

Because the student in this case had initially sought relief at the administrative level after the *Smith* decision was rendered, the student petitioned the district court for attorney's fees. The district court found for the school district and the student appealed to the U.S. Court of Appeals, Ninth Circuit. The appeals court held that the district court had abused its discretion in denying attorney's fees to the handicapped student. When the parties settled, the student had no right to receive fees. Although the school district had no expectation of paying fees and might not have entered the settlement had it known it could be liable for fees, these reasons failed to justify the denial of attorney's fees. The HCPA applied retroactively to any action brought after July 3, 1984, the date of the *Smith* decision. The unfairness of retroactivity did not justify the denial of attorney's fees. The appeals court remanded the case to determine whether special circumstances existed which would allow denial of attorney fees under the EHA. *Abu-Sahyun v. Palo Alto Unified School Dist.*, 843 F.2d 1250 (9th Cir. 1988).

The parents of a handicapped child sued an Illinois school district under the EHA, seeking compensation for the education of their handicapped son. Their case was pending on July 4, 1984, and was resolved in March of 1986. In August, 1986, Congress passed an amendment to the HCPA which made attorney's fees available to litigants prevailing under the EHA if their cases were pending on July 4, 1984. The student's parents then sought attorney's fees in a federal district court. The district court awarded the parents attorney's fees and the school district appealed to the United States Court of Appeals, Seventh Circuit. The court of appeals held that the student was not barred from seeking attorney's fees which were initially not available when the case was decided. The student's original complaint had requested attorney's fees. However, the district court did not address that issue because there was no legal basis for an award of fees until Congress passed the amendments in August, 1986. Ordinarily, failing to rule on the request would have precluded it in later litigation. However, the U.S. Constitution permitted Congress to alter this principle by providing retroactive recovery of attorney's fees. The appeals court affirmed the district court's decision. *Max M. v. New Trier High School Dist. No. 203*, 859 F.2d 1297 (7th Cir. 1988).

A severely handicapped New York student attended a private school for the blind and retarded at public expense pursuant to the EHA. After the school closed, the student instituted administrative proceedings to obtain placement at another school. The administrative proceedings were protracted which caused the student to lose nearly two years of academic education. The New York State Commissioner of Education refused to provide compensatory education beyond the student's twenty-first birthday to make up for the delay. The student then appealed that decision to a federal district court claiming that the delays in the hearing process violated his rights under the EHA. The federal district court dismissed the case on the grounds that the Eleventh

Amendment barred the action. The U.S. Court of Appeals, Second Circuit, reversed the decision and granted the plaintiff one year of compensatory education past the age of twenty-one. The U.S. Supreme Court granted a writ of certiorari and remanded the case for consideration in light of its decision in *Dellmuth v. Muth*, 109 S.Ct. 2397 (1989). The Supreme Court held that the EHA did not itself state an intent to abrogate sovereign immunity. The second circuit reformed its prior holding and restated its judgment granting the student one year of compensatory education. The student then instituted an action to recover attorney's fees and costs of $100,000. The defendants argued that the attorney's fees should be substantially reduced and suggested the amount of $14,000.

Under the EHA, a plaintiff must be a prevailing party to recover attorney's fees. In regard to related claims, the court noted that even if they did not succeed on all the claims, the attorney's fees were to be awarded by looking at the case as a whole. The court noted that the accepted system for determining a reasonable fee was to start with the number of hours worked and multiply this by an appropriate hourly rate. Furthermore, the court noted that any errors due to recordkeeping were more than accounted for by discounting the billable hours. The court found that the fees charged by the plaintiff were a little excessive and reduced the amount to $96,000 plus costs. *Burr by Burr v. Sobol*, 748 F.Supp. 97 (S.D.N.Y.1990).

Two sets of parents of severely handicapped students sued the New York education commissioner for placement costs at an out-of-state facility for severely handicapped persons. A New York trial court agreed with the parents' decision to place the children at the out-of-state facility. Although the parents had failed to exhaust their administrative remedies, further appeal to the commissioner would have been futile given his previous refusal to implement each student's special committee recommendation. The parents then made a motion for attorney's fees under the HCPA. Both children's parents were represented by the same attorneys from the same law firm. The trial court granted the motion for attorney's fees totaling over $34,000 in the first case and $43,803.25 in the second. The commissioner appealed, claiming that HCPA counsel fees were not available under the EHA, and that the fees were improperly determined.

The appellate division court ruled that under the U.S. Supreme Court decision in *Honig v. Doe*, 108 S.Ct. 592, parents are permitted to seek EHA review by a court where the administrative process was futile or inadequate. Therefore, the parents had properly filed the matter in court. However, the parents' attorneys had failed to submit sufficient evidence to determine their fees. Because the attorneys had represented the parents of both children, there was a possibility that they were being paid twice for the same research. The court remanded the case to the trial court and directed the attorneys to submit their time sheets, taking precautions to protect confidential material. *Behavior Research Institute v. Ambach*, 535 N.Y.S.2d 465 (A.D.3d Dep't 1988).

In a second New York case, an emotionally disturbed student was enrolled at a private school at public expense for approximately five years. The New York City Board of Education committee recommended that he be reclassified as emotionally disturbed for the next school year. It also approved his private school enrollment. However, before the school year began, the state education director for handicapped children advised the city's board that the department would not approve the private school placement and directed a reevaluation. The city's committee reevaluated the student and changed his classification to mentally retarded. It also recommended placement in a public school retarded children's class. The student's parents reenrolled him at the private school at their expense and brought administrative procedures to challenge the reclassification. The hearing officer determined that the emotionally disturbed designation was correct and ruled that the private school placement was appropriate. The parents were found to be entitled to tuition reimbursement. The city board then applied to the education department for funds. Again the director stated that the department would not approve the student's private school placement.

The parents sued the state education commissioner, the handicapped director and the city board for an order to pay the student's tuition at the private school. The parents also sought attorney's fees. A New York trial court ruled for the parents, stating that the hearing officer's determination was final. It ordered that the hearing officer's determination be implemented and also ordered funding of the student's placement at the private school for the following school year. Meanwhile, Congress approved the HCPA. The parents applied for attorney's fees under the HCPA and the trial court made an attorney's fee award of over $16,000. The state education department contended that Congress was not authorized to make retroactive attorney's fee awards. The department also argued that the parents had not been "aggrieved" by the hearing officer's decision or any decision by a state education agency. The New York Supreme Court, Appellate Division, Third Department, disagreed, ruling that the parents had been aggrieved by the commissioner's determination to ignore the hearing officer's decision. However, the trial court erred in making an attorney's fee award on its own time estimates, rather than permitting the parents' attorneys to submit their own time records. The case was remanded to the trial court for redetermination of attorney's fees. *Sidney K. by Harry K. v. Ambach*, 535 N.Y.S.2d 468 (A.D.3 Dep't 1988).

An orthopedically handicapped student at the Louisiana Special Education Center (LSEC) was transferred to a hospital in March, 1985, to be treated for respiratory problems. When he attempted to return to the LSEC, it refused to admit him, arguing that it was not equipped to deal with his medical problems. The student subsequently sued the LSEC under the EHA. A federal district court ordered the school to admit the student who subsequently sought attorney's fees. The district court denied attorney's fees on the basis of *Smith v. Robinson*, in which the Supreme Court declared attorney's fees unavailable in EHA cases. He appealed, but before the appeal reached the court, Congress passed the Handicapped Children's Protection Act of 1986 which overruled the *Smith* decision by expressly providing for attorney's fees in EHA cases. The U.S. Court of Appeals, Fifth Circuit, ruled that he was entitled to attorney's fees and remanded the case to the district court. The district court awarded attorney's fees to the student in the amount of $9,300 and the LSEC appealed. He requested additional attorney's fees on appeal.

The court of appeals first determined that the LSEC could not avoid paying the attorney's fees on the ground that it had acted in good faith when it refused to admit the student. It also rejected the LSEC's argument that he could not sue for attorney's fees because the EHA allows payment of such fees only to "the parents or guardian of a handicapped child or youth." The student in this case was eighteen years or older while the suit was in progress and he therefore sought attorney's fees in his own name. The court declared that the EHA legislative history indicated that handicapped children can seek attorney's fees on their own behalf if they are old enough and are otherwise competent to bring suit. Because the district court had not abused its discretion in awarding attorney's fees, the award was proper. The court of appeals ruled in the student's favor and remanded the case to the district court for a determination of the amount of additional attorney's fees that he should receive for the appeal. *Fontenot v. Louisiana Bd. of Elementary & Secondary Educ.*, 835 F.2d 117 (5th Cir. 1988).

In another Louisiana case a group of handicapped children sued the state of Louisiana in a U.S. district court, seeking statewide extended year programs for handicapped students. The parties entered into a consent decree authorized by the court which provided for the extended year programs. Therefore, the handicapped children were prevailing parties under the EHA. The handicapped children then asked the court for an award of attorney's fees. They claimed that they were entitled to fees under EHA § 1415(e). The state contended that the U.S. Constitution's Eleventh Amendment barred recovery of attorney's fees because the state did not expressly waive its immunity from a federal lawsuit. The district court held for the handicapped children. The state had consented to the court's jurisdiction by entering into the consent decree thus waiving its Eleventh Amendment immunity. The court ordered the state to pay the handicapped childrens' attorney's fees under § 1415(e). *Laura I. v. Clausen*, 676 F.Supp. 717 (M.D.La. 1988).

In 1980, a U.S. district court held that the District of Columbia Board of Education's IEP for an autistic child was inadequate and ordered the board to place the child at a residential school in West Virginia. It also awarded attorney's fees to the child's parents under § 504 of the Rehabilitation Act. In 1984, however, the fee award was vacated in response to the U.S. Supreme Court's ruling in *Smith v. Robinson*. After the Handicapped Children's Protection Act (HCPA) was passed in 1986, the parents asked the district court to reinstate the attorney's fee award.

The court noted that the HCPA provides that courts may award attorney's fees to prevailing children or parents in EHA "actions or proceedings brought . . . after July 3, 1984, and actions or proceedings brought prior to July 4, 1984, . . . which were pending on July 4, 1984." The parents argued that since their earlier attorney's fee award had not been vacated until August 17, 1984, their action had still been "pending" on July 4, 1984. The district court agreed with the parents' interpretation. It rejected the board's arguments that the HCPA was unconstitutional retroactive legislation and ordered that the parents were entitled to $8,420, the amount of the previous fee award. *Capello v. Dist. of Columbia Bd. of Educ.*, 669 F.Supp. 14 (D.D.C. 1987).

In 1983, a U.S. district court held that Missouri's policy precluding educational programs for handicapped children in excess of the nine-month school year was discriminatory against the handicapped and was unenforceable.

However, under the authority of *Smith v. Robinson*, 104 S.Ct. 3457 (1984), the district court later denied a request by a handicapped student's parents for attorney's fees. After passage of the HCPA the parents sued their school district in U.S. district court. Once again they asked for attorney's fees. The school district argued that because the attorney's fees issue had already been finalized in its favor, it could not be held liable for attorney's fees now.

The court held that the parents could recover attorney's fees. It observed that federal court rules provided that parties could be relieved of final judgments against them when exceptional circumstances were present. The court reasoned that by authorizing attorney's fees in the HCPA and making such authorizations retroactive, Congress intended to reverse the affects of *Smith*. This reversal, stated the court, presented exceptional circumstances which favored the parents' case. The court rejected the school district's argument that a change in the law was not sufficient to provide relief when the judgment was final. It noted that although changes in court decisions cannot affect a final judgment, changes in statutory law (as in this case) can. The court reasoned that expressly retroactive changes in statutory law created new claims for parties seeking relief from previous judgments. This meant that the parents here had a new and viable claim for attorney's fees since the HCPA expressly provided for attorney's fees retroactive to cases pending on July 4, 1984.

The court also rejected the school district's argument that the Eleventh Amendment to the U.S. Constitution, which limits the power of federal courts in lawsuits against individual states, barred a retroactive award of attorney's fees against the state. It concluded that monetary awards against states were allowed when authorized by Congress in order to enforce the Fourteenth Amendment, which provides in part that states cannot infringe upon the privileges of its citizens. The court therefore awarded attorney's fees to the parents, payable by the state of Missouri. *Yaris v. Special School Dist.*, 661 F.Supp. 996 (E.D.Mo.1987).

II. ADMINISTRATIVE PROCEEDINGS

Where a student or parent prevails in an administrative proceeding, a lawsuit may be brought for the sole purpose of obtaining attorney's fees.

In two separate cases, the parents of two handicapped children sought to have them put in a residential setting for educational purposes. The respective school districts refused. For a while an attempt at education was made at the schools and when that proved ineffective, the children were placed in day schools specifically for the handicapped. Eventually the parents asked for an administrative hearing in which their requests were granted. They then sought attorney's fees, costs and expenses, which were denied. They filed suit in a California federal district court which ruled against them, and they appealed to the U.S. Court of Appeals, Ninth Circuit.

The court of appeals noted that at the time of the district courts' decisions, there were few cases available which spoke to the subject of attorney's fees. However, with the enactment of the Handicapped Children's Protection Act of 1986 cases had been decided which interpreted the Act. The court followed the Fifth Circuit's decision in *Duane M. v. Orleans Parish School Bd.*, 861 F.2d 115 (1988) and the Sixth Circuit's holding in *Eggers v. Bullitt County*

School District, 854 F.2d 892 (1988) and held that the parents could recover attorney's fees and appropriate costs plus expenses. The court recognized that the overwhelming majority of cases now supported awarding fees to parents who prevailed in administrative hearings as well as at trial. It thus reversed the district courts' decisions. *McSomebodies v. San Mateo City School Dist.*, 897 F.2d 975 (9th Cir. 1989) and *McSomebodies v. Burlingame Elementary School Dist.*, 897 F.2d 974 (9th Cir. 1989).

Several Washington, D.C., handicapped students and their parents instituted administrative proceedings in which they prevailed. They then instituted this action in a federal district court for recovery of attorney's fees and costs incurred in the administrative proceedings. The trial court found for the parents, and the school district appealed to the U.S. Court of Appeals, D.C. Circuit, which reversed. The parents then filed a suggestion for en banc consideration and the court decided to rehear the case.

On appeal, the court noted that the four circuit courts that have addressed the issue have concluded that the Handicapped Children's Protection Act (HCPA) does authorize an award of attorney's fees to a parent who prevails in an EHA administrative proceeding. The court, through an in-depth analysis of the statutory content and legislative history, determined that the HCPA does authorize an award of attorney's fees to a prevailing party. The court of appeals affirmed the trial court's decision to grant attorney's fees. *Moore v. District of Columbia*, 907 F.2d 165 (D.C.Cir. 1990).

A Georgia school district refused to permit a severely handicapped twelve-year-old to enter the public school system. The district recommended that the student's parents place her in a residential placement center. The parents enrolled her at a residential center on a temporary basis. The district failed to develop an IEP and the center did not provide licensed teachers. The student's parents requested a due process hearing. A regional hearing officer found that the district had failed to provide free and appropriate education as required under the EHA. The officer found, however, that the student could be taught at the center as long as educational standards were met and licensed teachers were provided during school days. The school district appealed to a state hearing officer which confirmed the regional hearing officer's decision. The parents then sought attorney's fees and costs. The state hearing officer determined that the parents could not petition administratively for attorney's fees but should seek relief from a federal court. The parents then sued the school district in a federal district court for attorney's fees. The district court granted summary judgment to the school district and the parents appealed to the U.S. Court of Appeals, Eleventh Circuit.

The court of appeals ruled that parties who prevail at the administrative level are entitled to attorney's fees for all EHA proceedings. The court found that the parents were "prevailing parties." The parents had achieved the most significant relief they sought, which was to ensure that the student received a free appropriate education. Because the hearing officer had directed the center to provide the student with instruction by licensed teachers during the school day, the parents' fundamental objective of training and education was met. The court of appeals reversed and remanded to the district court for a determination of reasonable attorney's fees. *Mitten v. Muscogee County School Dist.*, 877 F.2d 932 (11th Cir. 1989).

Nine learning disabled District of Columbia students prevailed in due process hearings under the Education of the Handicapped Act (EHA). The students were placed in private dayschools. The students requested reimbursement of attorney's fees and costs they had incurred in administrative proceedings. The District of Columbia rejected their requests and the students sued it in federal district court to obtain attorney's fees and costs. The district court held that § 1415(e)(4)(B) of the EHA authorized courts to award attorney's fees for services rendered during an administrative proceeding, where the lawsuit was brought solely for that purpose. The District of Columbia appealed to the U.S. Court of Appeals, District of Columbia Circuit.

The court of appeals held that the EHA did not authorize attorney's fees for administrative proceedings, in a lawsuit brought solely to obtain attorney's fees. It noted that attorney's fees may be awarded only to someone who has prevailed in an "action or proceeding" brought under § 1415(e). Although the students were prevailing parties in the administrative proceedings, this did not make them prevailing parties to whom EHA § 1415(e)(4)(B) authorized the award of attorney's fees. Attorney's fees were to be awarded as "part of the cost." If attorney's fees were awarded in a lawsuit brought solely to obtain the fee, the fee could not be awarded as "part of the cost" of the lawsuit since the fee was the sole objective of the lawsuit. The language Congress used in § 1415(e)(4)(B) provided for the award of attorney's fees only in cases in which a party who lost in the administrative proceedings brought a judicial action challenging the administrative decision and prevailed in the judicial action. The court of appeals reversed the district court's decision. *Moore v. Dist. of Columbia*, 866 F.2d 335 (D.C.Cir.1989).

A ten-year-old Washington student fell from a tree and suffered severe head injuries. He received developmental disability services and was placed at the State Department of Social and Health Services (DSHS) in the Division of Developmental Disabilities, Ranier School. Five years later, the division attempted to remove the student from school because of his improved functional level. At about the same time, a juvenile court found the student to be developmentally disabled because of neurological damage and ordered him committed to the Ranier school. The student then reapplied for developmental disability services. The division denied his application because he was "not mentally retarded." The student appealed the division's decision to an administrative law judge. The judge found that he did not have jurisdiction over juvenile court findings. The student then appealed to the DSHS Office of Hearings. The reviewing judge again dismissed the appeal for lack of jurisdiction, this time because the student had not yet turned eighteen. The student appealed the final decision to a state trial court. The court found that both administrative judges had erred in dismissing the student's appeals. It remanded the case to the administrative law judge and awarded the student attorney's fees. The DSHS then appealed to the Court of Appeals of Washington.

On appeal, the court held that the student was not entitled to the attorney's fees award. The only possible basis for attorney's fees was found in two Washington statutes which authorized attorney's fees and costs to applicants and recipients of public assistance who successfully challenged the DSHS's decisions. They applied only to financial need-based public assistance eligibility decisions and not to decisions concerning eligibility for developmental disability services. The trial court had no authority to order the DSHS division to pay the student's attorney's fees and the court of appeals reversed its decision. *Johnstun v. Dept. of Social & Health Serv.*, 766 P.2d 1104 (Wash. App.1988).

A Tennessee four-year-old was diagnosed as hearing impaired with speech and language disabilities. Her parents notified the local school board and negotiations began to determine the correct educational program. Following a multidisciplinary team meeting, the parents stated their dissatisfaction with the board's educational options and stated their preference for comprehensive full-day, five-day-a-week classes with specific therapies and services. The board then proposed that the student attend a public school where she would receive help from a deaf education specialist one hour per day, see a speech therapist for a half-hour three days a week, and consult a vision specialist twice a week. The parents rejected this proposal and requested a due process hearing, which resulted in a finding that the school board had denied the student special education and related services and had negligently attempted to identify and evaluate appropriate services. However, the hearing officer found that the board had not violated federal regulations for offering a placement not based on an IEP or for failing to maintain a continuum of alternative placements. Neither party appealed the hearing officer's decision, but the parents filed a lawsuit in a federal district court for their attorney's fees.

The district court outlined the appropriateness of attorney's fees under the Handicapped Children's Protection Act (HCPA). The HCPA permits reasonable attorney's fees to parents of handicapped children who are prevailing parties under the act. Because the hearing officer had ruled that the school board was negligent, the court stated that the student was the prevailing party. However, attorney's fees are unavailable for actions performed after a written offer of settlement if the final relief granted is no more favorable than a written offer of settlement. The court noted a letter from the board's special education services director offering the public school placement with speech therapy and other specialists which did not materially differ from the eventual result of the hearing. The court also noted that the attorney had delayed almost one month in rejecting the board's offer. Because the settlement offer was as favorable as the final award, the court disallowed attorney's fees and dismissed the lawsuit. *Hyden v. Bd. of Educ. of Wilson County*, 714 F.Supp. 290 (M.D.Tenn.1989).

The parents of a blind Rhode Island elementary school student objected to the school's use of an optometric consultant provided by the district. The consultant was neither certified to teach blind students nor certified to teach in the state of Rhode Island. The parents requested a hearing before the state special education board under the EHA and the Rehabilitation Act. When mediation failed, the parents filed a complaint against the school district with the U.S. Department of Education's Office of Civil Rights (OCR). Before the OCR reached a decision, the state department of education found the school district in violation of state handicapped student regulations. The department ordered the district to provide the student with a certified teacher.

The OCR then found that although the school district had violated regulations, it had remedied the situation.

The parents then sued the school district in a federal district court for attorney's fees under the EHA. The district argued that the parents were not a prevailing party under the act because there had been no actual administrative hearing. The district court disagreed, ruling that by requesting an administrative hearing and complaining to state and federal agencies, the parents had prevailed in their request to receive certified education for their daughter. Litigants who had obtained their major legal objectives were prevailing parties under the EHA despite the lack of an administrative hearing. Thus, the parents were entitled to attorney's fees. However, the parents in this case had claimed they were entitled to $19,310.95, which the court found excessive. The court reduced the attorney's fee award to $9,260.60. *Mr. D. v. Glocester School Comm.*, 711 F.Supp. 66 (D.R.I.1989).

The parents of a Massachusetts learning disabled student disapproved of the IEP proposed for the student by the Boston School Committee. The parents appealed the committee's IEP proposal to the Massachusetts Department of Education. The department rejected the IEP and granted the educational services the parents had requested. During the proceedings, the parents were represented by an attorney at a rate of $150 per hour for a total of 51.5 hours. The parents sued the committee in federal district court to recover attorney's fees under the 1986 Handicapped Children's Protection Act (HCPA).

The committee argued that the HCPA did not authorize the award of attorney's fees when parents prevailed only at the administrative level. It contended that the parents must be "aggrieved parties," unsuccessful in the administrative process, and must pursue their claim in federal district court before the court had jurisdiction to consider an award of attorney's fees. The court rejected the committee's argument and held that the parents were entitled to reasonable attorney's fees. The HCPA's legislative history demonstrated that Congress intended to award attorney's fees to parents for legal representation in any action or proceeding. Under the HCPA prevailing parties may recover reasonable fees based on rates prevailing in the community. The time the parents' attorney spent on the administrative process was found reasonable. However, the attorney did not submit supporting documentation concerning the prevailing hourly rate attorneys received in the community. The court found that the parents were therefore entitled to reasonable attorney's fees limited to $125 per hour. *Williams v. Boston School Comm.*, 709 F.Supp. 27 (D.Mass.1989).

A mildly retarded young adult initiated administrative proceedings against his Connecticut school district. He sought additional education as compensation for a two-year period during which he was hospitalized and received little or no education. After unsuccessful administrative hearings, the young adult appealed to a U.S. district court. The lawsuit was settled by a consent decree signed by both the state and the local school district. The decree granted the young adult two years of compensatory education at the state's expense. The young adult sued both the state and the school district in a U.S. district court after passage of the HCPA. He sought attorney's fees incurred in the earlier lawsuit at the administrative level. The court held that because the young adult had obtained limited success against the school district at the administrative level (in that the school district was fiscally responsible for the young adult's education during his two-year hospitalization) it was liable for twenty percent of the attorney's fees. The school district appealed to the U.S. Court of Appeals, Second Circuit.

The school district argued that attorney's fees were unavailable for administrative hearings under the HCPA. Furthermore, the young adult failed to prevail against it as required by the HCPA. The young adult argued that he was entitled to attorney's fees from both the state and the school district due to the "relative culpability" of both defendants. The court of appeals held for the school district although it rejected the district's argument that the HCPA failed to afford attorney's fees for work done in connection with administrative hearings. Under the HCPA a court may award attorney's fees to any handicapped youth who is a "prevailing party." A youth is considered a prevailing party if he or she succeeds on any significant issue in litigation. The young adult clearly prevailed against the state with respect to the consent decree but the court concluded that he did not prevail against the school district either at the administrative level or in the consent decree. Although a hearing officer found that the school district was fiscally responsible for the young adult's education during his hospitalization, she refused to award compensatory education. The consent decree imposed no obligations or expenses on the school district. The state alone was liable for attorney's fees. *Counsel v. Dow*, 849 F.2d 731 (2d Cir. 1988).

A Louisiana school board held a meeting to develop an IEP for an autistic student. The board decided to place the student in a special residential school. When school officials delayed the placement, the student's parents requested a due process hearing. Prior to that hearing, an additional IEP conference was held at which school officials decided to place the student in the Louisiana State Hospital. The parents disagreed with the school board's reappraisal and requested that the due process hearing go forward. The hearing officer found that placement in the hospital would be adequate. The parents appealed the decision to a state-level review panel. The panel overruled the hearing officer's decision. The parties then agreed to place the student in a class for high-functioning autistic children. The settlement did not mention attorney's fees.

The parents then sued the school board in a federal district court, seeking attorney's fees as provided under the HCPA. The court awarded attorney's fees and costs to the parents. The school board appealed to the United States Court of Appeals, Fifth Circuit. The court of appeals held that the HCPA authorized a separate suit for attorney's fees where costs were incurred in successful administrative proceedings. The parents had sought fees for their legal representation in the mandatory administrative proceedings. The HCPA legislative history demonstrated Congress' intent to award attorney's fees to parents for legal representation at due process hearings. The appeals court affirmed the district court's decision. *Duane M. v. Orleans Parish School Bd.*, 861 F.2d 115 (5th Cir. 1988).

The parents of a Kentucky student requested an administrative hearing from their school district when a dispute arose over their son's placement.

The parents were represented by attorneys from an independent state agency which represented those with developmental disabilities. The parents prevailed at the hearing. They were also successful when the district appealed to an appeals board. The parents then sought to recover attorney's fees from the district under the HCPA. The district refused to pay the fees and the parents sued the district in a Kentucky federal district court. It held for the school district because the parents had been represented by a publicly-funded state agency. The parents appealed to the U.S. Court of Appeals, Sixth Circuit.

One of the issues on appeal was whether the district court wrongfully denied an award of attorney's fees to the state agency which represented the parents. In reaching its decision, the appeals court noted that the HCPA provides for attorney's fees to parents prevailing at the administrative level. The appeals court held that an administrative hearing was an "action or proceeding" under the HCPA. The appeals court noted that the legislative history of the HCPA made no distinction between private and publicly-funded attorneys. Section 1988 of the HCPA established that "reasonable fees are to be calculated according to the prevailing market rates in the relevant community, regardless of whether plaintiff is represented by private or non-profit counsel." Thus, the school district was obligated to pay the attorney's fees award. *Eggers v. Bullet County School Dist.*, 854 F.2d 892 (6th Cir.1988).

An Indiana child attended a public school and was classified as physically handicapped. After the child entered the second grade, her parents, teacher, and other school officials met to develop her IEP. At that time, an agreement was reached on a number of issues, but there remained disagreements on others. Throughout that school year and the following summer, the teachers and the child's parents continued to disagree on several issues. The parents wanted full control over who was to deliver the physical therapy and occupational services given to their daughter. The school, however, offered to provide the physical and occupational therapy services through its own personnel. The parents filed for an administrative hearing. During the hearing, the school attempted to make an interim settlement. The school offered to have its occupational therapist work with the child. This was agreed to and for the first time, the school's occupational therapist was permitted to work with the child. The mother, however, would not allow the school's physical therapist to work with the child. She continued to have her own physical therapist work with her child. The administrative officer entered her decision which indicated that the parents could use their own physical therapist and that the school must reimburse them for the amount not covered by insurance. The parents, however, would be responsible for the costs of the private evaluations by their own physical therapist. The parents then sought reimbursement of the legal fees incurred in the administrative proceeding in a federal district court.

In order for the parents to recover their legal fees, they must show that they prevailed (i.e. in some way won) at the administrative level. At trial, the hearing officer who rendered the administrative decision stated that the decision was in favor of the school authorities because no significant relief was granted to the parents of the child. The district court, however, determined that the administrative decision was slightly in favor of the parents. The parents did not receive all the attorney's fees that they requested because their lawyer acted adversarially which the court determined to be unnecessary. The court then awarded reduced attorney's fees based on this decision. *Howey by Howey v. Tippecanoe School Corp.*, 734 F.Supp. 1485 (N.D.Ind.1990).

A severely handicapped New York student attended a private school for the blind and retarded at public expense pursuant to the EHA. After the school closed, the student instituted administrative proceedings to obtain placement at another school. The administrative proceedings were protracted which caused the student to lose nearly two years of academic education. The New York State Commissioner of Education refused to provide compensatory education beyond the student's twenty-first birthday to make up for the delay. The student then appealed that decision to a federal district court claiming that the delays in the hearing process violated his rights under the EHA. The federal district court dismissed the case on the grounds that the Eleventh Amendment barred the action. The U.S. Court of Appeals, Second Circuit, reversed the decision and granted the plaintiff one year of compensatory education past the age of twenty-one. The U.S. Supreme Court granted a writ of certiorari and remanded the case for consideration in light of its decision in *Dellmuth v. Muth*, 109 S.Ct. 2397 (1989). The Supreme Court held that the EHA did not itself state an intent to abrogate sovereign immunity. The second circuit reformed its prior holding and restated its judgment granting the student one year of compensatory education. The student then instituted an action to recover attorney's fees and costs of $100,000. The defendants argued that the attorney's fees should be substantially reduced and suggested the amount of $14,000.

Under the EHA, a plaintiff must be a prevailing party to recover attorney's fees. In regard to related claims, the court noted that even if they did not succeed on all the claims, the attorney's fees were to be awarded by looking at the case as a whole. The court noted that the accepted system for determining a reasonable fee was to start with the number of hours worked and multiply this by an appropriate hourly rate. Furthermore, the court noted that any errors due to recordkeeping were more than accounted for by discounting the billable hours. The court found that the fees charged by the plaintiff were a little excessive and reduced the amount to $96,000 plus costs. *Burr by Burr v. Sobol*, 748 F.Supp. 97 (S.D.N.Y.1990).

The parents of a handicapped public school student asked a Kansas school district to provide her with the related services of occupational and physical therapy. The district denied the request. An EHA due process hearing was held and the hearing officer ruled that the district must provide the services. Neither party appealed the decision and it became final in June, 1986. Congress enacted the HCPA in August, 1986. It authorized federal courts to award reasonable attorney's fees to prevailing parties in "actions or proceedings under the EHA commenced after July 3, 1984." The parents sued the school district in a U.S. district court for attorney's fees under the HCPA.

The school district contended that the HCPA [20 U.S.C. § 1415(e)(4)(B)] did not authorize an award of attorney's fees for work done solely at the administrative level. The district court held for the parents. The statutory language allowed an award of attorney's fees since the terms "action or proceeding" may include administrative hearings and appeals. The HCPA's legislative history demonstrated the legislative intent to allow fees at the administrative level. The retroactive attorney's fees award was constitutional because there was a legitimate and rational legislative purpose for retroactive awards. Prior to the Supreme Court decision in *Smith v. Robinson*, 104 S.Ct. 3457 (1984), Congress intended that attorney's fees be available for administrative proceedings. To advance this goal, Congress recognized the need to completely erase the effects of *Smith* by making the HCPA fee provision retroactive to the date *Smith* was decided. The court ordered the school district to pay for the parents' attorney's fees. *Unified School Dist. No. 259 v. Newton*, 673 F.Supp. 418 (D.Kan.1987).

A blind New York student sought admission to the New York Institute for the Education of the Blind. The institute rejected him and he appealed. A hearing officer appointed by the New York State Commissioner of Education ordered the student's admission to the institute and awarded him a year of free compensatory public education. The institute appealed the decision to the commissioner, who upheld the admission. However, he ruled against the student concerning the compensatory education. The student then sued the commissioner in a U.S. district court. The court dismissed the case. However, the student's claim for attorney's fees for the administrative level proceedings which resulted in his institute admission was still pending before the court. The commissioner contended that the HCPA provided no attorney's fees to parties who prevailed at the administrative level. He also claimed that he was not a party against whom the student prevailed at the administrative level. The student argued that he prevailed against the commissioner for the purpose of attorney's fees because the commissioner was the only official with the authority to appoint students to the institute.

The court held that the student was entitled to recover attorney's fees on the issue of admission to the institute, but was not entitled to recover attorney's fees from the commissioner. Even though the commissioner unlawfully reviewed the hearing officer's decision, it did not follow that the student was entitled to attorney's fees from him. The EHA does not contemplate an award of attorney's fees against a decisionmaker such as the commissioner. The student could only recover attorney's fees from the institute. *Burr v. Ambach*, 683 F.Supp. 46 (S.D.N.Y.1988). This case was overruled on other grounds. See page 197.

A group of parents challenged the Connecticut State Board of Education, alleging that it violated the due process rights of their handicapped children. They argued that the board had violated EHA regulations by failing to hold hearings and make decisions within forty-five days of receiving requests for hearings. The parents also claimed that the board repeatedly violated the EHA requirement of hearing officer independence. The parties agreed to a consent decree which defined the children's due process rights. The parents then asked a U.S. district court for an award of attorney's fees. The district court held for the parents. It observed that the parents were "prevailing parties" if they succeeded "on any significant issue in litigation which [achieved] some of the benefit the parties sought in bringing suit." The fact that the lawsuit resulted in a consent decree did not preclude the parents from claiming attorney's fees as prevailing parties. The consent decree established the most important of the parents' objectives. It forced the board to recognize its responsibility to hold hearings and render decisions within forty-five days of receiving a request. Because the parents had prevailed on an issue central to their lawsuit, the court awarded attorney's fees. *Barbara R. v. Tirozzi*, 665 F.Supp. 141 (D.Conn.1987).

After the father of a handicapped child disagreed with a local school district concerning an IEP for his child, he sought a due process hearing under the EHA. The hearing officer granted the IEP provisions he sought and the school district complied. However, the school district refused to pay the father for the attorney's fees he incurred in obtaining the IEP provisions. The father sued the school district in U.S. district court. The school district moved for dismissal claiming that the EHA did not authorize a parent who prevailed in a due process hearing to initiate a lawsuit in a federal court for the sole purpose of obtaining attorney's fees. The father contended that the EHA's legislative history indicated that it did authorize such lawsuits.

The court held that such lawsuits were authorized by the EHA due to passage of the Handicapped Children's Protection Act (HCPA). It observed that, although the language of the EHA was inconclusive as to whether a parent could recover attorney's fees in such cases, it was reasonable to read "action or proceeding" in EHA § 1415(e)(4)(B) as referring to both judicial actions and due process hearings. It also looked to the language of the legislative history of § 1415(e)(4)(B) and concluded that the legislative history clearly indicated that separate lawsuits for attorney's fees were permissible. The court dismissed the school district's motion and held that the father could sue in a federal court for attorney's fees incurred in the due process hearing. *Prescott v. Palos Verdes Peninsula Unified School Dist.*, 659 F.Supp. 921 (C.D.Cal.1987).

In another case a U.S. district court in Texas looked to the reasoning in *Prescott*. The case involved the parents of a handicapped child who were dissatisfied with the child's IEP. A hearing officer granted two of the parents' five requests and omitted a ruling on two others. They sued their school district seeking attorney's fees contending that they prevailed in the due process hearing. The school district moved to dismiss their request arguing that the court lacked authority to grant attorney's fees because the parents had not first sued the school district in the U.S. district court on the case itself. The school district also claimed that the parents were not entitled to attorney's fees because they were not prevailing parties.

The district court held that the parents were entitled to attorney's fees. It observed that several district courts have found that an award of attorney's fees for work done with regard to due process hearings was proper where the case never reached the district court level. It accepted *Prescott's* reasoning that the legislative history of § 1415(e)(4)(B) compelled a conclusion that such awards were intended by Congress. It also reasoned that the parents were prevailing parties because they acquired substantive changes in their child's IEP at the due process hearing. The court dismissed the school district's motion and held that the parents were entitled to attorney's fees. *Kristi W. v. Graham Indep. School Dist.*, 663 F.Supp. 86 (N.D.Tex.1987).

A lawsuit to recover EHA attorney's fees was instituted in a U.S. district court in the District of Columbia. The plaintiffs had successfully pursued an administrative action and sought the fees pursuant to the Handicapped Children's Protection Act of 1986 (HCPA). The HCPA effectively overturned the

U.S. Supreme Court's holding in *Smith v. Robinson* that attorney's fees were not available to the prevailing party in special education cases.

The defendants in this case, the District of Columbia and others, argued 1) that the HCPA should not have been applied retroactively by Congress and 2) that attorney's fees should not be available for EHA administrative proceedings. The court stated that neither of these arguments had merit and therefore ruled in favor of the plaintiffs.

As to the retroactivity argument, the court stated that it is within the authority of Congress to pass retroactive legislation, especially where, as here, the legislators are attempting to explicate what they intended in an earlier version of the law. By the later, retroactive Act, Congress was expressing its explicit approval of attorney's fee awards after the Supreme Court had denied the award of such fees. This type of retroactive clarification is clearly within congressional authority and does not offend the U.S. Constitution.

As to the second argument regarding attorney's fees for parents who prevail at an administrative level, the court said that Congress has manifested its intention in the clear words of the HCPA that attorney's fees be recoverable for administrative proceedings. New EHA section 1415(e)(4)(B) reads, "in any action or proceeding brought under this subsection, the court, in its discretion, may award reasonable attorneys' fees. . . ." Thus, stated the court, the words of the statute support the plaintiffs' position that fees are recoverable for administrative proceedings. *Moore v. Dist. of Columbia*, 666 F.Supp. 263 (D.D.C.1987).

After the Cambridge, Massachusetts, School Department proposed an individualized education program (IEP) for a handicapped boy that his mother deemed inappropriate she appealed to the state Bureau of Special Education Appeals (BSEA). The BSEA ruled for her and ordered the school department to provide residential special education for her son. After passage of the Handicapped Children's Protection Act of 1986 (HCPA) the mother and her son sued the school department seeking attorney's fees due to their status as prevailing parties at the due process hearing. A U.S. district court held that parents who prevailed at an EHA due process hearing may later bring a lawsuit solely to obtain an award of attorney's fees.

The court looked to the language of the HCPA, which amended EHA § 1415(e)(4). The new language provides that "in any action or proceeding brought under this subsection" a court may award attorney's fees. It held that "proceeding" referred to both judicial and administrative proceedings, rather than only judicial proceedings as the school department argued. The court concluded that a "close reading of [§ 1415(e)] indicates that it contemplates the award of attorney's fees for parties who prevail at the administrative hearing level."

The court also noted that § 1415(e)(4)(D) provided that parents may not obtain attorney's fees if "the court or administrative officer finds that the relief finally obtained by the parent" was less than any rejected settlement offer. This provision contemplated that fees could be awarded for administrative level hearings. The court also noted that the legislative history of the HCPA supported its decision. A Senate Committee Report stated that the HCPA allows "the award of reasonable attorney's fees to prevailing parents in [EHA] civil actions and in administrative proceedings to parents in certain specified circumstances." Thus, the court held that the parent in this case was entitled to a fee award. *Michael F. v. Cambridge School Dep't*, Civ. No. 86-2532-C (D.Mass.3/5/87).

Parents of a handicapped child filed a complaint with the Division of Community Programs of the Wyoming Department of Health and Social Services alleging that a county children's center had failed to properly develop an Individualized Educational Plan (IEP) for their child. After an administrative hearing, the hearing officer issued a final decision in favor of the parents and ordered that a teacher trained to teach deaf students be employed on a regular basis by the children's center to serve as a consultant. The parents then petitioned the Division for an award of attorney's fees incurred in the administrative hearing process. The Division's administrator denied the request on the ground that they could only be awarded by a court. The parents filed a lawsuit in a U.S. district court seeking attorney's fees.

The district court noted that the lawsuit was not an appeal from the Division administrator's decision. It was instead an independent action for attorney's fees following the administrator's determination that he was not empowered to award them. The issue, therefore, was not whether the administrator had decided wrongly, but whether the parents could recover attorney's fees despite the fact that the IEP dispute was resolved at the administrative level rather than in court. Also at issue was whether the separate lawsuit for attorney's fees was proper.

The court of appeals noted that the EHA, as amended by HCPA provides that "In any action or proceeding brought under [the EHA], the court, in its discretion, may award reasonable attorneys' fees as part of the costs to the parents or guardian of a handicapped child or youth who is the prevailing party." The court determined that this provision placed the decision of whether to award attorney's fees at the discretion of the federal district courts. This interpretation was supported by the legislative history of the HCPA.

The court of appeals also determined that Congress did not intend that EHA lawsuits would have to be decided in federal court as a prerequisite to an award of attorney's fees. The EHA allows an award of reasonable attorney's fees to parents if they are successful in "any action or proceeding" under the EHA. This language indicated that awards of attorney's fees are allowed when favorable results are achieved in lawsuits or administrative proceedings. The court awarded $3,000 to the parents as reasonable attorney's fees. *Mathern v. Campbell County Children's Center*, 674 F.Supp. 816 (D. Wyo.1987).

An emotionally disturbed New Jersey student required a shared-time program to meet the goals set out in his IEP. The student was involved in several incidents which resulted in indefinite suspension. The parents then retained an attorney and sought to have the student readmitted to the shared-time program through an administrative hearing. Prior to the hearing the administrative law judge met with the parties and facilitated the reaching of a settlement. The settlement provided that the student would be admitted to a shared-time program with a different high school and also provided other relief. The parents then instituted this action in a federal district court solely for the purpose of recovering attorney's fees in connection with the settlement, the administrative hearing and the instant action. The parents moved for summary judgment.

The court noted that a prevailing party must "succeed on any significant issue in the proceedings that achieved some of the benefit plaintiff sought from administrative review." Since the parents' main objective was to have their son readmitted to a shared-time program, they were deemed to be prevailing parties under the HCPA. The court thus awarded reasonable attorney's fees. *E.P. by P.Q. v. Union County Reg. High Sch. Dist. 1*, 741 F.Supp. 1144 (D.N.J.1989).

In 1985, the U.S. Court of Appeals, Fourth Circuit, held that a school board wrongly expelled a student for behavior which resulted from his handicap. After the passage of the Handicapped Children's Protection Act of 1986 (HCPA) his parents asked the court of appeals for an award of attorney's fees. The HCPA provides that a court may award reasonable attorney's fees to parents of handicapped children who are prevailing parties under EHA § 1415(e)(4)(B)-(D). The court of appeals remanded the question to a U.S. district court in Virginia.

The school board resisted the application of the HCPA on several theories. It contended that a violation of the separation of powers doctrine would occur if the HCPA's retroactive application formed the basis of a decision in a pending case. It also argued that retroactive application of the HCPA to award attorney's fees to the parents would exceed the spending power of Congress. Specifically, it argued that Congress' power to impose liabilities on recipients of federal aid was limited since attorney's fees had not been available to parents when the board accepted EHA funds. It also claimed that the parents were too late in filing their request for attorney's fees. Finally, it contended that the HCPA only provided for an award of attorney's fees to parties who prevailed in court proceedings as opposed to those who prevailed in due process hearings.

Concerning the school board's separation of powers argument, the court observed that here the law was changed only generally. Although the change had broad application, it only affected this case incidentally (i.e. attorney's fees, not the decision itself). The court held that the only limitation on Congress' power to impose liabilities on federal aid recipients was that Congress must do so unambiguously as it did here. The court also concluded that the parents had requested attorney's fees three months after passage of the HCPA which was not an unreasonable period of time. Finally, the court held that the HCPA only clearly prohibited an award of attorney's fees when court-obtained relief was less than any settlement offer. It also noted that the HCPA provided for fee awards in "any action or proceeding," implying the possibility of fee recovery for due process hearings. The court therefore ordered that the parents recover attorney's fees. *School Bd. v. Malone*, 662 F.Supp. 999 (E.D.Va.1987).

The parents of two handicapped children in New Hampshire were successful in securing relief for their children in administrative due process hearings. After passage of the HCPA they requested payment of attorney's fees from the Manchester School District (MSD). MSD refused and the parents sued MSD in U.S. district court. MSD moved for dismissal. The court observed that although the Supreme Court held in *Smith v. Robinson* that the EHA was the exclusive source of rights and remedies in special education cases, Congress effectively overruled *Smith v. Robinson* by passing the HCPA. It held that the HCPA permits a court to award attorney's fees for success at either the administrative or judicial level. MSD's motion to dismiss was denied, and the court held that it was liable for attorney's fees. *Burpee v. Manchester School Dist.*, 661 F.Supp. 731 (D.N.H.1987).

After the parents of four handicapped children were successful in challenging a decision by the New York Commissioner of Education to terminate their children's placement, they moved in a New York trial court for an order awarding attorney's fees under EHA § 1415(e)(4)(B). This subsection is part of the Handicapped Children's Protection Act of 1986. The commissioner contended that § 1415 did not authorize any fees in this case since the original lawsuit was not brought under it. Specifically, he claimed that the administrative action attacked in the original lawsuit did not involve a determination made by the commissioner after an appeal to him, but rather dealt with a claim that the commissioner's wrong interpretation of New York law was denying the students the placement they deserved under the EHA. Such a distinction required the denial of attorney's fees according to the commissioner.

The court disagreed, concluding that, because the commissioner had recognized from the outset of the original lawsuit (according to statements made by his attorney) that the theory behind the lawsuit was a violation of the EHA he was therefore liable for attorney's fees. The court also ruled that the EHA should be broadly construed to "effect its purpose of providing appropriate free public education for handicapped students" and that any remedy (including attorney's fees) which encouraged parents to protect the child's interests should be "viewed expansively." The trial court awarded attorney's fees to the parents. *Esther C. by Ephraim C. v. Ambach*, 515 N.Y.S.2d 997 (Sup.1987). Both parties then appealed the attorney's fee issue to the New York Supreme Court, Appellate Division, Third Department. The court noted that Congress enacted the Handicapped Children's Protection Act (HCPA) specifically to award attorney's fees to parents prevailing in EHA lawsuits. Although the trial court had awarded over $11,000 in attorney's fees to the parents, it had awarded only $750 for its appeal to the court for attorney's fees despite the parents' allegation that their attorneys had worked over thirty hours on the application. The appellate division court assessed the trial court's determination of a $90 hourly rate as reasonable and modified the trial court's decision to reflect attorney's fees on that basis. The appellate court remanded the case to the trial court for further proceedings to determine appropriate attorney's fees. *Esther C. by Ephraim C. v. Ambach*, 535 N.Y.S.2d 462 (A.D.3d Dep't 1988).

At least one federal court has held that attorney's fees are not recoverable for those who prevail at the administrative level. A U.S. district court held that the Delaware State Board of Education was liable for attorney's fees to the parents of a handicapped child whose private school placement had been wrongly changed to a public school. It also ruled that the local board of education was not liable for attorney's fees since the parents had not prevailed against it in a court proceeding. The parents moved for reargument contending that in enacting the HCPA, Congress intended to permit attorney's fees for plaintiffs who prevailed in due process hearings. Specifically, the parents argued that legislative history and case law mandated that plaintiffs who prevailed in due process hearings under the EHA may bring a lawsuit for the sole purpose of recovering attorney's fees.

The district court disagreed citing two reasons for its decision. First, it noted that in cases involving other federal civil rights laws, the U.S. Supreme Court has held that plaintiffs may not recover fees for prevailing in administrative hearings. Second, the parents in the present case had not succeeded on any significant issue in the due process hearings. Nothing in the record suggested that the parents had sought or had benefited from the prospective change in procedures ordered by the due process hearing officer or that any attorney time was spent on that issue. The district court denied the parents' motion for reargument. *Rollison v. Biggs*, 660 F.Supp. 875 (D.Del.1987).

A New Jersey special education lay advocate sued the New Jersey State Board of Education in a U.S. district court. She sought compensation for her services. The court held that she was not entitled to compensation for her services as a lay advocate in due process hearings under the EHA. She then appealed to the U.S. Court of Appeals, Third Circuit.

On appeal she contended that the EHA preempted a New Jersey Court Rule which required that lay advocates represent the handicapped free of charge. The no-fee provision was preempted because it hindered the fulfillment of the goals set out by Congress in the EHA. The advocate argued that because the EHA gave parents the right to representation by lay advocates, Congress intended that lay advocates charge fees. She also claimed that the no-fee provision violated her rights under the Equal Protection Clause of the U.S. Constitution.

The court of appeals upheld the district court decision. The EHA did not support the advocate's contention that Congress intended no distinction between lay advocates and attorneys. The EHA, which permitted a prevailing party to recover attorney's fees, contained no express provision granting fees to lay advocates.

The advocate's equal protection argument failed because the court found the New Jersey no-fee provision rationally related to New Jersey's interest in maintaining high ethical and fiduciary standards among attorneys. According to the court, permitting lay advocates to charge fees for their representation would likely encourage an abundance of unlicensed legal practitioners to the detriment of the public. *Arons v. New Jersey State Bd. of Educ.*, 842 F.2d 58 (3d Cir.1988).

CHAPTER SEVEN
SCHOOL LIABILITY

I. LIABILITY FOR INJURIES

Courts have generally held schools and their agents liable for injuries received by disabled students during the course of the regular school day which resulted from the schools' or their agents' failure to provide a reasonably safe environment, failure to warn participants of known hazards or to remove known dangers where possible, failure to properly instruct participants in an activity, or failure to provide supervision adequate for the type of activity, the ages of the participants involved and their physical and mental capabilities.

A. Negligent Supervision

A twenty-one-year-old mentally disabled Tennessee student traveled regularly with his class to the YMCA to use its swimming pool. The trips were supervised by a teacher and an aide, both school employees, and while at the pool, by a YMCA lifeguard. Some of the trips involved Special Olympics training. The student's mother had signed a document which released county employees from liability as a result of any injuries that might occur in connection with the Special Olympics Program. Near the end of a training excursion at the YMCA, the teacher instructed all of the students to get out of the pool. No one saw the student exit from the pool and he was later found on the floor of the pool. The lifeguard revived the student and he was taken to the hospital. The student suffered injuries and incurred medical expenses as a result of the incident. The student and his parents sued the county and the county board of education in a Tennessee trial court alleging negligent student supervision. The trial court found for the county. The student and his parents appealed to the Court of Appeals of Tennessee.

The court of appeals held that the county was negligent in failing to adequately supervise the student. The evidence indicated that neither the teacher, aide or lifeguard were watching the student after he was told to get out of the pool. The court also found that the release signed by the mother relieved the county of liability, but did not waive the student's rights. Under state law a guardian cannot waive the rights of an infant or incompetent. The student's mother could not execute a valid release of the rights of her son against the Special Olympics or anyone else. The court of appeals ruled the release void and remanded the case for further proceedings. *Childress v. Madison County*, 777 S.W.2d 1 (Tenn.App.1989).

In a similar case involving negligent supervision, a Florida man was instructed by school administrators to enroll his nine-year-old son in a particular elementary school for special speech therapy classes. The district promised the man that bus transportation would be provided for the child. The bus transportation did not materialize so the man took his son to a public bus stop. After two weeks the man let the child go to the bus stop alone and the child was killed while crossing an intersection. The man sued the school, asserting that it had negligently supervised his son. The court granted summary judgment for the school because the parent had also failed to supervise his son. The father appealed to the Court of Appeal of Florida.

On appeal, the issue was whether the school could be held liable for negligent supervision even if the father was found to be negligent. The court of appeal reversed and ordered a trial since the failure of the man to supervise his son could not preclude liability for negligent supervision on the part of the school district. *Brunson v. Dade County Sch. Bd.*, 559 So.2d 646 (Fla. App.3d Dist.1990).

An Illinois student suffered from spinal muscle atrophy with scoliosis and was confined to a wheelchair. She attended a school which was owned and operated by the school district. Across the street from the school was the school's playground which the district also controlled and maintained. While being transported in her wheelchair by a classmate on a walkway between the school and the playground, the student's chair hit a crevice. The student was thrown on the pavement and was injured. Although the student's parents had advised the district to always secure the student in the wheelchair they had provided, the student's seatbelt had not been fastened. The student sued the school district and the city in an Illinois trial court alleging that the district had negligently failed to provide adequate equipment and that it was guilty of wilful and wanton misconduct. The student also claimed that the city had been negligent in failing to keep the walkway in a reasonably safe condition. The city filed a counterclaim against the school district for contribution. The trial court dismissed the student's claim against the school district and the city's counterclaim for contribution. The student and the city appealed to the Appellate Court of Illinois, Fifth Circuit.

The appellate court held that the student had a claim against the district based on the district's alleged failure to furnish adequate equipment. If the equipment provided by the parents was not adequate for a particular activity, the district was required to provide alternative adequate equipment. The appellate court also ruled that the trial court erred when it dismissed the claim based on wilful and wanton misconduct. The district had been notified that the student must be fastened in her wheelchair whenever she was moved. The district, however, had allowed the student to be pushed by a classmate without being secured with the seatbelt. The court also found that the city's allegations sufficiently alleged a cause of action for contribution based on the district's wilful and wanton misconduct. The appellate court reversed the trial court's decision and remanded for further proceedings. *Bertetto v. Sparta Comm. Unit Dist. 140*, 544 N.E.2d 1140 (Ill.App.5th Dist.1989).

In a case arising in the state of Washington, a mentally handicapped high school student was seriously burned during metal shop class. The eighteen-year-old student's shirt had ignited while he stood with his back to the forge. He sued the school district and shop instructor for his injuries, claiming negligent supervision. At trial, the evidence established that the student had a mental age of eleven. He sought a jury instruction that he should only be held to the standard of care of a child. The trial judge instead instructed the jury that the student should be held to the standard of care of any reasonable person. The jury reached a verdict in favor of the student, awarding him $50,000 in damages for his injuries. However, based upon the "reasonable person" standard of care, the jury also found that the student had been seventy percent contributorily negligent, which reduced his damages to $15,000. The student appealed, seeking a new trial on the issue of damages.

The Washington Court of Appeals ruled against the student, stating that the trial judge's instruction to the jury was correct and hence the reduction of the damage award was proper. Although he had a mental age of eleven, holding him to the reduced standard of care of a child would have been improper in light of the following Washington statute: "Except as otherwise provided by law, all persons should be deemed and taken to be of full age for all purposes at the age of eighteen years." Because the student had already reached the chronological age of eighteen, he was not entitled to a jury instruction imposing only the standard of care of a child. The reduction of the damage award to $15,000 due to the student's contributory negligence was affirmed. *Higgins v. East Valley School Dist.*, 704 P.2d 630 (Wash.App. 1985).

A twelve-year-old student enrolled in a school for trainable mentally retarded children was discovered during recess lying face down at the foot of a set of steps leading back into the school's classrooms. As a result of his probable fall, the student suffered extensive head injuries. He sued the New York board of education and his teacher, whom he alleged negligently failed to supervise the children in her care. The teacher testified before the trial court that she was aware of the student's perceptual motor difficulties and poor eye-hand coordination. She also testified that the student and another boy with whom he had been running on the day of the accident often played a chasing game called "monster" during recess. An expert witness testified that purposeless, "freestyle" running during school hours was dangerous and should never be permitted for any child, and was especially hazardous where mentally retarded children were concerned. She further testified that the proper procedure for a teacher to follow under the circumstances would have been to stop the children either by word or physical act. The trial court held that the school board was liable for damages for personal injuries the child suffered. The school board appealed to the New York Supreme Court, Appellate Division, which held that the student had established a *prima facie* case of negligence on the part of the teacher for failing to supervise her students. The trial court ruling was affirmed. *Rodriguez v. Bd. of Educ., City of New York*, 480 N.Y.S.2d 901 (A.D.2d Dept.1984).

Schools may be found liable for injuries caused by the criminal acts of others where supervision is inadequate. A nineteen-year-old mentally retarded student, who functioned at a five-year-old level, was a student at a Louisiana residential training school operated by a Roman Catholic diocese. The girl participated in a co-educational training program for mentally handicapped students offered at a nearby parish school. When at the parish school, the students were under the supervision of the school's employees and took regularly scheduled breaks. At the beginning of a break, the boys and girls were taken separately to the bathroom and were supposed to be under constant supervision. One afternoon after assembling the boys for a break, the boy's supervisor left and went to the office which had a glass wall to allow observation. When he looked back, he noticed two of the boys missing. He found one of the students guarding a door and the other inside leaning over the nineteen-year-old girl with his pants down. The girl was returned to the residence home and examined by a nurse who did not check for signs of sexual activity. After the girl's guardians removed her from the home a few weeks later, she was withdrawn, seemed afraid of men, had nightmares, crying spells, and suffered a loss of appetite. As a result, the girl's guardians sought counseling for her. The guardians then filed this suit against the parish school board, the residence training school and the Roman Catholic diocese in a state trial court for the costs of the counseling and other damages. The trial judge dismissed the claims because the guardians had failed to prove sexual intercourse occurred. The guardians appealed to the Court of Appeal of Louisiana.

The appellate court disagreed, stating that it was not necessary to prove actual intercourse under a negligence theory. The guardians only needed to prove that as a result of the defendants' negligence the girl suffered harm. The guardians met this requirement because the symptoms occurred after the incident. The court reversed the trial court's decision and found the parish school board negligent. The appellate court affirmed the trial court's decision with respect to the training school and the Roman Catholic diocese because they were not the cause of the girl's injuries. *Guidry v. Parish School Bd.*, 560 So.2d 125 (La.App.3d Cir.1990).

An emotionally handicapped male student at a Florida public school was mixed with regular students in a shop class as part of the federal mainstreaming requirement. On a day when a substitute teacher was entrusted with supervision of the shop class the student was sexually assaulted in class by another student. The assailant was a youth who was known by school officials to be prone to sexually assaultive behavior. The handicapped student was forced into performing oral sex on the assailant for ten minutes at the rear of the classroom. The substitute teacher claimed that he was unaware of this incident but that he had been diligently monitoring the classroom at the time of the assault. The assaulted student sued the school district in state court contending that the district had breached its duty of reasonable care owed to him. The jury found in favor of the student. However, the trial judge threw out the verdict and the student appealed. The Florida District Court of Appeal reversed the trial judge and reinstated the jury verdict in favor of the student. Only when there is no evidence upon which a jury could properly rely should its verdict be set aside. The case was remanded to the trial court with orders to reinstate the jury verdict and to act on other post-trial motions. *Collins v. School Bd. of Broward County,* 471 So.2d 560 (Fla.App.4th Dist.1985).

Several Missouri handicapped students complained to their school district that their bus driver had physically and sexually abused them. They sued the district in a Missouri federal district court for violating their constitutional right to privacy and bodily security. They alleged that the district failed to take sufficient action to prevent the bus driver from continuing his abusive behavior. The district sought to have the suit dismissed by claiming that district officials had not been deliberately indifferent to the driver's acts. Nor did the district have a policy of ignoring and failing to act upon these types of complaints.

In considering the dismissal motion the court noted that the district's negligence in supervision was not sufficient to establish liability. It also noted that in order to impose personal liability on district officials, students would have to show that the officials were personally involved in the violation. The students asserted that the officials' inaction made them liable. The officials argued that their failure to act did not amount to a deliberate indifference or to tacit authorization of the alleged abuse. The court determined that most of the complaints failed to establish the necessary pattern of unconstitutional conduct. The court also noted that the officials responded to the complaints by questioning the bus driver and counseling him about physical interaction with children. The court dismissed the case against the officials in their individual capacities and the suit against the district. The students failed to show that the district had an official policy or custom which led to the harm caused. Thus, the school district's dismissal motion was granted. *Jane Doe (A) v. Special School Dist. of St. Louis County,* 682 F.Supp. 451 (E.D.Mo. 1988).

The parents appealed to the U.S. Court of Appeals, Eighth Circuit. They contended that the school district's official policy did not allow the officials to adequately investigate prior complaints of the bus driver's conduct. The court, however, determined that the school district did not have any knowledge of, nor had the district been indifferent to, the rights of the handicapped children. The parents further contended that the individual defendants failed to adequately respond to a known risk of physical and emotional harm by the bus driver. Individual defendants will be subject to liability only if it can be proven that they received notice, demonstrated indifference, failed to take sufficient action and that such failure caused the injury to the children. The court determined that the evidence did not support a finding that the individual defendants had notice of a pattern of unlawful acts by the bus driver. The school district and its officials were at most guilty of negligence. The court of appeals affirmed the trial court's decision, granting summary judgment to the school district. *Jane Doe A v. Special School District,* 901 F.2d 642 (8th Cir.1990).

Liability may also arise from a school's failure to detect or treat students' injuries. In a New York case, a fourteen-year-old deaf girl contracted rheumatic fever while attending a summer camp operated by the National Council of Beth Jacob Schools. Due to the camp's negligence, the girl's disease was neither detected nor treated until she returned home at the end of the summer. As a result, she developed polyarthritis, an enlarged heart, a heart murmur and a leakage of her aortic valve. The girl was forced to miss two and one-half months of school. At the time the case went to trial (three years after she contracted the disease) the girl tired easily and had a susceptibility to heart problems. Her medical expenses totaled $2,900. The trial court, sitting without a jury, awarded the girl $30,000 in damages and her mother $2,000. The girl's mother appealed, contending that the trial court's award of damages was insufficient. The New York Supreme Court, Appellate Division, noted that under state law, nonjury damage awards are freely reviewable by an appellate court. It agreed with the mother's contentions and modified the award to $50,000 for the child and $5,000 for the mother. The appellate court reasoned that the trial court's award was inadequate because the child, who already had been afflicted with one handicap, now had to deal with a heart condition that showed no signs of improving. *Berman v. Nat'l Council of Beth Jacob Schools, Inc.,* 501 N.Y.S.2d 413 (A.D.2d Dept.1986).

A nineteen-year-old New York student was injured while participating in a work study program. The student was learning disabled and his mother persuaded him to join a work study program so that he would have enough credits to graduate. He worked with lumber under the direct supervision of a company. During his work study the student severed two of his fingers and injured a third one when using a saw he was familiar with. Alleging negligent supervision, the student sued the school in a New York trial court.

The school asserted that it had no duty to exercise control over the student because he was of majority age and because his mother encouraged him to participate in the program. The New York state court held that schools were not insurers for the safety of students. Further, the court stated that a less demanding standard of reasonable care was warranted when a student was nineteen years old. The court also stated that there was no evidence that any of the machinery was unfit. Thus, the trial court ruled in favor of the school. *Kennedy v. Waterville Cent. Sch. Dist.,* 555 N.Y.S.2d 224 (Sup.1990).

A Louisiana student attended a school for the mentally handicapped. While walking toward his bus, the student was struck in the jaw by another student who was a foster child in the custody of the Louisiana Department of Health and Human Resources (DHHR). Upon arriving at home, the student began to experience pain in his jawbone which subsequently required surgery. The student sued the state of Louisiana, through the DHHR, its insurer, the school board and the foster child. A Louisiana trial court directed a verdict for the state and the school board. The student then appealed to the Court of Appeal of Louisiana, Third Circuit.

On appeal, the student argued that the DHHR and its insurer were strictly liable for the foster child and that the school board, through its employees, negligently failed to supervise the bus loading procedures. The court found that the state was not strictly liable. There was no language under state law which suggested that the state could be held strictly liable for the acts of a foster child. The court also found that the school board was not negligent in failing to prevent the foster child from striking the student. The incident was of a sudden and unforeseeable nature and therefore unavoidable. There was no reason to anticipate any trouble between the two students. Because the altercation happened so quickly teachers who were assigned to supervise the boarding of the buses were unable to prevent the injury. The spontaneous, unpredictable act of the foster child did not create liability on behalf of the school board or its employees. The court of appeal affirmed the trial court's decision. *Gooden v. State DHHR*, 546 So.2d 279 (La.App.3d Cir.1989).

A New York school for self-sufficient mentally retarded adults operated daily weekday sessions from 8:00 a.m. to 3:00 p.m. The school was not responsible for its students' travel arrangements. At the end of the day the students would walk one block to the public bus stop. While at the bus stop, one student pushed another student into a pedestrian. The pedestrian was seriously injured and sued the school in a New York trial court to recover damages.

The pedestrian contended that the school was negligent in its failure to supervise the activities of its students. The school moved for summary judgment, arguing that its duty to third parties for the activities of its students ceased at the end of the school day. The court held that the school was not liable to the pedestrian. It noted that a school's duty to supervise students terminated once the students were outside the school's control. Once the school had discharged the students it no longer had physical control and thus owed no duty to the pedestrian. The court entered summary judgment for the school. *Bodaness v. Staten Island Aid*, 544 N.Y.S.2d 115 (Sup.1989).

In a Pennsylvania case, the mother of a nine-year-old diabetic fifth grade girl met with the nurse at her daughter's elementary school. She explained the nature of her daughter's medical condition to the school nurse, and she and the nurse distributed written materials to school personnel describing the special care she needed. One day approximately three months later, while attending reading class, the student had a hypoglycemic reaction. She informed her reading class teacher that she needed to see the school nurse. The teacher refused to allow her to leave the room until class was over nearly forty-five minutes later.

By the time the student reached the nurses' office, she was having difficulty maintaining consciousness and was unable to inform the nurse that she needed her medication. She received no medical care for nearly two hours. Eventually school officials contacted her grandmother, who instructed them to take the girl to a hospital. She was in the hospital for six days.

The student sued the school district, the elementary school's principal, the nurse and the reading class teacher in U.S. district court under § 1983 of the federal Civil Rights Act. She claimed that the defendants had deprived her of needed medical attention in violation of the Fourteenth Amendment's Equal Protection and Due Process clauses, as well as the EHA. The defendants asked the court to dismiss the student's claims.

First, the court held that because the school officials had not been acting pursuant to any established school district policy on the day of the incident, the school district itself could not be held liable under § 1983.

Second, the girl's Equal Protection Clause claim was dismissed because, with regard to handicapped students, all equal protection claims are subsumed within the EHA.

Third, the court dismissed the student's due process claim. It held that even though she had a constitutional right to be free of interference by school officials in seeking needed medical attention, § 1983 was of no help to her. This was because imposing "additional administrative safeguards as a constitutional requirement would significantly intrude into the area of educational responsibility that lies primarily with public school authorities." The court stated that rather than attempting to prove a violation of her constitutional rights, the student should have relied upon traditional state common-law negligence principles.

Finally, the court dismissed her EHA claims, pointing out that she had proceeded directly to federal court and had bypassed the administrative remedies set forth in the EHA. Concluding that this was impermissible, the court dismissed the entire lawsuit. *DeFalco v. Deer Lake School Dist.*, 663 F.Supp. 1108 (W.D.Pa.1987).

A severely handicapped New York infant was placed on a bus equipped for handicapped children and then taken to a school for mentally retarded children. Although the child could not communicate by speech, he cried or whined when he was in pain. On the day in question, the child did not cry or whine either in school or on the bus. However, when the mother put the infant to bed right after he returned from school, she noticed that the child had a broken leg. She sued the school district and the bus company in a New York trial court alleging negligence in her son's care. The defendants moved to dismiss the complaint.

The mother relied on a legal principle (res ipsa loquitur) that allows recovery for negligence even if one cannot point to the exact person or persons responsible for the negligence. The three requirements which must be proved are as follows: the event must be of a kind which ordinarily does not occur in the absence of negligence, it must be caused by an agency or instrumentality (i.e. source of injury) within the exclusive control of the defendant, and it must not have been due to any voluntary action or contribution on the part of the injured plaintiff. Although the mother met the first and third requirements, she did not meet the second. The court noted that in this case neither the injury nor the circumstances pointed to the instrumentality. Therefore, in the absence of proof of negligence, the mother could not recover and the trial court dismissed the case. *Rabena v. City of New York*, 556 N.Y.S.2d 807 (N.Y.C.Civ.Ct.1990).

A quadriplegic student at the Southwest Louisiana State School brought a negligence lawsuit against the school after suffering a spiral-type fracture of his right femur. On the morning of the injury the student's mother bathed him, fed him and strapped him into his wheelchair. She then gave him his usual dosage of phenobarbital. The school bus arrived and he was wheeled out to meet it without apparent incident. The bus driver testified that the student was in his usual good spirits as he transported him to the State School. He said that he strapped the student's wheelchair down securely that morning. Upon his arrival at the State School, the student, who weighed only thirty-two pounds, was wheeled into class where two of his instructors noticed that he was "crying and fussing." They sought to alleviate his discomfort by placing him on a mat. When this proved unsuccessful, one instructor lifted him off the mat and placed him on a table. She testified that as she did so, she heard a loud "pop." The student was immediately taken to a doctor, and the spiral fracture was diagnosed. He was hospitalized for three weeks and he recovered completely. Believing that the State School and its employees had somehow been negligent, causing the student's injury, his parents brought a lawsuit in state district court. They pointed to a statement one of the teachers had made immediately after taking the student to the doctor. She had said that she did not understand how the student's leg could have broken unless she had accidently knelt on it.

However, evidence was also presented of an incident which occurred one year after the original fracture. The student, while strapped in his wheelchair at home, became excited and pushed his leg until it became caught in the chair, then twisted it, causing the same type of spiral fracture as had occurred the previous year. He was using the same wheelchair at the time of this later incident. In light of this evidence, the district court ruled in favor of the State School and its employees, stating that a number of other explanations existed for the student's injury besides negligence on the part of a State School employee. On appeal by the parents, the Louisiana Court of Appeal upheld this ruling. Stated the court: "The mere fact that an accident occurred does not necessarily mean that someone was negligent." The court held that the parents had failed to meet their burden of proving by a preponderance of the evidence that a State School employee had caused their son's injury. *Henry v. State*, 482 So.2d 962 (La.App.3d Cir.1986).

B. Negligent Placement

In a Maryland case, as part of a handicapped female student's new IEP she was placed in a regular eighth grade physical education class, with no restrictions placed upon her participation. Her parents failed to express any dissatisfaction or challenge this new IEP. Midway through the school year she was seriously injured while maneuvering on a "Swedish Box." Her parents filed suit in state court against the school board and the physical education teacher, claiming that they had been negligent in placing the student in a regular physical education class without adequate safeguards. The parent's complaint did not allege negligent supervision, but negligent placement in the class.

The circuit court ruled that the parents could not base their lawsuit on negligent placement. The parents had not contested the revised IEP when it was initially implemented, and thus they were barred from contesting it now in a civil lawsuit. The court's ruling was based on the elaborate state procedural system through which disputes over special education placements could be contested. The parents had not availed themselves of this system and the circuit court refused to allow the parents to do in a civil lawsuit what they should have done through established procedures. This ruling effectively destroyed the parents' case since they would now have to prove that the teacher failed to use "reasonable care" in supervising the student. The circuit court therefore rendered a decision in favor of the school board and teacher.

The parents appealed to the Maryland Court of Special Appeals, which affirmed the circuit court decision. When the parents failed to contest the

IEP which placed the student in the regular physical education class, they placed her in the same legal position as any other student in the class and no suit for "negligent placement" would be possible. Because the parents were unable to prove that the teacher had failed to exercise reasonable care in the supervision of the student the appeals court upheld the lower court's ruling against the parents. *Alban v. Bd. of Educ. of Harford County*, 494 A.2d 745 (Md.App.1985).

In a New York case, a severely disabled individual sustained serious injuries after being placed in a residential facility. Suit was brought on his behalf, alleging negligence on the part of the facility's employees. The suit alleged that employees at the residential facility had allowed the individual to participate in a normalization program designed to allow familiarization with tasks of daily living. During the program he accidently overturned a covered pot of hot water used to demonstrate the preparation of tea and coffee, causing him to be severely burned.

Reversing a lower court, the New York Court of Appeals dismissed the claim that employees had negligently placed him in the therapy program, stating that the decision to place him in the program involved medical judgment for which no liability could be imposed. The lower court's ruling that the use of a covered pot of hot water to instruct severely disabled persons was so negligent that a trial was not even necessary was reversed by the Court of Appeals, which stated that while a residential facility owes a duty of reasonable care to severely disabled persons, it is not required to maintain constant surveillance of each individual. After noting that "there are certain risks inherent in any therapeutic program, especially, as in this case, one which is designed to provide a normal homelike setting," the Court of Appeals remanded the case to the lower court for reconsideration of whether the lawsuit should be allowed to proceed. *Killen v. State*, 498 N.Y.S.2d 358 (1985).

The Supreme Court of Montana affirmed the dismissal of a lawsuit for wrongful placement in a special education program. The suit was brought in 1980 by a student against her school board and various state and local officials, alleging that she had suffered irreparable emotional harm as a result of her placement in 1973 in a special education program. The evidence showed that she was required to repeat a year of school, was called a "retard" and was taunted about flunking. When the trial court dismissed the case the student appealed. The Supreme Court of Montana upheld the trial court's decision, stating that insufficient evidence had been presented to prove that the student had suffered compensable emotional damage. In a suit for wrongful placement, expert testimony was necessary to prove that emotional harm had occurred. Because the only evidence offered to the trial court was the testimony of the student and her mother, the suit was properly dismissed. *Berger v. State*, 698 P.2d 399 (Mont.1985).

The mother of a blind, deaf and mute student in the District of Columbia, who had been sexually assaulted by the coordinator of a program for blind and deaf students, sued the coordinator and the District of Columbia. She contended that the district was liable for damages arising from the assault on her daughter due to the district's negligence in hiring or failing to supervise the coordinator. The District of Columbia Court of Appeals affirmed a trial court ruling in favor of the school district. The court of appeals found that although an employer may be held liable for the acts of employees committed within the scope of their employment, there was no showing that the coordinator's assault of the child was within that scope.

The court rejected the mother's argument that the assault was a direct result of the coordinator's job assignment since his employment necessarily included some physical contact with the child. The mother argued that a deaf, blind and mute child can be taught only through the sense of touch and, therefore, the fact that physical touching was necessarily a part of the teacher-student relationship made it foreseeable that sexual assaults would occur. The court found that a sexual assault cannot be deemed a direct result of a school official's authorization to take a student by the hand or arm in guiding her past obstacles in the building. Here, the attack was "unprovoked," had not arisen from the coordinator's instructions or job assignment and was not an integral part of the school's activities, interests or objectives. The coordinator's acts could not be viewed as being within the scope of his employment, and thus the school district was not liable. *Boykin v. Dist. of Columbia*, 484 A.2d 560 (D.C.App.1984).

II. GOVERNMENTAL IMMUNITY

Governmental immunity is a doctrine which prohibits a lawsuit against any governmental entity or its officials. The doctrine, which has its roots deep in Anglo-American common law, has suffered a great decline in the last century. While some states retain the doctrine in full force, others have partially or completely eliminated it by legislative or judicial decision. Congress has at least partially authorized lawsuits against the U.S. Government through passage of the Federal Tort Claims Act.

A. Eleventh Amendment Immunity

Where a lawsuit is brought against state officials in *federal* court, the Eleventh Amendment to the U.S. Constitution comes into play. Generally, a private citizen is barred by the Eleventh Amendment from seeking in federal court an award of money damages against a state or against state officials in their official capacities. However, the federal courts may issue injunctions ordering states and state officials to conform their future conduct to the dictates of federal law; this is known as "prospective relief" and is not barred by the Eleventh Amendment.

Local political subdivisions, unlike states and official state departments, are fully subject to lawsuits brought by private citizens in federal court because they are not considered "states" under the Eleventh Amendment. Further, the Eleventh Amendment is inapplicable to suits brought by the federal government against a state, and is inapplicable to any lawsuit brought in a state court.

In 1989, the Supreme Court ruled that while local school districts could be sued under the EHA, states were immune from EHA liability under the Eleventh Amendment. A handicapped student with a language learning disability and emotional problems was enrolled in a Pennsylvania public school. His father requested an administrative hearing to challenge the student's individualized education program (IEP). Meanwhile, the father enrolled the student in a private school for learning disabled students. The hearing examiner determined that the original IEP was inappropriate. The school district and father both appealed to the Pennsylvania Secretary of Education, which remanded the case to the hearing officer with instructions to revise the IEP. After the revisions were made, the hearing officer determined that the revised IEP was appropriate. The secretary affirmed this decision.

The father sued the school district and the secretary of education in a federal district court. He contended that the district's revised IEP was inappropriate and that the state's administrative proceedings violated the EHA because the secretary had not been impartial and extensive delays had occurred because of the remand. The court ruled in the father's favor, stating that he was entitled to reimbursement for the student's private school tuition plus attorney's fees. The court determined that the Commonwealth of Pennsylvania, as well as the school district, were jointly and severally liable under the EHA. According to the court, the EHA abrogated the state's Eleventh Amendment immunity from damage suits.

The secretary appealed to the U.S. Court of Appeals, Third Circuit. The court affirmed the district court's decision and the secretary appealed to the U.S. Supreme Court, which agreed to hear the case. The Court noted that Congress does not abrogate sovereign immunity unless it specifically states so within a legislative act. The EHA did not specify an intent to abrogate state immunity from lawsuit. Although the Handicapped Children's Protection Act, a 1986 amendment to the EHA, specifically provided for reduction of attorney's fees if the state or local educational agency unreasonably protracts the resolution of an EHA action, the EHA did not itself state an intent to abrogate sovereign immunity. The Eleventh Amendment barred the father's attempt to collect tuition reimbursement from the Commonwealth of Pennsylvania. The Court reversed and remanded the court of appeals' decision. *Dellmuth v. Muth*, 109 S.Ct. 2397 (1989).

However, the Eleventh Amendment does not bar claims against state officials in their individual capacities. A New York paraplegic student had been a client of the Office of Vocational Rehabilitation (OVR). OVR operated rehabilitation programs established under the Federal Vocational Rehabilitation Act of 1983. The purpose of the Act was the development and implementation of programs of vocational rehabilitation for disabled individuals, designed to help them obtain employment. The Act required states receiving funding under the Act to develop an individualized written rehabilitation program (IWRP) for each person in the program. The IWRP was to be tailored to each client's individual needs and potential with an emphasis placed on the determination and achievement of a vocational goal. The student maintained that since his IWRP had employment as a practicing attorney as his goal, the OVR should have funded his higher education, including law school. The OVR funded the student's undergraduate tuition and living expenses. However, during law school the OVR then limited its expenditures on behalf of each of its clients to $1,500 for tuition and $1,300 for maintenance per year. As a result, the student had to borrow more than $25,000 to cover the costs of law school. The student then commenced this action based on his belief that the OVR was required to individualize service to rehabilitation clients. He sued the state agency and state officials in a federal district court claiming an equal protection violation of the Rehabilitation Act and a violation of § 1983 of the Civil Rights Act. After the defendants moved to dismiss the action, the motion was referred to a magistrate for a recommendation.

The magistrate determined that all claims but the § 1983 claim against the individual defendants were barred by the Eleventh Amendment. Under the Eleventh Amendment, a private person may not sue a state agency in a federal court. The court agreed with the magistrate's decision except that it determined that the other claims against the officials in their individual capacities did not constitute a suit against the state and were therefore not barred by the Eleventh Amendment. Accordingly, the trial court denied the motion to dismiss. *McGuire v. Switzer*, 734 F.Supp. 99 (S.D.N.Y.1990).

A Navajo student, suffering from severe arthritis, was confined to a wheelchair at the age of thirteen. She successfully completed her junior high school education without any delays resulting from her illness, and she then sought admission to the only high school in her neighborhood. The school was administered by the U.S. Bureau of Indian Affairs. School officials allegedly denied admission to the student for four consecutive academic years because the school's facilities could not accommodate her handicap. During her attempts to attend the local high school, she attended a high school ten miles away along poorly surfaced roads which, due to her severe arthritis, caused her great pain. The roads also became impassable in bad weather and the student eventually withdrew from school because of poor academic performance brought on by excessive absences. She then sued the federal school officials in an Arizona federal district court. The court ordered her admittance to the school and she finally graduated two years later than she should have. However, she continued her lawsuit against the officials, asserting claims under the Education of the Handicapped Act (EHA), under the Rehabilitation Act and under the Fifth Amendment due process clause.

The school officials sought to dismiss the student's claims on the grounds of sovereign immunity. Further, they argued that the Rehabilitation Act did not place the burden of making schools accessible on individual defendants. They also argued that the student's Fifth Amendment due process claim should be dismissed because the EHA was the student's exclusive remedy. The court, however, disagreed. It first stated that because the student sought damages against the officials in their individual rather than representative capacities, her claims were not directed against the United States. Thus, the officials were not entitled to sovereign immunity. The court also noted that congress had intended other claims to be pursued in conjunction with the EHA and that the student's constitutional claim should not be dismissed. However, the court noted that mere negligence would not be sufficient to hold the school officials liable under the due process clause. The court thus held that there were material questions of fact to be determined and denied the school officials' motion to dismiss the case. *Begay v. Hodel*, 730 F.Supp. 1001 (D.Ariz.1990).

A group of handicapped children and their parents brought suit against Oregon state and local education officials to enjoin their school district from discontinuing an educational program provided to handicapped children. A U.S. district court held in favor of the children and their parents, ruling that 1) the state defendants and, in particular, the Oregon Department of Education, were in violation of the EHA for failure to ensure that the plaintiffs would receive free appropriate public educations, and 2) the defendant school districts were not in violation of the EHA because they had no legal responsibility under Oregon law to provide the plaintiffs with free appropriate public educations under the EHA. The court also stated that in deference to the Oregon legislature, which has the responsibility and the expertise to resolve the problem, it would decline at that time to consider the remedy of injunctive relief, but it did enter a temporary, ninety-day injunction pursuant to the consent of all parties. The court further stated that during that ninety-day period the parties should meet and attempt to agree upon a plan to resolve the dispute. It then said that at the end of ninety days, if the matter had not been resolved, it would make a further determination as to what steps and procedures should then be taken.

Because no agreement was reached between the parties at the end of ninety days, a supplemental opinion was then issued by the court, which addressed the Eleventh Amendment issue and forced action upon the parties. The Eleventh Amendment issue was raised by the state of Oregon, which claimed absolute immunity from suit under that amendment. However, the court observed that the EHA had been enacted pursuant to § 5 of the Fourteenth Amendment, and thus constituted a congressional abrogation of Oregon's immunity from suit in federal court. Since the Eleventh Amendment did not bar suit and in light of the court's earlier ruling, the court held that the state of Oregon's receipt of federal funds for assistance in educating the plaintiffs required the state to comply with its part of the bargain—namely, to provide sufficient funds to cover the full cost of their educations. Budgetary constraints could not excuse the state from the obligations arising from the acceptance of federal funds. In other words, the Oregon legislature could not refuse or neglect to enact a legislative program—in whatever manner it should deem to be appropriate—to provide funding for the full cost of the plaintiffs' educations. The court ordered the parties to act in accordance with its decision. *Kerr Center Parents Ass'n v. Charles*, 581 F.Supp. 166 (D.Or. 1983).

The state of Oregon then appealed to the U.S. Court of Appeals, Ninth Circuit. The appeals court rejected the state's argument that the students were unilaterally placed at the private facility. Although the students were placed at the facility for medical, not educational reasons, their placement was not unrelated to the goal of providing them a free appropriate education. In conclusion, the appeals court agreed that the school district could not provide the required education unless the state department of education provided it with appropriate funds. In turn, the education department could not fulfill its responsibility unless the state legislature adequately funded handicapped students' education. Because of a "subject to the availability of funds" clause, the legislature was free to provide adequate funding however it saw fit. But it could not refuse to appropriate sufficient funds to meet that responsibility. The appeals court sent the case back to the district court to determine if the state was immune from liability. If the state did not have immunity, it would have to provide sufficient funding for the students. *Kerr Center Parents Assoc. v. Charles*, 842 F.2d 1052 (9th Cir.1988).

In an Illinois case, a handicapped student and his parents brought suit against the governor of Illinois and state and local education officials, charging violations of the officials' legal duties created by the child's condition as a handicapped child. The officials moved for partial dismissal of the parents' complaint on four grounds. First, argued the officials, there was no basis for joining the governor as a defendant. Nothing the governor does, continued the argument, is asserted to have caused the alleged harm suffered by the parents and the child. Second, the parents should not be allowed to assert a Rehabilitation Act claim, as this Act was not a predicate for the relief sought. Third, the parents should not be allowed to assert their state law claim under an Illinois statute governing identification, evaluation and placement of handicapped children in special education in light of the U.S. Supreme Court's recent decision interpreting the Eleventh Amendment, *Pennhurst State School & Hospital v. Halderman*, 104 S.Ct. 900 (1984). Fourth, the officials claimed that once the Rehabilitation Act claim was gone, their request for attorney's fees should vanish with it because the EHA does not embody such relief. A U.S. district court in Illinois agreed with the officials' arguments and granted all four of their requests. Thus, the parents were allowed to proceed with their complaint only as narrowed. *Hayward v. Thompson*, 593 F.Supp, 57 (N.D.Ill.1984).

A U.S. district court in Wisconsin applied the doctrine of Eleventh Amendment governmental immunity in a claim against the Milwaukee public school system. A handicapped child brought suit in federal court against the school system on behalf of himself and all other similarly situated children in Milwaukee who were placed in day treatment facilities. After the state proposed termination of the day service placements, the parents of the children alleged that their children were being denied educational facilities in violation of the EHA. The court held that the parents' claim for damages against the Wisconsin state superintendent of public instruction was essentially a claim against state funds, and that no congressional authorization existed to abrogate the state's Eleventh Amendment immunity from retroactive monetary claims payable from the state treasury. However, the court did grant an injunction to the children against the superintendent of public instruction in her official capacity. The injunction restrained the Milwaukee public schools from terminating the current placement of the children and removing the children from those schools until completion of a full and impartial evaluation of their education needs. The injunction, said the court, was prospective in nature and thus was not barred by governmental immunity. *M.R. v. Milwaukee Public Schools*, 495 F.Supp. 864 (E.D.Wis.1980).

Georgia hearing procedures were successfully attacked by a handicapped child who, through her father, sued the Georgia Superintendent of the Georgia State Board of Education alleging that the procedures were in violation of the EHA. Specifically, the child alleged that in Georgia, the decision of a state educational agency, which should have been treated as final, was subject to "veto" by the state board of education. The U.S. Court of Appeals, Fifth Circuit, held that Eleventh Amendment immunity does not bar a federal court from enjoining state officials to conform their future conduct to the requirements of federal law. Accordingly, the state of Georgia was ordered to alter its procedures to conform to the provisions of the EHA, which provide that the decision of a state education agency is final. *Helms v. McDaniel*, 657 F.2d 800 (5th Cir.1981).

In a Michigan case, the parents of a handicapped child brought suit against a local school district alleging that the district had misdiagnosed their child's language impairment. The school district's motion for summary judgment was granted by the court on the ground that the school, in its operation of a speech therapy program, was involved in a government program and thus entitled to governmental immunity. In handing down its decision, the court outlined the guidelines it used in deciding whether a particular function is entitled to immunity. The court stated that it examines the precise activity giving rise to the plaintiff's claim, rather than the overall department operations. In this situation the examination and diagnosis of students in a public school was "intended to promote the general public health and [is] exercised for the common good of all." The court held, therefore, that the school district was immune from liability in performing the function. *Brosnan v. Livonia Pub. Schools*, 333 N.W.2d 288 (Mich.App.1983).

In a New Hampshire case, the parents of a handicapped child brought suit in federal court under the EHA seeking reimbursement for the cost of maintaining their child in a private residential facility. The federal judge certified two questions to the Supreme Court of New Hampshire: first, has that state waived its defense of sovereign immunity in cases involving tuition reimbursement for handicapped children, and second, has the state waived its privileges under the Eleventh Amendment to the U.S. Constitution, thus consenting to be sued in federal court? A unanimous supreme court answered both questions in the negative. As to the first question, the state of New Hampshire had implemented a program under the EHA by which its local school districts shouldered financial responsibility for the education of handicapped children. Thus, although a lawsuit against a school district could be brought in state or federal court, the state itself could not be named as a defendant.

As to the second question, the supreme court held that the state also could not be sued under the EHA in federal court. However, parents could bring a proceeding in federal court to review a state agency or court decision. The court explained that while New Hampshire had received federal funds under the EHA, the state had left the actual provision of special educational services to the local school districts. Therefore, the supreme court held that the state of New Hampshire had not become involved in the provision of special educational services to such an extent as to waive its immunity from suit in federal court. The case was sent back to the U.S. district court with both certified questions answered in the negative.

The U.S. district court however, decided to disregard the state supreme court's legal conclusions. Instead, it made the following observations. The parents' claim involved an alleged state violation of the EHA made under the authority of New Hampshire law. Congress has stated that the EHA's purpose was to assist states in providing appropriate educations to handicapped children. Congress then allowed a citizen to sue a state for violation of the EHA. Thus, the court ruled that because a citizen is allowed to file a suit against the state under the EHA, the citizen should also be allowed to file a claim under a state law passed to carry out the EHA's purposes. The federal district court ruled that the state was not immune from suit. *John H. v. Brunelle*, 631 F.Supp. 208 (D.N.H.1986).

B. Qualified Immunity

The doctrine of qualified immunity shields government officials, whether local, state or federal, from liability arising out of their discretionary acts. This immunity generally extends only to officials acting at the planning level, not the operational level.

A Connecticut eight-year-old suffered from a seizure disorder, learning disabilities and behavioral disturbances that rendered him handicapped within the meaning of the EHA. The student was admitted to the Greater Bridgeport Children's Services Center (GBCSC) for psychiatric treatment. In order to provide educational services to children residing in or receiving day treatment at the institution the state had established Unified School District No. 2, known as the family school. A child became eligible to attend the family school upon admission to GBCSC. Once the treatment team determined that a handicapped child no longer required GBCSC care, he was discharged and became ineligible for services from the family school. The student remained at the family school for the 1984-85 school year. He was discharged from the medical facility at the end of the school year and became ineligible for services at the family school. His parents then demanded an administrative hearing to review the discharge decision and requested that he be allowed to attend the family school pending the conclusion of the hearing. This request was denied and his parents filed a lawsuit alleging that the medical and school officials violated the student's rights under the EHA. The district court granted summary judgment to the defendants holding that, although the EHA was applicable to the family school, the defendants were entitled to qualified immunity. The district court also awarded the parents attorney's fees. Both parties appealed to the U.S. Court of Appeals, Second Circuit.

Government officials performing discretionary functions generally are shielded from liability for civil damages insofar as their conduct does not violate clearly established statutory or constitutional rights of which a reasonable person would have known. The defendants maintained that it was not clear when this action arose that the EHA applied to GBCSC discharge decisions. The court agreed. The court noted that the student's discharge was not from the family school but from the GBCSC, a medical facility. Therefore, the court determined that since the law was not clearly established at the time of the discharge the defendants were entitled to the protection of qualified immunity. The court, however, reversed the order for reimbursement of attorney's fees as the parents were not prevailing parties. *Christopher P. by Norma P. v. Marcus*, 915 F.2d 794 (2d Cir. 1990).

A mildly retarded Vermont young man had been in the custody of the state since the age of three. He had lived in nine foster homes and schools prior to turning eighteen. After his eighteenth birthday, he was placed under the guardianship of the Department of Mental Health (state). While in a foster home, the man threatened a member of the household with a screwdriver and then stayed away overnight. The caretakers notified the state that they could not handle the student and that he would have to leave within two days. The man was uncooperative, so the state ordered the police to transport the man pursuant to Vermont's emergency admissions procedure law. An administrative hearing was held to determine if the statutory requirements for short term emergency admission to the residential educational facility had been met. Admission was denied. Because the state did not have a residential placement available, he remained at the school for approximately two years. He received only sporadic educational services largely because he resisted attempts to develop an individual education program for him. This action was filed on his behalf seeking a declaratory judgment and injunction requiring state officials to place him in an appropriate, professionally supervised community facility and develop a long range treatment, residential and educational plan. The state officials moved to dismiss the case against them citing their qualified immunity. The federal district court denied the motion for summary judgment. The defendants then appealed to the U.S. Court of Appeals, Second Circuit.

Qualified immunity is the doctrine that shields government officials performing discretionary functions from liability for civil damages. The mentally retarded young man claimed that the EHA was violated because his ability to succeed educationally was linked to his residential placement and frequent changes in residence led to inconsistent and sporadic schooling that limited his ability to receive an appropriate education. In order to defeat a qualified immunity defense, the man was required to show that his right was clearly established. The court determined that it was not clearly established that state employees had any duty to provide a consistent residential placement. The EHA requires the local education agency to provide for appropriate education but makes no mention of any other state agencies or their possible duty. Therefore, the court of appeals granted qualified immunity to the defendants and reversed the district court's decision. *P.C. v. McLaughlin*, 913 F.2d 1033 (2d Cir. 1990).

An Indiana special education student was subjected to at least three incidents of sexual abuse by other students in her classes. The incidents occurred in separate years, culminating with an attempt by another student to have sexual intercourse with her on a field trip. The teacher in charge of the field trip had permitted the student to accompany three male students to the lavatory unsupervised. In both of the previous instances, the teacher had notified parents of the students involved, and in this case the teacher wrote letters to the students' parents and punished the students. The abused student was transferred to a private school by her parents the following year. None of the incidents were ever reported to the county welfare department or law enforcement agency. Indiana law directs individuals with knowledge that children are victims of abuse to make oral reports to local child protection or law enforcement agencies.

The student sued the school corporation, the teacher, the principal and other officials in an Indiana trial court for the expense of psychological counseling following the third incident. The school corporation initially responded with a request for a jury trial, then amended its answer with a motion for summary judgment. The student responded with a motion to strike the corporation's governmental immunity defense because it had not been raised in the initial answer. The court granted the school corporation's summary judgment motion as a final judgment in favor of the corporation and officials. The student appealed to the Indiana Court of Appeals, Third District.

The appeals court ruled that the student was not prejudiced by the corporation's failure to raise the affirmative defense of governmental immunity in its initial answer. It also rejected the student's argument that the corporation must be liable for the sexual abuse incidents because of its prior knowledge of past incidents. The school corporation had not violated a duty of care to the student. However, the teacher's and principal's actions were not protected under any governmental immunity doctrine. Although Indiana statutes required reporting of child abuse, they did not provide a basis for civil lawsuits against governmental officials. The case was remanded for determination of whether the teacher breached a duty to reasonably supervise the students, and whether the principal had failed to reasonably supervise students. In neither case would civil liability be premised upon the child abuse reporting statute. *Borne v. Northwest Allen County School Corp.*, 532 N.E.2d 1196 (Ind.App.3d Dist.1989).

C. State Statutory Immunity

Congress has enacted the Federal Tort Claims Act which allows individuals to sue the federal government in limited circumstances. Many states have enacted similar legislation wherein they effectively consent to be sued in certain instances.

A Wyoming student suffered from physical and mental handicaps. He and his family resided within the boundaries of a school district which had entered into a special education residential services agreement with the Board of Cooperative Educational Services (BOCES). BOCES members were selected by the board of trustees of participating school districts. Its purpose was to provide special educational services for member school districts. BOCES agreed to pay for the student's education including room and board. The student was placed at a facility owned and operated by BOCES. At BOCES the student was severely burned while being bathed by a staff member. The student's parents sued the school district in a Wyoming district court. The district court held that BOCES employees were not employees of the school district and the school district could not be liable for acts of BOCES employees. The student's parents appealed to the Supreme Court of Wyoming.

On appeal, the school district argued that BOCES was a governmental agency. The student's parents contended that although BOCES was an agent of the school district, this relationship did not make it a governmental entity under the Wyoming Governmental Claims Act. The court found that under the act, a governmental entity was any local government unit including school districts and their agents. BOCES was a governmental entity and its employees were immune from liability. The school district was not liable for BOCES employees' acts. The district court's decision was affirmed. *Sykes v. Lincoln County School Dist. 1 & 2*, 763 P.2d 1263 (Wyo.1988).

An educable mentally handicapped (EMH) student in Chicago was struck by a chalkboard clip thrown by another EMH student and was injured. The incident occurred during a twenty-minute recess break, during which the regular EMH classroom teacher was absent. The class was unsupervised at the time because a teacher's aide who was assigned to simultaneously supervise both the regular classroom and the EMH classroom was not in the room. The student sued the teacher's aide, the teacher and the city board of education in an Illinois trial court. The teacher's aide testified that during the recess period she went back and forth between the classrooms, leaving each class unattended for only a minute at a time. She also stated that when she heard yelling from the EMH classroom she immediately returned. Some of the students in the classroom testified that there had been no supervision in the EMH classroom for one half-hour before and twenty minutes after the accident occurred. There was no evidence that the student who threw the chalkboard clip had prior behavioral problems. The school psychologist testified that EMH students were placed there because of low I.Q. and not for behavioral disorders. The trial court granted the school district and officials' summary judgment motion, applying a wilful and wanton standard for the conduct of school board personnel. The injured student appealed to the Illinois Appellate Court.

The court noted that under Illinois law, teachers and other educational employees who are responsible for supervising students were immune from negligent conduct. Because the teacher and assistant were immune from liability for ordinarily negligent conduct, it was required to show that they had been wilful or wanton in order to impute liability to them. Thus, the trial court had applied the proper legal standard for evaluating school employees' conduct. The court rejected the injured student's argument that this standard should not apply to EMH classroom settings. The court also noted that teaching assistants were entitled to immunity from lawsuit and were protected from liability under the Local Governmental and Governmental Employees Tort Immunity Act. Illinois courts consistently have held that there is no wilful or wanton misconduct where the teacher merely leaves children unsupervised. The requisite standard was for injured parties to show that the teacher or school was aware of a high probability of serious harm or unreasonable risk of harm. Because there was no such evidence in this case, no factual question existed about whether the school or its employees should have known of a high probability of impending danger to the EMH students. The appellate court affirmed the trial court's summary judgment for the school board and its employees. *Jackson v. Chicago Bd. of Educ.*, 549 N.E.2d 829 (Ill.App.1st Dist.1989).

A behaviorally disturbed Kansas student was injured in a high school industrial arts class while using a table saw. The school district had developed an IEP which included enrollment in regular classes. The student's woodworking teacher was allegedly notified that he was a special education student and advised of his particular problem. However, the teacher denied receiving any such notice. The student's father sued the school district and its employees in a federal district court. The father contended that the district and the teacher had failed to take reasonable steps to protect the safety of the student and were negligent in failing to properly supervise him in the woodworking class. The school district moved for summary judgment, arguing that its actions were discretionary and that it was therefore entitled to immunity under the Kansas Tort Claims Act.

The court found that under the Tort Claims Act a governmental entity or its employee shall not be liable for damages resulting from any claim based upon the exercise, performance or failure to perform a discretionary function or duty. The school board was entitled to immunity only if its actions were not governed by any readily ascertainable standard, or if no legal duty existed to act in a certain manner. The court held that the school district and the teacher were under a legal duty to properly supervise the student in the woodworking class. They also had to take reasonable steps to protect his safety, including properly instructing him on safety procedures and providing proper guards and warning signs. These matters were not discretionary and the teacher and the school district were not entitled to immunity. In addition, the district would not have been immune if it failed to notify the teacher of the student's IEP, as it was under a legal duty to do so. The district court denied the school district's motion for summary judgment. *Greider v. Shawnee Mission Unified School Dist.*, 710 F.Supp. 296 (D.Kan.1989).

A Texas elementary school student who suffered from cerebral palsy was pushed into a stack of chairs and sustained a head injury while a group of students were left unsupervised. The student had mild convulsions, developed cold sweats and became dazed and incoherent, but the teacher did not call for help or send her to the school nurse. When the student was later taken to the nurse by an occupational therapist, the nurse told her to stay in school. On the way to her daycare center on a school bus at the end of the day the student suffered severe convulsions. The bus driver contacted his supervisor requesting that a school nurse be provided at the next stop, but he was told to take the student to the daycare center, where she finally received medical treatment. The student's mother filed a lawsuit against the school district and school employees alleging that their grossly negligent failure to provide adequate care decreased the student's life expectancy. After the lawsuit was dismissed before trial the mother appealed.

The Texas Supreme Court considered whether the lawsuit was barred by the Texas Tort Claims Act. The court noted that the act provides an exception from immunity for professional school employees when in "disciplining a student the employee uses excessive force or negligence which results in bodily injury to the student." The mother argued that under this exception school employees could be held liable both for using excessive force when disciplining a student *and* for any "negligence which results in bodily injury to the student." Although the language of the exception was ambiguous because negligence isn't "used," the court observed that it has been interpreted by Texas courts to apply only when a student's bodily injury is a result of some form of punishment. Because the student in this case was not being punished when she incurred her injuries, the court determined that the exception did not apply.

The court next turned to the mother's assertion that the student's injuries fell within another exception to sovereign immunity for damages arising from the "use or operation of a motor vehicle." The court concluded that this exception did not apply because although the girl suffered convulsions on the school bus, those convulsions were not "the proximate result of the use or operation of the school bus." The supreme court affirmed the dismissal of the case. *Hopkins v. Spring Indep. School Dist.*, 736 S.W.2d 617 (Tex.1987).

D. Exceptions

A physically-handicapped Pennsylvania student with cerebral palsy fell backwards after refusing to use his walker and struck his head on the sidewalk. The accident occurred under a classroom aide's supervision on school grounds. His injuries included permanent paralysis and respiratory disability. The student's parents sued the school, claiming the injuries resulted from the dangerous condition of the school property. The school moved to have the case dismissed by claiming governmental immunity under § 8542(b) of the Judicial Code. The trial court found the allegations made by the parents to amount to no more than "a claim for negligent supervision which had been repeatedly denied as a cause of action under § 8542." The court dismissed the case and the parents appealed.

On appeal, the parents argued that the school had not adapted the school grounds so that it would be safe for use by handicapped students. The failure to do so resulted in a "dangerous condition" which fell within an exception to the governmental immunity doctrine. The court held that the exception could only be applied where the alleged negligence made the property itself unsafe for activities for which it was used. The student's fall was not caused by the condition of the school's property. It was not connected in any way to the property, sidewalk or street. There had been no prior incidents which would have placed the school on notice that a dangerous condition existed which required correction. The school was entitled to dismissal of the case on the basis of governmental immunity under § 8542(b). *Houston v. Cent. Bucks School Auth.*, 546 A.2d 1286 (Pa.Cmwlth.1988).

A Pennsylvania student who was mentally retarded drowned in a Pennsylvania university's pool while he was participating in a Recreation for Exceptional Citizens Program (REC). He was eighteen-years-old and suffered from cerebral palsy since birth. The student's parents sued the university and the REC in a Pennsylvania trial court for negligently creating a dangerous condition on real property and for not following proper safety procedures for a swimming pool. The trial court ruled in favor of the university and the organization stating that the pool, unattended by a lifeguard, was not a dangerous condition created by the school's negligence. The parents then appealed to the Pennsylvania Supreme Court.

The university and the REC asserted the defense of sovereign immunity. However, the parents alleged that their claim fell within the real property exception to sovereign immunity. The court stated that the real property exception extended to injuries arising out of the care, custody or control of real estate. Thus, the exception did not apply to claims of negligent supervision. Since the swimming pool itself did not cause the injury, the school and the REC were not liable. The supreme court affirmed the trial court's decision. *Nusheno v. Lock Haven Univ.*, 574 A.2d 129 (Pa.Cmwlth.1990).

III. REMEDIES AVAILABLE TO STUDENTS UNDER THE EHA

Upon violations of the EHA, students may seek either monetary or equitable relief (in the nature of an injunction). Relief may be awarded by an administrative officer or it may come from the courts. Generally, monetary damages are disfavored, but they can be awarded in proper circumstances.

A. Monetary Damages

In January, 1984, a handicapped Mississippi boy was suspended from school for unbuttoning a girl's blouse and he was sent to a state hospital for evaluation and treatment with his mother's consent. After the boy returned home he was refused admission to school but his mother was not informed officially of the refusal. The boy was refused admission again in September, 1984, and the mother filed complaints with local and state education authorities but received no satisfaction. She sued the school board in a U.S. district court alleging that the boy's due process rights were violated. She also sought a court order to readmit her son to school.

The district court held a due process hearing in December, 1984, in which it upheld an October, 1984, school board IEP determination that the boy should be placed in a residential setting. The U.S. Court of Appeals, Fifth Circuit, upheld the decision and after further proceedings in the district court the mother appealed again to the court of appeals. She contended that the boy's due process rights were violated when he was excluded from school in the winter and fall of 1984.

The court of appeals held that when the school board failed to convene an IEP conference in the spring of 1984 it violated the EHA. The EHA specifically required that "written prior notice to the parents" be provided whenever the school proposes to initiate or change . . . the . . . educational placement of the child. . . ." The U.S. Supreme Court has held that even a short suspension of ten days requires notice and some type of formal hearing. Also, both the EHA and the Fourteenth Amendment require the school to provide the boy with notice and a hearing regarding his continued exclusion from school. The court held that this procedural violation gave rise to a claim by the boy for compensatory damages under the "due process" exception to *Smith v. Robinson*. It also observed that the Handicapped Children's Protection Act of 1986 provides for compensatory damages. The case was remanded to the district court to determine the extent of the boy's loss caused by the school's failure to provide notice and a hearing in April and August, 1984. The court of appeals also instructed the district court to determine what damages, either monetary or in remedial educational services, would be appropriate for the boy. *Jackson v. Franklin County School Bd.*, 806 F.2d 623 (5th Cir. 1986).

A California state hospital patient was developmentally disabled. Between 1977 and 1981, California received federal funds to provide education to handicapped children under the EHA. However, between 1977 and 1981 the state allocated no EHA funds for eligible students in the state hospital system, including the hospital in which the patient resided. The patient was a child during those years. He instituted a class action lawsuit against the state of California. He alleged that the state's failure to allocate EHA funds for the education of children in state hospitals deprived members of the class of their "liberty interests" in a free appropriate public education. This allegedly violated the due process clauses of the state and federal constitutions. He sought $20 million in damages and attorney's fees under the Civil Rights Act for violations of the EHA.

One of the issues before a California appellate court was whether money damages were an appropriate remedy if he proved that he and his class were unlawfully excluded from EHA services. The patient claimed the Handicapped Children's Protection Act (HCPA) provided for money damages. The court rejected the patient's argument. Compensatory educational services were available to the patient and other members of the class. The court noted that if the patient's parents had furnished the special education services he claimed he was wrongfully denied between 1977 and 1981, the decision in *Burlington School Comm. v. Dep't of Educ.* authorized reimbursement. *Burlington* required that compensatory educational services be furnished to handicapped children who were entitled to EHA services but were now beyond the age of ordinary entitlement. Money damages were inconsistent with Congress' intent to allow the limited financial resources of states to be spent on the education of handicapped children rather than damages. Although the HCPA provided for the retroactive award of attorney's fees, it expressly excluded the retroactive recovery of money damages. The patient could not obtain money damages if he prevailed on his civil rights claims. *White v. State*, 240 Cal.Rptr. 732 (Cal.App.3d Dist.1987).

A Connecticut case demonstrates other circumstances where monetary damages are allowed under pre-1986 law. It involved a multi-handicapped boy who required a highly structured but flexible school program. A June, 1982, study found that the boy was making no academic progress in the Trumbull, Connecticut Public School program and recommended placement in the Foundation School. The parents unilaterally placed the boy in the Foundation School in December, 1982. When Trumbull proposed a new program for the boy for the 1983-84 school year, which was modeled after Foundation's program, a hearing officer found it to be appropriate but the parents insisted on leaving him at Foundation. They sued Trumbull seeking a court order requiring the school board to pay reasonable costs of tuition and transportation for the boy's attendance at Foundation. They also requested that the board be required to maintain the boy in his Foundation School placement during the pendency of the court proceedings. They sought damages of $10 million and costs incurred by the exhaustion of their EHA remedies. The board moved for a dismissal before a hearing officer who denied the motion, and the board then appealed to a U.S. district court.

The issue before the court was whether the parents were entitled to money damages under § 1983 of the federal Civil Rights Act and § 504 of the Rehabilitation Act of 1973. The court noted that prior to passage of the Handicapped Children's Protection Act of 1986, (Pub.L. No. 99-372, 100 Stat. 796) the exclusive remedy of the parents was the EHA, but that is no longer true. The court therefore had to determine whether the 1986 legislation should be given retroactive application in this case. Applying the law in effect at the time it rendered its decision would be appropriate, held the court, unless doing so would result in injustice or if there was statutory direction or legislative history to the contrary. All three exceptions were operative here. Congress did not intend to give retroactive effect to § 3 of the Handicapped Children's Protection Act of 1986 which provides that plaintiffs must exhaust all administrative procedures before seeking resolution in a civil action. The parents had to rely on prior law for relief. The motion to dismiss with respect to the parents' § 3 claim was granted to Trumbull.

The court noted that under pre-1986 law, monetary damages are generally denied but are allowed under two exceptional circumstances: (1) "where the child's physical health would have been endangered if the parents had not made alternative arrangements; and (2) where defendants acted in bad faith by failing, in an egregious fashion, to comply with the procedural provisions of the [EHA]." The court reasoned that the parents may qualify for the "bad faith" exception and accordingly it refused to dismiss this portion of the parents' lawsuit. *Silano v. Tirozzi*, 651 F.Supp. 1021 (D.Conn.1987).

In a Georgia case, a young child, through his parents, brought an action against his school district, board of education and certain of its administrators seeking declaratory, injunctive and monetary relief for alleged violations of the EHA. When the child started school he was tested and it was determined by school authorities that he should be assigned to a self-contained learning disability classroom. The parents agreed to this placement. Approximately one year later the child's progress was reviewed and placement was changed to "research learning disability" which gave him part-time assistance. Again, the parents approved. Shortly thereafter, the parents insisted that their child be placed in a regular first grade class without resource assistance. This request was denied by the school board.

A hearing was later held at which the hearing officer determined that assistance was unnecessary, thus clearing the way for regular classroom placement. The school rejected this decision, prompting an automatic appeal to the state board of education. That board determined that the current school board placement was appropriate. Suit was then filed in federal court by the child and his parents. During pendency of the suit, the child was placed in a regular classroom. The trial court entered summary judgment for the local school board, a decision appealed to the U.S. Court of Appeals, Eleventh Circuit, which ruled that the parents' monetary claims under the EHA were moot due to the child's removal from all special education during pendency of the action. *Powell v. Defore*, 699 F.2d 1078 (11th Cir.1983).

The parents of a high school freshman in Illinois sued a local school district seeking relief for their child who had been placed in a special education program. The child was referred to the district's Department of Special Education which recommended outside intensive psychotherapy. An IEP which did not include psychotherapy, was developed without participation by the child's parents. The child's condition worsened; nonetheless, the school district later issued the child a diploma. The parents brought suit seeking a revocation of the diploma, a court order directing remedial education for their child in a private residential facility, reimbursement for costs expended in providing services to their child under his independently prepared IEP, and $1,000,000 in general damages for alleged violations of the EHA.

In ruling against the parents, a U.S. district court cited Illinois law which requires that the state provide tuition-free education, but held that that did not require the state to provide psychotherapy. Further, general money damages are not available under the EHA. The attempt to have the diploma revoked was likewise dismissed since it would make no sense to revoke the diploma if the state was not required to provide the educational placement the parents sought. *Max M. v. Thompson*, 566 F.Supp. 1330 (N.D.Ill.1983). The case was appealed to the U.S. Court of Appeals, Seventh Circuit, which affirmed the district court ruling. The district court, however, was asked to reconsider its prior holding dismissing the child's claim for a compensatory education, and the case was remanded.

The Court of Appeals pointed out to the district court that shortly after it had rendered its opinion dismissing the child's claim for compensatory services, *Timms v. Metropolitan School District of Wabash County*, 722 F.2d 1310 (7th Cir.1983), was decided. That case denied a handicapped student's claim for a compensatory education on the ground that her parents failed to exhaust their administrative remedies prior to bringing suit. However, the court of appeals in *Timms* stated that an obligation placed upon the state to correct the effects of past educational shortcomings would not "fall afoul" of the Eleventh Amendment, which serves to bar lawsuits against public officials (see § III, below). Further, because compensatory services in *Timms* were recharacterized as prospective, they were allowable under the EHA. The district court, hearing the case for a second time, held that the *Timms* decision was controlling and reinstated the student's claim for compensatory services. *Max M. v. Thompson*, 585 F.Supp. 317 (N.D.Ill.1984).

Money damages were allowed in a case in New York. The parents of a seventeen-year-old deaf child brought suit in a U.S. district court, seeking to compel their local school district and the New York State Commissioner of Education to pay for their child's education since 1973-1974 at a special school for the deaf in Massachusetts. The suit was brought under the EHA with the parents claiming that the defendants' failure to bear such costs deprived their child of a free appropriate public education in violation of the Act. Up to the time of the suit the parents paid the expenses of sending the child to the school. The defendants claimed that adequate schools existed in New York, that the Massachusetts school was not approved by the Commissioner and that money damages may not be awarded in an action under the Act.

The court disagreed and held that money damages may be awarded under the Act, "at least to the extent of reimbursement for tuition and expenses related to providing an appropriate educational placement for the handicapped child. The statute's language authorizing the court to fashion such relief as it determines to be 'appropriate' grants a substantial amount of discretion to the court." However, the court did state that such damages could be awarded against the school district only and not against the Commissioner. The mere fact that the school was not approved by the commissioner did not necessarily preclude the plaintiffs from maintaining the present action but they were told by the court that they could not maintain an action for school years for which they had not made prior request that the school district pay. The net result of the lawsuit was that a motion by the defendants to dismiss was denied but the parents were required to undergo additional administrative proceedings to further clarify the issues involved. In the meantime, court action was stayed. *Matthews v. Ambach*, 552 F.Supp. 1273 (W.D. N.Y.1982).

B. Compensatory Education

Although compensatory education is not usually awarded under the EHA, it may be awarded where benefits which Congress intended to protect under the EHA were not granted. A handicapped student does not have a right to demand public education beyond age twenty-one, unless the student is found entitled to educational services to compensate for the deprivation of a free appropriate education.

In a Pennsylvania case, a profoundly retarded student was afflicted with severe behavior problems. The school district, the student's mother and the Delaware County intermediate unit agreed that he should be placed at a special education day facility, known as Summit School. He remained at Summit throughout the year and progressed with his IEP. The next fall, the student's behavior deteriorated significantly. Summit officials and the student's teacher determined that he could no longer be provided with an appropriate education and they recommended that he be placed in a residential program. After three years of inappropriate education, the student's parents contacted the Department of Education requesting that it assist in locating an appropriate special education program for the student. The bureau suggested that the student be placed in an out of state residential school. Meanwhile, the student's mother filed a declaratory judgment action against the Commonwealth of Pennsylvania, the Secretary of Education and the school district. A federal district court awarded the student compensatory education. The school district appealed to the U.S. Court of Appeals, Third Circuit.

The school district contended that a compensatory remedy required the court to ascertain the student's future educational needs and that these needs were not ripe for decision. The appellate court, however, noted that the trial court had merely determined that it was unable to predict the student's future, specific educational needs and left the components of the instructional program to be determined once he reached the age of twenty-one. Next the district contended that it was entitled to Eleventh Amendment immunity from the student's EHA claims. The court determined, however, that although there was a significant amount of state funding it was not established that the district was acting under color of state law. The district acted in an independent nature in determining special education services and other educational services. Therefore, the school district did not fall within the state's Eleventh Amendment immunity. Finally, the district contended that compensatory education was not a remedy available under the EHA. The court concluded that Congress empowered the courts to grant a compensatory remedy. And since the school district did not place the student in an appropriate school, the student was harmed by its failure to do so. The U.S. Court of Appeals upheld the district court's decision and granted the student a compensatory education of two and one-half years beyond age twenty-one. *Lester H. by Octavia P. v. Gilhool*, 916 F.2d 865 (3d Cir.1990).

A Blind New York student sought admission to the state institute for the education of the blind. When the institute rejected his application, the student appealed to the state commissioner of education. A hearing officer determined that the student should be admitted to the institute with a year of free compensatory public education. The commissioner upheld the admission in a subsequent administrative appeal brought by the institute, but determined that the student was not entitled to compensatory education. The student then sued the commissioner in a federal district court, which dismissed the part of the complaint concerning compensatory education, but allowed the student to recover attorney's fees from the institute. The student appealed to the U.S. Court of Appeals, Second Circuit.

The court of appeals ruled that the student was entitled to a year and one-half of compensatory education. The court remanded the case to the district court to vacate the commissioner's decision. The U.S. Supreme Court granted the New York education commissioner's petition for a writ of certiorari. The Court vacated and remanded the case to the court of appeals for further consideration in light of its decision in *Dellmuth v. Muth*, 109 S.Ct. 2397. In *Dellmuth*, the Court ruled that states could not be liable for tuition reimbursement in lawsuits filed under the Education of the Handicapped Act due to the Eleventh Amendment of the Constitution.

On remand, the court of appeals noted that in its previous decision, it had reinstated the compensatory education award to the student despite the fact that he was over the age of twenty-one. This was because he had been denied his right to a free appropriate education during the extensive delays caused by the state administrative hearings. The appeals court stated that it did not base its previous holding in this case on the abrogation of a state's Eleventh Amendment immunity because it did not believe that argument was necessary to reach its outcome. Rather, its decision had merely vacated a decision by the state commissioner of education. The relief granted was prospective in nature and would be permissible despite the Eleventh Amendment. The court reaffirmed its previous holding. *Burr by Burr v. Sobol*, 888 F.2d 258 (2d Cir. 1989).

In January, 1990, attorneys for the New York State Commissioner of Education filed a new petition for certiorari with the U.S. Supreme Court, again arguing that the award of compensatory education imposed against the state violated the Eleventh Amendment. The Court vacated the court of appeals decision and remanded the case for further consideration in light of *Dellmuth v. Muth*, see Section II, above. *Sobol v. Burr*, 109 S.Ct. 3209 (1990).

In 1979, the parents of a handicapped girl sued the state of Missouri alleging that several state and local government agencies denied their daughter the educational services she desired. Two U.S. district court orders dismissed the parents' complaint and they appealed to the U.S. Court of Appeals, Eighth Circuit, seeking a compensatory education for their twenty-four year old daughter.

On appeal the parents claimed that an earlier Eighth Circuit decision dismissing their claim was wrong since the compensatory educational services they sought were not damages as the court had earlier concluded. The court of appeals observed that the U.S. Supreme Court's ruling in *Burlington School Committee v. Department of Education of Massachusetts* had altered its understanding of what are "damages" under the EHA. The parents were seeking to recover educational services (which they could not afford to provide) that their daughter would have received during the three years she was in the Youth Center of the St. Louis State Hospital. The court of appeals stated that ". . . Congress did not intend the child's entitlement to a *free* education to turn upon her parent's ability to 'front' its costs." The parents were seeking the recovery of compensatory educational services in order to remedy denial of the benefit Congress sought to protect through the EHA. It held that the parents would be entitled to recover compensatory educational services for their daughter if they prevailed on their claim that the state denied their daughter a free appropriate education in violation of the EHA. The compensatory education issue was remanded to the district court for further proceedings. *Miener v. State of Missouri*, 800 F.2d 749 (8th Cir.1986).

In November, 1985, a mildly retarded young adult sued his local school district and the state of Connecticut. He claimed that he was being denied his right to an education under the EHA. The case was settled through a consent decree which was signed by both the state and local defendants. The consent decree granted the young adult two years of compensatory education at the state's expense.

After passage of the Handicapped Children's Protection Act of 1986 (HCPA), the young adult sued both the school district and the state seeking the attorney's fees he incurred in the earlier lawsuit ($2,633). The school district argued that because the state had to pay the expense of the young adult's compensatory education he had "prevailed" only against the state and not against the school district. According to the district, this meant that the state was solely liable for the young adult's attorney's fees.

The court rejected the school district's arguments. It observed that the young adult did obtain limited success against the school district at the administrative level. Before filing the lawsuit, he had sought a compensatory education through the EHA's due process hearing procedures. The school district was involved in that administrative process. Even though a hearing officer denied the young adult's request for a compensatory education, that denial resulted in the lawsuit which in turn produced the consent decree favorable to him. Therefore, the young adult was deemed to have "prevailed" in the administrative process. The court ruled that the school district should pay twenty percent, and the state eighty percent, of the young adult's attorney's fees. *Counsel v. Dow*, 666 F.Supp. 366 (D.Conn.1987).

The school district then appealed to the U.S. Court of Appeals, Second Circuit. The school district argued that attorney's fees were unavailable for administrative hearings under the HCPA. Furthermore, the young adult failed to prevail against it as required by the HCPA. The young adult argued that he was entitled to attorney's fees from both the state and the school district due to the "relative culpability" of both defendants. The court of appeals held for the school district although it rejected the district's argument that the HCPA failed to afford attorney's fees for work done in connection with administrative hearings. Under the HCPA a court may award attorney's fees to any handicapped youth who is a "prevailing party." A youth is considered a prevailing party if he or she succeeds on any significant issue in litigation. The young adult clearly prevailed against the state with respect to the consent decree but the court concluded that he did not prevail against the school district either at the administrative level or in the consent decree. Although a hearing officer found that the school district was fiscally responsible for the young adult's education during his hospitalization, she refused to award compensatory education. The consent decree imposed no obligations or expenses on the school district. The state alone was liable for attorney's fees. *Counsel v. Dow*, 849 F.2d 731 (2d Cir.1988).

A twenty-five-year-old California man with Down's syndrome brought suit against the California education commissioner on the grounds that he had been excluded from the educational system prior to 1973. The lawsuit alleged that for several years his mother had unsuccessfully tried to enroll him in a San Francisco public school special education class. In 1973, at the age of twelve, he was finally allowed to enroll in the special education program. When he reached the age of twenty-one, his school district sought to terminate his placement in the special education program as provided by section 1415(b)(2) of the EHA. He claimed, however, that he should be allowed to stay in the program to compensate for the seven years he was wrongfully denied a special education prior to 1973. A federal district court denied his request, and he appealed to the U.S. Court of Appeals, Ninth Circuit, which affirmed the district court's decision.

The appeals court ruled that even though the man had been denied access to a special education prior to the enactment of the EHA in 1975, he was barred from bringing suit under any other statute, including the Rehabilitation Act. The court cited the U.S. Supreme Court's 1984 decision of *Smith v. Robinson*, 104 S.Ct. 3457 (1984), which stated that all special education lawsuits must be brought under the EHA. In *Smith* the Supreme Court held that Congress, having passed the EHA, had removed all other Acts as possible bases for special education lawsuits. Extending this doctrine to lawsuits which arose even before 1975, the court of appeals held that the man could make no claim under any Act but the EHA. Since the EHA contains no provision authorizing "compensatory educations" for pre-1975 denials of special educational services, and explicitly states that persons over the age of twenty-one are not entitled to such services, the man's lawsuit was dismissed. *Alexopulos v. Riles*, 784 F.2d 1408 (9th Cir. 1986).

The parents of a profoundly mentally handicapped twenty-year-old girl in Indiana who had received one and one-half hours of educational instruction per day from 1976 to 1980 requested, in 1979, that their daughter be placed in a full-day instructional program in the hope that she would respond to increased attention. The school district denied the request because of a belief that there was a correlation between the girl's self-abusive behavior and increased attention. After exhausting their administrative remedies the parents brought suit in a U.S. district court, which held in favor of the school district. On appeal to the U.S. Court of Appeals, Seventh Circuit, the parents sought an injunction to prohibit the school district from excluding their daughter from a full school day and, in addition, asking for one full year of day-long instruction to compensate for the 1979-80 school year during which she received one and one-half hours of instruction. The Court of Appeals held that the request for an injunction was moot because the girl was past the age at which the school district was required to provide educational services. The court also denied a compensatory education on the ground that since neither the EHA nor the Rehabilitation Act provide for general money damages for an alleged inadequate IEP, except in cases of bad faith refusal to abide by the procedures set out in those acts, the remedy of a compensatory education also could not be implied. *Timms v. Metropolitan School Dist. of Wabash County*, 718 F.2d 212 (7th Cir. 1983).

The parents of a handicapped student in Georgia sought in federal court a compensatory education for their child, whom they claimed was inappropriately placed. The child had been attending a special education program which had been recommended by his school district. The parents insisted that he be placed in a regular classroom. A series of administrative appeals resulted in a determination that a special education environment would be best for the child. However, the parents disagreed and filed suit in a U.S. district court, which entered summary judgment for the local school board. The parents appealed to the U.S. Court of Appeals, Eleventh Circuit, arguing that their child was entitled to a compensatory education so he could catch up to his age group, having fallen behind his nonhandicapped peers because of a year spent in the special education program. The court ruled against the parents, stating that there is nothing in the EHA requiring a school board to remediate a previously handicapped child. *Powell v. Defore*, 699 F.2d 1078 (11th Cir. 1983).

The governor of Illinois and state education officials appealed a court order reinstating the parents' claim for a compensatory education for their child. The officials alleged that the order should be amended on four grounds: 1) the parents' failure to assert the compensatory educational claim at the state level administrative hearing; 2) the requested relief was moot because the child had turned twenty-one and was no longer eligible for special education services; 3) the parents failed to allege sufficient wrongdoing on the part of the school district, i.e., that the school district had acted in bad faith; and 4) state educational officials should not be held legally responsible for the acts of a local educational agency.

A U.S. district court held that the record of the administrative proceedings revealed that the parents did raise the compensatory education issue at the state level hearing. Second, the issue was not moot because Congress did not intend to prevent compensatory educational relief in cases where a child may have passed the age where he is legally entitled to special education services. A contrary holding, said the court, could result in school districts intentionally delaying services until the districts are no longer responsible for the child's education. Third, the state's argument that the plaintiffs had failed to allege sufficient wrongdoing on the part of the state was invalid. The court held that the pre-*Burlington* "exceptional circumstances" test, where parents are entitled to reimbursement only when a school district has acted in bad faith or somehow endangered or threatened the health and safety of the child, did not apply. Here, the parents were asking for prospective relief, and the exceptional circumstances test applied only when retroactive relief is requested.

Finally, the court did not absolve the state defendants from liability for the local school district's actions. The court noted that Congress intended that responsibility for the implementation of all services under the EHA be at the state level. However, the plaintiffs could only sue the state defendants in their official, not individual, capacity. The court held that there was no basis for holding the governor liable. The state's motion to amend the previous order was thus granted in part and denied in part. *Max M. v. Thompson*, 592 F.Supp. 1450 (N.D.Ill.1984). See also *Max M. v. Thompson*, 592 F.Supp. 1437 (N.D.Ill.1984).

CHAPTER EIGHT
SCHOOL DISTRICT OPERATIONS

I. EMPLOYMENT

The following cases address issues involving special education employees. Employee misconduct, discrimination, teachers' constitutional privacy rights, hiring practices, salary, termination, seniority, tenure, and unemployment compensation benefits represent the range of special education employee-related concerns which have been before the courts.

A. Dismissals for Cause

The following cases involve dismissals of special education employees due to budgetary reasons, alleged misconduct or incompetence. The first group of cases deals with employee misconduct.

An assistant teacher was employed at a Florida residential treatment center for emotionally disturbed and mentally handicapped children. Two months after he was hired, the teacher struck a student with a pointer. He was cited for violations of school policy and child abuse, and given a final written warning which stated that similar actions would be grounds for immediate dismissal. Nine months later the teacher was involved in another incident in which he threw a cup of coffee at a student. The teacher was dismissed for child abuse. He then applied for unemployment compensation benefits which an appeals referee denied because he had been dismissed for misconduct. Under a Florida statute misconduct was defined as a "substantial disregard of the employer's interests." The teacher contended that his actions did not constitute misconduct and that he should not have been denied benefits. The Florida Unemployment Appeals Commission affirmed the referee's denial of benefits. The teacher then appealed to the District Court of Appeal of Florida, claiming that the referee's decision was not supported by substantial evidence.

The court noted that the appeals referee had found that the teacher exhibited blatant disregard of his employer's interests. This constituted misconduct which warranted denial of unemployment benefits. The court held that the appeals referee's conclusion was supported by substantial evidence, and it upheld the appeals referee's decision. *Sturaitis v. Montanari Clinical School*, 522 So.2d 429 (Fla.App.4th Dist.1988).

In a Maryland case, reinstatement was ordered for a teacher who was also a Catholic priest. The teacher, who had taught in Japan for over twenty years, took employment teaching groundskeeping and home maintenance to severely retarded males of secondary school age at a center for the mentally handicapped. His teaching objective was to train students to enter the employment market as handymen or custodial workers. The teaching program consisted of working with a small group of students in the classroom for several days a week, and at various outdoor worksites on the remaining school days.

One day, without authorization, the teacher left four of his six students under a teaching aide's supervision at a recreational center, where they were to clean the building and the adjacent grounds. He took the two remaining students with him to work on other groundskeeping projects. When it began to snow the teacher took the boys to a work shed located behind his home and directed them to work on a project at this site. One of the boys became disruptive and began throwing glass bottles and mishandling the saw he was using. The teacher ordered him to stop his disruptive behavior but to no avail. At this point, the teacher decided that the boy needed to be "timed out," a behavior modification technique used by some special education teachers whereby a misbehaving student is isolated and kept still, in order to calm him and to cause him to reflect on his misbehavior. The teacher ordered the boy to leave the shed and kneel outside on two wooden blocks under a plastic-covered picnic table for an extended period in below-freezing snowy weather. Throughout the incident, the other boy remained inside the shed shivering and shaking from the cold. A neighbor who witnessed the episode called the police, who found the boy sobbing and crying.

The County Board of Education terminated the teacher's employment and the teacher appealed to the State Board of Education, which modified the disciplinary sanction from dismissal to suspension. The County Board appealed and the case finally reached the Court of Appeals of Maryland, which held that the dismissal was not warranted and that the State Board did not exceed its statutory power in imposing a lengthy suspension instead of dismissal. The court took note of the teacher's excellent teaching record and stated that the teacher's action, although improper, was motivated by and intended to modify the behavior of a student whom he could not reach by verbal direction. *Bd. of Educ. of Prince George's County v. Waeldner*, 470 A.2d 332 (Md.1984).

A woman taught in a Missouri school district for thirty-six years. In the 1983-84 academic year she taught remedial math in an elementary school during which there were in effect board of education regulations, which included a provision regarding corporal punishment of students. Teachers were only to administer corporal punishment by blows to the child's "fleshy posterior" in the presence of the principal or a principal's designee. The provision also stated that a teacher should never hit a child on the head. These regulations were placed in the teacher's lounge and/or library of each school building in the district.

In the fall of 1983, the principal received a report from a mother that the teacher had slapped her ten-year-old son. The principal also received at least one other complaint from a parent who stated that the teacher had struck her son in the back with her hand. In March, 1984, the district superintendent sent a letter to the teacher alleging that she had violated the board's corporal punishment regulations by striking children without the presence of the principal and by hitting students about the head. It further stated that if any of the shortcomings still existed by May 1, 1984, the teacher's contract would be terminated. After receiving another similar letter from the superintendent the teacher requested a school board hearing on the matter. The board found that the teacher had persistently violated the corporal punishment regulations and her teaching contract was terminated as of October 30, 1984. The teacher appealed the decision to a Missouri circuit court, which ruled for the school board. She appealed this decision to the Missouri Court of Appeals.

The teacher argued that because the warning letter did not meet the requirements of Missouri law and because all the actions charged occurred before the warning letter was sent, she was denied the opportunity to avoid firing through the improvement of her performance. The court of appeals rejected this argument observing that a warning letter is not necessary in order to terminate a teaching contract on the grounds of wilful or persistent violation of regulations.

The teacher also argued that her contract should not be terminated since the principal promulgated corporal punishment policies that contradicted the board of education regulations posted in the teacher's lounge. The principal allegedly told his teachers that if any of them had a disciplinary problem with children to "bop them in the mouth." The principal had also prepared and distributed to the teachers a handbook that sanctioned spanking in front of another teacher which was in conflict with the board of education regulation. The court reasoned that even though the principal's statement and handbook were inconsistent with the board regulation, the teacher's testimony clearly indicated that she had not relied on the principal's statement because she denied hitting the children at all. The board's decision to terminate the teacher's contract was valid. The lower court decision was upheld. *Shepard v. South Harrison R-II School Dist.*, 718 S.W.2d 195 (Mo.App.1986).

The Orange County, Florida, school board operated the Woodlands School for learning disabled, physically handicapped and multi-handicapped children. The school was located on the campus of the Sunland State Hospital and was a tenant of the hospital. Due to the Woodland School's location on the grounds of the State Hospital, work-release prisoners sometimes were present at Woodlands. Hospital rules expressly prohibited any fraternization by employees with work-release prisoners.

Beginning in 1979, a woman was employed by the school board as a non-certified special education teacher's aide at Woodlands on a series of ten-month contracts. In March, 1982, her principal recommended that her contract for the following year not be renewed due to numerous minor problems: excessive absenteeism, reading magazines on the job, wearing inappropriate shoes, failure to require her guests to check in when visiting her, and inability to get along with other teacher's aides. The superintendent and the school board concurred. After the teacher's aide was informed of the decision not to renew, she was reprimanded for fraternizing on the job with work-release prisoners. She began harassing the teacher who reported her infractions of the no-fraternization rule, and on one occasion chased the teacher to her home in her car. The board immediately relieved the teacher's aide with pay for the remaining two weeks of her contract. She then brought suit alleging that a number of her constitutional rights had been violated, but a federal district court ruled against her on all counts.

First, the court rejected her due process claim because she had not achieved tenure; she had been employed under a fixed-term contract. Also, the board had not deprived her of her right to a good reputation because she had admitted to fraternizing with the prisoners while at work. Second, her First Amendment right to freedom of association did not include a right to engage in social contact with prisoners while on the job in violation of official written policy. The court's decision was made easier by the fact that the teacher's aide admitted that her contact with prisoners was purely social in nature. Political association is more vigorously protected by the First Amendment. In any event, she had failed to prove that the board's decision not to renew her teacher's aide contract was based upon her fraternization with prisoners. Finding no constitutional violation, the court dismissed the suit. *Brew v. School Bd. of Orange County*, 626 F.Supp. 709 (M.D.Fla.1985).

A Pennsylvania school board's decision to dismiss a school psychologist because of incompetency has been upheld by the Commonwealth Court of Pennsylvania. The psychologist argued that her dismissal should have been based on provisions contained in the Public School Code which states that, in evaluating school personnel, due consideration shall be given to "personality, preparation, technique and pupil reaction." She maintained that her dismissal did not relate to these concerns. The court, in rejecting that argument, stated that the fact that consideration should be given to the qualities mentioned in the statute does not mean that other matters, such as lack of judgment or simple ability, may not also be considered. The school board's dismissal order was affirmed. *Grant v. Bd. of School Directors of the Centennial School Dist.*, 471 A.2d 1292 (Pa.Cmwlth.1984).

An Oregon teacher was discharged for gross unfitness and sexual misconduct. He sought reinstatement from the Teachers Standards and Practices Commission. The commission found that the teacher lacked good moral character to serve as a teacher and to hold an Oregon Teaching Certificate.

The lack of good moral character was evidenced by the teacher's repeated acts of inappropriate contact with female students. The commission denied his application for reinstatement. The teacher appealed to the Court of Appeals of Oregon.

On appeal, the teacher contended that the commission had not defined its interpretation of "good moral character." The court concluded, however, that the commission offered a "reasoned interpretation" of the term by reference to gross unfitness and to gross neglect of duty. The teacher next contended that the commission erred because the students who complained about him were not called to testify, but rather, the students' allegations were admitted through police reports and testimony of others. Oregon admitted evidence in administrative proceedings of a type commonly relied upon by reasonably prudent persons. The court determined that the hearsay evidence of students' complaints and statements was admissible because it could be relied on by reasonably prudent persons. The court affirmed the commission's decision and denied the teacher reinstatement. *Reguero v. Teachers Standards and Practices*, 789 P.2d 11 (Or.App.1990).

The next cases involve qualification requirements.

An Indiana psycometrist was employed under annual contracts with a city school system for five consecutive years. She was then laid off under an administrative reduction policy adopted by the city school board. The reduction policy eliminated guidance counselor and psycometrist positions and created a new combined position for psycometrist/counselors. However, the school district's attorneys advised the district to reemploy the psycometrist for the following school year because proper cancellation procedures were not followed. Having served five successive yearly contracts, the psycometrist had achieved permanent teacher status under Indiana education law. The district again notified the psycometrist that it would consider her termination at a board meeting. The reasons it stated for termination were declining student enrollment, uncertain funding and lack of seniority. The board based its termination findings on the rescinded administrative reduction policy of the previous year, in which psycometrists were required to obtain certification both as psycometrists and guidance counselors in order to perform in the new job designation. At the same time the psycometrist's contact was cancelled a second time, the school district retained two nontenured employees in psycometrist/counselor positions, allegedly because they both had classroom teacher licenses. The psycometrist appealed her contract cancellation to an Indiana trial court which affirmed the school board's decision. The psycometrist appealed to the Indiana Court of Appeals.

The court found that the school board had illegally created new licensing requirements for its teachers. Under Indiana law, this responsibility was exclusively the state board of education's. The appeals court overturned the trial court's conclusion that the psycometrist was less qualified than the two retained employees. The psycometrist's license satisfied the requirements of the state Commission on Teacher Training and Licensing for School Psychologists I and she was therefore a "teacher" under the state's statutory definition. The two retained employees were not properly licensed and the psycometrist's contract should not have been cancelled. Because the board had cancelled the psycometrist's contract arbitrarily, it had deprived her of a property interest secured by the Due Process Clause of the Fourteenth Amendment. She was entitled to damages and equitable relief under § 1983 of the Civil Rights Act, along with attorney's fees under § 1988 of the same act. The court reversed and remanded the trial court's decision. *Stewart v. Fort Wayne Comm. Schools*, 545 N.E.2d 7 (Ind.App.3d Dist.1989).

A Montana man began his teaching career in 1963. He taught until 1981 when his position was changed to school psychologist. Problems between the psychologist and certain school district employees arose and these problems eventually culminated in his termination by the board of trustees. The psychologist appealed his termination and eventually won a settlement in which he was awarded back pay and fringe benefits due to the improper discharge procedures used by the school district. A proper termination hearing was then held and the board of trustees voted to terminate the psychologist for incompetence. The psychologist appealed to the Montana Supreme Court after a Montana trial court affirmed the board of trustees' decision.

The psychologist contended that the district was required to offer him a teaching position in other areas of his certification. The psychologist was certified to teach science, biology, chemistry and guidance counseling. The court noted that it would be against public policy to require the district to reinstate the psychologist to another teaching position. The district would have been required to terminate a nontenured teacher to make room for the psychologist. The court determined that the goals of the state in educating its students would not be served by such a result. The psychologist next contended that there was insufficient evidence to determine that he was incompetent. The court, however, noted that there was sufficient evidence to support the conclusion of incompetency in his position as school psychologist. Numerous complaints had been lodged by teachers and parents concerning his work. The other psychologist employed by the district reviewed the psychological evaluations, and noted deficiencies in his psychological reports. Four experts reviewed 109 of the 400 cases prepared by the psychologist. As a result of their review, all the experts agreed that the psychologist was incompetent. Therefore, the Supreme Court of Montana upheld the trial court's decision. *Harris v. Bailey*, 798 P.2d 96 (Mont.1990).

A Lutheran school for the deaf in New York hired a female art teacher in March, 1979. She possessed permanent certification as an art teacher, but was not certified as a teacher for the deaf as required by state law. At the time she was hired, she was told that in order to waive the certification requirement she would have to pursue courses toward deaf education certification. At the close of the 1980-81 academic year, however, the teacher had taken only two courses toward certification. In November, 1981, she left to have a baby and began her child-rearing leave in January, 1982. In March, 1982, school officials wrote to the woman and again informed her that in order to waive certification she must pursue at least six semester hours of study per year. She then met with the school superintendent, assuring him that she would continue to work toward certification. She was also granted an additional year of child-rearing leave.

In March, 1983, the superintendent asked the woman if she intended to return to her position in the fall. He refused to extend her child-rearing leave but told her that if she became pregnant again she would have "no trouble" in receiving additional pregnancy leave. At this time the woman told the superintendent that she had taken only three semester hours of courses toward certification in the past year. One month later she told the principal that she was pregnant. This prompted him to offer her a woodworking teacher position instead of art because when she would be forced to leave again in the fall a woodworking teacher's sudden absence would be less disruptive to the learning process. The woman refused this offer and one month later she was dismissed.

She sued in U.S. district court, alleging unlawful discrimination due to pregnancy. The court disagreed with her claims, holding that the school had proven that the decision to terminate her employment was based upon her lack of deaf education certification. It was entirely proper for school officials to show concern for the continuity and quality of instruction at the school in the face of the woman's lack of certification and lengthy child-rearing leaves. The court noted that while pregnancy leaves are protected by the Civil Rights Act, child-rearing leaves are not. Because no unlawful discrimination was proven, the court dismissed the woman's complaint. *Record v. Mill Neck Manor Lutheran School for the Deaf*, 611 F.Supp. 905 (E.D.N.Y.1985).

Since 1975, a Louisiana school board had employed a woman as special education supervisor. In 1982, after becoming dissatisfied with her performance, the board obtained an opinion from the Louisiana Attorney General which stated that because the supervisor was not certified for the position, she was not tenured under the state's tenure laws. The board then notified her that her contract would not be renewed for the following year. No dismissal hearing was held. She sued the board in state court, contending that she was tenured, and the court ordered that the board hold a dismissal hearing. When it was done the board once again voted to dismiss, but failed to follow proper procedures. Once again the supervisor successfully sued the board, winning reinstatement and back pay. She then commenced the present lawsuit in federal court, claiming that her federal civil rights had been violated by the board's failure to adhere to state notice and hearing requirements. In essence, she claimed that this failure had deprived her of her federal due process rights.

The U.S. Court of Appeals, Fifth Circuit, disagreed with her claims. The fact that the state courts had forced the board to hold a dismissal hearing completely satisfied all federal due process requirements. Under the U.S. Constitution, due process requires only compliance with minimal notice and hearing requirements; the fact that state law provided greater protection was irrelevant. The court stated: "There is not a violation of due process every time a . . . government entity violates its own rules. Such action may constitute a breach of contract or violation of state law, but unless the conduct trespasses on federal constitutional safeguards, there is no constitutional deprivation." The dismissal of the special education supervisor's federal claims was thus affirmed. *Franceski v. Plaquemines Parish School Bd.*, 772 F.2d 197 (5th Cir.1985).

The special rules applicable to administrators are the subject of the next two cases.

A California school administrator was reassigned from the position of Coordinator of Special Education Services of Alverd Unified School to a classroom teaching position. At the time she was reassigned, she was given notice and a list of thirty reasons for the reassignment. The school district maintained that the administrator was reassigned because she was unwilling to maintain a professional demeanor. The administrator claimed that the reassignment was based on allegations of incompetency. California Education Code § 44896 requires that an administrator be given an evaluation before he or she may be demoted to a teaching position if the demotion is based on incompetency. The administrator requested and was granted a hearing before the district's school board. The board concluded that the reassignment was appropriate and affirmed the decision. After five months, the administrator sued the district in a California trial court, seeking reinstatement. The trial court ruled in favor of the school district.

The administrator appealed to the California Court of Appeal, Fourth District. The court of appeal found that the reassignment was based on allegations of incompetency, as evidenced by the list of thirty reasons. By failing to provide the administrator with the required statutory evaluation, the school district had violated the Education Code. The court ruled, however, that a violation of § 44896 did not require reinstatement of the administrator to her former position. The Education Code was intended to establish a uniform performance evaluation system for district personnel. Performance evaluations were mandatory at specified intervals. The administrator had no right to reinstatement. She merely had the right to receive a competency reevaluation giving her the true reasons for reassignment, as well as compensation for any wrongful salary reduction. The court of appeal reversed the trial court's decision and granted the administrator's request for an order directing the school district to conduct a reevaluation and determine any improper salary loss. *Hahn v. Alverd Unified Sch. Dist.*, 252 Cal.Rptr. 471 (Cal.App. 4th Dist.1988).

A Massachusetts state school facility for the mentally disabled hired a unit director. At the time the director took over the unit, the facility was in danger of being decertified by the Department of Public Health. The director was praised by the facility's superintendent for the progress she had made in addressing the unit's problems. However, the director and the superintendent later disagreed about the reorganization of the facility. The director opposed a plan in which the power at the facility would be centralized in the superintendent. Shortly thereafter, the superintendent informed the director that if she did not resign she would be discharged. He gave as his reason his dissatisfaction with her administrative performance. The director was dismissed and she sued the superintendent claiming that her termination violated public policy. The Superior Court, Middlesex County, found for the director and the superintendent appealed to the Supreme Judicial Court of Massachusetts, Middlesex.

The court held that the dismissal of an at-will employee did not violate public policy. Redress for at-will employees based on public policy was allowed only in certain circumstances, such as for termination for asserting a legally guaranteed right, doing what the law requires, or for refusing to break the law. The director was an at-will employee and public policy exceptions to the at-will employment doctrine did not apply to her situation. It was the superintendent's job to make policy decisions and to run the facility. The director, who simply disagreed with her employer's policy decisions, could not seek redress in the courts. The lower court's decision was reversed and the court held for the superintendent. *Smith-Pfeffer v. Fernald State School*, 533 N.E.2d 1368 (Mass.1989).

The last cases in this section deal with specific legal issues involved in terminating an employee.

The Arizona State School for the Deaf and Blind (ASDB) placed a physical education instructor on administrative leave pending investigation by the superintendent of schools. The instructor was then sent a letter notifying him of possible termination for improper attitude, inefficiency and physical assault. The instructor responded by mail rebutting each allegation. However, he was terminated for cause one month later. He then requested a post-termination hearing. The school denied his request. He filed a complaint in an Arizona trial court. The trial court denied the instructor's request for a post termination hearing and the instructor appealed to the Court of Appeals of Arizona.

On appeal, the instructor contended that the trial court abused its discretion in denying him the right to a post termination hearing. Before a public employee can invoke the Fourteenth Amendment's guarantee of procedural due process, he must first assert a constitutionally protected interest. Continued employment with a state agency has been recognized as a constitutionally protected claim. The Supreme Court in *Cleveland Bd. of Educ. v. Loudermill*, 470 U.S. 532 (1985), held that before termination, at a minimum, an employee is entitled to oral or written notice of the charges against him, an explanation of the employer's evidence, and an opportunity to present his side of the story. In *Loudermill*, the court held that due process was satisfied if informal pre-termination procedures were followed by a full post-termination hearing. The court determined that the ASDB would be required to provide adequate notice and a hearing before it fired the instructor. Therefore, the instructor was entitled to a due process post-termination hearing. *Deuel v. ASDB*, 799 P.2d 865 (Ariz.App.1990).

A probationary Wisconsin special education teacher's contract was not renewed. The teacher sued for reinstatement and money damages in a Wisconsin trial court. She asserted that the board violated a provision of the law providing for a private conference between the members of the board and the affected teacher prior to the nonrenewal. The teacher also claimed bias on the part of a board member who was also the parent of a special education student in the teacher's class. The trial court granted summary judgment to the school district, dismissing the complaint. She appealed to the Court of Appeals of Wisconsin.

The appellate court determined that the board was immune from suit for damages because the acts complained of were discretionary rather than ministerial. However, the court determined that there were material issues of fact precluding summary judgment on the claim for reinstatement. A Wisconsin statute provides that a teacher has a right to a private conference with the board prior to nonrenewal of his or her contract. Her complaint alleged that one of the board members voting with the four to three majority not to renew her contract was a student's mother. Therefore, the court concluded that the teacher was entitled to a trial on her claim for reinstatement. Her complaint raised issues of disputed fact material to her claim that the private conference provisions were not properly followed and that there may have been bias on the part of a board member. *Harkness v. Palmyra-Eagle School Dist.*, 460 N.W.2d 769 (Wis.App.1990).

In an Arkansas case, the state's supreme court refused to set aside a tenured special education teacher's dismissal, where her attorney did not adequately prove the case in the lower court. Here a special education teacher had been employed in a school district for thirteen years. She had never received an unsatisfactory evaluation and in the past had been used as a model for new teachers. However, soon after a new principal arrived at her school he informed her that her performance was inadequate. He recommended dismissal, and her employment was terminated by the school board shortly thereafter. The teacher sued in county court seeking reinstatement to her position on the ground that her dismissal had been politically motivated. Evidence was presented that the teacher's husband had been a former school employee and had twice engaged in disputes with the superintendent. Also, her husband had twice (unsuccessfully) run for the school board, and a board member had once stated that he wanted to "get a shot" at the teacher. The county court, however, found that the school board had acted out of dissatisfaction with the special education teacher's classroom performance, and she appealed.

The Arkansas Supreme Court upheld the county court. Although admitting that the teacher's attorney had presented strong evidence of political reasons for her dismissal, he had not sufficiently explored during trial the bases for her principal's unsatisfactory evaluations. Without proof that the principal had possessed political motives, the school board was entitled to rely upon his recommendation of dismissal. The Supreme Court declined to intervene. *Kirtley v. Dardanelle Pub. Schools*, 702 S.W.2d 25 (Ark.1986).

After the New York City Board of Education caused the A.C.J. Transportation Corp., a private contractor providing private bus transportation to handicapped children on behalf of the board, to terminate the contract of a male bus driver following complaints of sexual misconduct, a federal court jury awarded him $15,000 in damages plus attorney's fees. The U.S. Court of Appeals, Second Circuit, reversed the damage award and sent the case back to the district court with instructions to award only nominal damages to the bus driver.

The U.S. Court of Appeals upheld the determination that the bus driver had been deprived of due process, but reversed the award of damages. The district court had acted improperly when it failed to consider that even if the bureau had afforded due process to the handicapped student bus driver, he probably would have been fired anyway. Thus, the compensation for lost salary may have been erroneous. The court of appeals remanded the case for further proceedings with instructions that if the district court concluded that the bus driver would have been fired even if a proper hearing notice had been given to him, the court could award him nominal damages only. *Stein v. Bd. of Educ. of City of New York*, 792 F.2d 13 (2d Cir.1986).

Eleven New York special education teaching assistants were employed by Onondaga-Cortland-Madison Board of Cooperative Educational Services (OCM). OCM contracted with area school districts to provide special education services to the area's handicapped students. In 1989, the school districts discontinued their contracts with OCM and provided their own special education programs. Eleven teaching assistants brought Article 78 proceedings against the school district in the Supreme Court of New York. Both parties moved to dismiss the case.

On appeal, the teaching assistants claimed that they were protected from termination based on New York Education Laws. They relied on Education Law § 3014-b which provides that when a school district takes over a program formerly provided by a cooperative, each teacher employed by the cooperative shall be considered an employee of the school district and given the teaching positions available at the school on a tenure basis. Those teachers not assigned to the school district's new program would be placed on an eligibility list. The trial court, however, relied on Education Law § 3001 which states that the qualifications required of teachers are very different from those required of teaching assistants. Teachers are required to have a college degree and a teaching certificate. Alternatively, teaching assistants are only required to have six semester hours of college coursework. Thus, the court ruled that there was no authority to extend the statutory protection afforded teachers under § 3014-b to teaching assistants and dismissed the case. *Anderson v. Cortland City School Dist.*, 554 N.Y.S.2d 769 (Sup. 1990).

B. Employment Discrimination

Under Title VII of the Civil Rights Act of 1964 (42 U.S.C. § 2000e *et seq.*), a plaintiff has the initial burden to establish that he or she was not hired or promoted due to racial or sexual discrimination by the employer. The plaintiff must show that he or she 1) is a member of a protected minority class; 2) applied and was qualified for the position sought; 3) was not hired or promoted; and 4) that a non-minority was hired or promoted to the position the plaintiff was seeking. Once the plaintiff makes this initial showing, the burden shifts to the employer to articulate a legitimate, nondiscriminatory reason for not hiring the plaintiff. If the employer is able to do so, then the courts will rule in favor of the employer.

Discrimination on the basis of handicap by employers receiving federal financial assistance is prohibited by § 504 of the Rehabilitation Act. Such employers must "reasonably accommodate" handicapped individuals who are "otherwise qualified" for employment.

The U.S. Supreme Court ruled that tuberculosis is a handicap under § 504 of the Rehabilitation Act. Federal law defines a handicapped individual as "any person who (i) has a physical or mental impairment which substantially limits one or more of such person's major life activities, (ii) has a record of such impairment or (iii) is regarded as having such an impairment." It defines "physical impairment" as disorders affecting, among other things, the respiratory system and defines "major life activities" as "functions such as caring for one's self . . . and working."

The case involved a Florida elementary school teacher who was discharged because of the continued recurrence of tuberculosis. The teacher sued the school board under § 504 but a U.S. district court dismissed her claims. However, the U.S. Court of Appeals, Eleventh Circuit, reversed the district court's decision and held that persons with contagious diseases fall within § 504's coverage. The school board appealed to the U.S. Supreme Court.

The Supreme Court ruled that tuberculosis was a handicap under § 504 because it affected the respiratory system and affected her ability to work. The school board contended that in defining a handicapped individual under § 504, the contagious effects of a disease can be distinguished from the disease's physical effects. However, the Court reasoned that the teacher's contagion and her physical impairment both resulted from the same condition: tuberculosis. It would be unfair to allow an employer to distinguish between a disease's potential effect on others and its effect on the afflicted employee in order to justify discriminatory treatment. Allowing discrimination based on the contagious effects of a physical impairment would be inconsistent with the underlying purpose of § 504. That purpose is to ensure that handicapped persons are not denied jobs because of prejudice or ignorance. The Court noted that society's myths and fears about disability and disease are as handicapping as the physical limitations that result from physical impairment, and concluded that contagion cannot remove a person from § 504 coverage. The Supreme Court remanded the case to the district court to determine whether the teacher was "otherwise qualified" for her job and whether the school board could reasonably accommodate her as an employee. *School Bd. of Nassau County v. Arline*, 107 S.Ct. 1123 (1987).

On remand, the Florida federal district court held that the teacher was "otherwise qualified" to teach. The teacher posed no threat of spreading tuberculosis to her students in 1978. When she was on medication, medical tests indicated a limited number of negative cultures. Her family members tested negative and she had limited contact with students. The court ordered reinstatement or front-pay in the amount of $768,724 for earnings until retirement. *Arline v. School Bd. of Nassau County*, 692 F.Supp. 1286 (M.D. Fla.1988).

A Nebraska human services agency which provided services to mentally disabled persons adopted a chronic infectious disease policy. Personnel having the most frequent contact with clients were required to take blood tests for AIDS and hepatitis B viruses. It also required employees to notify personnel officers when they knew or suspected that they had one of the diseases. The agency justified the policy by stating that it was concerned that clients might become infected by biting or scratching infected employees. Employees of a county subagency challenged the policy in a federal district court, claiming it violated their constitutional rights. The court accepted evidence that the chances of transmission from staff members to clients from the clients' scratching or biting or from employees' personal hygiene was near zero. There was no evidence of drug abuse or sexual abuse by the agency's personnel. The agency appealed to the U.S. Court of Appeals, Eighth Circuit.

The appeals court ruled that mandatory blood testing was a search or seizure under the Fourth Amendment which must comply with its reasonableness standard. This required balancing the personnel members' privacy rights against public and client interests and safety. The court rejected the agency's argument that employees had a reduced expectation of privacy because they worked in a highly-regulated state agency. It also accepted the district court's finding that the risk of transmission from employees to clients was miniscule. Therefore, the agency's blood testing policy was unreasonable from its inception and was unjustifiable under the Constitution. The appeals court affirmed the district court's order preventing the policy's enforcement. *Glover v. Eastern Nebraska Comm. Office of Retardation*, 867 F.2d 461 (8th Cir. 1989).

The U.S. Court of Appeals, Ninth Circuit, applied *Arline* in a recent case. A teacher of hearing-impaired children was relegated to an administrative position when the school district discovered that he had AIDS. The teacher sued the school board asserting that it had violated his rights under the Rehabilitation Act of 1973 by removing him from the classroom. The teacher's request for a preliminary injunction which would have allowed him to teach until the court could hold a trial and issue a ruling was denied by a U.S. district court. The U.S. Court of Appeals, Ninth Circuit, reversed and issued the preliminary injunction. The court of appeals later issued a decision which sets out the reasons for the issuance of the preliminary injunction.

The court noted that to acquire the preliminary injunction the teacher had to demonstrate a combination of probable success at trial and a possibility of irreparable injury. Under the Rehabilitation Act the teacher could not be dismissed because of his handicapping condition (AIDS) if he was otherwise qualified to teach. The court then applied a test devised by the U.S. Supreme Court in *Arline*. The test provided that "[a] person who poses a significant risk of communicating an infectious disease to others in the workplace will not be otherwise qualified for his or her job if reasonable accommodations will not eliminate that risk." The court then pointed out the district court's finding that transmission of AIDS was unlikely to occur in the classroom. The court held that the teacher was otherwise qualified for his position because his presence in the classroom would not pose "a significant risk of communicating an infectious disease to others." This finding meant that the teacher would probably succeed at trial.

The court then noted that although the teacher's salary was not reduced when he was transferred to the administrative position, the transfer removed him from a job for which he had developed special skills and from which he derived "tremendous personal satisfaction and joy." The administrative position, on the other hand, involved no student contact and did not utilize the teacher's skills, training or experience. The court also observed that the teacher's ability to work would surely be affected in time by AIDS which has proved fatal in all reported cases. The court concluded that any delay in returning the teacher to the classroom caused an irretrievable loss of the teacher's productive time. This established the possibility of irreparable injury if the preliminary injunction was not awarded.

Because the teacher had shown 1) that he would probably succeed at trial, and 2) that the denial of a preliminary injunction in his favor could cause him irreparable injury the court awarded the preliminary injunction. The teacher was returned to the classroom. *Chalk v. U.S. Dist. Court*, 840 F.2d 701 (9th Cir. 1988).

A sixty-one-year-old speech pathologist for the Ohio Mental Retardation and Developmental Disabilities Board became ill, and the board determined that she could no longer perform her job. Because of her age, her supervisor told her that under Ohio law she had only two options: an unpaid medical leave, which would not entitle her to any benefits, or a length-of-service retirement, which would entitle her to a monthly payment. Had she been under sixty, the Ohio plan would have given her a third option: disability benefits with the possibility of returning to work if her condition sufficiently improved. Under this third option, she would have been entitled to receive double the amount of money per month as she would have under the retirement option. Faced with the two choices put to her, she chose the length-of-service retirement. She sued the board in federal district court claiming age discrimination. The district court determined that the employer's conduct constituted "involuntary retirement" because of age. The board appealed to the U.S. Court of Appeals, Sixth Circuit.

The school board contended that the speech therapist was retiring in order to obtain health benefits and that this was not actionable. The court, however, concluded that she was not retiring because of health reasons but that her benefits were limited because of her age. The court of appeals determined that in administering retirement plans employers may not force older workers involuntarily into less desirable retirement programs on the basis of age. The court of appeals affirmed the trial court's decision. *Betts v. Hamilton County*, 897 F.2d 1380 (6th Cir. 1990).

The Pennsylvania Department of Transportation revoked the driving privileges of a school bus driver who had worked for eighteen years at a public school district. The license revocation occurred nearly two years after the driver was diagnosed as a diabetic and found incompetent to drive a school bus under a Pennsylvania statute. The driver appealed to a Pennsylvania trial court, which ruled that the transportation department's action violated § 504 of the Rehabilitation Act of 1973, 29 U.S.C. § 794. The court reinstated the driver's driving privileges, but also ordered that the district perform a blood prick test on the driver each day she was scheduled to drive and to suspend her immediately if her condition was not under control. The district was also ordered to supply copies of blood tests to the transportation department. The department appealed to the Pennsylvania Commonwealth Court.

The commonwealth court considered the trial court's decision in view of the U.S. Supreme Court's decision in *School Bd. of Nassau County v. Arline*, above. The *Arline* case held that in Rehabilitation Act cases, courts were to evaluate the condition of the individual handicapped person who was otherwise qualified to perform the job duties. The transportation department's argument that diabetics presented a risk to the safety of bus passengers was speculative and inappropriate. In each case, the inquiry must be into whether the employee was able to perform the job duties. In this case, the driver's diabetes had been under control since her release from the hospital. Because the school district and transportation department would not suffer a great burden by accommodating the school bus driver, the trial court had properly reinstated her. However, because the transportation department was solely authorized to make department testing regulations, the commonwealth court affirmed the driver's reinstatement but not the extra testing requirements. *Comm. of Pennsylvania v. Tinsley*, 564 A.2d 286 (Pa.Cmwlth. 1989).

A blind District of Columbia man was hired by the Department of Health, Education and Welfare as a public affairs assistant. The employee was then transferred to the same position in the Department of Education (DOE). He was originally hired to transcribe printed matter into Braille. Upon his transfer, however, his duties consisted of analyzing and answering correspondence. The employee sued the DOE, claiming it had not reasonably accommodated his handicap. Thereafter the employee received a notice from his supervisor stating that his job performance and attitude were unsatisfactory. He was advised that he had thirty days to improve his performance or face termination. Four months later his employment was terminated. The employee sued the DOE under § 501 of the Rehabilitation Act in a federal district court. The district court held for the DOE. It found that the employee had been provided reasonable accommodation for the performance of his duties. The employee then appealed to the U.S. Court of Appeals, District of Columbia Circuit.

The appeals court held that the DOE had accommodated the employee's visual handicap. The position required only very basic skills such as making phone calls to obtain information in order to answer the correspondence. The employee was provided two part-time readers and efforts had been made to secure a full-time reader. Even after the DOE provided a reader, the employee's work continued to be unsatisfactory. While other people in the office drafted up to twelve letters per week, the employee's workload was reduced to six letters per week. The department provided accommodations which made it possible for the employee to perform his essential duties. The court of appeals affirmed the lower court's decision. *Carter v. Bennett*, 840 F.2d 63 (D.C.Cir.1988).

A physically disabled Nevada student received a teaching degree in special education and was then licensed by the state of Nevada as a special education teacher. She applied for a teaching position with a Nevada school district and also placed herself on the list of persons available for substitute teaching. She worked as a substitute teacher for over three years and received high praise for her performance. However, she was not offered permanent employment. She then worked as a substitute teacher under a federally-funded temporary contract at another school. The following spring the school had four teaching positions available and offered the teacher a temporary contract. When the teacher received her one-year temporary contract, a permanent position was open in the school district but was given to a student teacher with no teaching experience. The teacher received the most difficult and demanding class assignment at the school. She then filed a discrimination lawsuit against the school district in a U.S. district court.

The court found that under § 794 of the Rehabilitation Act, an otherwise qualified handicapped individual could not be discriminated against under any program or activity receiving federal financial assistance. The teacher fell within the Act's definition of a handicapped person and was otherwise qualified to serve as a special education teacher. The court found that the school district never made an affirmative effort to recognize the teacher's handicaps or to accommodate them. Thus she was discriminated against solely on the basis of her handicap. The court found for the teacher and awarded her compensatory damages. *Recanzone v. Washoe County School Dist.*, 696 F.Supp. 1372 (D.Nev.1988).

A disabled black teacher began to work for an Oregon school district in 1971. She had suffered from a degenerative condition in her hip since childhood. By 1979 she required a total hip replacement. In 1980 and 1981, she was injured when students ran into her at work. These injuries aggravated her hip condition but she was able to continue teaching. She missed the last three weeks of the 1981 school year because of the injuries. From August to November of 1981, the teacher was "loaned" to the United Way. She then worked for the school district in a nonteaching position until June, 1982, when funding for her position expired. The teacher then requested that the school district place her in another nonteaching position with no student contact. She was not reinstated until July, 1985 when a position in the teacher's support center became available. She worked in that position until 1986 when she voluntarily resigned. Meanwhile, the teacher had filed a lawsuit in an Oregon trial court, alleging unlawful employment practices and discrimination based on her race, gender and handicap. The court held for the school district, but denied the school district's demand for attorney's fees. Both parties then appealed to the Oregon Court of Appeals.

The court of appeals upheld the lower court's decision. The school was required to offer the injured teacher a suitable job as soon as one became available. In this case the available jobs required either student contact, which was unacceptable to the teacher, or an advanced degree or certification, which she did not hold. The court found that the school did not commit unlawful employment practices by failing to reinstate the teacher since none of the positions were suitable. The court also denied the school's claim for attorney's fees as it did not find the teacher's claims to be frivolous, unreasonable or without foundation. *Robinson v. School Dist. No. 1*, 759 P.2d 1116 (Or.App.1988).

An applicant for a special education teaching position in Iowa sued a local education agency under the federal Rehabilitation Act and Iowa law alleging that the agency refused to hire him due to his physical disability. The teacher, a resident of Vermont, suffered from several severe handicaps but was able to walk without assistance and to lift children and drive. The teacher applied to the Iowa agency for a job, and was scheduled for an interview in Iowa at his own expense, with possible reimbursement if he were hired.

After arranging the interview, the teacher became concerned that he had not disclosed his handicaps. Because of limited financial resources, he did not wish to fly to Iowa only to be rejected because of his handicaps. He called the Iowa school, explained his handicaps and was told that the job involved transporting children which, in turn, required a bus driver's permit that the teacher probably could not get because of his handicaps. The agency suggested a trip to Iowa would probably be futile.

The teacher then sued in a U.S. district court, which found in his favor. The test of proof for a discrimination claim under the Rehabilitation Act is: 1) that the plaintiff is a handicapped individual under the terms of the Act; 2) that the plaintiff is otherwise qualified to participate in the program or activity at issue; 3) that the plaintiff was excluded from the program or activity solely by reason of her or his handicap; and 4) that the program or activity receives federal financial assistance.

Here, there was no dispute that the plaintiff was a handicapped individual within the meaning of the Rehabilitation Act. The court also had little difficulty in finding that the plaintiff was otherwise qualified for the position, because of his superior credentials. The court also found that the plaintiff had satisfied the third and fourth prongs of the test, in that the defendant agency was a recipient of federal financial assistance, including funds received pursuant to the EAHCA and that, with a minimum of accommodation, the school district could have arranged an alternative situation whereby the teacher would not have had to transport children. The court awarded the teacher $1,000 damages for mental anguish, and $5,150 for loss of earnings. *Fitzgerald v. Green Valley Educ. Agency*, 589 F.Supp. 1130 (S.D.Iowa 1984).

A Kansas school district employed a high school principal who served as its principal for grades seven through twelve. The district also employed the principal's wife, who had contracts to drive a school bus and to sell concessions at school sporting events. The principal had been employed for a period of almost nine years. In the middle of a two-year contract for employment, the district authorized the principal to take a leave of absence due to his alcohol-related problems. The principal was admitted to a hospital for drug and alcohol rehabilitation. He underwent treatment until he received a work release permit nearly two months later. The school board decided to pay the principal for his leave of absence. However, within two months, the school board adopted a resolution consolidating the school district into a one-principal system and resolving not to renew the principal's contract. The board notified the principal that his position had been abolished for economic reasons. The principal accused the board of failing to renew his contract because of his status as a recovering alcoholic. Within several months of the district's nonrenewal of the principal's contract, it advised his wife that her bus driving position had also been eliminated. This was because her bus route had been combined with another route for the following school year. The district also stated that concessions would be operated by high school students and that her contract to sell concessions at sporting events for the school year was terminated.

The couple filed a lawsuit against the district in a federal district court, claiming that it had wrongfully discharged both of them. The lawsuit was filed under several federal statutes, including the Rehabilitation Act of 1973, 29 U.S.C. § 794. The husband stated that the reasons given for nonrenewal by the district were pretextual and that the termination constituted unlawful discrimination under the Rehabilitation Act. The school district filed a motion for summary judgment, stating that the husband and wife had failed to state any claims upon which relief could be granted. According to the court, a party claiming discrimination under the Rehabilitation Act must prove that he is a handicapped person under the act, that he is otherwise qualified for the position sought, that he is being excluded from the position solely by reason of his handicap, and that the program or activity maintaining the position received federal funding. The principal's claims failed because he did not claim that he had been dismissed solely because of his alcoholism. The principal himself had stated other issues, including general dissatisfaction by the district about his job performance. Therefore, the court granted the district's motion for summary judgment. It also dismissed his state law claims for wrongful discharge and the wife's complaint that she had been discriminated against for associating with a person with alcohol-related problems.

Noting that the district had not violated the constitutional rights of either the husband or wife, the court granted the district's motions to dismiss the lawsuit. *Pierce v. Engle*, 726 F.Supp. 1231 (D.Kan.1989).

The last cases in this section involve alleged racial discrimination. The process followed by the court is the same as outlined in the above cases.

A black Maryland speech and language pathologist indicated she wished to become an elementary school principal. She had been working as a fulltime speech pathologist, dividing her time between two elementary schools. She had never held a position that involved administrative or supervisory duties. After she received her doctoral degree, she submitted an application to the Elementary Principal Assessment Center (center) which was the first stepping stone for persons interested in becoming an elementary school principal. Applications were reviewed by a screening committee. The committee members worked independently and were not told the names or races of the applicants. The speech pathologist was ranked very low and not admitted to the center. She then filed this suit in a federal district court alleging race discrimination and that her failure to be accepted was in retaliation for her previous filing of a discrimination lawsuit. The school moved for summary judgment.

The court noted that in order to succeed on a claim of retaliation the plaintiff must prove that there was some causal connection between the failure to be accepted and the protected activity. Since members of the selection committee did not know of her previous claims, there was no connection to her nonacceptance. To succeed on her discrimination claim the speech pathologist must show that she was not hired even though she was qualified. At this point the defendant must articulate a legitimate, nondiscriminatory reason for its action, and then the plaintiff must show that the reason given was pretextual. The court noted that the school district showed that it had a non-discriminatory reason for not admitting the speech pathologist. The race-neutral selection process produced far better qualified applicants which included twenty-six percent minorities. Since the speech pathologist failed to produce evidence indicating that the reason given was pretextual, she failed to establish a case of race discrimination. The court granted summary judgment to the school. *Featherson v. Montgomery County Public Schools*, 739 F.Supp. 1021 (D.Md.1990).

The Pulaski County, Arkansas, Special School District decided to have a "head teacher" serve as a liaison to represent the needs of special education students. Two teachers from the special education staff applied for the position: a black male and a white female. When the white female was awarded the head teacher position after being recommended by a two-person selection committee, the black male sued the school district in a U.S. district court claiming racial discrimination. After the district court ruled for the school district the man appealed to the U.S. Court of Appeals, Eighth Circuit.

The court of appeals observed that the district court had determined that the school district selected the white female teacher for legitimate, nondiscriminatory reasons. The school district relied on her prior experiences as a head teacher, the higher evaluations of her overall teaching skills, her flexibility and superior grasp of the fundamentals of developing individualized educational plans. The appellate court observed that the district court's choice to believe an employer's account of its motivations is a factual finding which may be overturned on appeal only if that decision was "clearly erroneous." The court was convinced that the district court carefully considered all the testimony and exhibits and that its findings had ample support in the trial court record. In ruling that the district court's decision was not clearly erroneous the court of appeals stated that "[a] factfinder's choice between two permissible views of the evidence cannot be clearly erroneous."

The man also argued that the district court was wrong in ruling that the ultimate burden of proving intentional discrimination remained with him. He said that in light of the school district's past history of racial discrimination, the district court should have shifted the burden to the district to prove by clear and convincing evidence that the reasons were nondiscriminatory for its selection of the white female. The court of appeals refused to apply the higher standard.

A further argument presented by the man was that the district court mistakenly admitted into evidence teacher evaluations of the two teachers made *after* the selection of the white female as head teacher. The court of appeals ruled, however, that even if it was a mistake to admit the postdecision evaluations into evidence, the district court did not consider them in making its findings. Instead, it relied on the testimony of the selection committee members concerning the areas in which they felt the white female was superior. The decision of the district court denying the man's racial discrimination claim was upheld. *Nelson v. Pulaski County Special School Dist.*, 803 F.2d 961 (8th Cir.1986).

An Alabama sex and race discrimination case concluded with a federal judge's dismissal of the case. The plaintiff, a black female teacher at a school for handicapped children, applied for the position of principal. The selection committee interviewed a total of twenty individuals for the principal position, including sixteen white males, one black female, one oriental female and two white females. The committee selected a white male for the job, citing his superior academic credentials, his experience in securing government grants, his extensive managerial experience and his experience with multi-handicapped children. The black female applicant brought suit in U.S. district court under Title VII of the Civil Rights Act, claiming sex and race discrimination. The court disagreed with her contentions. Although the selection committee was dominated by white males, the two black females on the committee had ranked the white male applicant higher than the plaintiff. The evidence established that he was clearly better qualified for the position than the plaintiff. The court also took notice of evidence that the plaintiff's attitudes were "too rigid." This put her at a disadvantage in seeking promotion to a position where she would be required to deal continuously with handicapped children and "their justifiably distressed parents." The case was dismissed due to the lack of evidence of any discrimination in the principal selection process. *Love v. Alabama Institute for the Deaf and Blind*, 613 F.Supp. 436 (N.D.Ala.1984).

A black woman who was employed by a Missouri school board as an assistant special education teacher sued the board in U.S. district court alleging that the board had failed to promote her to the position of teacher because of her race. The court ruled in favor of the school board holding that the board had articulated legitimate, nondiscriminatory reasons for not hiring the woman as a full teacher. Her superiors, including one other black woman, had conducted periodic evaluations of her abilities and had interviewed her. The evaluations revealed that she was unable to speak clearly and correctly and that her writing style was grammatically incorrect. The court agreed that these alone were grave deficiencies in an applicant for the position of special education teacher. Furthermore, the woman's interviews revealed that she had never given any diagnostic tests while she was employed as an assistant teacher, and she could not tell the interviewers how any of these tests were used. The court held that these deficiencies constituted sufficient grounds for the school board to refuse to promote her to the position of teacher. Judgment was rendered for the school board in all respects. *Love v. Special School Dist. of St. Louis County*, 606 F.Supp. 1320 (E.D.Mo.1985).

C. Right to Privacy

Public employees have a reasonable expectation of privacy guaranteed by the U.S. Constitution.

A U.S. district court in Washington, D.C., declared that school bus attendants may not be subjected to mandatory urine testing unless there is probable cause to suspect that the attendant has engaged in drug use. In this case, a school bus attendant for handicapped children was forced to give a urine sample as part of a program instituted by the Washington school district to ferret out drug use by its transportation employees. When the bus attendant's urine tested positive, her employment was terminated. She sued in U.S. district court, contending that the school district's urinalysis program violated her Fourth Amendment rights.

The court first ruled that the test results were flawed. Although the manufacturers of the urinalysis test used, the EMIT Cannabinoid Assay Test, recommended that the test results be verified through an alternate testing method, the school district had not obtained such verification. After the bus attendant's first urinalysis test, effected by computer, showed that THC metabolites (indicative of marijuana use) were present in her urine, the school district ran the same test manually to verify that result. No alternative test was performed. Having disregarded the instructions of the manufacturers of the EMIT test, the school district could not use the results as a ground for termination.

Next, the court held that urinalysis testing could not be required without probable cause to suspect the bus attendant of drug use. Unlike school bus drivers or mechanics, who expect that their privacy rights will be limited by public safety considerations, school bus attendants legitimately expect a zone of personal privacy. Urine testing imposes upon this expectation of privacy. Therefore, the court stated, urine testing of school bus attendants is a "search" under the Fourth Amendment to the U.S. Constitution and requires probable cause. Since the school district had no probable cause to suspect that the bus attendant had ever used drugs, the board's decision to terminate her employment was reversed. Full back pay and reinstatement were ordered. *Jones v. McKenzie*, 628 F.Supp. 1500 (D.D.C.1986).

A Massachusetts public school teacher was suspended for two days and involuntarily transferred from her teaching position after being found guilty of insubordination and conduct unbecoming a teacher. The teacher had disagreed with her principal regarding the treatment of a handicapped boy. She wrote a case study paper for a night class that she was taking, which described the boy's situation and which was highly critical of the principal. Shortly thereafter, at a meeting held to evaluate the boy's progress, the teacher gave her paper to the special education supervisor at her school. She did not tell him that her case study paper contained confidential material. The supervisor never read her paper and returned it to the teacher the same day.

On the following day the principal requested that the teacher turn over a copy of the paper, claiming that it was part of the boy's official file which the principal had a duty to examine. The teacher refused and the principal informed her that she was being insubordinate. Two weeks later she turned over a copy of the paper, but the principal left the question of disciplinary action open until a later date. Several months later, on Parent's Night, the teacher posted copies of her correspondence with the principal concerning the allegedly insubordinate refusal to immediately turn over her case study paper. A parent later complained to school officials regarding the teacher's public display of this correspondence. The teacher was then suspended for two days and involuntarily transferred from her teaching post as a result of her insubordination in refusing to promptly furnish the principal with a copy of her paper, and for engaging in conduct unbecoming a teacher by posting the letters on Parents' Night.

Concluding that her constitutional rights had been violated, the teacher sued her school district in U.S. district court. The court held in favor of the school district and the U.S. Court of Appeals, First Circuit, affirmed. The appeals court held that the teacher had no Fourth Amendment privacy interest in her paper because she had given it to the special education supervisor. Therefore, when the principal demanded the paper she could not assert her right to privacy. The court further held that her act of posting the principal's letters to her concerning the paper were unprotected as well since the matter was primarily an employment dispute, and not a matter of public interest. The disciplinary sanctions against the teacher were, therefore, held not to violate the teacher's constitutional rights. *Alinovi v. Worcester School Comm.*, 777 F.2d 776 (1st Cir.1985).

D. Collective Bargaining

A tenured teacher was laid off because of a staff reduction in a Michigan school district. She was covered by a collective bargaining agreement which contained a provision governing layoff/recall procedures and qualification standards. During her layoff she completed all state requirements for learning disabilities certification. The teacher sent the school district a teaching certificate showing a new learning disabilities endorsement. The teacher filed petitions with the State Tenure Commission, contending that she should have been recalled to learning disabilities positions which were given to probationary teachers with less seniority and for whom the school district had to seek temporary approval. The commission found that the school district was obligated to recall the teacher for learning disabilities positions before applying for a permit or a renewal for temporary approval of probationary teachers. Both parties sought review of the commissioner's decision in a Michigan circuit court, which affirmed the decision and remanded the matter to the commission for further administrative proceedings. Both parties then appealed to the Court of Appeals of Michigan.

The court held that the school district could fill a position with a person on "temporary approval" only when a fully certified teacher was unavailable. Because the teacher was fully certified she should have been chosen for any learning disabilities positions ahead of any temporarily approved candidate. Michigan law further provided that a tenured teacher who had been terminated because of a reduction in staff should be appointed to the first vacancy for which she was certified and qualified. A teacher could not waive any of these rights and privileges under state law by signing a collective bargaining agreement. The appeals court affirmed the commission's decision and remanded the matter to the commission for further administrative proceedings. *Hodgeson v. Bd. of Educ. of Buena Vista*, 438 N.W.2d 295 (Mich.App. 1989).

An Illinois private school received funding from the state to operate a special education and therapy program for its students. The school also received federal funding to operate a Head Start program. The funds received were kept separate and the school operated each program independent of the other. The school employed forty-five individuals, of which approximately twenty were assigned to work in the school's therapeutic program. The National Labor Relations Board (NLRB) found that the school had violated the National Labor Relations Act by threatening and then discharging two psychotherapists because they had repeatedly protested the school's delay in paying their wages and the announcement of imminent layoffs. The school did not dispute these facts but contended that the NLRB lacked jurisdiction over the school's operations since the school received funding from state and federal sources. The NLRB petitioned the U.S. Court of Appeals, Seventh Circuit, for enforcement of the NLRB's order requiring the private school to remedy its unfair labor practices.

The court of appeals held that the school's relationship to state agencies for funding purposes was insufficient to deprive the NLRB of jurisdiction. The unfair labor practices at issue evolved from the state funded therapeutic day-school program which was independently operated, funded from separate revenues and staffed with their own employees. The NLRB's jurisdiction was not limited by the fact that the school was operated in part through public funds. The court of appeals ordered enforcement of the NLRB's order requiring the private school to remedy its unfair labor practices. *NLRB v. Potential School for Exceptional Children*, 883 F.2d 560 (7th Cir.1989).

A Louisiana woman was employed as a teacher's aide for handicapped students. The aide used her own car to transport the students from their homes to school. She was reimbursed for her mileage expenses. The school purchased a bus and the aide assumed the duties of an attendant during the ride. She received no compensation for this additional work until several years later when she requested additional wages. She was then paid additional wages equivalent to two hours a day at her teacher's aide salary. The aide sued the school board in a Louisiana trial court for retroactive wages for the previous three years. The trial court dismissed the lawsuit and the aide appealed to the Court of Appeal of Louisiana, Third Circuit.

The court of appeal held that the aide was not entitled to additional wages for the time period before she entered into the agreement with the board to be compensated for her additional bus attendant duties. The court noted that compensation for bus attendants was not part of the aide's original contract but was an integral part of her job as a teacher's aide. The aide had accepted the job as offered. When she requested additional compensation for her bus attendant duties, she was compensated in the amount requested. The court of appeal affirmed the trial court's decision denying additional wages. *Cormier v. Acadia Parish School Bd.*, 548 So.2d 73 (La.App.3d Cir.1989).

After a collective bargaining agreement between a teachers' union and a school district expired, a series of selective teacher strikes was called by the union. The school district asked for a preliminary injunction prohibiting further strikes which was granted by a Pennsylvania common pleas court. The union appealed to the Commonwealth Court of Pennsylvania, which ruled that the common pleas court was wrong in holding that the strike activity posed a threat to the health, safety or welfare of the public. The school district had argued that the strike infringed upon the right to an education guaranteed to all handicapped children under the EAHCA. Although the selective strikes did not violate the rights of handicapped students in this case, the commonwealth court conceded that the same facts could become aggravated by "some unexpected circumstances or [if] continued for such a period of time" so as to violate the rights of handicapped students. Such circumstances, however, were not yet present, and the lower court decision favoring the school district was reversed. *Wilkes-Barre Area Educ. Ass'n v. Wilkes-Barre Area School Dist.*, 523 A.2d 1183 (Pa.Cmwlth.1987).

A group of West Virginia teachers began a strike to protest the failure of the local government to enact a wage and benefit package to their satisfaction. The local board of education filed suit in a West Virginia trial court and the judge granted it injunctive relief. The teachers then appealed to the Supreme Court of Appeals of West Virginia.

The court noted that the trial court had ruled correctly on the current law in West Virginia, and looked to see if it was now time to change that law. The current law held that the strike was illegal in the absence of legislation requiring the public employer to recognize the association as a union. Other jurisdictions outside West Virginia had recently changed their laws allowing public employees to form unions. In the jurisdictions allowing unions, contracts were usually formed by negotiation. In West Virginia contracts are formed solely by the legislative body. When contracts are formed this way, allowing public employees to strike would give them excessive bargaining leverage and threatened the public welfare. These factors would continue to be problems in West Virginia unless a legislative act changed the process. In order to avoid irreparable harm to the public welfare, teachers in West Virginia would not be recognized as a union and therefore would not be allowed to strike. The supreme court upheld the decision of the trial court. *Jefferson Cty. Bd. of Educ. v. Educ. Ass'n*, 393 S.E.2d 653 (W.Va.1990).

A probationary Wisconsin special education teacher's contract was not re-newed. The teacher sued for reinstatement and money damages in a Wisconsin trial court. She asserted that the board violated a provision of the law providing for a private conference between the members of the board and the affected teacher prior to the nonrenewal. The teacher also claimed bias on the part of a board member who was also the parent of a special education student in the teacher's class. The trial court granted summary judgment to the school district, dismissing the complaint. She appealed to the Court of Appeals of Wisconsin.

The appellate court determined that the board was immune from suit for damages because the acts complained of were discretionary rather than min-isterial. However, the court determined that there were material issues of fact precluding summary judgment on the claim for reinstatement. A Wisconsin statute provides that a teacher has a right to a private conference with the board prior to nonrenewal of his or her contract. Her complaint alleged that one of the board members voting with the four to three majority not to renew her contract was a student's mother. Therefore, the court concluded that the teacher was entitled to a trial on her claim for reinstatement. Her complaint raised issues of disputed fact material to her claim that the private conference provisions were not properly followed and that there may have been bias on the part of a board member. *Harkness v. Palmyra-Eagle School Dist.*, 460 N.W.2d 769 (Wis.App.1990).

In 1978, the Leonard Kirtz Mahoning County School for the Retarded hired a woman as a special education teacher. She was assigned to Develop-mental Classroom I, which consisted of students who were the least fortunate in terms of educational potential. After three years she discovered that three teachers for students with the most potential were leaving the school. She made a request to both the superintendent and the principal that she be trans-ferred to one of the vacant positions. However, the county board denied her request and immediately transferred two other teachers, neither of whom had requested reassignment, and hired one new teacher, in order to fill the three vacancies.

The Ohio Supreme Court rebuked the county board for its blatant disre-gard of its own collective bargaining agreement. Reversing an errant lower court, the Supreme Court reinstated an arbitrator's ruling that because the agreement required the county board to respect a teacher's transfer requests, the board was bound to transfer her. Held the court: "The board argues, and the court of appeals decided, that collective bargaining agreements are not as binding upon public employers as they are upon private employers. It is time to put an end to that notion and categorically reject the argument. Today's decision gives notice that negotiated collective bargaining agreements are just as binding upon public employers as they are upon private employers." The county board was ordered to honor its contractual obligation to the teacher. *Mahoning County Bd. of Mental Retardation and Developmental Disabili-ties v. Mahoning County TMR Educ. Ass'n*, 488 N.E.2d 872 (Ohio 1986).

The Supreme Judicial Court of Massachusetts vacated a preliminary in-junction entered by a three-judge panel of the Superior Court, which had enjoined a strike by bus drivers for special needs children. The case arose when several bus companies, with whom the Boston School Committee had contracted, and their bus drivers, failed to negotiate a mutually acceptable collective bargaining agreement. The bus drivers, who were affiliated with the AFL-CIO, declined to work without a contract. Parents of handicapped children were left to make their own arrangements for their children's transportation to and from school. As a result, the parents commenced a class action suit and asked the Superior Court for an injunction ordering the striking school bus drivers back to work, which was granted. On appeal by the school bus drivers' union, the Supreme Judicial Court reversed and held that under Massachusetts law [M.G.L.A. ch. 150E, sec. 9A(b)] the parents could not sue to enjoin the strike because the bus drivers, although ostensibly employed by private bus companies, were public employees. As such, only the public employer could petition the court to enjoin the strike. The court also noted that although state law clearly outlaws any strike by public employees, it just as clearly forbids anyone but the relevant public employer from seeking a back-to-work order. The Superior Court's injunction was therefore vacated. *Allen v. School Comm. of Boston*, 487 N.E.2d 529 (Mass.1986).

The Board of Trustees of the Florida School for the Deaf and the Blind entered into a three-year collective bargaining agreement with its teachers' union, effective July 1, 1983, to June 30, 1986. The agreement contained annual reopeners on salary, insurance benefits and any other two articles chosen by each. Less than one year after the contract had been in effect, the Board of Trustees and the teachers' union reached an impasse over the number of hours teachers were to work each day. A special master was consulted in an attempt to work out a solution, but the board rejected his report. Under Florida law, the board was required to submit the dispute to its legislative body for resolution [F.S.A. sec. 447.403(4)]. The term "legislative body" is defined as the state legislature, any county board of commissioners, any district school board, or the governing body of any municipality. The term also includes any body having authority to make appropriations of public funds [447.203(10)]. The Board of Trustees informed the teachers' union that in its opinion the board itself was a legislative body. The board claimed that since it transferred monies between categories of appropriations, it was a body that appropriates public funds. Therefore the Board of Trustees unilaterally changed the working hours of its special education teachers from seven to seven and one-half hours per day.

The teachers' union filed a complaint with the Public Employees' Relations Commission and received a ruling that the board had committed an unfair labor practice by unilaterally increasing the working hours of its special education teachers. On appeal, this ruling was affirmed. The court stated that just because the Board of Trustees transferred monies into different categories did not mean it was a legislative body. The board only acted pursuant to statutory authority; it was the legislature itself which did the actual appropriating. Since it was not a "legislative body," the Board of Trustees was without authority to unilaterally modify the collective bargaining agreement with the special education teachers' union. The court upheld the Commission's award of penalties and attorney's fees against the board. *Florida School for the Deaf and the Blind v. Florida School for the Deaf and the Blind, Teachers United, FTP-NEA*, 483 So.2d 58 (Fla.App.1st Dist.1986).

E. Tenure, Seniority, Salary and Benefits

The first cases in this section demonstrate the difficulty in determining tenure status.

A Michigan county school district decided to reorganize its special education services for hearing-impaired students. Prior to the reorganization, two constituent school districts had provided these services. After the reorganization, the services were discontinued and the Dearborn Board of Education provided them. Five special education teachers who had lost their jobs in the reorganization were hired by the board of education. The teachers were given credit for seniority earned with other districts. A teachers' union representative challenged the propriety of granting teachers credit for seniority earned in other districts. The trial court held in favor of the board of education and the union appealed to the Court of Appeals of Michigan.

The appeals court noted that the Michigan State School Aid Act provided that if special education personnel were transferred from one district to another they would be "entitled to the rights, benefits and tenure to which the person would otherwise be entitled had that person been employed by the receiving district originally." The overall statutory scheme did not recognize a transfer procedure different from the arrangement used in this case. Thus the five teachers were "transferred" within the meaning of the statute and they were entitled to benefits including retention of their seniority. The court of appeals affirmed the trial court's decision. *Local 681 v. Dearborn Bd. of Educ.*, 431 N.W.2d 253 (Mich.App.1988).

In 1977, a Louisiana teacher began teaching remedial reading and math to slow learners in the fifth and sixth grades. She was employed under the funding of a federal program called Chapter I. In 1985, school authorities were advised of budget cuts in the program. They were given permission to cut Chapter I expenses immediately for the upcoming school year. The principal informed the teacher she would be dismissed; however, the cut was reconsidered. The next spring the teacher received a letter from the school superintendent telling her that her position would be eliminated due to spending cuts in the Chapter I program. After she unsuccessfully contacted principals of other schools for employment, the teacher formally requested employment by writing a letter to the superintendent. The superintendent offered her an opportunity to present her grievances at a school board meeting. At the meeting, the teacher complained of her dismissal, but the school board refused to change its procedure for removing probationary teachers. The teacher then filed suit in a Louisiana trial court, alleging the board had failed to follow the procedure required by state law for removing tenured teachers. She also alleged discrimination and sought damages for her injured reputation. In addition, she claimed that if she was not a tenured teacher, the board had not followed its "reduction in force" policy when it terminated her. The trial court found that the teacher was not tenured for purposes of state law. However, the court determined that she was not a probationary teacher, either. She was in a separate category of teachers, each employed under a federal grant. Thus, she was not entitled to the termination procedures under state law. The teacher appealed to the Louisiana Court of Appeal.

The court of appeal held for the school board and affirmed the trial court's decision. It held that she was neither a tenured nor probationary teacher. Therefore, state requirements did not apply. The court also held that the board's "reduction in force" policy also did not apply. The policy required that layoffs be used as a last resort, based on seniority, qualifications and performance. The teacher was in a special position, having been employed under a federal grant. The court upheld the trial court decision, affirming the layoff. *Abbott v. Claiborne Parish School Bd.*, 550 So.2d 294 (La.App.2d Cir.1989).

A Louisiana civil service employee taught special education classes at a state school operated by the state Department of Health and Human Resources (DHHR). A year after the commencement of her employment by the DHHR, the state legislature created a special school district into which all state special schools were consolidated. The special school district was governed by the state Board of Elementary and Secondary Education (BESE). After the legislative change, state school employees were given the option of remaining classified civil service personnel or becoming probationary teachers under the BESE. The latter option, which the special education instructor selected, would bring the employees under the state tenure laws, which generally require probationary terms of three contract years in order to obtain tenure. Under the statute the word "teacher" implied a certified employee at a special school who had served the mandatory three contract years. Probationary employees were not entitled to the tenure protection afforded to "teachers" and untenured employees could be terminated upon a simple recommendation of a supervisor. Tenured status required a notice and hearing before any termination action could commence accompanied by valid reasons.

The special education employee served for two years under the BESE, when her employment was terminated. She sued BESE in a Louisiana trial court, asserting that she had served in the same position for over three years. She claimed that her year of service under the DHHR should be considered a contract year with BESE and credited toward her acquisition of tenure. The court granted the BESE's motion for summary judgment and the employee appealed to the Louisiana Court of Appeal. The court of appeal refused to consider the employee's argument that her year of service with DHHR should be considered a contract year. The court specifically found that the employee was not a "teacher" as defined by Louisiana education law. The tenure provisions of the Louisiana statute applied only to teachers who were certified and met the other requirements of state law. In this case the DHHR employment did not require a teaching certificate and the employee had not served the mandatory three years of contract service to become a "teacher" in Louisiana. The BESE's motion for summary judgment was correct and the court of appeal affirmed it. *Perkins v. State Bd. of Elem. and Secondary Educ.*, 552 So.2d 735 (La.App.1st Cir.1989).

A Louisiana school district implemented a compensatory education program in compliance with a state law known as the Louisiana Compensatory or Remedial Education Plan. The program contained two job designations, but in later years, the positions were abolished due to budget considerations.

Some employees had their work years reduced. The state legislature then eliminated all appropriations for the state's remedial program and the district's remedial employees were returned to regular teaching positions. However, some employees were placed in nonteaching positions which required a longer work week and loss of a pay supplement which they had received under the remedial program. Seven employees, including a special education assessment consultant, social worker, school psychologist, speech and language consultant, an adaptive physical education coordinator and a remedial reading specialist sued the school board in a Louisiana trial court seeking recovery of lost wages and reinstatement under the state tenure law. The court awarded the specialists compensation for lost wages and administrative fees but denied their application for a declaratory judgment under the tenure law. The specialists appealed to the Louisiana Court of Appeal.

The court first considered the Louisiana statute which prohibited school districts from paying supervisors, principals or other administrative personnel salaries which were less than they had received in the preceding year. The district argued that the specialists were not administrative personnel under the statute and therefore were not entitled to recover their salary supplements. The court disagreed, finding that the specialists were administrative personnel under the act. The trial court had also been correct in finding that the specialists were not protected under the Louisiana Tenure Law, which protected permanent teachers only on specified grounds and with prescribed constitutional safeguards. The statute only applied to removal from office, and was not implicated in this case, where it was not shown that the specialists had suffered a loss of rank or status within the school district. The court of appeal affirmed the trial court's decision. *Brooks v. Orleans Parish School Bd.*, 550 So.2d 1267 (La.App.4th Cir.1989).

The next cases deal with transferring tenure status.

An Indiana teacher held a public school teacher's certificate with elementary and handicapped endorsements. The teacher signed a regular teacher's contract with an Indiana school. The school board assigned the teacher to a special education class. A month later the teacher requested medical leave from the special education position because of stress related problems. The leave was to last only as long as it took to reassign her to a regular education class. The board denied the teacher's request to be transferred, but approved her request for immediate medical leave. After the board failed to assign her to a regular class which became available in January, she sued the board in an Indiana trial court. The court found for the teacher and the board appealed to the Court of Appeals of Indiana, Third District.

The court of appeals held that the teacher was entitled to compensation for the salary she would have received had the board assigned her to the elementary teaching position. The court noted that state law required that where a board had granted a leave of absence, the teacher had the right to return to a teaching position for which she was certified. The teacher was certified, qualified and had a statutory right to return to the elementary teaching position. Because the board did not transfer her to the open position, it had failed to honor her statutory right. The court of appeals affirmed the trial court's decision. *Jay School Corp. v. Cheeseman*, 540 N.E.2d 1248 (Ind.App.3d Dist.1989).

When an Arkansas school district delayed and hindered the implementation of a special education program, the principal of a school and several teachers discussed these problems with the administrator of the program, then with school district administrators and the school board. When these efforts proved fruitless, the principal and teachers sent a letter to the state department of education. The letter enumerated instances of failure to follow established procedures relating to the education of handicapped students. The department of education conducted an investigation which resulted in a conclusion that the school district had not followed proper procedures in the placement of handicapped students.

Afterward, several of the teachers' contracts were not renewed and the principal and one teacher resigned under pressure by the school district. The principal and teachers sued the school district and various administrators seeking money damages for the retaliation they suffered in response to the letter. They claimed the retaliation was a violation of their First Amendment right of free speech on a matter of public concern in their community. When a U.S. district court ruled in favor of the principal and teachers, the school district and administrators appealed.

The U.S. Court of Appeals, Eighth Circuit, determined that the letter concerned the quality of education in the community and the school district's observance of federal policy as prescribed by Congress for the welfare of handicapped children. The letter therefore involved a matter of public concern and was protected by the First Amendment. The lower court's ruling was upheld. *Southside Pub. Schools v. Hill*, 827 F.2d 270 (8th Cir.1987).

The following case illustrates that, for purposes of tenure, a transfer from a position not related to special education to one involving special education responsibilities is not a lateral transfer. After an "excessed" elementary school principal in New York was assigned to a position as assistant to the director of special education he filed suit against the school district claiming that his tenure rights had been violated. Following dismissal of his case by a lower court, he appealed to the Supreme Court, Appellate Division. The major issue before the appellate court was whether the new assignment, which would have required the principal to serve a 3-year probationary term, was outside the area in which he was granted tenure. The school district argued that the two positions were essentially the same because both included implementation of the curriculum and supervision of the teachers. The court rejected this argument, pointing to the unique responsibilities in special education and the need to focus on the remedial needs of certain groups of students in accordance with federal and state law. The court ordered the plaintiff appointed to a suitable position. *Cowan v. Bd. of Educ. of Brentwood Union*, 472 N.Y.S.2d 429 (A.D.2d Dept.1984).

Disputes over salary are the subject of the following two cases.

A learning disabilities consultant was hired in March, 1980 by the Trenton, New Jersey, Board of Education. At the time of hiring he was placed at step eleven of the learning consultants' salary guide. Beginning in the fall of 1980, and for each academic year thereafter, the consultant was moved up one step on the salary guide. By 1983 he was at step 15, was being paid an annual salary of $27,227 and was scheduled for an increase to $28,569.

The school board and the teacher's association, however, had negotiated an agreement before the learning disabilities consultant was hired which provided that any employee hired after February 1 of any year would remain at his or her step on the salary guide during the following academic year. The school district, which had erroneously advanced the consultant on the salary guide in the fall of 1980 even though he had been hired after February 1, did not realize its error for three years; it then reduced the teacher to step fourteen and made a reduction in his salary from $28,569 to $27,751 a year. When the consultant received his first reduced check he contacted the personnel office immediately. His check was not corrected. On January 30, 1984, he informed the Board of Education that he had retained an attorney and requested back pay and reinstatement to his proper salary level. On February 8, 1984, the board sent him a letter refusing his request.

The consultant filed a complaint with the New Jersey Commissioner of Education. The case was heard by an administrative law judge (ALJ), who ruled that the complaint had not been filed within the required ninety days of the date the consultant first received notice of his salary reduction. The ALJ held that notice of the salary reduction had been accomplished by the consultant's receipt of his paycheck. The State Board of Education affirmed the ALJ's decision, and the consultant appealed to the New Jersey Superior Court, Appellate Division.

The court found that under the New Jersey Teacher Tenure Act the consultant had a vested right in his salary. Therefore, it held that the unilateral decision by the school district to reduce his salary violated his rights under the Act. It said that the fact that the consultant's paycheck was less than what he expected did not constitute proper notice that his salary was being reduced. It was not until the school board's letter of February 8, 1984, denying his requests for back pay and reinstatement to his proper salary that he was put on notice that a "dispute" existed. The court remanded the case to the Commissioner of Education for resolution of the dispute on the merits. *Stockton v. Bd. of Educ. of City of Trenton*, 509 A.2d 264 (N.J.Super. A.D. 1986).

Salary errors were alleged in a Louisiana case, where two special education teachers brought suit against their school board alleging that the board had wrongly calculated their salary supplements. Under a former statute, special education teachers were to be paid ten percent of their base salary. That statute was later amended, making the ten percent supplement discretionary, but mandating that no teacher currently receiving the supplement shall suffer a loss in pay. The lower court granted summary judgment to the board, stating that after passage of the amendment the plaintiffs had suffered no loss in pay. The Louisiana Court of Appeal overturned the lower court's judgment, stating that the amendment had no bearing on the factual issue of whether the plaintiffs' salaries were miscalculated. The case was remanded for further factual development. *Wattigney v. Jefferson Parish School Bd.*, 445 So.2d 1318 (La.App.5th Cir.1984).

The last cases deal with benefits from seniority or tenure.

Special education employees in New York challenged the infringement of their seniority rights in the following two cases. In the first, two tenured teachers employed by the New York Board of Cooperative Educational Services (BOCES) in the special education area brought suit alleging that after two school districts for which BOCES provided special education services established their own special education programs, no longer utilizing the BOCES program, BOCES improperly dismissed them. The teachers were hired as of the date of their dismissal by the respective school districts as teachers in their programs. The teachers sought to have themselves reinstated to their former positions as tenured BOCES teachers. The court held that because BOCES retained teachers in the special education tenure area having less seniority that the dismissed teachers, the abolition of the teachers' positions may have violated teacher tenure law. The New York Supreme Court, Appellate Division, reversed a lower court ruling dismissing the teachers' complaint and remanded the case to the lower court, which was to reinstate the teachers if it found that teachers with less seniority than the dismissed teachers were retained by BOCES, in violation of New York tenure law. BOCES would then be directed to follow an appropriate procedure for correctly determining the teachers with less seniority to be made eligible for hiring by the school districts which had established their own special education program. *Koch v. Putnam-Northern Westchester Bd. of Coop. Educ. Serv.*, 470 N.Y.S.2d 651 (A.D.2d Dept.1984).

In a later case, a dispute arose after a school district and four other component districts took over part of a learning achievement program which had formerly been operated by BOCES. Two special education teachers who had been employed by BOCES sought to fill the new positions created but their applications were rejected. They brought suit against the school district claiming that they had a right, at their option, to claim such positions under a statute defining teachers' rights as a result of a school district taking over a program formerly operated by BOCES. The New York Supreme Court, Appellate Division, disagreed, saying that absent a showing that the teachers had been "excessed," the school district was not required by statute to hire them. *Buenzow v. Lewiston-Porter Cent. School Dist.*, 474 N.Y.S.2d 161 (A.D.4th Dept.1984).

The Director of Special Education Services for a local school district in South Dakota alleged that the board of education acted illegally in not finding him another position in the district after his position was eliminated due to economic necessity. The director argued before the state Supreme Court that the board was obligated to follow the state's staff reduction policy. Under the statute, he argued, he was classified as a "teacher" and thus was protected from termination under the circumstances. The board insisted that despite the fact that the director held a teaching certificate and was employed under a "Teaching Contract," only certain provisions of the statute were applicable to him because his employment was administrative in nature. The director, continued the board, was an "other administrative employee" under the statute. The director's other certifications, claimed the board, were not taken into account. The court held in the director's favor. The board acted illegally in not following the staff reduction procedures applicable to continuing contract teachers. Though the director may have been classed as an "other administrative employee" under the statute, the statute also provided that such persons were "teachers" for purposes of tenure. *Burke v. Lead-Deadwood School Dist. No. 40-1*, 347 N.W.2d 343 (S.D.1984).

A different result was reached by the Supreme Court of Iowa in a case involving a teacher who had filled a special education teaching vacancy for one year. The teacher was not special education-certified but was given special permission by the State Department of Public Instruction to teach a special education class, because of the school district's inability to find a replacement for a special education teacher who had resigned. At the close of the school year, the "substitute" teacher expressed an interest in returning the following year either in the same capacity or as a regular classroom teacher. He also offered to receive special education training over the summer months. However, he was not reemployed. The state Supreme Court affirmed a lower court ruling in the district's favor, finding that the teacher was a "temporary substitute" and therefore did not have probationary teaching status. The statutory tenure provisions thus did not apply to the teacher and his termination was upheld. *Fitzgerald v. Saydel Consol. School Dist.*, 345 N.W.2d 101 (Iowa 1984).

In a case arising in the state of Washington, unemployment compensation benefits were claimed by employees of a state school for the deaf and blind. The noninstructional employees appealed a decision of the Washington Commissioner of the Department of Employment Security who denied them unemployment benefits during the summer closure of the schools. Washington Unemployment Compensation law prescribes that to deny unemployment benefits to an employee off work during the summer months, written notices to the employee must state that he or she will perform services at the end of the summer months. The civil service employees claimed that written notices they received advising them of the summer closure of the schools, informing them that they were being placed on "leave without pay," and stating that they would be expected to resume their positions at a time to be specified later, were ineffective when applied to civil service employees to exempt them from the unemployment compensation statute. The schools argued that the employees were noninstructional employees rendering services for an educational institution, thus making them ineligible for unemployment benefits while not working during summer recess. The Court of Appeals of Washington was persuaded by the schools' argument and found that the employees were not entitled to unemployment benefits. The written notices the employees received satisfied the unemployment compensation statute's exemption requirement by being "reasonable assurances" of reemployment and were consistent with civil service law. *Alexander v. Employment Security Dep't of the State of Washington*, 688 P.2d 516 (Wash.App.1984).

II. BUDGET AND FINANCE

The following cases concern litigation over special education budget and finance. The first cases deal with disputes concerning state and federal funding.

The U.S. Department of Education regulates funds allocated to states under the Education of the Handicapped Act (EHA). A state receives federal funds based on the number of handicapped children receiving special education and related services. The EHA also includes provisions to ensure that federal funds are used to defray the excess costs of educating handicapped children and to supplement the amount spent by the state for this purpose. The Spokane School District received federal funds for the purpose of educating its handicapped children. Prior to the 1980-81 school year, Spokane taught handicapped children in self-contained classrooms. Because self-contained classrooms were not available in all schools, extensive transportation was necessary. The Association of Retarded Citizens challenged the use of self-contained classrooms as a violation of the EHA requirement of the "least restrictive environment." In response, Spokane changed its system to teach all but the most severely handicapped children in regular classrooms. As a result, the district spent less for the special education of handicapped children in the 1981-82 school year than in the 1980-81 school year. In 1983, the Department of Education audited Spokane's use of the federal funds and determined that the federal funds were used to "supplant" state funds rather than supplement them because the amount spent in 1981-82 was less than in 1980-81. The district appealed to the U.S. Court of Appeals, Ninth Circuit.

On appeal, Spokane contended that so long as it did not use federal funds to displace state funds for particular costs, the statute was satisfied. The Department of Education, however, argued that the statute prohibited local agencies from using federal funds without using state funds in a particular program and further required local agencies to maintain the same level of funding efforts each year. The court determined that Spokane's interpretation would allow a local agency to reduce its own expenditures for educating handicapped children without losing federal funds by simply eliminating particular programs. Therefore, the court determined that this reading of the statute was unreasonable. The court affirmed the Department of Education's decision to require maintenance of local funding efforts each year. *State of Washington v. U.S. Dep't of Educ.*, 905 F.2d 274 (9th Cir. 1990).

Before the passage of an amendment to the Louisiana constitution, the state's public educational system was under the control of the state superintendent of education. The amendment created the Board of Elementary and Secondary Education (BESE). The board was supposed to take over most of the superintendent's duties, but power conflicts between the two often arose. Before the superintendent's position was eliminated in 1988, the BESE and the superintendent jointly applied to the U.S. Department of Education (DOE) for funds under the Education for the Handicapped Act (EHA). After the DOE approved the funds, they were distributed, as was customary, to the superintendent. The BESE discovered that the superintendent planned to use the funds on a program it believed did not fulfill federal requirements. The BESE contacted the DOE about the alleged misexpenditures. After the DOE completed an audit, it ordered the BESE to repay the funds, concluding they had been misspent. The BESE contended that it was not responsible because it had not received the funds. After the Education Appeal Board ordered it to return the funds, the BESE appealed to the U.S. Court of Appeals, Fifth Circuit.

The court of appeals affirmed the order. It held that since the BESE was a "recipient" under applicable regulations, the DOE could order it to repay the funds. The BESE had significantly not denied the finding that the funds had been misspent. DOE could not be estopped from ordering repayment because the BESE had warned it that the funds were going to the superintendent. *Louisiana State Bd. of Educ. v. U.S. Dept. of Education*, 881 F.2d 204 (5th Cir.1989).

The U.S. Department of Education (DOE) awarded funds to the Michigan Department of Education under a grant program administered by the DOE's Rehabilitative Services Administration. The grant was intended to fund vocational rehabilitation and independent living programs to help handicapped individuals find employment. The DOE inspector general's office conducted an audit of the Michigan education department and determined that thirteen of 259 audited authorizations for client service expenditures were to be disallowed. On the basis of the audit, the DOE demanded a refund of $465,732. The amount demanded reflected a recalculation for possible error. The Michigan department challenged the audit determination in an administrative hearing conducted by the DOE's Education Appeals Board (EAB). The EAB upheld the audit and the Michigan education department appealed to the U.S. Court of Appeals, Sixth Circuit.

On appeal, the Michigan department argued that the DOE's determination was without authority. It also complained that the audit was based upon an erroneous sampling and that the refund demand was incorrect as a result. The DOE argued that its decision was supported by substantial evidence and that its random sampling technique was appropriate. The appeals court agreed with the DOE. The administrative hearing was supported by substantial evidence and was within the Rehabilitation Act's statutory scheme. It would be impossible for the EAB to audit the over 6,600 cases coming under the grant. The amount demanded had been reduced to compensate for possible errors and the state had had an opportunity to present its own evidence of possible errors in the administrative hearing. Because the administrator had not used an arbitrary statistical sample for the audit, there was no basis for disallowing it. The court affirmed the decision for the DOE. *Michigan Dep't of Educ. v. U.S. Dep't of Educ.*, 875 F.2d 1196 (6th Cir.1989).

State educational agencies must allocate federal funds in a timely fashion or risk forfeiture. Under the EHA, states receive grants of federal funding which are then subgranted to qualified local educational authorities (LEAs) for use in providing educational services to handicapped children. Each LEA is entitled to a share of the state's grant based on its proportionate share of the state's population of handicapped children. If an LEA does not spend its subgrant in a timely fashion, the funds revert to the state. Also, if the state fails to obligate funds to LEAs by the end of the fiscal year succeeding the fiscal year for which the funds were appropriated, those funds have to be returned to the U.S. Department of Education.

Several LEAs returned unspent 1979 funds to the state of Massachusetts four days before the deadline for state obligation of funds to LEAs. The state, however, directed these funds to LEAs which had received only partial subgrants for 1979 after the obligation period had ended. Because these LEAs had been less than fully funded by 1979 subgrants the state allowed them to apply the reallocated funds to expenditures that they had paid for themselves prior to the deadline. The U.S. Department of Education determined that Massachusetts had impermissibly retained and reallocated the funds and Massachusetts petitioned for review of this determination in the U.S. Court of Appeals, First Circuit. The court noted that the department's interpretation was reasonable and "entirely consistent" with the EHA plan for fund allotment. The court upheld the department's decision that Massachusetts had impermissibly retained and reallocated the funds. *Massachusetts Dept. of Educ. v. U.S. Dept. of Educ.*, 837 F.2d 536 (1st Cir.1988).

The U.S. Department of Education audited the California State Department of Education (CSDE). It found that the CSDE had finalized its financial status reports before receiving all expenditure reports from its local educational agencies and had improperly transferred funds. The U.S. Secretary of Education issued an audit letter and ordered the CSDE to refund $1.2 million to the department. The funds, allocated under Part B of the EHA, were the annual appropriation for special education students. EHA-B funds are allocated to states on a per capita basis to each state's educational agency which must then comply with EHA-B distribution requirements. Funds received by states are required to be "linked" to expenditures. Distribution of EHA-B funds must also comply with the Tydings Amendment, 20 U.S.C. § 1225(b), which has been construed to permit state educational agencies twenty-seven months in which to commit funds to local educational agencies.

CSDE filed an application for review of the audit with the Education Appeal Board. The parties stipulated that expenditures had been committed to local educational agencies within the Tydings period and that the appeal board would consider only whether the CSDE had "linked" its expenditures with specific federal funding. However, the appeal board held that the CSDE had not properly reallocated the funds within the Tydings period and that it must refund $1.2 million to the department. The education secretary permitted the board's decision to become final. The CSDE appealed to the U.S. Court of Appeals, Ninth Circuit.

On appeal, the CSDE contended that the appeal board had exceeded the education department's jurisdiction. The CSDE also alleged that the secretary had violated the CSDE's due process rights by failing to adequately explain the issues on appeal. The appeals court agreed, ruling that the state should have been given an opportunity to understand that the Tydings period issue might determine the case's outcome. The secretary's audit letter might have been construed to concern a general failure by the state to comply with obligating its funds within the Tydings period. However, because of the stipulation by the parties it might also be reasonable to conclude that the state had relied on the narrow linkage issue framed by the final audit letter rather than whether funds had been allocated within the Tydings period.

According to the appeals court, the appeal board had also endorsed this narrow interpretation of the audit in its decision. Therefore, the secretary's final decision went beyond the issue defined in the initial notice of hearing. The final decision was void for lack of jurisdiction because it pertained only to the Tydings compliance issue. Because the appeal board had already determined the linkage issue in the state's favor, the secretary was not entitled to the refund. The appeals court reversed the appeal board's decision. *Dep't of Educ. of State of California v. Bennett*, 864 F.2d 655 (9th Cir.1988).

The second group of cases explain some solutions to residence disputes.

Disputes have arisen when a child is temporarily institutionalized within the boundaries of one school district and the parents reside in another. The parents of a boy with Down's syndrome placed the boy in a family home in Edmeston, New York. The parents' school district (the Bedford school district) paid for the boy's education but when his parents moved to Massachusetts, the Bedford school district claimed that the burden of paying for the boy's education was upon the Massachusetts district. After the Massachusetts district declined responsibility his parents sued the New York Commissioner of Education and the Edmeston school district. A U.S. district court held for the parents ruling that the boy was a resident of the Edmeston district and therefore his educational costs were the responsibility of the commissioner and the Edmeston school district. The commissioner and the Edmeston school district appealed to the U.S. Court of Appeals, Second Circuit.

The controversy centered on the commissioner's interpretation of New York Education Law § 3202(4)(b) which stated that "Children cared for in free family homes and . . . family homes at board, when such family homes shall be the actual and only residence of such children and when such children are not supported and maintained at the expense of a social services district or of a state department or agency, shall be deemed residents of the school district in which the family home is located." The commissioner claimed that a presumption arose that the child's residence was that of the child's natural parents. He further contended that the presumption could be overcome by showing that the parents neither exercised control over the child nor were financially responsible for the child. The parents argued that § 3202(4)(b) made no mention of the "presumption" or of the information necessary for rebuttal. Because the controlling issue concerned the interpretation of the term "actual and only residence," the court of appeals held that the district court should have abstained from deciding the issue (i.e., the state courts should decide it). The fact that the commissioner went beyond the terms of § 3202(4)(b) to further define "residence" indicated ambiguity, observed the court. *Catlin v. Ambach*, 820 F.2d 588 (2d Cir.1987).

The case was then removed to the Albany County Supreme Court. The supreme court held that the student was a resident of Edmeston for the purposes of tuition-free education. While a child's residence was presumed to be that of his parents, § 3202(4)(b) created a class of children presumed not to reside with their parents. These children included those who were cared for in a "family home at board" not supported or maintained at the expense of a social service district or a state agency. These children were considered residents of the "family home at board," not residents of their parents' home. The student was entitled to tuition-free education. *Catlin by Catlin v. Sobol*, 532 N.Y.S.2d 1006 (Sup.Ct.1988).

A Pennsylvania statute established an irrebuttable presumption that students were residents of the school district in which their parents resided. The act provided no opportunity for a hearing to contest the presumption. Although state regulations permitted parents of exceptional children to challenge the type of education received, the regulations did not permit a challenge to the denial of tuition-free education because of the nonresidency presumption. A New York student moved to Pennsylvania and began public school attendance. His parents paid tuition, but soon commenced a class action suit in a federal district court challenging the statute.

The court considered U.S. Supreme Court cases dealing with school district residency requirements. It determined that the Pennsylvania statute was identical to a Connecticut statute which the Supreme Court had found unconstitutional. This was because there were reasonable alternatives for determining residency besides an irrebuttable presumption of nonresidence based upon parental residence. Under the Supreme Court cases, residence in the school context required only physical presence and an intention to remain in the school district. A Texas statute upheld by the Supreme Court permitted free education regardless of parental residence so long as the student could establish that transfer to the school district was not for the primary purpose of obtaining a free public education there. The court noted that Pennsylvania was permitted to establish reasonable criteria for determining in-state status. The Pennsylvania statute was unconstitutional because it denied the class members their procedural due process rights. The court ordered the state education secretary to convene a residency hearing as well as to consider all the complaining students' Rehabilitation Act and EHA complaints. Other class members were also to be afforded individual opportunities to establish residency. *Steven M. v. Gilhool*, 700 F.Supp. 261 (E.D.Pa.1988).

In a New York case the New York Supreme Court, Appellate Division, has issued a ruling which interprets section 4004(2)(a) of that state's Education Law. This section declares that "[t]he school district in which a child resided at the time the social services district . . . assumed responsibility for the support and maintenance of the child . . . [shall] reimburse the state toward the state's expenditure on behalf of such child." The dispute in this case arose when custody of a handicapped child was surrendered by his mother to a county social services department. He was later returned to the custody of his mother. At that time he began to attend school in the Brentwood school district, his district of residence.

When the mother once again surrendered custody of her child to the county social services department, the state sought reimbursement from the Brentwood district. Brentwood refused, arguing that the school district where the child resided at the time of his first placement with the social services department was his school district of origin for the purpose of section 4004(2)(a). This interpretation would mean that any subsequent residence was irrelevant. The state Commissioner of Education had previously ruled that "when a child is returned to the custody of his parents and then subsequently replaced with the Department of Social Services, the financial burden of such care falls on the school district in which the child resided at the time of placement, regardless of his residence at the time of any earlier placement." The Appellate Division agreed with the Commissioner, holding that section 4004(2)(a) requires that whatever school district in which a child resides at the time of his placement in a social services program must bear the financial burden. The five-judge panel concluded that the Commissioner's ruling that Brentwood reimburse the state was practical because it "relieves a [former] school district of the responsibility for underwriting the expenses of a subsequently relocated child with whom the district may not have had any contact for years." *Brentwood Union Free School Dist. v. Ambach*, 495 N.Y.S.2d 513 (A.D.3d Dept.1985).

In a New Hampshire case a declaratory judgment action was brought to determine which school district was liable for the special education expenses of an educationally handicapped child. The child had lived for nearly one year with a married couple who wished to adopt him. However, later the couple decided not to adopt him and the child then became a patient at a New Hampshire state hospital. He later lived at a group home and at a training center in Massachusetts. A New Hampshire trial court placed all responsibility for the child's educational expenses on the school district in which the child had lived with the couple who had wished to adopt him. The school district appealed to the Supreme Court of New Hampshire, which affirmed the trial court ruling, saying that a state statute which obligated "the district in which the child last resided" to pay his special education expenses referred to the place where a child actually lived outside of a facility. Because the evidence was sufficient to support a finding that the child's residence for nearly one year with the couple who had wished to adopt him was bona fide, that district was liable for his special education expenses incurred after his leaving the couple's home. *In re Gary B.*, 466 A.2d 929 (N.H.1983).

A Massachusetts town providing special educational services to a child brought suit challenging the burden imposed upon it to pay the child's expenses. The town sought reimbursement from another town in which the child's natural parent resided. However, the child was temporarily in the custody of the Department of Social Services (DSS) and the town from which reimbursement was sought argued that the DSS should assume the child's residential and educational expenses. The Supreme Judicial Court of Massachusetts found this argument without merit. The agency with custody, found the court, has the power to determine the child's place of abode, medical care and education. However, quoting Massachusetts law, the court stated that an acceptance of a child into DSS custody "shall entail no abrogation of parental rights or responsibilities, [rather, it is] a temporary delegation of certain rights and responsibilities necessary to provide foster care . . . agreed upon by both and terminable by either." The purpose of the child's transfer to DSS custody was only to aid him in obtaining appropriate residential care and educational services, not to place full legal responsibility on the agency. The DSS, therefore, was not a parent for purposes of Massachusetts law and thus was not liable for the child's expenses. *Town of Northbridge v. Town of Natick*, 474 N.E.2d 551 (Mass.1985).

In a Colorado case, a juvenile court terminated the parent-child relationship between an emotionally handicapped child and his parents and granted custody of the child to the Denver Department of Social Services (DDSS). The department then placed the child with a set of foster parents. The child was enrolled in a special education program for children with emotional disorders in the school district in which he resided with his foster parents. Because the child experienced great difficulty in school adjustment, the school district recommended that he be placed in a twenty-four hour residential child care facility. The foster parents objected to this proposal because they believed he was doing well living in their home and because they believed it would destroy the bonding which had developed between them and the child. The foster parents unilaterally enrolled the child in the Denver Academy, a private day school specializing in the treatment of children with learning disabilities. The child's guardian ad litem then filed a motion with the juvenile court seeking to compel the DDSS to pay the $5,400 annual tuition at the Denver Academy. The juvenile court held that it lacked authority to consider such matters and the guardian ad litem appealed.

The Colorado Court of Appeals affirmed the juvenile court's ruling. The child's guardian ad litem argued that since the juvenile court had placed the child in the custody of the department, the court had authority to review all aspects of the child's care, including his educational program. This argument was rejected on the ground that Colorado's Exceptional Children's Act provides that a student's school district of residence is completely responsible for providing and paying for special educational services. Thus, although the juvenile court had jurisdiction over the child's welfare, the responsibility for his special education lay with his school district. The DDSS was not the responsible party and could not be compelled to fund the child's education at the private academy. *A.C.B. v. Denver Dep't of Social Servs.*, 725 P.2d 94 (Colo.App.1986).

III. HANDICAPPED STUDENTS IN SCHOOL ATHLETICS

Handicapped students may not be excluded from any athletic activity conducted by a school receiving federal financial assistance as long as the student is "otherwise qualified" to participate. "Otherwise qualified" means that the student is qualified to participate in spite of his or her disability.

The first cases in this section explore some dispute resolutions concerning handicapped athletes' eligibility.

A Tennessee learning disabled tenth grade student transferred from a Christian school to a metropolitan public school. The executive director of the Tennessee Secondary Schools Athletic Association (TSSAA) ruled that the student was ineligible to participate in interscholastic sports for a period of twelve months. The student submitted an appeal asking that the TSSAA grant a hardship request, which was denied. The student appealed to a number of authorities, but all his appeals were denied. After the first four games, the student's parents filed suit in a federal district court claiming that the student's ineligibility for participation in athletics deprived him of his rights under the Education of the Handicapped Act (EHA). The court concluded that a student who transfers from one school to another for the purpose of receiving a free appropriate education under the EHA could not be prohibited from participating in extracurricular activities since such a prohibition would amount to discrimination based on the handicap. The court found that it was necessary to determine the reason for the student's transfer and that the determination was to be made by the local education agency. Pending that determination, the court determined that the TSSAA could not invalidate any contest in which the student participated. The TSSAA and officials appealed to the U.S. Court of Appeals, Sixth Circuit. The court noted that in EHA cases, federal courts were available only to parties aggrieved by an administrative proceeding result. Direct access to federal courts was not permitted under the EHA without an administrative proceeding. In this case, the parents had failed to exhaust their administrative remedies. The Tennessee education commissioner was in compliance with EHA procedural requirements, and the state provided adequate procedures. There was no merit to the parents' complaint that state administrative procedures were unavailable because the state had delegated authority to the TSSAA regarding access to varsity sports. The parents should have challenged their son's IEP and obtained a hearing rather than going to federal court. Therefore, the court dissolved the district court's injunction and dismissed the lawsuit. *Crocker v. Tennessee Secondary School Athletic Ass'n*, 873 F.2d 933 (6th Cir.1989).

The parents then requested an EHA due process hearing. The hearing officer ruled that the TSSAA had discriminated against the student in prohibiting him from participating in interscholastic athletics by failing to grant a hardship exception to the TSSAA transfer rule. The parents filed a suit alleging that TSSAA had deprived the student of his rights secured him by the EHA. The student asked the court to issue a temporary restraining order to prevent TSSAA from all acts which might prevent or prohibit the high school from allowing the student to participate in interscholastic athletics pending further order of the court. In order to grant preliminary injunctive relief the court must consider four factors: 1) whether the plaintiff has shown a strong likelihood of success on the merits; 2) whether the plaintiff has shown irreparable harm; 3) whether the issuance of a preliminary injunction would cause substantial harm to others; and 4) where the public interest lies. To determine if the student would have a likelihood of success on the merits under 42 U.S.C. § 1983, the student would have to establish that he had been deprived of a right created by federal law and that the TSSAA acted under color of state law. The court noted that the student fulfilled both of these requirements. Second, since the student would only have one opportunity to participate in high school athletics, the court determined he would suffer irreparable harm. Third, the court then noted that TSSAA would not be substantially harmed if the preliminary injunction were granted because it would only be required to refrain from any reprisals. And fourth, the court also noted that the public interest in "reinforcing the respectability of the judicial systems of the United States and Tennessee," provided the public interest requirement for a preliminary injunction. Therefore, the court granted the preliminary injunction to the student. *Crocker v. Tennessee Secondary School Athletic Ass'n*, 735 F.Supp. 753 (N.D.Tenn.1990).

An Illinois student confined to a wheelchair wished to compete against regular students in track and field. The school district granted the parents' request for a due process hearing. The hearing officer concluded that the student must be allowed to compete on the school's teams. When safety warranted it, the student should participate in a separate wheelchair division. The hearing officer ruled that the district was under no obligation to provide services beyond those offered to nonhandicapped students. The officer ordered the school district to establish a wheelchair division for any sport offered to nonhandicapped students in the district. The district held a multidisciplinary conference (MDC) to decide whether the student could safely participate with nonhandicapped athletes. The MDC participants determined that the student could only compete with nonhandicapped students in golf and tennis. His participation at track events should be limited to a wheelchair division.

The student filed a lawsuit against the school district in a federal district court, claiming violation of 42 U.S.C. § 1983 and the Education of the Handicapped Act (EHA). The court noted a number of procedural deficiencies in the administrative proceedings. The court also noted that most of the MDC participants were not knowledgeable about wheelchair athletics and many were unfamiliar with the student's disabilities. The EHA's regulations permitted persons having significant information regarding the student to participate in MDCs. This included parents. The school district had not sought out such evidence. The district had violated the hearing officer's order for a case study and medical examination. The MDC lacked qualified personnel and failed to comply with the hearing officer's order. The district violated the student's rights under the EHA and § 1983. *Hollenbeck v. Bd. of Educ. of Rochelle Township*, 699 F.Supp. 658 (N.D.Ill.1988).

A New York school district attempted to prevent a junior high school girl from participating in contact sports by reason of her visual impairment, which resulted from a congenital cataract. New York law provides that upon a school district's determination that a student shall not be permitted to participate in an athletic program by reason of physical impairment, the student may commence a special proceeding to enjoin the school district from prohibiting such participation. Further, if the court finds that it is in the best interests of the student to participate in the athletic program and that it is reasonably safe to do so, the court shall grant permission to participate. The law further protects a school district from liability for any injury sustained by a student participating pursuant to such a court determination.

In this case, the lower court determined that with protective eyewear it would be reasonably safe for this student to participate in the athletic program, but denied her application on the grounds that it would not be in her best interests to participate, because of the immunity from liability granted to the school district should an injury occur. The New York Supreme Court, Appellate Division, rejected this lower court finding and granted the student permission to participate. Whatever immunity from liability is enjoyed by a school district is not to be weighed by the court in considering the best interests of the student. Here, ample evidence suggested that with protective eyewear it would be in the best interests of this student to participate in the athletic program. *Kampmeier v. Harris*, 411 N.Y.S.2d 744 (A.D.4th Dept. 1978).

The second group of cases provide guidance in the application of a transfer rule or age restriction.

The Michigan Court of Appeals held that a placement decision made when a handicapped student was in fourth grade barred the student from playing varsity basketball. The student suffered from a severe hearing impairment and attended special education classes in his local school district. In 1976 he was placed in a regular education class as part of his school district's commitment to mainstreaming. However, when the student was mainstreamed he was placed in a regular education classroom one grade level below what his age would normally require. This mainstreaming decision presented no difficulties until it was discovered that the student would turn nineteen just before the beginning of his senior year, the 1984-85 academic year. He was declared ineligible to play varsity basketball during his senior year due to an age rule established by the Michigan High School Athletic Association (MHSAA).

The rule prohibited students who reach their nineteenth birthday before September 1 of the academic year in question from participating in interscholastic athletics. The student sued his school district in a state circuit court, claiming that the enforcement of the age rule violated his Fourteenth Amendment right to due process and equal protection of the laws. Shortly after the beginning of the student's senior year the circuit court entered a ruling in favor of the school district and the student appealed.

In upholding the circuit court's decision, the Michigan Court of Appeals rejected each of the student's three constitutional claims. First, the student argued that he had been denied due process of law because no hearing had been held at the time he was mainstreamed. Under Michigan law the student and his parents could have requested a hearing to contest the student's placement in a grade level below the grade in which he would normally be placed. However, they had not sought a hearing. The court held that the failure to request a hearing at the time of the mainstreaming decision precluded a subsequent due process claim. The student's second contention was that he was denied equal protection by the MHSAA's refusal to grant him an exception to its age rule. The MHSAA's rules provide that it will consider waiving the age rule if a school district requests a waiver on behalf of a student. The court held that because the student never asked his school district to request a waiver from the MHSAA, his equal protection claim was barred. Finally, the student claimed that the age rule was discriminatory, arbitrary and capricious. This claim was also rejected by the court which observed that the rule was applied equally to all students regardless of sex, race, national origin or handicap. The rule also prevented the "red shirting" (holding back) of students for athletic purposes and reduced the opportunity for mismatches between older and younger athletes. Furthermore, if the September 1 age cutoff date was declared arbitrary and a new date such as August 1 established, then students turning nineteen on July 30 would seek to have the new date declared arbitrary as well. The September 1 cutoff date was a reasonable exercise of school authority. The circuit court's ruling against the student was upheld. *Nichols v. Farmington Pub. Schools,* 389 N.W.2d 480 (Mich.App. 1986).

A high school athletic regulatory agency in Texas barred a male high school student from participating in high school football because he had moved to another district to live with his grandparents. The student had suffered emotional problems and was handicapped within the meaning of the Rehabilitation Act. The student sued alleging that there were compelling medical reasons why he should be permitted to participate in the football program. The U.S. district court issued a preliminary injunction restraining the athletic regulatory agency from enforcing its rule. The court said that the purpose of the rule was to prevent recruiting abuses and to prevent an athlete from irresponsibly shopping around for a school or coach. These evils were not present here. To deny the student the opportunity to play football would violate his rights as a handicapped individual. *Doe v. Marshall*, 459 F.Supp. 1190 (S.D.Tex.1978).

A nineteen-year-old neurologically impaired high school senior challenged a New York Department of Education regulation prohibiting students over eighteen years of age from participating in interscholastic athletics. The boy had entered the public school system at the ninth grade level after leaving a private school, where he had failed the ninth grade. His participation in wrestling from the ninth grade until his senior year appeared to have significantly improved his self image. The boy brought suit in U.S. district court, alleging he had been discriminated against on the basis of his handicap and had been unlawfully denied the opportunity to participate in interscholastic wrestling in violation of the equal protection provisions of the U.S. Constitution and the Rehabilitation Act. The court held that because the student had reached the age of nineteen and had not been treated any differently than any other nonphysically handicapped nineteen-year-old student, there was no violation of equal protection, nor was there unfair discrimination. *Cavallaro v. Ambach*, 575 F.Supp. 171 (W.D.N.Y.1983).

IV. STUDENT RECORDS

Generally, access to handicapped students' records will not be allowed when the privacy interest of the students outweighs the asserted need for inspection of the records.

A fourteen-year-old handicapped New York student was allegedly sexually abused by her step-grandfather. The student told a school district social worker who worked in her high school about the alleged abuse. The social worker telephoned the Albany Child Protective Central Service Registry and filed a written report with the County Department of Child Protective Services. The social worker forwarded her file on the student to the school's internal committee on the handicapped. The Department of Social Services determined that the allegations of sexual abuse were unfounded. The step-grandfather then sued the social worker and school district in a New York trial court to recover damages for publication of the report. The court found that the report should not have been circulated to the committee. Any qualified privilege which the social worker and school district might have had was destroyed. The social worker and school district appealed to the New York Supreme Court, Appellate Division, Second Department.

The appellate court held that the school's internal committee was authorized to receive the report. The school district's and social worker's qualified privilege was not destroyed when the report was delivered to the committee. The committee had a duty to review all relevant information pertinent to each student. The committee was obligated to recommend appropriate educational programs suited to help the student. The allegations of sexual abuse were relevant to the student's case and necessary for the committee's informed recommendation of a suitable program. Thus the information was privileged and immunized the school district and social worker from civil liability. The lower court's decision was reversed. *Dunajewski v. Bellmore-Merrick Cent. High*, 526 N.Y.S.2d 139 (A.D.2 Dept.1988).

A human rights advocacy committee in Florida petitioned for access to confidential school records which it considered pertinent to its investigation of the alleged abuse of four developmentally disabled students by public school personnel. A Florida trial court denied the committee's request and appeal was taken to the District Court of Appeal of Florida. The court affirmed the trial court rulings. It found that the committee was not entitled to

access to the confidential school records of the students because a state statute limited the committee's area of jurisdiction, for the purpose of obtaining
client records, to matters occurring solely within a program or facility operated, funded or regulated by the Department of Health and Rehabilitative
Services. The court also based its decision on a school code provision protecting the privacy interests of every student with regard to his or her educational
records. *Human Rights Advocacy Comm. v. Lee County School Bd.*, 457
So.2d 522 (Fla.App.2d Dist.1984).

The Human Rights Authority of the State of Illinois Guardianship and
Advocacy Commission appealed an order of an Illinois district court denying
the enforcement of a subpoena issued by the commission. Acting on a complaint which alleged that a local school district was not providing occupational and physical therapy for its students, the commission began an
investigation and asked the district superintendent to produce the students'
educational program records. The records were to be masked so as to delete
any information by which students could be identified. When the school district failed to turn over the information, the commission issued a subpoena
for the masked records. Again, the school district refused to comply. The
commission then sought judicial enforcement of the subpoena.

The district court ruled that the commission had no right to examine the
records because it did not satisfy the access requirements of Illinois state law
regarding student records. After the commission appealed to the Appellate
Court of Illinois, the school district argued that, along with the access provisions of the Student Records Act, the commission had no authority to investigate or review special education programs, and that the commission's right to
investigate did not apply to all of the handicapped students in a school district, but was limited to individual cases. The thrust of the school district's
first argument was that the commission was somehow usurping the role of
the State Board of Education by investigating the special education program
of the school district. The commission's inquiry was "tantamount to the control and direction of special education which makes local school authorities
accountable to the [Commission] rather than the State Board of Education as
required by the School Code."

The appellate court disagreed. The statutory authority of the commission
to investigate complaints concerning violations of the rights of handicapped
persons, including the right to special education programs, was not subordinate to that of the State Board of Education. Further, the commission's investigation of the school district's overall special education program, and not
merely individual students, was within the bounds of the commission's statutory authority. *Human Rights Authority of the State of Illinois Guardianship
Comm. v. Miller*, 464 N.E.2d 833 (Ill.App.3d Dist.1984).

V. SPECIAL EDUCATION FOR PRESCHOOL CHILDREN
AND CHILDREN OVER EIGHTEEN YEARS OF AGE

**The EHA requires that states provide a free appropriate education to chil-
dren between the ages of three and twenty-one. However, section 1412(B) of
the Act states that with respect to handicapped children aged three to five and
eighteen to twenty-one, the requirement to provide an education shall not
apply if to do so would conflict with state law regarding public education for**

such age groups. Additionally, a 1986 EHA amendment established a discretionary funding program encouraging states to develop "early intervention services" for handicapped children from birth until their third birthday. The 1986 amendment also established a new preschool grant program which created incentives for states to ensure that all handicapped children ages three to five receive special education services.

A twenty-three-year-old Texas handicapped student received special education services in a Houston, Texas, school district until she was twenty-one-years-old. The school district implemented the student's individualized education plan (IEP) which indicated specific goals for her educational and behavioral progress. The child never attained these goals. Since the child had reached twenty-one, she was due to graduate from school. The parents then instituted a due process hearing to determine if their child had received an appropriate education. The hearing officer determined that the child did not make any significant educational progress and that her behavioral problems had not been adequately addressed. The parents then sued the school district in a federal district court alleging civil rights and EHA violations. The parents claimed that the school district denied the student a free appropriate education under the EHA and that it also failed to provide an adequate IEP for their child. The defendant moved to dismiss the case.

The court dismissed all claims against the school district, noting three factors in its ruling. First, the statute of limitations barred all claims before 1986, and the parents had not provided any reason why the statute of limitations should be tolled. Next, the court discussed the parents' § 1983 claim. Specifically, the parents contended that the student had made no significant educational progress and that her behavioral problems were not addressed; therefore, she was discriminated against due to her handicap. The court, however, determined that it was not enough to show a failure of an educational program. The plaintiff must show that the educators failed to adequately administer a program based on a bias because the plaintiff was handicapped. Since these allegations were not made and no evidence was given in support of the claim, the student could not recover on the discrimination claim. Further, the court dismissed the EHA claim stating that due to the U.S. Supreme Court's decision in *Honig v. Doe*, 484 U.S. 305 (1988), the twenty-three-year-old's claims were moot. The *Honig* court stated that because the plaintiff was twenty-four-years-old, he was "no longer entitled to the protections and benefits of the EHA which limits eligibility to disabled children under twenty-one." Since this student was twenty-three-years-old, she was no longer entitled to the protections of the EHA and the court dismissed all the claims. *McDowell v. Fort Bend Indep. Sch. Dist.*, 737 F.Supp. 386 (S.D.Tex.1990).

The Wyoming Supreme Court considered three cases in which handicapped students over the age of twenty-one attempted to secure public funding to complete their educations.

In the first case, a multiply-handicapped student filed a complaint with the state school superintendent for a due process hearing five weeks before she reached the age of twenty-one. The school district advised the student that she would no longer be eligible for free public education after her twenty-first birthday. She sought an order from the state superintendent which would require her school district to continue her free education. Although the hearing occurred after the student's twenty-first birthday, the hearing officer ruled that the school district must provide her with free education until her twenty-second birthday. The school district then sought a ruling on state funding. The superintendent ruled that the school district could use federal funds to comply with the hearing officer's decision, but no state funds were to be expended. The school district appealed to the Wyoming County Court, which sent the appeal to the Wyoming Supreme Court.

The supreme court noted that the EHA adopted state educational standards to determine an individual state's obligation to provide free appropriate public education. The Wyoming constitution acknowledged the right to an education and state statutes required free and appropriate education for handicapped students of school age. The language did not apply to adults who had reached age twenty-one. The student was not entitled to a due process hearing and was not entitled to any relief. School districts were not permitted to expend either federal or state funds for students over twenty-one-years-old. The district's policy stated that handicapped students could be considered for graduation whenever the IEP had been completed or upon reaching age twenty-one. The hearing officer had incorrectly ruled that because the student had a continuing need for educational services, the district was committed to continue her free education. The district was not responsible for the student's failure to complete the district's handicapped students' graduation requirements. The court reversed the hearing officer's decision. *Natrona County School Dist. 1 v. Ryan*, 764 P.2d 1019 (Wyo. 1988).

In the second case, the supreme court considered a handicapped student who had finished his education after reaching age twenty-one. He submitted a claim for maintenance and tuition costs for his vocational activity program after his twenty-first birthday. The hearing officer determined that the state obligation ended at his twenty-first birthday. His parents appealed to a Wyoming county court which reversed the hearing officer's decision and ruled that the state had contracted for an additional year's educational costs, and that the school district had an obligation to continue funding. During the course of the administrative proceedings, the student completed his educational program. When the matter came before the Wyoming Supreme Court, the court noted that the disposition in the *Ryan* case (above) prohibited expenditure of funds on a student over twenty-one. However, as the student had completed his educational program the court determined that the educational expenses should be allocated between the school district and the state board as if the services had been rendered before his twenty-first birthday. *State v. Cochran*, 764 P.2d 1037 (Wyo.1988).

The third case involved a twenty-one-year-old student who had the academic level of a two-year-old after fifteen years of education and rehabilitation efforts by his school district. After several years of placement in the district's educable and trainable handicapped children's programs, he was placed in a high-tuition private handicapped facility located in Rhode Island.

The student was later moved from the handicapped facility to a private institution in Arizona.

Following a hearing at which the parents disputed the removal from the Rhode Island facility, the school district agreed to continue the Rhode Island schooling. From 1977 until 1988, the school district expended over $653,000 on placement in the private facilities. In 1987, the district received notice from the state education board that handicapped students over twenty-one were not eligible for funding. The student's parents requested another hearing. They claimed that compensation was due for the period when he was removed from the Rhode Island facility. The hearing officer ruled that the student was eligible for compensatory education beyond age twenty-one where he had been denied free appropriate education in the past. The hearing officer ordered the district to pay for thirty-seven months of compensatory education at the Rhode Island facility. The district appealed the hearing officer's decision to a Wyoming trial court which certified the appeal to the Wyoming Supreme Court.

The supreme court ruled that neither the state nor any school district may undertake educational responsibility for any student over twenty-one. The court noted that the parents' argument was essentially an educational malpractice argument which, if accepted, could serve as the legal basis for a lawsuit by any student who failed to graduate form Wyoming schools. Normal public education ended at age eighteen and the additional three years served as adequate compensation to underachievers or handicapped students. The court reversed the hearing officer's determination in all respects. *Natrona County School Dist. 1 v. McKnight*, 764 P.2d 1039 (Wyo.1988).

A Nebraska special education student petitioned the state education department, claiming he was entitled to remain in his school district's special education programs until his twenty-second birthday. The education department's hearing officer dismissed the petition because the student had already reached age twenty-one. The student appealed to a Nebraska trial court, which affirmed the hearing officer's decision but permitted the student to stay in school pending further appeal. The student appealed to the Nebraska Supreme Court.

On appeal, the student claimed that the Rehabilitation Act required school districts using federal funds to provide free education to persons over twenty-one years old. The district claimed that the trial court, by allowing the student to stay in school pending appeal, had erroneously required it to maintain the student's placement beyond his twenty-first birthday. The supreme court ruled that according to the applicable Nebraska statutes and the state constitution, free instruction was mandated for all persons between the ages of five and twenty-one years but not to students over twenty-one years old. The court also ruled that EHA regulations specifically required that state law determine public education age groups. States had the right to determine when educational services to handicapped students could terminate. The supreme court affirmed the trial court's decision. Because Nebraska law stated that free education to handicapped students was available only until the student's twenty-first birthday the district was not required to maintain the student in a special education program. *Monahan v. School Dist. 1 of Douglas County*, 425 N.W.2d 624 (Neb.1988).

In 1978, the state of New York agreed to pay the tuition costs of a schizo-phrenic boy who had been placed in a residential psychiatric hospital which operated an accredited academic high school. Behavioral problems prevented the boy from attending the high school, but he continued to reside at the hospital. His doctors hoped that the behavior problems could be overcome. The boy's parents, after petitioning state officials in vain, sought to compel the state to pay the cost of the boy's residential care at the hospital from the time of his placement, July, 1978, through June, 1983, when the boy turned twenty-one years old.

The state contended before a U.S. district court that as long as the child's behavioral problems prevented him from attending the high school at the institution, he was in effect uneducable and therefore the state had no re-sponsibility for any of his expenses. The court ruled that once the state placed the boy at the psychiatric hospital, it became obligated to pay the entire ex-pense of the placement. The state could not escape its responsibility for costs of the boy's residential care simply by stating that those costs did not directly address educational problems. As long as the boy could be educated (how-ever little) through a residential placement, the state remained responsible for the cost of that placement until the boy became twenty-one. *Vander Malle v. Ambach*, 667 F.Supp. 1015 (S.D.N.Y. 1987).

The U.S. Court of Appeals ruled that a twenty-three year old man had no EHA claims. The case involved a Michigan man, born in 1954, who was able to communicate only through limited use of sign language. He was enrolled in three different special education programs from 1973 until he reached the age of twenty-five in 1979. The man was never excluded from attending any of the schools or from participating in special education programs, and he was never enrolled in a program that received federal financial assistance. He sued the three school districts in a U.S. district court alleging that the school districts had deprived him of a meaningful education. Specifically, the man claimed that his due process and equal protection rights under the Fourteenth Amendment had been violated. He also claimed that the school districts had failed to afford him a free appropriate education according to the EHA and the Rehabilitation Act. The district court ruled against the man and he ap-pealed to the U.S. Court of Appeals, Sixth Circuit.

At the time, the EHA was the exclusive avenue through which a person could assert an equal protection claim to a publicly financed special educa-tion. The court had to determine whether the EHA had been available to the young man. The man claimed that the EHA became effective in 1975 but the court found that the EHA's requirement to make a free appropriate public education available did not become effective until 1977. It also noted that when the man entered one of the school district's programs in the fall of 1977 he was twenty-three years old. The EHA only requires an appropriate public education for handicapped children between ages three and twenty-one. The man thus had no legitimate equal protection claims under the EHA.

The court of appeals stated that in order to establish a deprivation of an interest protected by the due process clause, the man had to show that he was excluded from the school districts' special education programs. He argued that he was in effect excluded from the districts' programs because he had no communicative skills and sat in classrooms where he was unaware of what was happening. In ruling for the school district, the court noted that other courts have repeatedly rejected the idea that the due process clause secures a right to the "most appropriate" education. Even though the man was limited in what he gained from the special education classes he was not excluded from those classes and did receive an appropriate education. Thus, the school district did not infringe upon the man's due process rights.

The court also denied the man's Rehabilitation Act claim since none of the programs that he participated in received federal financial assistance. It was not enough to show that the schools that the man attended were federally financed because the most common standard applied is whether the specific program was federally financed. The EHA and Rehabilitation Act claims were inapplicable and the court found no constitutional violations. The district court decision against the man was upheld. *Gallagher v. Pontiac School Dist.*, 807 F.2d 75 (6th Cir. 1986).

A handicapped child in Oklahoma who was about to be graduated by her school district brought suit against the school district alleging that she was in the tenth, not the twelfth, grade and was therefore entitled to two additional years of special education. The school district argued that any notations in the student's individual education program (IEP) or her report card indicating that she was in the tenth grade were a mistake and that the child was in the twelfth grade and thus eligible for graduation. The district further argued that Oklahoma state law did not obligate school districts to provide education to handicapped students from eighteen through twenty-one years of age nor did the EHA impose such a requirement. A U.S. district court in Oklahoma held in the child's favor and the school district appealed.

The U.S. Court of Appeals, Tenth Circuit, affirmed the district court ruling finding that since nonhandicapped children in the eighteen to twenty-one age group may be entitled to additional years of education when one or more grades are failed, handicapped children within this age group are similarly entitled to continue their education.

The court found evidence of the school district's different methods used to determine when handicapped and nonhandicapped children are in the twelfth grade and found that certain standards for the evaluation of handicapped children, as with nonhandicapped children must be met before a handicapped child can be deemed to have advanced a grade. A nonhandicapped student's performance was evaluated by standardized course content whereas a handicapped student's progress was measured by whether the goals in his or her IEP were met. The court found that the EHA contemplates that a handicapped child's progress in school should be measured by objective, if not standardized, criteria. It would make a farce of the clear intent of Congress to interpret the EHA as allowing a handicapped child to fail to meet his or her IEP objectives and yet advance a grade level. Here, the court found a failure on the part of the school district to adequately measure the child's progress. A notation in the child's IEP and in her report card indicating that she was in tenth grade prompted the court to rule that the child was entitled to two additional years of special education. *Helms v. Indep. School Dist. No. 3*, 750 F.2d 820 (10th Cir. 1985).

VI. GIFTED PROGRAMS

A Pennsylvania school district devised an IEP for an exceptional student. It recommended that the district include the student in its "enrichment" program. The enrichment program added certain materials to the regular curriculum but did not attempt to provide accelerated instruction. The student's parents requested a due process hearing in which they asserted that the enrichment program was insufficient. The hearing officer concluded that the student should be given specialized instruction in addition to the enrichment program. Both the state secretary of education and the Pennsylvania Commonwealth Court affirmed the hearing officer's decision. The school district appealed to the Pennsylvania Supreme Court.

The issue before the supreme court was whether the secretary and the commonwealth court had exceeded the provisions of the Pennsylvania Public School Code in requiring the school district to provide the student with an IEP beyond the enrichment program. The code required that schools provide gifted students with plans for individualized instruction designed to meet the "unique needs of the child." The school district argued that this subjective standard would lead to its bankruptcy. It argued that providing a program for exceptional children which addressed their needs to some degree was sufficient. The supreme court affirmed the lower court and administrative decisions. Public school code regulations promulgated by the state education board required individualized planning and education for exceptional children. School districts were required to prepare an IEP for each exceptional child. However, districts were not required to provide individual tutors for exclusive individual programs outside the school district's existing special education curriculum. The student was entitled to specialized instruction beyond the enrichment program. *Centennial School Dist. v. Commonwealth Dep't of Educ.*, 539 A.2d 785 (Pa.1988).

In Pennsylvania a student who had scored 121 on an I.Q. test sued her school district in U.S. district court claiming that her exclusion from a gifted student program violated her rights under the EHA. Pennsylvania law provides that "Persons shall be assigned to a program for the gifted when they have an IQ of 130 or higher. A limited number of persons with IQ scores lower than 130 *may* be admitted to gifted programs when other educational criteria in the profile of the person strongly indicates gifted ability." In addressing the student's arguments, the district court held that although Pennsylvania law extended the same due process guarantees to gifted students as it did to handicapped students, the student was not entitled to EHA procedural protections as a matter of federal law. The court also rejected the student's claim that she had been denied due process of law under the Fourteenth Amendment. It reasoned that because she had not achieved an I.Q. score of 130 or higher, the student had no "property interest" in being admitted to the gifted student program. Although under Pennsylvania law a student with a I.Q. score of less than 130 "may" be admitted to a gifted student program, this did not mean that such a student was entitled to admittance. Also, the court rejected the argument that the student's equal protection rights had been violated by the school district. It observed that because there is no fundamental right to an education under the U.S. Constitution, Pennsylvania's I.Q. regulations were only required to be "rationally related" to some legitimate state purpose. Accordingly, the district court ruled in favor of the school district. *Student Roe v. Commonwealth*, 638 F.Supp. 929 (E.D.Pa. 1986).

A "placement lottery" was recently upheld by a New York appeals court. In this case a school district established a talented and gifted (TAG) program for its elementary school students. Although it identified 109 children as being gifted, it established a full-time TAG program with space available for only 27 students. The school district then used the lottery method to determine which of the 109 children would be admitted to the full-time TAG program. Consequently, the parents of a gifted child whose name was not chosen sued the school district, contending that the lottery was an arbitrary and capricious method of selection. The New York Supreme Court, Appellate Division, rejected this contention due to the fact that there is no constitutional right to a "gifted or talented" education. The parents' attempt to analogize their case to one in which a lottery was employed to select children for a handicapped student program was rejected by the court. The lottery method was upheld as a valid, reasonable way for the school district to solve its space limitation problem. *Bennett v. City School Dist.*, 497 N.Y.S.2d 72 (A.D.2d Dept.1985).

In the 1982-83 school year, a Pennsylvania school district organized a special program for gifted elementary students. The program was for public and nonpublic students and provided instruction one-half day per week in one of the district's public school buildings. Nonpublic school students were transported to the public schools by the school district. In the 1983-84 school year, the district reorganized its gifted student program. Instruction was offered in each public school and teachers traveled to each school on scheduled days, which eliminated the need for any student transportation. The parents of the nonpublic school students filed a lawsuit in the Commonwealth Court of Pennsylvania arguing that their children's right to a special education was violated. The Pennsylvania Department of Education investigated and found that the district was in violation of state law and directed the district to provide midday transportation to the nonpublic school students. Both the school district and the Department sought a court decision determining what their respective obligations were in providing midday transportation for the nonpublic school students.

The court stated that the issue was whether the district had an obligation to provide midday transportation to the nonpublic school students. The school district contended that its only transportation obligation to the gifted students arose out of a state statute which required school districts to provide identical transportation services to public and nonpublic school students. The Department argued that a different, more specific statute was controlling. The court observed that when a general provision in a statute is in conflict with a special provision in the same or other statute, the special provisions prevail, and the two will be construed, if possible, so that effect may be given to both statutes.

The court agreed with the Department that the controlling provision for the transportation of exceptional students was the more specific section of the code. The court said that the statute applied to the nonpublic elementary school gifted students since they were exceptional children and were regularly enrolled in an approved "special class" operated by the school district. The school district was required to furnish free transportation to the exceptional students enrolled in the nonpublic schools. *Woodland Hills School Dist. v. Commonwealth*, 516 A.2d 875 (Pa.Cmwlth.1986).

VII. CASES ARISING UNDER STATE LAW

The EHA, while paramount in the field of special education, leaves many issues to state law. The cases which follow were decided on the basis of state law. The subjects of these cases vary widely.

An emotionally disturbed Texas sixth grader who attended special classes for emotionally handicapped children and had a history of aggressive behavioral problems became disruptive during classroom instruction. The teacher then sent the student to the principal's office. The student received corporal punishment from the school's principal for misbehaving in class. Shortly after the child returned home, he complained of pain and of having been beaten by the principal. The parents called the sheriff's department and a police officer took pictures of the welts and scrapes on the child's body. The sheriff's department investigated the incident, but no criminal action was instituted. The parents claimed the injuries were the result of the corporal punishment. They filed an action against the school's principal, teacher and the school district in a federal district court. The court dismissed all claims except the state law excessive-force charge directed at the principal. It then remanded the case to the state court. The parents appealed to the U.S. Court of Appeals, Fifth Circuit.

Fifth Circuit cases dictated that injuries sustained incidentally to corporal punishment do not implicate the due process clause if the state affords post-punishment remedies for the student. The court noted that Texas law has authorized educators to impose a reasonable measure of corporal punishment upon students when necessary to maintain school discipline, and the state affords students post-punishment criminal or civil remedies if teachers are unfaithful to this obligation. The parents contended that the Fifth Circuit had an overly rigid rule and did not contemplate cases of student discipline such as physical disfigurement or severe emotional injury. The court held that Texas law provided adequate post-punishment relief in favor of students. The court of appeals thus affirmed the trial court's decision and remanded the claim to state court. *Fee v. Herndon*, 900 F.2d 804 (5th Cir.1990).

A Rhode Island boys' home provided private residential facilities for dependent and neglected children. The students residing in the home were provided an on-grounds educational program conducted through an elementary and special education school. The state Department of Children and Their Families (DCF) contracted with the home to provide tutorial and remedial help when appropriate. However, no agreement was made for providing speech therapy services. The DCF and the home requested a local public school to provide speech therapy services. The school initially agreed to allow the children to participate in its speech therapy program, but later discontinued the services. The home's director requested a hearing to determine whether the children residing in the home had the right to participate in speech therapy services conducted through the public school system.

The State Commissioner of Education ruled that the public school was not required to allow children to participate in speech therapy services. He claimed that the home was a "closed facility" because some children were not allowed to enroll as fulltime students in the public school system. Under a state statute, the public school was relieved of its obligation to provide speech therapy services whenever children were "confined" to a state-supported or state-operated "closed" facility. The DCF appealed the commissioner's decision to a Rhode Island trial court which vacated the previous decision and found that the home was not a "closed" facility under the statute. The children were entitled to the public school system's speech therapy services. The school then appealed to the Supreme Court of Rhode Island.

The supreme court held that the home was not a "closed" facility within the meaning of the statute. The fact that the children were not allowed to enroll fulltime in the public school system did not, by itself, make the home a closed facility. There was no evidence that the children were unable to leave the facility. Some students had been enrolled parttime outside the facility in the public school system. The court held that only when students are unable to leave a facility to attend public schools, even on a parttime basis, will a facility be "closed" within the scope of the statute. The school was obligated to provide the students with speech therapy services. The supreme court affirmed the trial court's decision. *In re Children Res. at St. Aloysius Home*, 556 A.2d 552 (R.I.1989).

A fifty-eight-year-old mentally disabled woman had resided at a Vermont training school since 1949. In 1983, she was conditionally discharged from the school and placed in a staffed apartment unit. Six months later, she broke her hip and was hospitalized. She was then placed in a convalescent center by her guardian and the state department of mental health. Following her conditional discharge from the center, the mental health department filed a petition with a Vermont trial court to determine the appropriateness of discharge from the training school. No action was taken until 1986, when the trial court reactivated its review. The court found the training school placement insufficient, citing a lack of an individual program plan to meet her needs. An individual program plan resembles an IEP for adults. The mental health department's commissioner then unconditionally discharged the student from the training school without a hearing. The trial court dismissed the proceedings and the department ended its support services. The student then sued the department for review of the absolute discharge, claiming that the department had failed to fulfill its duty to provide adequate care. The department then made a motion to dismiss the matter, which the court denied. However, the court granted the department's motion for appeal to the Vermont Supreme Court.

The supreme court noted an insufficient record for it to make a decision since the court had not previously interpreted the Vermont statute under which the case was filed. Additionally, it had never ruled on the question of arbitrary discharge from care, or on the argument that the department had failed to meet a legal duty to provide adequate care. The court dismissed the appeal, and remanded the case to the trial court for further consideration. *In re A.G.*, 559 A.2d 656 (Vt.1989).

The New Hampshire Department of Health and Human Services (HHS) is responsible for ensuring that services are provided to the developmentally disabled. The Department of Education (DOE) is responsible for ensuring that schools give handicapped children a free appropriate education. Because a person may be both developmentally disabled and educationally handicapped, the HHS and DOE regulations may overlap. The New Hampshire legislature ordered the commissioners of each agency to enter into an agreement defining each other's procedural role. Two developmentally disabled and educationally handicapped students sued to force the commissioners to settle the procedural dispute between the two officials. Each had been turned down for residential placement at public expense. After a New Hampshire trial court dismissed their complaint, they appealed to the New Hampshire Supreme Court.

The court upheld the dismissal. It refused to issue an order forcing the commissioners to settle the dispute, holding that such discretionary acts could not be ordered. It held that the students' opportunity for review by the state agencies did not violate the EHA because they could directly appeal to a federal court, instead of following the state agency's route of appeal. Thus, the state procedure for dealing with inter-agency disputes did not violate the EHA. *Guy v. Comm'r, New Hampshire Dep't of Educ.*, 565 A.2d 397 (N.H. 1989).

In 1989, the New York legislature passed a law transferring the responsibility of determining the special educational needs of three-to-four-year-olds from the family court to a local preschool special education committee (CPSE). The statute provides that although the law becomes effective July 1, 1989, the family court retains jurisdiction over petitions filed with it prior to August 1, 1989. A petition for special educational services for a three-year-old preschooler was not received until August 8, 1989. The family court determined it no longer had jurisdiction to decide the case, given the date it had received the petition. It acknowledged that although the child's placement would be significantly delayed as a result, the legislature's decree must be followed. The family court referred the case to the local CPSE. *Matter of Martin K.*, 545 N.Y.S.2d 897 (Fam.Ct.1989).

In 1967, a student entered the Philadelphia public school system and was diagnosed by school officials as being educable mentally retarded (EMR). She was placed in an EMR classroom, and although she was reevaluated every other year she remained an EMR student until her departure in 1980. In 1981, she sued the Philadelphia school district alleging that it had negligently diagnosed her as EMR when, in fact, she was learning disabled (LD). A Pennsylvania common pleas court characterized the student's claims as an educational malpractice lawsuit. Stating that educational malpractice was not recognized in Pennsylvania, the court dismissed her suit.

On appeal before the Pennsylvania Commonwealth Court, the student attempted to characterize her lawsuit as one claiming negligence rather than educational malpractice. The commonwealth court, however, agreed with the lower court and held that the student was limited to the legal remedies provided in the Pennsylvania Public School Code, which did not recognize educational malpractice claims.

The commonwealth court further observed that school districts were not required by the school code to devise educational programs which made the best use of each student's abilities. They were only required to identify handicapped children and develop educational programs appropriate to their particular needs. Since the school code did not provide for any monetary damages remedy arising out of the breach of a school district's placement duties, the student's lawsuit was properly dismissed. *Agostine v. School Dist. of Philadelphia*, 527 A.2d 193 (Pa.Cmwlth.1987).

A second grade Pennsylvania student had difficulty reading and keeping up with her class. She was tested by school officials to determine if she was learning disabled. Some of the tests identified her as learning disabled. Her mother requested permission to teach her at home but the school district denied the request. The student suffered daily illnesses because of frustration about her problems. The mother unilaterally removed her from school and then sued school officials in a federal district court. She claimed the student had been denied equal protection under the Fourteenth Amendment because school officials had failed to provide her with an appropriate individualized educational program (IEP). She sought monetary damages for the alleged physical and emotional harm to the student and herself. The court dismissed the complaint, holding that the school officials violated no equal protection rights by failing to provide the student an IEP. Pennsylvania law clearly indicated that neither parents nor children who are not handicapped may bring a lawsuit for damages based on claims that the child received an inadequate or inappropriate education. Although the mother failed to rely upon the EHA the court stated that the case also would have been dismissed under the EHA, which does not provide for damages for physical or emotional harm. *Smith v. Philadelphia School Dist.*, 679 F.Supp. 479 (E.D.Pa.1988).

The next two cases concern awarding diplomas to handicapped students.

After the Illinois State Superintendent of Education ordered that several handicapped children be given their diplomas, an Illinois school district appealed to a U.S. district court challenging the order. The school district argued that the superintendent had allowed the issuance of the diplomas despite the fact that the children failed to pass a minimum competency test as required by the local school board. The district court held that school boards have the right to develop reasonable means to determine the effectiveness of their educational programs with respect to all individual students to whom they issue diplomas and the use of the minimum competency tests is a reasonable means of measuring that effectiveness. The court held that nothing in the EHA or other federal or state law stands in the way of such testing. The court did advise schools to modify tests in order to minimize the effect of physical capacity. To that end, the court suggested that a blind student not be given a competency test which was printed in a normal manner. However, the court stated that the test should not be modified to avoid measuring a student's mental capabilities since to do so would fail completely to measure the results of the educational process. *Brookhart v. Illinois State Bd. of Educ.*, 534 F.Supp. 725 (C.D.Ill.1982).

After the New York Commissioner of Education and a local board of education invalidated diplomas received by two handicapped students enrolled in public school, the students' guardian brought suit to enjoin the commissioner and the board of education from invalidating the diplomas. The guardian objected to the requirement of basic competency tests as a prerequisite to obtaining a high school diploma. The Court of Appeals of New York affirmed two lower court rulings in favor of the school. The court stated that the students had no reasonable expectation of receiving a high school diploma without passing the competency test. The competency testing program had been in effect for three years prior to the completion of the students' studies and, thus, the students were not denied adequate notice of the requirement. *Bd. of Educ. v. Ambach*, 457 N.E.2d 775 (N.Y.1983).

The following cases illustrate the principle that any state statutory scheme which assesses parents or guardians or other relatives and requires reimbursement to the state for educating a handicapped child will not stand as valid law. This is due to the EHA *free* appropriate education requirement for handicapped children and the supremacy of federal law over state law.

An Illinois child resided in facilities operated by the Illinois Department of Mental Health and Developmental Disabilities until his death. Prior to his death, his father was appointed guardian of his estate. The estate included a large sum of money obtained in a medical malpractice settlement. After the child's death, the department claimed $48,725 was due to it pursuant to the Illinois Mental Health and Developmental Disabilities Code. Under the code, the estates of handicapped educational services recipients were required to reimburse the department for its services. Reimbursement was based upon ability to pay. The father refused to pay. The department then filed a lawsuit against the state in an Illinois trial court, seeking reimbursement. The court held that the EHA prevented recovery by the department. The court dismissed the claim and the department appealed to the Appellate Court of Illinois, Fourth District.

The appellate court held that the EHA preempted state law. The department could not obtain reimbursement from the minor's guardianship account. The EHA assured all handicapped children the right to a free appropriate public education. Free education included the right to receive free nonmedical care and room and board if placement in a public or private residential program was necessary to provide special education and related services. The minor was in such programs in order to receive special education. The Appellate Court affirmed the lower court's decision. The state could not seek reimbursement under the EAHCA. *Matter of Guardianship Estate of Zarse*, 529 N.E.2d 50 (Ill.App.4th Dist.1988).

The parents of a handicapped child appealed from an order of the Illinois Department of Mental Health and Developmental Disabilities assessing them a "responsible relative liability charge" for the care of their child. The department's decision was based upon its belief that this was mandated by the Illinois Mental Health and Developmental Disabilities Code. The Appellate Court of Illinois upheld a lower court decision reversing the department's order, ruling that the department's decision was in violation of the EHA.

The court observed that federal law requires maintenance by the state of "a policy that assures all handicapped children the right to a free appropriate public education." This education is to include both "special education" and "related services." The state's contention was that federal statutes should not prevent the assessment of charges pursuant to state law. The court disagreed, observing that there is a strong insistence by federal law on the requirement that all expenditures of every kind for the education and welfare of the child are to be borne by the educational authorities of the state. The assessment was therefore prohibited. *Parks v. Illinois Dep't of Mental Health and Developmental Disabilities*, 441 N.E.2d 1209 (Ill.App.1st Dist.1982).

A U.S. district court held that an Illinois statute requiring relatives to reimburse the state for payments made to support the residential placement of developmentally disabled children was contrary to the EHA and invalid under the Supremacy Clause of the U.S. Constitution. The EHA requires that states provide handicapped children with a free appropriate public education, which includes both special educational and related services. The court characterized the Illinois scheme as a blatant violation of federal law. In overturning the "responsible relatives" statute, the court ordered that relatives who had paid prior assessments be reimbursed for the $100 monthly contribution fee they had paid (back to the year 1978) for the residential care of their developmentally disabled children.

On appeal by the state, the U.S. Court of Appeals, Seventh Circuit, affirmed the ruling that Illinois violated the EHA by requiring parents to pay any part of the living expenses of handicapped children who are placed in a private residential facility on the ground of developmental disability rather than of educational need. The court rejected the state's argument that the class of developmentally disabled children are placed in residential institutions for reasons other than education and, therefore, those children fall outside the EHA. It noted that "if the child is so far handicapped as to be unconscious, and is thus wholly uneducable, he falls outside the Act even though his handicap is more rather than less severe than that of the children protected by the Act." However, the court continued that "in light of the close connection between mental retardation and special educational need . . . developmental disability, far from being an exempted category, is an important subcategory of the handicaps covered by the Act." What Illinois had done, found the court, was to carve out a class of handicapped children and deny them the full reimbursement to which they were entitled.

The appellate court, however, reversed that portion of the district court's ruling which ordered the state to reimburse the parents for expenses they had paid back to the year 1978. The parents were only entitled to reimbursement necessary to clear outstanding bills, thus preventing the expulsion of children from their residential placements. *Parks v. Pavkovic*, 753 F.2d 1397 (7th Cir.1985).

New Jersey's department of education issued detailed regulations governing private schools which educate handicapped children. The regulations applied only to private schools to which local school boards sent handicapped children in order to satisfy the local board's educational obligations. These private schools were required to submit detailed budgets, establish strict bookkeeping and accounting procedures, submit to annual audits by the state, and most objectionably, a school's profit was limited to 2.5% of its per pupil costs. Several private school associations sued the department seeking to have the regulations declared invalid. They claimed that the regulations were "confiscatory" and had been enacted without proper authority.

The New Jersey Superior Court, Appellate Division, upheld the regulations as within the scope of the department's powers. Especially persuasive to the court was the argument that private schools, by choosing to accept handicapped students on referral from local school boards, should expect to relinquish a degree of privacy and autonomy over their affairs. The 2.5% profit ceiling is a reasonable exercise of department authority over private schools which, said the court, have voluntarily submitted to department control. However, the court left open the possibility that in the future, if a private school were able to show that due to its financial condition the regulations were unreasonable as applied to it, then a waiver of the regulations might be justified. *Council of Private Schools for Children with Special Needs v. Cooperman*, 501 A.2d 575 (N.J.Super.A.D.1985).

A private school in Pennsylvania alleged it was denied due process of law after the Pennsylvania Secretary of Education denied the school's application for status as an approved private school for socially and emotionally disturbed children. A hearing examiner determined that three State Board of Education standards were not met: first, the student interns used in the school classrooms did not provide full-time supportive assistance to the classroom teachers; second, the school lacked an immediately available supervisor or other competent and trained person to handle a student in a period of crisis and to remove that student, if necessary from the classroom; third, the school's behavior management systems did not permit its classroom teachers to control classroom conduct adequately. The school appealed to the Commonwealth Court of Pennsylvania, which affirmed the hearing examiner's decision. The school then appealed to the Supreme Court of Pennsylvania, which found that the evidence was sufficient to support a finding that the school failed to provide adequate staff assistance to classroom teachers. The court concluded that the hearing examiner's findings went to the heart of the Pennsylvania regulatory scheme of insuring that approved private schools were able to provide adequate and necessary training and education to handicapped children. *Wiley House v. Scanlon*, 465 A.2d 995 (Pa.1983).

CHAPTER NINE
HANDICAP DISCRIMINATION

The Rehabilitation Act of 1973 prohibits discrimination against the handicapped in programs receiving federal financial assistance. Under the Act, no otherwise qualified handicapped individual is to be excluded from employment, programs or services to which he or she is entitled. Additionally, claims for alleged discrimination are sometimes brought under the Equal Protection Clause of the U.S. Constitution, which also prohibits discrimination by guaranteeing that laws will be applied equally to all citizens.

I. DUTY NOT TO DISCRIMINATE AGAINST THE HANDICAPPED

The duty not to discriminate against handicapped individuals may arise by statute, and/or may be concomitant with the receipt of federal funding. Where a state's asserted interest in discriminating against the handicapped is outweighed by the liberty interests of the handicapped, the state must affirmatively act to eliminate the source of discrimination, or, in other cases, must refrain from acting when doing so would promote unfair discrimination.

A. Students, Patients, and Other Individuals under the Rehabilitation Act and the Equal Protection Clause

The U.S. Supreme Court ruled recently that mental retardation is not a "suspect classification" calling for heightened protection under the U.S. Constitution. This case arose when the operator of a proposed group home for mentally handicapped individuals was denied a building-use permit by the city council of Cleburne, Texas. The city council determined that the group home would be classified as a "hospital for the feebleminded" under the zoning laws and proceeded to deny a permit to the group home. The operator sued the city in federal court, claiming that the council's action unlawfully discriminated against mentally retarded citizens in violation of the Equal Protection Clause of the U.S. Constitution. # The Supreme Court, while ordering that the group home be granted a permit, held that government regulations regarding mentally retarded individuals are not to be subjected to rigorous judicial analysis as are classifications based on race, alienage or sex. The Equal Protection Clause, held the Court, does not afford the same protection to handicapped citizens as it does to minorities. Although in this case the group home won its building-use permit, the Supreme Court's holding limited the scope of the Equal Protection Clause to cases involving irrational, unfounded or arbitrary action against the handicapped. *City of Cleburne, Texas v. Cleburne Living Center*, 105 S.Ct. 3249, 473 U.S. 432 (1985).

A handicapped student enrolled in a college of optometry. He suffered from retinitis pigmentosis and an associated neurological condition. As a result he had a restricted field of vision and impaired motor skills, sense of touch and manual coordination. The college's policy was that each school year was governed by its current catalog. The student enrolled in the college, under the terms of a catalog effective for the 1978-79 academic year. The catalog language cautioned that it did not create a contract between the college and any student. During the student's first year of study, the college introduced a pathology clinic proficiency requirement involving use of special equipment. The clinic requirement was not listed in the 1978-79 catalog. The student failed his tests on the equipment, and requested a waiver. The college's board of trustees denied his request but granted him an extra quarter to practice on the equipment. Despite his extra practice, the student failed to satisfy the proficiency requirements. The college refused to award the student a degree.

The student sued the college in a federal district court, claiming that it violated § 504 of the Rehabilitation Act, 42 U.S.C. § 1983, and that the college breached his educational contract under state law. The court dismissed the § 1983 claim and conducted a trial on the other matters. The college prevailed in the § 504 claim, but the student prevailed on the breach of contract claim. The student appealed to the U.S. Court of Appeals, Sixth Circuit, on his § 504 claim and the college cross-appealed on the breach of contract claim. The student claimed that the college used the test as a pretext for discrimination because it applied a higher standard to him by requiring mechanical proficiency with equipment. The court held that the college could reasonably set standards for its program to ensure competence. Section 504 did not require the college to lower its academic requirements to accommodate handicapped students. The college had not failed to reasonably accommodate the student and it prevailed on the § 504 claim. The court also held that students should reasonably anticipate changes in academic requirements after enrolling. The college's addition of new degree requirements was reasonable. There was no evidence that the college had deliberately introduced the clinical proficiency requirement to prevent the student's graduation. The case was reversed in part and affirmed in part so that the college prevailed in all matters. *Doherty v. Southern College of Optometry*, 862 F.2d 570 (6th Cir. 1988).

In New Hampshire an unsuccessful discrimination claim was brought by the mother of a disabled child in U.S. district court, alleging discrimination under the federal Rehabilitation Act. She alleged that the New Hampshire Medical Assistance Program (NHMAP) unlawfully discriminated against her son solely on the basis of his handicap. The NHMAP provides medical assistance under the medical needs program only to persons under eighteen years of age who are blind, she pointed out, while denying benefits to persons under eighteen years of age who are handicapped by any other disability. The state moved to dismiss the action for failure to state a claim upon which relief could be granted and the motion was granted.

The court stated that the state's refusal to expand the eligibility requirements for medical assistance to include the plaintiff in this case was not so unreasonable and arbitrary as to constitute unlawful discrimination. It was noted that the plaintiffs did not allege that New Hampshire's exclusion of non-blind children from medical assistance was motivated by an animus against handicapped individuals. In fact, the statutory history revealed that the exclusion was based on congressional authorization designed to encourage continued state participation in the Medicaid program, through limitation of the state's financial commitment. In the absence of any statutory or regulatory requirement identifying as discriminatory the refusal to undertake affirmative action by extending additional services to the handicapped, the court held that it was not at liberty to fashion its own affirmative action requirements. Thus, in spite of the plaintiff's obvious need for medical assistance and the compelling nature of his request for medical assistance equal to that afforded other disabled persons under the NHMAP, the court determined it should not overrule the judgment of the state of New Hampshire and Congress on this matter of social policy. *Duquette v. Dupuis*, 582 F.Supp. 1365 (D.N.H. 1984).

An Illinois case resulted in a ruling that a handicapped student may not sue the U.S. Secretary of Education. Here, a graduate student pursuing an MBA at Chicago's Roosevelt University failed to inform university officials that he was handicapped, and did not tell them that he was learning disabled. Instead, the university thought that he was recovering from a serious illness. In view of the student's "illness," the university allowed him to continue in its MBA program even though he had received his third "C," which usually results in academic dismissal. Eventually, the student was unable to meet the MBA program's requirements. He attempted to bring suit under the Rehabilitation Act directly against the U.S. Secretary of Education, seeking damages due to the secretary's refusal to review his claim that the university had discriminated against him on the basis of his handicap.

The federal district court observed that the student had never informed the university that he was handicapped by a learning disability. Unquestionably, he had no claim against the university since the Rehabilitation Act imposes no duty upon institutions which are unaware of a person's handicap, said the court, and this no doubt explained why he had attempted to sue the secretary instead. The student's lawsuit was thus dismissed by the court, which stated: "There is no doubt that a recipient or applicant of federal funds has a cause of action against the Secretary under Section 603 [of the Rehabilitation Act]. There is also no doubt that a beneficiary in [the handicapped student's] position has a private right of action against the recipient institution. But no private cause of action exists under Section 504 [of the Act] for a beneficiary against the Secretary." The student's complaint against the secretary was dismissed and he appealed to the U.S. Court of Appeals, Seventh Circuit.

The question before the court was whether the student could force the secretary to review his case or force the secretary to cut off the university's federal funding. The court held that "a request for damages against administrative adjudicators is not supported by any statute. . . . A request for damages against the Secretary of Education, who personally played no role in the administrative adjudication, also is not provided by any other statute." The court concluded that a private person has no legal interest in public enforcement of matters such as the termination of federal funding. The student had to be content with his own remedies against the university. The lower court's ruling that the student could not maintain a lawsuit against the secretary of education was upheld. *Salvador v. Bennett*, 800 F.2d 97 (7th Cir.1986).

A group of students and would-be students at the University of Texas at Austin sought declaratory and injunctive relief in federal district court requiring the university to make its shuttle buses accessible to wheelchairs. The plaintiffs were all confined to wheelchairs and, therefore, were handicapped individuals under the Rehabilitation Act of 1973. They were required to pay a mandatory student services fee each semester, which was used in part to pay for the operation of the shuttle bus system. However, they could not use the system because the buses were not accessible to wheelchairs. They contended that the university's failure to provide them with accessible shuttle service limited their ability to fully participate in academic and extracurricular programs, and that this failure was in violation of federal law. They also contended that the failure to accommodate wheelchairs was a breach of their contract with the university to provide them with bus transportation in exchange for student service fees.

The district court disagreed with these contentions. It held that the shuttle bus system was not a program receiving federal financial assistance for purposes of the Rehabilitation Act and therefore was not subject to the requirements of the Act, that the university had no obligation under the Equal Protection Clause of the Fourteenth Amendment to make major expenditures of funds required to make the shuttle bus system accessible to wheelchairs, and that the university had not "contracted" to provide shuttle bus service to mobility-impaired students on the basis of statements made in the university general information booklet. The students' request for declaratory and injunctive relief was therefore denied. *Ferris v. Univ. of Texas at Austin*, 558 F.Supp. 536 (W.D.Tex.1983).

As a result of reports of patient abuse at the Pennhurst State Hospital, a Pennsylvania institution for the severely mentally retarded, a state police officer was assigned to become an undercover aide at the hospital. Several hospital employees were later indicted by a federal grand jury and a male aide was convicted of violating the right of severely retarded persons to personal security, a federal crime. The evidence showed that the aide frequently "punched, kicked, kneed, or shoved" patients for no reason and that he frequently flicked cigarette butts on the floor where he hoped that more severely retarded patients would ingest them. The U.S. Court of Appeals, Third Circuit, upheld his conviction. The aide had knowingly deprived the patients of their federally protected right to personal security while acting under the authority of state law. *United States v. Dise*, 763 F.2d 586 (3d Cir.1985).

A group of mentally retarded children brought suit against the Board of Education of the City of New York challenging a proposed plan to segregate within the public schools those retarded children who were carriers of hepatitis B virus. The board argued that the plan was valid because it was formulated pursuant to New York City health department guidelines. A federal district court held in favor of the children, saying that the health department guidelines were more "akin to general statements of policy than mandatory prescriptions." Thus, the guidelines would not be afforded "presumptive validity." The plan was also flawed because it violated the Rehabilitation Act and the EHA. The New York Board of Education had not shown that the hepatitis B carriers had actually engaged in unhygienic contacts. The court noted that the segregation plan would violate the EHA in that the children would not be educated in the "least restrictive environment." Finally, despite the fact that there were over one million school children in New York City's public school system, no group other than the mentally retarded students was tested for hepatitis B. This violated the children's equal protection rights under the U.S. Constitution. This decision was affirmed by the U.S. Court of Appeals, Second Circuit. *New York State Ass'n for Retarded Children v. Carey*, 612 F.2d 644 (2d Cir.1979).

A private school in Missouri refused to admit a blind mentally-disabled student who had hepatitis B. As a result of his physical and mental impairments, the student frequently exhibited maladaptive behavior, including biting, scratching and self abuse. The school argued that the burden and risk of admitting the student was too high since it would be forced to immunize its staff on a continuing basis. The student sued the school in a federal district court seeking an order to compel his admission. The court found that the school had discriminated against the student solely on the basis of his handicap in violation of § 504 of the Rehabilitation Act. It ordered the school to admit the student. The court ordered the school to immunize only those employees who would be in regular contact with the student. It stated that if this were done, the burden on the school would be minimized. The school appealed the order to the U.S. Court of Appeals, Eighth Circuit.

The appeals court noted that although the school had discriminated against the student solely on the basis of his handicap, he was not entitled to admission under the district court's plan. The court held that the inevitable exposure of unimmunized staff to a significant risk of infection was unacceptable. Therefore, regardless of the cost of the plan, a program of limited inoculation as ordered by the district court could not reasonably accommodate the student. The court of appeals reversed the district court's order and remanded the case for further proceedings. *Kohl v. Woodhaven Learning Center*, 865 F.2d 930 (8th Cir.1989).

The next two cases summarize how the courts treat alcoholism with respect to the Rehabilitation Act.

Two honorably discharged veterans who were recovering alcoholics sought an extension of the ten-year Veterans' Administration (V.A.) limitation for receipt of educational assistance under the G.I. Bill. The ten-year limitation on educational benefits can be extended by the V.A. if the veteran can show he was prevented from using his benefits earlier because of "physical or mental disability which was not the result of . . . [his] own willful misconduct." V.A. regulations state that the deliberate drinking of alcohol is considered willful misconduct.

Both veterans requested extension of benefits after expiration of their respective ten-year limitation periods. These requests were based on grounds that they were handicapped by alcoholism. The V.A. denied their requests, stating that their alcoholism was due to willful misconduct. One veteran sued the V.A. in a New York district court. The other veteran sought review in the District Court for the District of Columbia.

The New York district court held for the V.A., but its decision was reversed by the U.S. Court of Appeals, Second Circuit. The District of Columbia district court ruled that the V.A. regulation was contrary to the Rehabilitation Act. The act prohibits federal programs from discriminating against handicapped individuals solely because of their handicap. The District of Columbia Court of Appeals reversed the district court's decision.

Noting the disagreement between two federal courts of appeal, the U.S. Supreme Court granted review and heard the cases together. The Court held that the Rehabilitation Act does not preclude a lawsuit against the V.A. Congress had changed the time limit for benefits several times, most recently in 1977. However, the Rehabilitation Act did not repeal the wilful misconduct provision of the 1977 regulations. Nothing in the act required that any benefit extended to one category of handicapped persons also be extended to all other categories of handicapped persons. Congress had the right to establish the allocation priorities for veterans' benefits. The District of Columbia Court of Appeals decision was affirmed and the Second Circuit Court of Appeals decision was reversed. The V.A. prevailed in both matters. *Traynor v. Turnage*, 108 S.Ct. 1372 (1988).

A law student at the University of Wisconsin completed his first semester with below standard grades. He was dismissed during his second semester because he failed to furnish certification of his undergraduate degree. The school allowed him to return the following spring despite knowledge that he was an alcoholic. Sensing that he was doing poorly, the student asked to withdraw. The school later learned that while drunk, he had harassed and threatened a classmate. The school readmitted the student for a third time the following spring. He completed the semester with below standard grades and the school expelled him. The student sued the school in a Wisconsin federal court alleging § 504 violations of the Rehabilitation Act, by discriminating against him on account of alcoholism. The district court granted the school's dismissal motion because the student was not "otherwise qualified" to continue as a law student. He then appealed to the U.S. Court of Appeals, Seventh Circuit.

The appeals court noted that § 504 provided that an institution receiving federal funds may not discriminate against an "otherwise qualified handicapped individual." It also noted that previous cases had held that "[a]n otherwise qualified person is one who is able to meet all of a program's requirements in spite of his handicap." The Rehabilitation Act did not forbid decisions based on the actual attributes of the handicapped individual. It also recognized that the school's decision was based on evaluations of how the student had previously performed and how he could be expected to perform in the future. In this case the school acted on the basis of the student's past performance rather than his alcoholism. The appeals court upheld the district court decision to dismiss the case. *Anderson v. Univ. of Wisconsin*, 841 F.2d 737 (7th Cir.1988).

A Kansas school district used a 3′ x 5′ "time-out" room for in-school suspensions of a handicapped student. The student had a history of truancy, violent behavior and willful disobedience of school rules. The student was placed in the time-out room when he was disruptive so he could regain his composure and not disturb other students. He was to engage in classroom work while in the time-out room. The student sued the school district in a federal district court. He alleged that use of the time-out room violated his due process rights under the Fourteenth Amendment to the U.S. Constitution. He also claimed that use of the time-out room violated the Eighth Amendment's prohibition against cruel and inhumane punishment. The school district argued that the student's fundamental contention was that it had violated the EHA's change-in-placement provision. Therefore, the student's claim should fail because he had not exhausted his administrative remedies under the EHA.

The court held for the student concerning the exhaustion of remedies argument. The use of the time-out room was not an activity the EHA was intended to prevent. Therefore, the EHA was not the exclusive avenue through which the student could bring his lawsuit. The student could sue alleging deprivation of his constitutional rights under § 1983 of the Civil Rights Act.

The court also concluded that the use of the time-out room did not constitute cruel and inhumane punishment. The Supreme Court has held that the Eighth Amendment protection against such punishment should not be extended to lawsuits brought by public school students.

The court held for the school district regarding the student's due process claim. The student was not deprived of his constitutional interest in education when he was placed in the time-out room. In fact, the use of the time-out room ensured that the student would not be deprived of his right to a public education when he was suspended because it kept him in school during that time. The student was not deprived of due process because he was placed in the time-out room only after three documented disciplinary violations. He was given sufficient prior notice of the reason for placement in the time-out room. The school sent written notice to his parents when use of the time-out room was contemplated. His parents were notified about time-out room use in conferences with school officials. The school district was not liable for violating the student's constitutional rights. *Hayes v. Unified School Dist. No. 377*, 669 F.Supp. 1519 (D.Kan.1987).

Six years after a handicapped individual was denied admission to a California nursing school, a federal appeals court ruled that she was entitled to damages for unlawful discrimination. The prospective student suffered from Crohn's Disease, an inflammatory bowel disorder which causes loss of weight, nausea, vomiting and other complications. She had been accepted to the Los Angeles County Medical Center School of Nursing in April, 1979, and had attended an orientation session. Two days before classes were to begin she was told that due to an unacceptable physical examination, she was being denied admission to the school. She filed suit in federal district court under the Rehabilitation Act, seeking an order that the school be compelled to accept her.

After twice being denied relief by the district court, the case came before the U.S. Court of Appeals, Ninth Circuit. The appeals court found that the woman was a handicapped individual within the meaning of the Rehabilitation Act, and noted that the school's physician had recommended that her application for admission be rejected because, in his opinion, it would be "too stressful" for her to study at the school. The court stated that "[i]t is precisely this type of general assumption about a handicapped person's capility that [the Act] was designed to avoid." Finding that the woman had been denied admission solely on the basis of her handicap, the court remanded the case to the district court with instructions to award her monetary damages and attorney's fees. *Kling v. County of Los Angeles*, 769 F.2d 532 (9th Cir.1985).

In a Texas case, the parents of a mentally handicapped child, who was enrolled in a private school, contacted a public school district regarding a possible public school placement for their child. A meeting was held a year later at which the parents were not present and of which they had no knowledge. At the meeting, it was decided that the child should be placed in an EMR class in the public schools. When the parents were finally contacted they rejected the recommendation, saying that their son was not mentally retarded. The parents continued private school placement for their child.

Approximately two years later the school district started a public awareness "blitz" to reach handicapped children not then receiving a free appropriate public education. A year after they became aware of this "child find" program, the parents once again contacted the school district for a possible public school placement. The child was eventually enrolled in a public school program and the parents sought reimbursement for their private school tuition expenses in a federal district court.

The court held that the school district had been under an affirmative duty to determine what special services would be needed for the child and then to provide those services. In failing to do so, the school district had discriminated against the child in violation of section 504 of the Rehabilitation Act. The parents were not entitled to damages under the EHA but were entitled to private school tuition reimbursement under the Rehabilitation Act. However, the court found that the parents were not entitled to tuition reimbursement subsequent to the time they became aware of the "child find" program. *David H. v. Spring Branch Indep. School Dist.*, 569 F.Supp. 1324 (S.D.Tex. 1983).

B. Students, Parents, and Other Individuals under the EHA

A sixteen-year-old California high school student, suffering from cerebral palsy, learning disabilities and right side deafness, used a wheelchair for mobility. She participated in a two-week training program with an organization which trains service dogs for use by people with disabilities. At the end of the training period, she received a service dog of her own. She then sought to bring the dog to school with her, but the school district refused to allow her to do so. She sued the school district in a federal district court, seeking injunctive and declaratory relief, and emotional distress damages. The district sought to dismiss her claim, and she moved for a preliminary injunction to allow her, during the course of the trial, to be accompanied by her service dog at school.

The district court first determined that the student's claim should not be dismissed because of her failure to exhaust her administrative remedies. The student did not contend that the service dog was educationally necessary, but merely asserted that she had a right to be accompanied by her service dog in places of accommodation. Thus, the relief that she sought was not specifically available under the Education of the Handicapped Act (EHA). The court ruled that the student need not exhaust her EHA administrative remedies to bring the lawsuit. It then determined that facilities which were open to members of the general public, like schools, were required to make access equally available to disabled and able-bodied persons alike.

The court then looked to the student's motion for a preliminary injunction. It recognized that preliminary relief would require an alteration of the status quo and decided that if the student could show that she would likely be successful in her case, and that the harm she would suffer by not having her dog with her would be much greater than the harm to the school by the dog's presence, she would be entitled to preliminary relief. Here, the school was a facility required by law to be nondiscriminatory and the student's chances of success were good. Further, the school district had shown only that it would suffer a minor inconvenience by having to restructure the student's educational program to accommodate her service dog. The student's injuries would far outweigh those of the school and, accordingly, the court granted the preliminary injunction in favor of the student. *Sullivan v. Vallejo City Unified School District*, 731 F.Supp. 947 (E.D.Cal.1990).

A West Virginia man enrolled his two hearing-impaired children in a public school. Since there were no other hearing-impaired children in the school system, it did not have an adequate program for such children. When the children were not being privately taught by a speech therapist, they were placed in a regular classroom. The children were then placed in a school for the deaf and blind, until one child was expelled for behavioral problems. After another attempt to place the children in different hearing-impaired schools, the children were again placed in the same public school. School authorities determined that the children also had speech, learning and behavioral problems. After the father rejected the school's attempt to institutionalize the children, he filed a complaint with the state Human Rights Commission. He alleged his children had been denied an appropriate education and thus had been discriminated against. Pending a determination, the children were finally given individualized educational programs. The commission determined that the board had violated the human rights act by failing to provide an appropriate education. It ordered monetary damages and compensatory education until the children reached age twenty-four. After a West Virginia trial court vacated the order, the father appealed to the West Virginia Supreme Court of Appeals.

The court reinstated the commission's order. It held that the board was a "person" within the meaning of state law and thus had violated prohibitions against handicap discrimination. Further, state law imposed a duty on the board to establish an appropriate education for handicapped children. The federal Education of the Handicapped Act (EHA) also required placement of the children in the least restrictive environment. The board had not done so because it sought to send the children to out of state institutions. It had discriminated against the children on the basis of handicap. *Board of Education v. Human Rights Comm'n*, 385 S.E.2d 637 (W.Va.1989).

The deaf parents of two New York public school students who had normal hearing repeatedly requested the school district to provide qualified sign-language interpreters for school meetings. The district denied requests to provide or pay for interpreters to assist the parents in communicating with teachers and counselors. The parents claimed that they had been unable to participate in some school events and had expended $2,000 in one academic year for their own interpreter. They claimed that they were being denied equal access to school services in violation of the Rehabilitation Act of 1973, 29 U.S. § 794 and the Civil Rights Act, 42 U.S.C. § 1983. They sued the school district in a federal district court for declaratory, injunctive and monetary relief.

The court held that the parents were otherwise qualified handicapped persons who were entitled to meaningful access to school-initiated meetings. It also held that the superintendent of schools was entitled to qualified immunity from liability. The court refused to grant a school district motion to dismiss the case. It then held a trial to determine the extent of the school district's obligation under § 504 of the Rehabilitation Act. According to the court, the parents had been effectively barred from participation in school district programs for parents due to the lack of a sign language interpreter. The parents were entitled to an interpreter for all school-sponsored activities designed for parental involvement which focused on academic progress or discipline. The parents would have to provide their own interpreter for participation in voluntary extracurricular activities. *Rothschild v. Grottenthaler*, 725 F.Supp. 776 (S.D.N.Y.1989).

A New Hampshire father alleged that his daughter, a handicapped child, was not receiving a free appropriate education. He was granted an administrative due process hearing by the state. Dissatisfied with the results of the hearing, he sued the New Hampshire State Board of Education in a federal district court. After the state refused to provide him with a free written transcript of the administrative hearing, he brought a separate lawsuit against it in the same court. The court ruled that the state did not have to provide a free written transcript of the hearing so he appealed to the U.S. Court of Appeals, First Circuit.

The court of appeals observed that, although a written transcript of the hearing would be more helpful than a recording for purposes of an EHA lawsuit, EHA § 1415(d)(3) only granted the right to receive either a written *or* electronic verbatim record of the hearing. Since the state had provided an electronic verbatim record of the administrative due process hearing, it had fulfilled its responsibility. The father's claim that because he could not afford the $3,000 for a written transcript, his due process rights had been violated, was rejected by the court of appeals. It concluded that the administrative due process hearing itself satisfied the father's basic due process rights.

The father also contended that the failure to provide a transcript violated his rights under the Equal Protection Clause. He claimed that the refusal to provide the transcript was the result of unconstitutional discrimination based upon either his daughter's handicap or his lack of wealth. The court of appeals did not accept the first argument since the father had failed to show that the EHA provision infringed upon the rights of any "suspect class." A "suspect class" is a group of persons who are afforded special protection under the Equal Protection Clause (e.g. racial minorities). The U.S. Supreme Court has held in *City of Cleburne v. Cleburne Living Center*, 473 U.S. 432 (1985), that handicapped persons are not a suspect class. Thus, legislative classifications based upon handicaps will not be given rigorous examination by the courts. Further, the court of appeals held that a classification based upon indigence received closer examination only if indigents were "completely unable to pay for some desired benefit [which results in] an absolute deprivation of a meaningful opportunity to enjoy that benefit." Here, the alleged classification based upon wealth only made recourse to the courts more difficult rather than impossible. The district court's decision was upheld. *Edward B. v. Paul*, 814 F.2d 52 (1st Cir.1987).

A group of mentally retarded children in Virginia brought suit against the Virginia Commissioner of the Department of Welfare, and other state officials, seeking injunctive relief enjoining the defendants from maintaining them in an institution or state hospital. The children claimed that these placements were made in lieu of providing them with an appropriate education and services in a foster home or other community-based facility in their home communities. A federal district court held that the children had a valid claim under the Developmentally Disabled Assistance and Bill of Rights Act, the EHA and the Rehabilitation Act. These statutes afford personal civil rights to beneficiaries under the statutes, which were intended to promote equal treatment of and equal opportunity to the beneficiaries. The defendants' motion for summary judgment on the ground that the children had failed to state a valid claim was denied. *Medley v. Ginsberg*, 492 F.Supp. 1294 (S.D. W.Va.1980).

C. Teachers

Teachers and other school employees are also protected by the Rehabilitation Act against discrimination on the basis of handicap.

The U.S. Supreme Court ruled that tuberculosis is a handicap under § 504 of the Rehabilitation Act. The Act defines a handicapped individual as "any person who (i) has a physical or mental impairment which substantially limits one or more of such person's major life activities, (ii) has a record of such impairment or (iii) is regarded as having such an impairment." It defines "physical impairment" as disorders affecting, among other things, the respiratory system and defines "major life activities" as "functions such as caring for one's self . . . and working."

The case involved a Florida elementary school teacher who was discharged because of the continued recurrence of tuberculosis. The teacher sued the school board under § 504 but a federal district court dismissed her claims. However, the U.S. Court of Appeals, Eleventh Circuit, reversed the district court's decision and the school board appealed to the U.S. Supreme Court.

The Supreme Court ruled that tuberculosis was a handicap under § 504 because it affected the respiratory system and affected her ability to work. The school board contended that in defining a handicapped individual under § 504, the contagious effects of a disease can be distinguished from the disease's physical effects. However, the Court reasoned that the teacher's contagion and her physical impairment both resulted from the same condition: tuberculosis. It would be unfair to allow an employer to distinguish between a disease's potential effect on others and its effect on the afflicted employee in order to justify discriminatory treatment. Allowing discrimination based on the contagious effects of a physical impairment would be inconsistent with the underlying purpose of § 504. According to the Court, that purpose is to ensure that handicapped persons are not denied jobs because of prejudice or ignorance. It noted that society's myths and fears about disability and disease are as handicapping as the physical impairment, and concluded that contagion cannot remove a person from § 504 coverage. It remanded the case to the district court to determine whether the teacher was "otherwise qualified" for her job and whether the school board could reasonably accommodate her as an employee. *School Bd. of Nassau County v. Arline*, 107 S.Ct. 1123 (1987).

On remand, the Florida federal district court held that the teacher was "otherwise qualified" to teach. The teacher posed no threat of spreading tuberculosis to her students in 1978. When she was on medication, medical tests indicated a limited number of negative cultures. Her family members tested negative and she had limited contact with students. The court ordered reinstatement or front-pay in the amount of $768,724 for earnings until retirement. *Arline v. School Bd. of Nassau County*, 692 F.Supp. 1286 (M.D. Fla.1988).

A teacher of hearing-impaired children was relegated to an administrative position when the school district discovered that he had AIDS. The teacher sued the school board asserting that it had violated his rights under the Rehabilitation Act of 1973 by removing him from the classroom. The teacher's request for a preliminary injunction which would have allowed him to teach until the court could hold a trial and issue a ruling was denied by a U.S. district court. The U.S. Court of Appeals, Ninth Circuit, reversed and issued the preliminary injunction. The court of appeals has now issued a decision which sets out the reasons for the issuance of the preliminary injunction.

The court noted that to acquire the preliminary injunction the teacher had to demonstrate a combination of probable success at trial and a possibility of irreparable injury. Under the Rehabilitation Act the teacher could not be dismissed because of his handicapping condition (AIDS) if he was otherwise qualified to teach. The court then applied a test devised by the U.S. Supreme

Court in *School Board of Nassau County v. Arline*. The test provided that "[a] person who poses a significant risk of communicating an infectious disease to others in the workplace will not be otherwise qualified for his or her job if reasonable accommodations will not eliminate that risk." The court then pointed out the district court's finding that transmission of AIDS was unlikely to occur in the classroom. The court held that the teacher was otherwise qualified for his position because his presence in the classroom would not pose "a significant risk of communicating an infectious disease to others." This finding meant that the teacher would probably succeed at trial.

The court then noted that although the teacher's salary was not reduced when he was transferred to the administrative position, the transfer removed him from a job for which he had developed special skills and from which he derived "tremendous personal satisfaction and joy." The administrative position, on the other hand, involved no student contact and did not utilize the teacher's skills, training or experience. The court also observed that the teacher's ability to work would surely be affected in time by AIDS which has proved fatal in all reported cases. The court concluded that any delay in returning the teacher to the classroom caused an irretrievable loss of the teacher's productive time. This established the possibility of irreparable injury if the preliminary injunction was not awarded.

Because the teacher had shown 1) that he would probably succeed at trial, and 2) that the denial of a preliminary injunction in his favor could cause him irreparable injury the court awarded the preliminary injunction. The teacher was returned to the classroom. *Chalk v. U.S. District Court*, 840 F.2d 701 (9th Cir.1988).

A physically disabled Nevada student received a teaching degree in special education and was then licensed by the state of Nevada as a special education teacher. She applied for a teaching position with a Nevada school district and also placed herself on the list of persons available for substitute teaching. She worked as a substitute teacher for over three years and received high praise for her performance. However, she was not offered permanent employment. She then worked as a substitute teacher under a federally-funded temporary contract at another school. The following spring the school had four teaching positions available and offered the teacher a temporary contract. When the teacher received her one-year temporary contract, a permanent position was open in the school district but was given to a student teacher with no teaching experience. The teacher received the most difficult and demanding class assignment at the school. She then filed a discrimination lawsuit against the school district in a federal district court.

The court found that under § 794 of the Rehabilitation Act, an otherwise qualified handicapped individual could not be discriminated against under any program or activity receiving federal financial assistance. The teacher fell within the Act's definition of a handicapped person and was otherwise qualified to serve as a special education teacher. The court found that the school district never made an affirmative effort to recognize the teacher's handicaps or to accommodate them. Thus she was discriminated against solely on the basis of her handicap. The court found for the teacher and awarded her compensatory damages. *Recanzone v. Washoe County School Dist.*, 696 F.Supp. 1372 (D.Nev.1988).

An applicant for a special education teaching position in Iowa sued a local school district under both the federal Rehabilitation Act and Iowa law, alleging that the district refused to hire him due to his physical disability. The teacher, a resident of Vermont, suffered from several severe handicaps, but was able to walk without assistance and to lift children and drive. The teacher applied to the Iowa school district for a job and was scheduled for an interview in Iowa, at his own expense, with possible reimbursement if he were hired. After arranging the interview, the teacher became concerned that he had not disclosed his handicaps. Because of his limited financial resources, he did not wish to fly to Iowa, only to be rejected because of his handicaps. He called the school district and explained his handicaps. He was told that the job involved transporting children which, in turn, required a bus driver's permit that the teacher probably could not get because of his handicaps. The district suggested that a trip to Iowa would probably be futile. The teacher then sued in a federal district court, which found in his favor.

The court stated that the test of proof for a discrimination claim under the Rehabilitation Act is: 1) that the plaintiff is a handicapped individual under the terms of the statute; 2) that the plaintiff is otherwise qualified to participate in the program or activity at issue; 3) that the plaintiff was excluded from the program or activity solely by reason of her or his handicap; and 4) that the program or activity receives federal financial assistance. There was no dispute that the plaintiff was a "handicapped individual" within the meaning of the Rehabilitation Act, the court had little difficulty in finding that the plaintiff was "otherwise qualified" for the position because of his superior credentials. The court also found that the plaintiff had satisfied the third and fourth prongs of the test in that the district was a recipient of federal financial assistance, including funds received pursuant to the EHA and that, with a minimum of accommodation, the school district could have arranged an alternative situation whereby the teacher would not have had to transport children. The court awarded the teacher $1,000 damages for mental anguish, and $5,150 for loss of earnings. *Fitzgerald v. Green Valley Educ. Agency*, 589 F.Supp. 1130 (S.D.Iowa 1984).

A Louisiana hospital required a nurse to divulge medical information about his human immunodeficiency virus (HIV) status. The nurse had failed to report that he was a hepatitis B carrier and that he had once had a syphilis infection. The hospital suspended the nurse pending disclosure of the information and later discharged him when he refused to provide the information. The hospital's infection control policies required employees to report infectious or communicable diseases to its employee health service. The nurse claimed that the policy violated his rights under § 504 of the Rehabilitation Act, 29 U.S.C. 794. Section 504 provides that: "no otherwise qualified individual with handicaps . . . shall, solely by reason of his handicap, . . . be subjected to discrimination under any program or activity receiving federal financial assistance." Congress defined an "individual with handicaps" to include individuals who are perceived as being impaired as well as individuals who are actually impaired. The nurse claimed that the hospital perceived him as being HIV positive and thus handicapped. The nurse sued the hospital in federal district court.

According to the court, there was no evidence to show that the hospital had perceived the nurse to be HIV positive. The nurse was informed at the termination hearing that he was being discharged for failure to follow hospital policy. He was discharged because he had violated the hospital's infection control policies, not because he was regarded as HIV positive. The nurse's refusal to comply with the hospital's policies rendered him "not otherwise qualified" to perform his job. The court held that the discharge of the nurse for refusal to provide HIV test results did not violate § 504 of the Rehabilitation Act. *Leckelt v. Bd. of Comm'rs of Hospital Dist. No. 1*, 714 F.Supp. 1377 (E.D.La.1989).

In 1979, the Council for the Hearing Impaired of Long Island and others brought suit in a federal district court against the Commissioner of Education of the State of New York, and several federal officials, alleging that the offering of lower salaries at educational institutions for handicapped students was unlawful. Specifically, the plaintiffs contended that because teaching salaries at these institutions were lower than those found in other schools, there existed a relatively high staff turnover rate which had an adverse impact on handicapped students' educations. The plaintiffs charged that this violated the EHA, § 504 of the Rehabilitation Act, section 1983 of the Civil Rights Act, and the First and Ninth Amendments to the U.S. Constitution.

On a motion for summary judgment, the district court dismissed the claim that a high staff turnover rate violated the EHA, noting that nothing in the EHA requires that the education of handicapped children be "equal" to that of other children. All that is required is that handicapped children be provided with an "educational benefit." Also dismissed were the plaintiff's claims under the First and Ninth Amendments, since education is not guaranteed by the U.S. Constitution. However, the plaintiffs were allowed to proceed with their claims under the Rehabilitation Act and the Civil Rights Act, insofar as they alleged that the state of New York had unlawfully discriminated between handicapped and nonhandicapped children in the provision of educational services. The district court then proceeded to admonish the plaintiffs for failing to diligently prosecute their case, stating that they "have been content to file repetitive motions with this Court without developing the factual bases necessary to support their claims." The court stated that unless the plaintiffs brought new evidence establishing their claims, the case would be dismissed for lack of prosecution. *Council for the Hearing Impaired v. Ambach*, 610 F.Supp. 1051 (E.D.N.Y.1985).

II. RACIAL DISCRIMINATION IN PLACEMENT PROGRAMS

The de facto overrepresentation of minority students in special education programs, or underrepresentation of such students in gifted programs is insufficient to prove racial discrimination in placement programs. A plaintiff must prove that the alleged overrepresentation or underrepresentation is the result of purposeful discriminatory intention.

In 1976, a desegregation order made busing mandatory in Dallas, Texas. Despite the order, minority scores on national achievement tests remained low, and the Dallas area school districts wanted to improve minority education scores. However, they were ordered by the federal district court not to disturb the present levels of desegregation in the schools brought about by the 1976 order because the court deemed the levels acceptable. Three South Dallas Education Centers for remedial learning were then developed for minorities by the school districts and were approved by a federal district court and Court of Appeals as complying with the desegregation order.

The school districts made another proposal for four remedial education centers for West Dallas minority students. Students in the fourth through sixth grades who were currently being bused would attend a center in their own attendance zone. The centers would have a teacher-pupil ratio of 1:18 rather than the required 1:27. Although salaries would be higher, requirements for teachers in the centers would be more stringent. In order to avoid disruptions due to "pull outs" for special lessons and tutoring, students would attend the school for extended hours. In addition, enhanced programs in special fields such as science were also planned.

Opponents of the proposed centers questioned the progress that the school districts claimed to have made in the existing South Dallas Centers, contending that the methodology used to tabulate improvements among the students attending the centers was flawed. However, the district court approved the West Dallas plan in spite of the opponents' objections. The court determined that providing remedial learning did more to prevent segregation than busing because it improved the quality of minority education. Furthermore, stated the court, the centers were the best educational opportunity available to the students. The proposal for the remedial education centers was therefore approved. *Tasby v. Wright*, 630 F.Supp. 597 (N.D.Tex.1986).

The Georgia chapter of the NAACP commenced a class action lawsuit in a federal district court on behalf of all black children in the state, claiming that the Georgia State Board of Education and a number of local school districts were assigning black students to programs for the educable mentally retarded in a racially discriminatory manner. The NAACP produced uncontroverted statistical evidence that a disproportionately high number of black students had been taken out of regular classrooms and placed in EMR programs. Depending on the school district, this was done on the basis of state I.Q. tests, the Metropolitan Achievement Test, the Development Indicators for the Assessment of Learning Tests, the MacMillan Placement Test, as well as other familiar evaluation devices and procedures. The NAACP made two basic allegations: 1) the use of these placement methods was intended to produce intraschool racial segregation, and 2) black children were assigned to the EMR programs in a discriminatory manner. Thus, the essence of the plaintiff's lawsuit was that since a disproportionately large number of black children were assigned to EMR programs, racial segregation had been the inevitable result. The methods of assignment to the programs, as well as the programs themselves, were alleged to be in violation of the U.S. Constitution, the Civil Rights Act and the Rehabilitation Act. The district court ruled against the plaintiffs on all counts and an appeal was taken to the U.S. Court of Appeals, Eleventh Circuit.

The appellate court held that ability grouping *per se*, and placement of black students in special education programs, did not violate federal law "even when it results in racial disparity in a school district's classrooms." The problem, said the court of appeals, stemmed from past racial segregation. Georgia's black children had previously been confined to grossly inferior "black" schools, receiving substandard public educations. When integration took place, "lack of [prior] educational quality would predictably cause [black] students from the inferior system to immediately be resegregated" within special education classes. The court of appeals had previously struck down this practice, holding that a newly-integrated school district may not use ability groupings if the result is racial segregation.

However, in the present case none of the black children had ever attended racially segregated public schools; all of Georgia's public schools had been integrated since the early 1970's. Therefore, the black children in this case could not claim that they had been placed in special education classes due to their past attendance at substandard schools. Past segregation had not caused them to be assigned to special education classes. Indeed, the court found that "'family background' and 'hard work,' rather than race, had the most powerful and consistent relationship to scholastic success." Accordingly, the court declared that the grouping of students on the basis of ability or achievement was permissible, even if the impact of such ability grouping was not racially neutral, as long as the school district had operated a nonsegregated school system "for a period of at least several years."

The NAACP also argued that "ability grouping exacerbates, rather than relieves, the problem of disproportionately lower achievement by black students." This argument was dismissed by the court, which found that ability grouping was educationally sound and "permits more resources to be routed to lower achieving students in the form of lower pupil-teacher ratios and additional instructional materials." Although nearly all of the district court's rulings against the NAACP were affirmed, the court of appeals remanded the case to the district court for a hearing on whether the NAACP was entitled to relief under the Rehabilitation Act for the school district's misinterpretation of state I.Q. regulations. *Georgia State Conference of Branches of NAACP v. State of Georgia*, 775 F.2d 1403 (11th Cir.1985).

Black parents in Maryland sought to reopen a school desegregation case which had been decided in 1972. The parents, who had been plaintiffs in the earlier case, now alleged that the school district was not in compliance with the 1972 desegregation order. The parents claimed that the district was intentionally discriminating on racial grounds in the area of special education. They claimed that statistical evidence showed that racial imbalances existed in the district's special education and talented and gifted education programs.

The same federal district court held that despite the statistical overrepresentation of blacks in special education programs, the procedures followed by the school system in placing children in special education programs did not discriminate against black children. The district utilized a checklist which included physical, emotional and academic evaluations and from which, once a handicapping condition was verified, it formulated an individualized education program. If parents objected to the proposed IEP or any part of the process of identification, diagnosis or formulation of an IEP, they were afforded administrative hearings as required by the Education for All Handicapped Children Act. The court also upheld the district's use of the California Achievement Test and the Cognitive Abilities Test for admission into the district's gifted student program. It also found that there had been a constant effort on the part of the district's staff to include greater numbers of black children in the gifted program. Accordingly, it concluded that the district had not intentionally discriminated against black children in the area of special education.

The case was appealed to the U.S. Court of Appeals, Fourth Circuit, which partially upheld the district court. The lower court had properly noted that usually, where numerical racial disparities exist in special programs, it is presumed that such disparities are the result of "chance" and not illegal racial discrimination. However, the rule is different in school districts that have a past history of racial segregation. The appeals court held that in such districts, the burden of proof is on the district to show that the disparities in the number of minority youths assigned to special and gifted programs is not the result of racial discrimination. Because the Maryland school district in this case had, in the past, operated a racially segregated school system, the Court of Appeals remanded the case to the lower court with instructions to force the school district to meet its higher standard of proof in determining whether the placement of students in special programs was discriminatory. *Vaughs v. Bd. of Educ. of Prince George's County*, 758 F.2d 983 (4th Cir. 1985).

III. AVAILABILITY OF CIVIL RIGHTS REMEDIES

Section 1983 of the federal Civil Rights Act and the Rehabilitation Act of 1973 are sometimes invoked by plaintiffs as a remedy where the EHA does not provide one. Both Acts prohibit unfair discrimination against handicapped individuals. The 1984 U.S. Supreme Court case *Smith v. Robinson* barred recourse to the Rehabilitation Act in cases where the relief sought was available under the EHA. The Handicapped Children's Protection Act of 1986 reversed *Smith v. Robinson* by amending the EHA to state that the other federal civil rights laws may be relied upon by handicapped children.

A. When a Claim May be Brought

The cases in this section deal with when claims, other than under the EHA, may be brought.

Parents of handicapped children sued the Connecticut state board of education in a U.S. district court under § 1983 of the Civil Rights Act. They alleged that the board failed to make meaningful attempts to resolve their complaints against a local school district. In addition, they claimed that the school district had violated § 1983 by failing to provide an adequate psychologist and staff and by failing to conduct triennial evaluations of the handicapped children. They sought an injunction that would require the board to formulate and implement adequate complaint resolution procedures. The court ruled that since the EHA was a comprehensive remedial statute, the parents could not sue under § 1983. The parents appealed to the U.S. Court of Appeals, Second Circuit.

The state board argued that the parents failed to exhaust their EHA administrative remedies. It also contended that it had fully complied with EHA requirements. The court of appeals observed that the right of the parents to assert a § 1983 claim was limited by two exceptions. Section 1983 claims are not available when Congress has foreclosed enforcement of the statute in the statute itself or when a statutory remedial scheme provided an exclusive remedy. The court of appeals reversed the district court decision. The district court wrongly dismissed the parents' complaint on the ground that no civil rights lawsuit could be maintained by them outside the EHA. The Handicapped Children's Protection Act of 1986 (HCPA) codified a congressional purpose to provide for such lawsuits. In light of the HCPA's clear legislative history, the parents were entitled to bring a § 1983 lawsuit based on alleged EHA violations. *Mrs. W., Mrs. B. v. Tirozzi*, 832 F.2d 748 (2d Cir.1987).

On remand to a federal district court, the board moved for judgment on the pleadings, contending that the court of appeals had not addressed the main issue as to whether there was a right to the complaint resolution procedures (CRP) which could be enforced under § 1983. The district court held that the parents of the handicapped children had stated a § 1983 claim for violation of the EHA. The Connecticut Board of Education had failed to meaningfully attempt to resolve the parents' complaints and had failed to fully implement federally required informal CRP. Parents are allowed to pursue EHA violations by invoking procedures provided in § 1983. The board was required to provide CRP to address complaints of violations of federal law. The court found for the parents and denied the board's motion for judgment on the pleadings. *Mrs. W. v. Tirozzi*, 706 F.Supp. 164 (D.Conn.1989).

A handicapped student in Oregon sued his school district, seeking attorney's fees and civil rights remedies under the EHA, the Rehabilitation Act and § 1983 of the Civil Rights Act. A federal district court held for the school district because the EHA provided the only remedy available to the student when he commenced his lawsuit. However, the EHA did not afford the relief sought by the student. The student moved that the court reinstate his lawsuit due to passage of the Handicapped Children's Protection Act (HCPA). He claimed that the HCPA permitted him to sue for attorney's fees and for relief under § 1983. His motion was granted. The school district then moved that the court reconsider its decision to reinstate the student's lawsuit.

The school district claimed that the HCPA did not form the basis for reinstatement of the student's § 1983 claim. Because Congress specifically provided that § 2 of the HCPA (providing for attorney's fees awards) be retroactive, it intended that § 3 of the HCPA not be retroactive. Section 3 provided that handicapped students may sue state and local educational agencies under the Constitution, the Rehabilitation Act and other federal civil rights statutes (§ 1983). The court held for the student, citing *Jackson v. Franklin County School Bd.*, 806 F.2d 623 (5th Cir.1986) and *Bd. of Educ. v. Diamond*, 808 F.2d 987 (3d Cir.1986). Congressional silence regarding the retroactivity of § 3 was insufficient to imply congressional intent to limit retroactivity to § 2. Because § 3 had retroactive effect, the student's § 1983 civil rights claim could proceed to trial along with his § 2 claim for attorney's fees. The school district's motion was denied. *Dodds v. Simpson*, 676 F.Supp. 1045 (D.Or.1987).

The U.S. Court of Appeals, Eleventh Circuit, held that where a school district deprives a handicapped child of a due process hearing under the EHA a lawsuit may be brought under § 1983 of the Civil Rights Act. This case involved an emotionally and physically impaired high school girl in Florida who was placed in a county special education school pursuant to her IEP. Although the girl made excellent progress at school she fought incessantly with her family. As a result her mother decided that placement at an out-of-state residential facility was warranted, and she requested a due process hearing on this matter. The school district special education director forwarded the mother's request for a due process hearing to the school district attorney, but no hearing was provided within the Act's forty-five day limit.

The child's parents then unilaterally placed the girl in the private facility and filed suit against the school district seeking to recover their tuition costs and attorney's fees. The parents' lawsuit was based upon the EHA, the Rehabilitation Act and § 1983. A U.S. district court held that 1) the EHA cannot provide the basis for an award of compensatory damages; 2) the Rehabilitation Act provides no private cause of action for money damages; and 3) § 1983 is inapplicable to special education cases because Congress intended EHA remedies to be exclusive.

The parents appealed to the U.S. Court of Appeals, Eleventh Circuit, which reversed in part and affirmed in part. The court held that § 1983 may provide the basis for a lawsuit in special education cases where, as here, the plaintiff has been denied the procedural protections of the EHA. This was significant because of the relative ease of obtaining money damages and attorney's fees under section 1983. The appeals court affirmed the district court ruling with regard to the claim under the Rehabilitation Act and remanded the case to the district court for a determination of money damages. *Manecke v. School Bd. of Pinellas County, Florida*, 762 F.2d 912 (11th Cir. 1985).

A federal district court in Wisconsin rejected the claims of two handicapped children who contended that they had valid claims under the Rehabilitation Act even if they were precluded from recovering under the EHA. The court stated that a plaintiff cannot proceed with a claim under the latter statute—whether it is based on a substantive or a procedural challenge to state and local agency action—without having exhausted EHA administrative remedies. Although the plaintiffs asserted that their claim under the one statute was independent of the one under the other statute, the court disagreed, stating that since both claims came from the same set of facts, they must at least be considered parallel. A further assertion by the plaintiffs was that they had an independent right of action for violation of constitutional rights under federal civil rights statutes. This contention was also rejected by the court, which noted that a number of courts have addressed this issue and have concluded that exhaustion of EHA administrative procedures should be required before constitutional claims that parallel EHA claims can be pursued in federal court. The court concluded by granting the defendants' motion for summary judgment and dismissing both federal and state law claims. *M.R. v. Milwaukee Pub. Schools*, 584 F.Supp. 767 (E.D.Wis.1984).

The mother of a handicapped child in New York claimed that she and her son suffered damages as a result of a local school district's failure to evaluate the child and provide him the special education to which he was entitled. The child allegedly suffered damages to his intellect, emotional capacity and personality, and was impeded in acquiring necessary training. In addition, the mother alleged that she moved to a different school district to obtain the services her child needed and that she herself suffered emotional distress. A federal district court held in favor of the mother and child, and the school district appealed.

The U.S. Court of Appeals, Second Circuit, held that because the mother had not availed herself of her administrative remedies under the EHA, she was deprived of her means of relief under that Act. However, the court found it unthinkable that Congress would have intended that a parent in this situation, where the district had refused to evaluate the child, should be left without any remedy. Accordingly, the court permitted the Civil Rights Act to supply the remedy for the mother who had been denied EHA procedural safeguards. The court viewed the absence of any prescribed remedy in the EHA as a "gap" to be filled by § 1983 of the Civil Rights Act. The case was remanded to determine the amount of damages. *Quakenbush v. Johnson City School Dist.*, 716 F.2d 141 (2d Cir.1983).

The New Mexico Association for Retarded Citizens and others commenced a class action against the state of New Mexico, seeking declaratory and injunctive relief on behalf of handicapped children allegedly denied certain federally guaranteed special education services. The case, decided by the U.S. Court of Appeals, Tenth Circuit, involved the interpretation of § 504 of the Rehabilitation Act. Section 504 provides that "no otherwise qualified handicapped individual in the United States . . . shall, solely by reason of his handicap, be excluded from participation in, be denied the benefits of, or be subjected to discrimination under any program or activity receiving federal financial assistance." Under the regulations to this act schools are required to provide "free appropriate public education" to all handicapped students within their territorial jurisdiction.

The court of appeals observed that the U.S. Supreme Court has held, in interpreting § 504, that its purpose is to prohibit discrimination against the handicapped rather than mandate affirmative relief for them. This is distinguished from the affirmative duties required under the EHA, which makes the receipt of federal money contingent on a state's performing affirmative duties with respect to the education of the handicapped. The state of New Mexico had chosen not to participate in the EHA program. Against this legislative and regulatory backdrop, citizens in New Mexico contended that the state's entire program in dealing with the special needs of handicapped children was deficient. The court, while recognizing that discrimination against handicapped children could require the fashioning of a judicial remedy, remanded the case to a lower court, stating that § 504 violations must be evaluated in light of the Supreme Court's decision that the statute and its regulations are designed to prohibit discrimination rather than to require action. *New Mexico Ass'n for Retarded Citizens v. State of New Mexico*, 678 F.2d 847 (10th Cir.1982).

The mother of an eleven-year-old girl with cerebral palsy, who challenged the proposed transfer of her child from a traditional elementary school to an elementary school specially designed to meet the needs of handicapped children, was denied relief under the EHA and the Rehabilitation Act. In holding that the child could not receive a satisfactory education in a traditional school, even with the use of supplementary aids and services to the maximum extent possible, a federal District Court in Michigan stated that there was no valid claim under the Rehabilitation Act because, under this Act, there must be an intentional, bad faith denial of education resources, or a grossly negligent placement decision. This was not the case here. Thus, the transfer decision was upheld. *Johnston v. Ann Arbor Pub. Schools*, 569 F.Supp. 1502 (E.D.Mich.1983).

B. The Claim's Likelihood of Success

These cases address the likelihood of the claim's success.

A Texas first grade special education student was sexually abused by his bus driver on a number of occasions. Allegedly, the school principal knew that the driver was suspected of abusing the student, but took no action. When the student's mother learned what happened, she sued the principal and the school district under 42 U.S.C. § 1983 alleging that the district's policy of leaving the investigation of alleged sexual abuse to the discretion of the school principal violated the student's constitutional right to be free from such conduct. A federal district court found for the mother and the district appealed to the U.S. Court of Appeals, Fifth Circuit. The court of appeals stated that a school district cannot be held liable solely because it employs an individual. The court stated that the repetition of the student's injury was not caused by the district's policy. Instead it was caused by the failure of the employee to properly exercise the discretion given him by the district. The court of appeals reversed the district court's decision. *Spann v. Tyler Indep. School Dist.*, 876 F.2d 437 (5th Cir.1989).

After passage of the Handicapped Children's Protection Act of 1986 (HCPA) three handicapped children in New Hampshire asked a federal district court to reinstate their civil rights claims. The court held that since § 3 of the HCPA (which made § 1983 civil rights lawsuits and money damages available to handicapped students) was not expressly made retroactive, their civil rights claims could not be reinstated. On reconsideration, the district court found that § 3 of the HCPA was to be applied to cases that were pending as of the HCPA's effective date (August 5, 1986). It observed that "while section 3 is not to be applied retroactively, section 3 is to be applied to cases pending at the time of its enactment." It also noted that "a court is to apply the law in effect at the time it renders its decision, unless doing so would result in manifest injustice or there is statutory direction or legislative history to the contrary." Since no manifest injustice would occur if the handicapped children were allowed to reinstate their civil rights claims under § 1983, the court vacated its earlier decision not to reinstate the claims. It held that the children could bring a civil rights lawsuit against the local school officials. *Edward B. v. Brunelle*, 662 F.Supp. 1025 (D.N.H.1986).

In *Robinson v. Pinderhughes*, the U.S. Court of Appeals, Fourth Circuit, held that because the Baltimore City Schools failed to implement a hearing officer's decision in a timely manner and had not appealed the decision, it had violated the EHA. The court of appeals also concluded that since the EHA did not contain any provision for enforcing final administrative orders by a hearing officer, the student was entitled to a § 1983 claim. When the Baltimore City Schools refused to enforce the hearing officer's decision to put him in a residential placement the Baltimore City Schools had, under color of state law, violated the EHA. The district court was therefore wrong in dismissing the student's § 1983 claim. His § 1983 claim was remanded to the district court for further proceedings. *Robinson v. Pinderhughes*, 810 F.2d 1270 (4th Cir.1987).

The U.S. Court of Appeals, Ninth Circuit, upheld a federal district court's issuance of an injunction against various California education officials prohibiting the use by any public school of standardized I.Q. tests to aid in placing students in EMR (educable mentally retarded) classrooms. The opinion of the court of appeals also upheld the district court's order that any California school district with a black EMR enrollment greater than one standard statistical deviation above its white student EMR enrollment must prepare a plan to rectify the racial imbalance. The case was filed as a class action suit in 1971 two years after the rapid implementation by California education officials of standardized I.Q. testing for EMR placement purposes. The district court found that the overrepresentation of black children in California EMR classrooms violated the EHA, Title VI of the Civil Rights Act of 1964 and other state and federal laws. The State Education Superintendent's argument that the overrepresentation was due to a higher incidence of mental retardation in black children (due to their adverse socioeconomic positions) was discounted by the district court.

The case followed a tortuous procedural history and was eventually appealed to the U.S. Court of Appeals, Ninth Circuit, which held several hearings and rehearings and finally issued the present decision affirming the district court's judgment. The court of appeals agreed that the superintendent's explanation of the overrepresentation of black children in EMR classrooms was erroneous because extremely poor or culturally disadvantaged black children had the same level of EMR placement as black children generally. The court thus believed that the superintendent's logic was inconsistent, and it adopted the district court's conclusion that the standardized I.Q. testing mistakenly placed black children in EMR classes. It emphasized the evil inherent in disproportionate black student EMR placements and upheld the district court's order that standardized I.Q. testing for placement purposes be stopped. *Larry P. v. Riles*, 793 F.2d 969 (9th Cir.1984), as amended after denial of rehearing 6/25/86.

A fifteen-year-old New York girl, three and one-half feet tall with a partially amputated right arm, a functionally impaired left arm and hand, and legs of approximately one foot in length, asked for and received from her school district a special van to transport her to school and the help of an aide during the school day. The school sponsored a Spanish class trip to Spain for which this student was academically qualified. The trip involved tours of historical sites which required the students to walk many miles. The school denied this student permission to go on the trip on the ground that she would endanger herself by attending. She sued the school seeking to enjoin it from enforcing its ban on her attendance. She argued that because the school was receiving federal funding for this trip she could not be barred from going simply on the ground that she was handicapped.

A federal district court in New York noted that the Rehabilitation Act of 1973 specifically states that a handicapped student may not be excluded from participation in a program receiving federal funding solely on the basis of his or her handicap if that student is otherwise qualified. However, in this case, after the court itself witnessed the difficulty this child had even climbing onto the witness stand, it held that she was not otherwise qualified since she could not fulfill the physical requirements of the trip. Her complaint against the school district was dismissed. *Wolff v. South Colonie School Dist.*, 534 F.Supp. 758 (N.D.N.Y.1982).

APPENDIX A

THE INDIVIDUALS
WITH DISABILITIES
EDUCATION ACT

AS AMENDED THROUGH OCTOBER 30, 1990

*[The EHA, henceforth to be known as the IDEA, is
reproduced here in its entirety, fully compiled, as
amended by Congress through October 30, 1990. No
separate section on amendments is included in this volume because all amendments have been placed in the
appropriate location in the statutory text, and any repealed sections have been deleted from the text. The
Handicapped Children's Protection Act of 1986 appears in § 1415(e)(4) and § 1415(f). The major provisions of the Education of the Handicapped Act
Amendments of 1986 appear in §§ 1408, 1411, 1413,
1418, 1419, 1433, and 1471-85.]*

CHAPTER 33—THE INDIVIDUALS WITH DISABILITIES EDUCATION ACT

SUBCHAPTER I—GENERAL PROVISIONS

SUBCHAPTER II—ASSISTANCE FOR EDUCATION OF ALL HANDICAPPED INDIVIDUALS

SUBCHAPTER III—CENTERS AND SERVICES TO MEET SPECIAL NEEDS OF HANDICAPPED INDIVIDUALS

SUBCHAPTER I—GENERAL PROVISIONS

§ 1400. Congressional statements and declarations

(a) Short title

This title may be cited as the "Individuals with Disabilities Education Act".

(b) Findings

The Congress finds that—

(1) there are more than eight million children with disabilities in the United States today;

(2) the special educational needs of such children are not being fully met;

(3) more than half of the children with disabilities in the United States do not receive appropriate educational services which would enable them to have full equality of opportunity;

(4) one million of the children with disabilities in the United States are excluded entirely from the public school system and will not go through the educational process with their peers;

(5) there are many children with disabilities throughout the United States participating in regular school programs whose disabilities prevent them from having a successful educational experience because their disabilities are undetected;

(6) because of the lack of adequate services within the public school system, families are often forced to find services outside the public school system, often at great distance from their residence and at their own expense;

(7) developments in the training of teachers and in diagnostic and instructional procedures and methods have advanced to the point that, given appropriate funding, State and local educational agencies can and will provide effective special education and related services to meet the needs of children with disabilities;

(8) State and local educational agencies have a responsibility to provide education for all children with disabilities, but present financial resources are inadequate to meet the special educational needs of children with disabilities; and

(9) it is in the national interest that the Federal Government assist State and local efforts to provide programs to meet the educational needs of children with disabilities in order to assure equal protection of the law.

(c) Purpose

It is the purpose of this chapter to assure that all children with disabilities have available to them, within the time periods specified in section 1412(2)(B) of this title, a free appropriate public education which emphasizes special education and related services designed to meet their unique needs, to assure that the rights of children with disabilities and their parents or guardians are protected, to assist States and localities to provide for the education of all children with disabilities, and to assess and assure the effectiveness of efforts to educate children with disabilities.

§ 1401. Definitions

(a) As used in this chapter—
(1) The term "children with disabilities" means children—
(A) with mental retardation, hearing impairments including deafness, speech or language impairments, visual impairments including blindness, serious emotional disturbance, orthopedic impairments, autism, traumatic brain injury, other health impairments, or specific learning disabilities; and
(B) who, by reason thereof need special education and related services.
(2) Repealed. Pub. L. 98-199, § 2(2), Dec. 2, 1983, 97 Stat. 1357.
(3) Repealed. Pub. L. 100-630, § 101(a)(2), Nov. 7, 1988, 102 Stat. 3289.
(4) The term "construction", except where otherwise specified, means (A) erection of new or expansion of existing structures, and the acquisition and installation of equipment therefor; or (B) acquisition of existing structures not owned by any agency or institution making application for assistance under this chapter; or (C) remodeling or alteration (including the acquisition, installation, modernization, or replacement of equipment) of existing structures; or (D) acquisition of land in connection with activities in clauses (A), (B), and (C); or (E) a combination of any two or more of the foregoing.
(5) The term "equipment" includes machinery, utilities, and built-in equipment and any necessary enclosures or structures to house them, and includes all other items necessary for the functioning of a particular facility as a facility for the provision of educational services, including items such as instructional equipment and necessary furniture, printed, published, and audio-visual instructional materials, telecommunications, sensory, and other technological aids and devices, and books, periodicals, documents, and other related materials.
(6) The term "State" means any of the several States, the District of Columbia, the Commonwealth of Puerto Rico, the Virgin Islands, Guam, American Samoa, the Commonwealth of the Northern Mariana Islands, or the Trust Territory of the Pacific Islands.
(7) The term "State educational agency" means the State board of education or other agency or officer primarily responsible for the State supervision of public elementary and secondary schools, or, if there is no such officer or agency, an officer or agency designated by the Governor or by State law.
(8) The term "local educational agency" means a public board of education or other public authority legally constituted within a State for either administrative control or direction of, or to perform a service function for, public elementary or secondary schools in a city, county, township, school district, or other political subdivision of a State, or such combination of school districts or counties as are recognized in a State as

an administrative agency for its public elementary or secondary schools. Such term also includes any other public institution or agency having administrative control and direction of a public elementary or secondary school.

(9) The term "elementary school" means a day or residential school which provides elementary education, as determined under State law.

(10) The term "secondary school" means a day or residential school which provides secondary education, as determined under State law, except that it does not include any education provided beyond grade 12.

(11) The term "institution of higher education" means an educational institution in any State which—

(A) admits as regular students only individuals having a certificate of graduation from a high school, or the recognized equivalent of such a certificate;

(B) is legally authorized within such State to provide a program of education beyond high school;

(C) provides an educational program for which it awards a bachelor's degree, or provides not less than a two-year program which is acceptable for full credit toward such a degree, or offers a two-year program in engineering, mathematics, or the physical or biological sciences which is designed to prepare the student to work as a technician and at a semiprofessional level in engineering, scientific, or other technological fields which require the understanding and application of basic engineering, scientific, or mathematical principles or knowledge;

(D) is a public or other nonprofit institution; and

(E) is accredited by a nationally recognized accrediting agency or association listed by the Secretary pursuant to this paragraph or, if not so accredited, is an institution whose credits are accepted, on transfer, by not less than three institutions which are so accredited, for credit on the same basis as if transferred from an institution so accredited: *Provided, however,* That in the case of an institution offering a two-year program in engineering, mathematics, or the physical or biological sciences which is designed to prepare the student to work as a technician and at a semiprofessional level in engineering, scientific, or technological fields which require the understanding and application of basic engineering, scientific, or mathematical principles or knowledge, if the Secretary determines that there is no nationally recognized accrediting agency or association qualified to accredit such institutions, the Secretary shall appoint an advisory committee, composed of persons specially qualified to evaluate training provided by such institutions, which shall prescribe the standards of content, scope, and quality which must be met in order to qualify such institutions to participate under this Act and shall also determine whether particular institutions meet such standards. For the purposes of this paragraph the Secretary shall publish a list of nationally recognized accrediting agencies or associations which the Secretary determines to be reliable authority as to the quality of education or training offered.

The term includes community colleges receiving funding from the Secretary of the Interior under the Tribally Controlled Community College Assistance Act of 1978.

(12) The term "nonprofit" as applied to a school, agency, organiza-

tion, or institution means a school, agency, organization, or institution owned and operated by one or more non-profit corporations or associations no part of the net earnings of which inures, or may lawfully inure, to the benefit of any private shareholder or individual.

(13) The term "research and related purposes" means research, research training (including the payment of stipends and allowances), surveys, or demonstrations in the field of education of children with disabilities, or the dissemination of information derived therefrom, including (but without limitation) experimental schools.

(14) The term "Secretary" means the Secretary of Education.

(15) The term "children with specific learning disabilities" means those children who have a disorder in one or more of the basic psychological processes involved in understanding or in using language, spoken or written, which disorder may manifest itself in imperfect ability to listen, think, speak, read, write, spell, or do mathematical calculations. Such disorders include such conditions as perceptual disabilities, brain injury, minimal brain dysfunction, dyslexia, and developmental aphasia. Such term does not include children who have learning problems which are primarily the result of visual, hearing, or motor disabilities, of mental retardation, of emotional disturbance, or of environmental, cultural, or economic disadvantage.

(16) The term "special education" means specially designed instruction, at no cost to parents or guardians, to meet the unique needs of a child with a disability, including—

(A) instruction conducted in the classroom, in the home, in hospitals and institutions, and in other settings; and

(B) instruction in physical education.

(17) The term "related services" means transportation, and such developmental, corrective, and other supportive services (including speech pathology and audiology, psychological services, physical and occupational therapy, recreation, including therapeutic recreation and social work services, and medical and counseling services, including rehabilitation counseling, except that such medical services shall be for diagnostic and evaluation purposes only) as may be required to assist a child with a disability to benefit from special education, and includes the early identification and assessment of disabling conditions in children.

(18) The term "free appropriate public education" means special education and related services that—

(A) have been provided at public expense, under public supervision and direction, and without charge,

(B) meet the standards of the State educational agency,

(C) include an appropriate preschool, elementary, or secondary school education in the State involved, and

(D) are provided in conformity with the individualized education program required under section 614(a)(5).

(19) The term "transition services" means a coordinated set of activities for a student, designed within an outcome-oriented process, which promotes movement from school to post-school activities, including post-secondary education, vocational training, integrated employment (including supported employment), continuing and adult education, adult services, independent living, or community participation. The coordinated

set of activities shall be based upon the individual student's needs, taking into account the student's preferences and interests, and shall include instruction, community experiences, the development of employment and other post-school adult living objectives, and, when appropriate, acquisition of daily living skills and functional vocational evaluation.

(20) The term "individualized education program" means a written statement for each child with a disability developed in any meeting by a representative of the local educational agency or an intermediate educational unit who shall be qualified to provide, or supervise the provision of, specially designed instruction to meet the unique needs of children with disabilities, the teacher, the parents or guardian of such child, and, whenever appropriate, such child, which statement shall include—

(A) a statement of the present levels of educational performance of such child,

(B) a statement of annual goals, including short-term instructional objectives,

(C) a statement of the specific educational services to be provided to such child, and the extent to which such child will be able to participate in regular educational programs,

(D) a statement of the needed transition services for students beginning no later than age 16 and annually therafter (and, when determined appropriate for the individual, beginning at age 14 or younger), including, when appropriate, a statement of the interagency responsibilities or linkages (or both) before the student leaves the school setting.

(E) the projected date for initiation and anticipated duration of such services, and

(F) appropriate objective criteria and evaluation procedures and schedules for determining, on at least an annual basis, whether instructional objectives are being achieved. In the case where a participating agency, other than the educational agency, fails to provide agreed upon services, the educational agency shall reconvene the IEP team to identify alternative strategies to meet the transition objectives.

(21) The term "excess costs" means those costs which are in excess of the average annual per student expenditure in a local educational agency during the preceding school year for an elementary or secondary school student, as may be appropriate, and which shall be computed after deducting

(A) amounts received—

(i) under this part,

(ii) under chapter 1 of title I of the Elementary and Secondary Education Act of 1965, or

(iii) under title VII of the Elementary and Secondary Education Act of 1965, and

(B) any State or local funds expended for programs that would qualify for assistance under such part, chapter, or title.

(22) The term "native language" has the meaning given that term by section 703(a)(2) of the Bilingual Education Act [20 U.S.C. 3223(a)(2)].

(23) The term "intermediate educational unit" means any public authority, other than a local educational agency, which is under the general supervision of a State educational agency, which is established by State law

for the purpose of providing free public education on a regional basis, and which provides special education and related services to children with disabilities within that State.

(24)(A) The term "public or private nonprofit agency or organization" includes an Indian tribe and the Bureau of Indian Affairs of the Department of the Interior (when acting on behalf of schools operated by the Bureau for children and students on Indian reservations) and tribally controlled schools funded by the Department of the Interior.

(B) The terms "Indian", "American Indian", and "Indian American" mean an individual who is a member of an Indian tribe.

(C) The term "Indian tribe" means any Federal or State Indian tribe, band, rancheria, pueblo, colony, or community, including any Alaskan native village or regional village corporation (as defined in or established under the Alaska Native Claims Settlement Act).

(25) The term "assistive technology device" means any item, piece of equipment, or product system, whether acquired commercially off the shelf, modified, or customized, that is used to increase, maintain, or improve functional capabilities of individuals with disabilities.

(26) The term "assistive technology service" means any service that directly assists an individual with a disability in the selection, acquisition, or use of an assistive technology device. Such term includes—

(A) the evaluation of the needs of an individual with a disability, including a functional evaluation of the individual in the individual's customary environment;

(B) purchasing, leasing, or otherwise providing for the acquisition of assistive technology devices by individuals with disabilities;

(C) selection, designing, fitting, customizing, adapting, applying, maintaining, repairing, or replacing of assistive technology devices;

(D) coordinating and using other therapies, interventions, or services with assistive technology devices, such as those associated with existing education and rehabilitation plans and programs;

(E) training or technical assistance for an individual with disabilities, or, where appropriate, the family of an individual with disabilities; and

(F) training or technical assistance for professionals (including individuals providing education and rehabilitation services), employers, or other individuals who provide services to, employ, or are otherwise substantially involved in the major life functions of individuals with disabilities.

(b) For purposes of subchapter III of this chapter, "youth with disabilities" means any child with disabilities (as defined in subsection (a) (1) of this section) who

(1) is twelve years of age or older; or

(2) is enrolled in the seventh or higher grade in school.

§ 1402. Office of Special Education Programs

(a) Administration and execution of programs and activities

There shall be, within the Office of Special Education and Rehabilitation Services in the Department of Education, an Office of Special Education Programs which shall be the principal agency in the Department for administering and carrying out this and other programs and activities concerning the education and training of individuals with disabilities.

(b) Deputy Assistant Secretary: selection and supervision, General Schedule and Senior Executive Service status; Associate Deputy Assistant Secretary and minimum assistantships: establishment, General Schedule status

(1) The office established under subsection (a) of this section shall be headed by a Deputy Assistant Secretary who shall be selected by the Secretary and shall report directly to the Assistant Secretary for Special Education and Rehabilitative Services. The position of Deputy Assistant Secretary shall be in grade GS-18 of the General Schedule under section 5104 of Title 5 and shall be a Senior Executive Service position for the purposes of section 3132(a)(2) of such Title.

(2) In addition to such Deputy Assistant Secretary, there shall be established in such office not less than six positions for persons to assist the Deputy Assistant Secretary, including the position of the Associate Deputy Assistant Secretary. Each such position shall be in grade GS-15 of the General Schedule under section 5104 of Title 5.

§ 1403. Repealed.

A new section has been added which does not yet have a 1400 series number.

§ 604. Abrogation of sovereign immunity

(a) A State shall not be immune under the eleventh amendment to the Constitution of the United States from suit in Federal court for a violation of this Act.

(b) In a suit against a State for a violation of this Act, remedies (including remedies both at law and in equity) are available for such a violation to the same extent as such remedies are available for such a violation in the suit against any public entity other than a State.

(c) The provisions of subsections (a) and (b) shall take effect with respect to violations that occur in whole or part after the date of the enactment of the Education of the Handicapped Act Amendments of 1990.

§ 1404. Acquisition of equipment and construction of necessary facilities

(a) Authorization for use of funds

In the case of any program authorized by this chapter, if the Secretary determines that such program will be improved by permitting the funds authorized for such program to be used for the acquisition of equipment and the construction of necessary facilities, the Secretary may authorize the use of such funds for such purposes.

(b) Recovery of payments under certain conditions

If, within twenty years after the completion of any construction (except minor remodeling or alteration) for which funds have been paid pursuant to a grant or contract under this chapter the facility constructed ceases to be used for the purposes for which it was constructed, the United States, unless the Secretary determines that there is good cause for releasing the recipient of the funds from its obligation, shall be entitled to recover from the applicant or other owner of the facility an amount which bears the same ratio to the then value of the facility as the amount of such Federal funds bore to the cost of the portion of the facility financed with such funds. Such value shall be determined by agreement of the parties or by action brought in the United States district court for the district in which the facility is situated.

§ 1405. Employment of individuals with disabilities

The Secretary shall assure that each recipient of assistance under this chapter shall make positive efforts to employ and advance in employment qualified individuals with disabilities in programs assisted under this chapter.

§ 1406. Grants for removal of architectural barriers; authorization of appropriations

(a) The Secretary is authorized to make grants and to enter into cooperative agreements with the Secretary of the Interior and with State educational agencies to assist such agencies in making grants to local educational agencies or intermediate educational units to pay part or all of the cost of altering existing buildings and equipment in accordance with standards promulgated under the Act entitled 'An Act to insure that certain buildings financed with Federal funds are so designed and constructed as to be accessible to the physically handicapped', approved August 12, 1968.

(b) For the purposes of carrying out the provisions of this section, there are authorized to be appropriated such sums as may be necessary.

§ 1407. Regulation requirements

(a) Minimum period for comment before effective date

For purposes of complying with section 1232(b) of this title with respect to regulations promulgated under subchapter II of this chapter, the thirty-day period under such section shall be ninety days.

(b) Lessening of procedural or substantive protections as in effect on July 20, 1983, prohibited

The Secretary may not implement, or publish in final form, any regulation prescribed pursuant to this chapter which would procedurally or substantively lessen the protections provided to children with disabilities under this chapter, as embodied in regulations in effect on July 20, 1983 (particularly as such protections relate to parental consent to initial evaluation or initial placement in special education, least restrictive environment, related services, timelines,[1] attendance of evaluation personnel at individualized education program meetings, or qualifications of personnel), except to the extent that such regulation reflects the clear and unequivocal intent of the Congress in legislation.

(c) Repealed.

§ 1408. Eligibility for financial assistance

Effective for fiscal years for which the Secretary may make grants under section 1419(b)(1) of this title, no State or local educational agency or intermediate educational unit or other public institution or agency may receive a grant under subchapters III through VII of this chapter which relate exclusively to programs, projects, and activities pertaining to children aged three to five, inclusive, unless the State is eligible to receive a grant under section 1419(b)(1) of this title.

---

[1]Reproduced as enacted. Probably should be "timeliness."

SUBCHAPTER II—ASSISTANCE FOR EDUCATION OF ALL HANDICAPPED INDIVIDUALS

§ 1411. Entitlements and allocations

(a) Formula for determining maximum State entitlement

(1) Except as provided in paragraph (3) and in section 1419 of this title, the maximum amount of the grant to which a State is entitled under this subchapter for any fiscal year shall be equal to—
(A) the number of children with disabilities aged 3-5, inclusive, in a State who are receiving special education and related services as determined under paragraph (3) if the State is eligible for a grant under section 1419 of this title and the number of children with disabilities aged 6-21, inclusive, in a State who are receiving special education and related services as so determined;
multiplied by—
(B)(i) 5 per centum, for the fiscal year ending September 30, 1978, of the average per pupil expenditure in public elementary and secondary schools in the United States;
(ii) 10 per centum, for the fiscal year ending September 30, 1979, of the average per pupil expenditure in public elementary and secondary schools in the United States;
(iii) 20 per centum, for the fiscal year ending September 30, 1980, of the average per pupil expenditure in public elementary and secondary schools in the United States;
(iv) 30 per centum, for the fiscal year ending September 30, 1981, of the average per pupil expenditure in public elementary and secondary schools in the United States; and
(v) 40 per centum, for the fiscal year ending September 30, 1982, and for each fiscal year thereafter, of the average per pupil expenditure in public elementary and secondary schools in the United States:
except that no State shall receive an amount which is less than the amount which such State received under this subchapter for the fiscal year ending September 30, 1977.
(2) For the purpose of this subsection and subsection (b) through subsection (e) of this section, the term "State" does not include Guam, American Samoa, the Virgin Islands, the Commonwealth of the Northern Mariana Islands, and the Trust Territory of the Pacific Islands.
(3) The number of children with disabilities receiving special education and related services in any fiscal year shall be equal to number of such children receiving special education and related services on December 1 of the fiscal year preceding the fiscal year for which the determination is made.
(4) For purposes of paragraph (1)(B), the term "average per pupil expenditure" in the United States, means the aggregate current expenditures, during the second fiscal year preceding the fiscal year for which the computation is made (or, if satisfactory data for such year are not available at the time of computation, then during the most recent preceding fiscal year for which satisfactory data are available) of all local educational agencies in the United States (which, for purposes of this subsection, means the fifty States and the

District of Columbia), as the case may be, plus any direct expenditures by the State for operation of such agencies (without regard to the source of funds from which either of such expenditures are made), divided by the aggregate number of children in average daily attendance to whom such agencies provided free public education during such preceding year.

(5)(A) In determining the allotment of each State under paragraph (1), the Secretary may not count—

(i) children with disabilities aged three to seventeen, inclusive, in such State under paragraph (1)(A) to the extent the number of such children is greater than 12 percent of the number of all children aged three to seventeen, inclusive, in such State and the State serves all children with disabilities aged three to five, inclusive, in the State pursuant to State law or practice or the order of any court,

(ii) children with disabilities aged five to seventeen, inclusive, in such State under paragraph (1)(A) to the extent the number of such children is greater than 12 percent of the number of all children aged five to seventeen, inclusive, in such State and the State does not serve all children with disabilities aged three to five, inclusive, in the State pursuant to State law or practice or the order of any court; and

(iii) children with disabilities who are counted under subpart 2 of part D of chapter 1 of title 1 of this title.

(B) For purposes of subparagraph (A), the number of children aged three to seventeen inclusive, in any State shall be determined by the Secretary on the basis of the most recent satisfactory data available to the Secretary.

(b) Distribution and use of grant funds by States for fiscal year ending September 30, 1978

(1) Of the funds received under subsection (a) of this section by any State for the fiscal year ending September 30, 1978—

(A) 50 per centum of such funds may be used by such State in accordance with the provisions of paragraph (2); and

(B) 50 per centum of such funds shall be distributed by such State pursuant to subsection (d) of this section to local educational agencies and intermediate educational units in such State, for use in accordance with the priorities established under section 1412(3) of this title.

(2) Of the funds which any State may use under paragraph (1)(A)—

(A) an amount which is equal to the greater of—

(i) 5 per centum of the total amount of funds received under this subchapter by such State; or

(ii) $200,000;

may be used by such State for administrative costs related to carrying out sections 1412 and 1413 of this title;

(B) the remainder shall be used by such State to provide support services and direct services, in accordance with the priorities established under section 1412(3) of this title.

(c) Distribution and use of grant funds by States for fiscal years ending September 30, 1979, and thereafter

(1) Of the funds received under subsection (a) of this section by any State for the fiscal year ending September 30, 1979, and for each fiscal year thereafter—

(A) 25 per centum of such funds may be used by such State in accordance with the provisions of paragraph (2); and

(B) except as provided in paragraph (4), 75 per centum of such funds shall be distributed by such State pursuant to subsection (d) of this section to local educational agencies and intermediate educational units in such State, for use in accordance with priorities established under section 1412(3) of this title.

(2)(A) Subject to the provisions of subparagraph (B), of the funds which any State may use under paragraph (1)(A)—

(i) an amount which is equal to the greater of—

(I) 5 per centum of the total amount of funds received under this subchapter by such State; or

(II) $350,000;

may be used by such State for administrative costs related to carrying out the provisions of sections 1412 and 1413 of this title; and

(ii) the part remaining after use in accordance with clause (i) shall be used by the State (I) to provide support services and direct services in accordance with the priorities established under section 1412(3) of this title, and (II) for the administrative costs of monitoring and complaint investigation but only to the extent that such costs exceed the costs of administration incurred during fiscal year 1985.

(B) The amount expended by any State from the funds available to such State under paragraph (1)(A) in any fiscal year for the provisions of support services or for the provision of direct services shall be matched on a program basis by such State, from funds other than Federal funds, for the provision of support services or for the provision of direct services for the fiscal year involved.

(3) The provisions of section 1413(a)(9) of this title shall not apply with respect to amounts available for use by any State under paragraph (2).

(4)(A) No funds shall be distributed by any State under this subsection in any fiscal year to any local educational agency or intermediate educational unit in such State if—

(i) such local educational agency or intermediate educational unit is entitled, under subsection (d) of this section, to less than $7,500 for such fiscal year; or

(ii) such local educational agency or intermediate educational unit has not submitted an application for such funds which meets the requirements of section 1414 of this title.

(B) Whenever the provisions of subparagraph (A) apply, the State involved shall use such funds to assure the provision of a free appropriate education to children with disabilities residing in the area served by such local educational agency or such intermediate educational unit. The provisions of paragraph (2)(B) shall not apply to the use of such funds.

(d) Allocation of funds within States to local educational agencies and intermediate educational units

From the total amount of funds available to local educational agencies and intermediate educational units in any State under subsection (b)(1)(B) or subsection (c)(1)(B) of this section, as the case may be, each local educational agency or intermediate educational unit shall be entitled to an amount which bears the same ratio to the total amount available under subsection (b)(1)(B) or subsection (c)(1)(B) of this section, as the case may be, as the number of children with disabilities aged three to twenty-one, inclusive, receiving special education and related services in such local educational agency or intermediate educational unit bears to the aggregate number of children with disabilities aged three to twenty-one, inclusive, receiving special education and related services in all local educational agencies and intermediate educational units which apply to the State educational agency involved for funds under this subchapter.

(e) Territories and possessions

(1) The jurisdictions to which this subsection applies are Guam, American Samoa, the Virgin Islands, the Commonwealth of the Northern Mariana Islands, and the Trust Territory of the Pacific Islands.

(2) Each jurisdiction to which this subsection applies shall be entitled to a grant for the purposes set forth in section 1400(c) of this title in an amount equal to an amount determined by the Secretary in accordance with criteria based on respective needs, except that the aggregate of the amount to which such jurisdictions are so entitled for any fiscal year shall not exceed an amount equal to 1 per centum of the aggregate of the amounts available to all States under this subchapter for that fiscal year. If the aggregate of the amounts, determined by the Secretary pursuant to the preceding sentence, to be so needed for any fiscal year exceeds an amount equal to such 1 per centum limitation, the entitlement of each such jurisdiction shall be reduced proportionately until such aggregate does not exceed such 1 per centum limitation.

(3) The amount expended for administration by each jurisdiction under this subsection shall not exceed 5 per centum of the amount allotted to such jurisdiction for any fiscal year, or $35,000, whichever is greater.

(f) Indian reservations

(1) The Secretary shall make payments to the Secretary of the Interior according to the need for assistance for the education of children with disabilities on reservations (A) served by elementary and secondary schools operated for Indian children by the Department of the Interior. The amount of such payment for any fiscal year shall be 1.25 percent of the aggregate amounts available to all States under this section for that fiscal year, and (B) for whom services were provided through contract with an Indian tribe or organization prior to fiscal year 1989.

(2) The Secretary of the Interior may receive an allotment under paragraph (1) only after submitting to the Secretary an application which—

(A) meets the applicable requirements of sections 1412, 1413, and 1414(a) of this title,

(B) includes satisfactory assurance that all children with disabilities aged 3 to 5, inclusive, receive a free appropriate public education by or before the 1987-1988 school year,

(C) includes an assurance that there are public hearings, adequate notice of such hearings, and an opportunity for comment afforded to members of tribes, tribal governing bodies, and designated local school boards before adoption of the policies, programs, and procedures required under sections 1412, 1413, and 1414(a) of this title, and

(D) is approved by the Secretary.

Section 1416 of this title shall apply to any such application.

(3) Before March 1, 1991, the Secretary of the Interior shall submit to the appropriate Committees of the Congress a plan for the provision of services under this Act to all children with disabilities residing on reservations, whether or not such reservation is served by a B.I.A. funded school. Such plan shall provide for the coordination of services benefiting these children from whatever source, including Tribes, the State in which the child resides and entities of such State, the Indian Health Service, other B.I.A. divisions and other Federal agencies. In developing such a plan, the Secretary shall consult with all interested and involved parties. Such a plan may not be based upon a blanket assumption or interpretation that denies Federal or Interior responsibility for any group or class of children or settings, but shall be based upon the needs of the children and the system best suited for meeting those needs, and may involve the establishment of service agreements between the B.I.A. and other entities.

(g) Reductions or increases

(1) If the sums appropriated under subsection (h) of this section for any fiscal year for making payments to States under subsection (a) of this section are not sufficient to pay in full the total amounts which all States are entitled to receive under subsection (a) of this section for such fiscal year, the maximum amounts which all States are entitled to receive under subsection (a) of this section for such fiscal year shall be ratably reduced. In case additional funds become available for making such payments for any fiscal year during which the preceding sentence is applicable, such reduced amounts shall be increased on the same basis as they were reduced.

(2) In the case of any fiscal year in which the maximum amounts for which States are eligible have been reduced under the first sentence of paragraph (1), and in which additional funds have not been made avalable to pay in full the total of such maximum amounts under the last sentence of such paragraph, the State educational agency shall fix dates before which each local educational agency or intermediate educational unit shall report to the State educational agency on the amount of funds available to the local educational agency or intermediate educational unit, under the provisions of subsection (d) of this section, which it estimates that it will expend in accordance with the provisions of this section. The amounts so available to any local educational agency or intermediate educational unit, or any amount which would be available to any other local educational agency or intermediate educational unit if it were to submit a program meeting the requirements of this subchapter, which the State educational agency determines will not be used for the period of its availability, shall be available for allocation to those local educational agencies or intermediate educational units, in the manner provided by this section, which the State educational agency determines will need and be able to use additional funds to carry out approved programs.

(h) Authorization of appropriations.

For grants under subsection (a) of this section there are authorized to be appropriated such sums as may be necessary.

§ 1412. Eligibility requirements

In order to qualify for assistance under this subchapter in any fiscal year, a State shall demonstrate to the Secretary that the following conditions are met:

(1) The State has in effect a policy that assures all children with disabilities the right to a free appropriate public education.

(2) The State has developed a plan pursuant to section 1413(b) of this title in effect prior to November 29, 1975, and submitted not later than August 21, 1975, which will be amended so as to comply with the provisions of this paragraph. Each such amended plan shall set forth in detail the policies and procedures which the State will undertake or has undertaken in order to assure that—

(A) there is established (i) a goal of providing full educational opportunity to all children with disabilities, (ii) a detailed timetable for accomplishing such a goal, and (iii) a description of the kind and number of facilities, personnel, and services necessary throughout the State to meet such a goal;

(B) a free appropriate public education will be available for all children with disabilities between the ages of three and eighteen within the State not later than September 1, 1978, and for all children with disabilities between the ages of three and twenty-one within the State not later than September 1, 1980, except that, with respect to children with disabilities aged three to five and aged eighteen to twenty-one, inclusive, the requirements of this clause shall not be applied in any State if the application of such requirements would be inconsistent with State law or practice, or the order of any court, respecting public education within such age groups in the State;

(C) all children residing in the State who are disabled, regardless of the severity of their disability, and who are in need of special education and related services are identified, located, and evaluated, and that a practical method is developed and implemented to determine which children are currently receiving needed special education and related services and which children are not currently receiving needed special education and related services;

(D) policies and procedures are established in accordance with detailed criteria prescribed under section 417(c) of this title; and

(E) any amendment to the plan submitted by the State required by this section shall be available to parents, guardians, and other members of the general public at least thirty days prior to the date of submission of the amendment to the Secretary.

(3) The State has established priorities for providing a free appropriate public education to all children with disabilities, which priorities shall meet the timetables set forth in clause (B) of paragraph (2) of this section, first with respect to children with disabilities who are not receiving an

education, and second with respect to children with disabilities, within each disability category, with the most severe disabilities who are receiving an inadequate education, and has made adequate progress in meeting the timetables set forth in clause (B) of paragraph (2) of this section.

(4) Each local educational agency in the State will maintain records of the individualized education program for each child with a disability, and such program shall be established, reviewed, and revised as provided in section 1414(a)(5) of this title.

(5) The State has established (A) procedural safeguards as required by section 1415 of this title, (B) procedures to assure that, to the maximum extent appropriate, children with disabilities, including children in public or private institutions or other care facilities, are educated with children who are not disabled, and that special classes, separate schooling, or other removal of children with disabilities from the regular educational environment occurs only when the nature or severity of the disability is such that education in regular classes with the use of supplementary aids and services cannot be achieved satisfactorily, and (C) procedures to assure that testing and evaluation materials and procedures utilized for the purposes of evaluation and placement of children with disabilities will be selected and administered so as not to be racially or culturally discriminatory. Such materials or procedures shall be provided and administered in the child's native language or mode of communication, unless it clearly is not feasible to do so, and no single procedure shall be the sole criterion for determining an appropriate educational program for a child.

(6) The State educational agency shall be responsible for assuring that the requirements of this subchapter are carried out and that all educational programs for children with disabilities within the State, including all such programs administered by any other State or local agency, will be under the general supervision of the persons responsible for educational programs for children with disabilities in the State educational agency and shall meet education standards of the State educational agency. This paragraph shall not be construed to limit the responsibility of agencies other than educational agencies in a State from providing or paying for some or all of the costs of a free appropriate public education to be provided children with disabilities in the State.

(7) The State shall assure that (A) in carrying out the requirements of this section procedures are established for consultation with individuals involved in or concerned with the education of children with disabilities, including individuals with disabilities and parents or guardians of children with disabilities, and (B) there are public hearings, adequate notice of such hearings, and an opportunity for comment available to the general public prior to adoption of the policies, programs, and procedures required pursuant to the provisions of this section and section 1413 of this title.

§ 1413. State plans

(a) Requisite features

Any State meeting the eligibility requirements set forth in section 1412 of this title and desiring to participate in the program under this subchapter shall submit to the Secretary, through its State educational agency, a State plan at such time, in such manner, and containing or accompanied by such information, as the Secretary deems necessary. Each such plan shall—

(1) set forth policies and procedures designed to assure that funds paid to the State under this subchapter will be expended in accordance with the provisions of this subchapter, with particular attention given to the provisions of sections 1411(b), 1411(c), 1411(d), 1412(2), and 1412(3) of this title;

(2) provide that programs and procedures will be established to assure that funds received by the State or any of its political subdivisions under any other Federal program, including subpart 2 of part D of chapter 1 of title I of the Elementary and Secondary Education Act of 1965 and sction 202(1) of the Carl D. Perkins Vocational Education Act, of this title, under which there is specific authority for the provision of assistance for the education of children with disabilities, will be utilized by the State, or any of its political subdivisions, only in a manner consistent with the goal of providing a free appropriate public education for all children with disabilities, except that nothing in this clause shall be construed to limit the specific requirements of the laws governing such Federal programs;

(3) describe, consistent with the purposes of this Act, a comprehensive system of personnel development that shall include—

(A) a description of the procedures and activities the State will undertake to ensure an adequate supply of qualified special education and related services personnel, including—

(i) the development and maintenance of a system for determining, on an annual basis—

(I) the number and type of personnel, including leadership personnel, that are employed in the provision of special education and related services, by area of specialization, including the number of such personnel who are employed on an emergency, provisional, or other basis, who do not hold appropriate State certification or licensure; and

(II) the number and type of personnel, including leadership personnel, needed, and a projection of the numbers of such personnel that will be needed in five years, based on projections of individuals to be served, retirement and other leaving of personnel from the field, and other relevant factors;

(ii) the development and maintenance of a system for determining, on an annual basis, the institutions of higher education within the State that are preparing special education and related services personnel, including leadership personnel, by area of specialization, including—

(I) the numbers of students enrolled in such programs, and

(II) the number who graduated with certification or licensure, or with credentials to qualify for certification or licensure, during the past year; and

(iii) the development, updating, and implementation of a plan that—

(I) will address current and projected special education and related services personnel needs, including the need for leadership personnel; and

(II) coordinates and facilitates efforts among State and local educational agencies, institutions of higher education, and professional associations to recruit, prepare, and retain qualified personnel, including personnel from minority backgrounds, and personnel with disabilities; and

(B) a description of the procedures and activities the State will undertake to ensure that all personnel necessary to carry out this part are appropriately and adequately prepared, including—

(i) a system for the continuing education of regular and special education and related services personnel;

(ii) procedures for acquiring and disseminating to teachers, administrators, and related services personnel significant knowledge derived from education research and other sources; and

(iii) procedures for adopting, where appropriate, promising practices, materials, and technology.

(4) set forth policies and procedures to assure—

(A) that, to the extent consistent with the number and location of children with disabilities in the State who are enrolled in private elementary and secondary schools, provision is made for the participation of such children in the program assisted or carried out under this subchapter by providing for such children special education and related services; and

(B) that

(i) children with disabilities in private schools and facilities will be provided special education and related services (in conformance with an individualized education program as required by this part) at no cost to their parents or guardian, if such children are placed in or referred to such schools or facilities by the State or appropriate local educational agency as the means of carrying out the requirements of this part or any other applicable law requiring the provision of special education and related services to all children with disabilities within such State; and

(ii) in all such instances, the State educational agency shall determine whether such schools and facilities meet standards that apply to State and local educational agencies and that children so served have all the rights they would have if served by such agencies;

(5) set forth policies and procedures which assure that the State shall seek to recover any funds made available under this subchapter for services to any child who is determined to be erroneously classified as eligible to be counted under section 1411(a) or 1411(d) of this title;

(6) provide satisfactory assurance that the control of funds provided under this subchapter, and title to property derived therefrom, shall be in a public agency for the uses and purposes provided in this subchapter, and that a public agency will administer such funds and property;

(7) provide for—

(A) making such reports in such form and containing such information as the Secretary may require to carry out the Secretary's functions under this part, and

(B) keeping such records and affording such access thereto as the Secretary may find necessary to assure the correctness and verification of such reports and proper disbursement of Federal funds under this part;

(8) provide procedures to assure that final action with respect to any application submitted by a local educational agency or an intermediate educational unit shall not be taken without first affording the local educational agency or intermediate educational unit involved reasonable notice and op-

portunity for a hearing;

(9) provide satisfactory assurance that Federal funds made available under this part—

(A) will not be commingled with State funds, and

(B) will be so used as to supplement and increase the level of Federal, State, and local funds (including funds that are not under the direct control of State or local educational agencies) expended for special education and related services provided to children with disabilities under this part and in no case to supplant such Federal, State, and local funds, except that, where the State provides clear and convincing evidence that all children with disabilities have available to them a free appropriate public education, the Secretary may waive in part the requirement of this subparagraph if the Secretary concurs with the evidence provided by the State;

(10) provide, consistent with procedures prescribed pursuant to section 1417(a)(2) of this title, satisfactory assurance that such fiscal control and fund accounting procedures will be adopted as may be necessary to assure proper disbursement of, and accounting for, Federal funds paid under this subchapter to the State, including any such funds paid by the State to local educational agencies and intermediate educational units;

(11) provide for procedures for evaluation at least annually of the effectiveness of programs in meeting the educational needs of children with disabilities (including evaluation of individualized education programs), in accordance with such criteria that the Secretary shall prescribe pursuant to section 1417 of this title;

(12) provide that the State has an advisory panel, appointed by the Governor or any other official authorized under State law to make such appointments, composed of individuals involved in or concerned with the education of children with disabilities, including individuals with disabilities, teachers, parents or guardians of children with disabilities, State and local education officials, and administrators of programs for children with disabilities, which

(A) advises the State educational agency of unmet needs within the State in the education of children with disabilities,

(B) comments publicly on any rules or regulations proposed for issuance by the State regarding the education of children with disabilities and the procedures for distribution of funds under this part, and

(C) assists the State in developing and reporting such data and evaluations as may assist the Secretary in the performance of the responsibilities of the Secretary under section 1418 of this title;

(13) set forth policies and procedures for developing and implementing interagency agreements between the State educational agency and other appropriate State and local agencies to

(A) define the financial responsibility of each agency for providing children and youth with disabilities with free appropriate public education, and

(B) resolve interagency disputes, including procedures under which local educational agencies may initiate proceedings under the agreement in order to secure reimbursement from other agencies or otherwise implement the provisions of the agreement; and

(14) set forth policies and procedures relating to the establishment and

maintenance of standards to ensure that personnel necessary to carry out the purposes of this subchapter are appropriately and adequately prepared and trained, including—

(A) the establishment and maintenance of standards which are consistent with any State approved or recognized certification, licensing, registration, or other comparable requirements which apply to the area in which such personnel are providing special education or related services, and

(B) to the extent such standards are not based on the highest requirements in the State applicable to a specific profession or discipline, the steps the State is taking to require the retraining or hiring of personnel that meet appropriate professional requirements in the State.

(b) Additional assurances

Whenever a State educational agency provides free appropriate public education for children with disabilities, or provides direct services to such children, such State educational agency shall include, as part of the State plan required by subsection (a) of this section, such additional assurances not specified in such subsection (a) of this section as are contained in section 1414(a) of this title, except that funds available for the provision of such education or services may be expended without regard to the provisions relating to excess costs in section 1414(a) of this title.

(c) Notice and hearing prior to disapproval of plan

(1) The Secretary shall approve any State plan and any modification thereof which—

(A) is submitted by a State eligible in accordance with section 1412 of this title; and

(B) meets the requirements of subsection (a) and subsection (b) of this section.

(2) The Secretary shall disapprove any State plan which does not meet the requirements of paragraph (1), but shall not finally disapprove a State plan except after reasonable notice and opportunity for a hearing to the State.

(d) Participation of children with disabilities in private schools; payment of Federal amount; determinations of Secretary: notice and hearing; judicial review: jurisdiction of court of appeals, petition, record, conclusiveness of findings, remand, review by Supreme Court

(1) If, on December 2, 1983, a State educational agency is prohibited by law from providing for the participation in special programs of children with disabilities enrolled in private elementary and secondary schools as required by subsection (a)(4) of this section, the Secretary shall waive such requirement, and shall arrange for the provision of services to such children through arrangements which shall be subject to the requirements of subsection (a)(4) of this section.

(2)(A) When the Secretary arranges for services pursuant to this subsection, the Secretary, after consultation with the appropriate public and private school officials, shall pay to the provider of such services an amount per child which may not exceed the Federal amount provided per child under this subchapter to all children with disabilities enrolled in the State for services for the fiscal year preceding the fiscal year for which the determination is made.

(B) Pending final resolution of any investigation or complaint that could result in a determination under this subsection, the Secretary may withhold from the allocation of the affected State educational agency the amount the Secretary estimates would be necessary to pay the cost of such services.

(C) Any determination by the Secretary under this section shall continue in effect until the Secretary determines that there will no longer be any failure or inability on the part of the State educational agency to meet the requirements of subsection (a)(4) of this section.

(3)(A) The Secretary shall not take any final action under this subsection until the State educational agency affected by such action has had an opportunity, for at least 45 days after receiving written notice thereof, to submit written objections and to appear before the Secretary or the Secretary's designee to show cause why such action should not be taken.

(B) If a State educational agency is dissatisfied with the Secretary's final action after a proceeding under subparagraph (A) of this paragraph, it may, within 60 days after notice of such action, file with the United States court of appeals for the circuit in which such state is located a petition for review of that action. A copy of the petition shall be forthwith transmitted by the clerk of the court to the Secretary. The Secretary thereupon shall file in the court the record of the proceedings on which the Secretary based the Secretary's action, as provided in section 2112 of title 28.

(C) The findings of fact by the Secretary, if supported by substantial evidence, shall be conclusive; but the court, for good cause shown, may remand the case to the Secretary to take further evidence, and the Secretary may thereupon make new or modified findings of fact and may modify the Secretary's previous action, and shall file in the court the record of the further proceedings. Such new or modified findings of fact shall likewise be conclusive if supported by substantial evidence.

(D) Upon the filing of a petition under subparagraph (B), the court shall have jurisdiction to affirm the action of the Secretary or to set it aside, in whole or in part. The judgment of the court shall be subject to review by the Supreme Court of the United States upon certiorari or certification as provided in section 1254 of title 28.

(e) Reduction of medical and other assistance or alteration of eligibility under social security provisions prohibited.

This chapter shall not be construed to permit a State to reduce medical and other assistance available or to alter eligibility under titles V and XIX of the Social Security Act with respect to the provision of a free appropriate public education for children with disabilities within the State.

§ 1414. Application

(a) Requisite features

A local educational agency or an intermediate educational unit which desires to receive payments under section 1411(d) of this title for any fiscal year shall submit an application to the appropriate State educational agency. Such application shall—

(1) provide satisfactory assurance that payments under this subchapter will be used for excess costs directly attributable to programs which—

(A) provide that all children residing within the jurisdiction of the local educational agency or the intermediate educational unit who are disabled, regardless of the severity of their disability, and are in need of special education and related services will be identified, located, and evaluated, and provide for the inclusion of a practical method of determining which children are currently receiving needed special education and related services and which children are not currently receiving such education and services;

(B) establish policies and procedures in accordance with detailed criteria prescribed under section 1417(c) of this title;

(C) establish a goal of providing full educational opportunities to all children with disabilities, including—

(i) procedures for the implementation and use of the comprehensive system of personnel development established by the State educational agency under section 1413(a)(3) of this title;

(ii) the provision of, and the establishment of priorities for providing, a free appropriate public education to all children with disabilities, first with respect to children with disabilities who are not receiving an education, and second with respect to children with disabilities, within each disability, with the most severe disabilities who are receiving an inadequate education;

(iii) the participation and consultation of the parents or guardian of such children; and

(iv) to the maximum extent practicable and consistent with the provisions of section 1412(5)(B) of this title, the provision of special services to enable such children to participate in regular educational programs;

(D) establish a detailed timetable for accomplishing the goal described in subclause (C); and

(E) provide a description of the kind and number of facilities, personnel, and services necessary to meet the goal described in subclause (C);

(2) provide satisfactory assurance that—

(A) the control of funds provided under this part, and title to property derived from such funds, shall be in a public agency for the uses and purposes provided in this part, and that a public agency will administer such funds and property;

(B) Federal funds expended by local educational agencies and intermediate educational units for programs under this part—

(i) shall be used to pay only the excess costs directly attributable to the education of children with disabilities; and

(ii) shall be used to supplement and, to the extent practicable, increase the level of State and local funds expended for the education of children with disabilities, and in no case to supplant such State and local funds; and

(C) State and local funds will be used in the jurisdiction of the local educational agency or intermediate educational unit to provide services in program areas that, taken as a whole, are at least comparable to services being provided in areas of such jurisdiction that are not receiving funds under this part;

(3) provide for

(A) furnishing such information (which, in the case of reports relating to performance, is in accordance with specific performance criteria related to program objectives), as may be necessary to enable the State educational agency to perform its duties under this part, including information relating to the educational achievement of children with disabilities participating in programs carried out under this part; and

(B) keeping such records, and affording such access to such records, as the State educational agency may find necessary to assure the correctness and verification of such information furnished under subparagraph (A);

(4) provide for making the application and all pertinent documents related to such application available to parents, guardians, and other members of the general public, and provide that all evaluations and reports required under clause (3) shall be public information;

(5) provide assurances that the local educational agency or intermediate educational unit will establish or revise, whichever is appropriate, an individualized education program for each child with a disability at the beginning of each school year and will then review and, if appropriate, revise, its provisions periodically, but not less than annually;

(6) provide satisfactory assurance that policies and programs established and administered by the local educational agency or intermediate educational unit shall be consistent with the provisions of paragraph (1) through paragraph (7) of section 1412 and section 1413(a) of this title; and

(7) provide satisfactory assurance that the local educational agency or intermediate educational unit will establish and maintain procedural safeguards in accordance with the provisions of sections 1412(5)(B), 1412(5)(C), and 1415 of this title.

(b) Approval by State educational agencies of applications submitted by local educational agencies or intermediate educational units; notice and hearing

(1) A State educational agency shall approve any application submitted by a local educational agency or an intermediate educational unit under subsection (a) of this section if the State educational agency determines that such application meets the requirements of subsection (a) of this section, except that no such application may be approved until the State plan submitted by such State educational agency under subsection (a) of this section is approved by the Secretary under section 1413(c) of this title. A State educational agency shall disapprove any application submitted by a local educational agency or an intermediate educational unit under subsection (a) of this section if the State educational agency determines that such application does not meet the requirements of subsection (a) of this section.

(2)(A) Whenever a State educational agency, after reasonable notice and opportunity for a hearing, finds that a local educational agency or an intermediate educational unit, in the administration of an application approved by the State educational agency under paragraph (1), has failed to comply with any requirement set forth in such application, the State educational agency, after giving appropriate notice to the local educational agency or the intermediate educational unit, shall—

(i) make no further payments to such local educational agency or such intermediate educational unit under section 1420 of this title until the State educational agency is satisfied that there is no longer any failure to comply with the requirement involved; or

(ii) take such finding into account in its review of any application made by such local educational agency or such intermediate educational unit under subsection (a) of this section.

(B) The provisions of the last sentence of section 1416(a) of this title shall apply to any local educational agency or any intermediate educational unit receiving any notification from a State educational agency under this paragraph.

(3) In carrying out its functions under paragraph (1), each State educational agency shall consider any decision made pursuant to a hearing held under section 1415 of this title which is adverse to the local educational agency or intermediate educational unit involved in such decision.

(c) Consolidated applications

(1) A State educational agency may, for purposes of the consideration and approval of applications under this section, require local educational agencies to submit a consolidated application for payments if such State educational agency determines that any individual application submitted by any such local educational agency will be disapproved because such local educational agency is ineligible to receive payments because of the application of section 1411(c)(4)(A)(i) of this title or such local educational agency would be unable to establish and maintain programs of sufficient size and scope to effectively meet the educational needs of children with disabilities.

(2)(A) In any case in which a consolidated application of local educational agencies is approved by a State educational agency under paragraph (1), the payments which such local educational agencies may receive shall be equal to the sum of payments to which each such local educational agency would be entitled under section 1411(d) of this title if an individual application of any such local educational agency had been approved.

(B) The State educational agency shall prescribe rules and regulations with respect to consolidated applications submitted under this subsection which are consistent with the provisions of paragraph (1) through paragraph (7) of section 1412 and section 1413(a) of this title and which provide participating local educational agencies with joint responsibilities for implementing programs receiving payments under this subchapter.

(C) In any case in which an intermediate educational unit is required pursuant to State law to carry out the provisions of this subchapter, the joint responsibilities given to local educational agencies under subparagraph (B) shall not apply to the administration and disbursement of any payments received by such intermediate educational unit. Such responsibilities shall be carried out exclusively by such intermediate educational unit.

(d) Special education and related services provided directly by State educational agencies: regional or State centers

Whenever a State educational agency determines that a local educational agency—

(1) is unable or unwilling to establish and maintain programs of free appropriate public education which meet the requirements established in subsection (a) of this section;

(2) is unable or unwilling to be consolidated with other local educational agencies in order to establish and maintain such programs; or

(3) has one or more children with disabilities who can best be served by a regional or State center designed to meet the needs of such children;
the State educational agency shall use the payments which would have been available to such local educational agency to provide special education and related services directly to children with disabilities residing in the area served by such local educational agency. The State educational agency may provide such education and services in such manner, and at such locations (including regional or State centers), as it considers appropriate, except that the manner in which such education and services are provided shall be consistent with the requirements of this subchapter.

(e) Reallocation of funds

Whenever a State educational agency determines that a local educational agency is adequately providing a free appropriate public education to all children with disabilities residing in the area served by such agency with State and local funds otherwise available to such agency, the State educational agency may reallocate funds (or such portion of those funds as may not be required to provide such education and services) made available to such agency, pursuant to section 1411(d) of this title, to such other local educational agencies within the State as are not adequately providing special education and related services to all children with disabilities residing in the areas served by such other local educational agencies.

(f) Programs using State or local funds

Notwithstanding the provisions of subsection (a)(2)(B)(ii) of this section, any local educational agency which is required to carry out any program for the education of children with disabilities pursuant to a State law shall be entitled to receive payments under section 1411(d) of this title for use in carrying out such program, except that such payments may not be used to reduce the level of expenditures for such program made by such local educational agency from State or local funds below the level of such expenditures for the fiscal year prior to the fiscal year for which such local educational agency seeks such payments.

§ 1415. Procedural safeguards

(a) Establishment and maintenance

Any State educational agency, any local educational agency, and any intermediate educational unit which receives assistance under this subchapter shall establish and maintain procedures in accordance with subsection (b) through subsection (e) of this section to assure that children with disabilities and their parents or guardians are guaranteed procedural safeguards with respect to the provision of free appropriate public education by such agencies and units.

(b) Required procedures; hearing

(1) The procedures required by this section shall include, but shall not be limited to—

(A) an opportunity for the parents or guardian of a child with a disability to examine all relevant records with respect to the identification, evaluation, and educational placement of the child, and the provision of a free appropriate public education to such child, and to obtain an independent educational evaluation of the child;

(B) procedures to protect the rights of the child whenever the parents or guardian of the child are not known, unavailable, or the child is a ward of the State, including the assignment of an individual (who shall not be an employee of the State educational agency, local educational agency, or intermediate educational unit involved in the education or care of the child) to act as a surrogate for the parents or guardian;

(C) written prior notice to the parents or guardian of the child whenever such agency or unit—

(i) proposes to initiate or change, or

(ii) refuses to initiate or change,

the identification, evaluation, or educational placement of the child or the provision of a free appropriate public education to the child;

(D) procedures designed to assure that the notice required by clause (C) fully informs the parents or guardian, in the parents' or guardian's native language, unless it clearly is not feasible to do so, of all procedures available pursuant to this section; and

(E) an opportunity to present complaints with respect to any matter relating to the identification, evaluation, or educational placement of the child, or the provision of a free appropriate public education to such child.

(2) Whenever a complaint has been received under paragraph (1) of this subsection, the parents or guardian shall have an opportunity for an impartial due process hearing which shall be conducted by the State educational agency or by the local educational agency or intermediate educational unit, as determined by State law or by the State educational agency. No hearing conducted pursuant to the requirements of this paragraph shall be conducted by an employee of such agency or unit involved in the education or care of the child.

(c) Review of local decision by State education agency

If the hearing required in paragraph (2) of subsection (b) of this section is conducted by a local educational agency or an intermediate educational unit, any party aggrieved by the findings and decision rendered in such a hearing may appeal to the State educational agency which shall conduct an impartial review of such hearing. The officer conducting such review shall make an independent decision upon completion of such review.

(d) Enumeration of rights accorded parties to hearings

Any party to any hearing conducted pursuant to subsections (b) and (c) of this section shall be accorded
(1) the right to be accompanied and advised by counsel and by individuals with special knowledge or training with respect to the problems of children with disabilities,
(2) the right to present evidence and confront, cross-examine, and compel the attendance of witnesses,
(3) the right to a written or electronic verbatim record of such hearing, and
(4) the right to written findings of fact and decisions (which findings and decisions shall be made available to the public consistent with the requirements of section 1417(c) and shall also be transmitted to the advisory panel established pursuant to section 1413(a)(12)).

(e) Civil action; jurisdiction; attorney fees

(1) A decision made in a hearing conducted pursuant to paragraph (2) of subsection (b) of this section shall be final, except that any party involved in such hearing may appeal such decision under the provisions of subsection (c) and paragraph (2) of this subsection. A decision made under subsection (c) of this section shall be final, except that any party may bring an action under paragraph (2) of this subsection.

(2) Any party aggrieved by the findings and decision made under subsection (b) of this section who does not have the right to an appeal under subsection (c) of this section, and any party aggrieved by the findings and decision under subsection (c) of this section, shall have the right to bring a civil action with respect to the complaint presented pursuant to this section, which action may be brought in any State court of competent jurisdiction or in a district court of the United States without regard to the amount in controversy. In any action brought under this paragraph the court shall receive the records of the administrative proceedings, shall hear additional evidence at the request of a party, and, basing its decision of the preponderance of the evidence, shall grant such relief as the court determines is appropriate.

(3) During the pendency of any proceedings conducted pursuant to this section, unless the State or local educational agency and the parents or guardian otherwise agree, the child shall remain in the then current educational placement of such child, or, if applying for initial admission to a public school, shall, with the consent of the parents or guardian, be placed in the public school program until all such proceedings have been completed.

(4)(A) The district courts of the United States shall have jurisdiction of actions brought under this subsection without regard to the amount in controversy.

(B) In any action or proceeding brought under this subsection, the court, in its discretion, may award reasonable attorneys' fees as part of the costs to the parents or guardian of a child or youth with a disability who is the prevailing party.

(C) For the purpose of this subsection, fees awarded under this subsection shall be based on rates prevailing in the community in which the action or proceeding arose for the kind and quality of services furnished. No bonus or multiplier may be used in calculating the fees awarded under this subsection.

(D) No award of attorneys' fees and related costs may be made in any action or proceeding under this subsection for services performed subsequent to the time of a written offer of settlement to a parent or guardian, if—

(i) the offer is made within the time prescribed by Rule 68 of the Federal Rules of Civil Procedure or, in the case of an administrative proceeding, at any time more than ten days before the proceeding begins;

(ii) the offer is not accepted within ten days; and

(iii) the court or administrative officer finds that the relief finally obtained by the parents or guardian is not more favorable to the parents or guardian than the offer of settlement.

(E) Notwithstanding the provisions of subparagraph (D), an award of attorneys' fees and related costs may be made to a parent or guardian who is the prevailing party and who was substantially justified in rejecting the settlement offer.

(F) Whenever the court finds that—

(i) the parent or guardian, during the course of the action or proceeding, unreasonably protracted the final resolution of the controversy;

(ii) the amount of the attorneys' fees otherwise authorized to be awarded unreasonably exceeds the hourly rate prevailing in the community for similar services by attorneys of reasonably comparable skill, experience, and reputation; or

(iii) the time spent and legal services furnished were excessive considering the nature of the action or proceeding,

the court shall reduce, accordingly, the amount of the attorneys' fees awarded under this subsection.

(G) The provisions of subparagraph (F) shall not apply in any action or proceeding if the court finds that the State or local educational agency unreasonably protracted the final resolution of the action or proceeding or there was a violation of this section.

(f) Effect on other laws

Nothing in this chapter shall be construed to restrict or limit the rights, procedures, and remedies available under the Constitution, title V of the Rehabilitation Act of 1973 [29 U.S.C.A. § 790 et seq.], or other Federal statutes protecting the rights of children and youth with disabilities, except that before the filing of a civil action under such laws seeking relief that is also available under this subchapter, the procedures under subsections (b)(2) and (c) of this section shall be exhausted to the same extent as would be required had the action been brought under this subchapter.

Effective Date of 1986 Amendment. Section 5 of the HCPA, Pub.L. 99-372, provided that: "The amendment made by section 2 [amending 20 U.S.C. § 1415(e)(4)] shall apply with respect to actions or proceedings brought under section 615(e) of the Education of the Handicapped Act 20 U.S.C. § 1415(e) after July 3, 1984, and actions or proceedings brought prior to July 4, 1984, under such section which were pending on July 4, 1984."

§ 1416. Withholding of payments

(a) Failure to comply with this subchapter; limitations; public notice

Whenever the Secretary, after reasonable notice and opportunity for hearing to the State educational agency involved (and to any local educational agency or intermediate educational unit affected by any failure described in clause (2)), finds—

(1) that there has been a failure to comply substantially with any provision of section 1412 or section 1413 of this title, or

(2) that in the administration of the State plan there is a failure to comply with any provision of this subchapter or with any requirements set forth in the application of a local educational agency or intermediate educational unit approved by the State educational agency pursuant to the State plan, the Secretary—

(A) shall, after notifying the State educational agency, withhold any further payments to the State under this part, and

(B) may, after notifying the State educational agency, withhold further payments to the State under the Federal programs specified in section 613(a)(2) within the Secretary's jurisdiction, to the extent that funds under such programs are available for the provision of assistance for the education of children with disabilities.

If the Secretary withholds further payments under clause (A) or clause (B) the Secretary may determine that such withholding will be limited to programs or projects under the State plan, or portions thereof, affected by the failure, or that the State educational agency shall not make further payments under this subchapter to specified local educational agencies or intermediate educational units affected by the failure. Until the Secretary is satisfied that there is no longer any failure to comply with the provisions of this subchapter, as specified in clause (1) or clause (2), no further payments shall be made to the State under this subchapter or under the Federal programs specified in section 1413(a)(2) of this title within the Secretary's jurisdiction to the extent that funds under such programs are available for the provision of assistance for the education of children with disabilities, or payments by the State educational agency under this subchapter shall be limited to local educational agencies and intermediate educational units whose actions did not cause or were not involved in the failure, as the case may be. Any State educational agency, local educational agency, or intermediate educational unit in receipt of a notice pursuant to the first sentence of this subsection shall, by means of a public notice, take such measures as may be necessary to bring the pendency of an action pursuant to this subsection to the attention· of the public within the jurisdiction of such agency or unit.

(b) Judicial review

(1) If any State is dissatisfied with the Secretary's final action with respect to its State plan submitted under section 1413 of this title, such State may, within sixty days after notice of such action, file with the United States court of appeals for the circuit in which such State is located a petition for review of that action. A copy of the petition shall be forthwith transmitted by the clerk of the court to the Secretary. The Secretary thereupon shall file in the court the record of the proceedings upon which the Secretary's action was based, as provided in section 2112 of title 28.

(2) The findings of fact by the Secretary, if supported by substantial evidence, shall be conclusive; but the court, for good cause shown, may remand the case to the Secretary to take further evidence, and the Secretary may thereupon make new or modified findings of fact that may modify the Secretary's previous action, and shall file in the court the record of the further proceedings. Such new or modified findings of fact shall likewise be conclusive if supported by substantial evidence.

(3) Upon the filing of such petition, the court shall have jurisdiction to affirm the action of the Secretary or to set it aside, in whole or in pard. The judgment of the court shall be subject to review by the Supreme Court of the United States upon certiorari or certification as provided in section 1254 of title 28.

§ 1417. Administration

(a) Duties of Secretary

(1) In carrying out the Secretary's duties under this subchapter, the Secretary shall

(A) cooperate with, and furnish all technical assistance necessary, directly or by grant or contract, to the States in matters relating to the education of children with disabilities and the execution of the provisions of this subchapter;

(B) provide such short-term training programs and institutes as are necessary;

(C) disseminate information, and otherwise promote the education of all children with disabilities within the States; and

(D) assure that each State shall, within one year after November 29, 1975 and every year thereafter, provide certification of the actual number of children with disabilities receiving special education and related services in such State.

(2) As soon as practicable after November 29, 1975, the Secretary shall, by regulation, prescribe a uniform financial report to be utilized by State educational agencies in submitting State plans under this subchapter in order to assure equity among the States.

(b) Rules and regulations

In carrying out the provisions of this subchapter, the Secretary shall issue, not later than January 1, 1977, amend, and revoke such rules and regulations as may be necessary. No other less formal method of implementing such provisions is authorized.

(c) Protection of rights and privacy of parents and students

The Secretary shall take appropriate action, in accordance with the provisions of section 1232g of this title, to assure the protection of the confidentiality of any personally identifiable data, information, and records collected or maintained by the Secretary and by State and local educational agencies pursuant to the provisions of this subchapter.

(d) Hiring of qualified personnel

The Secretary is authorized to hire qualified personnel necessary to conduct data collection and evaluation activities required by subsections (b), (c) and (d) of section 1418 of this title and to carry out the Secretary's duties under subsection (a)(1) of this section without regard to the provisions of title 5 relating to appointments in the competitive service and without regard to chapter 51 and subchapter III of chapter 53 of such title relating to classification and general schedule pay rates except that no more than twenty such personnel shall be employed at any time.

§ 1418. Evaluation

(a) Duties of Secretary

The Secretary shall, directly or by grant, contract, or cooperative agreement, collect data and conduct studies, investigations, and evaluations—
(1) to assess progress in the implementation of this Act;
(2) to assess the impact and effectiveness of State and local efforts, and efforts by the Secretary of the Interior, to provide—
(A) free appropriate public education to children and youth with disabilities; and
(B) early intervention services to infants and toddlers with disabilities; and
(3) to provide—
(A) Congress with information relevant to policymaking; and
(B) State, local, and Federal agencies, including the Department of the Interior, with information relevant to program management, administration, and effectiveness with respect to such education and early intervention services.

(b) Collection of data on education of infants, toddlers, children and youth with disabilities; additional information

In carrying out subsection (a) of this section, the Secretary, on at least an annual basis, shall obtain data concerning programs and projects assisted under this chapter and under other Federal laws relating to infants, toddlers, children, and youth with disabilities, and such additional information, from State and local educational agencies, the Secretary of Interior, and other appropriate sources, as is necessary for the implementation of this chapter including—

(1) the number of infants, toddlers, children, and youth with disabilities in each State receiving a free appropriate public education or early intervention services—

(A) in age groups 0-2 and 3-5, and

(B) in age groups 6-11, 12-17, and 18-21,

by disability category,

(2) the number of children and youth with disabilities in each State who are participating in regular educational programs (consistent with the requirements of sections 1412(5)(B) of this title and 1414(a)(1)(C)(iv) of this title) by disability category, and the number of children and youth with disabilities in separate classes, separate schools or facilities, or public or private residential facilities, or who have been otherwise removed from the regular education environment,

(3) the number of children and youth with disabilities exiting the education system each year through program completion or otherwise—

(A) in age group 3-5, and

(B) in age groups 6-11, 12-17, and 18-21,

by disability category and anticipated services for the next year,

(4) the amount of Federal, State, and local funds expended in each State specifically for special education and related services and for early intervention services (which may be based upon a sampling of data from State agencies including State and local educational agencies),

(5) the number and type of personnel that are employed in the provision of special education and related services to children and youth with disabilities and early intervention services to infants and toddlers with disabilities by disability category served, and the estimated number and type of additional personnel by disability category needed to adequately carry out the policy established by this chapter, and

(6) a description of the special education and related services and early intervention services needed to fully implement this chapter throughout each State, including estimates of the number of infants and toddlers with disabilities in the 0-2 age group and estimates of the number of children and youth with disabilities—

(A) in age group 3-5, and

(B) in age groups 6-11, 12-17, and 18-21,

and by disability category.

(c) Evaluation studies by grant, contract, or cooperative agreement

The Secretary shall, by grant, contract, or cooperative agreement, provide for evaluation studies to determine the impact of this chapter. Each such evaluation shall include recommendations for improvement of the programs under this chapter. The Secretary shall, not later than July 1 of each year, submit to the appropriate committees of each House of the Congress and publish in the Federal Register proposed evaluation priorities for review and comment.

(d) Cooperative agreements with State educational agencies

(1) The Secretary may enter into cooperative agreements with State educational agencies and other State agencies to carry out studies to assess the impact and effectiveness of programs assisted under this chapter.

(2) An agreement under paragraph (1) shall—

(A) provide for the payment of not to exceed 60 percent of the total cost of studies conducted by a participating State agency to assess the impact and effectiveness of programs assisted under this chapter, and

(B) be developed in consultation with the State Advisory Panel established under this chapter, the local educational agencies, and ?taers involved in or concerned with the education of children and youth with disabilities and the provision of early intervention services to infants and toddlers with disabilities.

(3) The Secretary shall provide technical assistance to participating State agencies in the implementation of the study design, analysis, and reporting procedures.

(4) In addition, the Secretary shall disseminate information from such studies to State agencies, regional resource centers, and clearinghouses established by this chapter, and, as appropriate, to others involved in, or concerned with, the education of children and youth with disabilities and the provision of early intervention services to infants and toddlers with disabilities.

(e) Specifically mandated studies

(1) At least one study shall be a longitudinal study of a sample of students with disabilities, encompassing the full range of handicapping conditions, examining their educational progress while in special education and their occupational, educational, and independent living status after graduating from secondary school or otherwise leaving special education.

(2) At least one study shall focus on obtaining and compiling current information available, through State educational agencies and local educational agencies and other service providers, regarding State and local expenditures for educational services for students with disabilities (including special education and related services) and shall gather information needed in order to calculate a range of per pupil expenditures by handicapping condition.

(f) Annual report

(1) Not later than 120 days after the close of each fiscal year, the Secretary shall publish and disseminate an annual report on the progress being made toward the provision of a free appropriate public education to all children and youth with disabilities and early intervention services for infants and toddlers with disabilities. The annual report shall be transmitted to the appropriate committees of each House of Congress and published and disseminated in sufficient quantities to the education community at large and to other interested parties.

(2) The Secretary shall include in each annual report under paragraph (1)—

(A) a compilation and analysis of data gathered under subsection (b) of this section.

(B) an index and summary of each evaluation activity and results of studies conducted under subsection (c) of this section,

(C) a description of findings and determinations resulting from monitoring reviews of State implementation of this subchapter,

(D) an analysis and evaluation of the participation of children and youth with disabilities in vocational education programs and services,

(E) an analysis and evaluation of the effectiveness of procedures undertaken by each State educational agency, local educational agency, and intermediate educational unit to ensure that children and youth with disabilities receive special education and related services in the least restrictive environment commensurate with their needs and to improve programs of instruction for children and youth with disabilities in day or residential facilities, and

(F) any recommendation for change in the provisions of this chapter or any other Federal law providing support for the education of children and youth with disabilities.

(3) In the annual report under paragraph (1) for fiscal year 1985 which is published in 1986 and for every third year thereafter, the Secretary shall include in the annual report—

(A) an index of all current projects funded under subchapters III through VII of this chapter, and

(B) data reported under sections 1421, 1422, 1423, 1426, 1434, 1441, and 1461 of this title.

(4) In the annual report under paragraph (1) for fiscal year 1988 which is published in 1989, the Secretary shall include special sections addressing the provision of a free appropriate public education to—

(A) infants, toddlers, children, and youth with disabilities in rural areas and,

(B) migrants with disabilities,

(C) Indians with disabilities (particularly programs operated under section 1411(f)),

(D) Native Hawaiian (and other native Pacific basin) children and youth with disabilities, and

(E) infants, toddlers, children, and youth with disabilities with limited English proficiency.

(5) Beginning in 1986, in consultation with the National Council on Disability and the Bureau of Indian Affairs Advisory Committee for Exceptional Children, the Secretary shall include a description of the status of early intervention services for infants and toddlers with disabilities from birth through age two, inclusive, and special education and related services to children with disabilities from 3 through 5 years of age (including those receiving services through Head Start, Developmental Disabilities Programs, Crippled Children's Services, Mental Health/Mental Retardation Agency, and State child-development centers and private agencies under contract with local schools).

(g) Authorization of appropriations

There are authorized to be appropriated $3,800,000 for fiscal year 1987,

$4,000,000 for fiscal year 1988, and $4,200,000 for fiscal year 1989 to carry out this section.

§ 1419. Pre-school grants

(a) Grants for fiscal years 1987 through 1989; amount of grants

(1) For fiscal years 1987 through 1989 (or fiscal year 1990 if the Secretary makes a grant under this paragraph for such fiscal year) the Secretary shall make a grant to any State which—
    (A) has met the eligibility requirements of section 1412 of this title,
    (B) has a State plan approved under section 1413 of this title, and
    (C) provides special education and related services to children with disabilities aged three to five, inclusive.
    (2)(A) For fiscal year 1987 the amount of a grant to a State under paragraph (1) may not exceed—
    (i) $300 per child with a disability aged three to five, inclusive, who received special education and related services in such State as determined under section 1411(a)(3) of this section, or
    (ii) if the amount appropriated under subsection (e) of this section exceeds the product of $300 and the total number of children with disabilities aged three to five, inclusive, who received special education and related services as determined under section 1411(a)(3) of this title—
    (I) $300 per child with a disability aged three to five, inclusive, who received special education and related services in such State as determined under section 1411(a)(3) of this title, plus
    (II) an amount equal to the portion of the appropriation available after allocating funds to all States under subclause (I) (the excess appropriation) divided by the estimated increase, from the preceding fiscal year, in the number of children with disabilities aged three to five, inclusive, who will be receiving special education and related services in all States multiplied by the estimated increase in the number of such children in such State.
    (B) For fiscal year 1988, funds shall be distributed in accordance with clause (i) or (ii) of paragraph (2)(A), except that the amount specified therein shall be $400 instead of $300.
    (C) For fiscal year 1989, funds shall be distributed in accordance with clause (i) or (ii) of paragraph (2)(A), except that the amount specified therein shall be $500 instead of $300.
    (D) If the Secretary makes a grant under paragraph (1) for fiscal year 1990, the amount of a grant to a State under such paragraph may not exceed $1,000 per child with a disability aged three to five, inclusive, who received special education and related services in such State as determined under section 1411(a)(3) of this title.
    (E) If the actual number of additional children served in a fiscal year differs from the estimate made under subparagraph (A)(ii)(II), the Secretary shall adjust (upwards or downwards) a State's allotment in the subsequent fiscal year.
    (F)(i) The amount of a grant under subparagraph (A), (B), or (C) to any State for a fiscal year may not exceed $3,800 per estimated child with a dis-

ability aged three to five, inclusive, who will be receiving or child with a disability, age three to five, inclusive, who is receiving special education and related services in such State.

(ii) If the amount appropriated under subsection (e) of this section for any fiscal year exceeds the amount of grants which may be made to the States for such fiscal year, the excess amount appropriated shall remain available for obligation under this section for 2 succeeding fiscal years.

(3) To receive a grant under paragraph (1) a State shall make an application to the secretary at such time, in such manner, and containing or accompanied by such information as the Secretary may reasonably require.

(b) Grants for fiscal year 1990 and thereafter; amount of grants

(1) For fiscal year 1990 (or fiscal year 1991 if required by paragraph (2)) and fiscal years thereafter the Secretary shall make a grant to any State which—

(A) has met the eligibility requirements of section 1412 of this title, and

(B) has a State plan approved under section 1413 of this title which includes policies and procedures that assure the availability under the State law and practice of such State of a free appropriate public education for all children with disabilities aged three to five, inclusive.

(2) The Secretary may make a grant under paragraph (1) only for fiscal year 1990 and fiscal years thereafter, except that if—

(A) the aggregate amount that was appropriated under subsection (e) of this section for fiscal years 1987, 1988, and 1989 was less than $656,000,000, or

(B) the amount appropriated for fiscal year 1990 under subsection (e) of this section is less than $306,000,000,

the Secretary may not make a grant under paragraph (1) until fiscal year 1991 and shall make a grant under subsection (a)(1) of this section for fiscal year 1990.

(3) The amount of any grant to any State under paragraph (1) for any fiscal year may not exceed $1,000 for each child with a disability in such State aged three to five, inclusive.

(4) To receive a grant under paragraph (1) a State shall make an application to the Secretary at such time, in such manner, and containing or accompanied by such information as the Secretary may reasonably require.

(c) Distribution by State of received funds

(1) For fiscal year 1987, a State which receives a grant under subsection (a)(1) of this section shall—

(A) distribute at least 70 percent of such grant to local educational agencies and intermediate educational units in such State in accordance with paragraph (3), except that in applying such section only children with disabilities aged three to five, inclusive, shall be considered,

(B) use not more than 25 percent of such grant for the planning and development of a comprehensive delivery system for which a grant could have been made under section 1423(b) of this title in effect through fiscal year 1987 and for direct and support services for children with disabilities, and

(C) use not more than 5 percent of such grant for administrative expenses related to the grant.

(2) For fiscal years beginning after fiscal year 1987, a State which receives a grant under subsection (a)(1) of this section or (b)(1) of this section shall—

(A) distribute at least 75 percent of such grant to local educational agencies and intermediate educational units in such State in accordance with paragraph (3), except that in applying such section only children with disabilities aged three to five, inclusive, shall be considered.

(B) use not more than 20 percent of such grant for the planning and development of a comprehensive delivery system for which a grant could have been made under section 1423(b) of this title in effect through fiscal year 1987 and for direct and support services for children with disabilities, and

(C) use not more than 5 percent of such grant for administrative expenses related to the grant.

(3) From the amount of funds available to local educational agencies and intermediate educational units in any State under this section, each local educational agency or intermediate educational unit shall be entitled to—

(A) an amount which bears the same ratio to the amount available under subsection (a)(2)(A)(i) of this title or subsection (a)(2)(A)(ii)(I) of this title, as the case may be, as the number of children with disabilities aged three to five, inclusive, who received special education and related services as determined under section 1411(a)(3) of this title in such local educational agency or intermediate educational unit bears to the aggregate number of children with disabilities aged three to five, inclusive, who received special education and related services in all local educational agencies and intermediate educational units in the State entitled to funds under this section, and

(B) to the extent funds are available under subsection (a)(2)(A)(ii)(II) of this section, an amount which bears the same ratio to the amount of such funds of this section as the estimated number of additional children with disabilities aged three to five, inclusive, who will be receiving special education and related services in such local educational agency or intermediate educational unit bears to the aggregate number of such children in all local educational agencies and intermediate educational units in the State entitled to funds under this section.

(d) Insufficiency of appropriated amounts; reduction of maximum amounts receivable by States

If the sums appropriated under subsection (e) of this section for any fiscal year for making payments to States under subsection (a)(1) of this section or (b)(1) are not sufficient to pay in full the maximum amounts which all States may receive under such subsection for such fiscal year, the maximum amounts which all States may receive under such subsection for such fiscal year shall be ratably reduced by first ratably reducing amounts computed under the excess appropriation provision of subsection (a)(2)(A)(ii)(II) of this section. If additional funds become available for making such payments for any fiscal year during which the preceding sentence is applicable, the reduced maximum amounts shall be increased on the same basis as they were reduced.

(e) Authorization of appropriations

For grants under subsections (a)(1) of this section and (b)(1) of this section there are authorized to be appropriated such sums as may be necessary.

(f) Notwithstanding any other provision of law, unless enacted in express limitation of this subsection, amounts appropriated under this section for fiscal years 1987 and 1988 and received by a State whose allotment for the succeeding fiscal year is adjusted downwards under subsection (a)(2)(E) shall remain available for obligation by such State, and by local educational agencies and intermediate educational units in such State, during the 2 fiscal years succeeding the fiscal year for which such amounts were appropriated.

§ 1420. Payments

(a) Payments to States; distribution by States to local educational agencies and intermediate educational units

The Secretary shall make payments to each State in amounts which the State educational agency of such State is eligible to receive under this subchapter. Any State educational agency receiving payments under this subsection shall distribute payments to the local educational agencies and intermediate educational units of such State in amounts which such agencies and units are eligible to receive under this subchapter after the State educational agency has approved applications of such agencies or units for payments in accordance with section 1414(b) of this title.

(b) Advances, reimbursements, and installments

Payments under this subchapter may be made in advance or by way of reimbursement and in such installments as the Secretary may determine necessary.

SUBCHAPTER III—CENTERS AND SERVICES TO MEET SPECIAL NEEDS OF INDIVIDUALS WITH DISABILITIES

§ 1421. Regional resource centers

(a) Establishment; functions

The Secretary may make grants to, or enter into contracts or cooperative agreements with, institutions of higher education, public agencies, private nonprofit organizations, State educational agencies, or combinations of such agencies or institutions (which combinations may include one or more local educational agencies) within particular regions of the United States, to pay all or part of the cost of the establishment and operation of regional resource centers that focus on special education and related services and early intervention services. Each regional resource center shall provide consultation, technical assistance, and training, as requested, to State educational agencies and through such State educational agencies to local educational agencies and to other appropriate public agencies providing special education and related services and early intervention services. The services provided by a regional resource center shall be consistent with the priority needs identified by the States served by the center and the findings of the Secretary in monitoring reports prepared by the Secretary under section 1417 of this title. Each regional resource center shall—

(1) assist in identifying and solving persistent problems in providing quality special education and related services for children and youth with disabilities and early intervention services to infants and toddlers with disabilities and their families,

(2) assist in developing, identifying, and replicating successful programs and practices which will improve special education and related services to children and youth with disabilities and their families and early intervention services to infants and toddlers with disabilities and their families,

(3) gather and disseminate information to all State educational agencies within the region and coordinate activities with other centers assisted under this subsection and other relevant programs and projects conducted under parts C through G and by the Department of Education.

(4) assist in the improvement of information dissemination to and training activities for professionals and parents of infants, toddlers, children and youth with disabilities, and

(5) provide information to and training for agencies, institutions, and organizations, regarding techniques and approaches for submitting applications for grants, contracts, and cooperative agreements under this subchapter and subchapters IV through VII.

(b) Considerations governing approval of application

In determining whether to approve an application for a project under subsection (a) of this section, the Secretary shall utilize criteria for setting criteria that are consistent with the needs identified by States within the region served by such center, consistent with requirements established by the

Secretary under subsection (f), and, to the extent appropriate, consistent with requirements under section 610, and shall consider the need for such a center in the region to be served by the applicant and the capability of the applicant to fulfill the responsibilities under subsection (a) of this section.

(c) Annual report; summary of information

Each regional resource center shall report a summary of materials produced or developed and the summaries reported shall be included in the annual report to Congress required under section 1418 of this title.

(d) Coordination technical assistance center; establishment; duties

The Secretary may establish one coordinating technical assistance center focusing on national priorities established by the Secretary to assist the regional resource centers in the delivery of technical assistance, consistent with such national priorities. Such coordinating technical assistance center is authorized to—

(1) provide information to, and training for, agencies, institutions, and organizations, regarding techniques and approaches for submitting applications for grants, contracts, and cooperative agreements under this part and parts D through G, and shall make such information available to the regional resource centers on request;

(2) give priority to providing technical assistance concerning the education of children with disabilities from minority backgrounds;

(3) exchange information with, and, where appropriate, cooperate with, other centers addressing the needs of children with disabilities from minority backgrounds; and

(4) provide assistance to State educational agencies, through the regional resource centers, for the training of hearing officers.

(e) Amounts available for coordination technical assistance center

Before using funds made available in any fiscal year to carry out this section for purposes of subsection (d) of this section, not less than the amount made available in the previous fiscal year for regional resource centers under subsection (a) shall be made available for such centers of this section and in no case shall more than $500,000 be made available for the center under subsection (d) of this section.

(f) Guidelines for resource centers

(1) The Secretary shall develop guidelines and criteria for the operation of Regional and Federal Resource Centers. In developing such criteria and guidelines, the Secretary shall establish a panel representing the Office of Special Education Programs staff, State special education directors, representatives of disability advocates, and, when appropriate, consult with the regional resource center directors.

(2) Such guidelines and criteria shall include—

(A) a description of how the Federal and Regional Resource Centers Program will be administered by the Secretary;

(B) a description of the geographic region each Center is expected to serve;

(C) a description of the role of a Center in terms of expected leadership and dissemination efforts;

(D) a description of expected relationships with State agencies, research and demonstration centers, and with other entities deemed necessary;

(E) a description of how a Center will be evaluated; and

(F) other guidelines and criteria deemed necessary.

(3) The Secretary shall publish in the Federal Register by July 1, 1991, for review and comment, proposed and (then following such review and comment) final guidelines developed by the panel.

§ 1422. Services for deaf-blind children and youth

(a) Grant and contract authority; types and scope of programs; governing considerations

(1) The Secretary is authorized to make grants to, or to enter into cooperative agreements or contracts with, public or nonprofit private agencies, institutions, or organizations to assist State educational agencies to local agencies, and designated lead agencies under part H—

(A) assure deaf-blind infants, toddlers, children and youth provision of special education, early intervention, and related services as well as vocational and transitional services; and

(B) make available to deaf-blind youth (who are in the process of transitioning into adult services) programs, services, and supports to facilitate such transition, including assistance related to independent living and competitive employment.

(2) For purposes of this ection, the term "deaf-blind", with respect to children and youth, means having auditory and visual impairments, the combination of which creates such severe communication and other developmental and learning needs that they cannot be appropriately educated in special education programs solely for children and youth with hearing impairments, visual impairments, or severe disabilities, without supplementary assistance to address their educational needs due to these dual, concurrent disabilities.

(3)(A) A grant, cooperative agreement, or contract may be made under paragraph (1)(A) only for programs providing—

(i) technical assistance to agencies, institutions, or organizations providing educational or early intervention services to deaf-blind infants, toddlers, children, or youth;

(ii) preservice or inservice training to paraprofessionals, professionals, or related services personnel preparing to serve, or serving, deaf-blind infants, toddlers, children, or youth;

(iii) replication of successful innovative approaches to providing educational, early intervention, or related services to deaf-blind infants, toddlers, children, and youth;

(iv) pilot projects that are designed to—

(I) expand local educational agency capabilities by providing services to deaf-blind children and youth that supplement services already provided to children and youth through State and local resources; and

(II) encourage eventual assumption of funding responsibility by State and local authorities;

(v) the development, improvement, or demonstration of new or existing methods, approaches, or techniques that contribute to the adjustment and education of deaf-blind infants, toddlers, children, and youth; or

(vi) facilitation of parental involvement in the education of their deaf-blind infants, toddlers, children, and youth.

(B) The programs described in subparagraph (A) may include—

(i) the diagnosis and educational evaluation of infants, toddlers, children, and youth who are likely to be diagnosed as deaf-blind;

(ii) programs of adjustment, education, and orientation for deaf-blind infants, toddlers, children, and youth; and

(iii) consultative, counseling, and training services for the families of deaf-blind infants, toddlers, children, and youth.

(4) A grant, cooperative agreement, or contract pursuant to paragraph (1)(B) may be made only for programs providing (A) technical assistance to agencies, institutions, and organizations that are preparing deaf-blind adolescents for adult placements, or that are preparing to receive deaf-blind young adults into adult living and work environments, or that serve, or propose to serve, deaf-blind individuals; (B) training or inservice training to paraprofessionals or professionals serving, or preparing to serve, such individuals; and (C) assistance in the development or replication of successful innovative approaches to providing supervised rehabilitative, semisupervised, or independent living programs.

(5) In carrying out this subsection, the Secretary is authorized to enter into a number of grants or cooperative agreements to establish and support single and multi-State centers for the provision of technical assistance and pilot supplementary services, for the purposes of program development and expansion, for children and youth with deaf-blindness and their families.

(b) Contract authority for regional programs of technical assistance

The Secretary is also authorized to enter into a limited number of cooperative agreements or contracts to establish and support regional programs for the provision of technical assistance in the education of deaf-blind children and youth.

(c) Annual report to Secretary; examination of numbers and services and revision of numbers; annual report to Congress: summary of data

(1) Programs supported under this section shall report annually to the Secretary on (A) the numbers of deaf-blind children and youth served by age, severity, sex, and nature of deaf-blindness; (B) the number of paraprofessionals, professionals, and family members directly served by each activity; and (C) the types of services provided and the setting in which the services are provided.

(2) The Secretary shall examine the number of deaf-blind children and youth (A) reported under subparagraph (c)(1)(A) and by the States; (B) served by the programs under subchapter II of this chapter and subpart 2 of

part D of chapter 1 of title I of the Elementary and Secondary Education Act of 1965 [20 U.S.C. 3801 et seq.]); (C) the Deaf-Blind Registry of each State. The Secretary shall revise the count of deaf-blind children and youth to reflect the most accurate count and (D) student outcomes, where appropriate.

(3) The Secretary shall summarize these data for submission in the annual report required under section 1418 of this title.

(d) Dissemination of materials and information concerning working practices

The Secretary shall make a grant, or enter into a contract or cooperative agreement, for a national clearinghouse for children and youth with deaf-blindness—

(1) to identify, coordinate, and disseminate information on deaf-blindness, emphasizing information concerning effective practices in working with deaf-blind infants, toddlers, children, and youth;

(2) to interact with educators, professional groups, and parents to identify areas for programming, materials developemnt, training, and expansion of specific services;

(3) to maintain a computerized data base on local, regional and national resources; and

(4) to respond to information requests from professionals, parents, and members of the community.

(e) Extended school year demonstration programs

In carrying out this section, the Secretary shall take into consideration the availability and quality of existing services for deaf-blind infants, toddlers, children, and youth in the country, and to the extent practicable, ensure that all parts of the country have an opportunity to receive assistance under this section.

(f) Grants for purposes under other parts of this chapter

The Secretary may make grants to, or enter into contracts or cooperative agreements with organizations or public or nonprofit private agencies, as determined by the secretary to be appropriate, to address the needs of children and youth with deaf-blindness, for—

(1) research to identify and meet the full range of special needs of such children and youth; and

(2) the development and demonstration of new, or improvements in existing methods, approaches, or techniques that would contribute to the adjustment and education of children and youth with deaf-blindness.

§ 1423. Experimental, demonstration, and outreach preschool and intervention programs for children with disabilities

(a) Contracts, grants and cooperative agreements; purpose; community coordination programs; national dispersion in urban and rural areas; Federal share; non-Federal contributions; arrangements with Indian tribes

(1) The Secretary may arrange by contract, grant, or cooperative agreement with appropriate public and private nonprofit organizations, for the development and operation of experimental, demonstration, and outreach preschool and early intervention programs for children with disabilities which the Secretary determines show promise of promoting a comprehensive and strengthened approach to the special needs of such children. Such programs shall include activities and services designed to—

(A) facilitate the intellectual, emotional, physical, mental, social, speech or other communication mode and, language development, and self-help skills of such children,

(B) provide family education and include a parent or their representative of such child, as well as encourage the participation of the parents of such children in the development and operation of any such program,

(C) acquaint the community to be served by any such program with the special needs and potentialities of such children,

(D) offer training about exemplary models and practices including interdisciplinary models and practices, to State and local personnel who provide services to children with disabilities from birth through age 8 and to the parents of such children,

(E) support the adoption of exemplary models and practices in States and local communities, including the involvement of adult role models with disabilities at all levels of the program,

(F) facilitate and improve the early identification of infants and toddlers with disabilities or those infants and toddlers at risk of having developmental disabilities,

(G) facilitate the transition of infants with disabilities or infants at risk of having developmental delays, from medical care to early intervention services, and the transition from early intervention services to preschool special education or regular education services (especially where the lead agency for early intervention programs under part H is not the State educational agency),

(H) promote the use of assistive technology devices and assistive technology services, where appropriate, to enhance the development of infants and toddlers with disabilities, and

(I) increase the understanding of, and address, the early intervention and preschool needs of children exposed prenatally to maternal substance abuse.

(2) Programs authorized by paragraph (1) shall be coordinated with similar programs in the schools operated or supported by State or local educational agencies of the community to be served and with similar programs operated by other public agencies in such community.

(3) As much as is feasible, programs assisted under paragraph (1) shall be geographically dispersed throughout the Nation in urban as well as rural areas.

(4)(A) Except as provided in subparagraph (B), no arrangement under paragraph (1) shall provide for the payment of more than 90 percent of the total annual costs of development, operation, and evaluation of any program. Non-Federal contributions may be in cash or in kind, fairly evaluated, including plant, equipment, and services.

(B) The Secretary may waive the requirement of subparagraph (A) in the case of an arrangement entered into under paragraph (1) with governing bodies of Indian tribes located on Federal or State reservations and with consortia of such bodies.

(b) Technical assistance development programs

The Secretary shall arrange by contract, grant, or cooperative agreement with appropriate public agencies and private nonprofit organizations for the establishment of a technical assistance development system to assist entities operating experimental, demonstration, and outreach programs and to assist State agencies to expand and improve services provided to children with disabilities. This technical assistance development system shall provide assistance to parents of and advocates for infants, toddlers, and children with disabilities, as well as direct service and administrative personnel involved with such children. Information from the system should be aggressively disseminated through established information networks and other mechanisms to ensure both an impact and benefit at the community level. The Secretary shall ensure that the technical assistance provided under this subsection includes assistance to part H State agencies on procedures for use by primary referred sources in referring a child to the appropriate agency with the system for evaluation, assessment, or service.

(c) Early childhood research institutes

The Secretary shall arrange by contract, grant, or cooperative agreement with appropriate public agencies and private nonprofit organizations for the establishment of early childhood research institutes to carry on sustained research to generate and disseminate new information on preschool and early intervention for children with disabilities and their families. Substitutes shall disseminate this information in the manner proscribed in section 610(g).

(d) Grants or contracts with organizations to identify needs of children with disabilities and for training of personnel

The Secretary may make grants to, or enter into contracts or cooperative agreements under this section with, such organizations or institutions, as are determined by the Secretary to be appropriate, for research to identify and meet the full range of special needs of children with disabilities and for training of personnel for programs specifically designed for children with disabilities including programs to integrate children with disabilities into regular preschool programs.

(e) Notice in Federal Register of intent to accept applications for grants, contracts, etc.

At least one year before the termination of a grant, contract, or cooperative agreement made or entered into under subsections (b) and (c) of this section, the Secretary shall publish in the Federal Register a notice of intent to accept applications for such a grant, contract, or cooperative agreement contingent on the appropriation of sufficient funds by Congress.

(f) "Children with disabilities" defined

For purposes of this section the term "children with disabilities" includes children from birth through eight years of age including infants and toddlers with disabilities.

(g) Institutions and organizations whom are contracted with

The Secretary may make grants to, or enter into contracts or cooperative agreements with, institutions of higher education and nonprofit private organizations to synthesize the knowledge developed under this section and organize, integrate, and present such knowledge so it can be incorporated and imparted to parents, professionals, and others providing or preparing to provide preschool and early intervention services and to persons designing preschool and early intervention programs.

§ 1424. Programs for children with severe disabilities

(a) Grant and contract authority

The Secretary may make grants to, or enter into contracts or cooperative agreements with, appropriate public agencies and nonprofit organizations to address the special education, related services, early intervention, and integration needs of infants, toddlers, children, and youth with severe disabilities through—

(1) research to identify and meet the full range of special education, related services, and early intervention needs including transportation to and from school of such children and youth with disabilities,

(2) the development or demonstration of new, or improvements in existing, methods, approaches, or techniques which would contribute to the adjustment and education of such children and youth with disabilities,

(3) training of special and regular education, related services, and early intervention personnel for programs specifically designed for such infants, toddlers, children and youth, including training of regular teachers, instructors, and administrators in strategies (the goal of which is to serve infants, toddlers, children, and youth with disabilities) that include integrated settings for educating such children along side their nondisabled peers,

(4) dissemination of materials and information about practices found effective in working with such children and youth by utilizing existing networks as prescribed in section 610(g), and

(5) statewide projects, in conjunction with the State's plan under part B, to improve the quality of special education and related services for children and youth with severe disabilities, and to change the delivery of those services from segregated to integrated environments.

(b) Contract authority to institutions and organizations

The Secretary is authorized to make grants to, or enter into contracts or cooperative agreements with, public or private nonprofit private agencies, institutions, or organizations for the development and operation of extended school year demonstration programs for infants, toddlers, children, and youth with severe disabilities.

(c) Coordination of activities with similar activities under other parts of this chapter

In making grants and entering into contracts and cooperative agreements under subsection (a) of this section, the Secretary shall ensure that the activities funded under such grants, contracts, or cooperative agreements will be coordinated with similar activities funded from grants and contracts under other sections of this chapter.

(d) National geographic dispersion of programs in urban and rural areas

To the extent feasible, programs authorized by subsection (a) of this section shall be geographically dispersed throughout the Nation in urban and rural areas.

(e) Priority for programs that mainstream

In awarding such grants and contracts under this section, the Secretary shall include a priority on programs that increase the likelihood that these children and youth will be educated with their nondisabled peers.

§ 1424a. Postsecondary and other specially designed model programs

(a) Grants and contract authority; development, operation, and dissemination of postsecondary, vocational, technical, continuing, or adult education programs; priority of programs; notice in Federal Register of intent to accept application for grant or contract; national geographic dispersion in urban and rural areas; availability of sums for regional centers

(1) The Secretary may make grants to, or enter into contracts with, State educational agencies, institutions of higher education, junior and community colleges, vocational and technical institutions, and other appropriate non-profit educational agencies for the development, operation, and dissemination of specially designed model programs of postsecondary, vocational, technical, continuing, or adult education for individuals with a disability. Such model programs may include joint projects that coordinate with special education and transition services.

(2) In making grants or contracts on a competitive basis under paragraph (1), the Secretary shall give priority consideration to 4 regional centers for the deaf and to model programs for individuals with disabling conditions other than deafness—

(A) for developing and adapting programs of postsecondary, vocational, technical, continuing, or adult education to meet the special needs of handicapped individuals,

(B) for programs that coordinate, facilitate, and encourage education of individuals with a disability with their nondisabled peers, and

(C) for outreach activities that include the provision of technical assistance to strengthen efforts in the development, operation, and design of model programs that are adapted to the special needs of individuals with disabilities.

(3) Persons operating programs for disabled persons under a grant or contract under paragraph (1) must coordinate their efforts with and disseminate information about their activities to the clearinghouse on postsecondary programs established under section 1433(b) of this title.

(4) At least one year before the termination of a grant or contract with any of the 4 regional centers for the deaf, the Secretary shall publish in the Federal Register a notice of intent to accept applications for such grant or contract, contingent on the appropriation of sufficient funds by Congress.

(5) To the extent feasible, programs authorized by paragraph (1) shall be geographically dispersed throughout the Nation in urban and rural areas.

(6) Of the sums made available for programs under paragraph (1), not less than $4,000,000 shall first be available for the 4 regional centers for the deaf.

(b) "Individuals with disabilities" defined

For purposes of subsection (a), the term "individuals with disabilities" means individuals—

(1) with mental retardation, hearing impairments including deafness, speech or language impairments, visual impairments including blindness, serious emotional disturbance, orthopedic impairments, autism, traumatic brain injury, other health impairments, or specific learning disabilities; and

(2) who, by reason thereof, need special education and related services.

§ 1425. Secondary education and transitional services for youth with a disability

(a) Grant and contract authority; statement of purposes; national geographic dispersion in urban and rural areas

The Secretary may make grants to, or enter into contracts with, institutions of higher education, State educational agencies, local educational agencies, or other appropriate public and private nonprofit institutions or agencies (including the State job training coordinating councils and service delivery area administrative entities established under the Job Training Partnership Act [29 U.S.C.A. § 1501 et seq.]) to—

(1) strengthen and coordinate special education and related services for youth with a disability currently in school or who recently left school to assist them in the transition to postsecondary education, vocational

training, competitive employment (including supported employment), continuing education, independent and community living, or adult services,

(2) stimulate the improvement and development of programs for secondary special education, and

(3) stimulate the improvement of the vocational and life skills of handicapped students to enable them to be better prepared for transition to adult life and services.

To the extent feasible, such programs shall be geographically dispersed throughout the Nation in urban and rural areas.

(b) Description of specific projects

Projects assisted under subsection (a) of this section may include—

(1) developing strategies and techniques for transition to independent living, vocational training, vocational rehabilitation, postsecondary education, and competitive employment (including supported employment) for youth with a disability,

(2) establishing demonstration models for services, programs, and individualized education programs, which emphasize vocational training, independent living, transitional services, and placement for youth with a disability,

(3) conducting demographic studies which provide information on the numbers, age levels, types of disabling conditions, and services required for some youth with disabilities remain to complete school programs while others drop out, youth with a disability in need of transitional programs,

(4) specially designed vocational programs to increase the potential for competitive employment for youth with a disability,

(5) research and development projects for exemplary service delivery models and the replication and dissemination of successful models,

(6) initiating cooperative models among educational agencies and adult service agencies, including vocational rehabilitation, mental health, mental retardation, and public employment, and employers, which facilitate the planning and developing of transitional services for youth with a disability to postsecondary education, vocational training, employment, continuing education, and adult services,

(7) developing appropriate procedures for evaluating vocational training, placement, and transitional services for youth with a disability,

(8) conducting studies whch provide information on the numbers, age levels, types of disabling conditions and reasons why youth with a disability drop out of school,

(9) developing curriculum and instructional techniques in special education and related services that will improve disabled students' acquisition of the skills necessary for transition to adult life and services,

(10) specially designed or adapted physical education and therapeutic recreation programs to facilitate the full participation of youths with disabilities in community programs, and

(11) developing and disseminating exemplary programs and practices that meet the unique needs of students who utilize assistive technology devices and assistive technology services as such students make the transi-

tion to postsecondary education, vocational training, competitive employment (including supported employment), and continuing education or
adult services.

(c) Coordination of non-educational-agency applicant with State educational agency

For purposes of paragraphs (1) and (2) of subsection (b) of this section,
if an applicant is not an educational agency, such applicant shall coordinate
its activities with the State educational agency.

(d) Applications for assistance; contents

Applications for assistance under subsection (a) of this section other
than for the purpose of conducting studies or evaluations shall—
(1) describe the procedures to be used for disseminating relevant findings and data to regional resource centers, clearinghouses, and other interested persons, agencies, or organizations,
(2) describe the procedures that will be used for coordinating services
among agencies for which youth with a disability are or will be eligible,
and
(3) provide for the direct participation of handicapped students and
the parents of disabled students in the planning, development, and implementation of such projects.

(e) Application for one-time grant; contents

(1) The Secretary shall make one-time, 5-year grants, on a competitive basis, to States in which the State vocational rehabilitation agency and
State educational agency submit a joint application to develop, implement, and improve systems to provide transition services for youth with
disabilities from age 14 through the age they exit school.
(2) In the case of a State whose vocational rehabilitation agency does
not participate regarding a joint application described in paragraph (1),
the Secretary may make a grant under such paragraph to the State if a
joint application for the grant is submitted by the State educational agency
and one other State agency that provides transition services to individuals
who are leaving programs under this Act.
(3) States that receive grants shall use grant funds to:
(A) Increase the availability, access, and quality of transition assistance through the development and improvement of policies, procedures, systems, and other mechanisms for youth with disabilities and
their families as such youth prepare for and enter adult life.
(B) Improve the ability of professionals, parents, and advocates to
work with such youth in ways that promote the understanding of and
the capability to successfully make the transition from "student" to
"adult".
(C) Improve working relationships among education personnel,
both within LEAs and in postsecondary training programs, relevant
State agencies, the private sector (especially employers), rehabilitation
personnel, local and State employment agencies, local Private Industry

Councils (PICS) authorized by the Job Training Partnership Act (JTPA), and families of students with disabilities and their advocates to identify and achieve consensus on the general nature and specific application of transition services to meet the needs of youth with disabilities.

(D) Create an incentive for accessing and using the expertise and resources of programs, projects, and activities related to transition funded through this section and with other sources.

(4)(A) In order to receive funding under this subsection, a State vocational rehabilitation agency and State educational agency shall describe in their application how they will use the first year, if necessary, to plan how to implement transition services, the second through fourth years to develop and implement transition services, and the fifth year to evaluate transition services. The application shall describe how the grant funds will be used during the planning period and phased out during the evaluation period to ensure the continuation of transition services. Such applications shall also include—

(i) a description of the current availability, access, and quality of transition services for eligible youth and a description of how, over 5 years, the State will improve and expand the availability, access, and quality of transition services for youth with disabilities and their families as such youth prepare for and enter adult life;

(ii) a description of how the State will improve and increase the ability of professionals, parents, and advocates to work with such youth in ways that promote the understanding of and the capability to successfully make the transition from "student" to "adult";

(iii) a description of how the State will improve and increase working relationships among education personnel, both within LEAs and in postsecondary training programs, relevant State agencies, the private sector (especially employers), rehabilitation personnel, local and State employment agencies, local Private Industry Councils (PICS) authorized by the JTPA, and families of students with disabilities and their advocates to identify and achieve consensus on the general nature and specific application of transition services to meet the needs of youth with disabilities; and

(iv) a description of how the State will use grant funds as an incentive for accessing and using the expertise and resources of programs, projects, and activities related to transition funded through this section and with other sources.

(B) The Secretary shall give preference to those applications that, in addition to clearly addressing the requirements under subparagraph (A), describe how the State will—

(i) target resources to school settings, such as providing access to rehabilitation counselors for students with disabilities who are in school settings;

(ii) target a substantial amount of grant funds, received under this subsection, to case management, program evaluation and documentation of, and dissemination of information about transition services;

(iii) provide incentives for interagency and private sector resource pooling and otherwise investing in transition services especially in the form of cooperative agreements, particularly with PICS authorized by the JTPA and local branches of State employment agencies;

(iv) provide for early, ongoing information and training for those involved with or who could be involved with transition services—professionals, parents, youth with disabilities, including self-advocacy training for such youth, and advocates for such youth as well as PICS authorized by the JTPA and local branches of State employment agencies;

(v) provide for the early and direct involvement of all relevant parties, including PICS authorized by the JTPA and local branches of State employment agencies, in operating and planning improvements in transition services, and the early and direct involvement of all relevant parties in planning and implementing transition services for individual youth;

(vi) provide access to training for eligible youth that matches labor market needs in their communities;

(vii) integrate transition services with relevant opportunities in communities, including those sponsored by PICS authorized by the JTPA and local employment agencies;

(viii) use a transition services evaluation plan that is outcome oriented and that focuses on individual youth-focused benefits; and

(ix) ensure that, when appropriate and no later than age 22, eligible youth who participate in transition services under this program would be served as appropriate in the State section 110 and/or title VI, part C program authorized under the Rehabilitation Act of 1973.

(f) Development or demonstration of new or improvement in methods, approaches, or techniques

(1) The Secretary is authorized to make grants to, or to enter into contracts or cooperative agreements with, such organizations or institutions as are determined by the Secretary to be appropriate for the development or demonstration of new or improvements in existing methods, approaches, or techniques which will contribute to the adjustment and education of handicapped children and youth and the dissemination of materials and information concerning practices found effective in working with such children and youth.

(2) The Secretary shall fund one or more demonstration models designed to establish appropriate methods of providing, or continuing to provide, assistive technology devices and services to secondary school students as they make the transition to vocational rehabilitation, employment, postsecondary education, or adult services. Such demonstration models shall include, as appropriate—

(A) cooperative agreements with the Rehabilitation Services Administration and/or State vocational rehabilitation agencies that ensure continuity of funding for assistive technology devices and services to such students; and

(B) methods for dissemination of exemplary practices that can be adapted or adopted by transitional programs for secondary school students with disabilities.; and

(3)(A) The Secretary shall award one, five-year cooperative agreement through a separate competition to an institution of higher education, or nonprofit public or private organization. The purpose of this agreement will be to evaluate and document the approaches and outcomes of the projects funded under subsection (e). The results of this agreement shall be disseminated through the appropriate clearinghouses, networks, and through direct communication with Federal, State, and local agencies.

(B) The evaluation carried out pursuant to subparagraph (A) of transition services under subsection (e) shall include an evaluation of—

(i) the outcomes of the transition services provided under such subsection, including the effect of the services regarding postsecondary education, job training, employment, and other appropriate matters;

(ii) the impact of including in the individualized education program a statement of needed transition services (as required under section 602(a)(20)(D));

(iii) the extent to which, in the provision of the transition services, agencies are cooperating effectively, including evaluation of the extent of coordination of the staff of the agencies, of procedures regarding confidentiality, assessment of needs, and procedures regarding confidentiality, assessment of needs, and referrals, and coordination regarding data bases and training; referrals, and coordination regarding data bases and training;

(iv) the extent to which obstacles exist regarding cooperation and coordination among agencies in the provision of the transition services, and the extent to which Federal law creates disincentives to such cooperation and coordination; and

(v) the extent to which the transition services have been provided in a cost-effective manner.

(C) The evaluation carried out pursuant to subparagraph (A) shall include recommendations on the manner in which the program under subsection (e) can be improved.

(D) In the annual report required under section 618(g), the secretary shall include a report of the activities and results associated with the agreement under subparagraph (A).

(g) Coordination of educational programs with vocational rehabilitation projects

The Secretary, as appropriate, shall coordinate programs described under subsection (a) of this section with projects developed under section 777a of Title 29, the Job Training Partnership Act (JTPA), and the Carl D. Perkins Vocational and Applied Technology Education Act.

§ 1426. Programs for children and youth with serious emotional disturbance

(a) Criteria for grants regarding serious emotional disturbances

The Secretary is authorized to make grants to, or enter into contracts or cooperative agreements with, institutions of higher education, State and local educational agencies, and other appropriate public and private nonprofit institutions or agencies to establish projects for the purpose of improving special education and related services to children and youth with serious emotional disturbance. Such projects may include—

(1) studies regarding the present state of special education and related services to such children and youth and their families, including information and data to enable assessment of the status of such services over time;

(2) developing methodologies and curricula designed to improve special education and related serivces for these children and youth;

(3) developing and demonstrating strategies and approaches to reduce the use of out-of-community residential programs and the increased use of school district-based programs (which may include day treatment programs, after-school programs, and summer programs);

(4) developing the knowledge, skills, and strategies for effective collaboration among special education, regular education, related services, and other professionals and agencies; or

(5) developing and demonstrating innovative approaches to assist and to prevent children with emotional and behavioral problems from developing serious emotional disturbances that require the provision of special education and related services.

(b) Grants for demonstration projects

(1) The Secretary is authorized to make grants, on a competitive basis, to local educational agencies in collaboration with mental health entities to provide services for children and youth with serious emotional disturbance. Such demonstration projects shall—

(A) increase the availability, access, and quality of community services for such children and youth and their families and community mental health and other relevant personnel, families of such children and youth, and their advocates;

(B) improve working relationships among education, school and community mental health and other relevant personnel, families of such children and youth, and their advocates;

(C) target resources to school settings, such as providing access to school and/or community mental health professionals and other community resources for students with serious emotional disturbance who are in community school settings; and

(D) take into account the needs of minority children and youth in all phases of project activity.

(2) Funds received under this subsection may also be used to facilitate interagency and private sector resource pooling to improve services for such children and youth and to provide information and training for those involved with, or who could be involved with, such children and youth.

(c) Application for grants; contents

Each project assisted under this section shall—
(1) apply existing research outcomes from multi-disciplinary fields;
(2) use a grant evaluation plan that is outcome-oriented and that focuses on the benefits to individual children and youth;
(3) report on the effectiveness of such project; and
(4) disseminate the findings of such project, where appropriate, in accordance with section 610(g).

§ 1427. Authorization of appropriations

(a) There are authorized to be appropriated to carry out section 1421 $8,525,000 for fiscal year 1991, $9,300,000 for fiscal year 1992, $10,140,000 for fiscal year 1993, and $11,052,000 for fiscal year 1994.

(b) There are authorized to be appropriated to carry out section 1422 $21,900,000 for fiscal year 1991, $24,100,000 for fiscal year 1992, $26,500,000 for fiscal year 1993, and $29,200,000 for fiscal year 1994.

(c) There are authorized to be appropriated to carry out section 1423 $31,400,000 for fiscal year 1991, $34,235,000 for fiscal year 1992, $37,325,000 for fiscal year 1993, and $40,705,000 for fiscal year 1994.

(d) There are authorized to be appropriated to carry out section 1424 $9,500,000 for fiscal year 1991, $10,500,000 for fiscal year 1992, $11,600,000 for fiscal year 1993, and $12,700,000 for fiscal year 1994.

(e) There are authorized to be appropriated to carry out section 1425 $9,470,000 for fiscal year 1991, $10,230,000 for fiscal year 1992, $11,050,000 for fiscal year 1993, and $11,930,000 for fiscal year 1994.

(f) There are authorized to be appropriated to carry out section 1426 (except subsection (e)) $9,800,000 for fiscal year 1991, $10,800,000 for fiscal year 1992, $11,900,000 for fiscal year 1993, and $13,050,000 for fiscal year 1994.

(g) There are authorized to be appropriated to carry out section 1426(e) $27,500,000 for fiscal year 1991, $30,250,000 for fiscal year 1992, $33,275,000 for fiscal year 1993, and $36,602,000 for fiscal year 1994.

(h) There are authorized to be appropriated to carry out section 1427 $6,500,000 for fiscal year 1991, $8,000,000 for fiscal year 1992, $9,500,000 for fiscal year 1993, and $11,500,000 for fiscal year 1994.

SUBCHAPTER IV—TRAINING PERSONNEL FOR THE EDUCATION OF INDIVIDUALS WITH DISABILITIES

§ 1431. Grants for personnel training

(a) Careers in special education; personnel standards; training-study and fellowships-traineeships costs; contract authority for areas of personnel shortages

(1) The Secretary may make grants, which may include scholarships with necessary stipends and allowances, to institutions of higher education (including university affiliated programs and satellite centers participating in programs under part D of the Developmental Disabilities Assistance and Bill of Rights Act) and other appropriate nonprofit agencies to assist them in training personnel for careers in special education related services, and early intervention, including—

(A) special education teaching, including speech-language pathology and audiology, and adaptive physical education and instructional and assistive technology services,

(B) related services to children and youth with disabilities in educational settings, and other settings,

(C) special education and other careers in preschool and early intervention services for infants and toddlers with disabilities,

(D) special education leadership, including supervision and administration (at the advanced graduate, doctoral, and post-doctoral levels), special education research, and special education personnel preparation (at the doctoral and post-doctoral levels), and

(E) training of special education personnel and other personnel providing special services and pre-school and early intervention services for children with disabilities.

(2)(A) The Secretary shall base the award of grants under paragraph (1) on information relating to the present and projected need for special education, related services, early intervention, and other personnel to be trained based on identified State, regional, or national shortages, including the need for personnel in the provision of special education to children of limited English proficiency, and the capacity of the institution or agency to train qualified personnel, and other information considered appropriate by the Secretary.

(B) The Secretary shall ensure that grants are only made under paragraph (1) to applicant agencies and institutions that meet State and professionally recognized standards for the preparation of special education and related services personnel unless the grant is for the purpose of assisting the applicant agency of institution to meet such standards, and that include in their applications a detailed description of strategies that will be utilized to recruit and train members of minority groups and persons with disabilities.

(3) Grants under paragraph (1) may be used by institutions to assist in covering the cost of courses of training or study for such personnel and for establishing and maintaining fellowships or traineeships with such stipends and allowances as may be determined by the Secretary. Such institutions shall give priority consideration in the selection of qualified recipients of fellow-

ships and traineeships to individuals from disadvantaged backgrounds, including minorities and individuals with disabilities who are underrepresented in the teaching profession or in the specializations in which they are being trained.

(4) The Secretary in carrying out paragraph (1) may reserve a sum not to exceed 5 percent of the amount available for paragraph (1) in each fiscal year for contracts to prepare personnel in areas where shortages exist when a response to that need has not been adequately addressed by the grant process.

(5) In making grants under subsection (a)(1), the Secretary may determine that a portion of training supported through such grants shall be conducted on an interdisciplinary basis, and shall be designed to assist special educators in properly coordinating service provision with related services personnel. To the extent feasible, training programs funded under subsection (a)(1)(B) and (a)(1)(E) shall require practica to demonstrate the delivery of related services in an array of regular and special education and community settings.

(6) Nothing in this subsection shall be construed to prevent regular education or special education personnel from benefiting or participating in training activities conducted under this subsection on a preservice or inservice basis.

(7) The Secretary, in carrying out paragraph (1), shall make grants to Historically Black Colleges and Universities, and other institutions of higher education whose minority student enrollment is at least 25 percent.

(b) Special projects for preservice training, regular educators, and inservice training of special education personnel.

The Secretary may make grants to institutions of higher education, State agencies, and other appropriate nonprofit agencies and organizations to develop and demonstrate effective ways for preservice training programs to prepare regular educators to work with children and youth with disabilities and their families; for training teachers to work in community and school settings with school students with disabilities and their families; for inservice and preservice training of personnel to work with infants, toddlers, children, and youth with disabilities and their families; for inservice and preservice training of personnel to work with minority infants, toddlers, children, and youth with disabilities and their families; for preservice and inservice training of special education and related services personnel in the use of assistive and instructional technology to benefit infants, toddlers, children, and youth with disabilities; and for the recruitment and retention of special education, related services, and early intervention personnel. Both preservice and inservice training shall include a component that addresses the coordination among all service providers, including regular educators.

(c) Parent training and information programs

(1) The Secretary may make grants through a separate competition to private nonprofit organizations for the purpose of providing training and information to parents of infants, toddlers, children, and youth with disabilities and persons who work with parents to enable such individuals to partici-

pate more effectively with professionals in meeting the educational needs of children with disabilities. Such grants shall be designed to meet the unique training and information needs of parents of infants, toddlers, children, and youth with disabilities living in the area to be served by the grant, particularly those who are members of groups that have been traditionally underrepresented.

(2) In order to receive a grant under paragraph (1) a private nonprofit organization shall—

(A) be governed by a board of directors of which a majority of the members are parents of infants, toddlers, children, and youth with disabilities, particularly minority parents, and that includes members who are professionals, especially minority professionals, in the field of special education, early intervention, and related services, and individuals with disabilities, or, if the nonprofit private organization does not have such a board, such organization shall have a membership that represents the interests of individuals with disabilities, and shall establish a special governing committee of which a majority of the members are parents of infants, toddlers, children, and youth with disabilities, particularly parents of minority children, and which includes members who are professionals, especially minority professionals, in the field of special education, early intervention, and related services, to operate the training and information program under paragraph (1), and parents and professional membership of these boards or special governing committees shall be broadly representative of minority and other individuals and groups having an interest in special education, early intervention, and related services;

(B) serve the parents of infants, toddlers, children, and youth with the full range of disabling conditions under such grant program, and

(C) demonstrate the capacity and expertise to conduct effectively the training and information activities for which a grant may be made under paragraph (1). Nothing in subparagraph (A) shall be construed to authorize or permit the denial to any person of the due process of law required by the United States Constitution.

(3) The board of directors or special governing committee of a private nonprofit organization receiving a grant under paragraph (1) shall meet at least once in each calendar quarter to review the parent training and information activities for which the grant is made, and each such committee shall advise the governing board directly of its views and recommendations. Whenever a private nonprofit organization requests the renewal of a grant under paragraph (1) for a fiscal year, the board of directors or the special governing committee shall submit to the Secretary a written review of the parent training and information program conducted by that private nonprofit organization during the preceding fiscal year, and, for purposes of paragraph (1), network with clearinghouses, including those established under § 633 and other organizations and agencies, and network with other established national, State, and local parent groups representing the full range of parents of infants, toddlers, children, and youth with disabilities, especially parents of minority children.

(4) The Secretary shall ensure that grants under paragraph (1) will—

(A) be distributed geographically to the greatest extent possible throughout all the States and give priority to grants which involve unserved areas,

(B) be targeted to parents of handicapped children in both urban and rural areas or on a State or regional basis, and

(C) serve parents of minority children with disabilities representative to the proportion of the minority population in the areas being served, and

(D) be funded at a sufficient size, scope, and quality to ensure that the program is adequate to serve the parents in the area.

(5) Parent training and information programs assisted under paragraph (1) shall assist parents to—

(A) better understand the nature and needs of the disabling conditions of children,

(B) provide followup support for educational programs of children with disabilities,

(C) communicate more effectively with special and regular educators, administrators, related services personnel, and other relevant professionals,

(D) participate in educational decisionmaking processes including the development of the individualized educational program of a child with a disability,

(E) obtain appropriate information about the range of options, programs, services, and resources available at the national, State, and local levels to assist infants, toddlers, children, and youth with disabilities and their families, and

(F) understand the provisions for the education of infants, toddlers, children, and youth with disabilities under this Act.

(6) Parent training and information programs may, at a grant recipients discretion, include State or local educational personnel where such participation will further an objective of the program assisted by the grant.

(7) Each private nonprofit organization operating a program receiving a grant under paragraph (1) shall consult and network with appropriate national, State, regional, and local agencies and organizations, such as protection and advocacy agencies, that serve or assist infants, toddlers, children, and youth with disabilities and their families and are located in the jurisdictions served by the program.

(8) The Secretary shall provide technical assistance, by grant or contract, for establishing, developing, and coordinating parent training and information programs.

(9) After the establishment in each State of a parent training and information center, the Secretary shall provide for the establishment of 3 experimental centers to serve large numbers of parents of children with disabilities located in high density areas that do not have such centers and 2 such centers to serve large numbers of parents of children with disabilities located in rural areas.

(10) Effective for fiscal year 1991 and every year thereafter, the Secretary shall obtain data concerning programs and centers assisted under this subsection on—

(A) the number of parents provided information and training by disability category of their children,

(B) the types and modes of information or training provided,

(C) strategies used to reach and serve parents of minority infants, toddlers, children, and youth with disabilities,

(D) the number of parents served as a result of activities described under subparagraph (C),

(E) activities to network with other information clearinghouses and parent groups as required in subsection (c)(2)(C), and

(F) the number of agencies and organizations consulted with at the national, State, regional, and local levels.

The Secretary shall include a summary of this information in the annual report to Congress as required in section 618(g).

§ 1432. Grants to State educational agencies and institutions for traineeships

(a) The Secretary shall make a grant of sufficient size and scope to each State educational agency for the purposes described in subsection (c) and, in any State in which the State educational agency does not apply for such a grant, to an institution of higher education within such State for such purposes.

(b) The Secretary may also make a limited number of grants to State educational agencies on a competitive basis for the purposes described in subsection (c). In any fiscal year, the Secretary may not expend for purposes of this subsection an amount that exceeds 10 percent of the amount expended for purposes of this section in the preceding fiscal year.

(c) Grants made under this section shall be for the purpose of assisting States in establishing and maintaining preservice and inservice programs to prepare special and regular education, related services and early intervention personnel to meet the needs of handicapped infants, toddlers, children, and youth or supervisors of such persons, consistent with the personnel needs identified in the State's comprehensive system of personnel development under section 1413 and under section 1476(b)(8), and to assist the State in developing and maintaining such systems and conducting personnel recruitment and retention activities.

(d) the Secretary is authorized to provide directly or by grant, contract, or cooperative agreement, technical assistance to State educational agencies on matters pertaining to the effective implementation of section 613(a)(3).

§ 1433. Clearinghouses

(a) National clearinghouse on education of handicapped; establishment; other support projects; statement of objectives

The Secretary is authorized to make grants to, or enter into contracts or cooperative agreements with, public agencies or private nonprofit organizations or institutions for the establishment of three national clearinghouses: on children and youth with disabilities; on postsecondary education for individuals with disabilities; and on careers in special education, to—

(1) collect, develop, and disseminate information,

(2) provide technical assistance,

(3) conduct coordinated outreach activities,

(4) provide for the coordination and networking with other relevant

national, State, and local organizations and information and referral resources,

(5) respond to individuals and organizations seeking information, and

(6) provide for the synthesis of information for its effective utilization by parents, professionals, individuals with disabilities, and other interested parties.

(b) National clearinghouse on postsecondary for disabled; establishment; statement of purpose

The national clearinghouse for children and youth with disabilities shall:

(1) Collect and disseminate information (including the development of materials) on characteristics of infants, toddlers, children, and youth with disabilities and on programs, legislation, and services relating to their education under this Act and other Federal laws.

(2) Participate in programs and services related to disability issues for providing outreach, technical assistance, collection, and dissemination of information; and promoting networking of individuals with appropriate national, State, and local agencies and organizations.

(3) Establish a coordinated network and conduct outreach activities with relevant Federal, State, and local organizations and other sources for promoting public awareness of disability issues and the availability of information, programs, and services.

(4) Collect, disseminate, and develop information on current and future national, Federal, regional, and State needs for providing information to parents, professionals, individuals with disabilities, and other interested parties relating to the education and related services of individuals with disabilities.

(5) Provide technical assistance to national, Federal, regional, State and local agencies and organizations seeking to establish information and referral services for individuals with disabilities and their families.

(6) In carrying out the activities in this subsection, the clearinghouse will include strategies to disseminate information to underrepresented groups such as those with limited English proficiency.

(c) National clearinghouse to collect and disseminate information

The national clearinghouse on postsecondary education for individuals with disabilities shall:

(1) Collect and disseminate information nationally on characteristics of individuals entering and particiating in education and training programs after high school; legislation affecting such individuals and such programs; policies, procedures, and support services, as well as adaptations, and other resources available or recommended to facilitate the education of individuals with disabilities; available programs and services that include, or can be adapted to include, individuals with disabilities; and sources of financial aid for the education and training of individuals with disabilities.

(2) Identify areas of need for additional information.

(3) Develop new materials (in both print and nonprint form), especially by synthesizing information from a variety of fields affecting disability issues and the education, rehabilitation, and retraining of individuals with disabilities.

(4) Develop a coordinated network of professionals, related organizations and associations, mass media, other clearinghouses, and governmental agencies at the Federal, regional, State, and local level for the purposes of disseminating information and promoting awareness of issues relevant to the education of individuals with disabilities after high school and referring individuals who request information to local resources.

(5) Respond to requests from individuals with disabilities, their parents, and professionals who work with them, for information that will enable them to make appropriate decisions about postsecondary education and training.

(d) National clearinghouse to encourage careers and employment in fields relating to education of the disabled

The national clearinghouse designed to encourage students to seek careers and professional personnel to seek employment in the various fields relating to the education of children and youth with disabilities shall:

(1) Collect and disseminate information on current and future national, regional, and State needs for special education and related services personnel.

(2) Disseminate information to high school counselors and others concerning current career opportunities in special education, location of programs, and various forms of financial assistance (such as scholarships, stipends, and allowances).

(3) Identify training programs available around the country.

(4) Establish a network among local and State educational agencies and institutions of higher education concerning the supply of graduates and available openings.

(5) Provide technical assistance to institutions seeking to meet State and professionally recognized standards.

(e) Considerations governing awards

(1) In awarding grants, contracts, and cooperative agreements under this section, the Secretary shall give priority consideration to any applicant with demonstrated, proven effectiveness (at the national level) in performing the functions established in this section; and with the ability to conduct such projects, communicate with intended consumers of information, and maintain the necessary communication with national, regional, State, and local agencies and organizations.

(2) In awarding grants, contracts, and cooperative agreements under this section, the Secretary shall give priority consideration to any applicant with demonstrated, proven effectiveness (at the national level) in providing informational services to minorities and minority organizations.

(f) Application contents

(1) Beginning in fiscal year 1991, and for each year thereafter, the Secretary shall obtain information on each project assisted under this section, including—

(A) the number of individuals served by disability category, as appropriate, including parents, professionals, students, and individuals with disabilities;

(B) a description of responses utilized;

(C) a listing of new products developed and disseminated; and

(D) a description of strategies and activities utilized for outreach to urban and rural areas with populations of minorities and underrepresented groups.

(2) A summary of the data required by this subsection shall be included in the annual report to Congress required under section 618.

§ 1434. Reports to the Secretary

(a) Not more than sixty days after the end of any fiscal year, each recipient of a grant or contract under this subchapter during such fiscal year shall prepare and submit a report to the Secretary. Each such report shall be in such form and detail as the Secretary determines to be appropriate, and shall include—

(1) the number of individuals trained under the grant or contract, by category of training and level of training;

(2) the number of individuals trained under the grant or contract receiving degrees and certification, by category and level of training, and

(3) information described in section 631(c)(9) and section 633(f)(1), as applicable.

(b) A summary of the data required by this section shall be included in the annual report of the Secretary under section 1418 of this title.

§ 1435. Authorization of appropriations

(a) Subchapter IV, personnel recruitment, and opportunities for handicapped programs

(1) There are authorized to be appropriated to carry out this part (other than sections 631(a)(7), 631(c), and 633) $94,725,000 for fiscal year 1991, $103,255,000 for fiscal year 1992, $113,580,000 for fiscal year 1993, and $123,760,000 for fiscal year 1994.

(2) There are authorized to be appropriated to carry out section 631(a)(7) $19,250,000 for fiscal year 1991, $21,175,000 for fiscal year 1992, $23,292,500 for fiscal year 1993, and $25,621,750 for fiscal year 1994.

(3) There are authorized to be appropriated to carry out section 631(c) $11,000,000 for fiscal year 1991, $12,100,000 for fiscal year 1992, $13,300,000 for fiscal year 1993, and $14,600,000 for fiscal year 1994.

(4) There are authorized to be appropriated to carry out section 633 $2,900,000 for fiscal year 1991, $2,465,000 for fiscal year 1992, $2,710,000 for fiscal year 1993, and $2,960,000 for fiscal year 1994.

(b) Personnel training for careers in special education and early intervention

Of the funds appropriated pursuant to subsection (a) of this section for any fiscal year, the Secretary shall reserve not less than 65 per centum for activities described in subparagraphs (A) through (E) of section 1431(a)(1) of this section.

(c) Parent training and information programs

Of the funds appropriated under subsection (a) of this section for any fiscal year, the Secretary shall reserve 10 percent for activities under section 1431(c) of this title.

§ 1436. Omitted

SUBCHAPTER V—RESEARCH IN THE EDUCATION OF INDIVIDUALS WITH DISABILITIES

§ 1441. Research and related activities

(a) Grant and contract authority; statement of objectives; description of specific activities

The Secretary may make grants to, or enter into contracts or cooperative agreements with, State and local educational agencies, institutions of higher education, and other public agencies and nonprofit private organizations for the purpose of advancing and improving the knowledge base and improving the practice of professionals, parents, and others providing early intervention, special education, and related services, including professionals who work with children and youth with disabilities in regular education environments, to provide such children effective instruction and enable them to successfully learn. The activities supported under this section shall support innovation, development, exchange, and use of such advancements in knowledge and practice designed to contribute to the improvement of instruction and learning of infants, toddlers, children, and youth with disabilities. In carrying out this section, the Secretary may support a wide range of research and related activities designed to—

(1) advance knowledge regarding the provision of instruction and other interventions to infants, toddlers, children, and youth with disabilities including—

(A) the organization, synthesis, and interpretation of current knowledge and the identification of knowledge gaps;

(B) the identification of knowledge and skill competencies needed by personnel providing special education, related services, and early intervention services;

(C) the improvement of knowledge regarding the developmental and learning characteristics of infants, toddlers, children, and youth with disabilities in order to improve the design and effectiveness of interventions and instruction;

(D) the evaluation of approaches and interventions;

(E) the development of instructional strategies, techniques, and activities;

(F) the improvement of curricula and instructional tools such as textbooks, media, materials, and technology;

(G) the development of assessment techniques, instruments (including tests, inventories, and scales), and strategies for measurement of progress and the identification, location, and evaluation of infants, toddlers, children, and youth with disabilities for the purpose of determining eligibility, program planning, and placement for special education, related services, and early intervention services. Particular attention should be given to the development of alternative assessment procedures and processes for minority individuals and those with limited English proficiency;

(H) the testing of research findings in practice settings to determine the application, usability, effectiveness, and generalizability of such research findings;

(I) the improvement of knowledge regarding families, minorities, limited English proficiency, and disabling conditions; and

(J) the identification of environmental, organizational, resource, and other conditions necessary for effective professional practice; and

(2) advance the use of knowledge by personnel providing special education, related services, and early intervention services including—

(A) the improvement of knowledge regarding how such individuals learn new knowledge and skills, and strategies for effectively facilitating such learning in preservice, inservice, and continuing education;

(B) the organization, integration, and presentation of knowledge so that such knowledge can be incorporated and imparted in personnel preparation, continuing education programs, and other relevant training and communication vehicles; and

(C) the expansion and improvement of networks that exchange knowledge and practice information.

(b) Qualifications of applicant

In carrying out subsection (a), the Secretary shall consider the special education, related services, or early intervention and research experience of applicants.

(c) Publication of research priorities in Federal Register

The Secretary shall publish proposed priorities under this part in the Federal Register not later than 12 months preceding the fiscal year for which they are being announced, and shall allow a period of 60 days for public comments and suggestions. The Secretary shall, after analyzing and considering the public comments, publish final priorities in the Federal Register not later than 90 days after the close of the comment period.

(d) Reports of research projects; index of research projects for annual report; availability to interested parties

The Secretary shall provide an index (including the title of each project and the name and address of the funded organization) of all projects conducted under this part in the prior fiscal year in the annual report described under section 618.

(e) Coordination of related research priorities; information respecting research priorities to Federal entities

The Secretary shall—

(1) coordinate the priorities established under subsection (b) with research priorities established by the National Institute for Disability and Rehabilitation Research and other appropriate agencies conducting research pertaining to the education of individuals with disabilities; and

(2) provide information concerning priorities established under subsection (b) to the National Council on Disability and to the Bureau of Indian Affairs Advisory Committee for Exceptional Children.

(f) Organization of information respecting attention deficient disorder

(1) The Secretary shall make grants or enter into contracts or cooperative agreements for the establishment of a center or centers designed to organize, synthesize, and disseminate current knowledge relating to children with attention deficit disorder with respect to the following:

(A) Assessment techniques, instruments, and strategies used for identification, location, evaluation and for measurement of progress.

(B) Knowledge and skill competencies needed by professionals providing special and regular education and related services.

(C) Environmental, organizational, resource, and other conditions necessary for effective professional practice.

(D) Developmental and learning characteristics.

(E) Instructional strategies, techniques, and activities.

(F) Curricula and instructional tools such as textbooks, media, materials, and technology.

(G) Strategies, techniques, and activities related to involvement of families.

(2) In awarding grants, contracts, and cooperative agreements under paragraph (1), the Secretary shall give priority consideration to applicants with—

(A) demonstrated knowledge concerning the disorder;

(B) proven effectiveness in performing the functions established in this subsection; and

(C) the ability to—

(i) conduct such projects;

(ii) communicate with intended consumers of information; and

(iii) maintain the necessary communication with national, regional, State, and local agencies.

(g) Ombudsman services to facilitate an appropriate education

(1) The Secretary shall make grants, or enter into contracts or cooperative agreements, for the establishment of model demonstration programs, of which some will be school-based models, that provide the services of an ombudsman to assist in resolving problems that are barriers to appropriate educational, related services or other services for children and youth with disabilities.

(2) Programs under paragraph (1) shall provide or identify personnel to assist children and youth with disabilities, their parents or guardians, special and regular education teachers, State and local education administrators, and related services personnel to resolve problems in a timely manner through dispute mediation and other methods, notwithstanding due process procedures, in order to further the delivery of appropriate education and related services. Participation in this program does not preclude or delay due process under part B of this Act.

(3) Ombudsman services for programs under paragraph (1) shall be provided by social workers, parent advocates, psychologists, and persons with similar qualifications designated by the Secretary.

§ 1442. Research and demonstration projects in physical education and recreation for children with disabilities

The Secretary is authorized to make grants to States, State or local educational agencies, institutions of higher education, and other public or non-profit private educational or research agencies and organizations, and to make contracts with States, State or local educational agencies, institutions of higher education, and other public or private educational or research agencies and organizations, for research and related purposes relating to physical education or recreation for children with disabilities, including therapeutic recreation, and to conduct research, surveys, or demonstrations relating to physical education or recreation for children with disabilities, including therapeutic recreation.

§ 1443. Panels of experts

(a) Convention; composition

The Secretary shall convene, in accordance with subsection (b) of this section, panels of experts who are competent to evaluate proposals for projects under subchapters III through VII of this chapter. The panels shall be composed of—

(1) individuals from the field of special education for individuals with a disability and other relevant disciplines who have significant expertise and experience in the content areas and age levels addressed in the proposals, and

(2) individuals with a disability and parents of individuals with a disability when appropriate.

(b) Funding requests for which panel required to be convened; membership; expenses and fees

(1) The Secretary shall convene panels under subsection (a) of this section for any application which includes a total funding request exceeding $60,000 and may convene or otherwise appoint panels for applications which include funding requests that are less than such amount.

(2) Such panels shall include a majority of non-Federal members. Such non-Federal members shall be provided travel and per diem not to exceed the rate provided to other educational consultants used by the Department and shall be provided consultant fees at such a rate.

(c) Use of funds available under other parts of this chapter for payment of expenses and fees

The Secretary may use funds available under subchapters III to VII of this chapter to pay expenses and fees of non-Federal members under subsection (b) of this section.

SUBCHAPTER VI—INSTRUCTIONAL MEDIA
FOR INDIVIDUALS WITH DISABILITIES

§ 1451. Purposes

The purposes of this subchapter are to promote—

(1) the general welfare of deaf and hard of hearing individuals by—

(A) bringing to such individuals understanding and appreciation of those films and television programs that play such an important part in the general and cultural advancement of hearing individuals;

(B) providing through these films and television programs enriched educational and cultural experiences through which deaf and hard of hearing individuals can be brought into better touch with the realities of their environment;

(C) providing a wholesome and rewarding experience which deaf and hard of hearing individuals may share together; and

(D) utilizing educational media to help eliminate illiteracy among individuals with disabilities;

(2) the educational advancement of individuals with disabilities by—

(A) carrying on research in the use of educational media for individuals with disabilities;

(B) producing and distributing educational media for the use of individuals with disabilities, their parents, their actual or potential employers, and other individuals directly involved in work for the advancement of individuals with disabilities; and

(C) training persons in the use of educational media for the instruction of individuals with disabilities; and

(3) the general welfare of visually impaired individuals by—

(A) bringing to such individuals an understanding and appreciation of textbooks, films, television programs, video material, and other educational publications and materials that play such an important part in the general and cultural advancement of visually unimpaired individuals; and

(B) ensuring access to television programming and other video materials.

§ 1452. Captioned films, television, descriptive video and educational media for individuals with disabilities

(a) Establishment of loan service

The Secretary shall establish a loan service of captioned films, descriptive video and educational media for the purpose of making such materials available, in accordance with regulations, in the United States for nonprofit purposes to individuals with disabilities, parents of individuals with disabilities, and other individuals directly involved in activities for the advancement of individuals with disabilities, including for the purpose of addressing problems of illiteracy among individuals with disabilities.

(b) Authority of Secretary

The Secretary is authorized to—

(1) acquire films (or rights thereto) and other educational media by purchase, lease, or gift;

(2) acquire by lease or purchase equipment necessary for the administration of this subchapter;

(3) provide, by grant or contract, for the captioning for deaf and hard of hearing individuals and video description for the visually impaired, of films, television programs, and video materials;

(4) provide, by grant or contract, for the distribution of captioned and video-described films, video materials, and other educational media and equipment through State schools for individuals with disabilities, public libraries, and such other agencies or entities as the Secretary may deem appropriate to serve as local or regional centers for such distribution;

(5) provide, by grant or contract, for the conduct of research in the use of educational and training films and other educational media for individuals with disabilities, for the production and distribution of educational and training films and other educational media for individuals with disabilities and the training of individuals in the use of such films and media, including the payment to those individuals of such stipends (including allowances for travel and other expenses of such individuals and their dependents) as the Secretary may determine, which shall be consistent with prevailing practices under comparable federally supported programs;

(6) utilize the facilities and services of other governmental agencies;

(7) accept gifts, contributions, and voluntary and uncompensated services of individuals and organizations, and

(8) provide by grant or contract for educational media and materials for deaf and hard of hearing individuals.

(c) Cooperative agreements with National Theatre of the Deaf, Inc.

The Secretary may make grants to or enter into contracts or cooperative agreements with the National Theatre of the Deaf, Inc. and other appropriate non-profit organizations for the purpose of providing cultural experiences to—

(1) enrich the lives of deaf and hard of hearing children and adults,

(2) increase public awareness and understanding of deafness and of the artistic and intellectual achievements of deaf and hard of hearing individuals, and

(3) promote the integration of hearing and deaf and hard of hearing individuals through shared cultural, educational, and social experiences.

(d) Authorization to provide transcribed tapes through graduate school

(1) The Secretary is authorized to make a grant or enter into a contract for the purpose of providing current, free textbooks and other educational publications and materials to blind and other print-handicapped students in elementary, secondary, postsecondary, and graduate schools and other institutions of higher education through the medium of transcribed tapes and cassettes.

(2) For the purpose of this subsection, the term "print-handicapped" refers to any individual who is blind or severely visually impaired, or who, by reason of a physical or perceptual disability, is unable to read printed material unassisted.

§ 1453. Repealed.

§ 1454. Authorization of appropriations

For the purpose of carrying out section 652 there are authorized to be appropriated $20,010,000 for fiscal year 1991, $22,010,000 for fiscal year 1992, $24,200,000 for fiscal year 1993, and $26,600,000 for fiscal year 1994.

SUBCHAPTER VII—TECHNOLOGY, EDUCATIONAL MEDIA, AND MATERIALS FOR INDIVIDUALS WITH DISABILITIES

§ 1461. Authority of Secretary; purpose of projects or centers

(a) Authority to provide new technology, media and materials

The Secretary may make grants or enter into contracts or cooperative agreements with institutions of higher education, State and local educational agencies, or other appropriate agencies and organizations for the purpose of advancing the use of new technology, media, and materials in the education of students with disabilities and the provision of related services and early intervention services to infants and toddlers with disabilities. In carrying out this section, the Secretary may fund projects or centers for the purposes of—

(1) determining how technology, assistive technology, media, and materials are being used in the education of individuals with disabilities and how they can be used most effectively, efficiently, and appropriately,

(2) designing and adapting technology, assistive technology, media, and materials to improve the education of students with disabilities,

(3) assisting the public and private sectors in the development and marketing of technology, assistive technology, media, and materials for the education of individuals with disabilities,

(4) disseminating information on the availability and use of technology, assistive technology, media, and materials for the education of individuals with disabilities, where appropriate, to entities described in section 610(g), and

(5) increasing access to and use of assistive technology devices and assistive technology services in the education of infants, toddlers, children, and youth with disabilities, and other activities authorized under the Technology-Related Assistance for Individuals With Disabilities Act of 1988, as such Act relates to the education of students with disabilities, and

(6) examining how these purposes can address the problem of illiteracy among individuals with disabilities.

(b) Authority to provide assistance which is closed captioned

(1) With respect to new technology, media, and materials utilized with funds under this part to improve the education of students with disabilities, the Secretary shall make efforts to ensure that such instructional materials are closed captioned.

(2) The Secretary may not award a grant, contract, or cooperative agreement under paragraphs (1) through (4) of subsection (a) unless the applicant for such assistance agrees that activities carried out with the assistance will be coordinated, as appropriate, with the State entity receiving funds under title I of Public Law 100-407.

§ 1462. Authorization of appropriations

For the purpose of carrying out this part, there are authorized to be appropriated $11,900,000 for fiscal year 1991, $12,860,000 for fiscal year 1992, $13,890,000 for fiscal year 1993, and $15,000,000 for fiscal year 1994.

SUBCHAPTER VIII—INFANTS AND TODDLERS WITH DISABILITIES

§ 1471. Findings and policy

(a) Findings

The Congress finds that there is an urgent and substantial need—

(1) to enhance the development of infants and toddlers with disabilities and to minimize their potential for developmental delay,

(2) to reduce the educational costs to our society, including our Nation's schools, by minimizing the need for special education and related services after infants and toddlers with disabilities reach school age,

(3) to minimize the likelihood of institutionalization of individuals with disabilities and maximize the potential for their independent living in society, and

(4) to enhance the capacity of families to meet the special needs of their infants and toddlers with disabilities.

(b) Policy

It is therefore the policy of the United States to provide financial assistance to States—

(1) to develop and implement a statewide, comprehensive, coordinated, multidisciplinary, interagency program of early intervention services for infants and toddlers with disabilities and their families,

(2) to facilitate the coordination of payment for early intervention services from Federal, State, local, and private sources (including public and private insurance coverage), and

(3) to enhance their capacity to provide quality early intervention services and expand and improve existing early intervention services being provided to infants and toddlers with disabilities and their families.

§ 1472. Definitions

As used in this subchapter—

(1) The term "infants and toddlers with disabilities" means individuals from birth to age 2, inclusive, who need early intervention services because they—

(A) are experiencing developmental delays, as measured by appropriate diagnostic instruments and procedures in one or more of the following areas: cognitive development, physical development, language and speech development, psychosocial development, or self-help skills, or

(B) have a diagnosed physical or mental condition which has a high probability of resulting in developmental delay.

Such term may also include, at a State's discretion, individuals from birth to age 2, inclusive, who are at risk of having substantial developmental delays if early intervention services are not provided.

(2) The term "early intervention services" are developmental services which—

(A) are provided under public supervision,

(B) are provided at no cost except where Federal or State law provides for a system of payments by families, including a schedule of sliding fees,

(C) are designed to meet the developmental needs of an infant or toddler with a disability in any one or more of the following areas:

(i) physical development,

(ii) cognitive development,

(iii) language and speech development,

(iv) psychosocial development, or

(v) self-help skills,

(D) meet the standards of the State, including the requirements of this part,

(E) include—

(i) family training, counseling, and home visits,

(ii) special instruction,

(iii) speech pathology and audiology,

(iv) occupational therapy,

(v) physical therapy,

(vi) psychological services,

(vii) case management services,

(viii) medical services only for diagnostic or evaluation purposes,

(ix) early identification, screening and assessment services,

(x) health services necessary to enable the infant or toddler to benefit from the other early intervention services, and

(xi) social work services,

(F) are provided by qualified personnel, including—

(i) special educators,

(ii) speech and language pathologists and audiologists,

(iii) occupational therapists,

(iv) physical therapists,

(v) psychologists,

(vi) social workers,

(vii) nurses, and

(viii) nutritionists, and

(G) are provided in conformity with an individualized family service plan adopted in accordance with section 1477 of this title.

(3) The term "developmental delay" has the meaning given such term by a State under section 1476(b)(1) of this title.

(4) The term "Council" means the State Interagency Coordinating Council established under section 1482 of this title.

§ 1473. General authority

The Secretary shall, in accordance with this subchapter, make grants to States (from their allocations under section 1484 of this title) to assist each State to develop a statewide, comprehensive, coordinated, multidisciplinary, interagency system to provide early intervention services for infants and toddlers with disabilities and their families.

§ 1474. General eligibility

In order to be eligible for a grant under section 1473 of this title for any fiscal year, a State shall demonstrate to the Secretary (in its application under section 1478 of this title) that the State has established a State Interagency Coordinating Council which meets the requirements of section 1482 of this title.

§ 1475. Continuing eligibility

(a) First two years

In order to be eligible for a grant under section 1473 of this title for the first or second year of a State's participation under this subchapter, a State shall include in its application under section 1478 of this title for that year an assurance that funds received under section 1473 of this title shall be used to assist the State to plan, develop, and implement the statewide system required by section 1476 of this title.

(b) Third and fourth year

(1) In order to be eligible for a grant under section 1473 of this title for the third or fourth year of a State's participation under this subchapter, a State shall include in its application under section 1478 of this title for that year information and assurances demonstrating to the satisfaction of the Secretary that—

(A) the State has adopted a policy which incorporates all of the components of a statewide system in accordance with section 1476 of this title or obtained a waiver from the Secretary under paragraph (2).

(B) funds shall be used to plan, develop, and implement the statewide system required by section 1476 of this title, and

(C) such statewide system will be in effect no later than the beginning of the fourth year of the State's participation under section 1473 of this title, except that in order to comply with section 1476(b)(4) of this title, a State need only conduct multidisciplinary assessments, develop individualized family service plans, and make available case management services.

(2) Notwithstanding paragraph (1), the Secretary may permit a State to continue to receive assistance under section 1473 of this title during such third year even if the State has not adopted the policy required by paragraph (1)(A) before receiving assistance if the State demonstrates in its application—

(A) that the State has made a good faith effort to adopt such a policy,

(B) the reasons why it was unable to meet the timeline and the steps remaining before such a policy will be adopted, and

(C) an assurance that the policy will be adopted to go into effect before the fourth year of such assistance.

(c) Fifth and succeeding years

In order to be eligible for a grant under section 1473 of this title for a fifth and any succeeding year of a State's participation under this subchapter, a State shall include in its application under section 1478 of this title for that year information and assurances demonstrating to the satisfaction of the Secretary that the State has in effect the statewide system required by section 1476 of this title and a description of services to be provided under section 1476(b)(2) of this title.

(d) Exception

Notwithstanding subsections (a) and (b) of this section, a State which has in effect a State law, enacted before September 1, 1986, that requires the provision of free appropriate public education to children with disabilities from birth through age 2, inclusive, shall be eligible for a grant under section 1473 of this title for the first through fourth years of a State's participation under this subchapter.

§ 1476. Requirements for statewide system

(a) In general

A statewide system of coordinate, comprehensive, multidisciplinary, interagency programs providing appropriate early intervention services to all infants and toddlers with disabilities and their families shall include the minimum components under subsection (b) of this section.

(b) Minimum components

The statewide system required by subsection (a) of this section shall include, at a minimum—

(1) a definition of the term "developmentally delayed" that will be used by the State in carrying out programs under this subchapter,

(2) timetables for ensuring that appropriate early intervention services will be available to all infants and toddlers with disabilities in the State before the beginning of the fifth year of a State's participation under this subchapter,

(3) a timely, comprehensive, multidisciplinary evaluation of the functioning of each infant and toddler with a disability in the State and the needs of the families to appropriately assist in the development of the infant or toddler with a disability,

(4) for each infant and toddler with a disability in the State, an individualized family service plan in accordance with section 1477 of this title, including case management services in accordance with such service plan,

(5) a comprehensive child find system, consistent with subchapter II of this chapter, including a system for making referrals to service providers that includes timelines and provides for participation by primary referral sources,

(6) a public awareness program focusing on early identification of infants and toddlers with disabilities, including the preparation and dissemination by the lead agency to all primary referral sources of information materials for parents on the availability of early intervention services,

and procedures for determining the extent to which primary referral sources, especially hospitals and physicians, disseminate information on the availability of early intervention services as required under this paragraph to parents of infants with disabilities,

(7) a central directory which includes early intervention services, resources, and experts available in the State and research and demonstration projects being conducted in the State,

(8) a comprehensive system of personnel development, including training of primary referral sources respecting the basic components of early intervention services available in the State,

(9) a single line of responsibility in a lead agency designated or established by the Governor for carrying out—

(A) the general administration, supervision, and monitoring of programs and activities receiving assistance under section 1473 of this title to ensure compliance with this subchapter,

(B) the identification and coordination of all available resources within the State from Federal, State, local and private sources,

(C) the assignment of financial responsibility to the appropriate agency,

(D) the development of procedures to ensure that services are provided to infants and toddlers with disabilities and their families in a timely manner pending the resolution of any disputes among public agencies or service providers,

(E) the resolution of intra- and interagency disputes, and

(F) the entry into formal interagency agreements that define the financial responsibility of each agency for paying for early intervention services (consistent with State law) and procedures for resolving disputes and that include all additional components necessary to ensure meaningful cooperation and coordination.

(10) a policy pertaining to the contracting or making of other arrangements with service providers to provide early intervention services in the State, consistent with the provisions of this subchapter, including the contents of the application used and the conditions of the contract or other arrangements,

(11) a procedure for securing timely reimbursement of funds used under this subchapter in accordance with section 1481(a) of this title,

(12) procedural safeguards with respect to programs under this subchapter as required by section 1480 of this title,

(13) policies and procedures relating to the establishment and maintenance of standards to ensure that personnel necessary to carry out this subchapter are appropriately and adequately prepared and trained, including—

(A) the establishment and maintenance of standards which are consistent with any State approved or recognized certification, licensing, registration, or other comparable requirements which apply to the area in which such personnel are providing early intervention services, and

(B) to the extent such standards are not based on the highest requirements in the State applicable to a specific profession or discipline, the steps the State is taking to require the retraining or hiring of personnel that meet appropriate professional requirements in the State, and

(14) a system for compiling data on the numbers of infants and toddlers with disabilities and their families in the State in need of appropriate early intervention services (which may be based on a sampling of data), the numbers of such infants and toddlers and their families served, the types of services provided (which may be based on a sampling of data), and other information required by the Secretary.

§ 1477. Individualized family service plan

(a) Assessment and program development

Each infant or toddler with a disability and the infant's or toddler's family shall receive—
(1) a multidisciplinary assessment of unique needs and the identification of services appropriate to meet such needs, and
(2) a written individualized family service plan developed by a multidisciplinary team, including the parent or guardian, as required by subsection (d) of this section.

(b) Periodic review

The individualized family service plan shall be evaluated once a year and the family shall be provided a review of the plan at 6-month intervals (or more often where appropriate based on infant or toddler and family needs).

(c) Promptness after assessment

The individualized family service plan shall be developed within a reasonable time after the assessment required by subsection (a)(1) of this section is completed. With the parent's consent, early intervention services may commence prior to the completion of such assessment.

(d) Contents of plan

The individualized family service plan shall be in writing and contain—
(1) a statement of the infant's or toddler's present levels of physical development, cognitive development, language and speech development, psychosocial development, and self-help skills, based on acceptable objective criteria,
(2) a statement of the family's strengths and needs relating to enhancing the development of the family's infant or toddler with a disability,
(3) a statement of the major outcomes expected to be achieved for the infant or toddler and the family, and the criteria, procedures, and timelines used to determine the degree to which progress toward achieving the outcomes is being made and whether modifications or revisions of the outcomes or services are necessary,
(4) a statement of specific early intervention services necessary to meet the unique needs of the infant or toddler and the family, including the frequency, intensity, and the method of delivering services,

(5) the projected dates for initiation of services and the anticipated duration of such services,

(6) the name of the case manager from the profession most immediately relevant to the infant's or toddler's or family's needs who will be responsible for the implementation of the plan and coordination with other agencies and persons, and

(7) the steps to be taken supporting the transition of the toddler with a disability to services provided under subchapter II of this chapter to the extent such services are considered appropriate.

§ 1478. State application and assurances

(a) Application

Any State desiring to receive a grant under section 1473 of this title for any year shall submit an application to the Secretary at such time and in such manner as the Secretary may reasonably require by regulation. Such an application shall contain—

(1) a designation of the lead agency in the State that will be responsible for the administration of funds provided under section 1473 of this title,

(2) information demonstrating eligibility of the State under section 1474 of this title,

(3) the information or assurances required to demonstrate eligibility of the State for the particular year of participation under section 1475 of this title,

(4)(A) information demonstrating that the State has provided (i) public hearings, (ii) adequate notice of such hearings, and (iii) an opportunity for comment to the general public before the submission of such application and before the adoption by the State of the policies described in such application, and (B) a summary of the public comments and the State's responses,

(5) a description of the uses for which funds will be expended in accordance with this subchapter and, for the fifth and succeeding fiscal years, a description of the services to be provided,

(6) a description of the procedure used to ensure an equitable distribution of resources made available under this subchapter among all geographic areas within the State, and

(7) such other information and assurances as the Secretary may reasonably require by regulation.

(b) Statement of assurances

Any State desiring to receive a grant under section 1473 of this title shall file with the Secretary a statement at such time and in such manner as the Secretary may reasonably require by regulation. Such statement shall—

(1) assure that funds paid to the State under section 1473 of this title will be expended in accordance with this subchapter,

(2) contain assurances that the State will comply with the requirements of section 1481 of this title,

(3) provide satisfactory assurance that the control of funds provided under section 1473 of this title, and title to property derived therefrom, shall be in a public agency for the uses and purposes provided in this subchapter and that a public agency will administer such funds and property,

(4) provide for (A) making such reports in such form and containing such information as the Secretary may require to carry out the Secretary's functions under this subchapter, and (B) keeping such records and affording such access thereto as the Secretary may find necessary to assure the correctness and verification of such reports and proper disbursement of Federal funds under this subchapter,

(5) provide satisfactory assurance that Federal funds made available under section 1473(A) of this title will not be commingled with State funds, and (B) will be so used as to supplement and increase the level of State and local funds expended for infants and toddlers with disabilities and their families and in no case to supplant such State and local funds.

(6) provide satisfactory assurance that such fiscal control and fund accounting procedures will be adopted as may be necessary to assure proper disbursement of, and accounting for, Federal funds paid under section 1473 of this title to the State, and

(7) such other information and assurances as the Secretary may reasonably require by regulation.

(c) Approval of application and assurances required

No State may receive a grant under section 1473 of this title unless the Secretary has approved the application and statement of assurances of that State. The Secretary shall not disapprove such an application or statement of assurances unless the Secretary determines, after notice and opportunity for a hearing, that the application or statement of assurances fails to comply with the requirements of this section.

§ 1479. Use of funds

In addition to using funds provided under section 1473 of this title to plan, develop, and implement the statewide system required by section 1476 of this title, a State may use such funds—

(1) for direct services for infants and toddlers with disabilities and their families that are not otherwise provided from other public or private sources, and

(2) to expand and improve on services for infants and toddlers with disabilities and their families that are otherwise available.

§ 1480. Procedural safeguards

The procedural safeguards required to be included in a statewide system under section 1476(b)(12) of this title shall provide, at a minimum, the following:

(1) The timely administrative resolution of complaints by parents. Any party aggrieved by the findings and decision regarding an administrative complaint shall have the right to bring a civil action with respect to the complaint, which action may be brought in any State court of competent jurisdiction or in a district court of the United States without regard to the amount in controversy. In any action brought under this paragraph, the court shall receive the records of the administrative proceedings, shall hear additional evidence at the request of a party, and, basing its decision on the preponderance of the evidence, shall grant such relief as the court determines is appropriate.

(2) The right to confidentiality of personally identifiable information.

(3) The opportunity for parents or a guardian to examine records relating to assessment, screening, eligibility determinations, and the development and implementation of the individualized family service plan.

(4) Procedures to protect the rights of the infant or toddler with a disability whenever the parents or guardian of the child are not known or unavailable or the child is a ward of the State, including the assignment of an individual (who shall not be an employee of the State agency providing services) to act as a surrogate for the parents or guardian.

(5) Written prior notice to the parents or guardian of the infant or toddler with a disability whenever the State agency or service provider proposes to initiate or change or refuses to initiate or change the identification, evaluation, placement, or the provision of appropriate early intervention services to the infant or toddler with a disability.

(6) Procedures designed to assure that the notice required by paragraph (5) fully informs the parents or guardian, in the parents' or guardian's native language, unless it clearly is not feasible to do so, of all procedures available pursuant to this section.

(7) During the pendency of any proceeding or action involving a complaint, unless the State agency and the parents or guardian otherwise agree, the child shall continue to receive the appropriate early intervention services currently being provided or, if applying for initial services, shall receive the services not in dispute.

§ 1481. Payor of last resort

(a) Nonsubstitution

Funds provided under section 1473 of this title may not be used to satisfy a financial commitment for services which would have been paid for from another public or private source but for the enactment of this subchapter, except that whenever considered necessary to prevent a delay in the receipt of appropriate early intervention services by the infant or toddler or family in a timely fashion, funds provided under section 1473 of this title may be used to pay the provider of services pending reimbursement from the agency which has ultimate responsibility for the payment.

(b) Reduction of other benefits

Nothing in this subchapter shall be construed to permit the State to reduce medical or other assistance available or to alter eligibility under title V of the Social Security Act (relating to maternal and child health) or title XIX of the Social Security Act (relating to medicaid for infants and toddlers with disabilities) within the State.

§ 1482. State Interagency Coordinating Council

(a) Establishment

(1) Any State which desires to receive financial assistance under section 1473 of this title shall establish a State Interagency Coordinating Council composed of 15 members.

(2) The Council and the chairperson of the Council shall be appointed by the Governor. In making appointments to the Council, the Governor shall ensure that the membership of the Council reasonably represents the population of the State.

(b) Composition

The council shall be composed of—

(1) at least 3 parents of handicapped infants or toddlers or handicapped children aged 3 through 6, inclusive,

(2) at least 3 public or private providers of early intervention services,

(3) at least one representative from the State legislature,

(4) at least one person involved in personnel preparation,

(5) other members representing each of the appropriate agencies involved in the provision of or payment for early intervention services to handicapped infants and toddlers and their families, and

(6) others selected by the Governor.

(c) Meetings

The Council shall meet at least quarterly and in such places as it deems necessary. The meetings shall be publicly announced, and, to the extent appropriate, open and accessible to the general public.

(d) Management authority

Subject to the approval of the Governor, the Council may prepare and approve a budget using funds under this subchapter to hire staff, and obtain other services of such professional, technical, and clerical personnel as may be necessary to carry out its functions under this subchapter.

(e) Functions of Council

The Council shall—

(1) advise and assist the lead agency designated or established under section 1476(b)(9) of this title in the performance of the responsibilities set out in such section, particularly the identification of the sources of fiscal and other support for services for early intervention programs, assignment of financial responsibility to the appropriate agency, and the promotion of the interagency agreements,

(2) advise and assist the lead agency in the preparation of applications and amendments thereto, and

(3) prepare and submit an annual report to the Governor and to the Secretary on the status of early intervention programs for infants and toddlers with disabilities and their families operated within the State.

(f) Conflict of interest

No member of the Council shall cast a vote on any matter which would provide direct financial benefit to that member or otherwise give the appearance of a conflict of interest under State law.

(g) Use of existing Councils

To the extent that a State has established a Council before September 1, 1986, that is comparable to the Council described in this section, such Council shall be considered to be in compliance with this section. Within 4 years after the date the State accepts funds under section 1473 of this title, such State shall establish a council that complies in full with this section.

§ 1483. Federal administration

Sections 1416, 1417 and 1420 of this title shall, to the extent not inconsistent with this subchapter, apply to the program authorized by this subchapter, except that—

(1) any reference to a State educational agency shall be deemed to a reference to the State agency established or designated under section 1476(b)(9) of this section,

(2) any reference to the education of children with disabilities and the education of all children with disabilities and the provision of free public education to all children with disabilities shall be deemed to be a reference to the provision of services to infants and toddlers with disabilities in accordance with this subchapter, and

(3) any reference to local educational agencies and intermediate educational agencies shall be deemed to be a reference to local service providers under this subchapter.

§ 1484. Allocation of funds

(a) Territories and insular possessions

From the sums appropriated to carry out this subchapter for any fiscal year, the Secretary may reserve 1 percent for payments to Guam, American Samoa, the Virgin Islands, the Republic of the Marshall Islands, the Federated States of Micronesia, the Republic of Palau, and the Commonwealth of Northern Mariana Islands in accordance with their respective needs.

(b) Secretary of Interior for assistance to Indians

(1) The Secretary shall make payments to the Secretary of the Interior according to the need for such assistance for the provision of early intervention services to infants and toddlers with disabilities and their families on reservations serviced by the elementary and secondary schools operated for Indians by the Department of the Interior. The amount of such payment for any fiscal year shall be 1.25 percent of the aggregate of the amount available to all States under this subchapter for that fiscal year.

(2) The Secretary of the Interior may receive an allotment under paragraph (1) only after submitting to the Secretary an application which meets the requirements of section 1478 of this title and which is approved by the Secretary. Section 1416 of this title shall apply to any such application.

(c) States

(1) For each of the fiscal years 1987 through 1991 from the funds remaining after the reservation and payments under subsections (a) and (b) of this section, the Secretary shall allot to each State an amount which bears the same ratio to the amount of such remainder as the number of infants and toddlers in the State bears to the number of infants and toddlers in all States, except that no State shall receive less than 0.5 percent of such remainder.

(2) For the purpose of paragraph (1)—

(A) the terms "infants" and "toddlers" mean children from birth to age 2, inclusive, and

(B) the term "State" does not include the jurisdictions described in subsection (a) of this section.

(d) Election by State not to receive allotment

If any State elects not to receive it allotment under subsection (c)(1) of this section, the Secretary shall reallot, among the remaining States, amounts from such State in accordance with such subsection.

§ 1485. Authorization of appropriations

There are authorized to be appropriated to carry out this subchapter $50,000,000 for fiscal year 1987, $75,000,000 for fiscal year 1988, and such sums as may be necessary for each of the 3 succeeding fiscal years.

APPENDIX B

FEDERAL REGULATIONS
AND
AMENDMENTS THROUGH 1990

[The most important federal regulations and amendments affecting the education of handicapped children, Parts 300 and 104 of Title 34 of the Code of Federal Regulations, have been reproduced here in their entirety as promulgated by the U.S. Department of Education.]

PART 300—ASSISTANCE TO STATES FOR EDUCATION OF HANDICAPPED CHILDREN

Subpart A—General

PURPOSE, APPLICABILITY, AND GENERAL PROVISIONS REGULATIONS

Subpart B—State Annual Program Plans and Local Applications

ANNUAL PROGRAM PLANS—GENERAL

ANNUAL PROGRAM PLANS—CONTENTS

LOCAL EDUCATIONAL AGENCY APPLICATIONS—GENERAL

LOCAL EDUCATIONAL AGENCY APPLICATIONS—CONTENTS

*See 1989 Amendments to EAHCA Regulations

*See 1989 Amendments to EAHCA Regulations

*See 1989 Amendments to EAHCA Regulations

AUTHORITY: 20 U.S.C. 1411-1420, unless otherwise noted.

SOURCE: 42 FR 42476, Aug. 23, 1977, unless otherwise noted. Redesignated at 45 FR 77368, Nov. 21, 1980.

Subpart A—General

PURPOSE, APPLICABILITY, AND GENERAL PROVISIONS REGULATIONS

§ 300.1 Purpose.

The purpose of this part is:

(a) To insure that all handicapped children have available to them a free appropriate public education which includes special education and related services to meet their unique needs,

(b) To insure that the rights of handicapped children and their parents are protected,

(c) To assist States and localities to provide for the education of all handicapped children, and

(d) To assess and insure the effectiveness of efforts to educate those children.

(Authority: 20 U.S.C. 1401 Note)

§ 300.2 Applicability to State, local, and private agencies.

(a) *States.* This part applies to each State which receives payments under Part B of the Education of the Handicapped Act.

(b) *Public agencies within the State.* The annual program plan is submitted by the State educational agency on behalf of the State as a whole. Therefore, the provisions of this part apply to all political subdivisions of the State that are involved in the education of handicapped children. These would include:

(1) The State educational agency, (2) local educational agencies and intermediate educational units, (3) other State agencies and schools (such as Departments of Mental Health and Welfare and State schools for the deaf or blind), and (4) State correctional facilities.

(c) *Private schools and facilities.* Each public agency in the State is responsible for insuring that the rights and protections under this part are given to children referred to or placed in private schools and facilities by that public agency.

(See §§ 300.400–300.403)

(Authority: 20 U.S.C. 1412(1), (6); 1413(a); 1413(a)(4)(B))

Comment. The requirements of this part are binding on each public agency that has direct or delegated authority to provide special education and related services in a State that receives funds under Part B of the Act, regardless of whether that agency is receiving funds under Part B.

§ 300.3 Regulations that apply to assistance to States for education of handicapped children.

(a) *Regulations.* The following regulations apply to this program of Assistance to States for Education of Handicapped Children.

(1) The Education Department General Administrative Regulations (EDGAR) in 34 CFR Part 76 (State-Administered Programs) and Part 77 (Definitions).

(2) The regulations in this Part 300.

(b) *How to use regulations; how to apply for funds.* The "Introduction to Regulations of the Department" at the beginning of EDGAR includes general information to assist in—

(1) Using regulations that apply to Department programs; and

(2) Applying for assistance under a Department program.

(Authority: 20 U.S.C. 1221e-3(a)(1))

DEFINITIONS

Comment. Definitions of terms that are used throughout these regulations are included in this subpart. Other terms are defined in the specific subparts in which they are used. Below is a list of those terms and the specific sections and subparts in which they are defined:

Consent (§ 300.500 of Subpart E)
Destruction (§ 300.560 of Subpart E)
Direct services (§ 300.370(b)(1) of Subpart C)
Evaluation (§ 300.500 of Subpart E)

*See 1989 Amendments to EAHCA Regulations

First priority children (§ 300.320(a) of Subpart C)
Independent educational evaluation (§ 300.503 of Subpart E)
Individualized education program (§ 300.340 of Subpart C)
Participating agency (§ 300.560 of Subpart E)
Personally identifiable (§ 300.500 of Subpart E)
Private school handicapped children (§ 300.450 of Subpart D)
Public expense (§ 300.503 of Subpart E)
Second priority children (§ 300.320(b) of Subpart C)
Special definition of "State" (§ 300.700 of Subpart G)
Support services (§ 300.370(b)(2) of Subpart C)

[42 FR 42476, Aug. 23, 1977, as amended at 45 FR 22531, Apr. 3, 1980. Redesignated at 45 FR 77368, Nov. 21, 1980]

§ 300.4   Free appropriate public education.

As used in this part, the term "free appropriate public education" means special education and related services which:

(a) Are provided at public expense, under public supervision and direction, and without charge.

(b) Meet the standards of the State educational agency, including the requirements of this part,

(c) Include preschool, elementary school, or secondary school education in the State involved, and

(d) Are provided in conformity with an individualized education program which meets the requirements under §§ 300.340–300.349 of Subpart C.

(Authority: 20 U.S.C. 1401(18))

§ 300.5   Handicapped children.

(a) As used in this part, the term "handicapped children" means those children evaluated in accordance with §§ 300.530–300.534 as being mentally retarded, hard of hearing, deaf, speech impaired, visually handicapped, seriously emotionally disturbed, orthopedically impaired, other health impaired, deaf-blind, multi-handicapped, or as having specific learning disabilities, who because of those impairments need special education and related services.

(b) The terms used in this definition are defined as follows:

(1) "Deaf" means a hearing impairment which is so severe that the child is impaired in processing linguistic information through hearing, with or without amplification, which adversely affects educational performance.

(2) "Deaf-blind" means concomitant hearing and visual impairments, the combination of which causes such severe communication and other developmental and educational problems that they cannot be accommodated in special education programs solely for deaf or blind children.

(3) "Hard of Hearing" means a hearing impairment, whether permanent or fluctuating, which adversely affects a child's educational performance but which is not included under the definition of "deaf" in this section.

(4) "Mentally retarded" means significantly subaverage general intellectual functioning existing concurrently with deficits in adaptive behavior and manifested during the developmental period, which adversely affects a child's educational performance.

(5) "Multihandicapped" means concomitant impairments (such as mentally retarded—blind, mentally retarded-orthopedically impaired, etc.), the combination of which causes such severe educational problems that they cannot be accommodated in special education programs solely for one of the impairments. The term does not include deaf-blind children.

(6) "Orthopedically impaired" means a severe orthopedic impairment which adversely affects a child's educational performance. The term includes impairments caused by congenital anomaly (e.g., clubfoot, absence of some member, etc.), impairments caused by disease (e.g. poliomyelitis, bone tuberculosis, etc.), and impairments from other causes (e.g., cerebral palsy, amputations, and fractures or burns which cause contractures).

(7) "Other health impaired" means (i) having an autistic condition which is manifested by severe communication and other developmental and educational problems; or (ii) having limited strength, vitality or alertness, due to chronic or acute health problems such as a heart condition, tuberculosis, rhematic fever, nephritis, asthma, sickle cell anemia, hemophilia, epilepsy, lead poisoning, leukemia, or diabe-

tes, which adversely affects a child's educational performance.

(8) "Seriously emotionally disturbed" is defined as follows:

(i) The term means a condition exhibiting one or more of the following characteristics over a long period of time and to a marked degree, which adversely affects educational performance:

(A) An inability to learn which cannot be explained by intellectual, sensory, or health factors;

(B) An inability to build or maintain satisfactory interpersonal relationships with peers and teachers;

(C) Inappropriate types of behavior or feelings under normal circumstances;

(D) A general pervasive mood of unhappiness or depression; or

(E) A tendency to develop physical symptoms or fears associated with personal or school problems.

(ii) The term includes children who are schizophrenic. The term does not include children who are socially maladjusted, unless it is determined that they are seriously emotionally disturbed.

(9) "Specific learning disability" means a disorder in one or more of the basic psychological processes involved in understanding or in using language, spoken or written, which may manifest itself in an imperfect ability to listen, think, speak, read, write, spell, or to do mathematical calculations. The term includes such conditions as perceptual handicaps, brain injury, minimal brain disfunction, dyslexia, and developmental aphasia. The term does not include children who have learning problems which are primarily the result of visual, hearing, or motor handicaps, of mental retardation of emotional disturbance or of environmental, cultural, or economic disadvantage.

(10) "Speech impaired" means a communication disorder such as stuttering, impaired articulation, a language impairment, or a voice impairment, which adversely affects a child's educational performance.

(11) "Visually handicapped" means a visual impairment which, even with correction, adversely affects a child's educational performance. The term includes both partially seeing and blind children.

(Authority: 20 U.S.C. 1401(1), (15))

[42 FR 42476, Aug. 23, 1977, as amended at 42 FR 65083, Dec. 29, 1977. Redesignated at 45 FR 77368, Nov. 21, 1980, and further amended at 46 FR 3866, Jan. 16, 1981]

§ 300.6 Include.

As used in this part, the term "include" means that the items named are not all of the possible items that are covered, whether like or unlike the ones named.

(Authority: 20 U.S.C. 1417(b))

§ 300.7 Intermediate educational unit.

As used in this part, the term "intermediate educational unit" means any public authority, other than a local educational agency, which:

(a) Is under the general supervision of a State educational agency;

(b) Is established by State law for the purpose of providing free public education on a regional basis; and

(c) Provides special education and related services to handicapped children within that State.

(Authority: 20 U.S.C. 1401 (22))

§ 300.8 Local educational agency.

(a) [Reserved]

(b) For the purposes of this part, the term "local educational agency" also includes intermediate educational units.

(Authority: 20 U.S.C. 1401 (8))

[42 FR 42476, Aug. 23, 1977, as amended at 45 FR 22531, Apr. 3, 1980. Redesignated at 45 FR 77368, Nov. 21, 1980]

§ 300.9 Native language.

As used in this part, the term "native language" has the meaning given that term by section 703(a)(2) of the Bilingual Education Act, which provides as follows:

The term "native language", when used with reference to a person of limited English-speaking ability, means the language normally used by that person, or in the case of a child, the language normally used by the parents of the child.

(Authority: 20 U.S.C. 880b–1(a)(2); 1401(21))

Comment. Section 602(21) of the Education of the Handicapped Act states that the term "native language" has the same meaning as the definition from the Bilingual Education Act. (The term is used in the prior notice and evaluation sections under § 300.505(b)(2) and § 300.532(a)(1) of Subpart E.) In using the term, the Act does not prevent the following means of communication:

(1) In all direct contact with a child (including evaluation of the child), communication would be in the language normally used by the child and not that of the parents, if there is a difference between the two.

(2) If a person is deaf or blind, or has no written language, the mode of communication would be that normally used by the person (such as sign language, braille, or oral communication).

§ 300.10 Parent.

As used in this part, the term "parent" means a parent, a guardian, a person acting as a parent of a child, or a surrogate parent who has been appointed in accordance with § 300.514. The term does not include the State if the child is a ward of the State.

(Authority: 20 U.S.C. 1415)

Comment. The term "parent" is defined to include persons acting in the place of a parent, such as a grandmother or stepparent with whom a child lives, as well as persons who are legally responsible for a child's welfare.

§ 300.11 Public agency.

As used in this part, the term "public agency" includes the State educational agency, local educational agencies, intermediate educational units, and any other political subdivision of the State which are responsible for providing education to handicapped children.

(Authority: 20 U.S.C. 1412(2)(B); 1412(6); 1413(a))

§ 300.12 Qualified.

As used in this part, the term "qualified" means that a person has met State educational agency approved or recognized certification, licensing, registration, or other comparable requirements which apply to the area in which he or she is providing special education or related services.

(Authority: 20 U.S.C. 1417(b))

§ 300.13 Related services.

(a) As used in this part, the term "related services" means transportation and such developmental, corrective, and other supportive services as are required to assist a handicapped child to benefit from special education, and includes speech pathology and audiology, psychological services, physical and occupational therapy, recreation, early identification and assessment of disabilities in children, counseling services, and medical services for diagnostic or evaluation purposes. The term also includes school health services, social work services in schools, and parent counseling and training.

(b) The terms used in this definition are defined as follows:

(1) "Audiology" includes:

(i) Identification of children with hearing loss;

(ii) Determination of the range, nature, and degree of hearing loss, including referral for medical or other professional attention for the habilitation of hearing;

(iii) Provision of habilitative activities, such as language habilitation, auditory training, speech reading (lipreading), hearing evaluation, and speech conservation;

(iv) Creation and administration of programs for prevention of hearing loss;

(v) Counseling and guidance of pupils, parents, and teachers regarding hearing loss; and

(vi) Determination of the child's need for group and individual amplification, selecting and fitting an appropriate aid, and evaluating the effectiveness of amplification.

(2) "Counseling services" means services provided by qualified social workers, psychologists, guidance counselors, or other qualified personnel.

(3) "Early identification" means the implementation of a formal plan for identifying a disability as early as possible in a child's life.

(4) "Medical services" means services provided by a licensed physician to determine a child's medically related handicapping condition which results in the child's need for special education and related services.

(5) "Occupational therapy" includes:

(i) Improving, developing or restoring functions impaired or lost through illness, injury, or deprivation;

(ii) Improving ability to perform tasks for independent functioning when functions are impaired or lost; and

(iii) Preventing, through early intervention, initial or further impairment or loss of function.

(6) "Parent counseling and training" means assisting parents in understanding the special needs of their child and providing parents with information about child development.

(7) "Physical therapy" means services provided by a qualified physical therapist.

(8) "Psychological services" include:

(i) Administering psychological and educational tests, and other assessment procedures;

(ii) Interpreting assessment results;

(iii) Obtaining, integrating, and interpreting information about child behavior and conditions relating to learning.

(iv) Consulting with other staff members in planning school programs to meet the special needs of children as indicated by psychological tests, interviews, and behavioral evaluations; and

(v) Planning and managing a program of psychological services, including psychological counseling for children and parents.

(9) "Recreation" includes:

(i) Assessment of leisure function;

(ii) Therapeutic recreation services;

(iii) Recreation programs in schools and community agencies; and

(iv) Leisure education.

(10) "School health services" means services provided by a qualified school nurse or other qualified person.

(11) "Social work services in schools" include:

(i) Preparing a social or developmental history on a handicapped child;

(ii) Group and individual counseling with the child and family;

(iii) Working with those problems in a child's living situation (home, school, and community) that affect the child's adjustment in school; and

(iv) Mobilizing school and community resources to enable the child to receive maximum benefit from his or her educational program.

(12) "Speech pathology" includes:

(i) Identification of children with speech or language disorders;

(ii) Diagnosis and appraisal of specific speech or langue disorders;

(iii) Referral for medical or other professional attention necessary for the habilitation of speech or language disorders;

(iv) Provisions of speech and language services for the habilitation or prevention of communicative disorders; and

(v) Counseling and guidance of parents, children, and teachers regarding speech and language disorders.

(13) "Transportation" includes:

(i) Travel to and from school and between schools,

(ii) Travel in and around school buildings, and

(iii) Specialized equipment (such as special or adapted buses, lifts, and ramps), if required to provide special transportation for a handicapped child.

(Authority: 20 U.S.C. 1401 (17))

Comment. With respect to related services, the Senate Report states:

The Committee bill provides a definition of "related services," making clear that all such related services may not be required for each individual child and that such term includes early identification and assessment of handicapping conditions and the provision of services to minimize the effects of such conditions.

(Senate Report No. 94-168, p. 12 (1975))

The list of related services is not exhaustive and may include other developmental, corrective, or supportive services (such as artistic and cultural programs, and art, music, and dance therapy), if they are required to assist a handicapped child to benefit from special education.

There are certain kinds of services which might be provided by persons from varying professional backgrounds and with a variety of operational titles, depending upon requirements in individual States. For example, counseling services might be provided by social workers, psychologists, or guidance counselors; and psychological testing might be done by qualified psychological examiners, psychometrists, or psychologists, depending upon State standards.

Each related service defined under this part may include appropriate administrative and supervisory activities that are necessary for program planning, management, and evaluation.

§ 300.14 Special education.

(a) (1) As used in this part, the term "special education" means specially designed instruction, at no cost to the parent, to meet the unique needs of a handicapped child, including classroom instruction, instruction in physical education, home instruction, and instruction in hospitals and institutions.

(2) The term includes speech pathology, or any other related service, if the service consists of specially designed instruction, at no cost to the parents, to meet the unique needs of a handicapped child, and is considered "special education" rather than a "related service" under State standards.

(3) The term also includes vocational education if it consists of specially designed instruction, at no cost to the parents, to meet the unique needs of a handicapped child.

(b) The terms in this definition are defined as follows:

(1) "At no cost" means that all specially designed instruction is provided without charge, but does not preclude incidental fees which are normally charged to non-handicapped students or their parents as a part of the regular education program.

(2) "Physical education" is defined as follows:

(i) The term means the development of:

(A) Physical and motor fitness;

(B) Fundamental motor skills and patterns; and

(C) Skills in aquatics, dance, and individual and group games and sports (including intramural and lifetime sports).

(ii) The term includes special physical education, adapted physical education, movement education, and motor development.

(Authority: 20 U.S.C. 1401 (16))

(3) "Vocational education" means organized educational programs which are directly related to the preparation of individuals for paid or unpaid employment, or for additional preparation for a career requiring other than a baccalaureate or advanced degree.

(Authority: 20 U.S.C. 1401 (16))

Comment. (1) The definition of "special education" is a particularly important one under these regulations, since a child is not handicapped unless he or she needs special education. (See the definition of "handicapped children" in § 300.5.) The definition of "related services" (§ 300.13) also depends on this definition, since a related service must be necessary for a child to benefit from special education. Therefore, if a child does not need special education, there can be no "related services," and the child (because not "handicapped") is not covered under the Act.

(2) The above definition of vocational education is taken from the Vocational Education Act of 1963, as amended by Pub. L. 94–482. Under that Act, "vocational education" includes industrial arts and consumer and homemaking education programs.

Subpart B—State Annual Program Plans and Local Applications

ANNUAL PROGRAM PLANS—GENERAL

§ 300.110 Condition of assistance.

In order to receive funds under Part B of the Act for any fiscal year, a State must submit an annual program plan to the Secretary through its State educational agency.

(Authority: 20 U.S.C. 1232c(b), 1412, 1413)

§ 300.111 Contents of plan.

Each annual program plan must contain the provisions required in this subpart.

(Authority: 20 U.S.C. 1412, 1413, 1232c(b))

ANNUAL PROGRAM PLANS—CONTENTS

§ 300.121 Right to a free appropriate public education.

(a) Each annual program plan must include information which shows that the State has in effect a policy which insures that all handicapped children have the right to a free appropriate public education within the age ranges and timelines under § 300.122.

(b) The information must include a copy of each State statute, court order, State Attorney General opinion, and other State document that shows the source of the policy.

(c) The information must show that the policy:

(1) Applies to all public agencies in the State;

(2) Applies to all handicapped children;

(3) Implements the priorities established under § 300.127(a)(1) of this subpart; and

(4) Establishes timeliness for implementing the policy, in accordance with § 300.122.

(Authority: 20 U.S.C. 1412(1)(2)(B), (6); 1413(a)(3))

§ 300.122 Timeliness and ages for free appropriate public education.

(a) *General.* Each annual program plan must include in detail the policies and procedures which the State will undertake or has undertaken in order to insure that a free appropriate public education is available for all handicapped children aged three through eighteen within the State not later than September 1, 1978, and for all handicapped children aged three through twenty-one within the State not later than September 1, 1980.

(b) *Documents relating to timeliness.* Each annual program plan must include a copy of each statute, court order, attorney general decision, an other State document which demonstrates that the State has established timelines in accordance with paragraph (a) of this secton.

(c) *Exception.* The requirement in paragraph (a) of this section does not apply to a State with respect to handicapped children aged three, four, five, eighteen, nineteen, twenty, or twenty-one to the extent that the requirement would be inconsistent with State law or practice, or the order of any court, respecting public education for one or more of those age groups in the State.

(d) *Documents relating to exceptions.* Each annual program plan must:

(1) Describe in detail the extent to which the exception in paragraph (c) of this section applies to the State, and

(2) Include a copy of each State law, court order, and other document which provides a basis for the exception.

(Authority: 20 U.S.C. 1412(2)(B))

§ 300.123 Full educational opportunity goal.

Each annual program plan must include in detail the policies and procedures which the State will undertake, or has undertaken, in order to insure that the State has a goal of providing full educational opportunity to all handicapped children aged birth through twenty-one.

(Authority: 20 U.S.C. 1412(2)(A))

§ 300.124 Full educational opportunity goal—data requirement.

Beginning with school year 1978–1979, each annual program plan must contain the following information:

(a) The estimated number of handicapped children who need special education and related services.

(b) For the current school year:

(1) The number of handicapped children aged birth through two, who are receiving special education and related services; and

(2) The number of handicapped children:

(i) Who are receiving a free appropriate public education,

(ii) Who need, but are not receiving a free appropriate public education,

(iii) Who are enrolled in public private institutions who are receiving a free appropriate public education, and

(iv) Who are enrolled in public and private institutions and are not receiving a free appropriate public education.

(c) The estimated numbers of handicapped children who are expected to receive special education and related services during the next school year.

(d) A description of the basis used to determine the data required under this section.

(e) The data required by paragraphs (a), (b), and (c) of this section must be provided:

(1) For each disability category (except for children aged birth through two), and

(2) For each of the following age ranges: birth through two, three through five, six through seventeen, and eighteen through twenty-one.

(Authority: 20 U.S.C. 1412(2)(A))

Comment. In Part B of the Act, the term "disability" is used interchangeably with "handicapping condition". For consistency in this regulation, a child with a "disability" means a child with one of the impairments listed in the definition of "handicapped children" in § 300.5, if the child needs special education because of the impairment. In essence, there is a continuum of impairments. When an impairment is of such a nature that the child needs special education, it is referred to as a disability, in these regulations, and the child is a "handicapped" child.

States should note that data required under this section are not to be transmitted to the Secretary in personally identifiable form. Generally, except for such purposes as monitoring and auditing, neither the States nor the Federal Government should have to collect data under this part in personally identifiable form.

§ 300.125 Full educational opportunity goal—timetable.

(a) *General requirement.* Each annual program plan must contain a detailed timetable for accomplishing the goal of providing full educational opportunity for all handicapped children.

(b) *Content of timetable.* (1) The timetable must indicate what percent of the total estimated number of handicapped children the State expects to have full educational opportunity in each succeeding school year.

(2) The data required under this paragraph must be provided:

(i) For each disability category (except for children aged birth through two), and

(ii) For each of the following age ranges: birth through two, three through five, six through seventeen, and eighteen through twenty-one.

(Authority: 20 U.S.C. 1412(2)(A))

§ 300.126 Full educational opportunity goal—facilities, personnel, and services.

(a) *General requirement.* Each annual program plan must include a description of the kind and number of facilities, personnel, and services necessary throughout the State to meet the goal of providing full educational opportunity for all handicapped children. The State educational agency shall include the data required under paragraph (b) of this section and

whatever additional data are necessary to meet the requirement.

(b) *Statistical description.* Each annual program plan must include the following data:

(1) The number of additional special class teachers, resource room teachers, and intinerant or consultant teachers needed for each disability category and the number of each of these who are currently employed in the State.

(2) The number of other additional personnel needed, and the number currently employed in the State, including school psychologists, school social workers, occupational therapists, physical therapists, home-hospital teachers, speech-language pathologists, audiologists, teacher aides, vocational education teachers, work study coordinators, physical education teachers, therapeutic recreation specialists, diagnostic personnel, supervisors, and other instructional and noninstructional staff.

(3) The total number of personnel reported under paragraphs (b)(1) and (2) of this section, and the salary costs of those personnel.

(4) The number and kind of facilities needed for handicapped children and the number and kind currently in use in the State, including regular classes serving handicapped children, self-contained classes on a regular school campus, resource rooms, private special education day schools, public special education day schools, private special education residential schools, public special education residential schools, hospital programs, occupational therapy facilities, physical therapy facilities, public sheltered workshops, private sheltered workshops, and other types of facilities.

(5) The total number of transportation units needed for handicapped children, the number of transportation units designed for handicapped children which are in use in the State, and the number of handicapped children who use these units to benefit from special education.

(c) *Data categories.* The data required under paragraph (b) of this section must be provided as follows:

(1) Estimates for serving all handicapped children who require special education and related services,

(2) Current year data, based on the actual numbers of handicapped children receiving special education and related services (as reported under Subpart G), and

(3) Estimates for the next school year.

(d) *Rationale.* Each annual program plan must include a description of the means used to determine the number and salary costs of personnel.

(Authority: 20 U.S.C. 1412(2)(A))

§ 300.127   Priorities.

(a) *General requirement.* Each annual program plan must include information which shows that:

(1) The State has established priorities which meet the requirements under §§ 300.320–300.324 of Subpart C.

(2) The State priorities meet the timelines under § 300.122 of this subpart, and

(3) The State has made progress in meeting those timeliness.

(b) *Child data.* (1) Each annual program plan must show the number of handicapped children known by the State to be in each of the first two priority groups named in § 300.321 of Subpart C:

(i) By disability category, and

(ii) By the age ranges in § 300.124(e)(2) of this subpart.

(c) *Activities and resources.* Each annual program plan must show for each of the first two priority groups:

(1) The programs, services, and activities that are being carried out in the State,

(2) The Federal, State, and local resources that have been committed during the current school year, and

(3) The programs, services, activities, and resources that are to be provided during the next school year.

(Authority: 20 U.S.C. 1412(3))

§ 300.128   Identification,   location,   and evaluation of handicapped children.

(a) *General requirement.* Each annual program plan must include in detail the policies and procedures which the State will undertake or has undertaken to insure that:

(1) All children who are handicapped, regardless of the severity of their handicap, and who are in need of special education and related services are identified, located, and evaluated; and

(2) A practical method is developed and implemented to determine which children are currently receiving needed special education and related services and which children are not currently receiving needed special education and related services.

(b) *Information.* Each annual program plan must:

(1) Designate the State agency (if other than the State educational agency) responsible for coordinating the planning and implementation of the policies and procedures under paragraph (a) of this section;

(2) Name each agency that participates in the planning and implementation and describe the nature and extent of its participation;

(3) Describe the extent to which:

(i) The activities described in paragraph (a) of this section have been achieved under the current annual program plan, and

(ii) The resources named for these activities in that plan have been used;

(4) Describe each type of activity to be carried out during the next school year, including the role of the agency named under paragraph (b)(1) of this section, timelines for completing those activities, resources that will be used, and expected outcomes;

(5) Describe how the policies and procedures under paragraph (a) of this section will be monitored to insure that the State educational agency obtains:

(i) The number of handicapped children within each disability category that have been identified, located, and evaluated, and

(ii) Information adequate to evaluate the effectiveness of those policies and procedures; and

(6) Describe the method the State uses to determine which children are currently receiving special education and related services and which children are not receiving special education and related services.

(Authority: 20 U.S.C. 1412(2)(C))

Comment. The State is responsible for insuring that all handicapped children are identified, located, and evaluated, including children in all public and private agencies and institutions in the State. Collection and use of data are subject to the confidentiality requirements in §§ 300.560–300.576.

§ 300.129 Confidentiality of personally identifiable information.

(a) Each annual program plan must include in detail the policies and procedures which the State will undertake or has undertaken in order to insure the protection of the confidentiality of any personally identifiable information collected, used, or maintained under this part.

(b) The Secretary shall use the criteria in §§ 300.560–300.576 of Subpart E to evaluate the policies and procedures of the State under paragraph (a) of this section.

(Authority: 20 U.S.C. 1412(2)(D); 1417(c))

Comment. The confidentiality regulations were published in the FEDERAL REGISTER in final form on February 27, 1976 (41 FR 8603–8610), and met the requirements of Part B of the Act, as amended by Pub. L. 94–142. Those regulations are incorporated in §§ 300.560–300.576 of Subpart E.

§ 300.130 Individualized education programs.

(a) Each annual program plan must include information which shows that each public agency in the State maintains records of the individualized education program for each handicapped child, and each public agency establishes, reviews, and revises each program as provided in Subpart C.

(b) Each annual program plan must include:

(1) A copy of each State statute, policy, and standard that regulates the manner in which individualized education programs are developed, implemented, reviewed, and revised, and

(2) The procedures which the State educational agency follows in monitoring and evaluating those programs.

(Authority: 20 U.S.C. 1412(4))

§ 300.131 Procedural safeguards.

Each annual program plan must include procedural safeguards which insure that the requirements in §§ 300.500–300.514 of Subpart E are met.

(Authority: 20 U.S.C. 1412(5)(A))

§ 300.132 Least restrictive environment.

(a) Each annual program plan must include procedures which insure that the requirements in §§ 300.550–300.556 of Subpart E are met.

(b) Each annual program plan must include the following information:

(1) The number of handicapped children in the State, within each disability category, who are participating in regular education programs, consistent with §§ 300.550–300.556 of Subpart E.

(2) The number of handicapped children who are in separate classes or separate school facilities, or who are otherwise removed from the regular education environment.

(Authority: 20 U.S.C. 1412(5)(B))

§ 300.133 Protection in evaluation procedures.

Each annual program plan must include procedures which insure that the requirements in §§ 300.530–300.534 of Subpart E are met.

(Authority: 20 U.S.C. 1412(5)(C))

§ 300.134 Responsibility of State educational agency for all educational programs.

(a) Each annual program plan must include information which shows that the requirements in § 300.600 of Subpart F are met.

(b) The information under paragraph (a) of this section must include a copy of each State statute, State regulation, signed agreement between respective agency officials, and any other document that shows compliance with that paragraph.

(Authority: 20 U.S.C. 1412(6))

§ 300.135 [Reserved]

§ 300.136 Implementation procedures— State educational agency.

Each annual program plan must describe the procedures the State educational agency follows to inform each public agency of its responsibility for insuring effective implementation of procedural safeguards for the handicapped children served by that public agency.

(Authority: 20 U.S.C. 1412(6))

§ 300.137   Procedures for consultation.

Each annual program plan must include an assurance that in carrying out the requirements of section 612 of the Act, procedures are established for consultation with individuals involved in or concerned with the education of handicapped children, including handicapped individuals and parents of handicapped children.

(Authority: 20 U.S.C. 1412(7)(A))

*§ 300.138   Other Federal programs.

Each annual program plan must provide that programs and procedures are established to insure that funds received by the State or any public agency in the State under any other Federal program, including section 121 of the Elementary and Secondary Education Act of 1965 (20 U.S.C. 241e-2), section 305(b)(8) of that Act (20 U.S.C. 844a(b)(8)) or Title IV-C of that Act (20 U.S.C. 1831), and section 110(a) of the Vocational Education Act of 1963, under which there is specific authority for assistance for the education of handicapped children, are used by the State, or any public agency in the State, only in a manner consistent with the goal of providing free appropriate public education for all handicapped children, except that nothing in this section limits the specific requirements of the laws governing those Federal programs.

(Authority: 20 U.S.C. 1413(a)(2))

§ 300.139   Comprehensive system of personnel development.

Each annual program plan must include the material required under §§ 300.380–300.387 of Subpart C.

(Authority: 20 U.S.C. 1413(a)(3))

§ 300.140   Private schools.

Each annual program plan must include policies and procedures which insure that the requirements of Subpart D are met.

(Authority: 20 U.S.C. 1413(a)(4))

§ 300.141   Recovery of funds for misclassified children.

Each annual program plan must include policies and procedures which insure that the State seeks to recover any funds provided under Part B of the Act for services to a child who is determined to be erroneously classified as eligible to be counted under section 611 (a) or (d) of the Act.

(Authority: 20 U.S.C. 1413(a)(5))

§ 300.142—300.143   [Reserved]

§ 300.144   Hearing on application.

Each annual program plan must include procedures to insure that the State educational agency does not take any final action with respect to an application submitted by a local educational agency before giving the local educational agency reasonable notice and an opportunity for a hearing.

(Authority: 20 U.S.C. 1413(a)(8))

§ 300.145   Prohibition of commingling.

Each annual program plan must provide assurance satisfactory to the Secretary that funds provided under Part B of the Act are not commingled with State funds.

(Authority: 20 U.S.C. 1413(a)(9))

Comment. This assurance is satisfied by the use of a separate accounting system that includes an "audit trail" of the expenditure of the Part B funds. Separate bank accounts are not required. (See 34 CFR 76, Subpart F (Cash Depositories))

§ 300.146   Annual evaluation.

Each annual program plan must include procedures for evaluation at least annually of the effectivesness of programs in meeting the educational needs of handicapped children, including evaluation of individualized education programs.

(Authority: 20 U.S.C. 1413(a)(11))

§ 300.147   State advisory panel.

Each annual program plan must provide that the requirements of §§ 300.650–300.653 of Subpart F are met.

(Authority: 20 U.S.C. 1413(a)(12))

§ 300.148   Policies and procedures for use of Part B funds.

Each annual program plan must set forth policies and procedures designed

*See 1989 Amendments to EAHCA Regulations, page 431; § **300.138**.

to insure that funds paid to the State under Part B of the Act are spent in accordance with the provisions of Part B, with particular attention given to sections 611(b), 611(c), 611(d), 612(2), and 612(3) of the Act.

(Authority: 20 U.S.C. 1413(a)(1))

§ 300.149 Description of use of Part B funds.

(a) *State allocation.* Each annual program plan must include the following information about the State's use of funds under § 300.370 of Subpart C and § 300.620 of Subpart F:

(1) A list of administrative positions, and a description of duties for each person whose salary is paid in whole or in part with those funds.

(2) For each position, the percentage of salary paid with those funds.

(3) A description of each administrative activity the State educational agency will carry out during the next school year with those funds.

(4) A description of each direct service and each support service which the State educational agency will provide during the next school year with those funds, and the activities the State advisory panel will undertake during that period with those funds.

(b) *Local educational agency allocation.* Each annual program plan must include:

(1) An estimate of the number and percent of local educational agencies in the State which will receive an allocation under this part (other than local educational agencies which submit a consolidated application),

(2) An estimate of the number of local educational agencies which will receive an allocation under a consolidated application,

(3) An estimate of the number of consolidated applications and the average number of local educational agencies per application, and

(4) A description of direct services the State educational agency will provide under § 300.360 of Subpart C.

(Authority: 20 U.S.C. 1232c(b)(1)(B)(ii))

*§ 300.150   [Reserved]

§ 300.151 Additional information if the State educational agency provides direct services.

If a State educational agency provides free appropriate public education for handicapped children or provides them with direct services, its annual program plan must include the information required under §§ 300.226–300.228, 300.231, and 300.235.

(Authority: 20 U.S.C. 1413(b))   *

Local Educational Agency Applications—General

§ 300.180 Submission of application.

In order to receive payments under Part B of the Act for any fiscal year a local educational agency must submit an application to the State educational agency.

(Authority: 20 U.S.C. 1414(a))

§ 300.181 [Reserved]

§ 300.182 The excess cost requirement.

A local educational agency may only use funds under Part B of the Act for the excess costs of providing special education and related services for handicapped children.

(Authority: 20 U.S.C. 1414 (a)(1), (a)(2)(B)(i))

§ 300.183 Meeting the excess cost requirement.

(a) A local educational agency meets the excess cost requirement if it has on the average spent at least the amount determined under § 300.184 for the education of each of its handicapped children. This amount may not include capital outlay or debt service.

(Authority: 20 U.S.C. 1402(20); 1414(a)(1))

Comment. The excess cost requirement means that the local educational agency must spend a certain minimum amount for the education of its handicapped children before Part B funds are used. This insures that children served with Part B funds have at least the same average amount spent on them, from sources other than Part B, as do the children in the school district taken as a whole.

---

*See 1989 Amendments to EAHCA Regulations, page 423; § § **300.150, 300.152, 300.153.**

The minimum amount that must be spent for the education of handicapped children is computed under a statutory formula. Section 300.184 implements this formula and gives a step-by-step method to determine the minimum amount. Excess costs are those costs of special education and related services which exceed the minimum amount. Therefore, if a local educational agency can show that it has (on the average) spent the minimum amount for the education of each of its handicapped children, it has met the excess cost requirement, and all additional costs are excess costs. Part B funds can then be used to pay for these additional costs, subject to the other requirements of Part B (priorities, etc.). In the "Comment" under § 300.184, there is an example of how the minimum amount is computed.

[42 FR 42476, Aug. 23, 1977, as amended at 45 FR 22531, Apr. 3, 1980. Redesignated at 45 FR 77368, Nov. 21, 1980]

§ 300.184 Excess costs—computation of minimum amount.

The minimum average amount a local educational agency must spend under § 300.183 for the education of each of its handicapped children is computed as follows:

(a) Add all expenditures of the local educational agency in the preceding school year, except capital outlay and debt service:

(1) For elementary school students, if the handicapped child is an elementary school student, or

(2) For secondary school students, if the handicapped child is a secondary school student.

(b) From this amount, subtract the total of the following amounts spent for elementary school students or for secondary school students, as the case may be:

(1) Amounts the agency spent in the preceding school year from funds awarded under Part B of the Act and Titles I and VII of the Elementary and Secondary Education Act of 1965, and

(2) Amounts from State and local funds which the agency spent in the preceding school year for:

(i) Programs for handicapped children,

(ii) Programs to meet the special educational needs of educationally deprived children, and

(iii) Programs of bilingual education for children with limited English-speaking ability.

(c) Divide the result under paragraph (b) of this section by the average number of students enrolled in the agency in the preceding school year:

(1) In its elementary schools, if the handicapped child is an elementary school student, or

(2) In its secondary schools, if the handicapped child is a secondary school student.

(Authority: 20 U.S.C. 1414(a)(1))

Comment. The following is an example of how a local educational agency might compute the average minimum amount it must spend for the education of each of its handicapped children, under § 300.183. This example follows the formula in § 300.184. Under the statute and regulations, the local educational agency must make one computation for handicapped children in its elementary schools and a separate computation for handicapped children in its secondary schools. The computation for handicapped elementary school students would be done as follows:

a. First, the local educational agency must determine its total amount of expenditures for elementary school students from all sources—local, State, and Federal (including Part B)—in the preceding school year. Only capital outlay and debt service are excluded.

Example: A local educational agency spent the following amounts last year for elementary school students (including its handicapped elementary school students):

(1) From local tax funds	$2,750,000
(2) From State funds	7,000,000
(3) From Federal funds	750,000
	10,500,000

Of this total, $500,000 was for capital outlay and debt service relating to the education of elementary school students. This must be subtracted from total expenditures:

	$10,500,000
	−500,000
Total expenditures for elementary school students (less capital outlay and debt service)	= 10,000,000

b. Next, the local educational agency must subtract amounts spent for:

(1) Programs for handicapped children;

(2) Programs to meet the special educational needs of educationally deprived children; and

(3) Programs of bilingual education for children with limited English-speaking ability.

These are funds which the local edcational agency actually spent, not funds received last year but carried over for the current school year.

Example: The local educational agency spent the following amounts for elementary school students last year:

(1) From funds under Title I of the Elementary and Secondary Education Act of 1965	$300,000
(2) From a special State program for educationally deprived children	200,000
(3) From a grant under Part B	200,000
(4) From State funds for the education of handicapped children	500,000
(5) From a locally-funded program for handicapped children	250,000
(6) From a grant for a bilingual education program under Title VII of the Elementary and Secondary Education Act of 1965	150,000
Total	1,600,000

(A local educational agency would also include any other funds it spent from Federal, State, or local sources for the three basic purposes: Handicapped children, educationally deprived children, and bilingual education for children with limited English-speaking ability.)

This amount is subtracted from the local educational agency's total expenditure for elementary school students computed above:

$$\begin{array}{r} \$10,000,000 \\ -\ 1,600,000 \\ \hline 8,400,000 \end{array}$$

c. The local educational agency next must divide by the average number of students enrolled in the elementary schools of the agency last year (including its handicapped students).

Example: Last year, an average of 7,000 students were enrolled in the agency's elementary schools. This must be divided into the amount computed under the above paragraph:

$8,400,000/7,000$ students $= \$1,200$/student

This figure is in the minimum amount the local educational agency must spend (on the average) for the education of each of its handicapped students. Funds under Part B may be used only for costs over and above this minimum. In this example, if the local educational agency has 100 handicapped elementary school students, it must keep records adequate to show that it has spent at least $120,000 for the education of those students (100 students times $1,200/stu-

dent), not including capital outlay and debt service.

This $120,000 may come from any funds except funds under Part B, subject to any legal requirements that govern the use of those other funds.

If the local educational agency has handicapped secondary school students, it must do the same computation for them. However the amounts used in the computation would be those the local educational agency spent last year for the education of secondary school students, rather than for elementary school students.

§ 300.185   Computation of excess costs—consolidated application.

The minimum average amount under § 300.183 where two or more local educational agencies submit a consolidated application, is the average of the combined minimum average amounts determined under § 300.184 in those agencies for elementary or secondary school students, as the case may be.

(Authority: 20 U.S.C. 1414(a)(1))

§ 300.186   Excess costs—limitation on use of Part B funds.

(a) The excess cost requirement prevents a local educational agency from using funds provided under Part B of the Act to pay for all of the costs directly attributable to the education of a handicapped child, subject to paragraph (b) of this section.

(b) The excess cost requirement does not prevent a local educational agency from using Part B funds to pay for all of the costs directly attributable to the education of a handicapped child in any of the age ranges three, four, five, eighteen, nineteen, twenty, or twenty-one, if no local or State funds are available for non-handicapped children in that age range. However, the local educational agency must comply with the non-supplanting and other requirements of this part in providing the education and services.

(Authority: 20 U.S.C. 1402(20); 1414(a)(1))

§ 300.190   Consolidated applications.

(a) [Reserved]

(b) *Required applications.* A State educational agency may require local educational agencies to submit a consolidated application for payments under Part B of the Act if the State educational agency determines that an individual application submitted by a local educational agency will be disapproved because:

(1) The agency's entitlement is less than the $7,500 minimum required by section 611(c)(4)(A)(i) of the Act (§ 300.360(a)(1) of Subpart C); or

(2) The agency is unable to establish and maintain programs of sufficient size and scope to effectively meet the educational needs of handicapped children.

(c) *Size and scope of program.* The State educational agency shall establish standards and procedures for determinations under paragraph (b)(2) of this section.

(Authority: 20 U.S.C. 1414(c)(1))

[42 FR 42476, Aug. 23, 1977, as amended at 45 FR 22531, Apr. 3, 1980. Redesignated at 45 FR 77368, Nov. 21, 1980]

§ 300.191   [Reserved]

§ 300.192   State regulation of consolidated applications.

(a) The State educational agency shall issue regulations with respect to consolidated applications submitted under this part.

(b) The State educational agency's regulations must:

(1) Be consistent with section 612 (1)–(7) and section 613(a) of the Act, and

(2) Provide participating local educational agencies with joint responsibilities for implementing programs receiving payments under this part.

(Authority: 20 U.S.C. 1414(c)(2)(B))

(c) If an intermediate educational unit is required under State law to carry out this part, the joint responsibilities given to local educational agencies under paragraph (b)(2) of this section do not apply to the administration and disbursement of any payments received by the intermediate educational unit. Those administrative responsibilities must be carried out exclusively by the intermediate educational unit.

(Authority: 20 U.S.C. 1414(c)(2)(C))

§ 300.193   State educational agency approval; disapproval.

(a)–(b) [Reserved]

(c) In carrying out its functions under this section, each State educational agency shall consider any decision resulting from a hearing under §§ 300.506–300.513 of Subpart E which is adverse to the local educational agency involved in the decision.

(Authority: 20 U.S.C. 1414(b)(3))

[42 FR 42476, Aug. 23, 1977, as amended at 45 FR 22531, Apr. 3, 1980. Redesignated at 45 FR 77368, Nov. 21, 1980]

§ 300.194   Withholding.

(a) If a State educational agency, after giving reasonable notice and an opportunity for a hearing to a local educational agency, decides that the local educational agency in the administration of an application approved by the State educational agency has failed to comply with any requirement in the application, the State educational agency, after giving notice to the local educational agency, shall:

(1) Make no further payments to the local educational agency until the State educational agency is satisfied that there is no longer any failure to comply with the requirement; or

(2) Consider its decision in its review of any application made by the local educational agency under § 300.180;

(3) Or both.

(b) Any local educational agency receiving a notice from a State educational agency under paragraph (a) of this section is subject to the public notice provision in § 300.592.

(Authority: 20 U.S.C. 1414(b)(2))

LOCAL EDUCATIONAL AGENCY APPLICATIONS—CONTENTS

§ 300.220   Child identification.

Each application must include procedures which insure that all children residing within the jurisdiction of the local educational agency who are handicapped, regardless of the severity of their handicap, and who are in need of special education and related services are identified, located, and evaluated, including a practical method of determining which children are currently receiving needed special education and related services and which children are not currently receiving needed special education and related services.

(Authority: 20 U.S.C. 1414(a)(1)(A))

Comment. The local educational agency is responsible for insuring that all handicapped children within its jurisdiction are identified, located, and evaluated, including children in all public and private agencies and institutions within that jurisdiction. Collection and use of data are subject to the confidentiality requirements in §§ 300.560–300.576 of Subpart E.

§ 300.221 Confidentiality of personally identifiable information.

Each application must include policies and procedures which insure that the criteria in §§ 300.560–300.574 of Subpart E are met.

(Authority: 20 U.S.C. 1414(a)(1)(B))

§ 300.222 Full educational opportunitiy goal; timetable.

Each application must: (a) Include a goal of providing full educational opportunity to all handicapped children, aged birth through 21, and

(b) Include a detailed timetable for accomplishing the goal.

(Authority: 20 U.S.C. 1414(a)(1) (C), (D))

§ 300.223 Facilities, personnel, and services.

Each application must provide a description of the kind and number of facilities, personnel, and services necessary to meet the goal in § 300.222.

(Authority: 20 U.S.C. 1414(a)(1)(E))

§ 300.224 Personnel development.

Each application must include procedures for the implementation and use of the comprehensive system of personnel development established by the State educational agency under § 300.140.

(Authority: 20 U.S.C. 1414(a)(1)(C)(i))

§ 300.225 Priorities.

Each application must include priorities which meet the requirements of §§ 300.320–300.324.

(Authority: 20 U.S.C. 1414(a)(1)(C)(ii))

§ 300.226 Parent involvement.

Each application must include procedures to insure that, in meeting the goal under § 300.222, the local educational agency makes provision for participation of and consultation with parents or guardians of handicapped children.

(Authority: 20 U.S.C. 1414(a)(1)(C)(iii))

§ 300.227 Participation in regular education programs.

(a) Each application must include procedures to insure that to the maximum extent practicable, and consistent with §§ 300.550–300.553 of Subpart E, the local educational agency provides special services to enable handicapped children to participate in regular educational programs.

(b) Each application must describe:

(1) The types of alternative placements that are available for handicapped children, and

(2) The number of handicapped children within each disability category who are served in each type of placement.

(Authority: 20 U.S.C. 1414(a)(1)(C)(iv))

§ 300.228 [Reserved]

§ 300.229 Excess cost.

Each application must provide assurance satisfactory to the State educational agency that the local educational agency uses funds provided under Part B of the Act only for costs which exceed the amount computed under § 300.184 and which are directly attributable to the education of handicapped children.

(Authority: 20 U.S.C. 1414(a)(2)(B))

§ 300.230 Nonsupplanting.

(a) Each application must provide assurance satisfactory to the State educational agency that the local educational agency uses funds provided under Part B of the Act to supplement and, to the extent practicable, increase the level of State and local funds expended for the education of handicapped children, and in no case to supplant those State and local funds.

(b) To meet the requirement in paragraph (a) of this section:

(1) The total amount or average per capita amount of State and local school funds budgeted by the local educational agency for expenditures in the current fiscal year for the education of handicapped children must be at least equal to the total amount or average per capita amount of State and local school funds actually expended for the education of handicapped children in the most recent preceding fiscal year for which the information is available. Allowance may be made for:

(i) Decreases in enrollment of handicapped children; and

(ii) Unusually large amounts of funds expended for such long-term purposes as the acquisition of equipment and the construction of school facilities; and

(2) The local educational agency must not use Part B funds to displace State or local funds for any particular cost.

(Authority: 20 U.S.C. 1414(a)(2)(B))

Comment. Under statutes such as Title I of the Elementary and Secondary Education Act of 1965, as amended, the requirement is to not supplant funds that "would" have been expended if the Federal funds were not available. The requirement under Part B, however, is to not supplant funds which have been "expended." This use of the past tense suggests that the funds referred to are those which the State or local agency actually spent at some time before the use of the Part B funds. Therefore, in judging compliance with this requirement, the Secretary looks to see if Part B funds are used for any costs which were previously paid for with State or local funds.

The nonsupplanting requirement prohibits a local educational agency from supplanting State and local funds with Part B funds on either an aggregate basis or for a given expenditure. This means that if an LEA spent $100,000 for special education in FY 1977, it must budget at least $100,000 in FY 1978, unless one of the conditions in § 300.230(b)(1) applies.

Whether a local educational agency supplants with respect to a particular cost would depend on the circumstances of the expenditure. For example, if a teacher's salary has been switched from local funding to Part B funding, this would appear to be supplanting. However, if that teacher was taking over a different position (such as a resource room teacher, for example), it would not be supplanting. Moreover, it might be important to consider whether the particular action of a local educational agency led to an increase in services for handicapped children over that which previously existed. The intent of the requirement is to insure that Part B funds are used to increase State and local efforts and are not used to take their place. Compliance would be judged with this aim in mind. The supplanting requirement is not intended to inhibit better services to handicapped children.

§ 300.231   Comparable services.

(a) Each application must provide assurance satisfactory to the State educational agency that the local educational agency meets the requirements of this section.

(b) A local educational agency may not use funds under Part B of the Act to provide services to handicapped children unless the agency uses State and local funds to provide services to those children which, taken as a whole, are at least comparable to services provided to other handicapped children in that local educational agency.

(c) Each local educational agency shall maintain records which show that the agency meets the requirement in paragraph (b) of this section.

(Authority: 20 U.S.C. 1414(a)(2)(C))

Comment. Under the "comparability" requirement, if State and local funds are used to provide certain services, those services must be provided with State and local funds to all handicapped children in the local educational agency who need them. Part B funds may then be used to supplement existing services, or to provide additional services to meet special needs. This, of course, is subject to the other requirements of the Act, including the priorities under §§ 300.320–300.324.

§§ 300.232—300.234   [Reserved]

§ 300.235   Individualized education program.

Each application must include procedures to assure that the local educational agency complies with §§ 300.340–300.349 of Subpart C.

(Authority: 20 U.S.C. 1414(a)(5))

§ 300.236 [Reserved]

§ 300.237 Procedural safeguards.

Each application must provide assurance satisfactory to the State educational agency that the local educational agency has procedural safeguards which meet the requirements of §§ 300.500–300.514 of Subpart E.

(Authority: 20 U.S.C. 1414(a)(7))

§ 300.238 Use of Part B funds.

Each application must describe how the local educational agency will use the funds under Part B of the Act during the next school year.

(Authority: 20 U.S.C. 1414(a))

§ 300.239 [Reserved]

§ 300.240 Other requirements.

Each local application must include additional procedures and information which the State educational agency may require in order to meet the State annual program plan requirements under §§ 300.120–300.151.

(Authority: 20 U.S.C. 1414(a)(6))

APPLICATION FROM SECRETARY OF INTERIOR

*§ 300.260 Submission of annual application; approval.

In order to receive payments under this part, the Secretary of Interior shall submit an annual application which:

(a) Meets applicable requirements of section 614(a) of the Act;

(b) Includes monitoring procedures which are consistent with § 300.601; and

(c) Includes other material as agreed to by the Secretary and the Secretary of Interior.

(Authority: 20 U.S.C. 1411(f))

§ 300.261 Public participation.

In the development of the application for the Department of Interior, the Secretary of Interior shall provide for public participation consistent with §§ 300.280–300.284.

(Authority: 20 U.S.C. 1411(f))

§ 300.262 Use of Part B funds.

(a) The Department of the Interior may use five percent of its payment in any fiscal year, or $350,000, whichever is greater, for administrative costs in carrying out the provisions of this part.

(b) The remainder of the payments to the Secretary of the Interior in any fiscal year must be used in accordance with the priorities under §§ 300.320–300.324 of Subpart C.

(Authority: 20 U.S.C. 1411(f))

[42 FR 42476, Aug. 23, 1977. Redesignated at 45 FR 77368, Nov. 21, 1980 and amended at 51 FR 19311, May 28, 1986]

EFFECTIVE DATE NOTE: In § 300.262, paragraph (a) was revised at 51 FR 19311, May 28, 1986, effective July 23, 1986. For the convenience of the reader, the superseded text is set forth below.

§ 300.262 Use of Part B funds.

(a) The Department of Interior may use five percent of its payments in any fiscal year, or $200,000, whichever is greater, for administrative costs in carrying out the provisions of this part.

*   *   *   *   *

§ 300.263 Applicable regulations.

The Secretary of the Interior shall comply with the requirements under Subparts C, E, and F.

(Authority: 20 U.S.C. 1411(f)(2))

PUBLIC PARTICIPATION

§ 300.280 Public hearings before adopting an annual program plan.

(a) Prior to its adoption of an annual program plan, the State educational agency shall:

(1) Make the plan available to the general public,

(2) Hold public hearings, and

(3) Provide an opportunity for comment by the general public on the plan.

(Authority: 20 U.S.C. 1412(7))

§ 300.281 Notice.

(a) The State educational agency shall provide notice to the general public of the public hearings.

(b) The notice must be in sufficient detail to inform the public about:

*See 1989 Amendments to EAHCA Regulations, page 425; § **300.260.**

(1) The purpose and scope of the annual program plan and its relation to Part B of the Education of the Handicapped Act,

(2) The availability of the annual program plan,

(3) The date, time, and location of each public hearing,

(4) The procedures for submitting written comments about the plan, and

(5) The timetable for developing the final plan and submitting it to the Secretary for approval.

(c) The notice must be published or announced:

(1) In newspapers or other media, or both, with circulation adequate to notify the general public about the hearings, and

(2) Enough in advance of the date of the hearings to afford interested parties throughout the State a reasonable opportunity to participate.

(Authority: 20 U.S.C. 1412(7))

§ 300.282 Opportunity to participate; comment period.

(a) The State educational agency shall conduct the public hearings at times and places that afford interested parties throughout the State a reasonable opportunity to participate.

(b) The plan must be available for comment for a period of at least 30 days following the date of the notice under § 300.281.

(Authority: 20 U.S.C. 1412(7))

§ 300.283 Review of public comments before adopting plan.

Before adopting its annual program plan, the State educational agency shall:

(a) Review and consider all public comments, and

(b) Make any necessary modifications in the plan.

(Authority: 20 U.S.C. 1412(7))

§ 300.284 Publication and availability of approved plan.

After the Secretary approves an annual program plan, the State educational agency shall give notice in newspapers or other media, or both, that the plan is approved. The notice must name places throughout the State where the plan is available for access by any interested person.

(Authority: 20 U.S.C. 1412(7))

Subpart C—Services

FREE APPROPRIATE PUBLIC EDUCATION

*§ 300.300 Timeliness for free appropriate public education.

(a) *General.* Each State shall insure that free appropriate public education is available to all handicapped children aged three through eighteen within the State not later than September 1, 1978, and to all handicapped children aged three through twenty-one within the State not later than September 1, 1980.

(b) *Age ranges 3-5 and 18-21.* This paragraph provides rules for applying the requirement in paragraph (a) of this section to handicapped children aged three, four, five, eighteen, nineteen, twenty, and twenty-one:

(1) If State law or a court order requires the State to provide education for handicapped children in any disability category in any of these age groups, the State must make a free appropriate public education available to all handicapped children of the same age who have that disability.

(2) If a public agency provides education to non-handicapped children in any of these age groups, it must make a free appropriate public education available to at least a proportionate number of handicapped children of the same age.

(3) If a public agency provides education to 50 percent or more of its handicapped children in any disability category in any of these age groups, it must make a free appropriate public education available to all of its handicapped children of the same age who have that disability.

(4) If a public agency provides education to a handicapped child in any of these age groups, it must make a free appropriate public education available to that child and provide that child and his or her parents all of the rights under Part B of the Act and this part.

(5) A State is not required to make a free appropriate public education

*See 1989 Amendments to EAHCA Regulations, page 433; § **300.300**.

available to a handicapped child in one of these age groups if:

(i) State law expressly prohibits, or does not authorize, the expenditure of public funds to provide education to nonhandicapped children in that age group; or

(ii) The requirement is inconsistent with a court order which governs the provision of free public education to handicapped children in that State.

(Authority: 20 U.S.C. 1412(2)(B); Sen. Rept. No. 94-168 p. 19 (1975))

Comment. 1. The requirement to make free appropriate public education available applies to all handicapped children within the State who are in the age ranges required under § 300.300 and who need special education and related services. This includes handicapped children already in school and children with less severe handicaps, who are not covered under the priorities under § 300.321.

2. In order to be in compliance with § 300.300, each State must insure that the requirement to identify, locate, and evaluate all handicapped children is fully implemented by public agencies throughout the State. This means that before September 1, 1978, every child who has been referred or is on a waiting list for evaluation (including children in school as well as those not receiving an education) must be evaluated in accordance with §§ 300.530-300.533 of Subpart E. If, as a result of the evaluation, it is determined that a child needs special education and related services, an individualized education program must be developed for the child by September 1, 1978, and all other applicable requirements of this part must be met.

3. The requirement to identify, locate, and evaluate handicapped children (commonly referred to as the "child find system") was enacted on August 21, 1974, under Pub. L. 93-380. While each State needed time to establish and implement its child find system, the four year period between August 21, 1974, and September 1, 1978, is considered to be sufficient to insure that the system is fully operational and effective on a State-wide basis.

Under the statute, the age range for the child find requirement (0-21) is greater than the mandated age range for providing free appropriate public education (FAPE). One reason for the broader age requirement under "child find" is to enable States to be aware of and plan for younger children who will require special education and related services. It also ties in with the full educational opportunity goal requirement, which has the same age range as child find. Moreover, while a State is not required to provide

"FAPE" to handicapped children below the age ranges mandated under § 300.300, the State may, at its discretion, extend services to those children, subject to the requirements on priorities under §§ 300.320-300.324.

§ 300.301   Free appropriate public education—methods and payments.

(a) Each State may use whatever State, local, Federal, and private sources of support are available in the State to meet the requirements of this part. For example, when it is necessary to place a handicapped child in a residential facility, a State could use joint agreements between the agencies involved for sharing the cost of that placement.

(b) Nothing in this part relieves an insurer or similar third party from an otherwise valid obligation to provide or to pay for services provided to a handicapped child.

(Authority: 20 U.S.C. 1401 (18); 1412(2)(B))

§ 300.302   Residential placement.

If placement in a public or private residential program is necessary to provide special education and related services to a handicapped child, the program, including non-medical care and room and board, must be at no cost to the parents of the child.

(Authority: 20   U.S.C.   1412(2)(B); 1413(a)(4)(B))

Comment. This requirement applies to placements which are made by public agencies for educational purposes, and includes placements in State-operated schools for the handicapped, such as a State school for the deaf or blind.

§ 300.303   Proper functioning of hearing aids.

Each public agency shall insure that the hearing aids worn by deaf and hard of hearing children in school are functioning properly.

(Authority: 20 U.S.C. 1412(2)(B))

Comment. The report of the House of Representatives on the 1978 appropriation bill includes the following statement regarding hearing aids:

In its report on the 1976 appropriation bill the Committee expressed concern about the condition of hearing aids worn by children in public schools. A study done at the Committee's direction by the Bureau of Education for the Handicapped reveals that up to one-third of the hearing aids are malfunctioning. Obviously, the Committee expects the Office of Education will ensure that hearing impaired school children are receiving adequate professional assessment, follow-up and services.

(Authority: House Report No. 95-381, p. 67 (1977))

§ 300.304 Full educational opportunity goal.

(a) Each State educational agency shall insure that each public agency establishes and implements a goal of providing full educational opportunity to all handicapped children in the area served by the public agency.

(b) Subject to the priority requirements under §§ 300.320-300.324, a State or local educational agency may use Part B funds to provide facilities, personnel, and services necessary to meet the full educational opportunity goal.

(Authority: 20   U.S.C.   1412(2)(A); 1414(a)(1)(C))

Comment. In meeting the full educational opportunity goal, the Congress also encouraged local educational agencies to include artistic and cultural activities in programs supported under this part, subject to the priority requirements under §§ 300.320-300.324. This point is addressed in the following statements from the Senate Report on Pub. L. 94-142:

The use of the arts as a teaching tool for the handicapped has long been recognized as a viable, effective way not only of teaching special skills, but also of reaching youngsters who had otherwise been unteachable. The Committee envisions that programs under this bill could well include an arts component and, indeed, urges that local educational agencies include the arts in programs for the handicapped funded under this Act. Such a program could cover both appreciation of the arts by the handicapped youngsters, and the utilization of the arts as a teaching tool per se.

Museum settings have often been another effective tool in the teaching of handicapped children. For example, the Brooklyn Museum has been a leader in developing exhibits utilizing the heightened tactile sensory skill of the blind. therefore, in light of the national policy concerning the use of museums in federally supported education programs enunciated in the Education Amendments of 1974, the Committee also urges local educational agencies to include

museums in programs for the handicapped funded under this Act.

(Authority: Senate Report No. 94-168, p. 13 (1975))

§ 300.305 Program options.

Each public agency shall take steps to insure that its handicapped children have available to them the variety of educational programs and services available to non-handicapped children in the area served by the agency, including art, music, industrial arts, consumer and homemaking education, and vocational education.

(Authority: 20   U.S.C.   1412(2)(A); 1414(a)(1)(C))

Comment. The above list of program options is not exhaustive, and could include any program or activity in which nonhandicapped students participate. Moreover, vocational education programs must be specially designed if necessary to enable a handicapped student to benefits fully from those programs; and the set-aside funds under the Vocational Education Act of 1963, as amended by Pub. L. 94-482, may be used for this purpose. Part B funds may also be used, subject to the priority requirements under §§ 300.320-300.324.

§ 300.306 Nonacademic services.

(a) Each public agency shall take steps to provide nonacademic and extracurricular services and activities in such manner as is necessary to afford handicapped children an equal opportunity for participation in those services and activities.

(b) Nonacademic and extracurricular services and activities may include counseling services, athletics, transportation, health services, recreational activities, special interest groups or clubs sponsored by the public agency, referrals to agencies which provide assistance to handicapped persons, and employment of students, including both employment by the public agency and assistance in making outside employment available.

(Authority: 20   U.S.C.   1412(2)(A); 1414(a)(1)(C))

§ 300.307 Physical education.

(a) General. Physical education services, specially designed if necessary, must be made available to every handicapped child receiving a free appropriate public education.

(b) *Regular physical education.* Each handicapped child must be afforded the opportunity to participate in the regular physical education program available to non-handicapped children unless:

(1) The child is enrolled full time in a separate facility; or

(2) The child needs specially designed physical education, as prescribed in the child's individualized education program.

(c) *Special physical education.* If specially designed physical education is prescribed in a child's individualized education program, the public agency responsible for the education of that child shall provide the services directly, or make arrangements for it to be provided through other public or private programs.

(d) *Education in separate facilities.* The public agency responsible for the education of a handicapped child who is enrolled in a separate facility shall insure that the child receives appropriate physical education services in compliance with paragraphs (a) and (c) of this section.

(Authority: 20 U.S.C. 1401(16); 1412(5)(B); 1414(a)(6))

Comment. The Report of the House of Representatives on Pub. L. 94–142 includes the following statement regarding physical education:

Special education as set forth in the Committee bill includes instruction in physical education, which is provided as a matter of course to all non-handicapped children enrolled in public elementary and secondary schools. The Committee is concerned that although these services are available to and required of all children in our school systems, they are often viewed as a luxury for handicapped children.

*   *   *   *   *

The Committee expects the Commissioner of Education to take whatever action is necessary to assure that physical education services are available to all handicapped children, and has specifically included physical education within the definition of special education to make clear that the Committee expects such services, specially designed where necessary, to be provided as an integral part of the educational program of every handicapped child.

(Authority: House Report No. 94–332, p. 9 (1975))

PRIORITIES IN THE USE OF PART B FUNDS

§ 300.320 Definitions of "first priority children" and "second priority children."

For the purposes of §§ 300.321–300.324, the term:

(a) "First priority children" means handicapped children who:

(1) Are in an age group for which the State must make available free appropriate public education under § 300.300; and

(2) Are not receiving any education.

(b) "Second priority children" means handicapped children, within each disability, with the most severe handicaps who are receiving an inadequate education.

(Authority: 20 U.S.C. 1412(3))

Comment. After September 1, 1978, there should be no second priority children, since States must insure, as a condition of receiving Part B funds or fiscal year 1979, that all handicapped children will have available a free appropriate public education by that date.

NOTE: The term "free appropriate public education," as defined in § 300.4 of Subpart A, means "special education and related services which * * * are provided in conformity with an individualized education program * * *."

New "First priority children" will continue to be found by the State after September 1, 1978 through on-going efforts to identify, locate, and evaluate all handicapped children.

§ 300.321 Priorities.

(a) Each State and local educational agency shall use funds provided under Part B or the Act in the following order of priorities:

(1) To provide free appropriate public education to first priority children, including the identification, location, and evaluation of first priority children.

(2) To provide free appropriate public education to second priority children, including the identification, location, and evaluation of second priority children.

(3) To meet the other requirements in this part.

(b) The requirements of paragraph (a) of this section do not apply to funds which the State uses for administration under § 300.620.

(Authority: 20 U.S.C. 1411 (b)(1)(B), (b)(2)(B), (c)(1)(B), (c)(2)(A)(ii))

(c) State and local educational agencies may not use funds under Part B of the Act for preservice training.

(Authority: 20 U.S.C. 1413(a)(3); Senate Report No. 94-168, p. 34 (1975))

Comment. Note that a State educational agency as well as local educational agencies must use Part B funds (except the portion used for State administration) for the priorities. A State may have to set aside a portion of its Part B allotment to be able to serve newly identified first priority children.

After September 1, 1978, Part B funds may be used:

(1) To continue supporting child identification, location, and evaluation activities;

(2) To provide free appropriate public education to newly identified first priority children;

(3) To meet the full educational opportunities goal required under § 300.304, including employing additional personnel and providing inservice training, in order to increase the level, intensity and quality of services provided to individual handicapped children; and

(4) To meet the other requirements of Part B.

§ 300.322 First priority children—school year 1977-1978.

(a) In school year 1977-1978, if a major component of a first priority child's proposed educational program is not available (for example, there is no qualified teacher), the public agency responsible for the child's education shall:

(1) Provide an interim program of services for the child; and

(2) Develop an individualized education program for full implementation no later than September 1, 1978.

(b) A local educational agency may use Part B funds for training or other support services in school year 1977-1978 only if all of its first priority children have available to them at least an interim program of services.

(c) A State educational agency may use Part B funds for training or other support services in school year 1977-1978 only if all first priority children

in the State have available to them at least an interim program of services.

(Authority: 20 U.S.C. 1411 (b), (c))

Comment. This provision is intended to make it clear that a State or local educational agency may not delay placing a previously unserved (first priority) child until it has, for example, implemented an inservice training program. The child must be placed. After the child is in at least an interim program, the State or local educational agency may use Part B funds for training or other support services needed to provide that child with a free appropriate public education.

§ 300.323 Services to other children.

If a State or a local educational agency is providing free appropriate public education to all of its first priority children, that State or agency may use funds provided under Part B of the Act:

(a) To provide free appropriate public education to handicapped children who are not receiving any education and who are in the age groups not covered under § 300.300 in that State; or

(b) To provide free appropriate public education to second priority children; or

(c) Both.

(Authority: 20 U.S.C. 1411 (b)(1)(B), (b)(2)(B), (c)(2)(A)(ii))

§ 300.324 Application of local educational agency to use funds for the second priority.

A local educational agency may use funds provided under Part B of the Act for second priority children, if it provides assurance satisfactory to the State educational agency in its application (or an amendment to its application):

(a) That all first priority children have a free appropriate public education available to them;

(b) That the local educational agency has a system for the identification, location, and evaluation of handicapped children, as described in its application; and

(c) That whenever a first priority child is identified, located, and evaluated, the local educational agency makes available a free appropriate public education to the child.

(Authority: 20 U.S.C. 1411 (b)(1)(B), (c)(1)(B); 1414(a)(1)(C)(ii))

INDIVIDUALIZED EDUCATION PROGRAMS

§ 300.340   Definition.

As used in this part, the term "individualized education program" means a written statement for a handicapped child that is developed and implemented in accordance with §§ 300.341–300.349.

(Authority: 20 U.S.C. 1401(19))

§ 300.341   State educational agency responsibility.

(a) *Public agencies.* The State educational agency shall insure that each public agency develops and implements an individualized education program for each of its handicapped children.

(b) *Private schools and facilities.* The State educational agency shall insure that an individualized education program is developed and implemented for each handicapped child who:

(1) Is placed in or referred to a private school or facility by a public agency; or

(2) Is enrolled in a parochial or other private school and receives special education or related services from a public agency.

(Authority: 20 U.S.C. 1412 (4), (6); 1413(a)(4))

Comment. This section applies to all public agencies, including other State agencies (e.g., departments of mental health and welfare), which provide special education to a handicapped child either directly, by contract or through other arrangements. Thus, if a State welfare agency contracts with a private school or facility to provide special education to a handicapped child, that agency would be responsible for insuring that an individualized education program is developed for the child.

§ 300.342   When individualized education programs must be in effect.

(a) On October 1, 1977, and at the beginning of each school year thereafter, each public agency shall have in effect an individualized education program for every handicapped child who is receiving special education from that agency.

(b) An individualized education program must:

(1) Be in effect before special education and related services are provided to a child; and

(2) Be implemented as soon as possible following the meetings under § 300.343.

(Authority: 20 U.S.C. 1412 (2)(B), (4), (6); 1414(a)(5); Pub. L. 94–142, Sec. 8(c) (1975))

Comment. Under paragraph (b)(2), it is expected that a handicapped child's individualized education program (IEP) will be implemented immediately following the meetings under § 300.343. An exception to this would be (1) when the meetings occur during the summer or a vacation period, or (2) where there are circumstances which require a short delay (e.g., working out transportation arrangements). However, there can be no undue delay in providing special education and related services to the child.

§ 300.343   Meetings.

(a) *General.* Each public agency is responsible for initiating and conducting meetings for the purpose of developing, reviewing, and revising a handicapped child's individualized education program.

(b) *Handicapped children currently served.* If the public agency has determined that a handicapped child will receive special education during school year 1977–1978, a meeting must be held early enough to insure that an individualized education program is developed by October 1, 1977.

(c) *Other handicapped children.* For a handicapped child who is not included under paragraph (b) of this action, a meeting must be held within thirty calendar days of a determination that the child needs special education and related services.

(d) *Review.* Each public agency shall initiate and conduct meetings to periodically review each child's individualized education program and if appropriate revise its provisions. A meeting must be held for this purpose at least once a year.

(Authority: 20 U.S.C. 1412(2)(B), (4), (6); 1414(a)(5))

Comment. The dates on which agencies must have individualized education programs (IEPs) in effect are specified in

§ 300.342 (October 1, 1977, and the beginning of each school year thereafter). However, except for new handicapped children (i.e., those evaluated and determined to need special education after October 1, 1977), the timing of meetings to develop, review, and revise IEPs is left to the discretion of each agency.

In order to have IEPs in effect by the dates in § 300.342, agencies could hold meetings at the end of the school year or during the summer preceding those dates. In meeting the October 1, 1977 timeline, meetings could be conducted up through the October 1 date. Thereafter, meetings may be held any time throughout the year, as long as IEPs are in effect at the beginning of each school year.

The statute requires agencies to hold a meeting at least once each year in order to review, and if appropriate revise, each child's IEP. The timing of those meetings could be on the anniversary date of the last IEP meeting on the child, but this is left to the discretion of the agency.

§ 300.344 Participants in meetings.

(a) *General.* The public agency shall insure that each meeting includes the following participants:

(1) A representative of the public agency, other than the child's teacher, who is qualified to provide, or supervise the provision of, special education.

(2) The child's teacher.

(3) One or both of the child's parents, subject to § 300.345.

(4) The child, where appropriate.

(5) Other individuals at the discretion of the parent or agency.

(b) *Evaluation personnel.* For a handicapped child who has been evaluated for the first time, the public agency shall insure:

(1) That a member of the evaluation team participates in the meeting; or

(2) That the representative of the public agency, the child's teacher, or some other person is present at the meeting, who is knowledgeable about the evaluation procedures used with the child and is familiar with the results of the evaluation.

(Authority: 20 U.S.C. 1401(19); 1412 (2)(B), (4), (6); 1414(a)(5))

Comment. 1. In deciding which teacher will participate in meetings on a child's individualized education program, the agency may wish to consider the following possibilities:

(a) For a handicapped child who is receiving special education, the "teacher" could be the child's special education teacher. If the child's handicap is a speech impairment, the "teacher" could be the speech-language pathologist.

(b) For a handicapped child who is being considered for placement in special education, the "teacher" could be the child's regular teacher, or a teacher qualified to provide education in the type of program in which the child may be placed, or both.

(c) If the child is not in school or has more than one teacher, the agency may designate which teacher will participate in the meeting.

2. Either the teacher or the agency representative should be qualified in the area of the child's suspected disability.

3. For a child whose primary handicap is a speech impairment, the evaluation personnel participating under paragraph (b)(1) of this section would normally be the speech-language pathologist.

§ 300.345 Parent participation.

(a) Each public agency shall take steps to insure that one or both of the parents of the handicapped child are present at each meeting or are afforded the opportunity to participate, including:

(1) Notifying parents of the meeting early enough to insure that they will have an opportunity to attend; and

(2) Scheduling the meeting at a mutually agreed on time and place.

(b) The notice under paragraph (a)(1) of this section must indicate the purpose, time, and location of the meeting, and who will be in attendance.

(c) If neither parent can attend, the public agency shall use other methods to insure parent participation, including individual or conference telephone calls.

(d) A meeting may be conducted without a parent in attendance if the public agency is unable to convince the parents that they should attend. In this case the public agency must have a record of its attempts to arrange a mutually agreed on time and place such as:

(1) Detailed records of telephone calls made or attempted and the results of those calls.

(2) Copies of correspondence sent to the parents and any responses received, and

(3) Detailed records of visits made to the parent's home or place of employment and the results of those visits.

(e) The public agency shall take whatever action is necessary to insure that the parent understands the proceedings at a meeting, including arranging for an interpreter for parents who are deaf or whose native language is other than English.

(f) The public agency shall give the parent, on request, a copy of the individualized education program.

(Authority: 20 U.S.C. 1401(19); 1412 (2)(B), (4), (6); 1414(a)(5))

Comment. The notice in paragraph (a) could also inform parents that they may bring other people to the meeting. As indicated in paragraph (c), the procedure used to notify parents (whether oral or written or both) is left to the discretion of the agency, but the agency must keep a record of its efforts to contact parents.

§ 300.346   Content of individualized education program.

The individualized education program for each child must include:

(a) A statement of the child's present levels of educational performance;

(b) A statement of annual goals, including short term instructional objectives;

(c) A statement of the specific special education and related services to be provided to the child, and the extent to which the child will be able to participate in regular educational programs;

(d) The projected dates for initiation of services and the anticipated duration of the services; and

(e) Appropriate objective criteria and evaluation procedures and schedules for determining, on at least an annual basis, whether the short term instructional objectives are being achieved.

(Authority: 20 U.S.C. 1401(19); 1412 (2)(B), (4), (6); 1414(a)(5); Senate Report No. 94-168, p. 11 (1975))

§ 300.347   Private school placements.

(a) *Developing individualized education programs.* (1) Before a public agency places a handicapped child in, or refers a child to, a private school or facility, the agency shall initiate and

conduct a meeting to develop an individualized education program for the child in accordance with § 300.343.

(2) The agency shall insure that a representative of the private school facility attends the meeting. If the representative cannot attend, the agency shall use other methods to insure participation by the private school or facility, including individual or conference telephone calls.

(3) The public agency shall also develop an individualized educational program for each handicapped child who was placed in a private school or facility by the agency before the effective date of these regulations.

(b) *Reviewing and revising individualized education programs.* (1) After a handicapped child enters a private school or facility, any meetings to review and revise the child's individualized education program may be initiated and conducted by the private school or facility at the discretion of the public agency.

(2) If the private school or facility initiates and conducts these meetings, the public agency shall insure that the parents and an agency representative:

(i) Are involved in any decision about the child's individualized education program; and

(ii) Agree to any proposed changes in the program before those changes are implemented.

(c) *Responsibility.* Even if a private school or facility implements a child's individualized education program, responsibility for compliance with this part remains with the public agency and the State educational agency.

(Authority: 20 U.S.C. 1413(a)(4)(B))

§ 300.348   Handicapped children in parochial or other private schools.

If a handicapped child is enrolled in a parochial or other private school and receives special education or related services from a public agency, the public agency shall:

(a) Initiate and conduct meetings to develop, review, and revise an individualized education program for the child, in accordance with § 300.343; and

(b) Insure that a representative of the parochial or other private school attends each meeting. If the representative cannot attend, the agency shall use other methods to insure participation by the private school, including individual or conference telephone calls.

(Authority: 20 U.S.C. 1413(a)(4)(A))

§ 300.349 Individualized education program—accountability.

Each public agency must provide special education and related services to a handicapped child in accordance with an individualized education program. However, Part B of the Act does not require that any agency, teacher, or other person be held accountable if a child does not achieve the growth projected in the annual goals and objectives.

(Authority: 20 U.S.C. 1412(2)(B); 1414(a) (5), (6); Cong. Rec. at H7152 (daily ed., July 21, 1975))

Comment. This section is intended to relieve concerns that the individualized education program constitutes a guarantee by the public agency and the teacher that a child will progress at a specified rate. However, this section does not relieve agencies and teachers from making good faith efforts to assist the child in achieving the objectives and goals listed in the individualized education program. Further, the section does not limit a parent's right to complain and ask for revisions of the child's program, or to invoke due process procedures, if the parent feels that these efforts are not being made.

DIRECT SERVICE BY THE STATE EDUCATIONAL AGENCY

§ 300.360 Use of local educational agency allocation for direct services.

(a) A State educational agency may not distribute funds to a local educational agency, and shall use those funds to insure the provision of a free appropriate public education to handicapped children residing in the area served by the local educational agency, if the local educational agency, in any fiscal year:

(1) Is entitled to less than $7,500 for that fiscal year (beginning with fiscal year 1979);

(2) Does not submit an application that meets the requirements of §§ 300.220–300.240;

(3) Is unable or unwilling to establish and maintain programs of free appropriate public education;

(4) Is unable or unwilling to be consolidated with other local educational agencies in order to establish and maintain those programs; or

(5) Has one or more handicapped children who can best be served by a regional or State center designed to meet the needs of those children.

(b) In meeting the requirements of paragraph (a) of this section, the State educational agency may provide special education and related services directly, by contract, or through other arrangements.

(c) The excess cost requirements under §§ 300.182–300.186 do not apply to the State educational agency.

(Authority: 20 U.S.C. 1411(c)(4); 1413(b); 1414(d))

Comment. Section 300.360 is a combination of three provisions in the statute (Sections 611(c)(4), 613(b), and 614(d)). This section focuses mainly on the State's administration and use of local entitlements under Part B.

The State educational agency, as a recipient of Part B funds is responsible for insuring that all public agencies in the State comply with the provisions of the Act, regardless of whether they receive Part B funds. If a local educational agency elects not to apply for its Part B entitlement, the State would be required to use those funds to insure that a free appropriate public education (FAPE) is made available to children residing in the area served by that local agency. However, if the local entitlement is not sufficient for this purpose, additional State or local funds would have to be expended in order to insure that "FAPE" and the other requirements of the Act are met.

Moreover, if the local educational agency is the recipient of any other Federal funds, it would have to be in compliance with Subpart D of the regulations for section 504 of the Rehabilitation Act of 1973 (34 CFR Part 104). It should be noted that the term "FAPE" has different meanings under Part B and section 504. For Example, under Part B, "FAPE" is a statutory term which requires special education and related services to be provided in accordance with an individualized education program (IEP). However, under section 504, each recipient must provide an education which includes services that are "designed to meet individual educational needs of handicapped persons as adequately as the needs of nonhandicapped persons are met * * *" Those regulations state that implementation of an IEP, in accordance with Part B, is one means of meeting the "FAPE" requirement.

§ 300.361   Nature and location of services.

The State educational agency may provide special education and related services under § 300.360(a) in the manner and at the location it considers appropriate. However, the manner in which the education and services are provided must be consistent with the requirements of this part (including the least restrictive environment provisions in §§ 300.550–300.556 of Subpart E).

(Authority: 20 U.S.C. 1414(d))

*§ 300.370   Use of State educational agency allocation for direct and support services.

(a) The State shall use the portion of its allocation it does not use for administration to provide support services and direct services in accordance with the priority requirements under §§ 300.320–300.324.

(b) For the purposes of paragraph (a) of this section:

(1) "Direct services" means services provided to a handicapped child by the State directly, by contract, or through other arrangements.

(2) "Support services" includes implementing the comprehensive system of personnel development under §§ 300.380–300.388, recruitment and training of hearing officers and surrogate parents, and public information and parent training activities relating to a free appropriate public education for handicapped children.

(Authority: 20 U.S.C. 1411(b)(2), (c)(2))

§ 300.371   State matching.

Beginning with the period July 1, 1978–June 30, 1979, and for each following year, the funds that a State uses for direct and support services under § 300.370 must be matched on a program basis by the State from funds other than Federal funds. This requirement does not apply to funds that the State uses under § 300.360.

(Authority: 20   U.S.C.   1411(c)(2)(B), (c)(4)(B))

Comment. The requirement in § 300.371 would be satisfied if the State can document

that the amount of State funds expended for each major program area (e.g., the comprehensive system of personnel development) is at least equal to the expenditure of Federal funds in that program area.

§ 300.372   Applicability of nonsupplanting requirement.

Beginning with funds appropriated for Fiscal Year 1979 and for each following Fiscal Year, the requirement in section 613(a)(9) of the Act, which prohibits supplanting with Federal funds, does not apply to funds that the State uses from its allocation under § 300.706(a) of Subpart G for administration, direct services, or support services.

(Authority: 20 U.S.C. 1411(c)(3))

COMPREHENSIVE SYSTEM OF PERSONNEL DEVELOPMENT

§ 300.380   Scope of system.

Each annual program plan must include a description of programs and procedures for the development and implementation of a comprehensive system of personnel development which includes:

(a) The inservice training of general and special educational instructional, related services, and support personnel;

(b) Procedures to insure that all personnel necessary to carry out the purposes of the Act are qualified (as defined in § 300.12 of Subpart A) and that activities sufficient to carry out this personnel development plan are scheduled; and

(c) Effective procedures for acquiring and disseminating to teachers and administrators of programs for handicapped children significant information derived from educational research, demonstration, and similar projects, and for adopting, where appropriate, promising educational practices and materials developed through those projects.

(Authority: 20 U.S.C. 1413(a)(3))

§ 300.381   Participation of other agencies and institutions.

(a) The State educational agency must insure that all public and private institutions of higher education, and

*See 1989 Amendments to EAHCA Regulations, page 433; § 300.370.

other agencies and organizations (including representatives of handicapped, parent, and other advocacy organizations) in the state which have an interest in the preparation of personnel for the education of handicapped children, have an opportunity to participate fully in the development, review, and annual updating of the comprehensive system of personnel development.

(b) The annual program plan must describe the nature and extent of participation under paragraph (a) of this section and must describe responsibilities of the State educational agency, local educational agencies, public and private institutions of higher education, and other agencies:

(1) With respect to the comprehensive system as a whole, and

(2) With respect to the personnel development plan under § 300.383.

(Authority: 20 U.S.C. 1412(7)(A); 1413(a)(3))

§ 300.382   Inservice training.

(a) As used in this section, "inservice training" means any training other than that received by an individual in a full-time program which leads to a degree.

(b) Each annual program plan must provide that the State educational agency:

(1) Conducts an annual needs assessment to determine if a sufficient number of qualified personnel are available in the State; and

(2) Initiates inservice personnel development programs based on the assessed needs of State-wide significance related to the implementation of the Act.

(c) Each annual program plan must include the results of the needs assessment under paragraph (b)(1) of this section, broken out by need for new personnel and need for retrained personnel.

(d) The State educational agency may enter into contracts with institutions of higher education, local educational agencies or other agencies, institutions, or organizations (which may include parent, handicapped, or other advocacy organizations), to carry out:

(1) Experimental or innovative personnel development programs;

(2) Development or modification of instructional materials; and

(3) Dissemination of significant information derived from educational research and demonstration projects.

(e) Each annual program plan must provide that the State educational agency insures that ongoing inservice training programs are available to all personnel who are engaged in the education of handicapped children, and that these programs include:

(1) The use of incentives which insure participation by teachers (such as released time, payment for participation, options for academic credit, salary step credit, certification renewal, or updating professional skills);

(2) The involvement of local staff; and

(3) The use of innovative practices which have been found to be effective.

(f) Each annual program plan must:

(1) Describe the process used in determining the inservice training needs of personnel engaged in the education of handicapped children;

(2) Identify the areas in which training is needed (such as individualized education programs, non-discriminatory testing, least restrictive environment, procedural safeguards, and surrogate parents);

(3) Specify the groups requiring training (such as special teachers, regular teachers, administrators, psychologists, speech-language pathologists, audiologists, physical education teachers, therapeutic recreation specialists, physical therapists, occupational therapists, medical personnel, parents, volunteers, hearing officers, and surrogate parents);

(4) Describe the content and nature of training for each area under paragraph (f)(2) of this section;

(5) Describe how the training will be provided in terms of (i) geographical scope (such as Statewide, regional, or local), and (ii) staff training source (such as college and university staffs, State and local educational agency personnel, and non-agency personnel);

(6) *Specify*: (i) The funding sources to be used, and

(ii) The time frame for providing it; and

(7) Specify procedures for effective evaluation of the extent to which program objectives are met.

(Authority: 20 U.S.C. 1413(a)(3))

§ 300.383   Personnel development plan.

Each annual program plan must: (a) Include a personnel development plan which provides a structure for personnel planning and focuses on preservice and inservice education needs;

(b) Describe the results of the needs assessment under § 300.382(b)(1) with respect to identifying needed areas of training, and assigning priorities to those areas; and

(c) Identify the target populations for personnel development, including general education and special education instructional and administrative personnel, support personnel, and other personnel (such as paraprofessionals, parents, surrogate parents, and volunteers).

(Authority: 20 U.S.C. 1413(a)(3))

§ 300.384   Dissemination.

(a) Each annual program plan must include a description of the State's procedures for acquiring, reviewing, and disseminating to general and special educational instructional and support personnel, administrators of programs for handicapped children, and other interested agencies and organizations (including parent, handicapped, and other advocacy organizations) significant information and promising practices derived from educational research, demonstration, and other projects.

(b) Dissemination includes:

(1) Making those personnel, administrators, agencies, and organizations aware of the information and practices;

(2) Training designed to enable the establishment of innovative programs and practices targeted on identified local needs; and

(3) Use of instructional materials and other media for personnel development and instructional programming.

(Authority: 20 U.S.C. 1413(a)(3))

§ 300.385   Adoption of educational practices.

(a) Each annual program plan must provide for a statewide system designed to adopt, where appropriate, promising educational practices and materials proven effective through research and demonstration.

(b) Each annual program plan must provide for thorough reassessment of educational practices used in the State.

(c) Each annual program plan must provide for the identification of State, local, and regional resources (human and material) which will assist in meeting the State's personnel preparation needs.

(Authority: 20 U.S.C. 1413(a)(3))

§ 300.386   [Reserved]

§ 300.387   Technical assistance to local educational agencies.

Each annual program plan must include a description of technical assistance that the State educational agency gives to local educational agencies in their implementation of the State's comprehensive system of personnel development.

(Authority: 20 U.S.C. 1413(a)(3))

Subpart D—Private Schools

HANDICAPPED CHILDREN IN PRIVATE SCHOOLS PLACED OR REFERRED BY PUBLIC AGENCIES

§ 300.400   Applicability   of   §§ 300.401–300.403.

Sections 300.401–300.403 apply only to handicapped children who are or have been placed in or referred to a private school or facility by a public agency as a means of providing special education and related services.

(Authority: 20 U.S.C. 1413(a)(4)(B))

§ 300.401   Responsibility of State educational agency.

Each State educational agency shall insure that a handicapped child who is placed in or referred to a private school or facility by a public agency:

(a) Is provided special education and related services:

(1) In conformance with an individualized education program which meets the requirements under §§ 300.340–300.349 of Subpart C;

(2) At no cost to the parents; and

(3) At a school or facility which meets the standards that apply to State and local educational agencies (including the requirements in this part); and

(b) Has all of the rights of a handicapped child who is served by a public agency.

(Authority: 20 U.S.C. 1413(a)(4)(B))

§ 300.402 Implementation by State educational agency.

In implementing § 300.401, the State educational agency shall:

(a) Monitor compliance through procedures such as written reports, on-site visits, and parent questionnaires;

(b) Disseminate copies of applicable standards to each private school and facility to which a public agency has referred or placed a handicapped child; and

(c) Provide an opportunity for those private schools and facilities to participate in the development and revision of State standards which apply to them.

(Authority: 20 U.S.C. 1413(a)(4)(B))

§ 300.403 Placement of children by parents.

(a) If a handicapped child has available a free appropriate public education and the parents choose to place the child in a private school or facility, the public agency is not required to pay for the child's education at the private school or facility. However, the public agency shall make services available to the child as provided under §§ 300.450–300.460.

(b) Disagreements between a parent and a public agency regarding the availability of a program appropriate for the child, and the question of financial responsibility, are subject to the due process procedures under §§ 300.500–300.514 of Subpart E.

(Authority: 20 U.S.C. 1412(2)(B); 1415)

HANDICAPPED CHILDREN IN PRIVATE SCHOOLS NOT PLACED OR REFERRED BY PUBLIC AGENCIES

§ 300.450 Definition of "private school handicapped children."

As used in this part, "private school handicapped children" means handicapped children enrolled in private schools or facilities other than handicapped children covered under §§ 300.400—300.402.

(Authority: 20 U.S.C. 1413(a)(4)(A))

[49 FR 48526, Dec. 12, 1984]

§ 300.451 State educational agency responsibility.

The State educational agency shall insure that—

(a) To the extent consistent with their number and location in the State, provision is made for the participation of private school handicapped children in the program assisted or carried out under this part by providing them with special education and related services; and

(b) The requirements in 34 CFR 76.651–76.663 of EDGAR are met.

(Authority: 20 U.S.C. 1413(a)(4)(A))

[45 FR 22531, Apr. 3, 1980. Redesignated at 45 FR 77368, Nov. 21, 1980]

§ 300.452 Local educational agency responsibility.

(a) Each local educational agency shall provide special education and related services designed to meet the needs of private school handicapped children residing in the jurisdiction of the agency.

(Authority: Sec. 1413(a)(4)(A); 1414(a)(6))

[42 FR 42476, Aug. 23, 1977, as amended at 45 FR 22531, Apr. 3, 1980. Redesignated at 45 FR 77368, Nov. 21, 1980]

PROCEDURES FOR BY-PASS

§ 300.480 By-pass—general.

(a) The Secretary implements a by-pass if a State educational agency is and was on December 2, 1983, prohibited by law from providing for the participation of private school handicapped children in the program assisted or carried out under this part, as re quired by section 613(a)(4)(A) of the Act and by §§ 300.451–300.452.

(b) The Secretary waives the requirement of section 613(a)(4)(A) of the Act and of §§ 300.451–300.452 if the Secretary implements a by-pass.

(Authority: 20 U.S.C. 1413(d)(1))

[49 FR 48526, Dec. 12, 1984]

§ 300.481   Provisions for services under a by-pass.

(a) Before implementing a by-pass, the Secretary consults with appropriate public and private school officials, including State educational agency officials, in the affected State to consider matters such as—

(1) The prohibition imposed by State law which results in the need for a by-pass;

(2) The scope and nature of the services required by private school handicapped children in the State, and the number of children to be served under the by-pass; and

(3) The establishment of policies and procedures to ensure that private school handicapped children receive services consistent with the requirements of section 613(a)(4)(A) of the Act, §§ 300.451–300.452, and 34 CFR 76.651–76.662.

(b) After determining that a by-pass is required, the Secretary arranges for the provision of services to private school handicapped children in the State in a manner consistent with the requirements of section 613(a)(4)(A) of the Act and §§ 300.451—300.452 by providing services through one or more agreements with appropriate parties.

(c) For any fiscal year in which a by-pass is implemented, the Secretary determines the maximum amount to be paid to the providers of services by multiplying—

(1) A per child amount, which may not exceed the amount per child provided by the Secretary under this part for all handicapped children in the State for the preceding fiscal year; by

(2) The number of private school handicapped children (as defined by §§ 300.5(a) and 300.450) in the State, as determined by the Secretary on the basis of the most recent satisfactory data available, which may include an estimate of the number of those handicapped children.

(d) The Secretary deducts from the State's allocation under this part the amount the Secretary determines is necessary to implement a by-pass and pays that amount to the provider of services. The Secretary may withhold this amount from the State's allocation pending final resolution of any investigation or complaint that could result in a determination that a by-pass must be implemented.

(Authority: 20 U.S.C. 1413(d)(2))

[49 FR 48526, Dec. 12, 1984]

DUE PROCESS PROCEDURES

SOURCE: Sections 300.482 through 300.486 appear at 49 FR 48526, Dec. 12, 1984, unless otherwise noted.

§ 300.482   Notice of intent to implement a by-pass.

(a) Before taking any final action to implement a by-pass, the Secretary provides the affected State educational agency with written notice.

(b) In the written notice, the Secretary—

(1) States the reasons for the proposed by-pass in sufficient detail to allow the State educational agency to respond;

(2) Advises the State educational agency that it has a specific period of time (at least 45 days) from receipt of the written notice to submit written objections to the proposed by-pass and that it may request in writing the opportunity for a hearing to show cause why a by-pass should not be implemented.

(c) The Secretary sends the notice to the State educational agency by certified mail with return receipt requested.

(Authority: 20 U.S.C. 1413(d)(3)(A))

§ 300.483   Request to show cause.

A State educational agency seeking an opportunity to show cause why a by-pass should not be implemented shall submit a written request for a show cause hearing to the Secretary.

(Authority: 20 U.S.C. 1413(d)(3)(A))

§ 300.484 Show cause hearing.

(a) If a show cause hearing is requested, the Secretary—

(1) Notifies the State educational agency and other appropriate public and private school officials of the time and place for the hearing; and

(2) Designates a person to conduct the show cause hearing. The designee must not have had any responsibility for the matter brought for a hearing.

(b) At the show cause hearing, the designee considers matters such as—

(1) The necessity for implementing a by-pass;

(2) Possible factual errors in the written notice of intent to implement a by-pass; and

(3) The objections raised by public and private school representatives.

(c) The designee may regulate the course of the proceedings and the conduct of parties during the pendency of the proceedings. The designee takes all steps necessary to conduct a fair and impartial proceeding, to avoid delay, and to maintain order, including procedures such as those established in 34 CFR 78.61(a), *Authority and Responsibilities of Panels.*

(d) The designee may interpret applicable statutes and regulations, but may not waive them or rule on their validity.

(e) The designee arranges for the preparation, retention, and, if appropriate, dissemination of the record of the hearing.

(Authority: 20 U.S.C. 1413(d)(3)(A))

§ 300.485 Decision.

(a) The designee who conducts the show cause hearing—

(1) Issues a written decision which includes a statement of findings; and

(2) Submits a copy of the decision to the Secretary and sends a copy to each party by certified mail with return receipt requested.

(b) Each party may submit comments and recommendations on the designee's decision to the Secretary within 15 days of the date the party receives the designee's decision.

(c) The Secretary adopts, reverses, or modifies the designee's decision and notifies the State educational agency of the Secretary's final action. That notice is sent by certified mail with return receipt requested.

(Authority: 20 U.S.C. 1413(d)(3)(A))

§ 300.486 Judicial review.

If dissatisfied with the Secretary's final action, the State educational agency may, within 60 days after notice of that action, file a petition for review with the United States court of appeals for the circuit in which the State is located. The procedures for judicial review are described in section 613(d)(3)(B)—(D) of the Act.

(Authority: 20 U.S.C. 1413(d)(3)(B)—(D)))

Subpart E—Procedural Safeguards

DUE PROCESS PROCEDURES FOR PARENTS AND CHILDREN

§ 300.500 Definitions of "consent", "evaluation", and "personally identifiable".

As used in this part: "Consent" means that:

(a) The parent has been fully informed of all information relevant to the activity for which consent is sought, in his or her native language, or other mode of communication;

(b) The parent understands and agrees in writing to the carrying out of the activity for which his or her consent is sought, and the consent describes that activity and lists the records (if any) which will be released and to whom; and

(c) The parent understands that the granting of consent is voluntary on the part of the parent and may be revoked at any time.,

"Evaluation" means procedures used in accordance with §§ 300.530–300.534 to determine whether a child is handicapped and the nature and extent of the special education and related services that the child needs. The term means procedures used selectively with an individual child and does not include basic tests administered to or procedures used with all children in a school, grade, or class.

"Personally identifiable" means that information includes:

(a) The name of the child, the child's parent, or other family member;

(b) The address of the child;

(c) A personal identifier, such as the child's social security number or student number; or

(d) A list of personal characteristics or other information which would make it possible to identify the child with reasonable certainty.

(Authority: 20 U.S.C. 1415, 1417(c))

§ 300.501   General responsibility of public agencies.

Each State educational agency shall insure that each public agency establishes and implements procedural safeguards which meet the requirements of §§ 300.500–300.514.

(Authority: 20 U.S.C. 1415(a))

§ 300.502   Opportunity to examine records.

The parents of a handicapped child shall be afforded, in accordance with the procedures in §§ 300.562–300.569 an opportunity to inspect and review all education records with respect to:

(a) The identification, evaluation, and educational placement of the child, and

(b) The provision of a free appropriate public education to the child.

(Authority: 20 U.S.C. 1415(b)(1)(A))

§ 300.503   Independent educational evaluation.

(a) *General.* (1) The parents of a handicapped child have the right under this part to obtain an independent educational evaluation of the child, subject to paragraphs (b) through (e) of this section.

(2) Each public agency shall provide to parents, on request, information about where an independent educational evaluation may be obtained.

(3) For the purposes of this part:

(i) "Independent educational evaluation" means an evaluation conducted by a qualified examiner who is not employed by the public agency responsible for the education of the child in question.

(ii) "Public expense" means that the public agency either pays for the full cost of the evaluation or insures that the evaluation is otherwise provided at no cost to the parent, consistent with § 300.301 of Subpart C.

(b) *Parent right to evaluation at public expense.* A parent has the right to an independent educational evaluation at public expense if the parent disagrees with an evaluation obtained by the public agency. However, the public agency may initiate a hearing under § 300.506 of this subpart to show that its evaluation is appropriate. If the final decision is that the evaluation is appropriate, the parent still has the right to an independent educational evaluation, but not at public expense.

(c) *Parent initiated evaluations.* If the parent obtains an independent educational evaluation at private expense, the results of the evaluation:

(1) Must be considered by the public agency in any decision made with respect to the provision of a free appropriate public education to the child, and

(2) May be presented as evidence at a hearing under this subpart regarding that child.

(d) *Requests for evaluations by hearing officers.* If a hearing officer requests an independent educational evaluation as part of a hearing, the cost of the evaluation must be at public expense.

(e) *Agency criteria.* Whenever an independent evaluation is at public expense, the criteria under which the evaluation is obtained, including the location of the evaluation and the qualifications of the examiner, must be the same as the criteria which the public agency uses when it initiates an evaluation.

(Authority: 20 U.S.C. 1415(b)(1)(A))

§ 300.504   Prior notice; parent consent.

(a) *Notice.* Written notice which meets the requirements under § 300.505 must be given to the parents of a handicapped child a reasonable time before the public agency:

(1) Proposes to initiate or change the identification, evaluation, or educational placement of the child or the provision of a free appropriate public education to the child, or

(2) Refuses to initiate or change the identification, evaluation, or educational placement of the child or the

provision of a free appropriate public education to the child.

(b) *Consent.* (1) Parental consent must be obtained before:

(i) Conducting a preplacement evaluation; and

(ii) Initial placement of a handicapped child in a program providing special education and related services.

(2) Except for preplacement evaluation and initial placement, consent may not be required as a condition of any benefit to the parent or child.

(c) *Procedures where parent refuses consent.* (1) Where State law requires parental consent before a handicapped child is evaluated or initially provided special education and related services, State procedures govern the public agency in overriding a parent's refusal to consent.

(2) (i) Where there is no State law requiring consent before a handicapped child is evaluated or initially provided special education and related services, the public agency may use the hearing procedures in §§ 300.506–300.508 to determine if the child may be evaluated or initially provided special education and related services without parental consent.

(ii) If the hearing officer upholds the agency, the agency may evaluate or initially provide special education and related services to the child without the parent's consent, subject to the parent's rights under §§ 300.510–300.513.

(Authority: 20 U.S.C. 1415(b)(1)(C), (D))

Comment. 1. Any changes in a child's special education program, after the initial placement, are not subject to parental consent under Part B, but are subject to the prior notice requirement in paragraph (a) and the individualized education program requirements in Subpart C.

2. Paragraph (c) means that where State law requires parental consent before evaluation or before special education and related services are initially provided, and the parent refuses (or otherwise withholds) consent, State procedures, such as obtaining a court order authorizing the public agency to conduct the evaluation or provide the education and related services, must be followed.

If, however, there is no legal requirement for consent outside of these regulations, the public agency may use the due process procedures under this subpart to obtain a decision to allow the evaluation or services without parental consent. The agency must notify the parent of its actions, and the parent has appeal rights as well as rights at the hearing itself.

§ 300.505 Content of notice.

(a) The notice under § 300.504 must include:

(1) A full explanation of all of the procedural safeguards available to the parents under Subpart E;

(2) A description of the action proposed or refused by the agency, an explanation of why the agency proposes or refuses to take the action, and a description of any options the agency considered and the reasons why those options were rejected;

(3) A description of each evaluation procedure, test, record, or report the agency uses as a basis for the proposal or refusal; and

(4) A description of any other factors which are relevant to the agency's proposal or refusal.

(b) The notice must be:

(1) Written in language understandable to the general public, and

(2) Provided in the native language of the parent or other mode of communication used by the parent, unless it is clearly not feasible to do so.

(c) If the native language or other mode of communication of the parent is not a written language, the State or local educational agency shall take steps to insure:

(1) That the notice is translated orally or by other means to the parent in his or her native language or other mode of communication;

(2) That the parent understands the content of the notice, and

(3) That there is written evidence that the requirements in paragraphs (c) (1) and (2) of this section have been met.

(Authority: 20 U.S.C. 1415(b)(1)(D))

§ 300.506 Impartial due process hearing.

(a) A parent or a public educational agency may initiate a hearing on any of the matters described in § 300.504(a) (1) and (2).

(b) The hearing must be conducted by the State educational agency or the public agency directly responsible for the education of the child, as determined under State statute, State regulation, or a written policy of the State educational agency.

(c) The public agency shall inform the parent of any free or low-cost legal and other relevant services available in the area if:

(1) The parent requests the information; or

(2) The parent or the agency initiates a hearing under this section.

(Authority: 20 U.S.C. 1416(b)(2))

Comment: Many States have pointed to the success of using mediation as an intervening step prior to conducting a formal due process hearing. Although the process of mediation is not required by the statute or these regulations, an agency may wish to suggest mediation in disputes concerning the identification, evaluation, and educational placement of handicapped children, and the provision of a free appropriate public education to those children. Mediations have been conducted by members of State educational agencies or local educational agency personnel who were not previously involved in the particular case. In many cases, mediation leads to resolution of differences between parents and agencies without the development of an adversarial relationship and with minimal emotional stress. However, mediation may not be used to deny or delay a parent's rights under this subpart.

§ 300.507 Impartial hearing officer.

(a) A hearing may not be conducted:

(1) By a person who is an employee of a public agency which is involved in the education or care of the child, or

(2) By any person having a personal or professional interest which would conflict with his or her objectivity in the hearing.

(b) A person who otherwise qualifies to conduct a hearing under paragraph (a) of this section is not an employee of the agency solely because he or she is paid by the agency to serve as a hearing officer.

(c) Each public agency shall keep a list of the persons who serve as hearing officers. The list must include a statement of the qualifications of each of those persons.

(Authority: 20 U.S.C. 1414(b)(2))

§ 300.508 Hearing rights.

(a) Any party to a hearing has the right to:

(1) Be accompanied and advised by counsel and by individuals with special knowledge or training with respect to the problems of handicapped children;

(2) Present evidence and confront, cross-examine, and compel the attendance of witnesses;

(3) Prohibit the introduction of any evidence at the hearing that has not been disclosed to that party at least five days before the hearing;

(4) Obtain a written or electronic verbatim record of the hearing;

(5) Obtain written findings of fact and decisions. (The public agency shall transmit those findings and decisions, after deleting any personally identifiable information, to the State advisory panel established under Subpart F).

(b) Parents involved in hearings must be given the right to:

(1) Have the child who is the subject of the hearing present; and

(2) Open the hearing to the public.

(Authority: 20 U.S.C. 1415(d))

§ 300.509 Hearing decision; appeal.

A decision made in a hearing conducted under this subpart is final, unless a party to the hearing appeals the decision under § 300.510 or § 300.511.

(Authority: 20 U.S.C. 1415(c))

§ 300.510 Administrative appeal; impartial review.

(a) If the hearing is conducted by a public agency other than the State educational agency, any party aggrieved by the findings and decision in the hearing may appeal to the State educational agency.

(b) If there is an appeal, the State educational agency shall conduct an impartial review of the hearing. The official conducting the review shall:

(1) Examine the entire hearing record;

(2) Insure that the procedures at the hearing were consistent with the requirements of due process;

(3) Seek additional evidence if necessary. If a hearing is held to receive additional evidence, the rights in § 300.508 apply;

(4) Afford the parties an opportunity for oral or written argument, or both, at the discretion of the reviewing official;

(5) Make an independent decision on completion of the review; and

(6) Give a copy of written findings and the decision to the parties.

(c) The decision made by the reviewing official is final, unless a party brings a civil action under § 300.512.

(Authority: 20 U.S.C. 1415 (c), (d); H. Rep. No. 94–664, at p. 49 (1975))

Comment. 1. The State educational agency may conduct its review either directly or through another State agency acting on its behalf. However, the State educational agency remains responsible for the final decision on review.

2. All parties have the right to continue to be represented by counsel at the State administrative review level, whether or not the reviewing official determines that a further hearing is necessary. If the reviewing official decides to hold a hearing to receive additional evidence, the other rights in § 300.508, relating to hearings, also apply.

§ 300.511   Civil action.

Any party aggrieved by the findings and decision made in a hearing who does not have the right to appeal under § 300.510 of this subpart, and any party aggrieved by the decision of a reviewing officer under § 300.510 has the right to bring a civil action under section 615(e)(2) of the Act.

(Authority: 20 U.S.C. 1415)

§ 300.512   Timeliness and convenience of hearings and reviews.

(a) The public agency shall insure that not later than 45 days after the receipt of a request for a hearing:

(1) A final decision is reached in the hearing; and

(2) A copy of the decision is mailed to each of the parties.

(b) The State educational agency shall insure that not later than 30 days after the receipt of a request for a review:

(1) A final decision is reached in the review; and

(2) A copy of the decision is mailed to each of the parties.

(c) A hearing or reviewing officer may grant specific extensions of time beyond the periods set out in paragraphs (a) and (b) of this section at the request of either party.

(d) Each hearing and each review involving oral arguments must be conducted at a time and place which is reasonably convenient to the parents and child involved.

(Authority: 20 U.S.C. 1415)

§ 300.513   Child's status during proceedings.

(a) During the pendency of any administrative or judicial proceeding regarding a complaint, unless the public agency and the parents of the child agree otherwise, the child involved in the complaint must remain in his or her present educational placement.

(b) If the complaint involves an application for initial admission to public school, the child, with the consent of the parents, must be placed in the public school program until the completion of all the proceedings.

(Authority: 20 U.S.C. 1415(e)(3))

Comment. Section 300.513 does not permit a child's placement to be chaged during a complaint proceeding, unless the parents and agency agree otherwise. While the placement may not be changed, this does not preclude the agency from using its normal procedures for dealing with children who are endangering themselves or others.

§ 300.514   Surrogate parents.

(a) *General.* Each public agency shall insure that the rights of a child are protected when:

(1) No parent (as defined in § 300.10) can be identified;

(2) The public agency, after reasonable efforts, cannot discover the whereabouts of a parent; or

(3) The child is a ward of the State under the laws of that State.

(b) *Duty of public agency.* The duty of a public agency under paragraph (a) of this section includes the assignment of an individual to act as a surrogate for the parents. This must include a method (1) for determining whether a child needs a surrogate parent, and (2) for assigning a surrogate parent to the child.

(c) *Criteria for selection of surrogates.* (1) The public agency may select a surrogate parent in any way permitted under State law.

(2) Public agencies shall insure that a person selected as a surrogate:

(i) Has no interest that conflicts with the interest of the child he or she represents; and

(ii) Has knowledge and skills, that insure adequate representation of the child.

(d) *Non-employee requirement; compensation.* (1) A person assigned as a surrogate may not be an employee of a public agency which is involved in the education or care of the child.

(2) A person who otherwise qualifies to be a surrogate parent under paragraphs (c) and (d)(1) of this section, is not an employee of the agency solely because he or she is paid by the agency to serve as a surrogate parent.

(e) *Responsibilities.* The surrogate parent may represent the child in all matters relating to:

(1) The identification, evaluation, and educational placement of the child, and

(2) The provision of a free appropriate public education to the child.

(Authority: 20 U.S.C. 1415(b)(1)(B))

PROTECTION IN EVALUATION
PROCEDURES

§ 300.530   General.

(a) Each State educational agency shall insure that each public agency establishes and implements procedures which meet the requirements of §§ 300.530–300.534.

(b) Testing and evaluation materials and procedures used for the purposes of evaluation and placement of handicapped children must be selected and administered so as not to be racially or culturally discriminatory.

(Authority: 20 U.S.C. 1412(5)(C))

§ 300.531   Preplacement evaluation.

Before any action is taken with respect to the initial placement of a handicapped child in a special education program, a full and individual evaluation of the child's educational needs must be conducted in accordance with the requirements of § 300.532.

(Authority: 20 U.S.C. 1412(5)(C))

§ 300.532   Evaluation procedures.

State and local educational agencies shall insure, at a minimum, that:

(a) Tests and other evaluation materials:

(1) Are provided and administered in the child's native language or other mode of communication, unless it is clearly not feasible to do so;

(2) Have been validated for the specific purpose for which they are used; and

(3) Are administered by trained personnel in conformance with the instructions provided by their producer;

(b) Tests and other evaluation materials include those tailored to assess specific areas of educational need and not merely those which are designed to provide a single general intelligence quotient;

(c) Tests are selected and administered so as best to ensure that when a test is administered to a child with impaired sensory, manual, or speaking skills, the test results accurately reflect the child's aptitude or achievement level or whatever other factors the test purports to measure, rather than reflecting the child's impaired sensory, manual, or speaking skills (except where those skills are the factors which the test purports to measure);

(d) No single procedure is used as the sole criterion for determining an appropriate educational program for a child; and

(e) The evaluation is made by a multidisciplinary team or group of persons, including at least one teacher or other specialist with knowledge in the area of suspected disability.

(f) The child is assessed in all areas related to the suspected disability, including, where appropriate, health, vision, hearing, social and emotional status, general intelligence, academic performance, communicative status, and motor abilities.

(Authority: 20 U.S.C. 1412(5)(C))

Comment. Children who have a speech impairment as their primary handicap may not need a complete battery of assessments (e.g., psychological, physical, or adaptive behavior). However, a qualified speech-language pathologist would (1) evaluate each speech impaired child using procedures that are appropriate for the diagnosis and appraisal of speech and language disorders, and (2) where necessary, make referrals for additional assessments needed to make an appropriate placement decision.

§ 300.533   Placement procedures.

(a) In interpreting evaluation data and in making placement decisions, each public agency shall:

(1) Draw upon information from a variety of sources, including aptitude and achievement tests, teacher recommendations, physical condition, social or cultural background, and adaptive behavior;

(2) Insure that information obtained from all of these sources is documented and carefully considered;

(3) Insure that the placement decision is made by a group of persons, including persons knowledgeable about the child, the meaning of the evaluation data, and the placement options; and

(4) Insure that the placement decision is made in conformity with the least restrictive environment rules in §§ 300.550–300.554.

(b) If a determination is made that a child is handicapped and needs special education and related services, an individualized education program must be developed for the child in accordance with §§ 300.340–300.349 of Subpart C.

(Authority: 20 U.S.C. 1412(5)(C); 1414(a)(5))

Comment. Paragraph (a)(1) includes a list of examples of sources that may be used by a public agency in making placement decisions. The agency would not have to use all the sources in every instance. The point of the requirement is to insure that more than one source is used in interpreting evaluation data and in making placement decisions. For example, while all of the named sources would have to be used for a child whose suspected disability is mental retardation, they would not be necessary for certain other handicapped children, such as a child who has a severe articulation disorder as his primary handicap. For such a child, the speech-language pathologist, in complying with the multisource requirement, might use (1) a standardized test of articulation, and (2) observation of the child's articulation behavior in conversational speech.

§ 300.534   Reevaluation.

Each State and local educational agency shall insure:

(a) That each handicapped child's individualized education program is reviewed in accordance with §§ 300.340–300.349 of Subpart C, and

(b) That an evaluation of the child, based on procedures which meet the requirements under § 300.532, is conducted every three years or more frequently if conditions warrant or if the child's parent or teacher requests an evaluation.

(Authority: 20 U.S.C. 1412(5)(c))

ADDITIONAL PROCEDURES FOR EVALUATING SPECIFIC LEARNING DISABILITIES

§ 300.540   Additional team members.

In evaluating a child suspected of having a specific learning disability, in addition to the requirements of § 300.532, each public agency shall include on the multidisciplinary evaluation team:

(a) (1) The child's regular teacher; or

(2) If the child does not have a regular teacher, a regular classroom teacher qualified to teach a child of his or her age; or

(3) For a child of less than school age, an individual qualified by the State educational agency to teach a child of his or her age; and

(b) At least one person qualified to conduct individual diagnostic examinations of children, such as a school psychologist, speech-language pathologist, or remedial reading teacher.

(Authority: 20 U.S.C. 1411 note)

[42 FR 65083, Dec. 29, 1977. Redesignated at 45 FR 77368, Nov. 21, 1980]

§ 300.541   Criteria for determining the existence of a specific learning disability.

(a) A team may determine that a child has a specific learning disability if:

(1) The child does not achieve commensurate with his or her age and ability levels in one or more of the areas listed in paragraph (a)(2) of this section, when provided with learning experiences appropriate for the child's age and ability levels; and

(2) The team finds that a child has a severe discrepancy between achieve-

ment and intellectual ability in one or more of the following areas:

(i) Oral expression;
(ii) Listening comprehension;
(iii) Written expression;
(iv) Basic reading skill;
(v) Reading comprehension;
(vi) Mathematics calculation; or
(vii) Mathematics reasoning.

(b) The team may not identify a child as having a specific learning disability if the severe discrepancy between ability and achievement is primarily the result of:

(1) A visual, hearing, or motor handicap;
(2) Mental retardation;
(3) Emotional disturbance; or
(4) Environmental, cultural or economic disadvantage.

(Authority: 20 U.S.C. 1411 note)

[42 FR 65083, Dec. 29, 1977. Redesignated at 45 FR 77368, Nov. 21, 1980]

§ 300.542   Observation.

(a) At least one team member other than the child's regular teacher shall observe the child's academic performance in the regular classroom setting.

(b) In the case of a child of less than school age or out of school, a team member shall observe the child in an environment appropriate for a child of that age.

(Authority: 20 U.S.C. 1411 note)

[42 FR 65083, Dec. 29, 1977. Redesignated at 45 FR 77368, Nov. 21, 1980]

§ 300.543   Written report.

(a) The team shall prepare a written report of the results of the evaluation.

(b) The report must include a statement of:

(1) Whether the child has a specific learning disability;
(2) The basis for making the determination;
(3) The relevant behavior noted during the observation of the child;
(4) The relationship of that behavior to the child's academic functioning;
(5) The educationally relevant medical findings, if any;
(6) Whether there is a severe discrepancy between achievement and ability which is not correctable without special education and related services; and

(7) The determination of the team concerning the effects of environmental, cultural, or economic disadvantage.

(c) Each team member shall certify in writing whether the report reflects his or her conclusion. If it does not reflect his or her conclusion, the team member must submit a separage statement presenting his or her conclusions.

(Authority: 20 U.S.C. 1411 note)

[42 FR 65083, Dec. 29, 1977. Redesignated at 45 FR 77368, Nov. 21, 1980]

LEAST RESTRICTIVE ENVIRONMENT

§ 300.550   General.

(a) Each State educational agency shall insure that each public agency establishes and implements procedures which meet the requirements of §§ 300.550–300.556.

(b) Each public agency shall insure:

(1) That to the maximum extent appropriate, handicapped children, including children in public or private institutions or other care facilities, are educated with children who are not handicapped, and

(2) That special classes, separate schooling or other removal of handicapped children from the regular educational environment occurs only when the nature or severity of the handicap is such that education in regular classes with the use of supplementary aids and services cannot be achieved satisfactorily.

(Authority: 20   U.S.C.   1412(5)(B); 1414(a)(1)(C)(iv))

§ 300.551   Continuum of alternative placements.

(a) Each public agency shall insure that a continuum of alternative placements is available to meet the needs of handicapped children for special education and related services.

(b) The continuum required under paragraph (a) of this section must:

(1) Include the alternative placements listed in the definition of special education under § 300.13 of Subpart A (instruction in regular classes, special classes, special schools, home instruction, and instruction in hospitals and institutions), and

(2) Make provision for supplementary services (such as resource room or itinerant instruction) to be provided in conjunction with regular class placement.

(Authority: 20 U.S.C. 1412(5)(B))

*§ 300.552   **Placements.**

Each public agency shall insure that:

(a) Each handicapped child's educational placement: (1) Is determined at least annually,

(2) Is based on his or her individualized education program, and

(3) Is as close as possible to the child's home;

(b) The various alternative placements included under § 300.551 are available to the extent necessary to implement the individualized education program for each handicapped child;

(c) Unless a handicapped child's individualized education program requires some other arrangement, the child is educated in the school which he or she would attend if not handicapped; and

(d) In selecting the least restrictive environment, consideration is given to any potential harmful effect on the child or on the quality of services which he or she needs.

(Authority: 20 U.S.C. 1412(5)(B))

Comment. Section 300.552 includes some of the main factors which must be considered in determining the extent to which a handicapped child can be educated with children who are not handicapped. The overriding rule in this section is that placement decisions must be made on an individual basis. The section also requires each agency to have various alternative placements available in order to insure that each handicapped child receives an education which is appropriate to his or her individual needs.

The analysis of the regulations for Section 504 of the Rehabilitation Act of 1973 (34 CFR Part 104—Appendix, Paragraph 24) includes several points regarding educational placements of handicapped children which are pertinent to this section:

1. With respect to determining proper placements, the analysis states: "* * * it should be stressed that, where a handicapped child is so disruptive in a regular classroom that the education of other students is significantly impaired, the needs of the handicapped child cannot be met in that environment. Therefore regular place-

ment would not be appropriate to his or her needs * * *."

2. With respect to placing a handicapped child in an alternate setting, the analysis states that among the factors to be considered in placing a child is the need to place the child as close to home as possible. Recipients are required to take this factor into account in making placement decisions. The parent's right to challenge the placement of their child extends not only to placement in special classes or separate schools, but also to placement in a distant school, particularly in a residential program. An equally appropriate education program may exist closer to home; and this issue may be raised by the parent under the due process provisions of this subpart.

§ 300.553   **Nonacademic settings.**

In providing or arranging for the provision of nonacademic and extracurricular services and activities, including meals, recess periods, and the services and activities set forth in § 300.306 of Subpart C, each public agency shall insure that each handicapped child participates with nonhandicapped children in those services and activities to the maximum extent appropriate to the needs of that child.

(Authority: 20 U.S.C. 1412(5)(B))

Comment. Section 300.553 is taken from a new requirement in the final regulations for Section 504 of the Rehabilitation Act of 1973. With respect to this requirement, the analysis of the Section 504 Regulations includes the following statement: "[A new paragraph] specifies that handicapped children must also be provided nonacademic services in as integrated a setting as possible. This requirement is especially important for children whose educational needs necessitate their being solely with other handicapped children during most of each day. To the maximum extent appropriate, children in residential settings are also to be provided opportunities for participation with other children." (34 CFR Part 104—Appendix, Paragraph 24.)

§ 300.554   **Children in public or private institutions.**

Each State educational agency shall make arrangements with public and private institutions (such as a memorandum of agreement or special implementation procedures) as may be necessary to insure that § 300.550 is effectively implemented.

(Authority: 20 U.S.C. 1412(5)(B))

*See 1989 Amendments to EAHCA Regulations, page 433; § **300.552.**

Comment. Under section 612(5)(B) of the statute, the requirement to educate handicapped children with nonhandicapped children also applies to children in public and private institutions or other care facilities. Each State educational agency must insure that each applicable agency and institution in the State implements this requirement. Regardless of other reasons for institutional placement, no child in an institution who is capable of education in a regular public school setting may be denied access to an education in that setting.

§ 300.555   Technical assistance and training activities.

Each State educational agency shall carry out activities to insure that teachers and administrators in all public agencies:

(a) Are fully informed about their responsibilities for implementing § 300.550, and

(b) Are provided with technical assistance and training necessary to assist them in this effort.

(Authority: 20 U.S.C. 1412(5)(B))

§ 300.556   Monitoring activities.

(a) The State educational agency shall carry out activities to insure that § 300.550 is implemented by each public agency.

(b) If there is evidence that a public agency makes placements that are inconsistent with § 300.550 of this subpart, the State educational agency:

(1) Shall review the public agency's justification for its actions, and

(2) Shall assist in planning and implementing any necessary corrective action.

(Authority: 20 U.S.C. 1412(5)(B))

CONFIDENTIALITY OF INFORMATION

§ 300.560   Definitions.

As used in this subpart:

"Destruction" means physical destruction or removal of personal identifiers from information so that the information is no longer personally identifiable.

"Education records" means the type of records covered under the definition of "education records" in Part 99 of this title (the regulations implementing the Family Educational Rights and Privacy Act of 1974).

"Participating agency" means any agency or institution which collects, maintains, or uses personally identifiable information, or from which information is obtained, under this part.

(Authority: 20 U.S.C. 1412(2)(D); 1417(c))

§ 300.561   Notice to parents.

(a) The State educational agency shall give notice which is adequate to fully inform parents about the requirements under § 300.128 of Subpart B, including:

(1) A description of the extent to which the notice is given in the native languages of the various population groups in the State;

(2) A description of the children on whom personally identifiable information is maintained, the types of information sought, the methods the State intends to use in gathering the information (including the sources from whom information is gathered), and the uses to be made of the information;

(3) A summary of the policies and procedures which participating agencies must follow regarding storage, disclosure to third parties, retention, and destruction of personally identifiable information; and

(4) A description of all of the rights of parents and children regarding this information, including the rights under section 438 of the General Education Provisions Act and Part 99 of this title (the Family Educational Rights and Privacy Act of 1974, and implementing regulations).

(b) Before any major identification, location, or evaluation activity, the notice must be published or announced in newspapers or other media, or both, with circulation adequate to notify parents throughout the State of the activity.

(Authority: 20 U.S.C. 1412(2)(D); 1417(c))

§ 300.562   Access rights.

(a) Each participating agency shall permit parents to inspect and review any education records relating to their children which are collected, maintained, or used by the agency under this part. The agency shall comply with a request without unnecessary delay and before any meeting regarding an individualized education program or hearing relating to the identification, evaluation, or placement of the child, and in no case more than 45 days after the request has been made.

(b) The right to inspect and review education records under this section includes:

(1) The right to a response from the participating agency to reasonable requests for explanations and interpretations of the records;

(2) The right to request that the agency provide copies of the records containing the information if failure to provide those copies would effectively prevent the parent from exercising the right to inspect and review the records; and

(3) The right to have a representative of the parent inspect and review the records.

(c) An agency may presume that the parent has authority to inspect and review records relating to his or her child unless the agency has been advised that the parent does not have the authority under applicable State law governing such matters as guardianship, separation, and divorce.

(Authority: 20 U.S.C. 1412(2)(D); 1417(c))

§ 300.563   Record of access.

Each participating agency shall keep a record of parties obtaining access to education records collected, maintained, or used under this part (except access by parents and authorized employees of the participating agency), including the name of the party, the date access was given, and the purpose for which the party is authorized to use the records.

(Authority: 20 U.S.C. 1412(2)(D); 1417(c))

§ 300.564   Records on more than one child.

If any education record includes information on more than one child, the parents of those children shall have the right to inspect and review only the information relating to their child or to be informed of that specific information.

(Authority: 20 U.S.C. 1412(2)(D); 1417(c))

§ 300.565   List of types and locations of information.

Each participating agency shall provide parents on request a list of the types and locations of education records collected, maintained, or used by the agency.

(Authority: 20 U.S.C. 1412(2)(D); 1417(c))

§ 300.566   Fees.

(a) A participating education agency may charge a fee for copies of records which are made for parents under this part if the fee does not effectively prevent the parents from exercising their right to inspect and review those records.

(b) A participating agency may not charge a fee to search for or to retrieve information under this part.

(Authority: 20 U.S.C. 1412(2)(D); 1417(c))

§ 300.567   Amendment of records at parent's request.

(a) A parent who believes that information in education records collected, maintained, or used under this part is inaccurate or misleading or violates the privacy or other rights of the child, may request the participating agency which maintains the information to amend the information.

(b) The agency shall decide whether to amend the information in accordance with the request within a reasonable period of time of receipt of the request.

(c) If the agency decides to refuse to amend the information in accordance with the request it shall inform the parent of the refusal, and advise the parent of the right to a hearing under § 300.568.

(Authority: 20 U.S.C. 1412(2)(D); 1417(c))

§ 300.568   Opportunity for a hearing.

The agency shall, on request, provide an opportunity for a hearing to challenge information in education records to insure that it is not inaccurate, misleading, or otherwise in violation of the privacy or other rights of the child.

(Authority: 20 U.S.C. 1412(2)(D); 1417(c))

§ 300.569   Result of hearing.

(a) If, as a result of the hearing, the agency decides that the information is inaccurate, misleading or otherwise in violation of the privacy or other rights of the child, it shall amend the information accordingly and so inform the parent in writing.

(b) If, as a result of the hearing, the agency decides that the information is not inaccurate, misleading, or otherwise in violation of the privacy of other rights of the child, it shall inform the parent of the right to place in the records it maintains on the child a statement commenting on the information or setting forth any reasons for disagreeing with the decision of the agency.

(c) Any explanation placed in the records of the child under this section must:

(1) Be maintained by the agency as part of the records of the child as long as the record or contested portion is maintained by the agency; and

(2) If the records of the child or the contested portion is disclosed by the agency to any party, the explanation must also be disclosed to the party.

(Authority: 20 U.S.C. 1412(2)(D); 1417(c))

§ 300.570   Hearing procedures.

A hearing held under § 300.568 of this subpart must be conducted according to the procedures under § 99.22 of this title.

(Authority: 20 U.S.C. 1412(2)(D); 1417(c))

§ 300.571   Consent.

(a) Parental consent must be obtained before personally identifiable information is:

(1) Disclosed to anyone other than officials of participating agencies collecting or using the information under this part, subject to paragraph (b) of this section; or

(2) Used for any purpose other than meeting a requirement under this part.

(b) An educational agency or institution subject to Part 99 of this title may not release information from education records to participating agencies without parental consent unless authorized to do so under Part 99 of this title.

(c) The State educational agency shall include policies and procedures in its annual program plan which are used in the event that a parent refuses to provide consent under this section.

(Authority: 20 U.S.C. 1412(2)(D); 1417(c))

§ 300.572   Safeguards.

(a) Each participating agency shall protect the confidentiality of personally identifiable information at collection, storage, disclosure, and destruction stages.

(b) One official at each participating agency shall assume responsibility for insuring the confidentiality of any personally identifiable information.

(c) All persons collecting or using personally identifiable information must receive training or instruction regarding the State's policies and procedures under § 300.129 of Subpart B and Part 99 of this title.

(d) Each participating agency shall maintain, for public inspection, a current listing of the names and positions of those employees within the agency who may have access to personally identifiable information.

(Authority: 20 U.S.C. 1412(2)(D); 1417(c))

§ 300.573   Destruction of information.

(a) The public agency shall inform parents when personally identifiable information collected, maintained, or used under this part is no longer needed to provide educational services to the child.

(b) The information must be destroyed at the request of the parents. However, a permanent record of a student's name, address, and phone number, his or her grades, attendance record, classes attended, grade level completed, and year completed may be maintained without time limitation.

(Authority: 20 U.S.C. 1412(2)(D); 1417(c))

Comment. Under § 300.573, the personally identifiable information on a handicapped child may be retained permanently unless the parents request that it be destroyed. Destruction of records is the best protection against improper and unauthorized disclosure. However, the records may be needed for other purposes. In informing parents about their rights under this section, the agency should remind them that the records may be needed by the child or the parents for social security benefits or other purposes. If the parents request that the information be destroyed, the agency may retain the information in paragraph (b).

§ 300.574 Children's rights.

The State educational agency shall include policies and procedures in its annual program plan regarding the extent to which children are afforded rights of privacy similar to those afforded to parents, taking into consideration the age of the child and type or severity of disability.

(Authority: 20 U.S.C. 1412(2)(D); 1417(c))

Comment. Note that under the regulations for the Family Educational Rights and Privacy Act (45 CFR 99.4(a)), the rights of parents regarding education records are transferred to the student at age 18.

§ 300.575 Enforcement.

The State educational agency shall describe in its annual program plan the policies and procedures, including sanctions, which the State uses to insure that its policies and procedures are followed and that the requirements of the Act and the regulations in this part are met.

(Authority: 20 U.S.C. 1412(2)(D); 1417(c))

§ 300.576 Department.

If the Department or its authorized representatives collect any personally identifiable information regarding handicapped children which is not subject to 5 U.S.C. 552a (The Privacy Act of 1974), the Secretary shall apply the requirements of 5 U.S.C. section 552a (b) (1)–(2), (4)–(11); (c); (d); (e)(1); (2); (3)(A), (B), and (D), (5)–(10); (h); (m); and (n), and the regulations implementing those provisions in Part 5b of this title.

(Authority: 20 U.S.C. 1412(2)(D); 1417(c))

DEPARTMENT PROCEDURES

300.580 Opportunity for a hearing.

The Secretary gives a State educational agency reasonable notice and an opportunity for a hearing before taking any of the following actions:

(a) Disapproval of a State's annual program plan under § 300.113 of Subpart B.

(b) Withholding payments from a State under § 300.590 or under section 434(c) of the General Education Provisions Act.

(c) Waiving the requirement under § 300.589 of this subpart regarding supplementing and supplanting with funds provided under Part B of the Act.

(Authority: 20 U.S.C. 1232(c); 1413(a)(9)(b); 1413(c); 1416)

EFFECTIVE DATE NOTE: Section 300.580 was removed and reserved at 51 FR 17905, May 15, 1986, effective July 23, 1986.

§ 300.581 Disapproval of a State plan.

Before disapproving a State plan, the Secretary gives the State educational agency written notice and an opportunity for a hearing.

(Authority: 20 U.S.C. 1413(c))

[51 FR 17905, May 15, 1986]

EFFECTIVE DATE NOTE: Section 300.581 was added at 51 FR 17905, May 15, 1986, effective July 23, 1986.

§ 300.582 Content of notice.

(a) In the written notice, the Secretary—

(1) States the basis on which the Secretary proposes to disapprove the State plan;

(2) May describe possible options for resolving the issues;

(3) Advises the State educational agency that it may request a hearing and that the request for a hearing must be made not later than 30 calendar days after it receives the notice of proposed disapproval; and

(4) Provides information about the procedures followed for a hearing.

(b) The Secretary sends the written notice to the State educational agency by certified mail with return receipt requested.

(Authority: 20 U.S.C. 1413(c))

[51 FR 17905, May 15, 1986]

EFFECTIVE DATE NOTE: Section 300.582 was added at 51 FR 17905, May 15, 1986, effective July 23, 1986.

§ 300.583 Hearing official or panel.

(a) If the State educational agency requests a hearing, the Secretary designates one or more individuals, either from the Department or elsewhere, not responsible for or connected with the administration of the program under this part, to conduct a hearing.

(b) If more than one individual is designated, the Secretary designates one of those individuals as the Chief Hearing Official of the Hearing Panel. If one individual is designated, that individual is the Hearing Official.

(c) If the State has an appeal pending with the Education Appeal Board on a matter arising out of the same State plan, or on the same issue arising from a prior plan, the State may contest the disapproval of its plan before the Education Appeal Board in accordance with 34 CFR Part 78.

(Authority: 20 U.S.C. 1413(c))

[51 FR 17905, May 15, 1986]

EFFECTIVE DATE NOTE: Section 300.583 was added at 51 FR 17905, May 15, 1986, effective July 23, 1986.

§ 300.584   Hearing procedures.

(a) As used in §§ 300.581—300.586 the term "party" or "parties" means the following:

(1) A State educational agency that requests a hearing regarding the proposed disapproval of its State plan under this part.

(2) The Department of Education official who administers the program of financial assistance under this part.

(3) A person, group or agency with an interest in and having relevant information about the case who has applied for and been granted leave to intervene by the Hearing Official or Panel.

(b) Within 15 calendar days after receiving a request for a hearing, the Secretary designates a Hearing Official or Panel and notifies the parties.

(c) The Hearing Official or Panel may regulate the course of proceedings and the conduct of the parties during the proceedings. The Hearing Official or Panel takes all steps necessary to conduct a fair and impartial proceeding, to avoid delay, and to maintain order, including the following:

(1) The Hearing Official or Panel may hold conferences or other types of appropriate proceedings to clarify, simplify, or define the issues or to consider other matters that may aid in the disposition of the case.

(2) The Hearing Official or Panel may schedule a prehearing conference of the Hearing Official or Panel and parties.

(3) Any party may request the Hearing Official or Panel to schedule a prehearing or other conference. The Hearing Official or Panel decides whether a conference is necessary and notifies all parties.

(4) At a prehearing or other conference, the Hearing Official or Panel and the parties may consider subjects such as—

(i) Narrowing and clarifying issues;

(ii) Assisting the parties in reaching agreements and stipulations;

(iii) Clarifying the positions of the parties;

(iv) Determining whether an evidentiary hearing or oral argument should be held;

(v) Setting dates for—

(A) The exchange of written documents;

(B) The receipt of comments from the parties on the need for oral argument or evidentiary hearing;

(C) Further proceedings before the Hearing Official or Panel (including an evidentiary hearing or oral argument, if either is scheduled);

(D) Requesting the names of witnesses each party wishes to present at an evidentiary hearing and estimation of time for each presentation; or

(E) Completion of the review and the initial decision of the Hearing Official or Panel.

(5) A prehearing or other conference held under paragraph (b)(4) of this section may be conducted by telephone conference call.

(6) At a prehearing or other conference, the parties shall be prepared to discuss the subjects listed in paragraph (b)(4) of this section.

(7) Following a prehearing or other conference the Hearing Official or Panel may issue a written statement describing the issues raised, the action taken, and the stipulations and agreements reached by the parties.

(d) The Hearing Official or Panel may require parties to state their positions and to provide all or part of the evidence in writing.

(e) The Hearing Official or Panel may require parties to present testimony through affidavits and to conduct cross-examination through interrogatories.

(f) The Hearing Official or Panel may direct the parties to exchange relevant documents or information and lists of witnesses, and to send copies to the Hearing Official or Panel.

(g) The Hearing Official or Panel may receive, rule on, exclude, or limit evidence at any stage of the proceedings.

(h) The Hearing Official or Panel may rule on motions and other issues at any stage of the proceedings.

(i) The Hearing Official or Panel may examine witnesses.

(j) The Hearing Official or Panel may set reasonable time limits for submission of written documents.

(k) The Hearing Official or Panel may refuse to consider documents or other submissions if they are not submitted in a timely manner unless good cause is shown.

(l) The Hearing Official or Panel may interpret applicable statutes and regulations but may not waive them or rule on their validity.

(m)(1) The parties shall present their positions through briefs and the submission of other documents and may request an oral argument or evidentiary hearing. The Hearing Official or Panel shall determine whether an oral argument or an evidentiary hearing is needed to clarify the positions of the parties.

(2) The Hearing Official or Panel gives each party an opportunity to be represented by counsel.

(n) If the Hearing Official or Panel determines that an evidentiary hearing would materially assist the resolution of the matter, the Hearing Official or Panel gives each party, in addition to the opportunity to be represented by counsel—

(1) An opportunity to present witnesses on the party's behalf; and

(2) An opportunity to cross-examine witnesses either orally or with written questions.

(o) The Hearing Official or Panel accepts any evidence that it finds is relevant and material to the proceedings and is not unduly repetitious.

(p)(1) The Hearing Official or Panel—

(i) Arranges for the preparation of a transcript of each hearing;

(ii) Retains the original transcript as part of the record of the hearing; and

(iii) Provides one copy of the transcript to each party.

(2) Additional copies of the transcript are available on request and with payment of the reproduction fee.

(q) Each party shall file with the Hearing Official or Panel all written motions, briefs, and other documents and shall at the same time provide a copy to the other parties to the proceedings.

(Authority: 20 U.S.C. 1413(c))

[51 FR 17905, May 15, 1986]

EFFECTIVE DATE NOTE: Section 300.584 was added at 51 FR 17905, May 15, 1986, effective July 23, 1986.

§ 300.585   Initial decision; final decision.

(a) The Hearing Official or Panel prepares an initial written decision which addresses each of the points in the notice sent by the Secretary to the State educational agency under § 300.582.

(b) The initial decision of a Panel is made by a majority of Panel members.

(c) The Hearing Official or Panel mails by certified mail with return receipt requested a copy of the initial decision to each party (or to the party's counsel) and to the Secretary, with a notice stating that each party has an opportunity to submit written comments regarding the decision to the Secretary.

(d) Each party may file comments and recommendations on the initial decision with the Hearing Official or Panel within 15 calendar days of the date the party receives the Panel's decision.

(e) The Hearing Official or Panel sends a copy of a party's initial comments and recommendations to the other parties by certified mail with return receipt requested. Each party may file responsive comments and recommendations with the Hearing Official or Panel within seven calendar days of the date the party receives the initial comments and recommendations.

(f) The Hearing Official or Panel forwards the parties' initial and responsive comments on the initial decision to the Secretary who reviews the initial decision and issues a final decision.

(g) The initial decision of the Hearing Official or Panel becomes the final decision of the Secretary unless, within 25 calendar days after the end of the time for receipt of written comments, the Secretary informs the Hearing Official or Panel and the parties to a hearing in writing that the decision is being further reviewed for possible modification.

(h) The Secretary may reject or modify the initial decision of the Hearing Official or Panel if the Secretary finds that it is clearly erroneous.

(i) The Secretary conducts the review based on the initial decision, the written record, the Hearing Official's or Panel's proceedings, and written comments. The Secretary may remand the matter for further proceedings.

(j) The Secretary issues the final decision within 30 calendar days after notifying the Hearing Official or Panel that the initial decision is being further reviewed.

[51 FR 17906, May 15, 1986]

EFFECTIVE DATE NOTE: Section 300.585 was added at 51 FR 17906, May 15, 1986, effective July 23, 1986.

§ 300.586 Judicial review.

If a State is dissatisfied with the Secretary's final action with respect to its State plan, the State may, within 60 calendar days after notice of that action, file a petition for review with the United States court of appeals for the circuit in which the State is located.

(Authority: 20 U.S.C. 1416(b)(1))

[51 FR 17906, May 15, 1986]

EFFECTIVE DATE NOTE: Section 300.586 was added at 51 FR 17906, May 15, 1986, effective July 23, 1986.

§§ 300.587—300.588 [Reserved]

* § 300.589 Waiver of requirement regarding supplementing and supplanting with Part B funds.

(a) Under sections 613(a)(9)(B) and 614(a)(2)(B)(ii) of the Act, State and local educational agencies must insure that Federal funds provided under Part B of the Act are used to supplement the level of State and local funds expended for the education of handicapped children, and in no case to supplant those State and local funds. Beginning with funds appropriated for fiscal year 1979 and for each following fiscal year, the nonsupplanting requirement only applies to funds allocated to local educational agencies. (See § 300.372.)

(b) If the State provides clear and convincing evidence that all handicapped children have available to them a free appropriate public education, the Secretary may waive in part the requirement under sections 613(a)(9)(B) and 614(a)(2)(B)(ii) of the Act if the Secretary concurs with the evidence provided by the State.

(c) If a State wishes to request a waiver, it must inform the Secretary in writing. The Secretary then provides the State with a finance and membership report form which provides the basis for the request.

(d) In its request for a waiver, the State shall include the results of a special study made by the State to obtain evidence of the availability of a free appropriate public education to all handicapped children. The special study must include statements by a representative sample of organizations which deal with handicapped children, and parents and teachers of handicapped children, relating to the following areas:

(1) The adequacy and comprehensiveness of the State's system for locating, identifying, and evaluating handicapped children, and

(2) The cost to parents, if any, for education for children enrolled in public and private day schools, and in public and private residential schools and institutions, and

(3) The adequacy of the State's due process procedures.

(e) In its request for a waiver, the State shall include finance data relating to the availability of a free appropriate public education for all handicapped children, including:

(1) The total current expenditures for regular education programs and special education programs by function and by source of funds (State, local, and Federal) for the previous school year, and

*See 1989 Amendments to EAHCA Regulations, page 433; § **300.589**.

(2) The full-time equivalent membership of students enrolled in regular programs and in special programs in the previous school year.

(f) The Secretary considers the information which the State provides under paragraphs (d) and (e) of this section, along with any additional information he may request, or obtain through on-site reviews of the State's education programs and records, to determine if all children have available to them a free appropriate public education, and if so, the extent of the waiver.

(g) The State may request a hearing with regard to any final action by the Secretary under this section.

(Authority: 20   U.S.C.   1411(c)(3); 1413(a)(9)(B))

[42 FR 42476, Aug. 23, 1977. Redesignated at 45 FR 77368, Nov. 21, 1980 and amended at 51 FR 17906, May 15, 1986]

EFFECTIVE DATE NOTE: Section 300.589(g) was revised at 51 FR 17906, May 15, 1986, effective July 23, 1986. For the convenience of the reader, the superseded text is set forth below.

§ 300.589 Waiver of requirement regarding supplementing and supplanting with Part B funds.

*   *   *   *   *

(g) The State may request a hearing under §§ 300.580—300.583 with regard to any final action by the Secretary under this section.

Subpart F—State Administration

* STATE EDUCATIONAL AGENCY RESPONSIBILITIES: GENERAL

* § 300.600 Responsibility for all educational programs.

(a) The State educational agency is responsible for insuring;

(1) That the requirements of this part are carried out; and

(2) That each educational program for handicapped children administered within the State, including each program administered by any other public agency:

(i) Is under the general supervision of the persons responsible for educational programs for handicapped children in the State educational agency, and

(ii) Meets education standards of the State educational agency (including the requirements of this part).

(b) The State must comply with paragraph (a) of this section through State statute, State regulation, signed agreement between respective agency officials, or other documents.

(Authority: 20 U.S.C. 1412(6))

Comment. The requirement in § 300.600(a) is taken essentially verbatim from section 612(6) of the statute and reflects the desire of the Congress for a central point of responsibility and accountability in the education of handicapped children within each State. With respect to State educational agency responsibility, the Senate Report on Pub. L. 94-142 includes the following statements:

This provision is included specifically to assure a single line of responsibility with regard to the education of handicapped children, and to assure that in the implementation of all provisions of this Act and in carrying out the right to education for handicapped children, the State educational agency shall be the responsible agency * * *.

Without this requirement, there is an abdication of responsibility for the education of handicapped children. Presently, in many States, responsibility is divided, depending upon the age of the handicapped child, sources of funding, and type of services delivered. While the Committee understands that different agencies may, in fact, deliver services, the responsibility must remain in a central agency overseeing the education of handicapped children, so that failure to deliver services or the violation of the rights of handicapped children is squarely the responsibility of one agency. (Senate Report No. 94-168, p. 24 (1975))

In meeting the requirements of this section, there are a number of acceptable options which may be adopted, including the following:

(1) Written agreements are developed between respective State agencies concerning State educational agency standards and monitoring. These agreements are binding on the local or regional counterparts of each State agency.

(2) The Governor's Office issues an administrative directive establishing the State educational agency responsibility.

(3) State law, regulation, or policy designates the State educational agency as responsible for establishing standards for all educational programs for the handicapped, and includes responsibility for monitoring.

*See 1989 Amendments to EAHCA Regulations, page 434; § **300.600.**

(4) State law mandates that the State educational agency is responsible for all educational programs.

USE OF FUNDS

§ 300.620 Federal funds for State administration.

A State may use five percent of the total State allotment in any fiscal year under Part B of the Act, or $350,000, whichever is greater, for administrative costs related to carrying out sections 612 and 613 of the Act. However, this amount cannot be greater than twenty-five percent of the State's total allotment for the fiscal year under Part B of the Act.

(Authority: 20 U.S.C. 1411 (b), (c))

[51 FR 19311, May 28, 1986]

EFFECTIVE DATE NOTE: Section 300.620 was revised at 51 FR 19311, May 28, 1986, effective July 23, 1986. For the convenience of the reader, the superseded text is set forth below.

§ 300.620 Federal funds for State administration.

A State may use five percent of the total State allotment in any fiscal year under Part B of the Act, or $200,000, whichever is greater, for administrative costs related to carrying out sections 612 and 613 of the Act. However, this amount cannot be greater than the amount which the State may use under § 300.704 or § 300.705, as the case may be.

(Authority: 20 U.S.C. 1411 (b), (c))

§ 300.621 Allowable costs.

(a) The State educational agency may use funds under § 300.620 of this subpart for:
(1) Administration of the annual program plan and for planning at the State level, including planning, or assisting in the planning, of programs or projects for the education of handicapped children;
(2) Approval, supervision, monitoring, and evaluation of the effectiveness of local programs and projects for the education of handicapped children;
(3) Technical assistance to local educational agencies with respect to the requirements of this part;
(4) Leadership services for the program supervision and management of special education activities for handicapped children; and

(5) Other State leadership activities and consultative services.
(b) The State educational agency shall use the remainder of its funds under § 300.620 in accordance with § 300.370 of Subpart C.

(Authority: 20 U.S.C. 1411 (b), (c))

STATE ADVISORY PANEL

§ 300.650 Establishment.

(a) Each State shall establish, in accordance with the provisions of this subpart, a State advisory panel on the education of handicapped children.
(b) The advisory panel must be appointed by the Governor or any other official authorized under State law to make those appointments.
(c) If a State has an existing advisory panel that can perform the functions in § 300.652, the State may modify the existing panel so that it fulfills all of the requirements of this subpart, instead of establishing a new advisory panel.

(Authority: 20 U.S.C. 1413(a)(12))

§ 300.651 Membership.

(a) The membership of the State advisory panel must be composed of persons involved in or concerned with the education of handicapped children. The membership must include at least one person representative of each of the following groups:
(1) Handicapped individuals.
(2) Teachers of handicapped children.
(3) Parents of handicapped children.
(4) State and local educational officials.
(5) Special education program administrators.
(b) The State may expand the advisory panel to include additional persons in the groups listed in paragraph (a) of this section and representatives of other groups not listed.

(Authority: 20 U.S.C. 1413(a)(12))

Comment. The membership of the State advisory panel, as listed in paragraphs (a) (1)–(5), is required in section 613(a)(12) of the Act. As indicated in paragraph (b), the composition of the panel and the number of members may be expanded at the discretion

*See 1989 Amendments to EAHCA Regulations, page 434; § **300.601**.

of the State. In adding to the membership, consideration could be given to having:

(1) An appropriate balance between professional groups and consumers (i.e., parents, advocates, and handicapped individuals);

(2) Broad representation within the consumer-advocate groups, to insure that the interests and points of view of various parents, advocates and handicapped individuals are appropriately represented;

(3) Broad representation within professional groups (e.g., (a) regular education personnel, (b) special educators, including teachers, teacher trainers, and administrators, who can properly represent various dimensions in the education of handicapped children, and (c) appropriate related services personnel); and

(4) Representatives from other State advisory panels (such as vocational education).

If a State elects to maintain a small advisory panel (e.g., 10-15 members), the panel itself could take steps to insure that it (1) consults with and receives inputs from various consumer and special interest professional groups, and (2) establishes committees for particular short-term purposes composed of representatives from those input groups.

§ 300.652   Advisory panel functions.

The State advisory panel shall:

(a) Advise the State educational agency of unmet needs within the State in the education of handicapped children;

(b) Comment publicly on the State annual program plan and rules or regulations proposed for issuance by the State regarding the education of handicapped children and the procedures for distribution of funds under this part; and

(c) Assist the State in developing and reporting such information and evaluations as may assist the Secretary in the performance of his responsibilities under section 618.

(Authority: 20 U.S.C. 1413(a)(12))

§ 300.653   Advisory panel procedures.

(a) The advisory panel shall meet as often as necessary to conduct its business.

(b) By July 1 of each year, the advisory panel shall submit an annual report of panel activities and suggestions to the State educational agency. This report must be made available to the public in a manner consistent with

other public reporting requirements under this part.

(c) Official minutes must be kept on all panel meetings and shall be made available to the public on request.

(d) All advisory panel meetings and agenda items must be publicly announced prior to the meeting, and meetings must be open to the public.

(e) Interpreters and other necessary services must be provided at panel meetings for panel members or participants. The State may pay for these services from funds under § 300.620.

(f) The advisory panel shall serve without compensation but the State must reimburse the panel for reasonable and necessary expenses for attending meetings and performing duties. The State may use funds under § 300.620 for this purpose.

(Authority: 20 U.S.C. 1413(a)(12))

Subpart G—Allocation of Funds; Reports

ALLOCATIONS

§ 300.700   Special definition of the term State.

For the purposes of § 300.701, § 300.702, and §§ 300.704–300.708, the term "State" does not include Guam, American Samoa, the Virgin Islands, and the Trust Territory of the Pacific Islands.

(Authority: 20 U.S.C. 1411(a)(2))

*§ 300.701   State entitlement; formula.

(a) The maximum amount of the grant to which a State is entitled under section 611 of the Act in any fiscal year is equal to the number of handicapped children aged three through 21 in the State who are receiving special education and related services, multiplied by the applicable percentage, under paragraph (b) of this section, of the average per pupil expenditure in public elementary and secondary schools in the United States.

(b) For the purposes of the formula in paragraph (a) of this section, the applicable percentage of the average per pupil expenditure in public ele-

*See 1989 Amendments to EAHCA Regulations, page 434; § 300.701.

mentary and secondary schools in the United States for each fiscal year is:

(1) 1978—5 percent,
(2) 1979—10 percent,
(3) 1980—20 percent,
(4) 1981—30 percent, and
(5) 1982, and for each fiscal year after 1982, 40 percent.

(Authority: 20 U.S.C. 1411(a)(1))

(c) For the purposes of this section, the average per pupil expenditure in public elementary and secondary schools in the United States, means the aggregate expenditures during the second fiscal year preceding the fiscal year for which the computation is made (or if satisfactory data for that year are not available at the time of computation, then during the most recent preceding fiscal year for which satisfactory data are available) of all local educational agencies in the United States (which, for the purpose of this section, means the fifty States and the District of Columbia), plus any direct expenditures by the State for operation of those agencies (without regard to the source of funds from which either of those expenditures are made), divided by the aggregate number of children in average daily attendance to whom those agencies provided free public education during that preceding year.

(Authority: 20 U.S.C. 1411(a)(4))

* § 300.702   Limitations and exclusions.

(a) In determining the amount of a grant under § 300.701 of this subpart, the Secretary may not count:

(1) Handicapped children in a State to the extent that the number of those children is greater than 12 percent of the number of all children aged five through 17 in the State; and

(2) [Reserved]

(3) Handicapped children who are counted under section 121 of the Elementary and Secondary Education Act of 1965.

(b) For the purposes of paragraph (a) of this section, the number of children aged five through 17 in any State shall be determined by the Secretary on the basis of the most recent satisfactory data available to him.

(Authority: 20 U.S.C. 1411(a)(5))

[42 FR 42476, Aug. 23, 1977, as amended at 42 FR 65083, Dec. 29, 1977. Redesignated at 45 FR 77368, Nov. 21, 1980]

§ 300.703   Ratable reductions.

(a) *General.* If the sums appropriated for any fiscal year for making payments to States under section 611 of the Act are not sufficient to pay in full the total amounts to which all States are entitled to receive for that fiscal year, the maximum amount which all States are entitled to receive for that fiscal year shall be ratably reduced. In case additional funds become available for making payments for any fiscal year during which the preceding sentence is applicable, those reduced amounts shall be increased on the same basis they were reduced.

(Authority: 20 U.S.C. 1411(g)(1))

(b) *Reporting dates for local educational agencies and reallocations.* (1) In any fiscal year in which the State entitlements have been ratably reduced, and in which additional funds have not been made available to pay in full the total of the amounts under paragraph (a) of this section, the State educational agency shall fix dates before which each local educational agency shall report to the State the amount of funds available to it under this part which it estimates it will expend.

(2) The amounts available under paragraph (a)(1) of this section, or any amount which would be available to any other local educational agency if it were to submit an application meeting the requirements of this part, which the State educational agency determines will not be used for the period of its availability, shall be available for allocation to those local educational agencies, in the manner provided in § 300.707, which the State educational agency determines will need and be able to use additional funds to carry out approved programs.

(Authority: 20 U.S.C. 1411(g)(2))

§ 300.704   Hold harmless provision.

No State shall receive less than the amount it received under Part B of the Act for fiscal year 1977.

*See 1989 Amendments to EAHCA Regulations, page 434; § **300.702**.

(Authority: 20 U.S.C. 1411(a)(1))

§ 300.705 Allocation for State in which bypass is implemented for private school handicapped children.

In determining the allocation under §§ 300.700–300.703 of a State in which the Secretary will implement a by-pass for private school handicapped children under §§ 300.451–300.486, the Secretary includes in the State's child count—

(a) For the first year of a by-pass, the actual or estimated number of private school handicapped children (as defined in §§ 300.5(a) and 300.450 in the State, as of the preceding December 1; and

(b) For succeeding years of a by-pass, the number of private school handicapped children who received special education and related services under the by-pass in the preceding year.

(Authority: 20   U.S.C.   1411(a)(1)(A), 1411(a)(3), 1413(d))

[49 FR 48526, Dec. 12, 1984]

§ 300.706 Within-State distribution: Fiscal year 1979 and after.

Of   the   funds   received   under § 300.701 by any State for fiscal year 1979, and for each fiscal year after fiscal year 1979:

(a) 25 percent may be used by the State in accordance with § 300.620 of Subpart F and § 300.370 of Subpart C, and

(b) 75 percent shall be distributed to the local educational agencies in the State in accordance with § 300.707.

(Authority: 20 U.S.C. 1411(c)(1))

§ 300.707 Local educational agency entitlements; formula.

From the total amount of funds available to all local educational agencies, each local educational agency is entitled to an amount which bears the same ratio to the total amount as the number of handicapped children aged three through 21 in that agency who are receiving special education and related services bears to the aggregate number of handicapped children aged three through 21 receiving special education and related services in all local educational agencies which apply to the State educational agency for funds under Part B of the Act.

(Authority: 20 U.S.C. 1411(d))

§ 300.708 Reallocation of local educational agency funds.

If a State educational agency determines that a local educational agency is adequately providing a free appropriate public education to all handicapped children residing in the area served by the local agency with State and local funds otherwise available to the local agency, the State educational agency may reallocate funds (or portions of those funds which are not required to provide special education and related services) made available to the local agency under § 300.707, to other local educational agencies within the State which are not adequately providing special education and related services to all handicapped children residing in the areas served by the other local educational agencies.

(Authority: 20 U.S.C. 1414(e))

* § 300.709 Payments to Secretary of Interior.

(a) The Secretary is authorized to make payments to the Secretary of the Interior according to the need for that assistance for the education of handicapped children on reservations serviced by elementary and secondary schools operated for Indian children by the Department of the Interior.

(b) The amount of those payments for any fiscal year shall not exceed one percent of the aggregate amounts available to all States for that fiscal year under Part B of the Act.

(Authority: 20 U.S.C. 1411(f)(1))

§ 300.710 Entitlements to jurisdictions.

(a) The jurisdictions to which this section applies are Guam, American Samoa, the Virgin Islands, and the Trust Territory of the Pacific Islands.

(b) Each jurisdiction under paragraph (a) of this section is entitled to a grant for the purposes set forth in section 601(c) of the Act. The amount to which those jurisdictions are so en-

---

*See 1989 Amendments to EAHCA Regulations, page 435; § 300.709.

titled for any fiscal year shall not exceed an amount equal to 1 percent of the aggregate of the amounts available to all States under this part for that fiscal year. Funds appropriated for those jurisdictions shall be allocated proportionately among them on the basis of the number of children aged three through twenty-one in each jurisdiction. However, no jurisdiction shall receive less than $150,000, and other allocations shall be ratably reduced if necessary to insure that each jurisdiction receives at least that amount.

(c) The amount expended for administration by each jurisdiction under this section shall not exceed 5 percent of the amount allotted to the jurisdiction for any fiscal year, or $35,000, whichever is greater.

(Authority: 20 U.S.C. 1411(e))

REPORTS

*§ 300.750 Annual report of children served—report requirement.

(a) The State educational agency shall report to the Secretary no later than February 1 of each year the number of handicapped children aged three through 21 residing in the State who are receiving special education and related services.

(Authority: 20 U.S.C. 1411(a)(3))

(b) The State educational agency shall submit the report on forms provided by the Secretary.

(Authority: 20 U.S.C. 1411(a)(3))

Comment. It is very important to understand that this report and the requirements that relate to it are solely for allocation purposes. The population of children the State may count for allocation purposes may differ from the population of children to whom the State must make available a free appropriate public education. For example, while section 611(a)(5) of the Act limits the number of children who may be counted for allocation purposes to 12 percent of the general school population aged five through seventeen, a State might find that 14 percent (or some other percentage) of its children are handicapped. In that case, the State must make free appropriate public education available to all of those handicapped children.

[42 FR 42476, Aug. 23, 1977, as amended at 45 FR 7551, Feb. 4, 1980. Redesignated at 45 FR 77368, Nov. 21, 1980]

*§ 300.751 Annual report of children served—information required in the report.

(a) In its report, the State educational agency shall include a table which shows:

(1) The number of handicapped children receiving special education and related services on December 1 of that school year;

(2) The number of those handicapped children within each disability category, as defined in the definition of "handicapped children" in § 300.5 of Subpart A; and

(3) The number of those handicapped children aged three through twenty-one for each year of age (three, four, five, etc.). For fiscal year 1985, a State educational agency that does not currently collect information in this manner may report the number of those handicapped children within each of the following age groups:

(i) Three through five.

(ii) Six through eleven.

(iii) Twelve through seventeen.

(iv) Eighteen through twenty-one.

(b) For the purpose of this part, a child's age is the child's actual age on the date of the child count: December 1.

(c) The State educational agency may not report a child under more than one disability category.

(d) If a handicapped child has more than one disability, the State educational agency shall report that child in accordance with the following procedure:

(1) A child who is both deaf and blind must be reported as "deaf-blind."

(2) A child who has more than one disability (other than a deaf-blind child) must be reported as "multihandicapped."

(The information collection requirements contained in paragraphs (a)(3) and (b) were approved by the Office of Management and Budget under control number 1820–0043)

(Authority: 20   U.S.C.   1411(a)(3); 1411(a)(5)(A)(ii); 1418(b))

[42 FR 42476, Aug. 23, 1977, as amended at 45 FR 7551, Feb. 4, 1980. Redesignated at 45

*See 1989 Amendments to EAHCA Regulations, page 435; § § **300.750, 300.751.**

FR 77368, Nov. 21, 1980; 49 FR 48525, Dec. 12, 1984]

§ 300.752 Annual report of children served—certification.

The State educational agency shall include in its report a certification signed by an authorized official of the agency that the information provided is an accurate and unduplicated count of handicapped children receiving special education and related services on the dates in question.

(Authority: 20 U.S.C. 1411(a)(3); 1417(b))

*§ 300.753 Annual report of children served—criteria for counting children.

(a) The State educational agency may include handicapped children in its report who are enrolled in a school or program which is operated or supported by a public agency, and which either:

(1) Provides them with both special education and related services; or

(2) Provides them only with special education if they do not need related services to assist them in benefitting from that special education.

(b) The State educational agency may not include handicapped children in its report who:

(1) Are not enrolled in a school or program operated or supported by a public agency;

(2) Are not provided special education that meets State standards;

(3) Are not provided with a related service that they need to assist them in benefitting from special education;

(4) Are counted by a State agency under section 121 of the Elementary and Secondary Education Act of 1965, as amended; or

(5) Are receiving special education funded solely by the Federal Government. However, the State may count children covered under § 300.186(b) of Subpart B.

(Authority: 20 U.S.C. 1411(a)(3); 1417(b))

Comment. 1. Under paragraph (a), the State may count handicapped children in a Head Start or other preschool program operated or supported by a public agency if those children are provided special education that meets State standards.

2. "Special education," by statutory definition, must be at no cost to parents. As of September 1, 1978, under the free appropri-

ate public education requirement, both special education and related services must be at no cost to parents.

There may be some situations, however, where a child receives special education from a public source at no cost, but whose parents pay for the basic or regular education. This child may be counted. The Department expects that there would only be limited situations where special education would be clearly separate from regular education—generally, where speech therapy is the only special education required by the child. For example, the child might be in a regular program in a parochial or other private school but receiving speech therapy in a program funded by the local educational agency. Allowing these children to be counted will provide incentives (in addition to complying with the legal requirement in section 613(a)(4)(A) of the Act regarding private schools) to public agencies to provide services to children in private schools, since funds are generated in part on the basis of the number of children provided special education and related services. Agencies should understand, however, that where a handicapped child is placed in or referred to a public or private school for educational purposes, special education includes the entire educational program provided to the child. In that case, parents may not be charged for any part of the child's education.

A State may not count Indian children on or near reservations and children on military facilities if it provides them no special education. If a State or local educational agency is responsible for serving these children, and does provide them special education and related services, they may be counted.

§ 300.754 Annual report of children served—other responsibilities of the State educational agency.

In addition to meeting the other requirements in this subpart, the State educational agency shall:

(a) Establish procedures to be used by local educational agencies and other educational institutions in counting the number of handicapped children receiving special education and related services;

(b) Set dates by which those agencies and institutions must report to the State educational agency to insure that the State complies with § 300.750(a);

(c) Obtain certification from each agency and institution that an unduplicated and accurate count has been made;

(d) Aggregate the data from the count obtained from each agency and institution, and prepare the reports required under this subpart; and

(e) Insure that documentation is maintained which enables the State and the Secretary to audit the accuracy of the count.

(Authority: 20 U.S.C. 1411(a)(3); 1417(b))

Comment. States should note that the data required in the annual report of children served are not to be transmitted to the Secretary in personally identifiable form. States are encouraged to collect these data in non-personally identifiable form.

1989 AMENDMENTS TO EAHCA REGULATIONS

PART 300—ASSISTANCE TO STATES FOR EDUCATION OF HANDI-CAPPED CHILDREN

1. The authority citation for Part 300 continues to read as follows:

Authority: 20 U.S.C. 1411-1420, unless otherwise noted.

§ 300.138   [Amended]

2. Section 300.138 is amended by removing "section 121 of the Elementary and Secondary Education Act of 1965 (20 U.S.C. 241e-2) section 305(b)(8) of that Act (20 U.S.C. 844a(b)(8)) or Title IV-C of that Act (20 U.S.C. 1831), and section 110(a) of the Vocational Education Act of 1963," and adding in its place "subpart 2 of part D of Chapter 1 of Title I of the Elementary and Secondary Education Act of 1965 and section 202(1) of the Carl D. Perkins Vocational Education Act."

3. Subpart B is amended by adding a new § 300.150 to read as follows:

§ 300.150   State-level nonsupplanting.

Each program plan must provide assurance satisfactory to the Secretary that funds provided under this part will be used so as to supplement and increase the level of Federal (other than funds available under this part), State, and local funds—including funds that are not under the direct control of State or local educational agencies—expended for special education and related services provided to handicapped children under this part and in no case to supplant those Federal (other than funds available under this part), State, and local funds unless a waiver is granted in accordance with § 300.589.

(Authority: 20 U.S.C. 1413(a)(9))

Comment. This requirement is distinct from the supplanting provision already contained in these regulations at § 300.230. Under this provision, the State must assure that Part B funds distributed to local educational agencies and intermediate educational units will be used to supplement and not supplant other Federal, State, and local funds (including funds not under the control of educational agencies) that would have been expended for special education and related services provided to handicapped children in the absence of the Part B funds. The portion of Part B funds that are not distributed to local educational agencies or intermediate educational units under the statutory formula (20 U.S.C. 1411(d)) are not subject to this supplanting provision. *See* 20 U.S.C. 1411(c)(3). States may not permit local educational agencies or intermediate educational units to use Part B funds to satisfy a financial commitment for services that would have been paid for by a health or other agency pursuant to policy or practice but for the fact that these services are now included in handicapped children's individualized education programs.

(H.R. Rep. No. 860, 99th Cong., 21-22 (1986))

4. Subpart B is further amended by adding new § § 300.152 and 300.153 to read as follows:

§ 300.152   Interagency agreements.

(a) Each State plan must set forth policies and procedures for developing and implementing interagency agreements between—

(1) The State educational agency; and

(2) All other State and local agencies that provide or pay for services required under this part for handicapped children.

(b) The policies and procedures referred to in paragraph (a) of this section must—

(1) Describe the role that each of those agencies plays in providing or paying for services required under this part for handicapped children; and

(2) Provide for the development and implementation of interagency agreements that—

(i) Define the financial responsibility of each agency for providing handicapped children with free appropriate public education;

(ii) Establish procedures for resolving interagency disputes among agencies that are parties to the agreements; and

(iii) Establish procedures under which local educational agencies may initiate proceedings in order to secure reimbursement from agencies that are parties to the agreement or otherwise implement the provisions of the agreement.

(Authority: 20 U.S.C. 1413 (a)(13))
(Approved by the Office of Management and Budget under control number 1820-0030)

§ 300.153   Personnel standards

(a) As used in this part:

(1) "Appropriate professional requirements in the State" means entry level requirements that—

(i) Are based on the highest requirements in the State applicable to the profession or discipline in which a person is providing special education or related services; and

(ii) Establish suitable qualifications for personnel providing special education and related services under this part to children and youth with handicaps who are served by State, local, and private agencies (*see* § 300.2);

(2) "Highest requirements in the State applicable to a specific profession or discipline" means the highest entry-level academic degree needed for any State approved or recognized certification, licensing, registration, or other comparable requirements that apply to that profession or discipline;

(3) "Profession or discipline" means a specific occupational category that—

(i) Provides special education and related services to handicapped children under this part;

(ii) Has been established or designated by the State; and

(iii) Has a required scope of responsibility and degree of supervision.

(4) "State approved or recognized certification, licensing, registration, or other comparable requirements" means the requirements that a State legislature either has enacted or has authorized a State agency to promulgate through rules to establish the entry-level standards for employment in a specific profession or discipline in that State.

(b)(1) Each State plan must include policies and procedures relating to the establishment and maintenance of standards to ensure that personnel necessary to carry out the purposes of this part are appropriately and adequately prepared and trained.

(2) The policies and procedures required in paragraph (b)(1) of this section must provide for the establishment and maintenance of standards that are consistent with any State approved or recognized certification, licensing, or other comparable requirements that apply to the profession or discipline in which a person is providing special education or related services.

(c) To the extent that a State's standards for a profession or discipline, including standards for temporary or emergency certification, are not based on the highest requirements in the State applicable to a specific profession or discipline, the State plan must include the steps the State is taking and the procedures for notifying public agencies and personnel of those steps and the timelines it has established for the retraining or hiring of personnel to meet appropriate professional requirements in the State.

(d)(1) In meeting the requirements in paragraphs (b) and (c) of this section, a determination must be made about the status of personnel standards in the State. That determination must be based on current information that accurately describes, for each profession or discipline in which personnel are providing special education or related services, whether the applicable standards are consistent with the highest requirements in the State for that profession or discipline.

(2) The information required in paragraph (d)(1) of this section must be on file in the State educational agency, and available to the public.

(e) In identifying the "highest requirements in the State" for purposes of this section, the requirements of all State statutes and the rules of all State agencies applicable to serving children and youth with handicaps must be considered.

(Authority: 20 U.S.C. 1413(a)(14))
(Approved by the Office of Management and Budget under control number 1820-0030)

Comment. The regulations require that the State use its own existing highest requirements to determine the standards appropriate to personnel who provide special education and related services under this part. The regulations do not require States to set any specified training standard, such as a master's degree, for employment of personnel who provide services under this part. In some instances, States will be required to show that they are taking steps to retrain or to hire personnel to meet the standards adopted by the State educational agency that are based on requirements for practice in a specific profession or discipline that were established by other State agencies. States in this position need not, however, require personnel providing services under this part to apply for and obtain the license, registration, or other comparable credential required by other agencies of individuals in that profession or discipline. The regulations permit each State to determine the specific occupational categories required to provide special education and related services and to revise or expand these categories as needed. The professions or disciplines defined by the State need not be limited to traditional occupational categories.

5. Section 300.260 is revised to read as follows:

§ 300.260 Submission of application; approval.

(a) In order to receive a grant under this part, the Secretary of the Interior shall submit an application that—

(1) Meets the requirements in section 612(1), 612(2)(A), 612(2)(C)-(E), 612(4), 612(5), 612(6), and 612(7) of the Act;

(2) Meets the requirements in section 613(a), 613(b), 613(c), and 613(e) of the Act;

(3) Meets the requirements of section 614(a) of the Act;

(4) Meets the requirements of this part that implement the sections of the Act listed in paragraphs (a)(1)-(a)(3) of this section; and

(5) Includes an assurance that there have been public hearings on the application, adequate notice of the public hearings, and an opportunity for members of tribes, tribal governing bodies, and designated local school boards to comment on the application before the adoption of the policies, programs, and procedures required under sections 612, 613, and 614(a) of the Act.

(b) Sections 300.580-300.586 apply to grants available to the Secretary of the Interior under this part.

(Authority: 20 U.S.C. 1411(f))
(Approved by the Office of Management and Budget under control number 1820-0030)

6. In § 300.300 paragraph (b)(3) is revised to read as follows:

§ 300.300 Timelines for free appropriate public education.

*   *   *   *   *

(b) * * *

(3) If a public agency provides education to 50 percent or more of its handicapped children in any disability category in any of these age groups, it must make a free appropriate public education available to all its handicapped children of the same age who have that disability. This provision does not apply to children aged three through five for any fiscal year for which the State receives a grant under section 619(a)(1) of the Act.

*   *   *   *   *

7. Section 300.370 is amended by revising the section title and paragraph (a) to read as follows:

§ 300.370 Use of State agency allocations.

(a) The State may use the portion of its allocation that it does not use for administration under § § 300.620-300.621—

(1) For support services and direct services in accordance with the priority requirements under § § 300.320-300.324; and

(2) For the administrative costs of the State's monitoring activities and complaint investigations, to the extent that these costs exceed the administrative costs for monitoring and complaint investigations incurred during fiscal year 1985.

*   *   *   *   *

8. Section 300.552 is amended by adding a new second and third paragraphs in the comment to read as follows:

§ 300.552 Placements.

*   *   *   *   *

The requirements of § 300.552, as well as the other requirements of § § 300.550-300.556, apply to all preschool handicapped children who are entitled to receive a free appropriate public education. Public agencies that provide preschool programs for non-handicapped children must ensure that the requirements of § 300.552(c) are met. Public agencies that do not operate programs for non-handicapped preschool children are not required to initiate such programs solely to satisfy the requirements regarding placement in the least restrictive environment embodied in § § 300.550-300.556. For these public agencies, some alternative methods for meeting the requirements of § § 300.550-300.556 include:

(1) Providing opportunities for the participation (even part-time) of preschool handicapped children in other preschool programs operated by public agencies (such as Head Start);

(2) Placing handicapped children in private school programs for non-handicapped preschool children or private school preschool programs that integrate handicapped and non-handicapped children; and

(3) Locating classes for handicapped preschool children in regular elementary schools.

In each case the public agency must ensure that each child's placement is in the least restrictive environment in which the unique needs of that child can be met, based upon the child's individualized education program, and meets all of the other requirements of § § 300.340-300.349 and § § 300.550-300.556.

10. Section 300.589 is amended by revising paragraph (a) to read as follows:

§ 300.589   Waiver of requirement regarding supplement and supplanting with Part B funds.

(a) Under sections 613(a)(9)(B) and 614(a)(2)(B)(ii) of the Act, State and local educational agencies must insure that Federal funds provided under this part are used to supplement and increase the level of Federal, State, and local funds (including funds that are not under the direct control of State or local educational agencies) expended for special education and related services provided to handicapped children under this part and in no case to supplant those Federal, State, and local funds. The nonsupplanting requirement applies only to funds allocated to local educational agencies (*See* § 300.372).

*   *   *   *   *

11. The center heading preceding § 300.600 is revised to read as follows:

General

12. Section 300.600 is amended by adding a new paragraph (c) to read as follows:

§ 300.600   Responsibility for all educational programs.

*   *   *   *   *

(c) This part may not be construed to limit the responsibility of agencies other than educational agencies for providing or paying some or all of the costs of a free appropriate public education to handicapped children in the State.

*   *   *   *   *

13. Subpart F is amended by adding a new § 300.601 to read as follows:

§ 300.601   Relation of Part B to other Federal programs.

This part may not be construed to permit a State to reduce medical and other assistance available to handicapped children, or to alter a handicapped child's eligibility, under Title V (Maternal and Child Health) or Title XIX (Medicaid) of the Social Security Act, to receive services that are also part of a free appropriate public education.

(Authority: 20 U.S.C. 1413(e))

14. Section 300.701 is amended by revising paragraph (a) to read as follows and removing and reserving paragraph (b).

§ 300.701   State entitlement, formula.

(a) The Secretary calculates the maximum amount of the grant to which a State is entitled under section 611 of the Act in any fiscal year as follows:

(1) If the State is eligible for a grant under section 619 of the Act, the maximum entitlement is equal to the number of handicapped children aged three through 21 in the State who are receiving special education and related services, multiplied by 40 percent of the average per pupil expenditure in public elementary and secondary schools in the United States.

(2) If the State is not eligible for a grant under section 619 of the Act, the maximum entitlement is equal to the number of handicapped children aged six through 21 in the State who are receiving special education and related services, multiplied by 40 percent of the average per pupil expenditure in public elementary and secondary schools in the United States.

(Authority: 20 U.S.C. 1411(a)(1))

(b) [Reserved]

*   *   *   *   *

15. Section 300.702 is amended by revising paragraphs (a)(1), (a)(3), and (b) and adding a new paragraph (a)(2). As revised, § 300.702 reads as follows:

§ 300.702   Limitation and exclusions.

(a) In determining the amount of a grant under § 300.701—

(1) If a State serves all handicapped children aged three through five in the State, the Secretary does not count handicapped children aged three through 17 in the State to the extent that the number of those children is greater than 12 percent of the number of all children aged three through 17 in the State;

(2) If a State does not serve all handicapped children aged three through five in the State, the Secretary does not count handicapped children aged five through 17 to the extent that the number of those children is greater than 12 percent of the number of all children aged five through 17 in the State; and

(3) The Secretary does not count handicapped children who are counted under

subpart 2 of Part D of Chapter 1 of title I of the Augustus F. Hawkins – Robert J. Stafford Elementary and Secondary School Improvement Amendments of 1988.

(b) For the purposes of paragraph (a) of this section, the number of children aged three through 17 and five through 17 in any State is determined by the Secretary on the basis of the most recent satisfactory data available.

(Authority: 20 U.S.C. 1411(a)(5))

16. Section 300.709 is amended by revising paragraph (b) to read as follows:

§ 300.709 Payments to the Secretary of Interior.

*   *   *   *   *

(b) The amount of those payments for any fiscal year is 1.25 percent of the aggregate amounts available to all States for that fiscal year under this part.

(Authority: 20 U.S.C. 1411(f)(1))

17. Section 300.750 is amended by revising the comment to read as follows:

§ 300.750 Annual report of children served—report requirement.

*   *   *   *   *

Comment. It is very important to understand that this report and the requirements that relate to it are solely for allocation purposes. The population of children the State may count for allocation purposes may differ from the population of children to whom the State must make available a free appropriate public education. For example, while section 611(a)(5) of the Act limits the number of children who may be counted for allocation purposes to 12 percent of the general school population aged three through 17 (in States that serve all handicapped children aged three through five) or five through 17 (in States that do not serve all handicapped children aged three through five), a State might find that 14 percent (or some other percentage) of its children are handicapped. In that case, the State must make a free appropriate public education available to all of those handicapped children.

18. Section 300.751 is amended by adding a new paragraph (a)(2), and revising paragraphs (a)(3), (a)(4), (c), and (d) to read as follows:

§ 300.751 Annual report of children served—information required in the report.

(a) In its report, the State educational agency shall include a table which shows:

*   *   *   *   *

(2) The number of handicapped children aged three through five who are receiving a free appropriate public education;

(3) The number of those handicapped children aged six through 21 within each disability category, as defined in the definition of "handicapped children" in § 300.5 of Subpart A; and

(4) The number of those handicapped children aged three through 21 for each year of age (three, four, five, etc.).

*   *   *   *   *

(c) The State educational agency may not report a child aged six through 21 under more than one disability category.

(d) If a handicapped child aged six through 21 has more than one disability, the State educational agency shall report that child in accordance with the following procedure:

(1) A child who is both deaf and blind must be reported as "deaf-blind."

(2) A child who has more than one disability (other than a deaf-blind) must be reported as "multihandicapped."

*   *   *   *   *

(Authority: 20 U.S.C. 1411(a)(3); 1411(a)(5)(A)(ii); 1418(b))

(Approved by the Office of Management and Budget under control number 1820-0043)

§ 300.753 [Amended]

19. In § 300.753, paragraph (b)(4) is amended by removing "section 121" and adding, in its place, "subpart 2 of part D of Chapter 1 of title 1".

PART 104—NONDISCRIMINATION ON THE BASIS OF HANDICAP IN PROGRAMS AND ACTIVITIES RECEIVING OR BENEFITING FROM FEDERAL FINANCIAL ASSISTANCE

AUTHORITY: Sec. 504, Rehabilitation Act of 1973, Pub. L. 93–112, 87 Stat. 394 (29 U.S.C. 794); sec. 111(a), Rehabilitation Act Amendments of 1974, Pub. L. 93–516, 88 Stat. 1619 (29 U.S.C. 706); sec. 606, Education of the Handicapped Act (20 U.S.C. 1405), as amended by Pub. L. 94–142, 89 Stat. 795.

Subpart A—General Provisions

§ 104.1 Purpose.

The purpose of this part is to effectuate section 504 of the Rehabilitation Act of 1973, which is designed to eliminate discrimination on the basis of handicap in any program or activity receiving Federal financial assistance.

§ 104.2 Application.

This part applies to each recipient of Federal financial assistance from the Department of Education and to each program or activity that receives or benefits from such assistance.

§ 104.3 Definitions.

As used in this part, the term:

(a) "The Act" means the Rehabilitation Act of 1973, Pub. L. 93–112, as amended by the Rehabilitation Act Amendments of 1974, Pub. L. 93–516, 29 U.S.C. 794.

(b) "Section 504" means section 504 of the Act.

(c) "Education of the Handicapped Act" means that statute as amended by the Education for all Handicapped Children Act of 1975, Pub. L. 94–142, 20 U.S.C. 1401 et seq.

(d) "Department" means the Department of Education.

(e) "Assistant Secretary" means the Assistant Secretary for Civil Rights of the Department of Education.

(f) "Recipient" means any state or its political subdivision, any instrumentality of a state or its political subdivision, any public or private agency, institution, organization, or other entity, or any person to which Federal financial assistance is extended directly or through another recipient, including any successor, assignee, or transferee of a recipient, but excluding the ultimate beneficiary of the assistance.

(g) "Applicant for assistance" means one who submits an application, request, or plan required to be approved by a Department official or by a recipient as a condition to becoming a recipient.

(h) "Federal financial assistance" means any grant, loan, contract (other than a procurement contract or a contract of insurance or guaranty), or any other arrangement by which the Department provides or otherwise makes available assistance in the form of:

(1) Funds;

(2) Services of Federal personnel; or

(3) Real and personal property or any interest in or use of such property, including:

(i) Transfers or leases of such property for less than fair market value or for reduced consideration; and

(ii) Proceeds from a subsequent transfer or lease of such property if the Federal share of its fair market value is not returned to the Federal Government.

(i) "Facility" means all or any portion of buildings, structures, equipment, roads, walks, parking lots, or other real or personal property or interest in such property.

(j) "Handicapped person." (1) "Handicapped persons" means any person who (i) has a physical or mental impairment which substantially limits one or more major life activities, (ii) has a record of such an impairment, or (iii) is regarded as having such an impairment.

(2) As used in paragraph (j)(1) of this section, the phrase:

(i) "Physical or mental impairment" means (A) any physiological disorder or condition, cosmetic disfigurement, or anatomical loss affecting one or more of the following body systems: neurological; musculoskeletal; special sense organs; respiratory, including speech organs; cardiovascular; reproductive, digestive, genito-urinary;

hemic and lymphatic; skin; and endocrine; or (B) any mental or psychological disorder, such as mental retardation, organic brain syndrome, emotional or mental illness, and specific learning disabilities.

(ii) "Major life activities" means functions such as caring for one's self, performing manual tasks, walking, seeing, hearing, speaking, breathing, learning, and working.

(iii) "Has a record of such an impairment" means has a history of, or has been misclassified as having, a mental or physical impairment that substantially limits one or more major life activities.

(iv) "Is regarded as having an impairment" means (A) has a physical or mental impairment that does not substantially limit major life activities but that is treated by a recipient as constituting such a limitation; (B) has a physical or mental impairment that substantially limits major life activities only as a result of the attitudes of others toward such impairment; or (C) has none of the impairments defined in paragraph (j)(2)(i) of this section but is treated by a recipient as having such an impairment.

(k) "Qualified handicapped person" means:

(1) With respect to employment, a handicapped person who, with reasonable accommodation, can perform the essential functions of the job in question;

(2) With respect to public preschool elementary, secondary, or adult educational services, a handicappped person (i) of an age during which nonhandicapped persons are provided such services, (ii) of any age during which it is mandatory under state law to provide such services to handicapped persons, or (iii) to whom a state is required to provide a free appropriate public education under section 612 of the Education of the Handicapped Act; and

(3) With respect to postsecondary and vocational education services, a handicapped person who meets the academic and technical standards requisite to admission or participation in the recipient's education program or activity;

(4) With respect to other services, a handicapped person who meets the es-

sential eligibility requirements for the receipt of such services.

(l) "Handicap" means any condition or characteristic that renders a person a handicapped person as defined in paragraph (j) of this section.

§ 104.4 Discrimination prohibited.

(a) *General.* No qualified handicapped person shall, on the basis of handicap, be excluded from participation in, be denied the benefits of, or otherwise be subjected to discrimination under any program or activitiy which receives or benefits from Federal financial assistance.

(b) *Discriminatory actions prohibited.* (1) A recipient, in providing any aid, benefit, or service, may not, directly or through contractual, licensing, or other arrangements, on the basis of handicap:

(i) Deny a qualified handicapped person the opportunity to participate in or benefit from the aid, benefit, or service;

(ii) Afford a qualified handicapped person an opportunity to participate in or benefit from the aid, benefit, or service that is not equal to that afforded others;

(iii) Provide a qualified handicapped person with an aid, benefit, or service that is not as effective as that provided to others;

(iv) Provide different or separate aid, benefits, or services to handicapped persons or to any class of handicapped persons unless such action is necessary to provide qualified handicapped persons with aid, benefits, or services that are as effective as those provided to others;

(v) Aid or perpetuate discrimination against a qualified handicapped person by providing significant assistance to an agency, organization, or person that discriminates on the basis of handicap in providing any aid, benefit, or service to beneficiaries of the recipients program;

(vi) Deny a qualified handicapped person the opportunity to participate as a member of planning or advisory boards; or

(vii) Otherwise limit a qualified handicapped person in the enjoyment of any right, privilege, advantage, or opportunity enjoyed by others receiving an aid, benefit, or service.

(2) For purposes of this part, aids, benefits, and services, to be equally effective, are not required to produce the identical result or level of achievement for handicapped and nonhandicapped persons, but must afford handicapped persons equal opportunity to obtain the same result, to gain the same benefit, or to reach the same level of achievement, in the most integrated setting appropriate to the person's needs.

(3) Despite the existence of separate or different programs or activities provided in accordance with this part, a recipient may not deny a qualified handicapped person the opportunity to participate in such programs or activities that are not separate or different.

(4) A recipient may not, directly or through contractual or other arrangements, utilize criteria or methods of administration (i) that have the effect of subjecting qualified handicapped persons to discrimination on the basis of handicap, (ii) that have the purpose or effect of defeating or substantially impairing accomplishment of the objectives of the recipient's program with respect to handicapped persons, or (iii) that perpetuate the discrimination of another recipient if both recipients are subject to common administrative control or are agencies of the same State.

(5) In determining the site or location of a facility, an applicant for assistance or a recipient may not make selections (i) that have the effect of excluding handicapped persons from, denying them the benefits of, or otherwise subjecting them to discrimination under any program or activity that receives or benefits from Federal financial assistance or (ii) that have the purpose or effect of defeating or substantially impairing the accomplishment of the objectives of the program or activity with respect to handicapped persons.

(6) As used in this section, the aid, benefit, or service provided under a program or activity receiving or benefiting from Federal financial assistance includes any aid, benefit, or service provided in or through a facility

that has been constructed, expanded, altered, leased or rented, or otherwise acquired, in whole or in part, with Federal financial assistance.

(c) *Programs limited by Federal law.* The exclusion of nonhandicapped persons from the benefits of a program limited by Federal statute or executive order to handicapped persons or the exclusion of a specific class of handicapped persons from a program limited by Federal statute or executive order to a different class of handicapped persons is not prohibited by this part.

§ 104.5 Assurances required.

(a) *Assurances.* An applicant for Federal financial assistance for a program or activity to which this part applies shall submit an assurance, on a form specified by the Assistant Secretary, that the program will be operated in compliance with this part. An applicant may incorporate these assurances by reference in subsequent applications to the Department.

(b) *Duration of obligation.* (1) In the case of Federal financial assistance extended in the form of real property or to provide real property or structures on the property, the assurance will obligate the recipient or, in the case of a subsequent transfer, the transferee, for the period during which the real property or structures are used for the purpose for which Federal financial assistance is extended or for another purpose involving the provision of similar services or benefits.

(2) In the case of Federal financial assistance extended to provide personal property, the assurance will obligate the recipient for the period during which it retains ownership or possession of the property.

(3) In all other cases the assurance will obligate the recipient for the period during which Federal financial assistance is extended.

(c) *Covenants.* (1) Where Federal financial assistance is provided in the form of real property or interest in the property from the Department, the instrument effecting or recording this transfer shall contain a covenant running with the land to assure nondiscrimination for the period during which the real property is used for a

purpose for which the Federal financial assistance is extended or for another purpose involving the provision of similar services or benefits.

(2) Where no transfer of property is involved but property is purchased or improved with Federal financial assistance, the recipient shall agree to include the covenant described in paragraph (b)(2) of this section in the instrument effecting or recording any subsequent transfer of the property.

(3) Where Federal financial assistance is provided in the form of real property or interest in the property from the Department, the covenant shall also include a condition coupled with a right to be reserved by the Department to revert title to the property in the event of a breach of the covenant. If a transferee of real property proposes to mortgage or otherwise encumber the real property as security for financing construction of new, or improvement of existing, facilities on the property for the purposes for which the property was transferred, the Assistant Secretary may, upon request of the transferee and if necessary to accomplish such financing and upon such conditions as he or she deems appropriate, agree to forbear the exercise of such right to revert title for so long as the lien of such mortgage or other encumbrance remains effective.

§ 104.6 Remedial action, voluntary action, and self-evaluation.

(a) *Remedial action.* (1) If the Assistant Secretary finds that a recipient has discriminated against persons on the basis of handicap in violation of section 504 or this part, the recipient shall take such remedial action as the Assistant Secretary deems necessary to overcome the effects of the discrimination.

(2) Where a recipient is found to have discriminated against persons on the basis of handicap in violation of section 504 or this part and where another recipient exercises control over the recipient that has discriminated, the Assistant Secretary, where appropriate, may require either or both recipients to take remedial action.

(3) The Assistant Secretary may, where necessary to overcome the effects of discrimination in violation of section 504 or this part, require a recipient to take remedial action (i) with respect to handicapped persons who are no longer participants in the recipient's program but who were participants in the program when such discrimination occurred or (ii) with respect to handicapped persons who would have been participants in the program had the discrimination not occurred.

(b) *Voluntary action.* A recipient may take steps, in addition to any action that is required by this part, to overcome the effects of conditions that resulted in limited participation in the recipient's program or activity by qualified handicapped persons.

(c) *Self-evaluation.* (1) A recipient shall, within one year of the effective date of this part:

(i) Evaluate, with the assistance of interested persons, including handicapped persons or organizations representing handicapped persons, its current policies and practices and the effects thereof that do not or may not meet the requirements of this part;

(ii) Modify, after consultation with interested persons, including handicapped persons or organizations representing handicapped persons, any policies and practices that do not meet the requirements of this part; and

(iii) Take, after consultation with interested persons, including handicapped persons or organizations representing handicapped persons, appropriate remedial steps to eliminate the effects of any discrimination that resulted from adherence to these policies and practices.

(2) A recipient that employs fifteen or more persons shall, for at least three years following completion of the evaluation required under paragraph (c)(1) of this section, maintain on file, make available for public inspection, and provide to the Assistant Secretary upon request: (i) A list of the interested persons consulted (ii) a description of areas examined and any problems identified, and (iii) a description of any modifications made and of any remedial steps taken.

§ 104.7   Designation of responsible employee and adoption of grievance procedures.

(a) *Designation of responsible employee.* A recipient that employs fifteen or more persons shall designate at least one person to coordinate its efforts to comply with this part.

(b) *Adoption of grievance procedures.* A recipient that employs fifteen or more persons shall adopt grievance procedures that incorporate appropriate due process standards and that provide for the prompt and equitable resolution of complaints alleging any action prohibited by this part. Such procedures need not be established with respect to complaints from applicants for employment or from applicants for admission to postsecondary educational institutions.

§ 104.8   Notice.

(a) A recipient that employs fifteen or more persons shall take appropriate initial and continuing steps to notify participants, beneficiaries, applicants, and employees, including those with impaired vision or hearing, and unions or professional organizations holding collective bargaining or professional agreements with the recipient that it does not discriminate on the basis of handicap in violation of section 504 and this part. The notification shall state, where appropriate, that the recipient does not discriminate in admission or access to, or treatment or employment in, its programs and activities. The notification shall also include an identification of the responsible employee designated pursuant to § 104.7(a). A recipient shall make the initial notification required by this paragraph within 90 days of the effective date of this part. Methods of initial and continuing notification may include the posting of notices, publication in newspapers and magazines, placement of notices in recipients' publication, and distribution of memoranda or other written communications.

(b) If a recipient publishes or uses recruitment materials or publications containing general information that it makes available to participants, beneficiaries, applicants, or employees, it shall include in those materials or publications a statement of the policy described in paragraph (a) of this section. A recipient may meet the requirement of this paragraph either by including appropriate inserts in existing materials and publications or by revising and reprinting the materials and publications.

§ 104.9   Administrative requirements for small recipients.

The Assistant Secretary may require any recipient with fewer than fifteen employees, or any class of such recipients, to comply with §§ 104.7 and 104.8, in whole or in part, when the Assistant Secretary finds a violation of this part or finds that such compliance will not significantly impair the ability of the recipient or class of recipients to provide benefits or services.

§ 104.10   Effect of state or local law or other requirements and effect of employment opportunities.

(a) The obligation to comply with this part is not obviated or alleviated by the existence of any state or local law or other requirement that, on the basis of handicap, imposes prohibitions or limits upon the eligibility of qualified handicapped persons to receive services or to practice any occupation or profession.

(b) The obligation to comply with this part is not obviated or alleviated because employment opportunities in any occupation or profession are or may be more limited for handicapped persons than for nonhandicapped persons.

Subpart B—Employment Practices

§ 104.11   Discrimination prohibited.

(a) *General.* (1) No qualified handicapped person shall, on the basis of handicap, be subjected to discrimination in employment under any program or activity to which this part applies.

(2) A recipient that receives assistance under the Education of the Handicapped Act shall take positive steps to employ and advance in employment qualified handicapped per-

sons in programs assisted under that Act.

(3) A recipient shall make all decisions concerning employment under any program or activity to which this part applies in a manner which ensures that discrimination on the basis of handicap does not occur and may not limit, segregate, or classify applicants or employees in any way that adversely affects their opportunities or status because of handicap.

(4) A recipient may not participate in a contractual or other relationship that has the effect of subjecting qualified handicapped applicants or employees to discrimination prohibited by this subpart. The relationships referred to in this paragraph include relationships with employment and referral agencies, with labor unions, with organizations providing or administering fringe benefits to employees of the recipient, and with organizations providing training and apprenticeship programs.

(b) *Specific activities.* The provisions of this subpart apply to:

(1) Recruitment, advertising, and the processing of applications for employment;

(2) Hiring, upgrading, promotion, award of tenure, demotion, transfer, layoff, termination, right of return from layoff and rehiring;

(3) Rates of pay or any other form of compensation and changes in compensation;

(4) Job assignments, job classifications, organizational structures, position descriptions, lines of progression, and seniority lists;

(5) Leaves of absense, sick leave, or any other leave;

(6) Fringe benefits available by virtue of employment, whether or not administered by the recipient;

(7) Selection and financial support for training, including apprenticeship, professional meetings, conferences, and other related activities, and selection for leaves of absence to pursue training;

(8) Employer sponsored activities, including social or recreational programs; and

(9) Any other term, condition, or privilege of employment.

(c) A recipient's obligation to comply with this subpart is not affected by any inconsistent term of any collective bargaining agreement to which it is a party.

§ 104.12   Reasonable accommodation.

(a) A recipient shall make reasonable accommodation to the known physical or mental limitations of an otherwise qualified handicapped applicant or employee unless the recipient can demonstrate that the accommodation would impose an undue hardship on the operation of its program.

(b) Reasonable accommodation may include: (1) Making facilities used by employees readily accessible to and usable by handicapped persons, and (2) job restructuring, part-time or modified work schedules, acquisition or modification of equipment or devices, the provision of readers or interpreters, and other similar actions.

(c) In determining pursuant to paragraph (a) of this section whether an accommodation would impose an undue hardship on the operation of a recipient's program, factors to be considered include:

(1) The overall size of the recipient's program with respect to number of employees, number and type of facilities, and size of budget;

(2) The type of the recipient's operation, including the composition and structure of the recipient's workforce; and

(3) The nature and cost of the accommodation needed.

(d) A recipient may not deny any employment opportunity to a qualified handicapped employee or applicant if the basis for the denial is the need to make reasonable accommodation to the physical or mental limitations of the employee or applicant.

§ 104.13   Employment criteria.

(a) A recipient may not make use of any employment test or other selection criterion that screens out or tends to screen out handicapped persons or any class of handicapped persons unless: (1) The test score or other selection criterion, as used by the recipient, is shown to be job-related for the position in question, and (2) alternative job-related tests or criteria that do not screen out or tend to screen out as many handicapped persons are not shown by the Director to be available.

(b) A recipient shall select and administer tests concerning employment so as best to ensure that, when administered to an applicant or employee who has a handicap that impairs sensory, manual, or speaking skills, the test results accurately reflect the applicant's or employee's job skills, aptitude, or whatever other factor the test purports to measure, rather than reflecting the applicant's or employee's impaired sensory, manual, or speaking skills (except where those skills are the factors that the test purports to measure).

§ 104.14   Preemployment inquiries.

(a) Except as provided in paragraphs (b) and (c) of this section, a recipient may not conduct a preemployment medical examination or may not make preemployment inquiry of an applicant as to whether the applicant is a handicapped person or as to the nature or severity of a handicap. A recipient may, however, make preemployment inquiry into an applicant's ability to perform job-related functions.

(b) When a recipient is taking remedial action to correct the effects of past discrimination pursuant to § 104.6 (a), when a recipient is taking voluntary action to overcome the effects of conditions that resulted in limited participation in its federally assisted program or activity pursuant to § 104.6(b), or when a recipient is taking affirmative action pursuant to section 503 of the Act, the recipient may invite applicants for employment to indicate whether and to what extent they are handicapped, *Provided,* That:

(1) The recipient states clearly on any written questionnaire used for this purpose or makes clear orally if no written questionnaire is used that the information requested is intended for use solely in connection with its remedial action obligations or its voluntary or affirmative action efforts; and

(2) The recipient states clearly that the information is being requested on a voluntary basis, that it will be kept confidential as provided in paragraph

(d) of this section, that refusal to provide it will not subject the applicant or employee to any adverse treatment, and that it will be used only in accordance with this part.

(c) Nothing in this section shall prohibit a recipient from conditioning an offer of employment on the results of a medical examination conducted prior to the employee's entrance on duty, *Provided,* That: (1) All entering employees are subjected to such an examination regardless of handicap, and (2) the results of such an examination are used only in accordance with the requirements of this part.

(d) Information obtained in accordance with this section as to the medical condition or history of the applicant shall be collected and maintained on separate forms that shall be accorded confidentiality as medical records, except that:

(1) Supervisors and managers may be informed regarding restrictions on the work or duties of handicapped persons and regarding necessary accommodations;

(2) First aid and safety personnel may be informed, where appropriate, if the condition might require emergency treatment; and

(3) Government officials investigating compliance with the Act shall be provided relevant information upon request.

Subpart C—Program Accessibility

§ 104.21 Discrimination prohibited.

No qualified handicapped person shall, because a recipient's facilities are inaccessible to or unusable by handicapped persons, be denied the benefits of, be excluded from participation in, or otherwise be subjected to discrimination under any program or activity to which this part applies.

§ 104.22 Existing facilities.

(a) *Program accessibility.* A recipient shall operate each program or activity to which this part applies so that the program or activity, when viewed in its entirety, is readily accessible to handicapped persons. This paragraph does not require a recipient to make each of its existing facilities or every part of a facility accessible to and usable by handicapped persons.

(b) *Methods.* A recipient may comply with the requirements of paragraph (a) of this section through such means as redesign of equipment, reassignment of classes or other services to accessible buildings, assignment of aides to beneficiaries, home visits, delivery of health, welfare, or other social services at alternate accessible sites, alteration of existing facilities and construction of new facilities in conformance with the requirements of § 104.23, or any other methods that result in making its program or activity accessible to handicapped persons. A recipient is not required to make structural changes in existing facilities where other methods are effective in achieving compliance with paragraph (a) of this section. In choosing among available methods for meeting the requirement of paragraph (a) of this section, a recipient shall give priority to those methods that offer programs and activities to handicapped persons in the most integrated setting appropriate.

(c) *Small health, welfare, or other social service providers.* If a recipient with fewer than fifteen employees that provides health, welfare, or other social services finds, after consultation with a handicapped person seeking its services, that there is no method of complying with paragraph (a) of this section other than making a significant alteration in its existing facilities, the recipient may, as an alternative, refer the handicapped person to other providers of those services that are accessible.

(d) *Time period.* A recipient shall comply with the requirement of paragraph (a) of this section within sixty days of the effective date of this part except that where structural changes in facilities are necessary, such changes shall be made within three years of the effective date of this part, but in any event as expeditiously as possible.

(e) *Transition plan.* In the event that structural changes to facilities are necessary to meet the requirement of paragraph (a) of this section, a recipient shall develop, within six months of the effective date of this part, a transition plan setting forth the steps necessary to complete such changes. The plan shall be developed with the assistance of interested persons, including handicapped persons or organizations representing handicapped persons. A copy of the transition plan shall be made available for public inspection. The plan shall, at a minimum:

(1) Identify physical obstacles in the recipient's facilities that limit the accessibility of its program or activity to handicappped persons;

(2) Describe in detail the methods that will be used to make the facilities accessible;

(3) Specify the schedule for taking the steps necessary to achieve full program accessibility and, if the time period of the transition plan is longer than one year, identify the steps of that will be taken during each year of the transition period; and

(4) Indicate the person responsible for implementation of the plan.

(f) *Notice.* The recipient shall adopt and implement procedures to ensure that interested persons, including persons with impaired vision or hearing, can obtain information as to the existence and location of services, activities, and facilities that are accessible to and usuable by handicapped persons.

§ 104.23 New construction.

(a) *Design and construction.* Each facility or part of a facility constructed by, on behalf of, or for the use of a recipient shall be designed and constructed in such manner that the facility or part of the facility is readily accessible to and usable by handicapped persons, if the construction was commenced after the effective date of this part.

(b) *Alteration.* Each facility or part of a facility which is altered by, on behalf of, or for the use of a recipient after the effective date of this part in a manner that affects or could affect the usability of the facility or part of the facility shall, to the maximum extent feasible, be altered in such manner that the altered portion of the facility is readily accessible to and usable by handicapped persons.

(c) *American National Standards Institute accessibility standards.* Design, construction, or alteration of facilities in conformance with the "American National Standard Specifications for Making Buildings and Facilities Accessible to, and Usable by, the Physically Handicapped," published by the American National Standards Institute, Inc. (ANSI A117.1-1961 (R1971)), which is incorporated by reference in this part, shall constitute compliance with paragraphs (a) and (b) of this section. Departures from particular requirements of those standards by the use of other methods shall be permitted when it is clearly evident that equivalent access to the facility or part of the facility is thereby provided. Incorporation by reference provisions approved by the Director of the Federal Register, May 27, 1975. Incorporated documents are on file at the Office of the Federal Register. Copies of the standards are obtainable from American National Standards Institute, Inc., 1430 Broadway, New York, N.Y. 10018.

[45 FR 30936, May 9, 1980; 45 FR 37426, June 3, 1980]

Subpart D—Preschool, Elementary, and Secondary Education

§ 104.31 Application of this subpart.

Subpart D applies to preschool, elementary, secondary, and adult education programs and activities that receive or benefit from Federal financial assistance and to recipients that operate, or that receive or benefit from Federal financial assistance for the operation of, such programs or activities.

§ 104.32 Location and notification.

A recipient that operates a public elementary or secondary education program shall annually:

(a) Undertake to identify and locate every qualified handicapped person residing in the recipient's jurisdiction who is not receiving a public education; and

(b) Take appropriate steps to notify handicapped persons and their parents or guardians of the recipient's duty under this subpart.

§ 104.33   Free appropriate public education.

(a) *General.* A recipient that operates a public elementary or secondary education program shall provide a free appropriate public education to each qualified handicapped person who is in the recipient's jurisdiction, regardless of the nature or severity of the person's handicap.

(b) *Appropriate education.* (1) For the purpose of this subpart, the provision of an appropriate education is the provision of regular or special education and related aids and services that (i) are designed to meet individual educational needs of handicapped persons as adequately as the needs of nonhandicapped persons are met and (ii) are based upon adherence to procedures that satisfy the requirements of §§ 104.34, 104.35, and 104.36.

(2) Implementation of an individualized education program developed in accordance with the Education of the Handicapped Act is one means of meeting the standard established in paragraph (b)(1)(i) of this section.

(3) A recipient may place a handicapped person in or refer such person to a program other than the one that it operates as its means of carrying out the requirements of this subpart. If so, the recipient remains responsible for ensuring that the requirements of this subpart are met with respect to any handicapped person so placed or referred.

(c) *Free education—*(1) *General.* For the purpose of this section, the provision of a free education is the provision of educational and related services without cost to the handicapped person or to his or her parents or guardian, except for those fees that are imposed on non-handicapped persons or their parents or guardian. It may consist either of the provision of free services or, if a recipient places a handicapped person in or refers such person to a program not operated by the recipient as its means of carrying out the requirements of this subpart, of payment for the costs of the program. Funds available from any public or private agency may be used to meet the requirements of this subpart. Nothing in this section shall be construed to relieve an insurer or similar third party from an otherwise valid obligation to provide or pay for services provided to a handicapped person.

(2) *Transportation.* If a recipient places a handicapped person in or refers such person to a program not operated by the recipient as its means of carrying out the requirements of this subpart, the recipient shall ensure that adequate transportation to and from the program is provided at no greater cost than would be incurred by the person or his or her parents or guardian if the person were placed in the program operated by the recipient.

(3) *Residential placement.* If placement in a public or private residential program is necessary to provide a free appropriate public education to a handicapped person because of his or her handicap, the program, including non-medical care and room and board, shall be provided at no cost to the person or his or her parents or guardian.

(4) *Placement of handicapped persons by parents.* If a recipient has made available, in conformance with the requirements of this section and § 104.34, a free appropriate public education to a handicapped person and the person's parents or guardian choose to place the person in a private school, the recipient is not required to pay for the person's education in the private school. Disagreements between a parent or guardian and a recipient regarding whether the recipient has made such a program available or otherwise regarding the question of financial responsibility are subject to the due process procedures of § 104.36.

(d) *Compliance.* A recipient may not exclude any qualified handicapped person from a public elementary or secondary education after the effective date of this part. A recipient that is not, on the effective date of this regulation, in full compliance with the other requirements of the preceding paragraphs of this section shall meet such requirements at the earliest practicable time and in no event later than September 1, 1978.

§ 104.34   Educational setting.

(a) *Academic setting.* A recipient to which this subpart applies shall educate, or shall provide for the education of, each qualified handicapped person in its jurisdiction with persons who are not handicapped to the maximum extent appropriate to the needs of the handicapped person. A recipient shall place a handicapped person in the regular educational environment operated by the recipient unless it is demonstrated by the recipient that the education of the person in the regular environment with the use of supplementary aids and services cannot be achieved satisfactorily. Whenever a recipient places a person in a setting other than the regular educational environment pursuant to this paragraph, it shall take into account the proximity of the alternate setting to the person's home.

(b) *Nonacademic settings.* In providing or arranging for the provision of nonacademic and extracurricular services and activities, including meals, recess periods, and the services and activities set forth in § 104.37(a)(2), a recipient shall ensure that handicapped persons participate with nonhandicapped persons in such activities and services to the maximum extent appropriate to the needs of the handicapped person in question.

(c) *Comparable facilities.* If a recipient, in compliance with paragraph (a) of this section, operates a facility that is identifiable as being for handicapped persons, the recipient shall ensure that the facility and the services and activities provided therein are comparable to the other facilities, services, and activities of the recipient.

§ 104.35 Evaluation and placement.

(a) *Preplacement evaluation.* A recipient that operates a public elementary or secondary education program shall conduct an evaluation in accordance with the requirements of paragraph (b) of this section of any person who, because of handicap, needs or is belived to need special education or related services before taking any action with respect to the initial placement of the person in a regular or special education program and any subsequent significant change in placement.

(b) *Evaluation procedures.* A recipient to which this subpart applies shall establish standards and procedures for

the evaluation and placement of persons who, because of handicap, need or are believed to need special education or related services which ensure that:

(1) Tests and other evaluation materials have been validated for the specific purpose for which they are used and are administered by trained personnel in conformance with the instructions provided by their producer;

(2) Tests and other evaluation materials include those tailored to assess specific areas of educational need and not merely those which are designed to provide a single general intelligence quotient; and

(3) Tests are selected and administered so as best to ensure that, when a test is administered to a student with impaired sensory, manual, or speaking skills, the test results accurately reflect the student's aptitude or achievement level or whatever other factor the test purports to measure, rather than reflecting the student's impaired sensory, manual, or speaking skills (except where those skills are the factors that the test purports to measure).

(c) *Placement procedures.* In interpreting evaluation data and in making placement decisions, a recipient shall (1) draw upon information from a variety of sources, including aptitude and achievement tests, teacher recommendations, physical condition, social or cultural background, and adaptive behavior, (2) establish procedures to ensure that information obtained from all such sources is documented and carefully considered, (3) ensure that the placement decision is made by a group of persons, including persons knowledgeable about the child, the meaning of the evaluation data, and the placement options, and (4) ensure that the placement decision is made in conformity with § 104.34.

(d) *Reevaluation.* A recipient to which this section applies shall establish procedures, in accordance with paragraph (b) of this section, for periodic reevaluation of students who have been provided special education and related services. A reevaluation procedure consistent with the Education for the Handicapped Act is one means of meeting this requirement.

§ 104.36 Procedural safeguards.

A recipient that operates a public elementary or secondary education program shall establish and implement, with respect to actions regarding the identification, evaluation, or educational placement of persons who, because of handicap, need or are believed to need special instruction or related services, a system of procedural safeguards that includes notice, an opportunity for the parents or guardian of the person to examine relevant records, an impartial hearing with opportunity for participation by the person's parents or guardian and representation by counsel, and a review procedure. Compliance with the procedural safeguards of section 615 of the Education of the Handicapped Act is one means of meeting this requirement.

§ 104.37 Nonacademic services.

(a) *General.* (1) A recipient to which this subpart applies shall provide nonacademic and extracurricular services and activities in such manner as is necessary to afford handicapped students an equal opportunity for participation in such services and activities.

(2) Nonacademic and extracurricular services and activities may include counseling services, physical recreational athletics, transportation, health services, recreational activities, special interest groups or clubs sponsored by the recipients, referrals to agencies which provide assistance to handicapped persons, and employment of students, including both employment by the recipient and assistance in making available outside employment.

(b) *Counseling services.* A recipient to which this subpart applies that provides personal, academic, or vocational counseling, guidance, or placement services to its students shall provide these services without discrimination on the basis of handicap. The recipient shall ensure that qualified handicapped students are not counseled toward more restrictive career objectives than are nonhandicapped students with similar interests and abilities.

(c) *Physical education and athletics.* (1) In providing physical education courses and athletics and similar programs and activities to any of its students, a recipient to which this subpart applies may not discriminate on the basis of handicap. A recipient that offers physical education courses or that operates or sponsors interscholastic, club, or intramural athletics shall provide to qualified handicapped students an equal opportunity for participation in these activities.

(2) A recipient may offer to handicapped students physical education and athletic activities that are separate or different from those offered to nonhandicapped students only if separation or differentiation is consistent with the requirements of § 104.34 and only if no qualified handicapped student is denied the opportunity to compete for teams or to participate in courses that are not separate or different.

§ 104.38 Preschool and adult education programs.

A recipient to which this subpart applies that operates a preschool education or day care program or activity or an adult education program or activity may not, on the basis of handicap, exclude qualified handicapped persons from the program or activity and shall take into account the needs of such persons in determining the aid, benefits, or services to be provided under the program or activity.

§ 104.39 Private education programs.

(a) A recipient that operates a private elementary or secondary education program may not, on the basis of handicap, exclude a qualified handicapped person from such program if the person can, with minor adjustments, be provided an appropriate education, as defined in § 104.33(b)(1), within the recipient's program.

(b) A recipient to which this section applies may not charge more for the provision of an appropriate education to handicapped persons than to nonhandicapped persons except to the extent that any additional charge is justified by a substantial increase in cost to the recipient.

(c) A recipient to which this section applies that operates special education programs shall operate such programs in accordance with the provisions of §§ 104.35 and 104.36. Each recipient to which this section applies is subject to the provisions of §§ 104.34, 104.37, and 104.38.

Subpart E—Postsecondary Education

§ 104.41   Application of this subpart.

Subpart E applies to postsecondary education programs and activities, including postsecondary vocational education programs and activities, that receive or benefit from Federal financial assistance and to recipients that operate, or that receive or benefit from Federal financial assistance for the operation of, such programs or activities.

§ 104.42   Admissions and recruitment.

(a) *General.* Qualified handicapped persons may not, on the basis of handicap, be denied admission or be subjected to discrimination in admission or recruitment by a recipient to which this subpart applies.

(b) *Admissions.* In administering its admission policies, a recipient to which this subpart applies:

(1) May not apply limitations upon the number or proportion of handicapped persons who may be admitted;

(2) May not make use of any test or criterion for admission that has a disproportionate, adverse effect on handicapped persons or any class of handicapped persons unless (i) the test or criterion, as used by the recipient, has been validated as a predictor of success in the education program or activity in question and (ii) alternate tests or criteria that have a less disproportionate, adverse effect are not shown by the Assistant Secretary to be available.

(3) Shall assure itself that (i) admissions tests are selected and administered so as best to ensure that, when a test is administered to an applicant who has a handicap that impairs sensory, manual, or speaking skills, the test results accurately reflect the applicant's aptitude or achievement level or whatever other factor the test purports to measure, rather than reflecting the applicant's impaired sensory, manual, or speaking skills (except where those skills are the factors that the test purports to measure); (ii) admissions tests that are designed for persons with impaired sensory, manual, or speaking skills are offered as often and in as timely a manner as are other admissions tests; and (iii) admissions tests are administered in facilities that, on the whole, are accessible to handicapped persons; and

(4) Except as provided in paragraph (c) of this section, may not make preadmission inquiry as to whether an applicant for admission is a handicapped person but, after admission, may make inquiries on a confidential basis as to handicaps that may require accommodation.

(c) *Preadmission inquiry exception.* When a recipient is taking remedial action to correct the effects of past discrimination pursuant to § 104.6(a) or when a recipient is taking voluntary action to overcome the effects of conditions that resulted in limited participation in its federally assisted program or activity pursuant to § 104.6(b), the recipient may invite applicants for admission to indicate whether and to what extent they are handicapped, *Provided,* That:

(1) The recipient states clearly on any written questionnaire used for this purpose or makes clear orally if no written questionnaire is used that the information requested is intended for use solely in connection with its remedial action obligations or its voluntary action efforts; and

(2) The recipient states clearly that the information is being requested on a voluntary basis, that it will be kept confidential, that refusal to provide it will not subject the applicant to any adverse treatment, and that it will be used only in accordance with this part.

(d) *Validity studies.* For the purpose of paragraph (b)(2) of this section, a recipient may base prediction equations on first year grades, but shall conduct periodic validity studies against the criterion of overall success in the education program or activity in question in order to monitor the general validity of the test scores.

§ 104.43   Treatment of students; general.

(a) No qualified handicapped student shall, on the basis of handicap, be excluded from participation in, be denied the benefits of, or otherwise be subjected to discrimination under any academic, research, occupational training, housing, health insurance, counseling, financial aid, physical education, athletics, recreation, transportation, other extracurricular, or other postsecondary education program or activity to which this subpart applies.

(b) A recipient to which this subpart applies that considers participation by students in education programs or activities not operated wholly by the recipient as part of, or equivalent to, and education program or activity operated by the recipient shall assure itself that the other education program or activity, as a whole, provides an equal opportunity for the participation of qualified handicapped persons.

(c) A recipient to which this subpart applies may not, on the basis of handicap, exclude any qualified handicapped student from any course, course of study, or other part of its education program or activity.

(d) A recipient to which this subpart applies shall operate its programs and activities in the most integrated setting appropriate.

§ 104.44 Academic adjustments.

(a) *Academic requirements.* A recipient to which this subpart applies shall make such modifications to its academic requirements as are necessary to ensure that such requirements do not discriminate or have the effect of discriminating, on the basis of handicap, against a qualified handicapped applicant or student. Academic requirements that the recipient can demonstrate are essential to the program of instruction being pursued by such student or to any directly related licensing requirement will not be regarded as discriminatory within the meaning of this section. Modifications may include changes in the length of time permitted for the completion of degree requirements, substitution of specific courses required for the completion of degree requirements, and adaptation of the manner in which specific courses are conducted.

(b) *Other rules.* A recipient to which this subpart applies may not impose upon handicapped students other rules, such as the prohibition of tape recorders in classrooms or of dog guides in campus buildings, that have the effect of limiting the participation of handicapped students in the recipient's education program or activity.

(c) *Course examinations.* In its course examinations or other procedures for evaluating students' academic achievement in its program, a recipient to which this subpart applies shall provide such methods for evaluating the achievement of students who have a handicap that impairs sensory, manual, or speaking skills as will best ensure that the results of the evaluation represents the student's achievement in the course, rather than reflecting the student's impaired sensory, manual, or speaking skills (except where such skills are the factors that the test purports to measure).

(d) *Auxiliary aids.* (1) A recipient to which this subpart applies shall take such steps as are necessary to ensure that no handicapped student is denied the benefits of, excluded from participation in, or otherwise subjected to discrimination under the education program or activity operated by the recipient because of the absence of educational auxiliary aids for students with impaired sensory, manual, or speaking skills.

(2) Auxiliary aids may include taped texts, interpreters or other effective methods of making orally delivered materials available to students with hearing impairments, readers in libraries for students with visual impairments, classroom equipment adapted for use by students with manual impairments, and other similar services and actions. Recipients need not provide attendants, individually prescribed devices, readers for personal use or study, or other devices or services of a personal nature.

§ 104.45 Housing.

(a) *Housing provided by the recipient.* A recipient that provides housing to its nonhandicapped students shall provide comparable, convenient, and accessible housing to handicapped students at the same cost as to others. At the end of the transition period provided for in Subpart C, such housing shall be available in sufficient quantity and variety so that the scope of handicapped students' choice of living accommodations is, as a whole, comparable to that of nonhandicapped students.

(b) *Other housing.* A recipient that assists any agency, organization, or person in making housing available to any of its students shall take such action as may be necessary to assure itself that such housing is, as a whole, made available in a manner that does not result in discrimination on the basis of handicap.

§ 104.46   Financial and employment assistance to students.

(a) *Provision of financial assistance.* (1) In providing financial assistance to qualified handicapped persons, a recipient to which this subpart applies may not (i), on the basis of handicap, provide less assistance than is provided to nonhandicapped persons, limit eligibility for assistance, or otherwise discriminate or (ii) assist any entity or person that provides assistance to any of the recipient's students in a manner that discriminates against qualified handicapped persons on the basis of handicap.

(2) A recipient may administer or assist in the administration of scholarships, fellowships, or other forms of financial assistance established under wills, trusts, bequests, or similar legal instruments that require awards to be made on the basis of factors that discriminate or have the effect of discriminating on the basis of handicap only if the overall effect of the award of scholarships, fellowships, and other forms of financial assistance is not discriminatory on the basis of handicap.

(b) *Assistance in making available outside employment.* A recipient that assists any agency, organization, or person in providing employment opportunities to any of its students shall assure itself that such employment opportunities, as a whole, are made available in a manner that would not violate Subpart B if they were provided by the recipient.

(c) *Employment of students by recipients.* A recipient that employs any

of its students may not do so in a manner that violates Subpart B.

§ 104.47   Nonacademic services.

(a) *Physical education and athletics.* (1) In providing physical education courses and athletics and similar programs and activities to any of its students, a recipient to which this subpart applies may not discriminate on the basis of handicap. A recipient that offers physical education courses or that operates or sponsors intercollegiate, club, or intramural athletics shall provide to qualified handicapped students an equal opportunity for participation in these activities.

(2) A recipient may offer to handicapped students physical education and athletic activities that are separate or different only if separation or differentiation is consistent with the requirements of § 104.43(d) and only if no qualified handicapped student is denied the opportunity to compete for teams or to participate in courses that are not separate or different.

(b) *Counseling and placement services.* A recipient to which this subpart applies that provides personal, academic, or vocational counseling, guidance, or placement services to its students shall provide these services without discrimination on the basis of handicap. The recipient shall ensure that qualified handicapped students are not counseled toward more restrictive career objectives than are nonhandicapped students with similar interests and abilities. This requirement does not preclude a recipient from providing factual information about licensing and certification requirements that may present obstacles to handicapped persons in their pursuit of particular careers.

(c) *Social organizations.* A recipient that provides significant assistance to fraternities, sororities, or similar organizations shall assure itself that the membership practices of such organizations do not permit discrimination otherwise prohibited by this subpart.

Subpart F—Health, Welfare, and Social Services

§ 104.51   Application of this subpart.

Subpart F applies to health, welfare, and other social service programs and activities that receive or benefit from Federal financial assistance and to recipients that operate, or that receive or benefit from Federal financial assistance for the operation of, such programs or activities.

§ 104.52   Health, welfare, and other social services.

(a) *General.* In providing health, welfare, or other social services or benefits, a recipient may not, on the basis of handicap:

(1) Deny a qualified handicapped person these benefits or services;

(2) Afford a qualified handicapped person an opportunity to receive benefits or services that is not equal to that offered nonhandicapped persons;

(3) Provide a qualified handicapped person with benefits or services that are not as effective (as defined in § 104.4(b)) as the benefits or services provided to others;

(4) Provide benefits or services in a manner that limits or has the effect of limiting the participation of qualified handicapped persons; or

(5) Provide different or separate benefits or services to handicapped persons except where necessary to provide qualified handicapped persons with benefits and services that are as effective as those provided to others.

(b) *Notice.* A recipient that provides notice concerning benefits or services or written material concerning waivers of rights or consent to treatment shall take such steps as are necessary to ensure that qualified handicapped persons, including those with impaired sensory or speaking skills, are not denied effective notice because of their handicap.

(c) *Emergency treatment for the hearing impaired.* A recipient hospital that provides health services or benefits shall establish a procedure for effective communication with persons with impaired hearing for the purpose of providing emergency health care.

(d) *Auxiliary aids.* (1) A recipient to which this subpart applies that employs fifteen or more persons shall provide appropriate auxiliary aids to persons with impaired sensory, manual, or speaking skills, where necessary to afford such persons an equal opportunity to benefit from the service in question.

(2) The Assistant Secretary may require recipients with fewer than fifteen employees to provide auxiliary aids where the provision of aids would not significantly impair the ability of the recipient to provide its benefits or services.

(3) For the purpose of this paragraph, auxiliary aids may include brailled and taped material, interpreters, and other aids for persons with impaired hearing or vision.

§ 104.53   Drug and alcohol addicts.

A recipient to which this subpart applies that operates a general hospital or outpatient facility may not discriminate in admission or treatment against a drug or alcohol abuser or alcoholic who is suffering from a medical condition, because of the person's drug or alcohol abuse or alcoholism.

§ 104.54   Education of institutionalized persons.

A recipient to which this subpart applies and that operates or supervises a program or activity for persons who are institutionalized because of handicap shall ensure that each qualified handicapped person, as defined in § 104.3(k)(2), in its program or activity is provided an appropriate education, as defined in § 104.33(b). Nothing in this section shall be interpreted as altering in any way the obligations of recipients under Subpart D.

Subpart G—Procedures

§ 104.61   Procedures.

The procedural provisions applicable to title VI of the Civil Rights Act of 1964 apply to this part. These procedures are found in §§ 100.6–100.10 and Part 101 of this title.

APPENDIX C

TABLE OF
SPECIAL EDUCATION CASES
DECIDED BY THE
U.S. SUPREME COURT

Title & Citation (in chronological order)

Southeastern Community College v. Davis, 442 U.S. 397 (1979).

University of Texas v. Camenisch, 451 U.S. 390 (1981).

Pennhurst State School and Hospital v. Halderman, 451 U.S. 1 (1981). (Pennhurst I)

Pennhurst State School and Hospital v. Halderman, 465 U.S. 89 (1984). (Pennhurst II)

Board of Education v. Rowley, 458 U.S. 176 (1982).

Irving Independent School District v. Tatro, 468 U.S. 883 (1984).

Smith v. Robinson, 468 U.S. 992 (1984).

Honig v. Students of California School for the Blind, 471 U.S. 148 (1985).

Burlington School Committee v. Department of Education of Massachusetts, 471 U.S. 359 (1985).

City of Cleburne, Texas v. Cleburne Living Center, 473 U.S. 432 (1985).

Witters v. Washington Department of Services for the Blind, 474 U.S. 481 (1986).

School Board of Nassau County v. Arline, 480 U.S. 273 (1987).

Honig v. Doe, 484 U.S. 305 (1988).

Traynor v. Turnage, —— U.S. ——, 108 S.Ct. 1372 (1988).

Dellmuth v. Muth, —— U.S. ——, 109 S.Ct. 2397 (1989).

APPENDIX D

U.S. SUPREME COURT CASES

Board of Education v. Rowley

U.S. Supreme Court, 458 U.S. 176, 102 S.Ct. 3034 (1982).

Syllabus*

The Education for All Handicapped Children Act of 1975 (Act) provides federal money to assist state and local agencies in educating handicapped children. To qualify for federal assistance, a State must demonstrate (through a detailed plan submitted for federal approval) that it has in effect a policy that assures all handicapped children the right to a "free appropriate public education," which must be tailored to the unique needs of the handicapped child by means of an "individualized educational program" (IEP). The IEP must be prepared (and reviewed at least annually) by school officials with participation by the child's parents or guardian. The Act also requires that a participating State provide specified administrative procedures by which the child's parents or guardian may challenge any change in the evaluation and education of the child. Any party aggrieved by the state administrative decisions is authorized to bring a civil action in either a state court or a federal district court. Respondents—a child with only minimal residual hearing who had been furnished by school authorities with a special hearing aid for use in the classroom and who was to receive additional instruction from tutors, and the child's parents—filed suit in Federal District Court to review New York administrative proceedings that had upheld the school administrators' denial of the parents' request that the child also be provided a qualified sign-language interpreter in all of her academic classes. Entering judgment for respondents, the District Court found that although the child performed better than the average child in her class and was advancing easily from grade to grade, she was not performing as well academically as she would without her handicap. Because of this disparity between the child's achievement and her potential, the court held that she was not receiving a "free appropriate public education," which the court defined as "an opportunity to achieve [her] full potential commensurate with the opportunity provided to other children." The Court of Appeals affirmed.

Held:

1. The Act's requirement of a "free appropriate public education" is satisfied when the State provides personalized instruction with sufficient support services to permit the handicapped child to benefit educationally from that instruction. Such instruction and services must be provided at public expense, must meet the State's educational standards, must approximate grade levels used in the State's regular education, and must comport with the child's IEP, as formulated in accordance with the Act's requirements. If the child is being educated in regular classrooms, as here, the IEP should be reasonably calculated to enable the child to achieve passing marks and advance from grade to grade.

(a) This interpretation is supported by the definitions contained in the Act, as well as by other provisions imposing procedural requirements and setting forth statutory findings and priorities for States to follow in extending educational services to handicapped children. The Act's language contains no express substantive standard prescribing the level of education to be accorded handicapped children.

---

*The syllabus constitutes no part of the opinion of the Court but has been prepared by the Reporter of Decisions for the convenience of the reader.

(b) The Act's legislative history shows that Congress sought to make public education available to handicapped children, but did not intend to impose upon the States any greater substantive educational standard than is necessary to make such access to public education meaningful. The Act's intent was more to open the door of public education to handicapped children by means of specialized educational services than to guarantee any particular substantive level of education once inside.

(c) While Congress sought to provide assistance to the States in carrying out their constitutional responsibilities to provide equal protection of the laws, it did not intend to achieve strict equality of opportunity or services for handicapped and nonhandicapped children, but rather sought primarily to identify and evaluate handicapped children, and to provide them with access to a free public education. The Act does not require a State to maximize the potential of each handicapped child commensurate with the opportunity provided nonhandicapped children.

2. In suits brought under the Act's judicial-review provisions, a court must first determine whether the State has complied with the statutory procedures, and must then determine whether the individualized program developed through such procedures is reasonably calculated to enable the child to receive educational benefits. If these requirements are met, the State has complied with the obligations imposed by Congress and the courts can require no more.

(a) Although the judicial-review provisions do not limit courts to ensuring that States have complied with the Act's procedural requirements, the Act's emphasis on procedural safeguards demonstrates the legislative conviction that adequate compliance with prescribed procedures will in most cases assure much, if not all, of what Congress wished in the way of substantive content in an IEP.

(b) The courts must be careful to avoid imposing their view of preferable educational methods upon the States. Once a court determines that the Act's requirements have been met, questions of methodology are for resolution by the States.

3. Entrusting a child's education to state and local agencies does not leave the child without protection. As demonstrated by this case, parents and guardians will not lack ardor in seeking to ensure that handicapped children receive all of the benefits to which they are entitled by the Act.

4. The Act does not require the provision of a sign-language interpreter here. Neither of the courts below found that there had been a failure to comply with the Act's procedures, and the findings of neither court will support a conclusion that the child's educational program failed to comply with the substantive requirements of the Act.

632 F. 2d 945, reversed and remanded.

REHNQUIST, J., delivered the opinion of the Court, in which BURGER, C.J., and POWELL, STEVENS, and O'CONNOR, JJ., joined. BLACKMUN, J., filed an opinion concurring in the judgment. WHITE, J., filed a dissenting opinion, in which BRENNAN and MARSHALL, JJ., joined.

JUSTICE REHNQUIST delivered the opinion of the Court.

This case presents a question of statutory interpretation. Petitioners contend that the Court of Appeals and the District Court misconstrued the requirements imposed by Congress upon States which receive federal funds under the Education for All Handicapped Children Act. We agree and reverse the judgment of the Court of Appeals.

I

The Education for All Handicapped Children Act of 1975 (Act), 20 U.S.C. § 1401 *et seq.*, provides federal money to assist state and local agencies in educating handicapped children, and conditions such funding upon a State's compliance with extensive goals and procedures. The Act represents an ambitious federal effort to promote the education of handicapped children, and was passed in response to Congress' perception that a majority of handicapped children in the United States "were either totally excluded from schools or [were] sitting idly in regular classrooms awaiting the time when they were old enough to 'drop out.' " H.R. Rep. No. 94-332, p. 2 (1975). The Act's evolution and major provisions shed light on the question of statutory interpretation which is at the heart of this case.

Congress first addressed the problem of educating the handicapped in 1966 when it amended the Elementary and Secondary Education Act of 1965 to establish a grant program "for the purpose of assisting the States in the initiation, expansion, and improvement of programs and projects . . . for the education of handicapped children." Pub. L. No. 89-750, § 161, 80 Stat. 1204 (1966). That program was repealed in 1970 by the Education for the Handicapped Act, Pub. L No. 91-230, 84 Stat. 175, Part B of which established a grant program similar in purpose to the repealed legislation. Neither the 1966 nor the 1970 legislation contained specific guidelines for state use of the grant money; both were aimed primarily at stimulating the States to develop educational resources and to train personnel for educating the handicapped.[1]

Dissatisfied with the progress being made under these earlier enactments, and spurred by two district court decisions holding that handicapped children should be given access to a public education,[2] Congress in 1974 greatly increased federal funding for education of the handicapped and for the first time required recipient States to adopt "a goal of providing full educational opportunities to all handicapped children." Pub. L. 93-380, 88 Stat. 579, 583 (1974) (the 1974 statute).

The 1974 statute was recognized as an interim measure only, adopted "in order to give the Congress an additional year in which to study what if any additional Federal assistance [was] required to enable the States to meet the needs of handicapped children." H.R. Rep. No. 94-332, *supra,* p. 4. The ensuing year of study produced the Education for All Handicapped Children Act of 1975.

In order to qualify for federal financial assistance under the Act, a State must demonstrate that it "has in effect a policy that assures all handicapped children the right to a free appropriate public education." 20 U. S. C. § 1412(1). That policy must be reflected in a state plan submitted to and

---

[1] See S. Rep. No. 94-168, p. 5 (1975); H.R. Rep. No. 94-332, pp. 2-3 (1975).

[2] Two cases, *Mills v. Board of Education of the District of Columbia,* 348 F. Supp. 866 (DC 1972), and *Pennsylvania Association for Retarded Children v. Commonwealth of Pennsylvania,* 334 F. Supp. 1257 (1971); 343 F. Supp. 279 (ED Pa 1972), were later identified as the most prominent of the cases contributing to Congress' enactment of the Act and the statutes which preceded it. H.R. Rep. No. 94-332, *supra,* at 3-4. Both decisions are discussed in Part III of this opinion, *infra.*

approved by the Commissioner of Education,[3] § 1413, which describes in detail the goals, programs, and timetables under which the State intends to educate handicapped children within its borders. §§ 1412, 1413. States receiving money under the Act must provide education to the handicapped by priority, first "to handicapped children who are not receiving an education" and second "to handicapped children . . . with the most severe handicaps who are receiving an inadequate education," § 1412(3), and "to the maximum extent appropriate" must educate handicapped children "with children who are not handicapped." § 1412(5).[4] The Act broadly defines "handicapped children" to include "mentally retarded, hard of hearing, deaf, speech impaired, visually handicapped, seriously emotionally disturbed, orthopedically impaired, [and] other health impaired children, [and] children with specific learning disabilities." § 1401(1).[5]

The "free appropriate public education" required by the Act is tailored to the unique needs of the handicapped child by means of an "individualized educational program" (IEP) § 1401(18). The IEP, which is prepared at a meeting between a qualified representative of the local educational agency, the child's teacher, the child's parents or guardian, and, where appropriate, the child, consists of a written document containing

> "(A) a statement of the present levels of educational performance of the child, (B) a statement of annual goals, including short-term instructional objectives, (C) a statement of the specific educational services to be provided to such child, and the extent to which such child will be able to participate in regular educational programs, (D) the projected date for initiation and anticipated duration of such service, and (E) appropriate objective criteria and evaluation procedures and schedules for determining, on at least an annual basis, whether instructional objectives are being achieved." § 1401(19).

Local or regional educational agencies must review, and where appropriate revise, each child's IEP at least annually. § 1404(a)(5). See also §§ 1413(a)(11), 1414(a)(5).

In addition to the state plan and the IEP already described, the Act imposes extensive procedural requirements upon States receiving federal funds under its provisions. Parents or guardians of handicapped children

---

[3]All functions of the Commissioner of Education, formerly an officer in the Department of Health, Education, and Welfare, were transferred to the Secretary of Education in 1979 when Congress passed the Department of Education Organization Act, 20 U. S. C. § 3401 *et seq.* See 20 U. S. C. § 3441(a)(1).

[4]Despite this preference for "mainstreaming" handicapped children—educating them with nonhandicapped children—Congress recognized that regular classrooms simply would not be a suitable setting for the education of many handicapped children. The Act expressly acknowledges that "the nature or severity of the handicap [may be] such that education in regular classes with the use of supplementary aids and services cannot be achieved satisfactorily." § 1412(5). The Act thus provides for the education of some handicapped children in separate classes or institutional settings. See *ibid.;* § 1413(a)(4).

[5]In addition to covering a wide variety of handicapping conditions, the Act requires special educational services for children "regardless of the severity of their handicap." §§ 1412(2)(C), 1414(a)(1)(A).

must be notified of any proposed change in "the identification, evaluation, or educational placement of the child or the provision of a free appropriate public education to the child," and must be permitted to bring a complaint about "any matter relating to" such evaluation and education. § 1415(b)(1)(D) and (E).[6] Complaints brought by parents or guardians must be resolved at "an impartial due process hearing," and appeal to the State educational agency must be provided if the initial hearing is held at the local or regional level. § 1415(b)(2) and (c).[7]

Thereafter, "[a]ny party aggrieved by the findings and decisions" of the state administrative hearing has "the right to bring a civil action with respect to the complaint . . . in any State court of competent jurisdiction or in a district court of the United States without regard to the amount in controversy." § 1415(e)(2).

Thus, although the Act leaves to the States the primary responsibility for developing and executing educational programs for handicapped children, it imposes significant requirements to be followed in the discharge of that responsibility. Compliance is assured by provisions permitting the withholding of federal funds upon determination that a participating state or local agency has failed to satisfy the requirements of the Act, §§ 1414(b)(2)(A), 1416, and by the provision for judicial review. At present, all States except New Mexico receive federal funds under the portions of the Act at issue today. Brief for the United States as *Amicus Curiae* 2, n. 2.

II

This case arose in connection with the education of Amy Rowley, a deaf student at the Furnace Woods School in the Hendrick Hudson Central School District, Peekskill, New York. Amy has minimal residual hearing and is an excellent lipreader. During the year before she began attending Furnace

---

[6] The requirements that parents be permitted to file complaints regarding their child's education, and be present when the child's IEP is formulated, represent only two examples of Congress' effort to maximize parental involvement in the education of each handicapped child. In addition, the Act requires that parents be permitted "to examine all relevant records with respect to the identification, evaluation, and educational placement of the child, and . . . to obtain an independent educational evaluation of the child." § 1415(b)(1)(A). See also §§ 1412(4), 1414(a)(4). State educational policies and the state plan submitted to the Commissioner of Education must be formulated in "consultation with individuals involved in or concerned with the education of handicapped children, including handicapped individuals and parents or guardians of handicapped children." § 1412(7). See also § 1412(2)(E). Local agencies, which receive funds under the Act by applying to the state agency, must submit applications which assure that they have developed procedures for "the participation and consultation of the parents or guardian[s] of [handicapped] children" in local educational programs, § 1414(a)(1)(C)(iii), and the application itself, along with "all pertinent documents related to such application," must be made "available to parents, guardians, and other members of the general public." § 1414(a)(4).

[7] "Any party" to a state or local administrative hearing must "be accorded (1) the right to be accompanied and advised by counsel and by individuals with special knowledge or training with respect to the problems of handicapped children, (2) the right to present evidence and confront, cross examine, and compel the attendance of witnesses, (3) the right to a written or electronic verbatim record of such hearing, and (4) the right to written findings of fact and decision." § 1415(d).

Woods, a meeting between her parents and school administrators resulted in a decision to place her in a regular kindergarten class in order to determine what supplemental services would be necessary to her education. Several members of the school administration prepared for Amy's arrival by attending a course in sign-language interpretation, and a teletype machine was installed in the principal's office to facilitate communication with her parents who are also deaf. At the end of the trial period it was determined that Amy should remain in the kindergarten class, but that she should be provided with an FM hearing aid which would amplify words spoken into a wireless receiver by the teacher or fellow students during certain classroom activities. Amy successfully completed her kindergarten year.

As required by the Act, an IEP was prepared for Amy during the fall of her first-grade year. The IEP provided that Amy should be educated in a regular classroom at Furnace Woods, should continue to use the FM hearing aid, and should receive instruction from a tutor for the deaf for one hour each day and from a speech therapist for three hours each week. The Rowleys agreed with the IEP but insisted that Amy also be provided a qualified sign-language interpreter in all of her academic classes. Such an interpreter had been placed in Amy's kindergarten class for a two-week experimental period, but the interpreter had reported that Amy did not need his services at that time. The school administrators likewise concluded that Amy did not need such an interpreter in her first-grade classroom. They reached this conclusion after consulting the school district's Committee on the Handicapped, which had received expert evidence from Amy's parents on the importance of a sign-language interpreter, received testimony from Amy's teacher and other persons familiar with her academic and social progress, and visited a class for the deaf.

When their request for an interpreter was denied, the Rowleys demanded and received a hearing before an independent examiner. After receiving evidence from both sides, the examiner agreed with the administrators' determination that an interpreter was not necessary because "Amy was achieving educationally, academically, and socially" without such assistance. App. to Pet. for Cert. F-22. The examiner's decision was affirmed on appeal by the New York Commissioner of Education on the basis of substantial evidence in the record. *Id.,* at E-4. Pursuant to the Act's provision for judicial review, the Rowleys then brought an action in the United States District Court for the Southern District of New York, claiming that the administrators' denial of the sign-language interpreter constituted a denial of the "free appropriate public education" guaranteed by the Act.

The District Court found that Amy "is a remarkably well-adjusted child" who interacts and communicates well with her classmates and has "developed an extraordinary rapport" with her teachers. 483 F. Supp. 528, 531. It also found that "she performs better than the average child in her class and is advancing easily from grade to grade," *id.* at 534, but "that she understands considerably less of what goes on in class than she would if she were not deaf" and thus "is not learning as much, or performing as well academically, as she would without her handicap," *id.,* at 532. This disparity between Amy's achievement and her potential led the court to decide that she was not receiving a "free appropriate public education," which the court defined as "an opportunity to achieve [her] full potential commensurate with the opportunity provided to other children." *Id.,* at 534. According to the

District Court, such a standard "requires that the potential of the handicapped child be measured and compared to his or her performance, and that the remaining differential or 'shortfall' be compared to the shortfall experienced by non-handicapped children." *Ibid.* The District Court's definition arose from its assumption that the responsibility for "giv[ing] content to the requirement of an 'appropriate education' " had "been left entirely to the federal courts and the hearing officers." *Id.,* at 533.[8]

A divided panel of the United States Court of Appeals for the Second Circuit affirmed. The Court of Appeals "agree[d] with the [D]istrict [C]ourt's conclusions of law," and held that its "findings of fact [were] not clearly erroneous." 632 F. 2d 945, 947 (1980).

We granted certiorari to review the lower courts' interpretation of the Act. 454 U.S. 961 (1981). Such review requires us to consider two questions: What is meant by the Act's requirement of a "free appropriate public education?" And what is the role of state and federal courts in exercising the review granted by § 1415 of the Act? We consider these questions separately.[9]

III

A

This is the first case in which this Court has been called upon to interpret any provision of the Act. As noted previously, the District Court and the Court of Appeals concluded that "[t]he Act itself does not define 'appropriate education,' " 483 F. Supp., at 533, but leaves "to the courts and the hearing officers" the responsibility of "giv[ing] content to the requirement of an appropriate education." *Ibid.* See also 632 F. 2d, at 947. Petitioners contend that the definition of the phrase "free appropriate public education" used by the courts below overlooks the definition of that phrase actually found in the Act. Respondents agree that the Act defines "free appropriate public education," but contend that the statutory definition is not "functional" and thus "offers judges no guidance in their consideration of controversies involving the 'identification, evaluation, or educational placement of

---

[8]For reasons that are not revealed in the record, the District Court concluded that "[t]he Act itself does not define 'appropriate education.' " 483 F. Supp., at 533. In fact, the Act expressly defines the phrase "free appropriate public education," see § 1401(18), to which the District Court was referring. See 483 F. Supp., at 533. After overlooking the statutory definition, the District Court sought guidance not from regulations interpreting the Act, but from regulations promulgated under Section 504 of the Rehabilitation Act. See 483 F. Supp., at 533, citing 45 CFR § 84.33(b).

[9]The IEP which respondents challenged in the District Court was created for the 1978-1979 school year. Petitioners contend that the District Court erred in reviewing that IEP after the school year had ended and before the school administrators were able to develop another IEP for subsequent years. We disagree. Judicial review invariably takes more than nine months to complete, not to mention the time consumed during the preceding state administrative hearings. The District Court thus correctly ruled that it retained jurisdiction to grant relief because the alleged deficiencies in the IEP were capable of repetition as to the parties before it yet evading review. *Rowley* v. *The Board of Education of the Hendrick Hudson Central School District,* 483 F. Supp. 536, 538 (1980). See *Murphy* v. *Hunt,* 455 U.S. 478, 482 (1982); *Weinstein* v. *Bradford,* 423 U.S. 147, 149 (1975).

the child or the provision of a free appropriate public education.' " Brief for Respondents 28. The United States, appearing as *amicus curiae* on behalf of respondents, states that "[a]lthough the Act includes definitions of 'free appropriate public education' and other related terms, the statutory definitions do not adequately explain what is meant by 'appropriate.' " Brief for United States as *Amicus Curiae* 13.

We are loath to conclude that Congress failed to offer any assistance in defining the meaning of the principal substantive phrase used in the Act. It is beyond dispute that, contrary to the conclusions of the courts below, the Act does expressly define "free appropriate public education":

> "The term 'free appropriate public education' means *special education* and *related services* which (A) have been provided at public expense, under public supervision and direction, and without charge, (B) meet the standards of the State educational agency, (C) include an appropriate preschool, elementary, or secondary school education in the State involved, and (D) are provided in conformity with the individualized education program required under section 1414(a)(5) of this title." § 1401(18) (emphasis added).

"Special education," as referred to in this definition, means "specially designed instruction, at no cost to parents or guardians, to meet the unique needs of a handicapped child, including classroom instruction, instruction in physical education, home instruction, and instruction in hospitals and institutions." § 1401(16). "Related services" are defined as "transportation, and such developmental, corrective, and other supportive services . . . as may be required to assist a handicapped child to benefit from special education." § 1401(17).[10]

Like many statutory definitions, this one tends toward the cryptic rather than the comprehensive, but that is scarcely a reason for abandoning the quest for legislative intent. Whether or not the definition is a "functional" one as respondents contend it is not, it is the principal tool which Congress has given us for parsing the critical phrase of the Act. We think more must be made of it than either respondents or the United States seems willing to admit.

According to the definitions contained in the Act, a "free appropriate public education" consists of educational instruction specially designed to meet the unique needs of the handicapped child, supported by such services as are necessary to permit the child "to benefit" from the instruction. Almost as a checklist for adequacy under the Act, the definition also requires that such instruction and services be provided at public expense and under public supervision, meet the State's educational standards, approximate the grade levels used in the State's regular education, and comport with the child's IEP. Thus, if personalized instruction is being provided with sufficient supportive services to permit the child to benefit from the instruction, and the other items on the definitional checklist are satisfied, the child is receiving a "free appropriate public education" as defined by the Act.

---

[10]Examples of "related services" identified in the Act are "speech pathology and audiology, psychological services, physical and occupational therapy, recreation, and medical and counseling services, except that such medical services shall be for diagnostic and evaluation purposes only" § 1401(17).

Other portions of the statute also shed light upon congressional intent. Congress found that of the roughly eight million handicapped children in the United States at the time of enactment, one million were "excluded entirely from the public school system" and more than half were receiving an inappropriate education. Note to § 1401. In addition, as mentioned in Part I, the Act requires States to extend educational services first to those children who are receiving no education and second to those children who are receiving an "inadequate education." § 1412(3). When these express statutory findings and priorities are read together with the Act's extensive procedural requirements and its definition of "free appropriate public education," the face of the statute evinces a congressional intent to bring previously excluded handicapped children into the public education systems of the States and to require the States to adopt *procedures* which would result in individualized consideration and instruction for each child.

Noticeably absent from the language of the statute is any substantive standard prescribing the level of education to be accorded handicapped children. Certainly the language of the statute contains no requirement like the one imposed by the lower courts—that States maximize the potential of handicapped children "commensurate with the opportunity provided to other children." 483 F. Supp., at 534. That standard was expounded by the District Court without reference to the statutory definitions or even to the legislative history of the Act. Although we find the statutory definition of "free appropriate public education" to be helpful in our interpretation of the Act, there remains the question of whether the legislative history indicates a congressional intent that such education meet some additional substantive standard. For an answer, we turn to that history.[11]

---

[11]The dissent, finding that "the standard of the courts below seems . . . to reflect the congressional purpose" of the Act, *post*, concludes that our answer to this question "is not a satisfactory one." *Id*. Presumably, the dissent also agrees with the District Court's conclusion that "it has been left entirely to the courts and the hearing officers to give content to the requirement of an 'appropriate education.'" 483 F. Supp., at 533. It thus seems that the dissent would give the courts carte blanche to impose upon the States whatever burden their various judgments indicate should be imposed. Indeed, the dissent clearly characterizes the requirement of an "appropriate education" as open-ended, noting that "if there are limits not evident from the face of the statute on what may be considered an 'appropriate education,' they must be found in the purpose of the statute or its legislative history." *Post*. Not only are we unable to find any suggestion from the face of the statute that the requirement of an "appropriate private education" was to be limitless, but we also view the dissent's approach as contrary to the fundamental proposition that Congress, when exercising its spending power, can impose no burden upon the States unless it does so unambiguously. See *infra*.

No one can doubt that this would have been an easier case if Congress had seen fit to provide a more comprehensive statutory definition of the phrase "free appropriate public education." But Congress did not do so, and "our problem is to construe what Congress has written. After all, Congress expresses its purpose by words. It is for us to ascertain—neither to add nor to subtract, neither to delete nor to distort." *62 Cases of Jam* v. *United States,* 340 U.S. 593, 596 (1951). We would be less than faithful to our obligation to construe what Congress has written if in this case we were to disregard the statutory language and legislative history of the Act by concluding that Congress had imposed upon the States a burden of unspecified proportions and weight, to be revealed only through case by case adjudication in the courts.

B

(i)

As suggested in Part I, federal support for education of the handicapped is a fairly recent development. Before passage of the Act some States had passed laws to improve the educational services afforded handicapped children,[12] but many of these children were excluded completely from any form of public education or were left to fend for themselves in classrooms designed for education of their nonhandicapped peers. The House Report begins by emphasizing this exclusion and misplacement, noting that millions of handicapped children "were either totally excluded from schools or [were] sitting idly in regular classrooms awaiting the time when they were old enough to 'drop out.' " H.R. Rep. No. 94-332, *supra,* at 2. See also S. Rep. No. 94-168, p. 8 (1975). One of the Act's two principal sponsors in the Senate urged its passage in similar terms:

"While much progress has been made in the last few years, we can take no solace in the progress until all handicapped children are, in fact, receiving an education. The most recent statistics provided by the Bureau of Education for the Handicapped estimate that . . . 1.75 million handicapped children do not receive any educational services, and 2.5 million handicapped children are not receiving an appropriate education." 121 Cong. Rec. 19486 (1975) (remarks of Sen. Williams).

This concern, stressed repeatedly throughout the legislative history,[13] confirms the impression conveyed by the language of the statute: By passing the Act, Congress sought primarily to make public education available to handicapped children. But in seeking to provide such access to public education, Congress did not impose upon the States any greater substantive educational standard than would be necessary to make such access meaningful. Indeed, Congress expressly "recognize[d] that in many instances the process of providing special education and related services to handicapped children is not guaranteed to produce any particular outcome." S. Rep. No. 94-168, *supra,* at 11. Thus, the intent of the Act was more to open the door of public education to handicapped children on appropriate terms than to guarantee any particular level of education once inside.

Both the House and the Senate reports attribute the impetus for the Act and its predecessors to two federal court judgments rendered in 1971 and 1972. As the Senate Report states, passage of the Act "followed a series of landmark court cases establishing in law the right to education for all handi-

---

[12]See H.R. Rep. No. 94-332, *supra,* at 10; Note, The Education of All Handicapped Children Act of 1975, Mich. J. L. Ref. 110, 119 (1976).

[13]See, e.g., 121 Cong. Rec. 19494 (1975) (remarks of Sen. Javits) ("all too often, our handicapped citizens have been denied the opportunity to receive an adequate education"); 121 Cong. Rec. 19502 (1975) (remarks of Sen. Cranston) (millions of handicapped "children are largely excluded from educational opportunities that we give to our other children"); 121 Cong. rec. 23708 (1975) (remarks of Rep. Mink) ("handicapped children . . . are denied access to public schools because of a lack of trained personnel").

capped children." S. Rep. No. 94-168, *supra,* at 6.[14] The first case, *Pennsylvania Association for Retarded Children* v. *Commonwealth of Pennsylvania (PARC),* 334 F. Supp. 1257 (1971), 343 F. Supp. 279 (ED Pa 1972), was a suit on behalf of retarded children challenging the constitutionality of a Pennsylvania statute which acted to exclude them from public education and training. The case ended in a consent decree which enjoined the State from "deny[ing] to any mentally retarded child *access* to a free public program of education and training." 334 F. Supp., at 1258 (emphasis added).

PARC was followed by *Mills* v. *Board of Education of the District of Columbia,* 348 F. Supp. 866 (DC 1972), a case in which the plaintiff handicapped children had been excluded from the District of Columbia public schools. The court's judgment, quoted at page 6 of the Senate Report on the Act, provided

> "[t]hat no [handicapped] child eligible for a publicly supported education in the District of Columbia public schools shall be *excluded* from a regular school assignment by a rule, policy, or practice of the Board of Education of the District of Columbia or its agents unless such child is provided (a) *adequate* alternative educational services suited to the child's needs, which may include special education or tuition grants, and (b) a constitutionally adequate prior hearing and periodic review of the child's status, progress, and the *adequacy* of any educational alternative." 348 F. Supp., at 878 (emphasis added).

Mills and *PARC* both held that handicapped children must be given access to an adequate, publicly supported education. Neither case purports to require any particular substantive level of education.[15] Rather, like the language of the Act, the cases set forth extensive procedures to be followed in formulating personalized educational programs for handicapped children.

---

[14]Similarly, the Senate Report states that it was an "[i]ncreased awareness of the educational needs of handicapped children and landmark court decisions establishing the right to education for handicapped children [that] pointed to the necessity of an expanded federal role." S. Rep. No. 94-168, *supra,* at 5. See also H.R. Rep. No. 94-332, *supra,* at 2-3.

[15]The only substantive standard which can be implied from these cases comports with the standard implicit in the Act. *PARC* states that each child must receive "access to a free public program of education and training *appropriate to his learning capacities,"* 334 F. Supp., at 1258, and that further state action is required when it appears that "the needs of the mentally retarded child are not being *adequately* served," *id.,* at 1266. (Emphasis added.) *Mills* also speaks in terms of "adequate" educational services, 348 F. Supp., at 878, and sets a realistic standard of providing *some* educational services to each child when every need cannot be met.

"If sufficient funds are not available to finance all of the services and programs that are needed and desirable in the system then the available funds must be expended equitably in such a manner that no child is entirely excluded from a publicly supported education consistent with his needs and ability to benefit therefrom. The inadequacies of the District of Columbia Public School System whether occasioned by insufficient funding or administrative inefficiency, certainly cannot be permitted to bear more heavily on the 'exceptional' or handicapped child than on the normal child." *Id.,* at 876.

See 348 F. Supp., at 878-883; 334 F. Supp., at 1258-1267.[16] The fact that both *PARC* and *Mills* are discussed at length in the legislative reports[17] suggests that the principles which they established are the principles which, to a significant extent, guided the drafters of the Act. Indeed, immediately after discussing these cases the Senate Report describes the 1974 statute as having "incorporated the major principles of the right to education cases." S. Rep. No. 94-168, *supra,* at 8. Those principles in turn became the basis of the Act, which itself was designed to effectuate the purposes of the 1974 statute. H.R. Rep. No. 94-332, *supra,* at 5.[18]

That the Act imposes no clear obligation upon recipient States beyond the requirement that handicapped children receive some form of specialized education is perhaps best demonstrated by the fact the Congress, in explaining the need for the Act, equated an "appropriate education" to the receipt of some specialized educational services. The Senate Report states: [T]he most recent statistics provided by the Bureau of Education for the Handicapped estimate that of the more than 8 million children . . . with handicapping conditions requiring special education and related services, only 3.9 million such children are receiving an appropriate education." S. Rep. No.

---

[16]Like the Act, *PARC* required the State to "identify, locate, [and] evaluate" handicapped children 334 F. Supp., at 1267, to create for each child an individual educational program, *id.,* at 1265, and to hold a hearing "on any change in educational assignment," *id.,* 1266. *Mills* also required the preparation of an individual educational program for each child. In addition, *Mills* permitted the child's parents to inspect records relevant to the child's education, to obtain an independent educational evaluation of the child, to object to the IEP and receive a hearing before an independent hearing officer, to be represented by counsel at the hearing, and to have the right confront and cross-examine adverse witnesses, all of which are also permitted by the Act. 348 F. Supp., at 879-881. Like the Act, *Mills* also required that the education of handicapped children be conducted pursuant to an overall plan prepared by the District of Columbia, and established a policy of educating handicapped children with nonhandicapped children whenever possible. *Ibid.*

[17]*See S. Rep. No. 94-168, supra,* at 6-7; H.R. Rep. No. 94-332, *supra,* at 3-4.

[18]The 1974 statute "incorporated the major principles of the right to education cases," by "add[ing] important new provisions to the Education of the Handicapped Act which require the States to: establish a goal of providing full educational opportunities to all handicapped children; provide procedures for insuring that handicapped children and their parents or guardians are guaranteed procedural safeguards in decisions regarding identification, evaluation, and education placement of handicapped children; establish procedures to insure that, to the maximum extent appropriate, handicapped children . . . are educated with children who are not handicapped; . . . and establish procedures to insure that testing and evaluation materials and procedures utilized for the purposes of classification and placement of handicapped children will be selected and administered so as not to be racially or culturally discriminatory," S. Rep. No. 94-168, *supra,* at 8.

The House Report explains that the Act simply incorporated these purposes of the 1974 statute: the Act intended "primarily to amend . . . the Education of the Handicapped Act in order to provide permanent authorization and a comprehensive mechanism which will insure that those provisions enacted during the 93rd Congress [the 1974 statute] will result in maximum benefits for handicapped children and their families." H.R. Rep. No. 94-332, *supra,* at 5. Thus, the 1974 statute's purpose of providing handicapped children *access* to a public education became the purpose of the Act.

94-168, *supra,* at 8.[19] This statement, which reveals Congress' view that 3.9 million handicapped children were "receiving an appropriate education" in 1975, is followed immediately in the Senate Report by a table showing that 3.9 million handicapped children were "served" in 1975 and a slightly larger number were "unserved." A similar statement and table appear in the House Report. H.R. Rep. No. 94-332, *supra,* at 11-12.

It is evident from the legislative history that the characterization of handicapped children as "served" referred to children who were receiving some form of specialized educational services from the States, and that the characterization of children as "unserved" referred to those who were receiving no specialized educational services. For example, a letter sent to the United State Commissioner of Education by the House Committee on Education and Labor, signed by two key sponsors of the Act in the House, asked the Commissioner to identify the number of handicapped "children served" in each State. The letter asked for statistics on the number of children "being served" in various types of "special education program[s]" and the number of children who were not "receiving education services." Hearings on S. 6 before the Subcommittee on the Handicapped of the Senate Committee on Labor and Public Welfare, 94th Cong., 1st Sess., 205-207 (1975). Similarly, Senator Randolph, one of the Act's principal sponsors in the Senate, noted that roughly one-half of the handicapped children in the United States "are receiving special educational services." *Id.,* at 1.[20] By characterizing the 3.9

---

[19]These statistics appear repeatedly throughout the legislative history of the Act, demonstrating a virtual consensus among legislators that 3.9 million handicapped children were receiving an appropriate education in 1975. See, e.g., 121 Cong. Rec. 19486 (1975) (remarks of Sen. Williams); 121 Cong. Rec. 19504 (1975) (remarks of Sen. Schweicker); 121 Cong. Rec. 23702 (1975) (remarks of Rep. Madden); 121 Cong. Rec. 23702 (1975) (remarks of Rep. Brademas); 121 Cong. Rec. 23709 (1975) (remarks of Rep. Minish); 121 Cong. Rec. 37024 (1975) (remarks of Rep. Brademas); 121 Cong. Rec. 37027 (1975) (remarks of Rep. Gude); 121 Cong. Rec. 37417 (1975) (remarks of Sen. Javits); 121 Cong., Rec. 37420 (1975) (remarks of Sen. Hathaway).

[20]Senator Randolph stated: "only 55 percent of the school-aged handicapped children and 22 percent of the pre-school-aged handicapped children are receiving special educational services." Hearings on S. 6 before the Subcommittee on the Handicapped of the Senate Committee on Labor and Public Welfare, 94th Cong., 1st Sess., 1 (1975). Although the figures differ slightly in various parts of the legislative history, the general thrust of congressional calculations was that roughly one-half of the handicapped children in the United States were not receiving specialized educational services, and thus were not "served." See, e.g., 121 Cong. Rec. 19494 (1975) (remarks of Sen. Javits) ("only 50 percent of the Nation's handicapped children received proper education services"); 121 Cong. Rec. 19504 (1975) (remark of Sen. Humphrey) ("[a]llmost 3 million handicapped children, while in school, receive none of the special services that they require in order to make education a meaningful experience"); 121 Cong. Rec. 23706 (1975) (remarks of Rep. Quie) ("only 55 percent [of handicapped children] were receiving a public education"); 121 Cong. Rec. 233709 (1975) (remarks of Rep. Biaggi) ("[o]ver 3 million [handicapped] children in this country are receiving either below par education or none at all").

Statements similar to those appearing in the text, which equate "served" as it appears in the Senate Report to "receiving special educational services," appear throughout the legislative history. See, e.g. 121 Cong. Rec. 19492 (1975) (remarks of Sen. Williams); 121 Cong. Rec. 19494 (1975) (remarks of Sen. Javits); 121 Cong. Rec. 19496 (1975) (remarks of Sen. Stone); 121 Cong. Rec. 19504-19505 (1975) (remarks of Sen. Humphrey); 121 Cong. Rec. 23703 (1975) (remarks of Rep. Brademas); Hearings million handicapped children who were "served" as children who were "receiving an appropriate education," the Senate and House reports unmistakably disclose Congress' perception of the type of education required by the Act: an "appropriate education" is provided when personalized educational services are provided.[21]

(ii)

Respondents contend that "the goal of the Act is to provide each handicapped child with an equal educational opportunity." Brief for Respondents 35. We think, however, that the requirement that a State provide specialized educational services to handicapped children generates no additional requirement that the services so provided be sufficient to maximize each child's potential "commensurate with the opportunity provided other children." Respondents and the United States correctly note that Congress sought "to provide assistance to the States in carrying out their responsibilities under . . . the Constitution of the United States to provide equal protection of the laws." S. Rep. No. 94-168, *supra,* at 13.[22] But we do not think that such

---

on H.R. 7217 before the Subcommittee on Select Education of the Committee on Education and Labor of the House of Representatives, 94th Cong., 1st Sess., 91, 150, 153 (1975); Hearings on H.R. 4199 before the Select Subcommittee on Education of the Committee on Education and Labor of the House of Representatives, 93rd Cong., 1st Sess., 130, 139 (1973). See also 45 CFR § 121a.343(b) (1980).

[21]In seeking to read more into the Act than its language or legislative history will permit, the United States focuses upon the word "appropriate," arguing that "the statutory definitions do not adequately explain what [it means]." Brief for the United States as *Amicus Curiae* 13. Whatever Congress meant by an "appropriate" education, it is clear that it did not mean a potential-maximizing education.

The term as used in reference to education the handicapped appears to have originated in the *PARC* decision, where the District Court required that handicapped children be provided with "education and training appropriate to [their] learning capacities." 334 F. Supp., at 1258. The word appears again in the *Mills* decision, The district Court at one point referring to the need for "an appropriate educational program," 348 F. Supp., at 879, and at another point speaking of a "suitable publicly-supported education," *id.,* at 878. Both cases also refer to the need for an "adequate" education. See 334 F. Supp., at 1266; 348 F. Supp., at 878.

The use of "appropriate" in the language of the Act, although by no means definitive, suggests that Congress used the word as much to describe the settings in which handicapped children should be educated as to prescribe the substantive content or supportive services of their education. For example, § 1412(5) requires that handicapped children be educated in classrooms with nonhandicapped children "to the maximum extent appropriate." Similarly, § 1401(19) provides that, "whenever appropriate," handicapped children should attend and participate in the meeting at which their IEP is drafted. In addition, the definition of "free appropriate public education" itself states that instruction given handicapped children should be at an "appropriate preschool, elementary, or secondary school" level. § 1401(18)(C). The Act's use of the word "appropriate" thus seems to reflect Congress' recognition that some settings simply are not suitable environments for the participation of some handicapped children. At the very least, these statutory uses of the word refute the contention that Congress used "appropriate" as a term of art which concisely expresses the standard found by the lower courts.

[22]See also 121 Cong. Rec. 19492(1975) (remarks of Sen. Williams); 121 Cong. Rec. 19504 (1975) (remarks of Sen. Humphrey).

statements imply a congressional intent to achieve strict equality of opportunity or services.

The educational opportunities provided by our public school systems undoubtedly differ from student to student, depending upon a myriad of factors that might affect a particular student's ability to assimilate information presented in the classroom. The requirement that States provide "equal" educational opportunities would thus seem to present an entirely unworkable standard requiring impossible measurements and comparisons. Similarly, furnishing handicapped children with only such services as are available to nonhandicapped children would in all probability fall short of the statutory requirement of "free appropriate public education;" to require, on the other hand, the furnishing of every special service necessary to maximize each handicapped child's potential is, we think, further than Congress intended to go. Thus to speak in terms of "equal" services in one instance gives less than what is required by the Act and in another instance more. The theme of the Act is "free appropriate public education," a phrase which is too complex to be captured by the word "equal" whether one is speaking of opportunities or services.

The legislative conception of the requirements of equal protection was undoubtedly informed by the two district court decisions referred to above. But cases such as *Mills* and *PARC* held simply that handicapped children may not be excluded entirely from public education. In *Mills,* the District Court said:

> "If sufficient funds are not available to finance all of the services and programs that are needed and desirable in the system then the available funds must be expended equitably in such a manner that no child is entirely excluded from a publicly supported education consistent with his needs and ability to benefit therefrom." 348 F. Supp., at 876

The *PARC* Court used similar language, saying "[i]t is the commonwealth's obligation to place each mentally retarded child in a free, public program of education and training appropriate to the child's capacity. . . ." 334 F. Supp., at 1260. The right of access to free public education enunciated by these cases is significant regardless of capacity. To the extent that Congress might have looked further than these cases which are mentioned in the legislative history, at the time of enactment of the Act this Court had held at least twice that the Equal Protection Clause of the Fourteenth Amendment does not require States to expend equal financial resources on the education of each child. *San Antonio School District* v. *Rodriguez,* 411 U. S. 1 (1975); *McInnis* v. *Shapiro,* 293 F. Supp. 327 (ND Ill. 1968), *aff'd sub nom, McInnis* v. *Ogilvie,* 394 U. S. 322 (1969).

In explaining the need for federal legislation, the House Report noted that "no congressional legislation, has required a precise guarantee for handicapped children, i.e. a basic floor of opportunity that would bring into compliance all school districts with the constitutional right of equal protection with respect to handicapped children." H.R. Rep. No. 94-332, *supra,* at 14. Assuming that the Act was designed to fill the need identified in the House Report—that is, to provide a "basic floor of opportunity" consistent with equal protection—neither the Act nor its history persuasively demonstrate that Congress thought that equal protection required anything more than equal access. Therefore, Congress' desire to provide specialized educational services, even in furtherance of "equality," cannot be read as imposing any particular substantive educational standard upon the States.

The District Court and the Court of Appeals thus erred when they held that the Act requires New York to maximize the potential of each handicapped child commensurate with the opportunity provided nonhandicapped children. Desirable though that goal might be, it is not the standard that Congress imposed upon States which receive funding under the Act. Rather, Congress sought primarily to identify and evaluate handicapped children, and to provide them with access to a free public education.

(iii)

Implicit in the congressional purpose of providing access to a "free appropriate public education" is the requirement that the education to which *access* is provided be sufficient to confer some educational benefit upon the handicapped child. It would do little good for Congress to spend millions of dollars in providing access to a public education only to have the handicapped child receive no benefit from that education. The statutory definition of "free appropriate public education," in addition to requiring that States provide each child with "specially designed instruction," expressly requires the provision of "such . . . supportive services . . . as may be required to assist a handicapped child to *benefit* from special education. § 1401(17) (emphasis added). We therefore conclude that the "basic floor of opportunity" provided by the Act consists of access to specialized instruction and related services which are individually designed to provide educational benefit to the handicapped child.[23]

---

[23]This view is supported by the congressional intention, frequently expressed in the legislative history, that handicapped children be enabled to achieve a reasonable degree of self sufficiency. After referring to statistics showing that many handicapped children were excluded from public education, the Senate Report states:

"The long range implications of these statistics are that public agencies and taxpayers will spend billions of dollars over the lifetimes of these individuals to maintain such persons as dependents and in a minimally acceptable lifestyle. With proper education services, many would be able to become productive citizens, contributing to society instead of being forced to remain burdens. Others, through such services, would increase their independence, thus reducing their dependence on society." S. Rep. No. 94-168, *supra,* at 9. See also H.R. Rep. No. 94-332, *supra,* at 11.

Similarly, one of the principal Senate sponsors of the Act stated that "providing appropriate educational services now means that many of these individuals will be able to become a contributing part of our society, and they will not have to depend on subsistence payments from public funds." 121 Cong. Rec. 19492 (1975) (remarks of Sen. Williams). See also 121 Cong. Rec. 25541 (1975) (remarks of Rep. Harkin); 121 Cong. Rec. 37024-37025 (1975) (remarks of Rep. Brademas); 121 Cong. Rec. 37027 (1975) (remarks of Rep. Gude); 121 Cong. Rec. 37410 (1975) (remarks of Sen. Randolph); 121 Cong. Rec. 37416 (1975) (Remarks of Sen. Williams).

The desire to provide handicapped children with an attainable degree of personal independence obviously anticipated that state educational programs would confer educational benefits upon such children. But at the same time, the goal of achieving some degree of self sufficiency in most cases is a good deal more modest than the potential-maximizing goal adopted by the lower courts.

Despite its frequent mention, we cannot conclude, as did the dissent in the Court of

The determination of when handicapped children are receiving sufficient educational benefits to satisfy the requirements of the Act presents a
more difficult problem. The Act requires participating States to educate a
wide spectrum of handicapped children, from the marginally hearing-impaired to the profoundly retarded and palsied. It is clear that the benefits
obtainable by children at one end of the spectrum will differ dramatically
from those obtained by children at the other end, with infinite variations in
between. One child may have little difficulty competing successfully in an
academic setting with nonhandicapped children while another child may en-
counter great difficulty in acquiring even the most basic of self-maintenance
skills. We do not attempt today to establish any one test for determining the
adequacy of educational benefits conferred upon all children covered by the
Act. Because in this case we are presented with a handicapped child who is
receiving substantial specialized instruction and related services, and who is
performing above average in the regular classrooms of a public school system, we confine our analysis to that situation.

The Act requires participating States to educate handicapped children
with nonhandicapped children whenever possible.[24] When that "mainstreaming" preference of the Act has been met and a child is being educated in the
regular classrooms of a public school system, the system itself monitors the
educational progress of the child. Regular examinations are administered,
grades are awarded, and yearly advancement to higher grade levels is permitted for those children who attain an adequate knowledge of the course material. The grading and advancement system thus constitutes an important
factor in determining educational benefit. Children who graduate from our
public school systems are considered by our society to have been "educated"
at least to the grade level they have completed, and access to an "education"
for handicapped children is precisely what Congress sought to provide in the
Act.[25]

Appeals, the self sufficiency was itself the substantive standard which Congress imposed upon the States. Because many mildly handicapped children will achieve self
sufficiency without state assistance while personal independence for the severely
handicapped may be an unreachable goal, "self sufficiency" as a substantive standard is at once an inadequate protection and an overly demanding requirement. We
thus view these references in the legislative history as evidence of Congress' intention
that the services provided handicapped children be educationally beneficial, whatever
the nature of severity of their handicap.

[24]Section 1412(5) of the Act requires that participating States establish "procedures
to assure that, to the maximum extent appropriate, handicapped children, including
children in public or private institutions or other care facilities, are educated with
children who are not handicapped, and that special classes, separate schooling, or
other removal of handicapped children from the regular educational environment
occurs only when the nature of severity of the handicap is such that education in
regular classes with the use of supplementary aids and services cannot be achieved
satisfactorily."

[25]We do not hold today that every handicapped child who is advancing from grade
to grade in a regular public school system is automatically receiving a "free appropriate public education." In this case, however, we find Amy's academic progress, when
considered with the special services and professional consideration accorded by the
Furnace Woods school administrators, to be dispositive.

C

When the language of the Act and its legislative history are considered together, the requirements imposed by Congress become tolerably clear. Insofar as a State is required to provide a handicapped child with a "free appropriate public education," we hold that it satisfies this requirement by providing personalized instruction with sufficient support services to permit the child to benefit educationally from that instruction. Such instruction and services must be provided at public expense, must meet the State's educational standards, must approximate the grade levels used in the State's regular education, and must comport with the child's IEP. In addition, the IEP, and therefore the personalized instruction, should be formulated in accordance with the requirements of the Act and, if the child is being educated in the regular classrooms of the public education system, should be reasonably calculated to enable the child to achieve passing marks and advance from grade to grade.[26]

IV

A

As mentioned in Part I, the Act permits "[a]ny party aggrieved by the findings and decision" of the state administrative hearings "to bring a civil action" in "any State court of competent jurisdiction or in a district court of the United States without regard to the amount in controversy." § 1415(e)(2). The complaint, and therefore the civil action, may concern "any matter relating to the identification, evaluation, or educational placement of the child, or the provision of a free appropriate public education to such child." § 1415(b)(1)(E). In reviewing the complaint, the Act provides that a court

---

[26]In defending the decisions of the District Court and the Court of Appeals, respondents and the United States rely upon isolated statements in the legislative history concerning the achievement of maximum potential, see H.R. Rep. No. 94-332, *supra*, at 13, as support for their contention that Congress intended to impose greater substantive requirements than we have found. These statements, however, are too thin a reed on which to base an interpretation of the Act which disregards both its language and the balance of its legislative history. "Passing references and isolated phrases are not controlling when analyzing a legislative history." *Department of State* v. *The Washington Post Co.,* 456 U.S. 595 (1982)

Moreover, even were we to agree that these statements evince a congressional intent to maximize each child's potential, we could not hold that Congress had successfully imposed that burden upon the States.

"[L]egislation enacted pursuant to the spending power is much in the nature of a contract: in return for federal funds, the States agree to comply with federally imposed conditions. The legitimacy of Congress' power to legislate under the spending power thus rests on whether the State voluntarily and knowingly accepts the terms of the 'contract.' . . . Accordingly, if Congress intends to impose a condition on the grant of federal moneys, it must do so unambiguously." *Pennhurst State School* v. *Halderman,* 451 U.S. 1, 17(1981).

As already demonstrated, the Act and its history impose no requirements on the States like those imposed by the District Court and the Court of Appeals. *A fortiori* Congress has not done so unambiguously, as required in the valid exercise of its spending power.

"shall receive the record of the [state] administrative proceeding, shall hear additional evidence at the request of a party, and, basing its decision on the preponderance of the evidence, shall grant such relief as the court determines is appropriate." § 1415(e)(2).

The parties disagree sharply over the meaning of these provisions, petitioners contending that courts are given only limited authority to review for state compliance with the Act's procedural requirements and no power to review the substance of the state program, and respondents contending that the Act requires courts to exercise *de novo* review over state educational decisions and policies. We find petitioners' contention unpersuasive, for Congress expressly rejected provisions that would have so severely restricted the role of reviewing courts. In substituting the current language of the statute for language that would have made state administrative findings conclusive if supported by substantial evidence, The Conference Committee explained that courts were to make "independent decision[s] based on a preponderance of the evidence." S. Cong. Rec. 37416 (1975) (remarks of Sen. Williams).

But although we find that this grant of authority is broader than claimed by petitioners, we think the fact that it is found in § 1415 of the Act, which is entitled "Procedural Safeguards," is not without significance. When the elaborate and highly specific procedural safeguards embodied in § 1415 are contrasted with the general and somewhat imprecise substantive admonitions contained in the Act, we think that the importance Congress attached to these procedural safeguards cannot be gainsaid. It seems to us no exaggeration to say that Congress placed every bit as much emphasis upon compliance with procedures giving parents and guardians a large measure of participation at every stage of the administrative process, see, e. g. § 1415(a)-(d), as it did upon the measurement of the resulting IEP against a substantive standard. We think that the Congressional emphasis upon full participation of concerned parties throughout the development of the IEP, as well as the requirements that state and local plans be submitted to the Commissioner for approval, demonstrate the legislative conviction that adequate compliance with the procedures prescribed would in most cases assure much if not all of what Congress wished in the way of substantive content in an IEP.

Thus the provision that a reviewing court base its decision on the "preponderance of the evidence" is by no means an invitation to the courts to substitute their own notions of sound educational policy for those of the school authorities which they review. The very importance which Congress has attached to compliance with certain procedures in the preparation of an IEP would be frustrated if a court were permitted simply to set state decisions at nought. The fact that § 1415(e) requires that the reviewing court "receive the records of the [state] administrative proceedings" carries with it the implied requirement that due weight shall be given to these proceedings. And we find nothing in the Act to suggest that merely because Congress was rather sketchy in establishing substantive requirements, as opposed to procedural requirements of the preparation of an IEP, it intended that reviewing courts should have a free hand to impose substantive standards of review which cannot be derived from the Act itself. In short, the statutory authorization to grant "such relief as the court determines is appropriate" cannot be read without reference to the obligations, largely procedural in nature, which are imposed upon recipient States by Congress.

Therefore, a court's inquiry in suits brought under § 1415(e)(2) is twofold. First, has the State complied with the procedures set forth in the Act?[27] And second, is the individualized educational program developed through the Act's procedures reasonably calculated to enable the child to receive educational benefits?[28] If these requirements are met, the State has complied with the obligations imposed by Congress and the Courts can require no more.

B

In assuring that the requirements of the Act have been met, courts must be careful to avoid imposing their view of preferable educational methods upon the States.[29] The primary responsibility for formulating the education to be accorded a handicapped child, and for choosing the educational method most suitable to the child's needs, was left by the Act to state and local educational agencies in cooperation with the parents or guardian of the child. The Act expressly charges States with the responsibility of "acquiring and disseminating to teachers and administrators of programs for handicapped children significant information derived from educational research, demonstration, and similar projects, and [of] adopting, where appropriate, promising educational practices and materials." § 1413(a)(3). In the face of such a clear statutory directive, it seems highly unlikely that Congress intended courts to overturn a State's choice of appropriate educational theories in a proceeding conducted pursuant to § 1415(e)(2).[30]

We previously have cautioned that courts lack the "specialized knowledge and experience" necessary to resolve "persistent and difficult questions of educational policy." *San Antonio School District* v. *Rodriguez,* 411 U. S. 1, 42 (1973). We think that Congress shared that view when it passed the Act. As already demonstrated, Congress' intention was not that the Act displace the primacy of States in the field of education, but that States receive funds to assist them in extending their educational systems to the handicapped.

---

[27]This inquiry will require a court not only to satisfy itself that the State has adopted the state plan, policies, and assurances required by the Act, but also to determine that the State has created an IEP for the child in question which conforms with the requirements of § 1401(19).

[28]When the handicapped child is being educated in the regular classrooms of a public school system, the achievement of passing marks and advancement from grade to grade will be one important factor in determining educational benefit. See Part III, *supra.*.

[29]In this case, for example, both the state hearing officer and the District Court were presented with evidence as to the best method for educating the deaf, a question long debated among scholars. See Large, Special Problems of the Deaf Under the Education for All Handicapped Children Act of 1975, 58 Washington U. L. Q. 213,229 (1980). The District Court accepted the testimony of respondents' experts that there was "a trend supported by studies showing the greater degree of success of students brought up in deaf households using [the method of communication used by the Rowleys]." 483 F. Supp., at 535.

[30]It is clear that Congress was aware of the States' traditional role in the formulation and execution of educational policy. "Historically, the States have had the primary responsibility for the education of children at the elementary and secondary level." 121 Cong. Rec. 19498 (1975) (remarks of Sen. Dole). See also *Epperson* v. *Arkansas,* 393 U. S. 97, 104 (1968) ("[b]y and large, public education in our Nation is committed to the control of state and local authorities").

Therefore, once a court determines that the requirements of the Act have been met, questions of methodology are for resolution by the States.

V

Entrusting a child's education to state and local agencies does not leave the child without protection. Congress sought to protect individual children by providing for parental involvement in the development of State plans and policies, *supra,* at 4-5 and n. 6, and in formulation of the child's individual educational program. As the Senate Report states:

> "The Committee recognizes that in many instances the process of providing special education and related services to handicapped children is not guaranteed to produce any particular outcome. By changing the language [of the provision relating to individualized educational programs] to emphasize the process of parent and child involvement and to provide a written record of reasonable expectations, the Committee intends to clarify that such individualized planning conferences are a way to provide parent involvement and protection to assure that appropriate services are provided to a handicapped child." S. Rep. No. 94-168, *supra,* at 11-12. See also S. Conf. Rep. No. 94-445, p. 30 (1975); 45 CFR § 121a.345 (1980).

As this very case demonstrates, parents and guardians will not lack ardor in seeking to ensure that handicapped children receive all of the benefits to which they are entitled by the Act.[31]

VI

Applying these principles to the facts of this case, we conclude that the Court of Appeals erred in affirming the decision of the District Court. Neither the District Court nor the Court of Appeals found that petitioners had failed to comply with the procedures of the Act, and the findings of neither court would support a conclusion that Amy's educational program failed to comply with the substantive requirements of the Act. On the contrary, the District Court found that the "evidence firmly establishes that Amy is receiving an 'adequate' education, since she performs better than the average child

---

[31]In addition to providing for extensive parental involvement in the formulation of state and local policies, as well as the preparation of individual educational programs, the Act ensures that States will receive the advice of experts in the field of educating handicapped children. As a condition for receiving federal funds under the Act, States must create "an advisory panel, appointed by the Governor or any other official authorized under State law to make such appointments, composed of individuals involved in or concerned with the education of handicapped children, including handicapped individuals, teachers, parents or guardians of handicapped children, State and local education officials, and administrators of programs for handicapped children, which (A) advises that State educational agency of unmet needs within the State in the education of handicapped children, [and] (B) comments publicly on any rules or regulations proposed for issuance by the State regarding the education of handicapped children." § 1413(a)(12).

in her class and is advancing easily from grade to grade." 483 F. Supp., at 534. In light of this finding, and of the fact that Amy was receiving personalized instruction and related services calculated by the Furnace Woods school administrators to meet her educational needs, the lower courts should not have concluded that the Act requires the provision of a sign-language interpreter. Accordingly, the decision of the Court of Appeals is reversed and the case is remanded for further proceedings consistent with this opinion.[32]

So ordered.

---

[32]Because the District Court declined to reach respondents' contention that petitioners had failed to comply with the Act's procedural requirements in developing Amy's IEP, 483 F. Supp., at 533, n. 8, the case must be remanded for further proceedings consistent with this opinion.

Irving Independent School District v. Tatro

U.S. Supreme Court, 468 U.S. 883, 104 S.Ct. 3371 (1984).

Syllabus*

Respondents' 8-year-old daughter was born with a defect known as spina bifida. As a result she suffers from orthopedic and speech impairments and a neurogenic bladder, which prevents her from emptying her bladder voluntarily. Consequently, she must be catheterized every three or four hours to avoid injury to her kidneys. To accomplish this, a procedure known as clean intermittent catheterization (CIC) was prescribed. This is a simple procedure that can be performed in a few minutes by a layperson with less than an hour's training. Since petitioner School District received federal funding under the Education of the Handicapped Act it was required to provide the child with "a free appropriate public education," which is defined in the Act to include "related services," which are defined in turn to include "supportive services (including . . . medical . . . services except that such medical services shall be for diagnostic and evaluation purposes only) as may be required to assist a handicapped child to benefit from special education." Pursuant to the Act, petitioner developed an individualized education program for the child, but the program made no provision for school personnel to administer CIC. After unsuccessfully pursuing administrative remedies to secure CIC services for the child during school hours, respondents brought an action against petitioner and others in Federal District Court, seeking injunctive relief, damages, and attorney's fees. Respondents invoked the Education of the Handicapped Act, arguing that CIC is one of the included "related services" under the statutory definition, and also invoked § 504 of the Rehabilitation Act of 1973, which forbids a person, by reason of a handicap, to be "excluded from the participation in, be denied the benefits of, or be subjected to discrimination under" any program receiving federal aid. After its initial denial of relief was reversed by the Court of Appeals, the District Court, on remand, held that CIC was a "related service" under the Education of the Handicapped Act, ordered that the child's education program be modified to include provision of CIC during school hours, and awarded compensatory damages against petitioner. The court further held that respondents had proved a violation of § 504 of the Rehabilitation Act, and awarded attorney's fees to respondents under § 505 of that Act. The Court of Appeals affirmed.

Held:

1. CIC is a "related service" under the Education of the Handicapped Act.

(a) CIC services qualify as a "supportive servic[e] . . . required to assist a handicapped child to benefit from special education," within the meaning of the Act. Without CIC services available during the school day, respondents' child cannot attend school and thereby "benefit from special education." Such services are no less related to the effort to educate than are services that enable a child to reach, enter, or exit a school.

(b) The provision of CIC is not subject to exclusion as a "medical service." The Department of Education regulations, which are entitled to deference, define "related services" for handicapped children to include "school health services," which are defined in turn as "services provided by a qualified school nurse or other qualified person," and define "medical services" as "ser-

---

*The syllabus constitutes no part of the opinion of the Court but has been prepared by the Reporter of Decisions for the convenience of the reader.

vices provided by a licensed physician." This definition of "medical services" is a reasonable interpretation of congressional intent to exclude physician's services as such and to impose an obligation to provide school nursing services.

2. Section 504 of the Rehabilitation Act is inapplicable when relief is available under the Education of the Handicapped Act to remedy a denial of educational service, *Smith* v. *Robinson, post,* p. ——, and therefore respondents are not entitled to any relief under § 504, including recovery of attorney's fees.

703 F. 2d 823, affirmed in part and reversed in part.

BURGER, C.J., delivered the opinion of the Court, in which WHITE, BLACKMUN, POWELL, REHNQUIST, and O'CONNOR, JJ., joined, and in all but Part III of which BRENNAN, MARSHALL, and STEVENS, JJ., joined. BRENNAN, J., filed an opinion concurring in part and dissenting in part, in which MARSHALL, J., joined. STEVENS, J., filed an opinion concurring in part and dissenting in part.

CHIEF JUSTICE BURGER delivered the opinion of the Court.

We granted certiorari to determine whether the Education of the Handicapped Act or the Rehabilitation Act of 1973 requires a school district to provide a handicapped child with clean intermittent catheterization during school hours.

I

Amber Tatro is an 8-year-old girl born with a defect known as spina bifida. As a result she suffers from orthopedic and speech impairments and a neurogenic bladder, which prevents her from emptying her bladder voluntarily. Consequently, she must be catheterized every three or four hours to avoid injury to her kidneys. In accordance with accepted medical practice, clean intermittent catheterization (CIC), a procedure involving the insertion of a catheter into the urethra to drain the bladder, has been prescribed. The procedure is a simple one that can be performed in a few minutes by a layperson with less than an hour's training. Amber's parents, babysitter, and teenage brother are all qualified to administer CIC, and Amber soon will be able to perform this procedure herself.

In 1979 petitioner Irving Independent School District agreed to provide special education for Amber, who was then three and one-half years old. In consultation with her parents, who are respondents here, petitioner developed an individualized education program for Amber under the requirements of the Education of the Handicapped Act, 84 Stat. 175, as amended significantly by the Education for All Handicapped Children Act of 1975, 89 Stat. 773, 20 U. S. C. §§ 1401(19), 1414(a)(5). The individualized education program provided that Amber would attend early childhood development classes and receive special services such as physical and occupational therapy. That program, however, made no provision for school personnel to administer CIC.

Respondents unsuccessfully pursued administrative remedies to secure

CIC services for Amber during school hours.[1] In October 1979 respondents brought the present action in District Court against petitioner, the State Board of Education, and others. See § 1415(e)(2). They sought an injunction ordering petitioner to provide Amber with CIC and sought damages and attorney's fees. First, respondents invoked the Education of the Handicapped Act. Because Texas received funding under that statute, petitioner was required to provide Amber with a "free appropriate public education," §§1412(1), 1414(a)(1)(C)(ii), which is defined to include "related services," § 1401(18). Respondents argued that CIC is one such "related service."[2] Second, respondents invoked § 504 of the Rehabilitation Act of 1973, 87 Stat. 394, as amended, 29 U. S. C. § 794, which forbids an individual, by reason of a handicap, to be "excluded from the participation in, be denied the benefits of, or be subjected to discrimination under" any program receiving federal aid.

The District Court denied respondents' request for a preliminary injunction. *Tatro* v. *Texas*, 481 F. Supp. 1224 (ND Tex. 1979). That court concluded that CIC was not a "related service" under the Education of the Handicapped Act because it did not serve a need arising from the effort to educate. It also held that § 504 of the Rehabilitation Act did not require "the setting up of governmental health care for people seeking to participate" in federally funded programs. *Id.*, at 1229.

The Court of Appeals reversed. *Tatro* v. *Texas*, 625 F. 2d 557 (CA5 1980) (*Tatro I*). First, it held that CIC was a "related service" under the Education of the Handicapped Act, 20 U. S. C. § 1401(17), because without the procedure Amber could not attend classes and benefit from special education. Second, it held that petitioner's refusal to provide CIC effectively excluded her from a federally funded educational program in violation of § 504 of the Rehabilitation Act. The Court of Appeals remanded for the District Court to develop a factual record and apply these legal principles.

On remand petitioner stressed the Education of the Handicapped Act's explicit provision that "medical services" could qualify as "related services" only when they served the purpose of diagnosis or evaluation. See n. 2, *supra*. The District Court held that under Texas law a nurse or other qualified person may administer CIC without engaging in the unauthorized practice of medicine, provided that a doctor prescribes and supervises the procedure. The District Court then held that, because a doctor was not needed to administer CIC, provision of the procedure was not a "medical service" for purposes of the Education of the Handicapped Act. Finding CIC to be a "related service" under that Act, the District Court ordered petitioner and the State Board of Education to modify Amber's individualized education program to include provision of CIC during school hours. It also awarded

---

[1]The Education of the Handicapped Act's procedures for administrative hearings are set out in 20 U. S. C. § 1415. In this case a hearing officer ruled that the Education of the Handicapped Act did require the school to provide CIC, and the Texas Commissioner of Education adopted the hearing officer's decision. The State Board of Education reversed, holding that the Act did not require petitioner to provide CIC.

[2]As discussed more fully later, the Education of the Handicapped Act defines "related services" to include "supportive services (including . . . medical and counseling services, except that such medical services shall be for diagnostic and evaluation purposes only) as may be required to assist a handicapped child to benefit from special education." 20 U. S. C. § 1401(17).

compensatory damages against petitioner.[3] *Tatro* v. *Texas*, 516 F. Supp. 968 (ND Tex. 1981).

On the authority of *Tatro I*, the District Court then held that respondents had proved a violation of § 504 of the Rehabilitation Act. Although the District Court did not rely on this holding to authorize any greater injunctive or compensatory relief, it did invoke the holding to award attorney's fees against petitioner and the State Board of Education.[4] 516 F. Supp., at 968; App. to Pet. for Cert. 55a-63a. The Rehabilitation Act, unlike the Education of the Handicapped Act, authorizes prevailing parties to recover attorney's fees. See 29 U. S. C. § 794a.

The Court of Appeals affirmed. *Tatro* v. *Texas*, 703 F. 2d 823 (CA5 1983) *(Tatro II)*. That court accepted the District Court's conclusion that state law permitted qualified persons to administer CIC without the physical presence of a doctor, and it affirmed the award of relief under the Education of the Handicapped Act. In affirming the award of attorney's fees based on a finding of liability under the Rehabilitation Act, the Court of Appeals held that no change of circumstances since *Tatro I* justified a different result.

We granted certiorari, 464 U. S. 1007 (1983), and we affirm in part and reverse in part.

II

This case poses two separate issues. The first is whether the Education of the Handicapped Act requires petitioner to provide CIC services to Amber. The second is whether § 504 of the Rehabilitation Act creates such an obligation. We first turn to the claim presented under the Education of the Handicapped Act.

States receiving funds under the Act are obliged to satisfy certain conditions. A primary condition is that the state implement a policy "that assures all handicapped children the right to a free appropriate public education." 20 U. S. C. § 1412(1). Each educational agency applying to a state for funding must provide assurances in turn that its program aims to provide "a free appropriate public education to all handicapped children." § 1414(a)(1)(C)(ii).

A "free appropriate public education" is explicitly defined as "special education and related services." § 1401(18).[5] The term "special education" means

---

[3]The District Court dismissed the claims against all defendants other than petitioner and the State Board, though it retained the members of the State Board "in their official capacities for the purpose of injunctive relief." 516 F. Supp., at 972-974.

[4]The District Court held that § 505 of the Rehabilitation Act, 29 U. S. C. § 794a, which authorizes attorney's fees as a part of a prevailing party's costs, abrogated the State Board's immunity under the Eleventh Amendment. See App. to Pet. for Cert. 56a-60a. The State Board did not petition for certiorari, and the Eleventh Amendment issue is not before us.

[5]Specifically, the "special education and related services" must

"(A) have been provided at public expense, under public supervision and direction, and without charge, (B) meet the standards of the State educational agency, (C) include an appropriate preschool, elementary, or secondary school education in the State involved, and (D) [be] provided in conformity with the individualized education program required under section 1414(a)(5) of this title." § 1401(18).

"specially designed instruction, at no cost to parents or guardians, to meet the unique needs of a handicapped child, including classroom instruction, instruction in physical education, home instruction, and instruction in hospitals and institutions." § 1401(16).

"Related service" are defined as

"transportation, and such developmental, corrective, and other *supportive services (including* speech pathology and audiology, psychological services, physical and occupational therapy, recreation, and *medical* and counseling *services, except that such medical services shall be for diagnostic and evaluation purposes only) as may be required to assist a handicapped child to benefit from special education*, and includes the early identification and assessment of handicapping conditions in children." § 1401(17)(emphasis added).

The issue in this case is whether CIC is a "related service" that petitioner is obliged to provide to Amber. We must answer two questions: first, whether CIC is a "supportive servic[e] . . . required to assist a handicapped child to benefit from special education"; and second, whether CIC is excluded from this definition as a "medical servic[e]" serving purposes other than diagnosis or evaluation.

A

The Court of Appeals was clearly correct in holding that CIC is a "supportive servic[e] . . . required to assist a handicapped child to benefit from special education."[6] It is clear on this record that, without having CIC services available during the school day, Amber cannot attend school and thereby "benefit from special education." CIC services therefore fall squarely within the definition of a "supportive service"[7]

As we have stated before, "Congress sought primarily to make public education available to handicapped children" and "to make such access

---

[6]Petitioner claims that courts deciding cases arising under the Education of the Handicapped Act are limited to inquiring whether a school district has followed the requirements of the state plan and has followed the Acts's procedural requirements. However, we held in *Board of Education of Hendrick Hudson Central School District v. Rowley*, 458 U. S. 176, 206, n. 27 (1982), that a court is required "not only to satisfy itself that the State has adopted the state plan, policies, and assurances required by the Act, but also to determine that the State has created an [individualized education plan] for the child in question which conforms with the requirements of § 1401(19) [defining such plans]." Judicial review is equally appropriate in this case, which presents the legal question of a school's substantive obligation under the "related services" requirement of § 1401(197).

[7]The Department of Education has agreed with this reasoning in an interpretive ruling that specifically found CIC to be a "related service." 46 Fed. Reg. 4912 (1981). Accord *Tokarcik* v. *Forest Hills School District*, 665 F. 2d 443 (CA3 1981), cert. denied *sub nom.* *Scanlon* v. *Tokarcik*, 458 U. S. 1121 (1982). The Secretary twice postponed temporarily the effective date of this interpretive ruling, see 46 Fed. Reg. 12495 (1981); *id.* at 18975, and later postponed it indefinitely, *id.* at 25614. But the Department presently does view CIC services as an allowable cost under Part B of the Act. *Ibid.*

meaningful." *Board of Education of Hendrick Hudson Central School District* v. *Rowley*, 458 U. S. 176, 192 (1982). A service that enables a handicapped child to remain at school during the day is an important means of providing the child with the meaningful access to education that Congress envisioned. The Act makes specific provision for services, like transportation, for example, that do no more than enable a child to be physically present in class, see 20 U. S. C. § 1401(17); and the Act specifically authorizes grants for schools to alter buildings and equipment to make them accessible to the handicapped, § 1406; see S. Rep, No. 94-168, p. 38 (1975); 121 Cong. Rec. 19483-19484 (1975) (remarks of Sen. Stafford). Services like CIC that permit a child to remain at school during the day are no less related to the effort to educate than are services that enable the child to reach, enter, or exit the school.

We hold that CIC services in this case qualify as a "supportive servic[e] . . . required to assist a handicapped child to benefit from special education."[8]

B

We also agree with the Court of Appeals that provision of CIC is not a "medical servic[e]," which a school is required to provide only for purposes of diagnosis or evaluation. See 20 U. S. C. § 1401(17). We begin with the regulations of the Department of Education, which are entitled to deference.[9] See, *e. g., Blum* v. *Bacon*, 457 U. S. 132, 141 (1982). The regulations define "related services" for handicapped children to include "school health services," 34 CFR § 300.13(a)(1983), which are defined in turn as "services provided by a qualified school nurse or other qualified person," § 300.13(b)(10). "Medical services" are defined as "services provided by a licensed physician." § 300.13(b)(4).[10] Thus, the Secretary has determined that the services of a school nurse otherwise qualifying as a "related service" are not subject to exclusion as a "medical service," but that the services of a physician are excludable as such.

---

[8]The obligation to provide special education and related services is expressly phrased as a "conditio[n]" for a state to receive funds under the Act. See 20 U. S. C. § 1412; see also S. Rep. No. 94-168, p. 16 (1975). This refutes petitioner's contention that the Act did not "impos[e] an obligation on the States to spend state money to fund certain rights as a condition of receiving federal moneys" but "spoke merely in precatory terms," *Pennhurst State School and Hospital* v. *Halderman*, 451 U. S. 1, 18 (1981).

[9]The Secretary of Education is empowered to issue such regulations as may be necessary to carry out the provisions of the Act. 20 U. S. C. § 1417(b). This function was initially vested in the Commissioner of Education of the Department of Health, Education, and Welfare, who promulgated the regulations in question. This function was transferred to the Secretary of Education when Congress created that position, see Department of Education Organization Act. §§ 301(a)(1), (2)(H), 93 Stat. 677, 20 U. S. C. §§ 3441(a)(1), (2)(H).

[10]The regulations actually define only those "medical services" that *are* owed to handicapped children: "services provided by a licensed physician to determine a child's medically related handicapping condition which results in the child's need for special education and related services." 34 CFR § 300.13(b)(4) (1983). Presumably this means that "medical services" *not* owed under the statute are those "services by a licensed physician" that serve other purposes.

This definition of "medical services" is a reasonable interpretation of congressional intent. Although Congress devoted little discussion to the "medical services" exclusion, the Secretary could reasonably have concluded that it was designed to spare schools from an obligation to provide a service that might well prove unduly expensive and beyond the range of their competence.[11] From this understanding of congressional purpose, the Secretary could reasonably have concluded that Congress intended to impose the obligation to provide school nursing services.

Congress plainly required schools to hire various specially trained personnel to help handicapped children, such as "trained occupational therapists, speech therapists, psychologists, social workers and other appropriately trained personnel." S. Rep. No. 94-168, *supra*, at 33. School nurses have long been a part of the educational system, and the Secretary could therefore reasonably conclude that school nursing services are not the sort of burden that Congress intended to exclude as a "medical service." By limiting the "medical services" exclusion to the services of a physician or hospital, both far more expensive, the Secretary has given a permissible construction to the provision.

Petitioner's contrary interpretation of the "medical services" exclusion is unconvincing. In petitioner's view, CIC is a "medical service," even though it may be provided by a nurse or trained layperson; that conclusion rests on its reading of Texas law that confines CIC to uses in accordance with a physician's prescription and under a physician's ultimate supervision. Aside from conflicting with the Secretary's reasonable interpretation of congressional intent, however, such a rule would be anomalous. Nurses in petitioner's school district are authorized to dispense oral medications and administer emergency injections in accordance with a physician's prescription. This kind of service for nonhandicapped children is difficult to distinguish from the provision of CIC to the handicapped.[12] It would be strange indeed if Congress, in attempting to extend special services to handicapped children, were unwilling to guarantee them services of a kind that are routinely provided to the nonhandicapped.

To keep in perspective the obligation to provide services that relate to both the health and educational needs of handicapped students, we note several limitations that should minimize the burden petitioner fears. First, to be entitled to related services, a child must be handicapped so as to require

---

[11]Children with serious medical needs are still entitled to an education. For example, the Act specifically includes instruction in hospitals and at home within the definition of "special education." See 20 U. S. C. § 1401(16).

[12]Petitioner attempts to distinguish the administration of prescription drugs from the administration of CIC on the ground that Texas law expressly limits the liability of school personnel performing the former, see Tex. Educ. Code Ann. § 21.914(c) (Supp. 1984), but not the latter. This distinction, however, bears no relation to whether CIC is a "related service." The introduction of handicapped children into a school creates numerous new possibilities for injury and liability. Many of these risks are more serious than that posed by CIC, which the courts below found is a safe procedure even when performed by a 9-year-old girl. Congress assumed that states receiving the generous grants under the Act were up to the job of managing these new risks. Whether petitioner decides to purchase more liability insurance or to persuade the state to extend the limitation on liability, the risks posed by CIC should not prove to be a large burden.

special education. See 20 U. S. C. § 1401(1); 34 CFR § 300.5 (1983). In the absence of a handicap that requires special education, the need for what otherwise might qualify as a related service does not create an obligation under the Act. See 34 CFR § 300.14, Comment (1) (1983).

Second, only those services necessary to aid a handicapped child to benefit from special education must be provided, regardless how easily a school nurse or layperson could furnish them. For example, if a particular medication or treatment may appropriately be administered to a handicapped child other than during the school day, a school is not required to provide nursing services to administer it.

Third, the regulations state that school nursing services must be provided only if they can be performed by a nurse or other qualified person, not if they must be performed by a physician. See 34 CFR §§/300.13(a), (b)(4), (b)(10) (1983). It bears mentioning that here not even the services of a nurse are required; as is conceded, a layperson with minimal training is qualified to provide CIC. See also, *e. g., Department of Education of Hawaii* v. *Katherine D.*, 727 F. 2d 809 (CA9 1983).

Finally, we note that respondents are not asking petitioner to provide *equipment* that Amber needs for CIC. Tr. of Oral Arg. 18-19. They seek only the *services* of a qualified person at the school.

We conclude that provision of CIC to Amber is not subject to exclusion as a "medical service," and we affirm the Court of Appeals' holding that CIC is a "related service" under the Education of the Handicapped Act.[13]

III

Respondents sought relief not only under the Education of the Handicapped Act but under § 504 of the Rehabilitation Act as well. After finding petitioner liable to provide CIC under the former, the District Court proceeded to hold that petitioner was similarly liable under § 504 and that respondents were therefore entitled to attorney's fees under § 505 of the Rehabilitation Act, 29 U. S. C. § 794a. We hold today, in *Smith* v. *Robinson,* 468 U. S. 992 (1984), that § 504 is inapplicable when relief is available under the Education of the Handicapped Act to remedy a denial of educational services. Respondents are therefore not entitled to relief under § 504, and we reverse the Court of Appeals' holding that respondents are entitled to recover attorney's fees. In all other respects, the judgment of the Court of Appeals is affirmed.

It is so ordered.

---

[13]We need not address respondents' claim that CIC, in addition to being a "related service," is a "supplementary ai[d] and servic[e]" that petitioner must provide to enable Amber to attend classes with nonhandicapped students under the Act's "mainstreaming" directive. See 20 U. S. C. § 1412(5)(B). Respondents have not sought an order prohibiting petitioner from educating Amber with handicapped children alone. Indeed, any request for such an order might not present a live controversy. Amber's present individualized education program provides for regular public school classes with nonhandicapped children. And petitioner has admitted that it would be far more costly to pay for Amber's instruction and CIC services at a private school, or to arrange for home tutoring, than to provide CIC at the regular public school placement provided in her current individualized education program. Tr. of Oral Arg. 12.

Burlington School Committee v. Department of Education of Massachusetts

U.S. Supreme Court, 471 U.S. 359, 105 S.Ct. 1996 (1985).

Syllabus*

The Education of the Handicapped Act requires participating state and local educational agencies to assure that handicapped children and their parents are guaranteed procedural safeguards with respect to the provision of free appropriate public education for such children. These procedures include the parents' right to participate in the development of an "individualized education program" (IEP) for the child and to challenge in administrative and court proceedings a proposed IEP with which they disagree. With respect to judicial review, the Act in 20 U. S. C. § 1415(e)(2) authorizes the reviewing court to "grant such relief as the court determines is appropriate." Section 1415(e)(3) provides that during the pendency of any review proceedings, unless the state or local educational agency and the parents otherwise agree, "the child shall remain in the then current educational placement of such child." Respondent father of a handicapped child rejected petitioner town's proposed IEP for the 1979-1980 school year calling for placement of the child in a certain public school, and sought review by respondent Massachusetts Department of Education's Bureau of Special Education Appeals (BSEA). Meanwhile, the father, at his own expense, enrolled the child in a state-approved private school for special education. The BSEA thereafter decided that the town's proposed IEP was inappropriate and that the private school was better suited for the child's educational needs, and ordered the town to pay the child's expenses at the private school for the 1979-1980 school year. The town then sought review in Federal District Court. Ultimately, after the town in the meantime had agreed to pay for the child's private-school placement for the 1980-1981 school year but refused to reimburse the father for the 1979-1980 school year as ordered by the BSEA, the court overturned the BSEA's decision, holding that the appropriate 1979-1980 placement was the one proposed in the IEP and that the town was not responsible for the costs at the private school for the 1979-1980 through 1981-1982 school years. The Court of Appeals, remanding, held that the father's unilateral change of the child's placement during the pendency of the administrative proceedings would not be a bar to reimbursement if such change were held to be appropriate.

Held:

1. The grant of authority to a reviewing court under § 1415(e)(2) includes the power to order school authorities to reimburse parents for their expenditures on private special education for a child if the court ultimately determines that such placement, rather than a proposed IEP, is proper under the Act. The ordinary meaning of the language in § 1415(e)(2) directing the court to "grant such relief as [it] determines is appropriate" confers broad discretion on the court. To deny such reimbursement would mean that the child's right to a free appropriate public education, the parents' right to participate fully in developing a proper IEP, and all of the procedural safeguards of the Act would be less than complete.

---

2. A parental violation of § 1415(e)(3) by changing the "then current educational placement" of their child during the pendency of proceedings to review a challenged proposed IEP does not constitute a waiver of the parents' right to reimbursement for expenses of the private placement. Otherwise, the parents would be forced to leave the child in what may turn out to be an inappropriate educational placement or to obtain the appropriate placement only by sacrificing any claim for reimbursement. But if the courts ultimately determine that the proposed IEP was appropriate, the parents would be barred from obtaining reimbursement for any interim period in which their child's placement violated § 1415(e)(3).

736 F. 2d 773, affirmed.

REHNQUIST, J., delivered the opinion for a unanimous Court.

JUSTICE REHNQUIST delivered the opinion of the Court.

The Education of the Handicapped Act (Act), 84 Stat. 175, as amended, 20 U. S. C. § 1401 *et seq.*, requires participating state and local educational agencies "to assure that handicapped children and their parents or guardians are guaranteed procedural safeguards with respect to the provision of free appropriate public education" to such handicapped children. § 1415(a). These procedures include the right of the parents to participate in the development of an "individualized education program" (IEP) for the child and to challenge in administrative and court proceedings a proposed IEP with which they disagree. §§ 1401(19), 1415(b),(d),(e). Where as in the present case review of a contested IEP takes years to run its course—years critical to the child's development—important practical questions arise concerning interim placement of the child and financial responsibility for that placement. This case requires us to address some of those questions.

Michael Panico, the son of respondent Robert Panico, was a first grader in the public school system of petitioner Town of Burlington, Massachusetts, when he began experiencing serious difficulties in school. It later became evident that he had "specific learning disabilities" and thus was "handicapped" within the meaning of the Act, 20 U. S. C. § 1401(1). This entitled him to receive at public expense specially designed instruction to meet his unique needs, as well as related transportation. §§ 1401(16), 1401(17). The negotiations and other proceedings between the Town and the Panicos, thus far spanning more than 8 years, are too involved to relate in full detail; the following are the parts relevant to the issues on which we granted certiorari.

In the spring of 1979, Michael attended the third grade of the Memorial School, a public school in Burlington, Mass., under an IEP calling for individual tutoring by a reading specialist for one hour a day and individual and group counselling. Michael's continued poor performance and the fact that Memorial School encompassed only grades K through 3 led to much discussion between his parents and Town school officials about his difficulties and his future schooling. Apparently the course of these discussions did not run smoothly; the upshot was that the Panicos and the Town agreed that Michael was generally of above average to superior intelligence, but had special educational needs calling for a placement in a school other than Memorial. They disagreed over the source and exact nature of Michael's learning difficulties, the Town believing the source to be emotional and the parents believing it to be neurological.

In late June, the Town presented the Panicos with a proposed IEP for Michael for the 1979-1980 academic year. It called for placing Michael in a highly structured class of six children with special academic and social needs, located at another Town public school, the Pine Glen School. On July 3, Michael's father rejected the proposed IEP and sought review under § 1415(b)(2) by respondent Massachusetts Department of Education's Bureau of Special Education Appeals (BSEA). A hearing was initially scheduled for August 8, but was apparently postponed in favor of a mediation session on August 17. The mediation efforts proved unsuccessful.

Meanwhile the Panicos received the results of the latest expert evaluation of Michael by specialists at Massachusetts General Hospital, who opined that Michael's "emotional difficulties are secondary to a rather severe learning disorder characterized by perceptual difficulties" and recommended "a highly specialized setting for children with learning handicaps . . . such as the Carroll School," a state approved private school for special education located in Lincoln, Mass. App. 26, 31. Believing that the Town's proposed placement of Michael at the Pine Glen school was inappropriate in light of Michael's needs, Mr. Panico enrolled Michael in the Carroll School in mid-August at his own expense, and Michael started there in September.

The BSEA held several hearings during the fall of 1979, and in January 1980 the hearing officer decided that the Town's proposed placement at the Pine Glen School was inappropriate and that the Carroll School was "the least restrictive adequate program within the record" for Michael's educational needs. The hearing officer ordered the Town to pay for Michael's tuition and transportation to the Carroll School for the 1979-1980 school year, including reimbursing the Panicos for their expenditures on these items for the school year to date.

The Town sought judicial review of the State's administrative decision in the United States District Court for the District of Massachusetts pursuant to 20 U. S. C. § 1415(e)(2) and a parallel state statute, naming Mr. Panico and the State Department of Education as defendants. In November 1980, the District Court granted summary judgment against the Town on the state-law claim under a "substantial evidence" standard of review, entering a final judgment on this claim under Federal Rule of Civil Procedure 54(b). The Court also set the federal claim for future trial. The Court of Appeals vacated the judgment on the state-law claim, holding that review under the state statute was pre-empted by § 1415(e)(2), which establishes a "preponderance of the evidence" standard of review and which permits the reviewing court to hear additional evidence.

In the meantime, the Town had refused to comply with the BSEA order, the District Court had denied a stay of that order, and the Panicos and the State had moved for preliminary injunctive relief. The State also had threatened outside of the judicial proceedings to freeze all of the Town's special education assistance unless it complied with the BSEA order. Apparently in response to this threat, the Town agreed in February 1981 to pay for Michael's Carroll School placement and related transportation for the 1980-1981 term, none of which had yet been paid, and to continue paying for these expenses until the case was decided. But the Town persisted in refusing to reimburse Mr. Panico for the expenses of the 1979-1980 school year. When the Court of Appeals disposed of the state claim, it also held that under this status quo none of the parties could show irreparable injury and thus none was entitled to a preliminary injunction. The court reasoned that the Town had not shown that Mr. Panico would not be able to repay the tuition and related costs borne by the Town if he ultimately lost on the merits, and Mr. Panico had not shown that he would be irreparably harmed if not reimbursed immediately for past payments which might ultimately be determined to be the Town's responsibility.

On remand, the District Court entered an extensive pretrial order on the Town's federal claim. In denying the Town summary judgment, it ruled that 20 U. S. C. § 1415(e)(3) did not bar reimbursement despite the Town's insistence that the Panicos violated that provision by changing Michael's placement to the Carroll School during the pendency of the administrative proceedings. The court reasoned that § 1415(e)(3) concerned the physical placement of the child and not the right to tuition reimbursement or to procedural review of a contested IEP. The court also dealt with the problem that no IEP had been developed for the 1980-1981 or 1981-1982 school years. It held that its power under § 1415(e)(A) to grant "appropriate" relief upon reviewing the contested IEP for the 1979-1980 school year included the power to grant relief for subsequent school years despite the lack of IEPs for those years. In this connection, however, the court interpreted the statute to place the burden of proof on the Town to upset the BSEA decision that the IEP was inappropriate for 1979-1980 and on the Panicos and the State to show that the relief for subsequent terms was appropriate.

After a 4-day trial, the District Court in August 1982 overturned the BSEA decision, holding that the appropriate 1979-1980 placement for Michael was the one proposed by the town in the IEP and that the parents had failed to show that this placement would not also have been appropriate for subsequent years. Accordingly, the court concluded that the Town was "not responsible for the cost of Michael's education at the Carroll School for the academic years 1979-80 through 1981-82."

In contesting the Town's proposed form of judgment embodying the court's conclusion, Mr. Panico argued that, despite finally losing on the merits of the IEP in August 1982, he should be reimbursed for his expenditures in 1979-1980, that the Town should finish paying for the recently completed 1981-1982 term, and that he should not be required to reimburse the Town for its payments to date, apparently because the school terms in question fell within the pendency of the administrative and judicial review contemplated by § 1415(e)(2). The case was transferred to another District Judge and consolidated with two other cases to resolve similar issues concerning the reimbursement for expenditures during the pendency of review proceedings.

In a decision on the consolidated case, the court rejected Mr. Panico's argument that the Carroll School was the "current educational placement" during the pendency of the review proceedings and thus that under § 1415(e)(3) the Town was obligated to maintain that placement. Doe v. Anrig, 561 F. Supp. 121 (1983). The court reasoned that the Panicos' unilateral action in placing Michael at the Carroll School without the Town's consent could not "confer thereon the imprimatur of continued placement," id., at 129, n. 5, even though strictly speaking there was no actual placement in effect during the summer of 1979 because all parties agreed Michael was finished with the Memorial School and the Town itself proposed in the IEP to transfer him to a new school in the fall.

The District Court next rejected an argument, apparently grounded at least in part on a state regulation, that the Panicos were entitled to rely on the BSEA decision upholding their placement contrary to the IEP, regardless of whether that decision were ultimately reversed by a court. With respect to the payments made by the Town after the BSEA decision, under the State's threat to cut off funding, the court criticized the State for resorting to extrajudicial pressure to enforce a decision subject to further review. Because this "was not a case where the town was legally obliged under section 1415(e)(3) to continue payments preserving the status quo," the State's coercion could not be viewed as "the basis for a final decision on liability" and it could only be "regarded as other than wrongful . . . on the assumption that the payments were to be returned if the order was ultimately reversed." *Id.*, at 130. The court entered a judgment ordering the Panicos to reimburse the Town for its payments for Michael's Carroll placement and related transportation in 1980-1981 and 1981-1982. The Panicos appealed.

In a broad opinion, most of which we do not review, the Court of Appeals for the First Circuit remanded the case a second time. 736 F. 2d 773 (1984). The court ruled, among other things, that the District Court erred in conducting a full trial *de novo*, that it gave insufficient weight to the BSEA findings, and that in other respects it did not properly evaluate the IEP. The court also considered several questions about the availability of reimbursement for interim placement. The Town argued that § 1415(e)(3) bars the Panicos from any reimbursement relief, even if on remand they were to prevail on the merits of the IEP, because of their unilateral change of Michael's placement during the pendency of the § 1415(e)(2) proceedings. The court held that such unilateral parental change of placement would not be "a bar to reimbursement of the parents if their actions are held to be appropriate at final judgment." *Id.*, at 799. In dictum the court suggested, however, that a lack of parental consultation with the Town or "attempt to achieve a negotiated compromise and agreement on a private placement," as contemplated by the Act, "may be taken into account in a district court's computation of an award of equitable reimbursement." *Ibid.* To guide the District Court on remand, the court stated that "whether to order reimbursement, and at what amount, is a question determined by balancing the equities." *Id.*, at 801. The court also held that the Panicos' reliance on the BSEA decision would estop the Town from obtaining reimbursement "for the period of reliance and requires that where parents have paid the bill for the period, they must be reimbursed." *Ibid.*

The Town filed a petition for a writ of certiorari in this Court challenging the decision of the Court of Appeals on numerous issues, including the scope of judicial review of the administrative decision and the relevance to the merits of an IEP of violations by local school authorities of the Act's procedural requirements. We granted certiorari, 469 U. S. — (1984), only to consider the following two issues: whether the potential relief available under § 1415(e)(2) includes reimbursement to parents for private school tuition and related expenses, and whether § 1415(e)(3) bars such reimbursement to parents who reject a proposed IEP and place a child in a private school without the consent of local school authorities. We express no opinion on any of the many other views stated by the Court of Appeals.

Congress stated the purpose of the Act in these words:

"to assure that all handicapped children have available to them . . . a free appropriate public education which emphasizes special education and related services designed to meet their unique needs [and] to assure that the rights of handicapped children and their parents or guardians are protected." 20 U. S. C. § 1400(c).

The Act defines a "free appropriate public education" to mean:

"special education and related services which (A) have been provided at public expense, under public supervision and direction, and without charge, (B) meet the standards of the State educational agency, (C) include an appropriate preschool, elementary, or secondary school education in the State involved, and (D) are provided in conformity with [an] individualized education program." 20 U. S. C. § 1401(18).

To accomplish this ambitious objective, the Act provides federal money to state and local educational agencies that undertake to implement the substantive and procedural requirements of the Act. See *Hendrick Hudson District Bd. of Education* v. *Rowley*, 458 U. S. 176, 179-184 (1982).

The *modus operandi* of the Act is the already mentioned "individualized educational program." The IEP is in brief a comprehensive statement of the educational needs of a handicapped child and the specially designed instruction and related services to be employed to meet those needs. § 1401(19). The IEP is to be developed jointly by a school official qualified in special education, the child's teacher, the parents or guardian, and, where appropriate, the child. In several places, the Act emphasizes the participation of the parents in developing the child's educational program and assessing its effectiveness. See §§ 1400(c), 1401(19), 1412(7), 1415(b)(1)(A), (C), (D), (E), and 1415(b)(2); 34 CFR § 300.345 (1984).

Apparently recognizing that this cooperative approach would not always produce a consensus between the school officials and the parents, and that in any disputes the school officials would have a natural advantage, Congress incorporated an elaborate set of what it labeled "procedural safeguards" to insure the full participation of the parents and proper resolution of substantive disagreements. Section 1415(b) entitles the parents "to examine all relevant records with respect to the identification, evaluation, and educational placement of the child," to obtain an independent educational evaluation of the child, to notice of any decision to initiate or change the identification, evaluation, or educational placement of the child, and to present complaints with respect to any of the above. The parents are further entitled to "an impartial due process hearing," which in the instant case was the BSEA hearing, to resolve their complaints.

The Act also provides for judicial review in state or federal court to "[a]ny party aggrieved by the findings and decision" made after the due process hearing. The Act confers on the reviewing court the following authority:

"[T]he court shall receive the records of the administrative proceedings, shall hear additional evidence at the request of a party, and, basing its decision of the preponderance of the evidence, shall grant such relief as the court determines is appropriate." § 1415(e)(2).

The first question on which we granted certiorari requires us to decide whether this grant of authority includes the power to order school authorities to reimburse parents for their expenditures on private special education for a child if the court ultimately determines that such placement, rather than a proposed IEP, is proper under the Act.

We conclude that the Act authorizes such reimbursement. The statute directs the court to "grant such relief as [it] determines is appropriate." The ordinary meaning of these words confers broad discretion on the court. The type of relief is not further specified, except that it must be "appropriate." Absent other reference, the only possible interpretation is that the relief is to be "appropriate" in light of the purpose of the Act. As already noted, this is principally to provide handicapped children with "a free appropriate public education which emphasizes special education and related services designed to meet their unique needs." The Act contemplates that such education will be provided where possible in regular public schools, with the child participating as much as possible in the same activities as nonhandicapped children, but the Act also provides for placement in private schools at public expense where this is not possible. See § 1412(5); 34 CFR §§ 300.132, 300.227, 300.307(b), 300.347 (1984). In a case where a court determines that a private placement desired by the parents was proper under the Act and that an IEP calling for placement in a public school was inappropriate, it seems clear beyond cavil that "appropriate" relief would include a prospective injunction directing the school officials to develop and implement at public expense an IEP placing the child in a private school.

If the administrative and judicial review under the Act could be completed in a matter of weeks, rather than years, it would be difficult to imagine a case in which such prospective injunctive relief would not be sufficient. As this case so vividly demonstrates, however, the review process is ponderous. A final judicial decision on the merits of an IEP will in most instances come a year or more after the school term covered by that IEP has passed. In the meantime, the parents who disagree with the proposed IEP are faced with a choice: go along with the IEP to the detriment of their child if it turns out to be inappropriate or pay for what they consider to be the appropriate placement. If they choose the latter course, which conscientious parents who have adequate means and who are reasonably confident of their assessment normally would, it would be an empty victory to have a court tell them several years later that they were right but that these expenditures could not in a proper case be reimbursed by the school officials. If that were the case, the child's right to a *free* appropriate public education, the parents' right to participate fully in developing a proper IEP, and all of the procedural safeguards would be less than complete. Because Congress undoubtedly did not intend this result, we are confident that by empowering the court to grant "appropriate" relief Congress meant to include retroactive reimbursement to parents as an available remedy in a proper case.

In this Court, the Town repeatedly characterizes reimbursement as "damages," but that simply is not the case. Reimbursement merely requires the Town to belatedly pay expenses that it should have paid all along and would have borne in the first instance had it developed a proper IEP. Such a *post-hoc* determination of financial responsibility was contemplated in the legislative history:

> "If a parent contends that he or she has been forced, at that parent's own expense, to seek private schooling for the child because an appropriate program does not exist within the local educational agency responsible for the child's education and the local educational agency disagrees, that disagreement and *the question of who remains financially responsible* is a matter to which the due process procedures established under [the predecessor to § 1415] appl[y]." S. Rep. No. 94-168, p. 32 (1975) (emphasis added).

See 34 CFR § 300.403(b)(1984) (disagreements and question of financial responsibility subject to the due process procedures).

Regardless of the availability of reimbursement as a form of relief in a proper case, the Town maintains that the Panicos have waived any right they otherwise might have to reimbursement because they violated § 1415(e)(3), which provides:

> "During the pendency of any proceedings conducted pursuant to [§ 1415], unless the State or local educational agency and the parents or guardian otherwise agree, the child shall remain in the then current educational placement of such child. . . ."

We need not resolve the academic question of what Michael's "then current placement" was in the summer of 1979, when both the Town and the parents had agreed that a new school was in order. For the purposes of our decision, we assume that the Pine Glen School, proposed in the IEP, was Michael's current placement and, therefore, that the Panicos did "change" his placement after they had rejected the IEP and had set the administrative review in motion. In so doing, the Panicos contravened the conditional command of § 1415(e)(3) that "the child shall remain in the then current educational placement."

As an initial matter, we note that the section calls for agreement by *either* the *State or* the *local educational agency.* The BSEA's decision in favor of the Panicos and the Carroll School placement would seem to constitute agreement by the State to the change of placement. The decision was issued in January 1980, so from then on the Panicos were no longer in violation of § 1415(e)(3). This conclusion, however, does not entirely resolve the instant dispute because the Panicos are also seeking reimbursement for Michael's expenses during the fall of 1979, prior to the State's concurrence in the Carroll School placement.

We do not agree with the Town that a parental violation of § 1415(e)(3) constitutes a waiver of reimbursement. The provision says nothing about financial responsibility, waiver, or parental right to reimbursement at the conclusion of judicial proceedings. Moreover, if the provision is interpreted to cut off parental rights to reimbursement, the principal purpose of the Act will in many cases be defeated in the same way as if reimbursement were never available. As in this case, parents will often notice a child's learning difficulties while the child is in a regular public school program. If the school officials disagree with the need for special education of the adequacy of the public school's program to meet the child's needs, it is unlikely they will agree to an interim private school placement while the review process runs its course. Thus, under the Town's reading of § 1415(e)(3), the parents are forced to leave the child in what may turn out to be an inappropriate educational placement or to obtain the appropriate placement only by sacrificing any claim for reimbursement. The Act was intended to give handicapped children both an appropriate education and a free one; it should not be interpreted to defeat one or the other of those objectives.

The legislative history supports this interpretation, favoring a proper interim placement pending the resolution of disagreements over the IEP:

> "The conferees are cognizant that an impartial due process hearing may be required to assure that the rights of the child have been completely protected. We did feel, however, that the placement, or change of placement should not be unnecessarily delayed while long and tedious administrative appeals were being exhausted. Thus the conference adopted a flexible approach to try to meet the needs of both the child and the State." 121 Cong. Rec. 37412 (1975) (Sen. Stafford).

We think at least one purpose of § 1415(e)(3) was to prevent school officials from removing a child from the regular public school classroom over the parents' objection pending completion of the review proceedings. As we observed in *Rowley*, 458 U. S., at 192, the impetus for the Act came from two federal court decisions, *Pennsylvania Assn. for Retarded Children* v. *Commonwealth*, 334 F. Supp. 1257 (ED Pa. 1971), and 343 F. Supp. 279 (1972), and *Mills* v. *Board of Education of District of Columbia*, 348 F. Supp. 866 (DC 1972), which arose from the efforts of parents of handicapped children to prevent the exclusion or expulsion of their children from the public schools. Congress was concerned about the apparently widespread practice of relegating handicapped children to private institutions or warehousing them in special classes. See § 1400(4); 34 CFR § 300.347(a) (1984). We also note that § 1415(e)(3) is located in a section detailing procedural safeguards which are largely for the benefit of the parents and the child.

This is not to say that § 1415(e)(3) has no effect on parents. While we doubt that this provision would authorize a court to order parents to leave their child in a particular placement, we think it operates in such a way that parents who unilaterally change their child's placement during the pendency of review proceedings, without the consent of state or local school officials, do so at their own financial risk. If the courts ultimately determine that the IEP proposed by the school officials was appropriate, the parents would be barred from obtaining reimbursement for any interim period in which their child's placement violated § 1415(e)(3). This conclusion is supported by the agency's interpretation of the Act's application to private placements by the parents:

> "(a) If a handicapped child has available a free appropriate public education and the parents choose to place the child in a private school or facility, the public agency is not required by this part to pay for the child's education at the private school or facility. . . .
>
> "(b) Disagreements between a parent and a public agency regarding the availability of a program appropriate for the child, and the

question of financial responsibility, are subject to the due process procedures under [§ 1415]." 34 CFR § 300.403 (1984).

We thus resolve the questions on which we granted certiorari; because the case is here in an interlocutory posture, we do not consider the estoppel ruling below or the specific equitable factors identified by the Court of Appeals for granting relief. We do think that the court was correct in concluding that "such relief as the court determines is appropriate," within the meaning of § 1415(e)(2), means that equitable considerations are relevant in fashioning relief.

The judgment of the Court of Appeals is

Affirmed.

School Board of Nassau County, Florida v. Arline

U.S. Supreme Court, 107 S.Ct. 1123 (1987).

Syllabus*

Section 504 of the Rehabilitation Act of 1973, 29 U. S. C. § 794, (Act) provides, *inter alia*, that no "otherwise qualified handicapped individual," as defined in 29 U. S. C. § 706(7), shall, solely by reason of his handicap, be excluded from participation in any program receiving federal financial assistance. Section 706(7)(B) defines "handicapped individual" to mean any person who "(i) has a physical . . . impairment which substantially limits one or more of [his] major life activities, (ii) has a record of such an impairment, or (iii) is regarded as having such an impairment." Department of Health and Human Services (HHS) regulations define "physical impairment" to mean, *inter alia*, any physiological disorder affecting the respiratory system, and define "major life activities" to include working. Respondent was hospitalized for tuberculosis in 1957. The disease went into remission for the next 20 years, during which time respondent began teaching elementary school in Florida. In 1977, March 1978, and November 1978, respondent had relapses, after the latter two of which she was suspended with pay for the rest of the school year. At the end of the 1978-1979 school year, petitioners discharged her after a hearing because of the continued recurrence of tuberculosis. After she was denied relief in state administrative proceedings, she brought suit in Federal District Court, alleging a violation of § 504. The District Court held that she was not a "handicapped person" under the Act, but that, even assuming she were, she was not "qualified" to teach elementary school. The Court of Appeals reversed, holding that persons with contagious diseases are within § 504's coverage, and remanded for further findings as to whether respondent was "otherwise qualified" for her job:

Held:

1. A person afflicted with the contagious disease of tuberculosis may be a "handicapped individual" within the meaning of § 504.

(a) Respondent is a "handicapped individual" as defined in § 706(7)(B) and the HHS regulations. Her hospitalization in 1957 for a disease that affected her respiratory system and that substantially limited "one or more of [her] major life activities" establishes that she has a "record of . . . impairment."

(b) The fact that a person with a record of impairment is also contagious does not remove that person from § 504's coverage. To allow an employer to justify discrimination by distinguishing between a disease's contagious effects on others and its physical effects on a patient would be unfair, would be contrary to § 706(7)(B)(iii) and the legislative history, which demonstrate Congress' concern about an impairment's effect on others, and would be inconsistent with § 504's basic purpose to ensure that handicapped individuals are not denied jobs because of the prejudice or ignorance of others. The Act replaces such fearful, reflexive reactions with actions based on reasoned and medically sound judgments as to whether contagious handicapped persons are "otherwise qualified" to do the job.

2. In most cases, in order to determine whether a person handicapped by contagious disease is "otherwise qualified" under § 504, the District Court must conduct an individualized inquiry and make appropriate findings of fact,

---

*The syllabus constitutes no part of the opinion of the Court but has been prepared by the Reporter of Decisions for the convenience of the reader.

based on reasonable medical judgments given the state of medical knowledge, about (a) the nature of the risk (*e. g.*, how the disease is transmitted), (b) the duration of the risk (how long is the carrier infectious), (c) the severity of the risk (what is the potential harm to third parties), and (d) the probabilities the disease will be transmitted and will cause varying degrees of harm. In making these findings, courts normally should defer to the reasonable medical judgments of public health officials. Courts must then determine, in light of these findings, whether any "reasonable accommodation" can be made by the employer under the established standards for that inquiry.

3. Because the District Court did not make appropriate findings, it is impossible for this Court to determine whether respondent is "otherwise qualified" for the job of elementary school teacher, and the case is remanded for additional findings of fact.

772 F. 2d 759, affirmed.

BRENNAN, J., delivered the opinion of the Court, in which WHITE, MARSHALL, BLACKMUN, POWELL, STEVENS, and O'CONNOR, JJ., joined. REHNQUIST, C. J., filed a dissenting opinion, in which SCALIA, J., joined.

JUSTICE BRENNAN delivered the opinion of the Court.

Section 504 of the Rehabilitation Act of 1973, 87 Stat. 394, as amended, 29 U. S. C. § 794 (Act), prohibits a federally funded state program from discriminating against a handicapped individual solely by reason of his or her handicap. This case presents the questions whether a person afflicted with tuberculosis, a contagious disease, may be considered a "handicapped individual" within the meaning of § 504 of the Act, and, if so, whether such an individual is "otherwise qualified" to teach elementary school.

I

From 1966 until 1979, respondent Gene Arline taught elementary school in Nassau County, Florida. She was discharged in 1979 after suffering a third relapse of tuberculosis within two years. After she was denied relief in state administrative proceedings, she brought suit in federal court, alleging that the School Board's decision to dismiss her because of her tuberculosis violated § 504 of the Act.[1]

A trial was held in the District Court, at which the principal medical evidence was provided by Marianne McEuen, M. D., an assistant director of the Community Tuberculosis Control Service of the Florida Department of Health and Rehabilitative Services. According to the medical records reviewed by Dr. McEuen, Arline was hospitalized for tuberculosis in 1957. App. 11-12. For the next twenty years, Arline's disease was in remission. *Id.*, at 32. Then, in 1977, a culture revealed that tuberculosis was again active in her system; cultures taken in March 1978 and in November 1978 were also positive. *Id.*, at 12.

---

[1]Respondent also sought relief under 42 U. S. C. § 1983 alleging that the Board denied her due process of law. Both the District Court and the Court of Appeals rejected this argument, and the respondent did not present the issue to this Court.

The superintendent of schools for Nassau County, Craig Marsh, then testified as to the School Board's response to Arline's medical reports. After both her second relapse, in the Spring of 1978, and her third relapse in November 1978, the School Board suspended Arline with pay for the remainder of the school year. *Id.*, at 49-51. At the end of the 1978-1979 school year, the School Board held a hearing, after which it discharged Arline, "not because she had done anything wrong," but because of the "continued reoccurrence [sic] of tuberculosis." *Id.*, at 49-52.

In her trial memorandum, Arline argued that it was "not disputed that the [School Board dismissed her] solely on the basis of her illness. Since the illness in this case qualifies the Plaintiff as a 'handicapped person' it is clear that she was dismissed solely as a result of her handicap in violation of Section 504." Record 119. The District Court held, however, that although there was "[n]o question that she suffers a handicap," Arline was nevertheless not "a handicapped person under the terms of that statute." App. to Pet. for Cert. C-2. The court found it "difficult . . . to conceive that Congress intended contagious diseases to be included within the definition of a handicapped person." The court then went on to state that, "even assuming" that a person with a contagious disease could be deemed a handicapped person, Arline was not "qualified" to teach elementary school. *Id.*, at C-2—C-3.

The Court of Appeals reversed, holding that "persons with contagious diseases are within the coverage of section 504," and that Arline's condition "falls . . . neatly within the statutory and regulatory framework" of the Act. 772 F. 2d 759, 764 (CA11 1985). The court remanded the case "for further findings as to whether the risks of infection precluded Mrs. Arline from being 'otherwise qualified' for her job and, if so, whether it was possible to make some reasonable accommodation for her in that teaching position" or in some other position. *Id.*, at 765 (footnote omitted). We granted certiorari, 475 U. S. —— (1986), and now affirm.

II

In enacting and amending the Act, Congress enlisted all programs receiving federal funds in an effort "to share with handicapped Americans the opportunities for an education, transportation, housing, health care, and jobs that other Americans take for granted." 123 Cong. Rec. 13515 (1977) (statement of Sen. Humphrey). To that end, Congress not only increased federal support for vocational rehabilitation, but also addressed the broader problem of discrimination against the handicapped by including § 504, an antidiscrimination provision patterned after Title VI of the Civil Rights of 1964.[2] Section 504 of the Rehabilitation Act reads in pertinent part:

---

[2] Congress' decision to pattern § 504 after Title VI is evident in the language of the statute, compare 29 U. S. C. § 794 with 42 U. S. C. § 2000d, and in the legislative history of § 504, see, *e. g.*, S. Rep. No. 93-1297, pp. 39-40 (1974); S. Rep. No. 95-890, p. 19 (1978). Cf. tenBroek & Matson, The Disabled and the Law of Welfare, 54 Cal. L. Rev. 809, 814-815 and nn. 21-22 (1966) (discussing theory and evidence that "negative attitudes and practices toward the disabled resemble those commonly attached to 'underprivileged ethnic and religious minority groups'"). The range of programs subject to § 504's prohibition is broader, however, than that covered by Title VI, because § 504 covers employment discrimination even in programs that receive federal aid with a primary objective other than the promotion of employment. See *Consolidated*

"No otherwise qualified handicapped individual in the United States, as defined in section 706(7) of this title, shall, solely by reason of his handicap, be excluded from participation in, be denied the benefits of, or be subjected to discrimination under any program or activity receiving Federal financial assistance . . . ." 29 U. S. C. § 794.

In 1974 Congress expanded the definition of "handicapped individual" for use in § 504 to read as follows:[3]

"[A]ny person who (i) has a physical or mental impairment which substantially limits one or more of such person's major life activities, (ii) has a record of such an impairment, or (iii) is regarded as having such an impairment." 29 U. S. C. § 706(7)(B).

The amended definition reflected Congress' concern with protecting the handicapped against discrimination stemming not only from simple prejudice, but from "archaic attitudes and laws" and from "the fact that the American people are simply unfamiliar with and insensitive to the difficulties confront[ing] individuals with handicaps." S. Rep. No. 93-1297, p. 50 (1974). To combat the effects of erroneous but nevertheless prevalent perceptions about the handicapped, Congress expanded the definition of "handicapped individual" so as to preclude discrimination against "[a] person who has a record of, or is regarded as having, an impairment [but who] may at present have no actual incapacity at all." *Southeastern Community College* v. *Davis*, 442 U. S. 397, 405-406, n. 6 (1979).[4]

In determining whether a particular individual is handicapped as defined by the Act, the regulations promulgated by the Department of Health and Human Services are of significant assistance. As we have previously recognized, these regulations were drafted with the oversight and approval of Congress, see *Consolidated Rail Corporation* v. *Darrone*, 465 U. S. 624, 634-635, and nn. 14-16 (1984); they provide "an important source of guidance on the

---

Rail Corporation v. *Darrone*, 465 U. S. 624 (1984); Note, Accommodating the Handicapped: Rehabilitating Section 504 after *Southeastern*, 80 Colum. L. Rev. 171, 174-175 and nn. 21 (1980).

[3]The primary focus of the 1973 Act was to increase federal support for vocational rehabilitation; the Act's original definition of the term "handicapped individual" reflected this focus by including only those whose disability limited their employability, and those who could be expected to benefit from vocational rehabilitation. After reviewing the Department of Health, Education, and Welfare's subsequent attempt to devise regulations to implement the Act, however, Congress concluded that the definition of "handicapped individual," while appropriate for the vocational rehabilitation provisions in Titles I and III of the Act, was too narrow to deal with the range of discriminatory practices in housing, education, and health care programs which stemmed from stereotypical attitudes and ignorance about the handicapped. S. Rep. No. 93-1297, pp. 16, 37-38, 50 (1974).

[4]See *id.*, at 39 ("This subsection includes within the protection of sections 503 and 504 those persons who do not in fact have the condition which they are perceived as having, as well as those persons whose mental or physical condition does not substantially limit their life activities and who thus are not technically within clause (A) in the new definition. Members of both of these groups may be subjected to discrimination on the basis of their being regarded as handicapped"); *id.*, at 37-39, 63-64; see also 120 Cong. Rec. 30531 (1974) (statement of Sen. Cranston).

meaning of § 504.'' *Alexander* v. *Choate*, 469 U. S. 287, 304, n. 24 (1985). The regulations are particularly significant here because they define two critical terms used in the statutory definition of handicapped individual.[5] "Physical impairment" is defined as follows:

> "[A]ny physiological disorder or condition, cosmetic disfigurement, or anatomical loss affecting one or more of the following body systems: neurological; musculoskeletal; special sense organs; respiratory, including speech organs; cardiovascular; reproductive, digestive, genito-urinary; hemic and lymphatic; skin; and endocrine.'' 45 CFR § 84.3(j)(2)(i) (1985).

In addition, the regulations define "major life activities" as:

> "functions such as caring for one's self, performing manual tasks, walking, seeing, hearing, speaking, breathing, learning, and working.'' § 84.3j(2)(ii).

III

Within this statutory and regulatory framework, then, we must consider whether Arline can be considered a handicapped individual. According to the testimony of Dr. McEuen, Arline suffered tuberculosis "in an acute form in such a degree that it affected her respiratory system," and was hospitalized for this condition. App. 11. Arline thus had a physical impairment as that term is defined by the regulations, since she had a "physiological disorder or condition . . . affecting [her] . . . respiratory [system].'' 45 CFR § 84.3(j)(2)(i) (1985). This impairment was serious enough to require hospitalization, a fact more than sufficient to establish that one or more of her major life activities were substantially limited by her impairment. Thus, Arline's hospitalization for tuberculosis in 1957 suffices to establish that she has a "record of . . . impairment" within the meaning of 29 U. S. C. § 706(7)(b)(ii), and is therefore a handicapped individual.

Petitioners concede that a contagious disease may constitute a handicapping condition to the extent that it leaves a person with "diminished physical or mental capabilities,'' Brief for Petitioners 15, and concede that Arline's

---

[5]In an appendix to these regulations, the Department of Health and Human Services explained that it chose not attempt to "set forth a list of specific diseases and conditions that constitute physical or mental impairments because of the difficulty of ensuring the comprehensiveness of any such list." 45 CFR pt. 84, App. A, p. 310 (1985). Nevertheless, the Department went on to state that "such diseases and conditions as orthopedic, visual, speech, and hearing impairments, cerebral palsy, epilepsy, muscular dystrophy, multiple sclerosis, cancer, heart disease, diabetes, mental retardation, [and] emotional illness" would be covered. *Ibid.* The Department also reinforced what a careful reading of the statute makes plain, "that a physical or mental impairment does not constitute a handicap for purposes of section 504 unless its severity is such that it results in a substantial limitation of one or more major life activities." *Ibid.* Although many of the comments on the regulations when first proposed suggested that the definition was unreasonably broad, the Department found that a broad definition, one not limited to so-called "traditional handicaps," is inherent in the statutory definition. *Ibid.*

hospitalization for tuberculosis in 1957 demonstrates that she has a record of a physical impairment, see Tr. of Oral Arg. 52-53. Petitioners maintain, however, Arline's record of impairment is irrelevant in this case, since the School Board dismissed Arline not because of her diminished physical capabilities, but because of the threat that her relapses of tuberculosis posed to the health of others.[6]

We do not agree with petitioners that, in defining a handicapped individual under § 504, the contagious effects of a disease can be meaningfully distinguished from the disease's physical effects on a claimant in a case such as this. Arline's contagiousness and her physical impairment each resulted from the same underlying condition, tuberculosis. It would be unfair to allow an employer to seize upon the distinction between the effects of a disease on others and the effects of a disease on a patient and use that distinction to justify discriminatory treatment.[7]

Nothing in the legislative history of § 504 suggests that Congress intended such a result. That history demonstrates that Congress was as concerned about the effect of an impairment on others as it was about its effect on the individual. Congress extended coverage, in 29 U. S. C. § 706(7)(B)(iii), to those individuals who are simply "regarded as having" a physical or mental impairment.[8] The Senate Report provides as an example of a person who would be covered under this subsection "a person with some kind of visible physical impairment which in fact does not substantially limit that person's functioning." S. Rep. No. 93-1297, p. 64 (1974).[9] Such an impairment might

---

[6]See Brief for Petitioners 15-16 (Act covers conditions that leave individuals with "diminished physical or mental capabilities," but not conditions that could "impair the health of others"); Pet. for Cert. 13-14 ("[T]he concept of a 'handicap' [should be limited] to physical and mental conditions which result in either a real or perceived diminution of an individual's capabilities. . . . [A]n individual suffering from a contagious disease may not necessarily suffer from any physical or mental impairments affecting his ability to perform the job in question. In other words, an employer's reluctance to hire such an individual is not due to any real or perceived inability on the individual's part, but rather because of the employer's reluctance to expose its other employees and its clientele to the threat of infection").

[7]The United States argues that it is possible for a person to be simply a carrier of a disease, that is, to be capable of spreading a disease without having a "physical impairment" or suffering from any other symptoms associated with the disease. The United States contends that this is true in the case of some carriers of the Acquired Immune Deficiency Syndrome (AIDS) virus. From this premise the United States concludes that discrimination solely on the basis of contagiousness is never discrimination on the basis of a handicap. The argument is misplaced in this case, because the handicap here, tuberculosis, gave rise both to a physical impairment *and* to contagiousness. This case does not present, and we therefore do not reach, the questions whether a carrier of a contagious disease such as AIDS could be considered to have a physical impairment, or whether such a person could be considered, solely on the basis of contagiousness, a handicapped person as defined by the Act.

[8]See n. 4, *supra.*

[9]Congress' desire to prohibit discrimination based on the effects a person's handicap may have on others was evident from the inception of the Act. For example, Representative Vanik, whose remarks constitute "a primary signpost on the road toward interpreting the legislative history of § 504," *Alexander* v. *Choate*, 469 U. S. 287, 295-296, and n. 13 (1985), cited as an example of improper handicap discrimination a case in which "a court ruled that a cerebral palsied child, who was not a

not diminish a person's physical or mental capabilities, but could nevertheless substantially limit that person's ability to work as a result of the negative reactions of others to the impairment.[10]

Allowing discrimination based on the contagious effects of a physical impairment would be inconsistent with the basic purpose of § 504, which is to ensure that handicapped individuals are not denied jobs or other benefits because of the prejudiced attitudes or the ignorance of others. By amending the definition of "handicapped individual" to include not only those who are actually physically impaired, but also those who are regarded as impaired and who, as a result, are substantially limited in a major life activity, Congress acknowledged that society's accumulated myths and fears about disability and disease are as handicapping as are the physical limitations that flow from actual impairment.[11] Few aspects of a handicap give rise to the same level of public fear and misapprehension as contagiousness.[12] Even those who suffer or have recovered from such noninfectious diseases as epilepsy or cancer have faced discrimination based on the irrational fear that they might be conta-

---

physical threat and was academically competitive, should be excluded from public school, because his teacher claimed his physical appearance 'produced a nauseating effect' on his classmates." 117 Cong. Rec. 45974 (1971). See also 118 Cong. Rec. 36761 (1972) (remarks of Sen. Mondale) (a woman "crippled by arthritis" was denied a job not because she could not do the work but because "college trustees [thought] 'normal students shouldn't see her.'"); *id.*, at 525 (remarks of Sen. Humphrey); cf. Macgregor, Some Psycho-Social Problems Associated with Facial Deformities, 16 Am. Sociological Rev. 629 (1961).

[10]The Department of Health and Human Services regulations, which include among the conditions illustrative of physical impairments covered by the Act "cosmetic disfigurement," lend further support to Arline's position that the effect of one's impairment on others is as relevant to a determination of whether one is handicapped as is the physical effect of one's handicap on oneself. 45 CFR § 84.3(j)(2)(i)(A) (1985). At oral argument, the Solicitor General took the position that a condition such as cosmetic disfigurement could not substantially limit a major life activity within the meaning of the statute, because the only major life activity that it would affect would be the ability to work. The Solicitor General recognized that "working" was one of the major life activities listed in the regulations, but said that to argue that a condition that impaired *only* the ability to work was a handicapping condition was to make "a totally circular argument which lifts itself by its bootstraps." Tr. or Oral Arg. 15-16. The argument is not circular, however, but direct. Congress plainly intended the Act to cover persons with a physical or mental impairment (whether actual, past, or perceived) that substantially limited one's ability to work. "[T]he primary goal of the Act is to increase employment of the handicapped." *Consolidated Rail Corporation* v. *Darrone*, 465 U. S., 633, at n. 13; see also *id.*, at 632 ("Indeed, enhancing employment of the handicapped was so much the focus of the 1973 legislation that Congress the next year felt it necessary to amend the statute to clarify whether § 504 was intended to prohibit other types of discrimination as well").

[11]S. Rep. No. 93-1297, p. 50 (1974); see n. 4, *supra*. See generally, tenBroek & Matson, 54 Cal. L. Rev., at 814; Strauss, Chronic Illness, in The Sociology of Health and Illness 138, 146-147 (P. Conrad & R. Kern eds.) (1981).

[12]The isolation of the chronically ill and of those perceived to be ill or contagious appears across cultures and centuries, as does the development of complex and often pernicious mythologies about the nature, cause, and transmission of illness. Tuberculosis is no exception. See R. Dubos & J. Dubos, The White Plague (1952); S. Sontag, Illness as Metaphor (1978).

gious.[13] The Act is carefully structured to replace such reflexive reactions to actual or perceived handicaps with actions based on reasoned and medically sound judgments: the definition of "handicapped individuals" is broad, but only those individuals who are both handicapped *and* otherwise qualified are eligible for relief. The fact that *some* persons who have contagious diseases may pose a serious health threat to others under certain circumstances does not justify excluding from the coverage of the Act *all* persons with actual or perceived contagious diseases. Such exclusion would mean that those accused of being contagious would never have the opportunity to have their condition evaluated in light of medical evidence and a determination made as to whether they were "otherwise qualified." Rather, they would be vulnerable to discrimination on the basis of mythology—precisely the type of injury Congress sought to prevent.[14] We conclude that the fact that a person with a record of a physical impairment is also contagious does not suffice to remove that person from coverage under § 504.[15]

---

[13]Senator Humphrey noted the "irrational fears or prejudice on the part of employers or fellow workers" that make it difficult for former cancer patients to secure employment. 123 Cong. Rec. 13515 (1977). See also Feldman, Wellness and Work, in Psychosocial Stress and Cancer 173-200 (C. Cooper ed. 1984) (documenting job discrimination against recovered cancer patients); S. Sontag, Illness as Metaphor 6 (1978) ("Any disease that is treated as a mystery and acutely enough feared will be felt to be morally, if not literally, contagious. Thus, a surprisingly large number of people with cancer find themselves being shunned by relatives and friends . . . as if cancer, like TB, were an infectious disease"); Dell, Social Dimensions of Epilepsy: Stigma and Response, in Psychopathology in Epilepsy: Social Dimensions 185-210 (S. Whitman & B. Hermann eds. 1986) (reviewing range of discrimination affecting epileptics); Brief for Epilepsy Foundation as *Amicus Curiae* 5-14 ("A review of the history of epilepsy provides a salient example that fear, rather than the handicap itself, is the major impetus for discrimination against persons with handicaps").

[14]Congress reaffirmed this approach in its 1978 amendments to the Act. There, Congress recognized that employers and other grantees might have legitimate reasons not to extend jobs or benefits to drug addicts and alcoholics, but also understood the danger of improper discrimination against such individuals if they were categorically excluded from coverage under the Act. Congress therefore rejected the original House proposal to exclude addicts and alcoholics from the definition of handicapped individual, and instead adopted the Senate proposal excluding only those alcoholics and drug abusers "whose current use of alcohol or drugs prevents such individual from performing the duties of the job in question or whose employment . . . would constitute a direct threat to property or the safety of others." 29 U. S. C. § 706(7)(B). See 124 Cong. Rec. 30322 (1978); Brief for Senator Cranston et al. as *Amici Curiae* 35-36; 43 Op. Atty. Gen. No. 12 (1977).

This approach is also consistent with that taken by courts that have addressed the question whether the Act covers persons suffering from conditions other than contagious diseases that render them a threat to the safety of others. See, *e. g., Strathie* v. *Department of Transportation*, 716 F. 2d 227, 232-234 (CA3 1983); *Doe* v. *New York University*, 666 F. 2d 761, 775 (CA2 1981).

[15]The dissent implies that our holding rests only on our "own sense of fairness and implied support from the Act," *post*, at 1, and that this holding is inconsistent with *Pennhurst State School and Hospital* v. *Halderman*, 451 U. S. 1 (1981). It is evident, however, that our holding is premised on the plain language of the Act, and on the detailed regulations that implement it, neither of which the dissent discusses and both of which support the conclusion that those with a contagious disease such as tuberculosis may be considered "handicapped" under the Act. We also find much support in

IV

The remaining question is whether Arline is otherwise qualified for the job of elementary school teacher. To answer this question in most cases, the District Court will need to conduct an individualized inquiry and make appropriate findings of fact. Such an inquiry is essential if § 504 is to achieve its goal of protecting handicapped individuals from deprivations based on prejudice, stereotypes, or unfounded fear, while giving appropriate weight to such legitimate concerns of grantees as avoiding exposing others to significant health and safety risks.[16] The basic factors to be considered in conducting this inquiry are well established.[17] In the context of the employment of a

_____

the legislative history, while the dissent is unable to find any evidence to support its view. Accordingly, the dissent's construction of the Act to exclude those afflicted with a contagious disease is not only arbitrary (and therefore unfair) but unfaithful to basic canons of statutory construction.

Nothing in *Pennhurst* requires such infidelity. The statutory provision at issue there was held to be "simply a general statement of 'findings'" and to express "no more than . . . a congressional preference for certain kinds of treatment." *Id.*, at 19. See *Wright* v. *Roanoke Redevelopment & Housing Auth.*, *ante* at ⸺ (slip op. at 5) ("In *Pennhurst* . . . the statutory provisions were thought to be only statements of 'findings' indicating no more than a congressional preference—at most a 'nudge in the preferred directio[n]'"). The contrast between the congressional preference at issue in *Pennhurst* and the antidiscrimination mandate of § 504 could not be more stark.

Nor is there any reason to think that today's decision will extend the Act beyond manageable bounds. Construing § 504 not to exclude those with contagious diseases will complement rather than complicate state efforts to enforce public health laws. As we state, *infra*, at 14, courts may reasonably be expected normally to defer to the judgments of public health officials in determining whether an individual is otherwise qualified unless those judgments are medically unsupportable. Conforming employment decisions with medically reasonable judgments can hardly be thought to threaten the States' regulation of communicable diseases. Indeed, because the Act requires employers to respond rationally to those handicapped by a contagious disease, the Act will assist local health officials by helping remove an important obstacle to preventing the spread of infectious diseases: the individual's reluctance to report his or her condition. It is not surprising, then, that in their brief as *amici curiae* in support of respondent, the States of California, Maryland, Michigan, Minnesota, New Jersey, New York, and Wisconsin conclude that "inclusion of communicable diseases within the ambit of Section 504 does not reorder the priorities of state regulatory agencies . . . [and] would not alter the balance between state and federal authority." Brief for State of California et al. 30.

[16]A person who poses a significant risk of communicating an infectious disease to others in the workplace will not be otherwise qualified for his or her job if reasonable accommodation will not eliminate that risk. The Act would not require a school board to place a teacher with active, contagious tuberculosis in a classroom with elementary school children. Respondent conceded as much at oral argument. Tr. of Oral Arg. 45.

[17]"An otherwise qualified person is one who is able to meet all of a program's requirements in spite of his handicap." *Southeastern Community College* v. *Davis*, 442 U. S. 397, 406 (1979). In the employment context, an otherwise qualified person is one who can perform "the essential functions" of the job in question. 45 CFR § 84.3(k) (1985). When a handicapped person is not able to perform the essential functions of the job, the court must also consider whether any "reasonable accommodation" by the employer would enable the handicapped person to perform those functions. *Ibid.* Accommodation is not reasonable if it either imposes "undue financial

person handicapped with a contagious disease, we agree with *amicus* American Medical Association that this inquiry should include:

> "[findings of] facts, based on reasonable medical judgments given the state of medical knowledge, about (a) the nature of the risk (how the disease is transmitted), (b) the duration of the risk (how long is the carrier infectious), (c) the severity of the risk (what is the potential harm to third parties) and (d) the probabilities the disease will be transmitted and will cause varying degrees of harm." Brief for American Medical Association as *Amicus Curiae* 19.

In making these findings, courts normally should defer to the reasonable medical judgments of public health officials.[18] The next step in the "otherwise-qualified" inquiry is for the court to evaluate, in light of these medical findings, whether the employer could reasonably accommodate the employee under the established standards for that inquiry. See *supra*, note 17.

Because of the paucity of factual findings by the District Court, we, like the Court of Appeals, are unable at this stage of the proceedings to resolve whether Arline is "otherwise qualified" for her job. The District Court made no findings as to the duration and severity of Arline's condition, nor as to the probability that she would transmit the disease. Nor did the court determine whether Arline was contagious at the time she was discharged, or whether the School Board could have reasonably accommodated her.[19] Accordingly, the resolution of whether Arline was otherwise qualified requires further findings of fact.

V

We hold that a person suffering from the contagious disease of tuberculosis can be a handicapped person within the meaning of the § 504 of the Rehabilitation Act of 1973, and that respondent Arline is such a person. We remand the case to the District Court to determine whether Arline is otherwise qualified for her position. The judgment of the Court of Appeals is

Affirmed.

---

and administrative burdens" on a grantee, *Southeastern Community College* v. *Davis, supra*, at 412, or requires "a fundamental alteration in the nature of [the] program" *id.*, at 410. See 45 CFR § 84.12(c) (1985) (listing factors to consider in determining whether accommodation would cause undue hardship); 45 CFR pt. 84, App. A, p. 315 (1985) ("where reasonable accommodation does not overcome the effects of a person's handicap, or where reasonable accommodation causes undue hardship to the employer, failure to hire or promote the handicapped person will not be considered discrimination"); *Davis, supra*, at 410-413; *Alexander* v. *Choate*, 469 U. S., at 299-301, and n. 19; *Strathie* v. *Department of Transportation, supra*, at 231.

[18]This case does not present, and we do not address, the question whether courts should also defer to the reasonable medical judgments of private physicians on which an employer has relied.

[19]Employers have an affirmative obligation to make a reasonable accommodation for a handicapped employee. Although they are not required to find another job for an employee who is not qualified for the job he or she was doing, they cannot deny an employee alternative employment opportunities reasonably available under the employer's existing policies. See n. 17, *supra*; 45 CFR § 84.12 and App. A, pp. 315-316 (1985).

Honig, California Superintendent of Public Instruction v. Doe

U.S. Supreme Court, 108 S.Ct. 592 (1988).

Syllabus*

In order to assure that States receiving federal financial assistance will provide a "free appropriate public education" for all disabled children, including those with serious emotional disturbances, the Education of the Handicapped Act (EHA or Act) establishes a comprehensive system of procedural safeguards designed to provide meaningful parental participation in all aspects of a child's educational placement, including an opportunity for an impartial due process hearing with respect to any complaints such parents have concerning their child's placement, and the right to seek administrative review of any decisions they think inappropriate. If that review proves unsatisfactory, either the parents or the local educational agency may file a civil action in any state or federal court for "appropriate" relief. 20 U. S. C. § 1415(e)(2). The Act's "stay-put" provision directs that a disabled child "shall remain in [his or her] then current educational placement" pending completion of any review proceedings, unless the parents and state or local educational agencies otherwise agree. § 1415(e)(3). Respondents Doe and Smith, who were emotionally disturbed students, were suspended indefinitely for violent and disruptive conduct related to their disabilities, pending the completion of expulsion proceedings by the San Francisco Unified School District (SFUSD). After unsuccessfully protesting the action against him, Doe filed a suit in Federal District Court, in which Smith intervened, alleging that the suspension and proposed expulsion violated the EHA, and seeking injunctive relief against SFUSD officials and petitioner, the State Superintendent of Public Instruction. The court entered summary judgment for respondents on their EHA claims and issued a permanent injunction. The Court of Appeals affirmed with slight modifications.

Held:

1. The case is moot as to respondent Doe, who is now 24 years old, since the Act limits eligibility to disabled children between the ages of 3 and 21. However, the case is justiciable with respect to respondent Smith, who continues to be eligible for EHA educational services since he is currently only 20 and has not yet completed high school. This Court has jurisdiction since there is a reasonable likelihood that Smith will again suffer the deprivation of EHA-mandated rights that gave rise to this suit. Given the evidence that he is unable to conform his conduct to socially acceptable norms, and the absence of any suggestion that he has overcome his behavioral problems, it is reasonable to expect that he will again engage in aggressive and disruptive classroom misconduct. Moreover, it is unreasonable to suppose that any future educational placement will so perfectly suit his emotional and academic needs that further disruptions on his part are improbable. If Smith does repeat the objectionable conduct, it is likely that he will again be subjected to the same type of unilateral school action in any California school district in which he is enrolled, in light of the lack of a statewide policy governing local school responses to disability-related misconduct, and petitioner's insistence that all local school district retain residual authority to exclude disabled children for dangerous conduct. In light of the

---

*The syllabus constitutes no part of the opinion of the Court but has been prepared by the Reporter of Decisions for the convenience of the reader.

ponderousness of review procedures under the Act, and the fact that an aggrieved student will often be finished with school or otherwise ineligible for EHA protections by the time review can be had in this Court, the conduct Smith complained of is "capable of repetition, yet evading review." Thus his EHA claims are not moot.

2. The "stay-put" provision prohibits state or local school authorities from unilaterally excluding disabled children from the classroom for dangerous or disruptive conduct growing out of their disabilities during the pendency of review proceedings. Section 1415(e)(3) is unequivocal in its mandate that "the child *shall* remain in the then current educational placement" (emphasis added), and demonstrates a congressional intent to strip school of the *unilateral* authority they had traditionally employed to exclude disabled students, particularly emotionally disturbed students, from school. This Court will not rewrite the statute to infer a "dangerousness" exception on the basis of obviousness or congressional inadvertence, since, in drafting the statute, Congress devoted close attention to *Mills* v. *Board of Education of District of Columbia*, 348 F. Supp. 866, and *Pennsylvania Assn. for Retarded Children* v. *Pennsylvania*, 334 F. Supp. 1257, and 343 F. Supp. 279, thereby establishing that the omission of an emergency exception for dangerous students was intentional. However, Congress did not leave school administrators powerless to deal with such students, since implementing regulations allow the use of normal, nonplacement-changing procedures, including temporary suspensions for up to 10 schooldays for students posing an immediate threat to others' safety, while the Act allows for interim placements where parents and school officials are able to agree, and authorizes officials to file a § 1415(e)(2) suit for "appropriate" injunctive relief where such an agreement cannot be reached. In such a suit, § 1415(e)(3) effectively creates a presumption in favor of the child's current educational placement which school officials can rebut only by showing that maintaining the current placement is substantially likely to result in injury to the student or to others. Here, the District Court properly balanced respondents' interests under the Act against the state and local school officials' safety interest, and both lower courts properly construed and applied § 1415(e)(3), except insofar as the Court of Appeals held that a suspension exceeding 10 schooldays does not constitute a prohibited change in placement. The Court of Appeals' judgment is modified to that extent.

3. Insofar as the Court of Appeals' judgment affirmed the District Court's order directing the State to provide services directly to a disabled child where the local agency has failed to do so, that judgment is affirmed by an equally divided Court.

793 F. 2d 1470, affirmed.

BRENNAN, J., delivered the opinion of the Court as to holdings number 1 and 2 above, in which REHNQUIST, C. J., and WHITE, MARSHALL, BLACKMUN, and STEVENS, JJ., joined. REHNQUIST, C. J., filed a concurring opinion. SCALIA, J., filed a dissenting opinion, in which O'CONNOR, J., joined.

JUSTICE BRENNAN delivered the opinion of the Court.

As a condition of federal financial assistance, the Education of the Handicapped Act requires States to ensure a "free appropriate public education" for all disabled children within their jurisdictions. In aid of this goal, the Act establishes a comprehensive system of procedural safeguards designed to ensure parental participation in decisions concerning the education of their disabled children and to provide administrative and judicial review of any decisions with which those parents disagree. Among these safeguards is the so-called "stay-put" provision, which directs that a disabled child "shall remain in [his or her] then current educational placement" pending completion of any review proceedings, unless the parents and state or local educational agencies otherwise agree. 20 U. S. C. § 1415(e)(3). Today we must decide whether, in the face of this statutory proscription, state or local school authorities may nevertheless unilaterally exclude disabled children from the classroom for dangerous or disruptive conduct growing out of their disabilities. In addition, we are called upon to decide whether a district court may, in the exercise of its equitable powers, order a State to provide educational services directly to a disabled child when the local agency fails to do so.

I

In the Education of the Handicapped Act (EHA or the Act), 84 Stat. 175, as amended, 20 U. S. C. § 1400 *et seq.*, Congress sought "to assure that all handicapped children have available to them . . . a free appropriate public education which emphasizes special education and related services designed to meet their unique needs, [and] to assure that the rights of handicapped children and their parents or guardians are protected." § 1400(c). When the law was passed in 1975, Congress had before it ample evidence that such legislative assurances were sorely needed: 21 years after this Court declared education to be "perhaps the most important function of state and local governments," *Brown* v. *Board of Education*, 347 U. S. 483 (1954), Congressional studies revealed that better than half of the Nation's eight million disabled children were not receiving appropriate educational services. § 1400(b)(3). Indeed, one out of every eight of these children was excluded from the public school system altogether, § 1400(b)(4); many others were simply "warehoused" in special classes or were neglectfully shepherded through the system until they were old enough to drop out. See H. R. Rep. No. 94-332, p. 2 (1975). Among the most poorly served of disabled students were emotionally disturbed children: Congressional statistics revealed that for the school year immediately preceding passage of the Act, the educational needs of 82 percent of all children with emotional disabilities went unmet. See S. Rep. No. 94-168, p. 8 (1975) (hereinafter S. Rep.).

Although these educational failings resulted in part from funding constraints, Congress recognized that the problem reflected more than a lack of financial resources at the state and local levels. Two federal-court decisions, which the Senate Report characterized as "landmark," see *id.*, at 6, demonstrated that many disabled children were excluded pursuant to state statutes or local rules and policies, typically without any consultation with, or even notice to, their parents. See *Mills* v. *Board of Education of District of Columbia*, 348 F. Supp. 866 (DC 1972); *Pennsylvania Assn. for Retarded Children* v. *Pennsylvania*, 334 F. Supp. 1257 (ED Pa. 1971), and 343 F. Supp. 279 (1972) (*PARC*). Indeed, by the time of the EHA's enactment, parents had brought legal challenges to similar exclusionary practices in 27 other states. See S. Rep., at 6.

In responding to these problems, Congress did not content itself with passage of a simple funding statute. Rather, the EHA confers upon disabled students an enforceable substantive right to public education in participating States, see *Board of Education of Hendrick Hudson Central School Dist.* v. *Rowley*, 458 U. S. 176 (1982),[1] and conditions federal financial assistance upon a State's compliance with the substantive and procedural goals of the Act. Accordingly, States seeking to qualify for federal funds must develop policies assuring all disabled children the "right to a free appropriate public education," and must file with the Secretary of Education formal plans mapping out in detail the programs, procedures and timetables under which they will effectuate these policies. 20 U. S. C. §§ 1412(1), 1413(a). Such plans must assure that, "to the maximum extent appropriate," States will "mainstream" disabled children, *i. e.*, that they will educate them with children who are not disabled, and that they will segregate or otherwise remove such children from the regular classroom setting "only when the nature or severity of the handicap is such that education in regular classes . . . cannot be achieved satisfactorily." § 1412(5).

The primary vehicle for implementing these congressional goals is the "individualized educational program" (IEP), which the EHA mandates for each disabled child. Prepared at meetings between a representative of the local school district, the child's teacher, the parents or guardians, and, whenever appropriate, the disabled child, the IEP sets out the child's present educational performance, establishes annual and short-term objectives for improvements in that performance, and describes the specially designed instruction and services that will enable the child to meet those objectives. § 1410(19). The IEP must be reviewed and, where necessary, revised at least once a year in order to ensure that local agencies tailor the statutorily required "free appropriate public education" to each child's unique needs. § 1414(a)(5).

Envisioning the IEP as the centerpiece of the statute's education delivery system for disabled children, and aware that schools had all too often denied such children appropriate educations without in any way consulting their parents, Congress repeatedly emphasized throughout the Act the importance and indeed the necessity of parental participation in both the development of the IEP and any subsequent assessments of its effectiveness. See §§ 1400(c), 1401(19), 1412(7), 1415(b)(1)(A), (C), (D), (E), and 1415(b)(2). Accordingly,

---

[1] Congress' earlier efforts to ensure that disabled students received adequate public education had failed in part because the measures it adopted were largely hortatory. In the 1966 amendments to the Elementary and Secondary Education Act of 1965, Congress established a grant program "for the purpose of assisting the States in the initiation, expansion, and improvement of programs and projects . . . for the education of handicapped children." Pub. L. 89-750, § 161, 80 Stat. 1204. It repealed that program four years later and replaced it with the original version of the Education of the Handicapped Act, Pub. L. 91-230, 84 Stat. 175, Part B of which contained a similar grant program. Neither statute, however, provided specific guidance as to how States were to use the funds, nor did they condition the availability of the grants on compliance with any procedural or substantive safeguards. In amending the EHA to its present form, Congress rejected its earlier policy of "merely establish[ing] an unenforceable goal requiring all children to be in school." 121 Cong. Rec. 37417 (1975) (remarks of Sen. Schweiker). Today, all 50 states and the District of Columbia receive funding assistance under the EHA. U. S. Dept. of Education, Ninth Annual Report to Congress on Implementation of Education of the Handicapped Act (1987).

the Act establishes various procedural safeguards that guarantee parents both an opportunity for meaningful input into all decisions affecting their child's education and the right to seek review of any decisions they think inappropriate. These safeguards include the right to examine all relevant records pertaining to the identification, evaluation and educational placement of their child; prior written notice whenever the responsible educational agency proposes (or refuses) to change the child's placement or program; an opportunity to present complaints concerning any aspect of the local agency's provision of a free appropriate public education; and an opportunity for "an impartial due process hearing" with respect to any such complaints. § 1415(b)(1), (2).

At the conclusion of any such hearing, both the parents and the local educational agency may seek further administrative review and, where that proves unsatisfactory, may file a civil action in any state or federal court. § 1415(c), (e)(2). In addition to reviewing the administrative record, courts are empowered to take additional evidence at the request of either party and to "grant such relief as [they] determine[] is appropriate." § 1415(e)(2). The "stay-put" provision at issue in this case governs the placement of a child while these often lengthy review procedures run their course. It directs that:

> "During the pendency of any proceedings conducted pursuant to [§ 1415], unless the State or local educational agency and the parents or guardian otherwise agree, the child shall remain in the then current educational placement of such child . . . ." § 1415(e)(3).

The present dispute grows out of the efforts of certain officials of the San Francisco Unified School District (SFUSD) to expel two emotionally disturbed children from school indefinitely for violent and disruptive conduct related to their disabilities. In November 1980, respondent John Doe assaulted another student at the Louise Lombard School, a developmental center for disabled children. Doe's April 1980 IEP identified him as a socially and physically awkward 17 year old who experienced considerable difficulty controlling his impulses and anger. Among the goals set out in his IEP was "[i]mprovement in [his] ability to relate to [his] peers [and to] cope with frustrating situations without resorting to aggressive acts." App. 17. Frustrating situations, however, were an unfortunately prominent feature of Doe's school career: physical abnormalities, speech difficulties, and poor grooming habits had made him the target of teasing and ridicule as early as the first grade, id., at 23; his 1980 IEP reflected his continuing difficulties with peers, noting that his social skills had deteriorated and that he could tolerate only minor frustration before exploding. Id., at 15-16.

On November 6, 1980, Doe responded to the taunts of a fellow student in precisely the explosive manner anticipated by his IEP: he choked the student with sufficient force to leave abrasions on the child's neck, and kicked out a school window while being escorted to the principal's office afterwards. Id., at 208. Doe admitted his misconduct and the school subsequently suspended him for five days. Thereafter, his principal referred the matter to the SFUSD Student Placement Committee (SPC or Committee) with the recommendation that Doe be expelled. On the day the suspension was to end, the SPC notified Doe's mother that it was proposing to exclude her child permanently from SFUSD and was therefore extending his suspension until such time as the expulsion proceedings were completed.[2] The Committee further advised her that she was entitled to attend the November 25 hearing at which it planned to discuss the proposed expulsion.

After unsuccessfully protesting these actions by letter, Doe brought this suit against a host of local school officials and the state superintendent of public education. Alleging that the suspension and proposed expulsion violated the EHA, he sought a temporary restraining order cancelling the SPC hearing and requiring school officials to convene an IEP meeting. The District Judge granted the requested injunctive relief and further ordered defendants to provide home tutoring for Doe on an interim basis; shortly thereafter, she issued a preliminary injunction directing defendants to return Doe to his then current educational placement at Louise Lombard School pending completion of the IEP review process. Doe re-entered school on December 15, 5½ weeks, and 24 school days, after his initial suspension.

Respondent Jack Smith was identified as an emotionally disturbed child by the time he entered the second grade in 1976. School records prepared that year indicated that he was unable "to control verbal or physical outburst[s]" and exhibited a "[s]evere disturbance in relationships with peers and adults." *Id.*, at 123. Further evaluations subsequently revealed that he had been physically and emotionally abused as an infant and young child and that, despite above average intelligence, he experienced academic and social difficulties as a result of extreme hyperactivity and low self-esteem. *Id.*, at 136, 139, 155, 176. Of particular concern was Smith's propensity for verbal hostility; one evaluator noted that the child reacted to stress by "attempt[ing] to cover his feelings of low self worth through aggressive behavior[,] . . . primarily verbal provocations." *Id.*, at 136.

Based on these evaluations, SFUSD placed Smith in a learning center for emotionally disturbed children. His grandparents, however, believed that his needs would be better served in the public school setting and, in September 1979, the school district acceded to their requests and enrolled him at A. P. Giannini Middle School. His February 1980 IEP recommended placement in a Learning Disability Group, stressing the need for close supervision and a highly structured environment. *Id.*, at 111. Like earlier evaluations, the February 1980 IEP noted that Smith was easily distracted, impulsive, and anxious; it therefore proposed a half-day schedule and suggested that the placement be undertaken on a trial basis. *Id.*, at 112, 115.

At the beginning of the next school year, Smith was assigned to a full-day program; almost immediately thereafter he began misbehaving. School officials met twice with his grandparents in October 1980 to discuss returning him to a half-day program; although the grandparents agreed to the reduction, they apparently were never apprised of their right to challenge the decision through EHA procedures. The school officials also warned them that if

---

[2]California law at the time empowered school principals to suspend students for no more than five consecutive school days, Cal. Educ. Code Ann. § 48903(a) (West 1978), but permitted school districts seeking to expel a suspended student to "extend the suspension until such time as [expulsion proceedings were completed]; provided, that [it] has determined that the presence of the pupil at the school or in an alternative school placement would cause a danger to persons or property or a threat of disrupting the instructional process." § 48903(h). The State subsequently amended the law to permit school districts to impose longer initial periods of suspension. See n. 3, *infra*.

the child continued his disruptive behavior—which included stealing, extorting money from fellow students, and making sexual comments to female classmates—they would seek to expel him. On November 14, they made good on this threat, suspending Smith for five days after he made further lewd comments. His principal referred the matter to the SPC, which recommended exclusion from SFUSD. As it did in John Doe's case, the Committee scheduled a hearing and extended the suspension indefinitely pending a final disposition in the matter. On November 28, Smith's counsel protested these actions on grounds essentially identical to those raised by Doe, and the SPC agreed to cancel the hearing and to return Smith to a half-day program at A. P. Giannini or to provide home tutoring. Smith's grandparents chose the latter option and the school began home instruction on December 10; on January 6, 1981, an IEP team convened to discuss alternative placements.

After learning of Doe's action, Smith sought and obtained leave to intervene in the suit. The District Court subsequently entered summary judgment in favor of respondents on their EHA claims and issued a permanent injunction. In a series of decisions, the District Judge found that the proposed expulsions and indefinite suspensions of respondents for conduct attributable to their disabilities deprived them of their congressionally mandated right to a free appropriate public education, as well as their right to have that education provided in accordance with the procedures set out in the EHA. The District Judge therefore permanently enjoined the school district from taking any disciplinary action other than a two- or five-day suspension against any disabled child for disability-related misconduct, or from effecting any other change in the educational placement of any such child without parental consent pending completion of any EHA proceedings. In addition, the judge barred the State from authorizing unilateral placement changes and directed it to establish an EHA compliance-monitoring system or, alternatively, to enact guidelines governing local school responses to disability-related misconduct. Finally, the judge ordered the State to provide services directly to disabled children when, in any individual case, the State determined that the local educational agency was unable or unwilling to do so.

On appeal, the Court of Appeals for the Ninth Circuit affirmed the orders with slight modifications. *Doe* v. *Maher*, 793 F. 2d 1470 (1986). Agreeing with the District Court that an indefinite suspension in aid of expulsion constitutes a prohibited "change in placement" under § 1415(e)(3), the Court of Appeals held that the stay-put provision admitted of no "dangerousness" exception and that the statute therefore rendered invalid those provisions of the California Education Code permitting the indefinite suspension or expulsion of disabled children for misconduct arising out of their disabilities. The court concluded, however, that fixed suspensions of up to 30 school days did not fall within the reach of § 1415(e)(3), and therefore upheld recent amendments to the state education code authorizing such suspensions.[3] Lastly, the court affirmed that portion of the injunction requiring the State

---

[3]In 1983, the State amended its Education Code to permit school districts to impose initial suspensions of 20, and in certain circumstances, 30 school days. Cal. Educ. Code Ann. §§ 48912(a), 48903 (West Supp. 1988). The legislature did not alter the indefinite suspension authority which the SPC exercised in this case, but simply incorporated the earlier provision into a new section. See § 48911(g).

to provide services directly to a disabled child when the local educational agency fails to do so.

Petitioner Bill Honig, California Superintendent of Public Instruction,[4] sought review in this Court, claiming that the Court of Appeals' construction of the stay-put provision conflicted with that of several other courts of appeals which had recognized a dangerousness exception, compare *Doe* v. *Maher*, 793 F. 2d 1470 (1986) (case below), with *Jackson* v. *Franklin County School Board*, 765 F. 2d 535, 538 (CA5 1985); *Victoria L.* v. *District School Bd. of Lee County, Fla.*, 741 F. 2d 369, 374 (CA11 1984); *S-1* v. *Turlington*, 635 F. 2d 342, 348, n. 9 (CA5), cert. denied, 454 U. S. 1030 (1981), and that the direct services ruling placed an intolerable burden on the State. We granted certiorari to resolve these questions, 479 U. S. —— (1987), and now affirm.

II

At the outset, we address the suggestion, raised for the first time during oral argument, that this case is moot.[5] Under Article III of the Constitution this Court may only adjudicate actual, ongoing controversies. *Nebraska Press Assn* v. *Stuart*, 427 U. S. 539, 546 (1976); *Preiser* v. *Newkirk*, 422 U. S. 395, 401 (1975). That the dispute between the parties was very much alive when suit was filed, or at the time the Court of Appeals rendered its judgment, cannot substitute for the actual case or controversy that an exercise of this Court's jurisdiction requires. *Steffel* v. *Thompson*, 415 U. S. 452, 459 n. 10 (1974); *Roe* v. *Wade*, 410 U. S. 113, 125 (1973). In the present case, we have jurisdiction if there is a reasonable likelihood that respondents will again suffer the deprivation of EHA-mandated rights that gave rise to this suit. We believe that, at least with respect to respondent Smith, such a possibility does in fact exist and that the case therefore remains justiciable.

Respondent John Doe is now 24 years old and, accordingly, is no longer entitled to the protections and benefits of the EHA, which limits eligibility to disabled children between the ages of three and 21. See 20 U. S. C. § 1412(2)(B). It is clear, therefore, that whatever rights to state educational services he may yet have as a ward of the State, see Tr. of Oral Arg. 23, 26, the Act would not govern the State's provision of those services, and thus the case is moot as to him. Respondent Jack Smith, however, is currently 20 and has not yet completed high school. Although at present he is not faced with any proposed expulsion or suspension proceedings, and indeed no longer even resides within the SFUSD, he remains a resident of California and is entitled to a "free appropriate public education" within that State. His claims under the EHA, therefore, are not moot if the conduct he originally complained of is "'capable of repetition, yet evading review.'" *Murphy* v. *Hunt*, 455 U. S. 478, 482 (1982). Given Smith's continued eligibility for edu-

---

[4]At the time respondent Doe initiated this suit, Wilson Riles was the California Superintendent of Public Instruction. Petitioner Honig succeeded him in office.

[5]We note that both petitioner and respondents believe that this case presents a live controversy. See Tr. of Oral Arg. 6, 27-31. Only the United States, appearing as *amicus curiae*, urges that the case is presently nonjusticiable. *Id.*, at 21.

cational services under the EHA,[6] the nature of his disability, and petitioner's insistence that all local school districts retain residual authority to exclude disabled children for dangerous conduct, we have little difficulty concluding that there is a "reasonable expectation," *ibid.*, that Smith would once again be subjected to a unilateral "change in placement" for conduct growing out of his disabilities were it not for the state-wide injunctive relief issued below.

Our cases reveal that, for purposes of assessing the likelihood that state authorities will re-inflict a given injury, we generally have been unwilling to assume that the party seeking relief will repeat the type of misconduct that would once again place him or her at risk of that injury. See *Los Angeles* v. *Lyons*, 461 U. S. 95, 105-106 (1983) (no threat that party seeking injunction

---

[6]Notwithstanding respondent's undisputed right to a free appropriate public education in California, JUSTICE SCALIA argues in dissent that there is no "demonstrated probability" that Smith will actually avail himself of that right because his counsel was unable to state affirmatively during oral argument that her client would seek to re-enter the state school system. See *post*, at 2. We believe the dissent overstates the stringency of the "capable of repetition" test. Although JUSTICE SCALIA equates "reasonable expectation" with "demonstrated probability," the very case he cites for this proposition described these standards in the disjunctive, see *Murphy* v. *Hunt*, 455 U. S., at 482 ("'[T]here must be a 'reasonable expectation' *or* a 'demonstrated probability' that the same controversy will recur" (emphasis added)), and in numerous cases decided both before and since *Hunt* we have found controversies capable of repetition based on expectations that, while reasonable, were hardly demonstrably probable. See *e. g.*, *Burlington Northern R. Co.* v. *Maintenance of Way Employees*, 481 U. S. ——, ——, n. 4 (1987) (parties "reasonably likely" to find themselves in future disputes over collective bargaining agreement); *California Coastal Comm'n* v. *Granite Rock Co.*, 480 U. S. ——, —— (1987) (O'CONNOR, J.) ("likely" that respondent would again submit mining plans that would trigger contested state permit requirement); *Press-Enterprise Co* v. *Superior Court of Cal., Riverside County*, 478 U. S. 1, 6 (1986) ("It can reasonably be assumed" that newspaper publisher will be subjected to similar closure order in the future); *Globe Newspaper Co.* v. *Superior Court of Norfolk County*, 457 U. S. 596, 603 (1982) (same); *United States Parole Comm'n* v. *Geraghty*, 445 U. S. 388, 398 (1980) (case not moot where litigant "faces some likelihood of becoming involved in same controversy in the future") (dicta). Our concern in these cases, as in all others involving potentially moot claims, was whether the controversy was *capable* of repetition and not, as the dissent seems to insist, whether the claimant had demonstrated that a recurrence of the dispute was more probable than not. Regardless, then, of whether respondent has established with mathematical precision the likelihood that he will enroll in public school during the next two years, we think there is at the very least a reasonable expectation that he will exercise his rights under the EHA. In this regard, we believe respondent's actions over the course of the last seven years speak louder than his counsel's momentary equivocation during oral argument. Since 1980, he has sought to vindicate his right to an appropriate public education that is not only free of charge, but free from the threat that school officials will unilaterally change his placement or exclude him from class altogether. As a disabled young man, he has as at least as great a need of a high school education and diploma as any of his peers, and his counsel advises us that he is awaiting the outcome of this case to decide whether to pursue his degree. Tr. Oral Arg. 23-24. Under these circumstances, we think it not only counterintuitive but unreasonable to assume that respondent will forgo the exercise of a right that he has for so long sought to defend. Certainly we have as much reason to expect that respondent will re-enter the California school system as we had to assume that Jane Roe would again both have an unwanted pregnancy and wish to exercise her right to an abortion. See *Roe* v. *Wade*, 410 U. S. 113, 125 (1973).

barring police use of chokeholds would be stopped again for traffic violation or other offense, or would resist arrest if stopped); *Hunt* v. *Murphy, supra,* at 484 (no reason to believe that party challenging denial of pretrial bail "will once again be in a position to demand bail"); *O'Shea* v. *Littleton,* 414 U. S. 488, 497 (1974) (unlikely that parties challenging discriminatory bond-setting, sentencing, and jury-fee practices would again violate valid criminal laws). No such reluctance, however, is warranted here. It is respondent Smith's very inability to conform his conduct to socially acceptable norms that renders him "handicapped" within the meaning of the EHA. See 20 U. S. C. § 1401(1); 34 CFR § 300.5(b)(8) (1987). As noted above, the record is replete with evidence that Smith is unable to govern his aggressive, impulsive behavior—indeed, his notice of suspension acknowledged that "Jack's actions seem beyond his control." App. 152. In the absence of any suggestion that respondent has overcome his earlier difficulties, it is certainly reasonable to expect, based on his prior history of behavioral problems, that he will again engage in classroom misconduct. Nor is it reasonable to suppose that Smith's future educational placement will so perfectly suit his emotional and academic needs that further disruptions on his part are improbable. Although JUSTICE SCALIA suggests in his dissent, *post,* that school officials are unlikely to place Smith in a setting where they cannot control his misbehavior, any efforts to ensure such total control must be tempered by the school system's statutory obligations to provide respondent with a free appropriate public education in "the least restrictive environment," 34 CFR § 300.552(d) (1987); to educate him, "to the maximum extent appropriate," with children who are not disabled, 20 U. S. C. § 1412(5); and to consult with his parents or guardians, and presumably with respondent himself, before choosing a placement. §§ 1401(19), 1415(b). Indeed, it is only by ignoring these mandates, as well as Congress' unquestioned desire to wrest from school officials their former unilateral authority to determine the placement of emotionally disturbed children, see *infra,* that the dissent can so readily assume that respondent's future placement will satisfactorily prevent any further dangerous conduct on his part. Overarching these statutory obligations, moreover, is the inescapable fact that the preparation of an IEP, like any other effort at predicting human behavior, is an inexact science at best. Given the unique circumstances and context of this case, therefore, we think it reasonable to expect that respondent will again engage in the type of misconduct that precipitated this suit.

We think it equally probable that, should he do so, respondent will again be subjected to the same unilateral school action for which he initially sought relief. In this regard, it matters not that Smith no longer resides within the SFUSD. While the actions of SFUSD officials first gave rise to this litigation, the District Judge expressly found that the lack of a state policy governing local school responses to disability-related misconduct had let to, and would continue to result in, EHA violations, and she therefore enjoined the state defendant from authorizing, among other things, unilateral placement changes. App. 247-248. She of course also issued injunctions directed at the local defendants, but they did not seek review of those orders in this Court. Only petitioner, the State Superintendent of Public Instruction, has invoked our jurisdiction, and he now urges us to hold that local school districts retain unilateral authority under the EHA to suspend or otherwise remove disabled children for dangerous conduct. Given these representations, we have every reason to believe that were it not for the injunction barring petitioner from authorizing such unilateral action, respondent would be faced with a real and substantial threat of such action in any California school district in which he enrolled. Cf. *Los Angeles* v. *Lyons, supra,* at 106 (respondent lacked standing to seek injunctive relief because he could not plausibly allege that police officers choked all persons whom they stopped, or that the City *"authorized* police officers to act in such manner" (emphasis added)). Certainly, if the SFUSD's past practice of unilateral exclusions was at odds with state policy and the practice of local school districts generally, petitioner would not now stand before us seeking to defend the right of all local school districts to engage in such aberrant behavior.[7]

We have previously noted that administrative and judicial review under the EHA is often "ponderous," *Burlington School Committee* v. *Massachusetts Dept. of Education,* 471 U. S. 359, 370 (1985), and this case, which has taken seven years to reach us, amply confirms that observation. For obvious reasons, the misconduct of an emotionally disturbed or otherwise disabled child who has not yet reached adolescence typically will not pose such a serious threat to the well-being of other students that school officials can only ensure classroom safety by excluding the child. Yet, the adolescent student improperly disciplined for misconduct that does pose such a threat will often be finished with school or otherwise ineligible for EHA protections by the time review can be had in this Court. Because we believe that respondent Smith has demonstrated both "a sufficient likelihood that he will again be wronged in a similar way," *Los Angeles* v. *Lyons,* 461 U. S., at 111, and that any resulting claim he may have for relief will surely evade our review, we turn to the merits of his case.

III

The language of § 1415(e)(3) is unequivocal. It states plainly that during the pendency of any proceedings initiated under the Act, unless the state or local educational agency and the parents or guardian of a disabled child otherwise agree, "the child *shall* remain in the then current educational placement." § 1415(e)(3) (emphasis added). Faced with this clear directive, petitioner asks us to read a "dangerousness" exception into the stay-put provision on the basis of either of two essentially inconsistent assumptions: first, that Congress thought the residual authority of school officials to exclude dangerous students from the classroom too obvious for comment; or second, that Congress inadvertently failed to provide such authority and this Court must therefore remedy the oversight. Because we cannot accept either premise, we decline petitioner's invitation to re-write the statute.

Petitioner's arguments proceed, he suggests, from a simple, common-sense proposition: Congress could not have intended the stay-put provision

---

[7]Petitioner concedes that the school district "made a number of procedural mistakes in its eagerness to protect other students from Doe and Smith." Reply Brief for Petitioner 6. According to petitioner, however, unilaterally excluding respondents from school was not among them; indeed, petitioner insists that the SFUSD acted properly in removing respondents and urges that the stay-put provision "should not be interpreted to require a school district to maintain such dangerous children with other children." *Id.*, at 6-7).

to be read literally, for such a construction leads to the clearly unintended, and untenable, result that school districts must return violent or dangerous students to school while the often lengthy EHA proceedings run their course. We think it clear, however, that Congress very much meant to strip schools of the *unilateral* authority they had traditionally employed to exclude disabled students, particularly emotionally disturbed students, from school. In so doing, Congress did not leave school administrators powerless to deal with dangerous students; it did, however, deny school officials their former right to "self-help," and directed that in the future the removal of disabled students could be accomplished only with the permission of the parents or, as a last resort, the courts.

As noted above, Congress passed the EHA after finding that school systems across the country had excluded one out of every eight disabled children from classes. In drafting the law, Congress was largely guided by the recent decisions in *Mills* v. *Board of Education of District of Columbia*, 348 F. Supp. 866 (1972), and *PARC*, 343 F. Supp. 279 (1972), both of which involved the exclusion of hard-to-handle disabled students. *Mills* in particular demonstrated the extent to which schools used disciplinary measures to bar children from the classroom. There, school officials had labeled four of the seven minor plaintiffs "behavioral problems," and had excluded them from classes without providing any alternative education to them or any notice to their parents. 348 F. Supp., at 869-870. After finding that this practice was not limited to the named plaintiffs but affected in one way or another an estimated class of 12,000 to 18,000 disabled students, *id.*, at 868-869, 875, the District Court enjoined future exclusions, suspensions, or expulsions "on grounds of discipline." *Id.*, at 880.

Congress attacked such exclusionary practices in a variety of ways. It required participating States to educate *all* disabled children, regardless of the severity of their disabilities, 20 U. S. C. § 1412(2)(C), and included within the definition of "handicapped" those children with serious emotional disturbances. § 1401(1). It further provided for meaningful parental participation in all aspects of a child's educational placement, and barred schools, through the stay-put provision, from changing that placement over the parent's objection until all review proceedings were completed. Recognizing that those proceedings might prove long and tedious, the Act's drafters did not intend § 1415(e)(3) to operate inflexibly, see 121 Cong. Rec. 37412 (1975) (remarks of Sen. Stafford), and they therefore allowed for interim placements where parents and school officials are able to agree on one. Conspicuously absent from § 1415(e)(3), however, is any emergency exception for dangerous students. This absence is all the more telling in light of the injunctive decree issued in *PARC*, which permitted school officials unilaterally to remove students in "'extraordinary circumstances.'" 343 F. Supp., at 301. Given the lack of any similar exception in *Mills*, and the close attention Congress devoted to these "landmark" decisions, see S. Rep., at 6, we can only conclude that the omission was intentional; we are therefore not at liberty to engraft onto the statute an exception Congress chose not to create.

Our conclusion that § 1415(e)(3) means what it says does not leave educators hamstrung. The Department of Education has observed that, "[w]hile the [child's] placement may not be changed [during any complaint proceeding], this does not preclude the agency from using its normal procedures for dealing with children who are endangering themselves or others." Comment following 34 CFR § 300.513 (1987). Such procedures may include the use of study carrels, timeouts, detention, or the restriction of privileges. More drastically, where a student poses an immediate threat to the safety of others, officials may temporarily suspend him or her for up to 10 school days.[8] This authority, which respondent in no way disputes, not only ensures that school administrators can protect the safety of others by promptly removing the most dangerous of students, it also provides a "cooling down" period during which officials can initiate IEP review and seek to persuade the child's parents to agree to an interim placement. And in those cases in which the parents of a truly dangerous child adamantly refuse to permit any change in placement, the 10-day respite gives school officials an opportunity to invoke the aid of the courts under § 1415(e)(2), which empowers courts to grant any appropriate relief.

Petitioner contends, however, that the availability of judicial relief is more illusory than real, because a party seeking review under § 1415(e)(2) must exhaust time-consuming administrative remedies, and because under the Court of Appeals' construction of § 1415(e)(3), courts are as bound by the stay-put provision's "automatic injunction," 793 F. 2d, at 1486, as are schools.[9] It is true that judicial review is normally not available under § 1415(e)(2) until all administrative proceedings are completed, but as we have previously noted, parents may by-pass the administrative process where

---

[8] The Department of Education has adopted the position first espoused in 1980 by its Office of Civil Rights that a suspension of up to 10 school days does not amount to a "change in placement" prohibited by § 1415(e)(3). U. S. Dept. of Education, Office of Special Education Programs, Policy Letter (Feb. 26, 1987), Ed. for Handicapped L. Rep. 211:437 (1987). The EHA nowhere defines the phrase "change in placement," nor does the statute's structure or legislative history provide any guidance as to how the term applies to fixed suspensions. Given this ambiguity, we defer to the construction adopted by the agency charged with monitoring and enforcing the statute. See *INS* v. *Cardoza-Fonseca*, 480 U. S. ——, —— (1987). Moreover, the agency's position comports fully with the purposes of the statute: Congress sought to prevent schools from permanently and unilaterally excluding disabled children by means of indefinite suspensions and expulsions; the power to impose fixed suspensions of short duration does not carry the potential for total exclusion that Congress found so objectionable. Indeed, despite its broad injunction, the District Court in *Mills* v. *Board of Education of District of Columbia*, 348 F. Supp. 866 (DC 1972), recognized that school officials could suspend disabled children on a short-term, temporary basis. See *id.*, at 880. Cf. *Goss* v. *Lopez*, 419 U. S. 565, 574-576, (1975) (suspension of 10 school days or more works a sufficient deprivation of property and liberty interests to trigger the protections of the Due Process Clause). Because we believe the agency correctly determined that a suspension in excess of 10 days does constitute a prohibited "change in placement," we conclude that the Court of Appeals erred to the extent it approved suspensions of 20 and 30 days' duration.

[9] Petitioner also notes that in California, schools may not suspend any given student for more than a total of 20, and in certain special circumstances 30, school days in a single year, see Cal. Educ. Code Ann. § 48903 (West Supp. 1988); he argues, therefore, that a school district may not have the option of imposing a 10-day suspension when dealing with an obstreperous child whose previous suspensions for the year total 18 or 19 days. The fact remains, however, that state law does not define the scope of § 1415(e)(3). There may be cases in which a suspension that is otherwise valid under the stay-put provision would violate local law. The effect of such a violation, however, is a question of state law upon which we express no view.

exhaustion would be futile or inadequate. See *Smith* v. *Robinson* 468 U. S. 992, 1014, n. 17 (1984) (citing cases); see also 121 Cong. Rec. 37416 (1975) (remarks of Sen. Williams) (''[E]xhaustion . . . should not be required . . . in cases where such exhaustion would be futile either as a legal or practical matter''). While many of the EHA's procedural safeguards protect the rights of parents and children, schools can and do seek redress through the administrative review process, and we have no reason to believe that Congress meant to require schools alone to exhaust in all cases, no matter how exigent the circumstances. The burden in such cases, of course, rests with the school to demonstrate the futility or inadequacy of administrative review, but nothing in § 1415(e)(2) suggests that schools are completely barred from attempting to make such a showing. Nor do we think that § 1415(e)(3) operates to limit the equitable powers of district courts such that they cannot, in appropriate cases, temporarily enjoin a dangerous disabled child from attending school. As the EHA's legislative history makes clear, one of the evils Congress sought to remedy was the unilateral exclusion of disabled children by *schools*, not courts, and one of the purposes of § 1415(e)(3), therefore, was ''to prevent *school* officials from removing a child from the regular public school classroom over the parents' objection pending completion of the review proceedings.'' *Burlington School Committee* v. *Massachusetts Dept. of Education*, 471 U. S., at 373 (emphasis added). The stay-put provision in no way purports to limit or pre-empt the authority conferred on courts by § 1415(e)(2), see *Doe* v. *Brookline School Committee*, 722 F. 2d 910, 917 (CA1 1983); indeed, it says nothing whatever about judicial power.

In short, then, we believe that school officials are entitled to seek injunctive relief under § 1415(e)(2) in appropriate cases. In any such action, § 1415(e)(3) effectively creates a presumption in favor of the child's current educational placement which school officials can overcome only by showing that maintaining the child in his or her current placement is substantially likely to result in injury either to himself or herself, or to others. In the present case, we are satisfied that the District Court, in enjoining the state and local defendants from indefinitely suspending respondent or otherwise unilaterally altering his then current placement, properly balanced respondent's interest in receiving a free appropriate public education in accordance with the procedures and requirements of the EHA against the interests of the state and local school officials in maintaining a safe learning environment for all their students.[10]

---

[10]We therefore reject the United States' contention that the District Judge abused her discretion in enjoining the local school officials from indefinitely suspending respondent pending completion of the expulsion proceedings. Contrary to the Government's suggestion, the District Judge did not view herself bound to enjoin any and all violations of the stay-put provision, but rather, consistent with the analysis we set out above, weighed the relative harms to the parties and found that the balance tipped decidedly in favor of respondent. App. 222-223. We of course do not sit to review the factual determinations underlying that conclusion. We do note, however, that in balancing the parties' respective interests, the District Judge gave proper consideration to respondent's rights under the EHA. While the Government complains that the District Court indulged an improper presumption of irreparable harm to respondent, we do not believe that school officials can escape the presumptive effect of the stay-put provision simply by violating it and forcing parents to petition for relief. In any suit brought by parents seeking injunctive relief for a violation of § 1415(e)(3), the burden

IV

We believe the courts below properly construed and applied § 1415(e)(3), except insofar as the Court of Appeals held that a suspension in excess of 10 school days does not constitute a "change in placement."[11] We therefore affirm the Court of Appeals' judgment on this issue as modified herein. Because we are equally divided on the question whether a court may order a State to provide services directly to a disabled child where the local agency has failed to do so, we affirm the Court of Appeals' judgment on this issue as well.

Affirmed.

---

rests with the school district to demonstrate that the educational status quo must be altered.

[11]See n. 8, *supra.*

APPENDIX E

SUBJECT MATTER TABLE
OF RECENT LAW REVIEW ARTICLES

AIDS

A basis for AIDS discrimination suits. [School Bd. of Nassau County v. Arline, 107 S.Ct. 1123 (1987)] 19 U.West.L.A.L.Rev. 203 (1987).

A major victory for AIDS employees under the Federal Rehabilitation Act of 1973. [Chalk v. U.S. Dist. Court, 840 F.2d 701, 9th Cir. (1988)] 22 Akron L.Rev. 241 (1988).

AIDS: a university's liability for failure to protect its students. 14 J.C.& U.L. 529 (1987).

AIDS: an insurable handicap. 9 Hamline J.Pub.L.& Pol'y 117 (1988).

AIDS and right to privacy. 16 S.U.L.Rev. 393 (1989).

AIDS as a handicap? Arline, tuberculosis and AIDS. 19 U.Tol.L.Rev. 859 (1988).

AIDS law: the impact of AIDS on American schools and prisons. 1987 Ann.Surv.Am.L. 117.

AIDS: legal issues in search of a cure. 14 Wm. Mitchell L. Rev. 575 (1988).

Associates of persons with AIDS: what are their rights? 57 UMKC L.Rev. 559 (1989).

Asymptomatic infection with the AIDS virus as a handicap under the Rehabilitation Act of 1973. 88 Colum.L.Rev. 563 (1988).

Baxley, James F. *Rehabilitating AIDS-based employment discrimination: HIV infection as a handicap under the Vocational Rehabilitation Act of 1973.* 19 Seton Hall L.Rev. 23 (1989).

Education and administrative law—education of health-impaired children and administrative due process—state Department of Education possesses statutory authority to promulgate administrative rules governing the admission to school of children afflicted with AIDS provided that department affords all parties appropriate procedural due process under those rules. [Bd. of Educ. v. Cooperman, 523 A.2d 655 (1987)] 19 Rutgers L.J. 483 (1988).

Enforcing the rights to a public education for children afflicted with AIDS. 36 Emory L.J. 603 (1987).

Fear and loathing in the classroom: AIDS and public education. 14 J.Legis. 87 (1987).

Keith, James A. *AIDS in the classroom.* 58 Miss.L.J. 349 (1988).

AIDS (continued)

Lally-Green, M.E. *Is AIDS a handicap under the Rehabilitation Act of 1973 after School Bd. v. Arline and the Civil Rights Restoration Act of 1987?* 19 U.Tol.L.Rev. 603 (1988).

Lawson, Gary. *AIDS, astrology and Arline: towards a causal interpretation of section 504.* 17 Hofstra L.Rev. 237 (1989).

O'Brien, Rev. Raymond C. *Discrimination: the difference with AIDS.* 6 J.Contemp.Health L.& Pol'y 93 (1990).

Opening the schoolhouse door for children with AIDS: the Education for All Handicapped Children Act. 13 B.C.Envtl.Aff. L.Rev. 583 (1986).

Protecting children with AIDS against arbitrary exclusion from school. 74 Calif.L.Rev. 1373 (1986).

Public schools and public health: exclusion of children with AIDS. 5 J.L.& Pol. 605 (1989).

Quick remediation for AIDS victims who cannot afford to wait. [Chalk v. U.S. Dist. Court, 840 F.2d 701, (9th Cir.1989)] 26 Hous.L.Rev. 1033 (1989).

Reading, writing, but no biting: isolating school children with AIDS. 37 Clev.St.L.Rev. 337 (1989).

Sullivan, Kathleen M. and Martha A. Field. *AIDS and the coercive power of the State.* 23 Harv.Civ.Rts.-Civ.Lib.L.Rev. 139 (1988).

The Rehabilitation Act's otherwise qualified requirements and the AIDS virus: protecting the public from AIDS-related health and safety hazards. 30 Ariz.L.Rev. 571 (1988).

Tuberculosis chapters: a model for future AIDS legislation? 32 St. Louis U.L.J. 1145 (1988).

Wasson, Robert P., Jr. *AIDS discrimination under federal, state and local law after Arline.* 15 Fla.St.U.L.Rev. 221 (1987).

Waters, Robert Craig. *AIDS and the perception of AIDS as handicaps under Florida law.* 17 Fla.St.U.L.Rev. 441 (1990).

Will AIDS fit the mold? [School Bd. of Nassau County, Florida v. Arline, 107 S.Ct. 1123 (1987)] 41 Ark.L.Rev. 639 (1988).

Without probable cause: the constitutional ramifications of mandatory AIDS testing in the workplace. 57 UMKC L.Rev. 863 (1989).

Attorney's Fees

Attorney fees in special education: sifting through the interpretive maze. 17 Cap.U.L.Rev. 597 (1989).

Civil rights—attorney's fees award—42 U.S.C. § 1988—the United States Supreme Court has held that an award of attorney's fees under 42 U.S.C. § 1988 is not required to be proportionate to the damages awarded a civil rights plaintiff, thus allowing a fee award seven times the amount of compensatory and punitive damages. [City of Riverside v. Rivera, 106 S.Ct. 2686 (1986)] 26 Duq.L.Rev. 139 (1987).

Education law—the Handicapped Children's Protection Act of 1986: the award of attorney's fees in litigation under the Education of the Handicapped Act. 11 S.Ill.U.L.J. 381 (1987).

Attorney's Fees (continued)

Guernsey, Thomas F. *The school pays the piper, but how much? Attorneys' fees in special education cases after the Handicapped Children's Protection Act of 1986.* 23 Wake Forest L.Rev. 237 (1988).

Schreck, Myron. *Attorneys' fees for administrative proceedings under the Education of the Handicapped Act: of Carey, Crest Street and congressional intent.* 60 Temp.L.Q. 599 (1987).

The Supreme Court's interpretation of section 1988 and awards of attorney's fees for work performed in administrative proceedings: a proposal for a result-oriented approach. [North Carolina Dep't of Transp. v. Crest Street Comm. Council, Inc., 107 S.Ct. 336 (1986)] 62 Wash.L.Rev. 889 (1987).

Classification and Identification

A contagious disease becomes a handicap. [School Bd. of Nassau County v. Arline, 107 S.Ct. 1123 (1987)] 34 Loy.L.Rev. 224 (1988).

AIDS: does it qualify as a "handicap" under the Rehabilitation Act of 1973? 61 Notre Dame L.Rev. 572 (1986).

Bennett, P.E. *The meaning of "mental illness" under the Michigan Mental Health Code.* 4 Cooley L.Rev. 65 (1986).

Garcia, Sandra Anderson, Eric Drogin, Robert Batey, and Richard E. Spana. *Institutionalized delinquent and maladjusted juveniles: a psycholegal systems analysis.* 68 Neb.L.Rev. 261 (1989).

Larson, David Allen. *Mental impairments and the Rehabilitation Act of 1973.* 48 La.L.Rev. 841 (1988).

Reinstitutionalization of the mentally retarded. 32 Wayne L.Rev. 1105 (1986).

The Education for All Handicapped Children Act: the benefits and burdens of mainstreaming capable handicapped children in a regular classroom. 38 Mercer L.Rev. 903 (1987).

The Rehabilitation Act of 1973; focusing the definition of a handicapped individual. 30 Wm.& Mary L.Rev. 149 (1988).

What's a handicap anyway? Analyzing handicap claims under the Rehabilitation Act of 1973 and analogous state statutes. 22 Willamette L.Rev. 529 (1986).

Discrimination

Administrative res judicata and section 1983: should the rule of preclusion apply to unreviewed state administrative decisions? 10 Nat'l Black L.J. 73 (1987).

An evolutionary step in equal protection analysis. [City of Cleburne v. Cleburne Living Center, 105 S.Ct. 3249 (1985)] 46 Md.L.Rev. 163 (1986).

Bacharach, Robert E. *Section 1983 and an administrative exhaustion requirement.* 40 Okla.L.Rev. 407 (1987).

A case of handicap discrimination, no transfer required. [Coffman v. W. Va. Bd. of Regents, No. 17904, slip op., (W.Va.June 2, 1989)] 91 W.Va.L.Rev. 487 (1989).

Discrimination (continued)

Citizens with mental retardation and the courts—new barriers for equal protection and due process? [Philadelphia Police and Fire Association for Handicapped Children, Inc. v. City of Philadelphia, 699 F.Supp. 1106 (E.D.Pa.1988, rev'd, 874 F.2d 156, 3d Cir.1989)] 43 Ark.L.Rev. 423 (1990).

Civil rights litigation I: developments under section 1983 and Title VII. 1986 Ann.Surv.Am.L. 795.

Civil rights litigation II: developments under section 1988. 1986 Ann.Surv.Am.L. 809.

Civil rights: mental disabilities included in Handicapped Discrimination Act's definition of disability. 23 Suffolk U.L.Rev. 421 (1989).

Civil rights—Rehabilitation Act—handicapped individual. [School Bd. of Nassau County, Florida v. Arline, 107 S.Ct. 1123 (1987)] 26 Duq.L.Rev. 511 (1987).

Civil rights—the Secretary of Health and Human Services is not authorized to dispense with the focus of section 504 of the Rehabilitation Act of 1973 to prevent discrimination and instead to employ federal resources to save the lives of handicapped newborns, without regard to whether they are victims of discrimination by recipients of federal funds. [Bowen v. American Hosp. Ass'n, 106 S.Ct. 2101 (1986)] 36 Drake L.Rev. 621 (1986-87).

Coleman, Jennifer A. *42 U.S.C. section 1988: a congressionally-mandated approach to the construction of section 1983.* 19 Ind. L.Rev. 665 (1986).

Constitutional law: although mentally retarded not a quasi-suspect class, denial of special use permit deprived applicants of constitutional right. [City of Cleburne v. Cleburne Living Center, 105 S.Ct. 3249 (1985)] 25 Washburn L.J. 575 (1986).

Constitutional law—equal protection—zoning ordinance excluding home for the mentally retarded fails the rational basis test. [City of Cleburne v. Cleburne Living Center, 105 S.Ct. 3249 (1985)] 8 U.Ark. Little Rock L.J. 721 (1985-86).

Constitutional law—mental health—the mentally handicapped do not constitute a "quasi-suspect" class for purposes of equal protection analysis. [City of Cleburne v. Cleburne Living Center, 105 S.Ct. 3249 (1985)] 62 N.D.L.Rev. 95 (1986).

Constitutional law—mental retardation is not a quasi-suspect classification. 17 St. Mary's L.J. 1053 (1986).

Contagiousness and the Rehabilitation Act of 1973. [School Bd. of Nassau County v. Arline, U.S., 107 S.Ct. 1123 (1987)] 14 N.Ky. L.Rev. 435 (1988).

Denial of quasi-suspect status for the mentally retarded and its effect on exclusionary zoning of group homes. [City of Cleburne v. Cleburne Living Center, 105 S.Ct. 3249 (1985)] 17 U.Tol.L.Rev. 1041 (1986).

Discrimination in the public schools: Dick and Jane have AIDS. 29 Wm.& Mary L.Rev. 881 (1988).

Discrimination (continued)

> *Employment discrimination against the handicapped: analysis of statutory and constitutional protection in Massachusetts.* 21 New Eng.L.Rev. 305 (1985-86).
>
> Engel, David M. and Alfred S. Konefsky. *Law students with disabilities: removing barriers in the law school community.* 38 Buffalo L.Rev. 551 (1990).
>
> *Equal protection and the mentally retarded: a denial of quasi-suspect status in . . .* [City of Cleburne v. Cleburne Living Center, 105 S.Ct. 3249 (1985)]. 72 Iowa L.Rev. 241 (1986).
>
> *Equal protection for the mentally retarded?* [City of Cleburne v. Cleburne Living Center, 105 S.Ct. 3249 (1985)] 9 Harv.J.L. & Pub.Pol'y 231 (1986).
>
> *Equal protection—mental retardation is not a quasi-suspect classification requiring heightened judicial scrutiny, but requiring a special use permit for the operation of a group home for the mentally retarded based on irrational prejudices fails even the rational basis test.* 36 Drake L.Rev. 201 (1986-87).
>
> *Extension within manageable bounds protecting the handicapped.* [School Bd. of Nassau County v. Arline, 408 So.2d 706 (Fla.App.1982)] 65 Denver U.L.Rev. 319 (1988).
>
> *Facial discrimination: extending handicap law to employment discrimination on the basis of physical appearance.* 100 Harv.L.Rev. 2035 (1987).
>
> Flaccus, Janet A. *Discrimination legislation for the handicapped: much ferment and the erosion of coverage.* 55 U.Cin.L.Rev. 81 (1986).
>
> Greene, Kenneth A. *Burdens of proving handicap discrimination using federal employment discrimination law: rational basis or undue burden?* 1989 Det.C.L.Rev. 1053.
>
> *Handicap and race discrimination in readmission procedures.* [Anderson v. Univ. of Wisconsin, 665 F.Supp. 1372 (W.D.Wis.1987)] 15 J.C.& U.L. 431 (1989).
>
> *Improving handicappers' civil rights in Michigan—preventing discrimination through accommodation.* 21 U.Mich.J.L.Ref. 283 (1987/88).
>
> *An individualized definition of "handicap" and its application to HIV.* 22 U.C.Davis L.Rev. 653 (1989).
>
> Kaufman, Michael J. *Federal and state handicapped discrimination laws: toward an accommodating legal framework.* 18 Loy.U. Chi.L.J. 1119 (1987).
>
> Larson, David D. *What disabilities are protected under the Rehabilitation Act of 1973?* 16 Mem.St.U.L.Rev. 229 (1986).
>
> Maffeo, Patricia A. *Making non-discriminatory fitness-for-duty decisions about persons with disabilities under the Rehabilitation Act and the Americans with Disabilities Act.* 16 Am.J.L. & Med. 279 (1990).
>
> Mims, William C. *The plight of the handicapped infant: The Federal Response.* 15 U.Balt.L.Rev. 449 (1986).

Discrimination (continued)

Minow, Martha. *When difference has its home: group homes for the mentally retarded, equal protection and legal treatment of difference.* 22 Harv.C.R. - C.L.L.Rev. 111 (1987).

Perras, Roichard A. and Walter C. Hunter. *Handicap discrimination in employment: the employer defense of future safety risk.* 6 J.L. & Com. 377 (1986).

Program specificity and section 504: making the best of a bad situation. 20 Loy.L.A.L.Rev. 1431 (1987).

Protecting children with AIDS against arbitrary exclusion from school. 74 Calif.L.Rev. 1373 (1986).

Rational basis review under the equal protection clause—a double standard of review. [City of Cleburne v. Cleburne Living Center, 105 S.Ct. 3249 (1985)] 55 Miss.L.J. 329 (1985).

Rational basis with a bite? [City of Cleburne v. Cleburne Living Center, 105 S.Ct. 3249 (1985)] 20 U.S.F.L.Rev. 927 (1986).

Real protection against discrimination for society's new outcasts? [School Bd. of Nassau County v. Arline, 107 S.Ct. 1123 (1987)] 17 Stetson L.Rev. 517 (1988).

Rebell, Michael A. *Structural discrimination and the rights of the disabled.* 74 Geo.L.J. 1435 (1986).

Rehabilitation Act—Department of Health and Human Services may not interfere in medical treatment decision regarding handicapped infants. [Bowen v. American Hosp. Ass'n, 106 S.Ct. 2101 (1986)] 16 Cum.L.Rev. 607 (1986).

Rothstein, Laura F. *Section 504 of the Rehabilitation Act: emerging issues for colleges and universities.* 13 J.C. & U.L. 229 (1986).

Safeguarding equality for the handicapped: compensatory relief under section 504 of the Rehabilitation Act. [Guardians Ass'n v. Civil Service Comm'n, 463 U.S. 582 (1983)] 1986 Duke L.J. 197.

Section 504 of the Rehabilitation Act: a re-examination of the civil rights declaration of the handicapped. 21 Suffolk U.L.Rev. 175 (1987).

Section 504 transportation regulations: molding civil rights legislation to meet the reality of economic constraints. 26 Washburn L.J. 558 (1987).

Shedding tiers for the mentally retarded. [City of Cleburne v. Cleburne Living Center, 105 S.Ct. 3249 (1985)] 35 DePaul L.Rev. 485 (1986).

Snelling, Phillip H. *Discrimination against children with special health care needs: Title V Crippled Children's Services programs and section 504 of the Rehabilitation Act of 1973.* 18 Loy.U. Chi.L.J. 995 (1987).

Tate, Kathryn W. *The federal employer's duties under the Rehabilitation Act: does reasonable accommodation or affirmative action include reassignment?* 67 Tex.L.Rev. 781 (1989).

Tucker, Bonnie P. *Section 504 of the Rehabilitation Act after ten years of enforcement: the past and the future.* 1989 U.Ill.L.Rev. 845.

Discrimination (continued)

> *Undoing a lesson of fear in the classroom: the legal recourse of AIDS-linked children.* 135 U.Pa.L.Rev. 193 (1986).
>
> *United States Commission on Civil Rights—medical discrimination against children with disabilities: an abstract.* 6 J.Contemp. Health L.& Pol'y 379 (1990).
>
> *What's a handicap anyway? Analyzing handicap claims under the Rehabilitation Act of 1973 and analogous state statutes.* 22 Willamette L.Rev. 529 (1986).

Education Generally

> Broadwell, Cathy A. and John C. Walden. *"Free appropriate public education" after Rowley: an analysis of recent court decisions.* 17 J.L.& Educ. 35 (1988).
>
> Cichon, Dennis E. *Educability and education: filling the cracks in service provision responsibility under the Education for All Handicapped Children Act of 1975.* 48 Ohio St.L.J. 1089 (1987).
>
> *Constitutional law—no free ride to the schoolhouse gate: equal protection analysis in . . .* [Kadrmas v. Dickinson Public Schools, 108 S.Ct. 2481 (1988)] 20 N.M.L.Rev. 161 (1990).
>
> *Education and administrative law—education of health-impaired children and administrative due process—state Department of Education possesses statutory authority to promulgate administrative rules governing the admission to school of children afflicted with AIDS provided that department affords all parties appropriate procedural due process under those rules.* [Bd. of Educ. v. Cooperman, 523 A.2d 655 (1987)] 19 Rutgers L.J. 483 (1988).
>
> Fleming, Evelyn R. and Donald C. Fleming. *Involvement of minors in special education decision-making.* 16 J.L.& Educ. 389 (1987).
>
> Guernsey, Thomas F. *When the teachers and parents can't agree, who really decides? Burdens of proof and standards of review under the EAHCA.* 36 Clev.St.L.Rev. 67 (1988).
>
> Hill, Kevin D. *Legal conflicts in special education: How competing paradigms in the Education for All Handicapped Children Act create litigation.* 64 U.Det.L.Rev. 129 (1986).
>
> *Inequality in Louisiana public school finance: should educational quality depend on a student's school district residency?* 60 Tul.L.Rev. 1269 (1986).
>
> Moss, Kary L. *Standardized tests as a tool of exclusion: improper use of the SAT in New York.* 4 Berkeley Women's L.J. 230 (1989-90).
>
> Stewart, Frank H., Abram S. Gordon and Andrew M. Ostrognai. *Ohio handicap law.* 13 U.Dayton L.Rev. 181 (1988).
>
> Wegner, Judith Welch. *Educational rights of handicapped children: three federal statutes and an evolving jurisprudence. Part I: the statutory maze.* 17 J.L.& Educ. 387 (1987).

Education of The Handicapped Act

> *Civil rights—Education of the Handicapped Act.* [Polk v. Cent. Susquehanna Intermediate Unit 16, 853 F.2d 171 (3d Cir.1988)] 62 Temp.L.Rev. 429 (1989).
>
> *Education law—right to a free and appropriate education—the Education for All Handicapped Children Act does not contain an implicit "dangerousness exception."* [Honig v. Doe, 108 S.Ct. 592 (1988)] 20 Rutgers L.J. 561 (1989).
>
> *Education law—Wyoming refuses to recognize compensatory education as a remedy under the Education for All Handicapped Children Act of 1975.* [Natrona County School Dist. No. 1 v. McKnight, 764 P.2d 1039 (Wyo.1988)] 24 Land & Water L.Rev. 529 (1989).
>
> Goldberg, Steven S. *The failure of legalization in education: alternative dispute resolution and the Education for All Handicapped Children Act of 1975.* 18 J.L.& Educ. 441 (1989).
>
> Guernsey, Thomas F. *The Education for All Handicapped Children Act, 42 U.S.C. § 1983, and § 504 of the Rehabilitation Act of 1973: statutory interaction following the Handicapped Children's Protection Act of 1986.* 68 Neb.L.Rev. 564 (1989).
>
> *Exhaustion of administrative remedies: exceptions and predictability.* 66 U.Det.L.Rev. 239 (1989).
>
> McMullen, Judith G. *Family support of the disabled: a legislative proposal to create incentives to support disabled family members.* 23 U.Mich. J.L.Rev. 439 (1990).
>
> *Mootness and the Education for All Handicapped Children Act: timely decision saves judicial and social costs.* [Honig v. Doe, 108 S.Ct. 592 (1988)] 57 U.Cin.L.Rev. 1101 (1989).

Eleventh Amendment

> *Congressional abrogation of state sovereign immunity and the Education for All Handicapped Children Act.* [Dellmuth v. Muth, 57 U.S.L.W. 4720 (U.S. June 13, 1989)] 57 Fordham L.Rev. 877 (1989).
>
> Rudovsky, David. *The qualified immunity doctrine in the Supreme Court: judicial activism and the restriction of constitutional rights.* 138 U.Pa.L.Rev. 23 (1989).
>
> *The Eleventh Amendment controversy continues: the availability and scope of relief against state entities under the Education of the Handicapped Act.* 22 Ind.L.Rev. 707 (1989).
>
> *The Eleventh Amendment pierces the legal shield of EHA protection.* [Dellmuth v. Muth, 109 S.Ct. 2398 (1989)] 23 J.Marshall L.Rev. 487 (1990).

Employment

> *After School Board of Nassau County v. Arline: employees with AIDS and the concerns of the "worried well."* [School Bd. of Nassau County v. Arline, 107 S.Ct. 1123 (1987)] 37 Am.U.L.Rev. 867 (1988).
>
> *AIDS and employment discrimination: should AIDS be considered a handicap?* 33 Wayne L.Rev. 1095 (1987).
>
> *Defining "handicap" for purposes of employment discrimination.* 30 Ariz.L.Rev. 633 (1988).

Employment (continued)

Employment discrimination and AIDS: is AIDS a handicap under section 504 of the Rehabilitation Act? 38 U.Fla.L.Rev. 649 (1986).

Handicap discrimination in the workplace: how to determine if a disability is related to the ability to work. [Father Flanagan's Boys' Home v. Goerke, 401 N.W.2d 731 (1987)] 21 Creighton L.Rev. 683 (1987-1988).

Handicap provision of Texas employment discrimination statute protects only those individuals whose disabilities severely limit them in performing work-related tasks in general. [Chevron v. Redmon, 745 S.W.2d 314 (Tex.1987)]. 19 Tex.Tech.L.Rev. 1485 (1988).

Handicapped workers: who should bear the burden of proving job qualifications? 38 Me.L.Rev. 135 (1986).

Mandatory AIDS testing—a Fourth Amendment analysis. [Glover v. Eastern Nebraska Community Office of Retardation, 867 F.2d 461 (8th Cir., cert. denied, 110 S.Ct. 321, 1989)] 23 Creighton L.Rev. 693 (1990).

Protection of AIDS victims from employment discrimination under the Rehabilitation Act. 1987 U.Ill.L.Rev. 355.

Finance

Inequality in Louisiana public school finance: should educational quality depend on a student's school district residency? 60 Tul.L.Rev. 1269 (1986).

First Amendment

Against a wall of strict separation: Missouri's Church-State doctrine and State provision of special education services to private schools. 53 Mo.L.Rev. 407 (1988).

An educational perspective on the evolution of Lemon. [Grand Rapids School District v. Ball, 105 S.Ct. 3216 (1985), and Aguilar v. Felton, 105 S.Ct. 3232 (1985)] 1986 B.Y.U.L.Rev. 489.

Bosmajian, Haig. *The judiciary's use of metaphors, metonymies and other tropes to give First Amendment protection to students and teachers.* 15 J.L. & Educ. 439 (1986).

Choper, Jesse H. *The establishment clause and aid to parochial schools—an update.* 75 Calif.L.Rev. 5 (1987).

Special education and the non-public school child: a handicap is a non-sectarian condition. 5 L.& Inequality 549 (1988).

Injuries

Henderson, Donald H. *Negligent liability suits emanating from the failure to provide adequate supervision: a critical issue for teachers and school boards.* 16 J.L. & Educ. 435 (1987).

Standard of care, duty & causation in failure to warn actions against mental health professionals. [Peck v. Counseling Service of Addison County, Inc., 499 A.2d 422 (Vt.1985)] 11 Vt.L.Rev. 343 (1986).

The use of closed-circuit television testing in child sexual abuse cases: a Twentieth Century solution to a Twentieth Century problem. 23 San Diego L.Rev. 919 (1986).

Injuries (continued)

> *The use of videotaped testimony of victims in cases involving child sexual abuse: a constitutional dilemma.* 14 Hofstra L.Rev. 291 (1986).

Medical Services

> Closen, Michael L., Susan Marie Connor, Howard L. Kaufman and Mark F. Wojcik. *AIDS: testing democracy—irrational responses to the public health crisis and the need for privacy in serologic testing.* 19 J.Marshall L.Rev. 835 (1986).
>
> *Establishing standards for treating children in mental institutions with psychotropic drugs.* 5 Pub.L.F. 215 (1986).
>
> *Joint ventures: for profit and nonprofit corporations as partners in providing mental health services.* 5 Pub.L.F. 201 (1986).
>
> *Law, Social Policy and Contagious Disease: a Symposium on Acquired Immune Deficiency Syndrome (AIDS).* 14 Hofstra L.Rev. 1 (1986).
>
> *Medical treatment of handicapped infants: who should make the decision?* 22 Tul.L.Rev. 259 (1986).
>
> Scott, Elizabeth S. *Sterilization of mentally retarded persons: reproductive rights and family privacy.* 1986 Duke L.J. 806.
>
> *Standard of care, duty & causation in failure to warn actions against mental health professionals.* [Peck v. Counseling Service of Addison County, Inc., 499 A.2d 422 (Vt.1985)] 11 Vt.L.Rev. 343 (1986).
>
> *Sterilization of the mentally disabled in Pennsylvania: three generations without legislative guidance are enough.* 92 Dick.L.Rev. 409 (1988).
>
> *The best interest standard in court-authorized sterilization of mentally retarded.* [In re Debra B., 495 A.2d 781 (Me.1985)] 38 Me.L.Rev. 209 (1987).
>
> *The Education for All Handicapped Children Act: trends and problems with the "related services" provision.* 18 Golden Gate U.L.Rev. 427 (1988).

Placement

> Huefner, Dixie Snow. *Special education residential placements under the Education for All Handicapped Children Act.* 18 J.L.& Educ. 441 (1989).
>
> *Retroactive reimbursement: the standard of review for a parent's unilateral placement under the Education for All Handicapped Children Act.* 10 Cardozo L.Rev. 2381 (1989).
>
> *Schools—Education for All Handicapped Children Act of 1975—school officials may not unilaterally change the current educational placement of a student protected under the Act.* [Honig v. Doe, 108 S.Ct. 592 (1988)] 58 Miss.L.J. 387 (1988).
>
> Tweedie, Jack. *Parental rights and accountability in public education: Special education and choice of school.* 7 Yale Law & Policy Rev. 396 (1989).
>
> Weber, Mark C. and Mary Binkelman. *Legal issues in the transition to public school for handicapped infants and children.* 19 J.L.& Educ. 193 (1990).

Student Rights

All aboard: accessible public transportation for disabled persons.
63 N.Y.U.L.Rev. 360 (1988).

An abused child's right to life, liberty and property in the home: constitutional approval of state inaction. [DeShaney v. Winnebago County Department of Social Services, 109 S.Ct. 998 (1989)] 92 W.Va.L.Rev. 205 (1989).

Administrative law—The Rehabilitation Act does not preclude the Veterans' Administration's denial of educational benefit extensions to primary alcoholics. [Traynor v. Turnage, 108 S.Ct. 1372 (1988)] 23 Suffolk U.L.Rev. 71 (1989).

Beyond least restrictive alternative: a constitutional right to treatment for mentally disabled persons in the community. 20 Loy. L.A.L.Rev. 1527 (1987).

Equal educational opportunity: the visually impaired and Public Law 94-142. [Education for All Handicapped Children Act of 1975] 33 UCLA L.Rev. 549 (1985).

Fleming, Evelyn R. and Donald C. Fleming. *Involvement of minors in special education decision-making.* 16 J.L.& Educ. 389 (1987).

Griffith, Frederick J., III. *New Jersey v. T.L.O. and its progeny: the Bill of Rights at school.* 5 Cooley L.Rev. 617 (1988).

Involuntary sterilization of mentally retarded minors in Nebraska. 68 Neb.L.Rev. 410 (1989).

Meeting the special educational needs of learning disabled juvenile delinquents. 31 Ariz.L.Rev. 615 (1989).

Perlin, Michael L. *Can mental health professionals predict judicial decisionmaking? Constitutional and tort liability aspects of the right of the institutionalized mentally disabled to refuse treatment: on the cutting edge.* 3 Touro L.Rev. 13 (1986).

Rethinking equality and difference: disability discrimination in public transportation. 97 Yale L.J. 863 (1988).

Ross, Stephen F. *Legislative enforcement of equal protection.* 72 Minn.L.Rev. 311 (1987).

Soifer, Aviam. *Moral ambition, formalism, and the "free world" of DeShaney.* 57 Geo.Wash.L.Rev. 1513 (1989).

State constitutions and statutes as sources of rights for the mentally disabled: the last frontier. 20 Loy.L.A.L.Rev. 1249 (1987).

Sterilization of the mentally disabled in Pennsylvania: three generations without legislative guidance are enough. 92 Dick.L.Rev. 409 (1988).

The Burlington decision: a vehicle to enforce free appropriate public education for the handicapped. [Burlington v. Dep't of Education, 105 S.Ct. 1996 (1985)] 19 Akron L.Rev. 311 (1985).

The handicapped in the classroom: the Supreme Court adopts a new standard for the protection of rights in . . . [Honig v. Doe, 108 S.Ct. 592 (1988)]. 24 Willamette L.Rev. 1141 (1988).

Underwood, Julie. *Special education discipline: changing practices after Honig v. Doe.* 17 J.L.& Educ. 375 (1988).

Suspension and Expulsion

Congress, Smith v. Robinson, *and the myth of attorney representation in special education hearings: is attorney representation desirable?* 37 Syracuse L.Rev. 1161 (1987).

Hartog-Rapp, Fay. *The legal standards for determining the relationship between a child's handicapping condition and misconduct charged in a school disciplinary proceeding.* 1985 S.Ill. U.L.Rev. 243.

The legal limits of school discipline for children with handicaps. 69 Or.L.Rev. 117 (1990).

Suspension and expulsion of handicapped children: an overview in light of . . . [Doe v. Maher, 793 F.2d 1470 (9th Cir.1986)]. 14 W.St.U.L.Rev. 341 (1986).

INDEX

553

Use the attached order cards to order your own or extra copies of **HANDI-CAPPED STUDENTS AND SPECIAL EDUCATION.**

Faculty lounge? Orientation workshops? School library? Your own office? Board members?

Order extra copies of **HANDICAPPED STUDENTS AND SPECIAL EDUCATION** now. The attached cards may be removed from the book for your order.

Please send me _____ copies of **HANDICAPPED STUDENTS AND SPECIAL EDUCATION,** Eighth Edition, at $77.00 per copy. Add $3.75 postage and handling. Total $80.75.

Name _____

Title/School _____

Address _____

City _____ **State** _____ **Zip** _____

Purchase Order Number_____ **Telephone Number** _____

Send order and check payable to: DATA RESEARCH, INC.,
P.O. BOX 490, ROSEMOUNT, MN 55068

Please send me _____ copies of **HANDICAPPED STUDENTS AND SPECIAL EDUCATION,** Eighth Edition, at $77.00 per copy. Add $3.75 postage and handling. Total $80.75.

Name _____

Title/School _____

Address _____

City _____ **State** _____ **Zip** _____

Purchase Order Number_____ **Telephone Number** _____

Send order and check payable to: DATA RESEARCH, INC.,
P.O. BOX 490, ROSEMOUNT, MN 55068

OUR GUARANTEE: If you are not satisfied with HANDICAPPED STUDENTS AND SPECIAL EDUCATION, for any reason, we'll refund your money.